AMERICAN DISASTERS

201 Calamities That Shook the Nation

AMERICAN DISASTERS

201 Calamities That Shook the Nation

BALLARD C. CAMPBELL, PH.D.

Professor of History
Northeastern University

Checkmark Books®
An imprint of Infobase Publishing

American Disasters: 201 Calamities That Shook the Nation

Copyright © 2008 by Infobase Publishing

All rights reserved. No part of this book may be reproduced or utilized in any form or by any means, electronic or mechanical, including photocopying, recording, or by any information storage or retrieval systems, without permission in writing from the publisher. For information contact:

Checkmark Books
An imprint of Infobase Publishing
132 West 31st Street
New York NY 10001

Library of Congress Cataloging-in-Publication

The Library of Congress has cataloged the hardcover edition as follows:
Campbell, Ballard C., 1940–
    Disasters, accidents, and crises in American history : a reference guide to the nation's most catastrophic events / Ballard C. Campbell.
        p. cm.
    Includes bibliographical references and index.
    ISBN-13: 978-0-8160-6603-2 (hc)—ISBN-13: 978-0-8160-7735-9 (pbk)
    ISBN-10: 0-8160-6603-5 (hc)—ISBN-10: 0-8160-7735-5 (pbk)
    1. Disasters—United States—History. 2. Disasters—Social aspects—United States. 3. Crises—United States—History. 4. Crises—Social aspects—United States. 5. Accidents—United States—History. 6. Accidents—Social aspects—United States. 7. United States—Social conditions. 8. United States—History—Anecdotes. I. Title.
E179.C27 2008
363.34'1—dc22   2007027688

Checkmark Books are available at special discounts when purchased in bulk quantities for businesses, associations, institutions, or sales promotions. Please call our Special Sales Department in New York at (212) 967-8800 or (800) 322-8755.

You can find Facts On File on the World Wide Web at http://www.factsonfile.com

Text design by Annie O'Donnell
Cover design by Salvatore Luongo
Illustrations by Accurate Art, Inc.
Photo research by Anne Burns Images

Printed in the United States of America

VB FOF 10 9 8 7 6 5 4 3 2 1

This book is printed on acid-free paper and contains 30 percent postconsumer recycled content.

◆ CONTENTS ◆

TOPICAL TABLE OF CONTENTS

◆ ACKNOWLEDGMENTS ◆

Thanks to Robert Cherny, Joe Conforti, Melanie Gustafson, Robert Hall, Peter Holloran, Alan Lessoff, David Rich Lewis, Kris Lindenmeyer, Clay McShane, William Shade, and John Wilson for suggesting disasters, accidents, and crises, and for recommending individuals to write about them. I am grateful to the contributors who took the time to contribute essays to the book. Special thanks also to Andrew Gyory, Executive Editor for History at Facts On File, who should be listed as a collaborator on the title page. Andrew partnered in selecting disasters to include in the book, was a sounding board for my ideas about the importance and impact of particular events, and labored tirelessly to smooth out prose. David O'Donnell performed admirably as my assistant on the project; besides writing five entries, he provided invaluable advice on the comparative impact of disasters. Anne Burns did a marvelous job locating pictures of catastrophic events. I am grateful to my wife Genie who kept her composure as I raced to the finish line.

Ballard C. Campbell
Portland, Maine

◆ INTRODUCTION ◆

Who can forget the pictures of the jet airliners slamming into the World Trade Center in 2001? Or the great clouds of billowing smoke when the Twin Towers collapsed? Images of this disaster, which millions saw on television, are permanently etched upon our memories. If the past is a guide to the future, the horrors of the terrorist attacks of 2001 will become a historical milestone, much in the way that other catastrophes have constituted turning points in American history. From the mass decimation of Native Americans beginning in 1492, the "starving time" at Jamestown in 1609–10, the Boston Massacre in 1770, and the Secession Crisis in 1860 to the explosion of the USS *Maine* in 1898, the Great Depression of the 1930s, the attack on Pearl Harbor in 1941, and the Columbine School Shooting in 1999, disasters and crises are symbols of their eras. Most of the great catastrophes in American history have triggered major changes in society. Like these earlier events, Hurricane Katrina—the most costly natural disaster in U.S. history—also seems destined to become imbedded in our collective memory. This great storm of 2005 did not directly affect most Americans, yet millions of people here and abroad watched the human tragedy unfold in New Orleans and along the Gulf coast. Katrina is one of the many significant catastrophes that we have assembled in *American Disasters*.

Crises and calamities occupy an integral place in American history. Catastrophes have occurred in all time periods and taken numerous forms over the past 500 years. The goal of this book is to describe the most destructive, influential, and fascinating of these events. We have collected stories about floods, hurricanes, epidemics, earthquakes, massacres, rebellions, fires, assassinations, financial panics and economic depressions, riots, explosions, shipwrecks, battles, bombings, strikes, avalanches, blizzards, train collisions, airplane crashes, political and business scandals, kidnappings, poisonings, health emergencies, dam and bridge collapses, tornadoes, oil spills, dust storms, and locust infestations, as well as several unusual occurrences that are not easily classified but nonetheless recognized as disastrous. Defining disasters broadly, we have selected events that touched natural, political, social, environmental, military, medical, and economic aspects of society. Some of these incidents are obvious candidates for inclusion because they are familiar to most Americans. The Salem witchcraft trials of 1692, the assassination of President Lincoln in 1865, and the Oklahoma City bombing in 1995 fall into this category. Other occurrences are less well known, such as the economic crisis of 1785, the Sand Creek massacre of 1864, and the smog tragedy at Donora in 1948. Still others are obscure, even a bit bizarre, such as the "dark day" of 1780, the "year without a summer" in 1816, the horse epizootic in 1872, and the *War of the Worlds* radio broadcast that caused panic in 1938. However diverse and unusual, the array of disasters, accidents, and crises portrayed in this book have had an immense impact on American civilization.

Extraordinary events burrow deeply into the human psyche. Many natives of the northeast retain strong recollections of the great New England hurricane of 1938, even if they did not live through it. Each region of the country can tell similar stories. Residents of the Gulf coast look back at the great hurricane that struck Galveston, Texas, in 1900, the measuring rod for tropical cyclones in the United States until Katrina struck in 2005. Californians see the San Francisco earthquake of 1906 as a powerful reminder that the Pacific Coast is prone to devastating geological disasters. The Loma Prieta quake of

1989 reinforced this historical lesson. Midwesterners realize that the Mississippi and other major rivers of their region have undergone "100-year" floods that caused tremendous damage, one in 1927 and one more recently in 1993. Floridians hardly need to be told that monster storms have battered their coast and are likely to do so again. Some disasters, such as the sinking of the *Titanic* in 1912, the disappearance of Amelia Earhart in 1937, and the heightened awareness of environmental degradation in the wake of the publication of *Silent Spring* in 1962 have no particular regional locus but remain firmly embedded in the national recollection.

Memories of natural disasters and accidents tend to dim with the passage of time. Political, diplomatic, and military crises, on the other hand, have greater staying power in the national recollection, in part because they are building blocks of the American civic tradition. These milestones in the nation's history are referenced time and again in books and films. Landmark crises between the American Revolution and World War I—the Battles of Lexington and Concord, the travail of Washington's army at Valley Forge, the burning of Washington, D.C., during the War of 1812, the assassination of President Lincoln, the sinking of the *Lusitania*—are part of a time line that has created a sense of the United States as a nation. The secession crisis of 1860, the crises over Korea and Vietnam, and the attack on 9/11, to cite several examples, are essential chapters in the history of a nation that has been shaped by the challenges it endured. Perhaps more than we realize, the national character has been molded by the way Americans have responded to disasters and crises.

These and other epic events examined in this book have a special claim on our attention. They fascinate us because of their unexpected randomness, their scale of destruction, and the seductiveness of their drama. The power unleashed in the great natural disasters confounds our comprehension. Horrible accidents that took hundreds of lives in minutes or seconds stun our senses. Society asks in the wake of these tragedies, How could it have happened? And how can we prevent this from happening again?

Crises are riveting because they hinge on irresolvable conflicts. The worst of these challenges, such as the Civil War and World War II, have threatened the existence of the nation. Political and diplomatic conflicts hinge on intractable opponents whose movements and actions are dramas that unfolded in unpredictable ways. Tension mounts until each crisis is resolved. The nation's four contested presidential elections in 1800, 1824, 1876, and 2000 created tense situations because their outcome was unknown but their resolution had immense influence on the affairs of state. Assassinations of four presidents—in 1865, 1881, 1901, and 1963—marked critical moments for our nation's government. Precursors of war, such as the British impressment of American seamen in 1807, the Compromise of 1850, the sinking of the *Lusitania* in 1915, and the bombing of Pearl Harbor in 1941, constituted a set of formidable challenges to the nation. The Tet Offensive and the My Lai Massacre in 1968 symbolize the country's dilemma over the Vietnam War. Great labor conflicts, such as the great railroad strike in 1877, the Haymarket Square incident in 1886, and the Pullman strike in 1894, rocked the foundations of society and suggested to the comfortable classes that the country was on the brink of revolution. Conflicts between European settlers and Native Americans, slaves and slaveholders, terrorists and law-abiding citizens, and invisible microbes and the human population embodied distinct challenges to American society.

Unlike the routine that characterizes our everyday lives, catastrophes are dramatic, memorable, and consequential. We have used all three of these criteria in our selection of the incidents presented in *American Disasters*. Each story represents an extraordinary moment in American history, many of which have had profound consequences on people's lives. We use the terms *disasters*, *accidents*, and *crises* to characterize these unusual events, but the reader should not insist on rigid distinctions between them. Some events fit several categories, or none of them, in unambiguous ways. Amelia Earhart's disappearance over the Pacific while on a round-the-world flight in 1937 is one of these hard-to-classify situations. We called her fated trip an accident, but what actually happened to the famed aviatrix is one of the 20th century's great mysteries. The Millerites' belief that the end of the world was coming on October 22, 1844, cannibalism among the Donner party in frontier California in 1846, and the FBI raid on the Branch Davidian compound in Waco, Texas, in 1993 likewise are difficult to classify. But there is little doubt that each incident posed a significant crisis. The great molasses spill in Boston in 1919, to cite another of our selections, was downright bizarre as well as a deadly accident. Our nation's history is strewn with airplane crashes and explosions, and *American Disasters* samples some of the more spectacular of them. Three of these accidents are eerily linked because they struck iconic symbols of the country: the B-25 bomber crash into the Empire State Building in 1945, the collision of two planes over the Grand Canyon in 1956, and the jetliners that terrorists flew into the Twin Towers in 2001. Similarly odd is the bunching of catastrophes in certain years. The year that Amelia Earhart disappeared, 1937, also dated the explosion of the airship *Hindenburg* in New Jersey, the "massacre" at Republic Steel in Chicago, the school explosion in New London, Texas, and the Elixir Sulfanilamide drug disaster that caused the deaths of more than 100 people nationwide. The years 1871–72, 1919, 1968, 1979–80, and 1993 are notable too for the bunching of catastrophes. In one instance, two major disasters occurred on the same day, and, oddly, both were fires: the Great Chicago Fire and the Peshtigo forest fire of October 8, 1871.

In addition to their hold on the American memory, we have selected the events for this book on the basis of their impact on society. Disasters have the capacity to change lives and institutions. As a rule of thumb, the larger the scope and scale of a catastrophe, the greater was its impact. Most major transportation accidents since the early 1800s have unleashed attempts to make travel safer. Great epidemics have encouraged local and federal governments to adopt measures to contain and eradicate these scourges, even before modern medical understanding developed. Political and economic crises drive officials and citizens to find solutions, which usually have significant consequences. The writing of the U.S. Constitution in 1787 in the wake of Shays's Rebellion, the impact of the assassination of President Lincoln on Reconstruction in the 1860s and 1870s, the formation of the New Deal in response to the Great Depression of the 1930s, and the use of atomic bombs in 1945 illustrate the influential power of these mega-events. In the 21st century, the attacks of 9/11 accelerated efforts to protect the nation from terrorists. *American Disasters* does not include global warming or the Iraq war, which some see as major

crises, but it is a good bet that these dilemmas will have long-lasting effects.

Most of the incidents covered in this book occurred on American soil. Some events that occurred overseas, however, are included, such as the sinking of both the steamship *Arctic* in 1854 and the USS *Maine* in 1898, the retreat from the Yalu River in Korea in 1950, and the Iran hostage crisis in 1979, because of the connection to American history. Other disasters that occurred beyond the nation's borders—such as the sinking of the *Titanic* in 1912, the tragic use of thalidomide, and the chemical spill at Bhopal, India, in 1984, involved the United States in some central way. And some events that severely affected the United States were also global developments, such as the flu pandemic of 1918, the major economic depressions of the 19th and 20th centuries, and the AIDS crisis at the end of the last century and into our own.

Pinpointing the consequences of an event is an art, not a science. We hope that this book generates discussion about the impact of disasters and calamities. The authors have reported the judgment of historians about the meaning of particular crises. Scholars see the Coercive Acts of 1774 as instrumental to the outbreak of the American Revolution in 1775. The Compromise of 1850 and John Brown's raid on the federal arsenal at Harper's Ferry in 1859 are commonly understood to have exacerbated the sectional tensions that led to the Civil War. Most historians recognize that the turmoil in 1968, evident in the Tet Offensive, the assassinations of Martin Luther King, Jr., and Robert F. Kennedy, and the 1968 Democratic Convention and riot, was instrumental in the election of Richard M. Nixon as president and the nation's shift to the right politically. Mega-crises of this order constitute an important criterion for our selection of events for the book.

In addition to listing the entries by the chronology of their occurrence in the table of contents, we have also sorted the stories into topical categories. Grouping events of a similar nature together helps in the interpretation of their significance. Although health crises are historically important in their own right, they also track the evolution of thinking about the reactions to disease over the generations, such as the smallpox epidemic that ravaged Boston in 1721, the cholera epidemic of 1832, or the ordeal of "Typhoid Mary" in the early 1900s. Since its colonial antecedents, the United States has endured repeated downturns in its economy. Each of these depressions has radiated shock waves through business, government, and society. Political crises in American history have engaged the great disputes of their era, such as securing national independence, slavery, race, civil rights, preservation of the federal union, the uses of presidential power, war, and the stability of the political order. Our greatest business scandals carried political and economic ramifications.

Some calamities had important symbolic as well as tangible impacts. The near extinction of the buffalo, the demise of chestnut and elm trees, and cheating in the 1919 World Series tug on our sensibilities as much as they diminished a physical entity. Major scandals in business, such as the Ponzi scheme in 1920 and Enron in 2001, and in government, such as the Credit Mobilier scandal in 1872, have sullied the reputation of essential American institutions. The immediate damage from killer smog in 1943 and 1948, the Santa Barbara Oil Spill in 1969, the discovery of harmful chemical wastes at Love Canal in 1978, and the accident at the Three Mile Island nuclear power plant in 1979 dissipated with time. Yet these and similar crises symbolized the diverse and apparently ever-present threats to the environment. The greatest disasters and crises contain both profound psychic *and* lasting tangible effects.

The third criterion used to select stories for *American Disasters* rested on the scope and scale of an event. In some instances, we used the number of fatalities to gauge the significance of an occurrence. In other instances, we took monetary costs and the displacement of people into account. These guidelines were helpful; however, they were not sufficient in themselves because historical records become less reliable the further back in time one travels. Generally speaking, most information about casualties, costs, and displacement of people from catastrophes before 1900 rests on estimates. Even for many recent catastrophes precise figures are hard to come by. Notwithstanding this limitation, suggestive evidence exists about all of the mega-events in American history.

Collecting stories about disasters prompts the question, which were the most significant? The question is fascinating in part because it has no definitive answer. Historical significance is essentially a subjective judgment. Assigning a rank order to extraordinary events can be misleading, partly because of

information gaps and partly because of the logical fallacy of comparing qualitatively different categories of phenomena. Given these constraints, a reasonable alternative is to identify the most significant events within similar categories of phenomena and to list them by their chronological occurrence. Our choice for the worst natural disasters are:

1871	Peshtigo Fire
1873	Locust Invasions across the Great Plains
1888	Blizzard of '88
1900	Galveston Hurricane
1906	San Francisco Earthquake and Fire
1935	Dust Bowl
1938	Great New England Hurricane
1980	Deadly Heat Wave
1993	Mississippi River Flood
2005	Hurricane Katrina

The most of important health crises have been:

1492	Decimation of Native Americans by European Diseases
1775	Smallpox Epidemic in the American Revolution
1832	Cholera Epidemic
1878	Yellow Fever Epidemic
1918	Influenza Pandemic
1952	Polio Epidemic
1981	AIDS Epidemic

The worst accidents in American history have been:

1865	Explosion of the *Sultana*
1871	Great Chicago Fire
1889	Johnstown Flood
1903	Iroquois Theater Fire
1904	*General Slocum* Disaster
1911	Triangle Shirtwaist Factory Fire
1912	Sinking of the *Titanic*
1915	Capsizing of the *Eastland*
1937	New London School Explosion
1979	Accident at Three Mile Island
1986	Shuttle *Challenger* Explosion
1989	*Exxon Valdez* Oil Spill

The most significant social disasters and labor crises are:

1609–10	Starving Time at Jamestown
1692	Salem Witchcraft Trials
1755	Exile of the Acadians
1831	Nat Turner Slave Rebellion
1838	Trail of Tears
1845	Irish Famine and Immigration
1846	The Donner Party
1877	Great Railroad Strike
1892	Lynching Tragedy
1894	Pullman Strike
1919	Chicago Race Riot
1967	Urban Riots
1995	Oklahoma City Bombing
1999	Columbine School Shooting

The most important political and economic crises have been:

1765	Stamp Act Crisis
1775	Battles of Lexington and Concord
1860	Secession Crisis
1865	Assassination of President Lincoln
1868	Impeachment of President Johnson
1893	Financial Panic and Depression
1933	The Great Depression
1968	Assassination of Martin Luther King, Jr.
1972	Watergate Scandal
1979	Iran Hostage Crisis
2001	9/11 Terrorist Attack

The most important of military disasters and crises are:

1675	King Philip's War
1777	Deprivation at Valley Forge
1814	Burning of Washington, D.C.
1836	Battle of the Alamo
1861	Battle of Bull Run
1898	Explosion of the USS *Maine*
1915	Sinking of the *Lusitania*
1941	Attack on Pearl Harbor
1945	Atomic Bombs Dropped on Japan

1950	Retreat from the Yalu
1968	Tet Offensive

These "most important of" selections represent one set of conjectures. We invite readers to draw up their own lists, and perhaps even to rank them, in light of the essays in this book and perusal of the "Further reading" suggestions that accompany each entry. Readers can also consult the appendix, which ranks certain catastrophes by fatalities and costs. The book features two tables of contents: The first lists articles by date—the way Americans experienced them in sequential order—and the second groups events by topic. In instances where a story was an unfolding process, such as the devastation of Native Americans from European disease and the demise of the buffalo, we picked a symbolic date to reference the entry. Each entry contains a Factbox that lists essential information about the incident. The Factbox gives readers a quick overview of the catastrophe and helps them to compare one event to another. Visual exhibits, including graphs and maps, offer further information about the catastrophe. In addition, we have included "sidebar" essays that profile agencies or entries—such as the Food and Drug Administration and Federal Emergency Management Agency—that have a special connection to particular disasters and crises.

We hope that readers have as much fun in using this book as Andrew Gyory, executive editor at Facts On File, and I had in putting it together. Selecting essays for the collection gave us an opportunity to ponder a cornucopia of tragic and influential events that mark the entire path of American history. We marveled at the endless number and extraordinary diversity of disasters and calamities that have occurred. Time and again we debated their significance and impact. Compiling these stories was a continuous learning process and an entertaining odyssey as well. American history, of course, is not just about disasters, accidents, and crises. But studying these great events reveals essential aspects of our past.

◆ CONTRIBUTORS ◆

Julie Arrison . . . . Northeastern University
Brendon Baillod. . . . . Independent scholar
Jennifer M. Balboni . . . . . Northeastern University
Robert Barde . . . . University of California, Berkeley
Michael Les Benedict. . . . . Ohio State University
Claude G. Berube . . . . Naval Academy, Annapolis
James C. Bradford . . . . . . Texas A & M University
Richard R. Brandt . . . . Salem State College
Roger D. Bridges . . . . Rutherford B. Hayes Center
Kevin C. Brown. . . . . Carnegie Mellon University
William Burgess . . . . . . Northeastern University
Charles W. Calhoun. . . . East Carolina University
Allison D. Carter . . . . . . Northeastern University
James M. Carter . . . . . . Texas A & M University, Corpus Christi
Philip Cash . . . . Emanuel College
Robert W. Cherny . San Francisco State University
Lauri Bauer Coleman. . . . . . . College of William and Mary
Frank T. Colon . . . . Lehigh University
Joseph Conforti . . . . University of Southern Maine
Timothy C. Coogan . . . . . LaGuardia Community College
Victoria H. Cummins . . . . Austin College
Gregory J. Dehler . . . . Front Range Community College
George Dehner . . . . Wichita State University
Diana Di Stefano . . . . Pacific Lutheran University
Susan Doll. . . . . Oakton Community College
Louise Nelson Dyble . . . . . University of Southern California
John E. Ebel. . . . . Boston College
Neenah Estrella-Luna . . . Northeastern University
C. Wyatt Evans . . . . Drew University
Curtis C. E. Fazen . . . . . Northeastern University
Karen Feldscher. . . . . . . Northeastern University
Richard A. Fournier. . . . . Boston University
Kevin M. Gannon . . . . Grand View College

Diana S. Grigsby . . . University of Illinois-Chicago
Mayumi Grigsby . . . . Independent scholar
William Gudelunas . . . . College of the Desert, California
Michael Gunther . . . . Lehigh University
Robert L. Hall . . . . Northeastern University
Madeleine Hall-Arber . . . . MIT Center for Marine Social Sciences
Mathias Hanses. . . . . . . Indiana State University
Gerald H. Herman. . . . . . Northeastern University
Elaine A. Hills. . . . . State University of New York, Albany
Peter C. Holloran. . . . . . . Worcester State College
Richard L. Hughes. . . . . . Illinois State University
James L. Huston . . . . . Oklahoma State University
Kathy Merlock Jackson . . . . . . Virginia Wesleyan College
Richard Jensen . . . . University of Illinois, Chicago
Jennifer A. Jovin . . . . . . Northeastern University
Marjoleine Kars. . . . . University of Maryland, Baltimore
Peter Knupfer . . . . Michigan State University
Michael Lafleur . . . . The Lowell Sun
Alan Lessoff . . . . Illinois State University
Kriste Lindenmeyer. . . . . University of Maryland, Baltimore
Marcos Luna . . . . Salem State College
Daniel S. Margolies . . . Virginia Wesleyan College
Clay McShane . . . . Northeastern University
David Morrow. . . . . Independent scholar
Matthew Mulcahy . . . . . Loyola College, Baltimore
William J. Nancarrow . . . . Curry College
Kathryn Newfont . . . . Mars Hill College
David A. Nichols . . . . Indiana State University
David G. O'Donnell. . . . . Northeastern University
Richard J. Orsi. . . . . . . California State University, Hayward
Katherine M. B. Osborn. . . . . Tennessee Technological University

John M. O'Toole . . . . Worcester State College

Lynn Hudson Parsons . . . . State University of New York, Brockport

Anthony N. Penna . . . . . . Northeastern University

Kimberly K. Porter . . . University of North Dakota

James Ralph . . . . Middlebury College

Kyle Renick . . . . Independent scholar

Pamela Riney-Kehrberg . . . . . Iowa State University

Dante J. Scala . . . . Saint Anselm College

Aaron Christopher Schab . . . . . University of Idaho

William G. Shade . . . . Lehigh University

Elizabeth M. Sharpe . . . . Independent scholar

Josh Sides . . . . California State University, Northridge

Sheila L. Skemp . . . . University of Mississippi

Mitchell Snay . . . . Denison University

Sheldon M. Stern . . . . John F. Kennedy Center

Anna Suranyi . . . . Northeastern University

Nancy C. Unger . . . . Santa Clara University

Julie Walsh . . . . . . American International College

Alex Wilson . . . . Northeastern University

Jeff Woods . . . . Arkansas Tech University

1492 ◆ CHRISTOPHER COLUMBUS'S FIRST VOYAGE

Christopher Columbus has been alternatively praised and attacked for his "discovery" of America—or at least of the islands he called the "West Indies"—on October 12, 1492. His unexpected landing in the Caribbean ranks as one of the greatest accidents—or unintentional events—in human history, one that profoundly transformed the planet. That his voyages, four in all, to the "New World" were of monumental importance cannot be denied. They began the process that would result in the European and English colonization of the Americas, including the United States. They led to the death—by warfare and even more by disease—of entire native populations on the Caribbean islands as well as on the mainland of North and South America. Columbus himself, however, never understood or accepted the implications of his feat. He went to his grave in 1506 convinced that he had reached his preferred destination of India, not an entirely separate continent. He refused to believe that Hispaniola, Cuba, and the coasts of Panama, Costa Rica, and Nicaragua were not a stone's throw away from Asia. Columbus had sailed west to reach the "East" and all of the riches that exotic land promised. His encounter with the islands was, from his perspective, an unfortunate accident. Centuries after his death, Europeans were still looking for a "passage to India"—a direct water route to Asia—on a land mass they continued to view as an obstacle rather than a destination.

Historians know less about Columbus than they would like. Although many nations have sought to claim the explorer as one of their own, the evidence indicates that he was born in about 1451 in the republic of Genoa to a family of weavers and merchants. He was, at one time or another, a wool worker, a sailor, a merchant, and a book seller. But sailing was his love. Before he left northern Italy for Portugal, he had already become familiar with the Mediterranean and had made short forays into the Atlantic. In Portugal, where adventurous seamen were in particular abundance thanks to an advantageous location and a supportive ruler, Columbus sailed ever further afield, going to England, Ireland, Africa, and

FACTBOX

PLACE Spain to the West Indies

DATE October 12, 1492

TYPE Unintentional "discovery" of America

DESCRIPTION Underestimating the size of the Atlantic Ocean, Christopher Columbus believed it was technologically and economically possible to sail west in order to reach the Asian mainland. His mathematical miscalculations led him to land accidentally on a continent that neither he nor anyone else in Europe knew existed.

CAUSE The European desire for a direct trade with India and China, as well as the desire to destroy Muslim influence

IMPACT The conquest, colonization, and resettling of North and South America, and ultimately the establishment of the United States

many Atlantic islands. He may even have sailed as far as Iceland. Hence, he was an experienced seaman when he began his preparations for his most famous voyage.

Columbus was extraordinary in his confidence and his zeal. But he was always a man of his times, and he built upon the achievements of his predecessors. By the 15th century, ships like the caravels on which he sailed had become larger and sturdier. Instruments such as the magnetic compass, the quadrant, and the astrolabe enabled seamen to navigate the seas without relying solely on the stars. Sailors—especially the Portuguese—had charted their course around the Horn of Africa and ventured far into the Atlantic, increasing the western world's knowledge of an ocean that seemed more hospitable and less mysterious all the time.

All schoolchildren have grown up believing that Christopher Columbus was a modern man, far ahead of his contemporaries, who resolutely faced down his stubbornly hidebound adversaries in his quest to reach the Indies by sailing across the Atlantic Ocean.

Although his landing in the Americas was accidental, Columbus's arrival in 1492 would transform world history. *(Library of Congress)*

He was, like Galileo (who was born a century later), a man of science in a society run by rigid religious fanatics. In particular, or so the legend goes, while nearly everyone thought that the earth was flat, and thus that sailors traveling too far from the European mainland would fall off the edge, Columbus somehow understood that the earth was round. Thus he succeeded where others would not even risk failure. The truth is more complicated, and more interesting, than that.

Columbus was a fascinating combination of the sacred and the profane. While he was in many ways a product of the Renaissance desire to expand human knowledge by exploring the world, he was also a deeply religious man. Like many of his counterparts, he was lured by his desire to tap the material resources of Africa and Asia. He hoped to gain direct access to Africa's gold and to Asia's herbs, spices, and silk. Still, although he may have hoped for untold wealth when he set sail for India, he saw himself above all else as divinely chosen to convert the world to Christi-

anity. He wanted to break the stranglehold of the Muslim world on Asian trade goods. But he also wanted to destroy the dominance of the Islamic religion once and for all. Indeed, he wanted to use the profits from his voyage to finance another crusade, wresting Jerusalem from the control of the Muslims.

Columbus's achievement, as monumental as it was, was the result of a huge miscalculation, not superior science. Virtually everyone in the 15th century believed that the earth was round, not flat. Few doubted that at least theoretically it was possible to reach India by sailing west. But most observers thought that the planet was too large to make a voyage across the ocean safe or economically feasible. It would simply cost too much money to equip a crew for so long an expedition. Nor were the technological developments of the time, while impressive, up to the task. Columbus disagreed. Relying on a combination of mathematical calculations and myth, carefully cherry-picking sources that supported him, finding in them what he so desperately hoped to find, he calculated that the earth was much smaller in circumference than anyone else thought it was. He also thought that Asia extended much further eastward than it actually did. Convinced that his estimations were correct, he finally persuaded Queen Isabella and King Ferdinand of Spain to finance his expedition. In fact, Columbus's calculations were wrong and his critics were right. Had the Americas not existed, Columbus and his crew would no doubt have sailed into oblivion, never to be heard from again.

Columbus sailed to the "Indies" three more times after 1492. But his first voyage was the one that captured the imagination of people in his own day and continued to fascinate scholars long after his death. Explorers, adventurers, and immigrants followed in his wake, searching for wealth, exploiting the native populations they encountered along the way. Columbus's accidental arrival in America marked a turning point in world history, spawning actions and events that continued to shape life for centuries to come. It is not altogether surprising that when the independent former colonies known as the United States of America decided to erect a national capital in the 1790s, they placed it in the newly named District of Columbia in honor of the man whose misguided ocean voyage was responsible for their nation's very existence.

Sheila Skemp

FURTHER READING:

Columbus, Christopher. *The Four Voyages of Christopher Columbus.* Edited and translated by J. M. Cohen. New York: Penguin Press, 1969.

Phillips, William D., Jr., and Carla Rahn Phillips. *The Worlds of Christopher Columbus.* Cambridge: Cambridge University Press, 1992.

West, Delno. "Christopher Columbus and His Enterprise to the Indies: Scholarship of the Last Quarter Century." *William and Mary Quarterly* 49 (April 1992): 254–277.

1492 ◆ DECIMATION OF NATIVE AMERICANS BY EUROPEAN DISEASES

Christopher Columbus first arrived in the Caribbean islands in 1492, expecting to meet Asian peoples. Instead, he and the conquerors who followed him encountered a variety of thriving indigenous societies throughout the Americas. These societies ranged from sophisticated civilizations that rivaled those of the Europeans, such as those of the Aztecs in present-day Mexico and the Inca peoples in Peru, to more loosely organized groups that relied on agriculture, hunting, and periodic migration, such as the peoples of the Caribbean and many of the native populations in what was to become the United States. Perhaps as many as 54 million people lived in the Americas in 1492, although estimates of the numbers of pre-Columbian indigenous peoples vary widely and are still much debated. By 1700, some 200 years after Europeans ventured into the Western Hemisphere, however, the number of Native Americans had dwindled to roughly 6 million, or approximately 11 percent of the estimated population size at the time that Columbus arrived. The peoples of the Caribbean islands, where the first contact occurred, virtually disappeared. It is sometimes believed that this demographic collapse was caused by massacres and ill treatment perpetrated by European conquerors and settlers, especially in the regions conquered by the Spaniards. This perception was supported by the so-called "Black Legend," an explanation initiated by the Spanish friar Bartolomé de Las Casas who detailed Spanish atrocities against Amerindians.

FACTBOX

PLACE Western Hemisphere

DATE October 12, 1492, to about 1700

TYPE Epidemic diseases

DESCRIPTION Unfamiliar European diseases brought to the Americas killed close to 90 percent of indigenous populations.

CAUSE Human pathogens carried across the Atlantic Ocean by Europeans infected native populations, who had not developed biological resistance to diseases common in the Eastern Hemisphere.

CASUALTIES An estimated 48 million deaths among Native Americans

IMPACT Massive reduction of indigenous populations greatly decreased their ability to resist European encroachment on their homelands.

While the stories of European atrocities contain substantial truth, the conquistadores were not in fact the primary cause of the disappearance of the tens of millions of indigenous Americans. Disease played a much larger role in this demographic disaster. Europeans and the African slaves they brought inadvertently carried bacteria and viruses across the Atlantic that Native Americans had never encountered. These pathogens included smallpox, measles, yellow fever, typhus, influenza, scarlet fever, malaria, bubonic and pneumonic plague, and diphtheria, among others. The resultant infections afflicted the Europeans and Africans as well, but with less devastating effect than the Amerindians experienced, because these diseases were commonplace in Europe, Africa, and Asia. Over the centuries, the peoples of these three continents had encountered these diseases many times and built up immunities. The first encounter with a particular illness usually resulted in an epidemic with a high rate of death, but individuals with the most resistant genes survived and passed on their resistance to their children. Later episodes of the disease usually came after 25- or 30-year remissions, coinciding with the growth of new generations who had never personally developed immunity. However, these were considerably diminished in impact as resistant genes spread throughout the population.

There appears initially to have been a much lower incidence of severe epidemic diseases in the pre-Columbian Americas than in Europe. The exception is syphilis. This affliction may have existed as a weaker strain in Europe, but when its more potent variation was first encountered by Europeans in the Americas, it had a virulence and killing power quite unlike its modern-day equivalent. Within a few decades, however, European populations became habituated to syphilis.

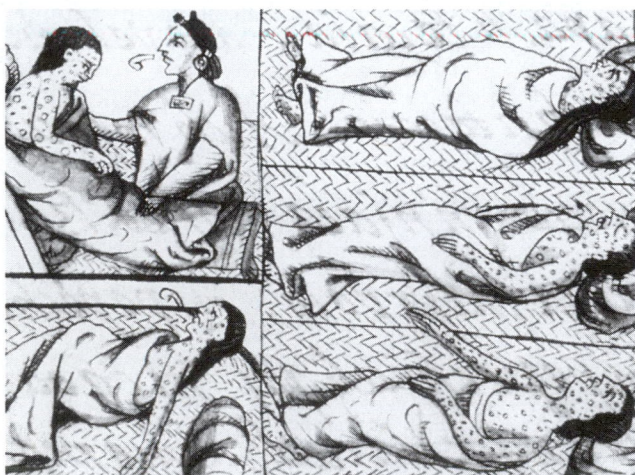

In this 16th-century illustration by an Aztec artist, the ravaging effects of smallpox—the deadliest disease Europeans brought to the Americas—are clearly evident. *(New York Public Library)*

Why the Americas had fewer disease-causing pathogens than the rest of the world remains a puzzle to scholars. One possibility is that the higher levels of animal domestication in the Eastern Hemisphere may have enabled more diseases to pass to humans from animal hosts. The peoples of the Americas had only domesticated dogs, turkeys, llamas, alpacas, and guinea pigs (and in most places only dogs), in comparison to the rest of the world, where people raised, tended, and owned at least two dozen species of animals. Domestic animals live in close proximity to humans and can easily spread disease. A number of pathogens that infect humans can be traced to common animals such as cattle, sheep, pigs, birds, and dogs. Over the centuries the peoples of the Eastern Hemisphere had become habituated to the diseases carried by their animals. While virulent, they only caused serious complications in a small percentage of the population. But the Amerindians had never encountered these pathogens before. Not only did the colonists bring germs and diseases to the Americas within their own bodies (often originally animal-borne), but they also brought with them additional reservoirs of disease in the form of cattle, pigs, and other domesticated animals, as well as their vermin, such as rats, mice, fleas, and mosquitoes, across the ocean.

When Europeans arrived in the Americas, they brought a number of different infectious microbes with them. Instead of encountering a single new disease, repeated waves of different illnesses hit native populations. A virulent infection such as smallpox or measles would strike a community, infecting and incapacitating a large percentage of the populace, in some instances as much as 70 to 90 percent. Examples include the Western Hemisphere's first smallpox epidemic, which took place on the island of Hispaniola in the Caribbean in 1507: likewise a severe epidemic, probably viral hepatitis, erupted in Massachusetts in 1616 before the arrival of the *Mayflower* in 1620. The Amerindians had little chance to recover, lacking the biological resistance that the Europeans had evolved over many centuries.

The force of such epidemics was often compounded because several new waves of infection would arrive in the Americas almost simultaneously. As sick individuals were recovering, another round of illness struck, and sometimes another, and then perhaps yet another affliction. The scope and scale of this demographic collapse meant that there were insufficient people to tend the sick or to cultivate the fields. Famine followed the epidemics, especially in densely settled areas such as the Aztec Empire. Such epidemics had emotional consequences in addition to physical suffering. Survivors could be demoralized and paralyzed by grief and fear. These psychological scars are recorded in native-language accounts written after the arrival of the Europeans.

Epidemics, rather than technological skill or military prowess, were responsible for the European conquests of the Aztecs and the Incas, the most technologically advanced societies in the Americas. Hernán Cortés, who subdued the Aztecs in 1521, persuaded their leader Moctezuma (also known as Montezuma) to allow Spaniards to enter the great city of Tenochtitlán (now Mexico City). When the conquistadores killed Moctezuma and perpetrated a massacre of unarmed worshippers, the Aztec warriors forcibly expelled the Spaniards from the city, causing severe losses. The Aztecs were clearly a military match for Spanish arms and technology. Yet when the Spaniards regrouped and returned to try to invade Tenochtitlán, likely an impossible task in normal circumstances, they entered a city where almost everyone was sick or dying, probably of smallpox. Bernardino de Sahagún, a friar who accompanied the conquistadores, described walking on the streets of the capital over the bodies of the sick and dying. Despite fierce fighting, Cortés was able to defeat the Aztecs, although the conquest of the outlying areas took years. Francisco Pizarro was likewise able to defeat the Inca Empire in Peru in 1532 with a contingent of only 158 men. Again, he encountered a state unable to resist. When he and his followers arrived in Peru, they found an unpopular usurper on the throne, while the empire was in the throes of a plague, likely also smallpox, that had spread to South America.

Although the Spaniards believed that their conquests had been won through military superiority, they eventually became aware of the devastation that disease was inflicting on the Native communities. They did not rejoice in this knowledge, both because they wanted the Natives alive as laborers and because they aimed to convert them to Catholicism. Consequently they sent doctors into the main towns to try to stem the surge of disease. Because

they were unaware of the actual vectors through which diseases traveled, Spanish medicine had little effect.

Disease traveled more slowly but wreaked the same havoc, through the less densely settled areas in the rest of South, Central, and North America, moving along trade and transportation routes. In New England in 1616, a devastating epidemic killed 90 percent of the Wampanoag Indians, persuading Massasoit, their leader, to seek friendly ties with the *Mayflower* colonists who landed in Massachusetts four years later. His aim in establishing an alliance was to oppose the relatively untouched Narragansett, the traditional enemies of the Wampanoag. This early alliance failed, however, for by the 1670s, the Wampanoag were at war with the English. By then the Narragansett had already met their own scourge in the smallpox epidemic of 1623.

The largely Protestant English settlers in the north responded very differently to the disease epidemics than had the Catholic Spanish settlers in the south. They interpreted the ravages of disease among the Amerindians as the will of God intent on wiping out wicked infidels. They were also not above attempting to further the course of events by practicing germ warfare, and they delivered smallpox-infected blankets to Indians during the 18th century, though the efficacy of these activities is unknown. By the 19th century, this tactic had largely been replaced by attempts to inoculate native groups against smallpox.

By 1700, about two centuries after the first contact, indigenous peoples in the Americas had begun to adapt to the introduced diseases, and by the 1800s, native populations began to recover, though their increase was slowed by the poor economic and social conditions under which Amerindians frequently lived. The depopulation and devastation wrought by disease—in sheer numbers perhaps the deadliest wave of epidemic and plague in human history—had already insured that effective resistance toward the Europeans who had claimed their lands was almost impossible.

Anna Suranyi

FURTHER READING:

Cook, Noble David. *Born to Die: Disease and New World Conquest, 1492–1650*. New York: Cambridge University Press, 1998.

Denevan, William M., ed. *The Native Population of the Americas in 1492.* Madison: University of Wisconsin Press, 1976.

Mann, Charles C. *1491: New Revelations of the Americas Before Columbus.* New York: Knopf, 2005.

Thornton, Russell. *American Indian Holocaust and Survival: A Population History since 1492.* Norman: University of Oklahoma Press, 1990.

Verano, John W., and Douglas H. Ubelaker, eds. *Disease and Demography in the Americas.* Washington, D.C.: Smithsonian Institution Press, 1992.

1590 ◆ LOST COLONY OF ROANOKE

Colonial leader John White was bewildered when he arrived on Roanoke Island on August 18, 1590. All the settlers he had left there three years earlier were gone, and all traces of them missing. Everyone he knew—including his daughter and granddaughter—had vanished. The Lost Colony of Roanoke remains one of the great mysteries of early American history. What had happened to the more than 100 inhabitants of Roanoke? Did Indians massacre them, or might they have been absorbed into an Indian group? Were they enslaved and taken into the interior of North America? Did marauding Spaniards kidnap them? Did they try to escape and drown? Or did environmental factors play a role in their disappearance?

The story of Roanoke actually began in 1584 when Philip Amadas and Arthur Barlowe led the first English expedition to North America. This initial group came not to colonize but to reconnoiter. They chose a site in Albemarle Sound in present-day North Carolina named Roanoke—after the Roanoac Indians who lived in the area—as a sheltered site from which to raid the Spanish treasure fleets. A year later Sir Richard Grenville established a military outpost on the island, but it soon failed because soldiers faced starvation and other hardships, partly because an Englishman had killed Wingina, the Roanoac chief. In retaliation, the Roanoac refused to help the settlers, which caused further suffering and unrest. Confronted with this calamity, Grenville placed some 75 men under the command of Ralph Lane, the new governor of Roanoke Island, and sailed back to England. While away, another leader, Sir Francis Drake, dropped anchor at Roanoke, helped the survivors with supplies, and offered them safe passage home.

FACTBOX

PLACE Roanoke Island, North Carolina

DATE 1587–90

TYPE Unexplained disappearance of colony

DESCRIPTION Upon returning after a three-year absence to the colony at Roanoke Island that he had helped found, John White discovered that all the settlers had vanished, including his daughter and granddaughter.

CASUALTIES More than 100 settlers disappeared.

IMPACT Deterred English attempts at colonization for almost a generation

Another enterprising adventurer, Sir Walter Raleigh—a high-ranking official in Elizabethan England—dispatched another group of settlers to North America. Led by artist John White, the appointed governor, the group arrived on the island on July 22, 1587. Numbering approximately 115, the new group grew a few weeks later when White's daughter gave birth to Virginia Dare, the first English child born in the present-day United States. As the colonists set to work building a palisade, a fort, and other structures, supplies dwindled quickly. White thereupon returned to England in August to secure more provisions. His return to Roanoke, however, was interrupted by the Spanish Armada, which attacked England in 1588, cutting off all overseas travel. Despite England's triumph over the Armada in 1588, the war with Spain seriously depleted England's financial resources, further delaying

White's return to Roanoke. Moreover, the Armada's defeat had weakened the Spanish navy, making it easier and more enticing to raid Spanish ships than to settle permanent colonies. English explorers and privateers like Raleigh became more interested in the pursuit of gold, glory, and adventure in South America than in colonizing North America.

Sailing with a privateering expedition, White left England in March 1590. After plundering several ships in the Caribbean, the privateers sailed toward the North Carolina coast in August in search of the colony. White arrived at Roanoke on August 18, only to find that the original settlers had all disappeared. Not a soul remained. The only clue the search party discovered was the word *Croatoan* carved on the palisade built around the settlement site and the letters *CRO* carved into a nearby tree. Could it be, thought White, that the colonists had moved to Croatoan Island? Or might their disappearance have had something to do with the nearby Croatan Indians? After looking all day, they came up empty-handed. The onset of a hurricane off the Carolina shore caused the group to suspend their search. Giving up on the idea of traveling to Croatoan Island, White's group abandoned further efforts to locate the lost colony. Running low on provisions, White returned to England rather than winter in the Caribbean as he had hoped.

According to the writings of contemporaries such as Thomas Harriot, Arthur Barlowe, and John White, Roanoke seemed at first an ideal place to plant an English colony in the mid-1580s. Tragically, by 1590, that sense of paradise had been lost. As far as historians know, John White never returned to America. Raleigh's interest in colonization also had waned. Although he did send another expedition to America a year later, no effort was made to find the colony. The mystery of the Lost Colony remains unsolved. Some historians have suggested that the colonists, desperate and hungry, abandoned their settlement and joined the Croatan. Others have theorized they were all killed, either by Indians or Spaniards. Recently environmentalists have claimed that a prolonged drought caused the collapse of the Lost Colony. This period of severe droughts, the driest spell in nearly a millennium, created a catastrophic climate that produced a shortage of water, severe reduction in food production, dangerous depletion of fresh water, malnutrition, and death. Without rejecting this theory outright, other historians contend that the colony moved wholesale and was later destroyed. Speculation abounds, yet one thing remains certain: The colonists were never seen again by any Europeans. England would not attempt to colonize America again until the early 17th century.

Timothy C. Coogan

FURTHER READING:

Kupperman, Karen Ordahl. *Roanoke: The Abandoned Colony.* Savage, Md.: Rowman and Littlefield, 1984.

Quinn, David Beers. *Set Fair for Roanoke: Voyages and Colonies, 1584–1606.* Chapel Hill: University of North Carolina Press, 1985.

1609–1610 ◆ STARVING TIME AT JAMESTOWN

On May 13, 1607, 104 English colonists established the first permanent English settlement in North America at Jamestown. By the following spring, only 38 settlers remained alive. The next two years would be no less devastating, with more than 400 colonists dying during the winter of 1609–10. Beset with disease, hunger, and antagonism from Algonquian tribes, the first European settlers at Jamestown faced tremendous adversity. Only a handful survived what became known as the "starving time."

Embarking on their journey to North America in December 1606, 144 intrepid colonists were instructed by the Virginia Company of London, which held the colony's charter, to establish kind relations with the Natives in order to facilitate trade and to secure a steady supply of food. Forty of the would-be settlers died at sea, leaving 104 colonists

FACTBOX

PLACE Jamestown, Virginia

DATE Winter 1609–10

TYPE Famine

DESCRIPTION Nearly all of the colonists at Jamestown, Virginia, died of starvation, and some turned to cannibalism.

CAUSE Lack of proper food supply, an increasing population, and a reluctance on the part of the colonists to cultivate their own food

CASUALTIES Approximately 440 of the colony's 500 inhabitants died.

IMPACT Despite being almost entirely wiped out, the survivors of the starving time in Jamestown became the nucleus of the first permanent English settlement in the Americas.

to establish the Virginia Company's colony in the Americas.

These first English settlers in Jamestown faced many difficulties. The brackish water of the James River—named, like the town itself, for King James of England—was unfit for drinking and was soon polluted by the colonists' waste, which bred diseases such as typhoid and dysentery. Because the colonists relied on trade with the natives and shipments of supplies from England for food, they had given insufficient attention to planting crops. They would pay dearly for their negligence.

In 1608, after barely surviving their first winter in Jamestown, the colonists were resupplied twice with people and provisions. When an additional 400 colonists arrived in August 1609, however, the population increase proved to be an unbearable burden for the burgeoning colony. Short on food, the colonists already at Jamestown were unprepared to support the additional settlers, who arrived starving and without provisions. The stage was set for the starving time of the winter of 1609–10.

During the course of the winter, the settlers ate dogs, cats, horses, rats and other vermin, even leather from their shoes and boots. When this proved insufficient, settlers turned to cannibalism, eventually eating the corpses of their fellow colonists. As one Jamestown official wrote, "One of our Colline murdered his wyfe

Ripped the Childe outt of her woambe and threwe itt into the River and after Chopped the Mother in pieces and salted her for his foode." Of the 500 that inhabited Jamestown in the fall of 1609, only 60 remained in the spring of 1610. All of the survivors had witnessed the deaths of their fellow colonists and no doubt wondered if they would be next. In addition to those who died of hunger, some colonists were executed for stealing provisions. Others were killed by the natives while foraging for food in the woods, and some starving colonists ran away to attempt to attain food from the Natives.

The Algonquian Indians in the region also played a critical role in starving their new neighbors. Seeking to rid the area of any English presence, Powhatan, their leader, ordered the slaughter of the colonists' livestock. The natives also killed colonists who left the settlement to forage for food and refused to provide food for the settlers.

In the spring of 1610, a ship from England arrived to find 60 emaciated colonists. Resolving to rescue these famished souls, the crew took the Jamestown settlers aboard the ship, abandoned the colony, and set sail for England. Their boat crossed paths with that of Captain Brewster and Lord De La Warre, who were on their way to Jamestown with provisions for the colonists. The departing vessel reversed course, returned to the colony, and set to the business of reestablishing a settlement in Jamestown.

The starving time at Jamestown was crucial to the future of North America. Had ships never arrived to save the colonists, Jamestown would have been the second failed attempt of the English to found a colony in the Americas, following the lost colony of Roanoke in the 1580s. The surviving settlers eventually took up the cultivation of tobacco, which provided the colony with an agricultural staple to secure its vitality as an imperial outpost. As the first successful English settlement in North America, Jamestown paved the way for the ensuing migration of people from throughout the world to North America.

See also 1620 FIRST WINTER AT PLYMOUTH.

Allison D. Carter

FURTHER READING:

Price, David A. *Love and Hate in Jamestown.* New York: Knopf, 2003.

Quitt, Martin H. "Trade and Acculturation at Jamestown, 1607–1609: The Limits of Understanding." *William and Mary Quarterly* 52, no. 2 (April 1995): 227–258.

1620 ◆ FIRST WINTER AT PLYMOUTH

The members of Plymouth Colony barely survived their first six months in America. After a slow and arduous journey across 3,000 miles of ocean from England, the settlers were ill-equipped to face the oncoming New England winter. Anchoring in Provincetown Harbor at the tip of Cape Cod in Massachusetts on November 9, 1620, 102 settlers endeavored to survive in a wilderness environment. By the spring of 1621, half of the group had died, including the colony's first governor, John Carver. In many ways, it was a miracle that any of these "Pilgrims"—as William Bradford, Carver's successor, had dubbed the adventurers—survived the first year. Their resiliency and faith were crucial, but Native Americans provided critical assistance when the colony was on the verge of extinction.

The Pilgrims were Separatists, a religious group that had renounced the Church of England. As a fringe sect, they were ostracized in their home village of Scrooby in England. In 1608, the group had fled to Holland, settling in Leiden. Conditions in that new home were better but hardly ideal. Opportunities for advancement were limited, and the Separatists had no desire for their children to become Dutch. Pastor John Robinson and Elder William Brewster, leaders of the band, resolved that God's will dictated migration to America, and the group received a patent from King James to settle the Virginia Colony.

This plan confronted the Pilgrims with two obstacles: capital to finance the journey and a durable ship. Thomas Weston, a London businessman, who represented a group of investors called the Merchant Adventurers, came to their aid, although the arrangement cost the Pilgrims critical time. A departure from Europe by early summer would have put the Pilgrims in America well ahead of winter. But Weston did not secure a dependable merchant ship, the *Mayflower,* until early August, when the Puritans departed from Southampton on the south coast of England for America. Hardly underway, both the *Mayflower* and the *Speedwell,* a smaller vessel commissioned to carry supplies, put in for repairs at Dartmouth, a mere 75 miles west of Southampton. Wasting precious time on this mishap, the *Speedwell* sprang another leak, leading the Pilgrims to abandon

FACTBOX

PLACE Plymouth, Massachusetts

DATE December 1620–March 1621

TYPE Settlers died from disease and starvation.

DESCRIPTION Lacking adequate provisions, starvation and disease took its toll on the colony, killing off more than half the settlers.

CAUSE Departing Europe late in the year and losing a supply ship en route, the Pilgrims lacked time to prepare for the New England winter.

CASUALTIES 52 of the 102 Pilgrims died.

IMPACT The colony's survival created a European foothold in New England, inspired more immigrants to come to America, and gave birth to Thanksgiving, one of the nation's most cherished holidays.

it—and the supplies on board. On September 6, 1620, the *Mayflower* cleared the British Isles.

Facing westerly gales and the Gulf Stream current, the *Mayflower* averaged a mere two miles per hour, a pace that consumed two months for the journey to America. The party landed well north of their intended destination, which had been the head of the Hudson River. Instead, the Pilgrims found themselves off Cape Cod, and on November 9, Master Christopher Jones, the captain of the vessel, decided to remain in Massachusetts. Because their patent from the king applied only to Virginia, the Pilgrims lacked a political agreement on how to administer the colony in Massachusetts. To rectify this, 41 men among the company signed the Mayflower Compact, which established a rule of law for "the general good of the colony." The Pilgrims had reached agreement on civic principles of their new society, but they still faced the harsh reality of New England winters. Seven colonists would die before year was out, most from disease. Dorothy Bradford, wife of William, perished in a freak accident on December 7 when she fell overboard and drowned. Many attributed her death to suicide, for the *Mayflower* was gently anchored at the time of her death.

Pilgrims give thanks before a meal. Half of the initial group that arrived on the *Mayflower* in 1620 died during the first winter. *(Library of Congress)*

On December 15, the colonists sailed from Provincetown Harbor and arrived five days later at an inlet on the far side of Cape Cod, where they planted their community of Plymouth. They opted for a large hillside—adjacent to an enormous rock—which Miles Standish, the Pilgrims' military leader, concluded was defensible to Indian attack. After construction of their village began on Christmas day, the bitter cold of January settled in. Malnourishment developed as freezing temperatures persisted and supplies dwindled. Scurvy ravaged the weakened colony. Forty more people perished between January and March 1621, 17 of them dying in February alone. Disease and exposure were the chief culprits. Plymouth colony's shelters were inadequate to shield their inhabitants from the unyielding cold. New England winters were colder in the 1620s than in the early 21st century, due to grip of the Little Ice Age on the Northern Hemisphere.

Extinction of the colony loomed as a real possibility. Only 18 women had made the journey, and 14 had died by the end of March. Three families—the Turners, Tinkers, and Rigsdales—had been completely wiped out. Recording this bleak moment in the colony's history, William Bradford wrote: "of all the hundred odd persons, scarcely fifty remained. . . . In the time of worse distress, there were but six or seven sound persons, who, to their great commendation be it spoken, spared no pains night or day." Moreover, the possibility of an Indian attack was a constant concern. By March, the Pilgrims lacked enough healthy bodies to mount a defense from an attack. When the alarm bell sounded, stricken men were literally carried from their sickbeds, propped against a tree, and armed with a rifle. Plymouth's fate hung in the balance.

Native Americans could have destroyed the settlement. Why they chose to help the beleaguered colonists is one of the more serendipitous surprises of American history. Massasoit, sachem of the neighboring Pokanoket, was responsible for this decision.

In March 1621, Massasoit sent two delegates to speak with the settlers. The envoy included Squanto, who spoke English because he had been kidnapped and taken to Europe years earlier but ultimately returned to Massachusetts. Massasoit determined that peace was the most prudent course, especially if European immigration continued, which he suspected it would. Regardless of his reasons, the Pilgrims were soon beholden to the Pokanoket, who showed the Pilgrims effective techniques of farming and fishing.

Although half the colonists had died, the spring brought warm weather and, with Pokanoket aid, the Pilgrims began to plant crops. In the fall of 1621, the Pokanoket and Pilgrims celebrated their friendship with a lavish feast. More than 200 years later, Americans began an annual commemoration of this event called Thanksgiving. But Massasoit's hope for peaceful coexistence faded as the immigration from Europe proceeded. Settlement of Boston commenced in 1630, and the newcomers' appetite for land would ultimately destroy the Native Americans' way of life. However, for the small group of separatists, an early alliance was possible. Without it, the Plymouth Colony never would have survived.

See also 1609–1610 STARVING TIME AT JAMESTOWN.

David G. O'Donnell

FURTHER READING:

Bradford, William. *Of Plymouth Plantation*. Edited by Samuel Eliot Morison. New York: Knopf, 1970.

Philbrick, Nathaniel. *Mayflower*. New York: Viking, 2006.

Willison, George F. *Saints and Strangers*. New York: Reynal and Hitchcock, 1945.

1622 ◆ MASSACRE AT JAMESTOWN

On the morning of March 22, 1622, Algonquian Indians attacked English colonists at Jamestown, murdering at least 347 of the settlers and wounding many others in an unexpected assault. Provoked by English incursion onto their native lands and the unaccommodating behavior of whites, the attack had major implications for the future relations between Indians and the English. Horrific in its violence and ferocity, the massacre of 1622 remains one of the most formative events in the history of Native and English relations in North America.

Prior to the establishment of the Jamestown colony in 1607, the English expressed both hopes of "civilizing" and fears of clashing with Native Americans. Their belief in their right to trade with natives was coupled with an arrogant assertion of their moral and cultural superiority over the Indian "savages." The English saw the natives as a threat to the safety and prosperity of the colony and as a great hindrance to their progress.

The Natives were willing to trade with the English but resisted settler attempts to convert them to Christianity. American Indians were concerned about the growing English population settled on

---

FACTBOX

PLACE Jamestown, Virginia

DATE March 22, 1622

TYPE Massacre

DESCRIPTION The Algonquian Indians slaughtered hundreds of English settlers at Jamestown.

CAUSE Accelerating English settlement on Indian lands and the settlers' disrespect for native religious beliefs and cultural practices

CASUALTIES At least 347 settlers died in the Indian attack; famine and epidemic in the following year claimed another 500–600 lives.

IMPACT The massacre shattered any hopes for a peaceful coexistence between Native Americans and the English and led to the complete separation of the two groups.

---

their lands, especially when it impinged on planting and hunting grounds. This tension caused sporadic warfare between Natives and the English from 1607 until a peace was reached in 1614.

A rapid rise in the colonists' population, however, led to increased encroachment on Native lands. Between 1619 and 1621, 42 ships arrived from England, raising the population of colonists to more than 1,200 people, an alarming increase since the arrival of the first 104 settlers in 1607. When Powhatan, leader of the Algonquian tribes of the region, died in 1618, he was eventually succeeded by his brother, Opechancanough. Expecting assistance from neighboring tribes, Opechancanough believed that a great assault on the colonists would be the Indians' best hope for regaining control of their lands and ridding Virginia of any English presence.

In a surprise attack at the beginning of spring in 1622, Native Americans killed at least 347 colonists, one-fourth of the colonists' population. The attack had other harrowing consequences for both the English and the Indians. Many white settlers died in the assault, and those who remained were reluctant to tend crops, as fighting between the natives and the English continued. Manpower devoted to defense diminished the labor force available to work in the fields. In face of the hostilities, colonists abandoned their far-flung plantations, consolidating their settlements in order to better defend themselves. Famine followed on the heels of these developments. The scarcity of food and epidemic disease killed another 500 to 600 people in the year after the massacre.

The colonists mounted a vicious counterattack against the natives in a campaign designed to eliminate the Indians from the entire region. A shipment of armaments from England, which arrived soon after the attack, facilitated this retaliatory war. While it is unclear how many, if any, Native Americans were killed in the initial massacre of 1622, hundreds died in the colonists' counterattack. After a decade of warfare, disease, and famine, a peace treaty was signed in 1632, which effectively separated Native and English lands.

The 1622 attack on the Jamestown settlement signaled the demise of the Virginia Company of London, who held the colony's charter. Criticized by the Crown for continuing to enlist new colonists from England in spite of food shortages and rampant disease in the new colony, the Virginia Company was disbanded and Virginia became the first royal colony in 1624. The massacre also led to a major shift in the policy toward Natives in English North America. English colonists abandoned attempts to cohabit peacefully with the natives. The news from Jamestown affected the colonists further north in Plymouth and, after its establishment in 1630, the Massachusetts Bay Colony, who were more cautious in their relations with neighboring Indians. The 1622 massacre was instrumental in causing English colonists to view all natives as enemies. Thereafter, white settlers and Natives withdrew to separate locales throughout the colonies, establishing a pattern for Indian-English relations that continued for decades and centuries.

See also 1704 DEERFIELD MASSACRE.

Allison D. Carter

The travails of European colonization of North America were emphasized by the massacre at Jamestown in 1622 when Native Americans killed at least 347 settlers. *(New York Public Library)*

FURTHER READING:

Price, David A. *Love and Hate in Jamestown.* New York: Knopf, 2003.

Vaughan, Alden T. "'Expulsion of the Salvages': English Policy and the Virginia Massacre of 1622." *William and Mary Quarterly* 35, no. 1 (January 1978): 57–84.

1675 ◆ KING PHILIP'S WAR

There have been certain times in American history when neighbors who had for years peacefully coexisted suddenly turned on each other with malice. King Philip's War (1675–76) is one particularly brutal example of warfare informed by unremitting cultural difference. The war echoes through American history because of the outrages committed on both sides, the cultural impact of the war experience on participants, and the portent of an evolving and expansive New England society where Indians would be made subject to colonial rule and culturally invisible.

The Wampanoag, an Algonquian tribe based in southeastern New England, had engaged in trade and diplomacy with English colonists for decades. An important sachem, Massasoit, had helped the Pilgrims survive their early years and negotiated a far-reaching peace with the Plymouth colony in 1621. He had also obtained symbolic European names for his two sons, Wamsutta, who became known as Alexander, and Metacom, who became known as Philip. It was this second son, Philip, who in 1675 initiated the first large-scale pan-Indian offensive against English colonists in New England. Father and son held different views on the expanding presence of the English in Wampanoag lives. Whereas Massasoit had fostered an alliance with Plymouth to counter his tribe's traditional enemies, Philip nursed grievances that were increasingly shared by other New England tribes. Massasoit's alliance with Plymouth and their tribe's increasing dependence on English trade goods combined to increase the pressure to sell tribal lands. This was exacerbated by the failure of colonial authorities to compel settlers to rein in their livestock, which competed with wild animals for forest nuts and trampled native fields. As the Wampanoag faced a looming subsistence crisis, Plymouth attempted with greater frequency to place limits on Indian autonomy, directing that Wampanoag land sales be made exclusively to Plymouth and calling for Philip's warriors to disarm.

King Philip's War began in the context of struggles over trade, land, and sovereignty that turned violent as a result of the John Sassamon case. Sassamon was a Wampanoag Christian convert and interpreter,

FACTBOX

PLACE New England

DATE 1675–76

TYPE Brutal warfare and massacre

DESCRIPTION King Philip's War was a brief but particularly bloody and consequential conflict.

CAUSE Though relations between the Wampanoag and the English colonists had deteriorated for a number of years, the immediate cause of war was the death of John Sassamon, a Christian Indian and interpreter. Plymouth judges tried and convicted three Wampanoag Indians for his death and hanged two of them, prompting the tribe to attack colonists.

CASUALTIES Roughly 4,000 Algonquian and 2,000 colonists (and allies) died, making King Philip's War per capita the most devastating in American history.

COST A Crown agent estimated that colonists spent £100,000 to prosecute the war and suffered £150,000 in property losses.

IMPACT The Wampanoag and their allies were virtually destroyed as tribal units. The tactics employed by both sides led to a deepening racial division in colonial New England; disease and the decimation of belligerent tribes opened much of southeastern and central New England to further European expansion.

a schoolteacher in missionary John Eliot's praying towns—communities of Indian converts—and subsequently secretary to Philip. In December 1674, Sassamon reported to Plymouth authorities that Philip was reaching out diplomatically to other tribes and planning to attack colonial settlements. Soon thereafter, he was found dead. Despite the fact that he was an Indian, and capital cases involving Indian victims were customarily left to the Indian justice system, Plymouth quickly tried and convicted three Wampanoag, hanging two of them on June 8, 1675. In a brief, fruitless round of diplomacy, Philip maintained his own innocence in Sassamon's death and refused Plymouth's demand to disarm. Then on June 24, a small band of Wampanoag attacked the outlying Plymouth town of Swansea, just 10 miles from Philip's home of Mount Hope and long an object of dispute. It is not known whether Philip ordered the attack, but the war quickly escalated, as Plymouth called on Massachusetts Bay and Connecticut for assistance. Philip's relatively small force escaped the colonial army's tentative early forays and traveled to the Massachusetts frontier, convincing the Nipmuck and some smaller Connecticut Valley tribes to join the rebellion.

Philip and his allies achieved many early victories, surprised and sacked nearly two dozen frontier communities, and terrified colonists with some of their tactics, including taking scalps and captives and torturing victims and, at times, settlers' livestock, a symbol of the threat of English colonization to their way of life. As Indian victories mounted, colonial anxiety rose to fever pitch. Neutral "praying Indians" were placed in internment camps, and colonial leaders eyed with suspicion the neutral Narragansett tribe of Rhode Island. The first colonial victory was the "Great Swamp Fight," directed against the main Narragansett community in southwestern Rhode Island. Guided by warriors from the Mohegan and Pequot tribes, allied to Connecticut, the colonists attacked on December 19, 1675, firing Narragansett homes and their fort, killing roughly 100 warriors and between 300 and 1,000 women and children at a cost of 220 casualties. It was a controversial victory against a neutral tribe that had reportedly harbored Wampanoag refugees, and it drove the desperate Narragansett to join Philip's rebellion.

The Algonquian resistance survived through the spring of 1676, but by the summer their cause was doomed, in large part due to the decision of the Iroquois League Mohawk of upstate New York to deny them aid and instead to attack their hereditary allies. The Mohegan Indians of Connecticut also provided key assistance to the colonies' army. On the run and unable to feed their families, waves of surviving Algonquian turned themselves in to colonial authorities—the ones who did so earlier could hire out their services as guides, but many of those who surrendered at war's end were sold into slavery. Some chose to flee northward where the war continued in sporadic form under the aegis of the Abenaki and the French for another eight decades. Philip returned to his homeland but was captured and killed in August 1676. The brief war destroyed the Wampanoag, Nipmuck, and Narragansett tribes, and it haunted New Englanders for years. Mary Rowlandson, for example, like many other captives, returned to a shattered community and wrote of her experiences, creating the first American captivity narrative. Ministers also pondered the providential meaning of the conflict for New England's future—some interpreted the war as punishment for their society's moral decay, while others were confident that "civilization" would prevail over "savagery." All agreed that the war marked a watershed in New England's history.

That Philip would utterly fail in his quest to maintain his tribe's autonomy does not lessen the significance of "King Philip's War" in American history. Roughly 4,000 Algonquian and 2,000 colonists (and allies) died, making King Philip's War per capita the most devastating war in American history. A Crown agent estimated that the colonists spent £100,000 to prosecute the war and suffered £150,000 in property losses. For the historian looking backward, the war marks in bold relief the frontier cycles of Native American accommodation, resistance, and defeat set against a web of ideas that would crystallize in the minds and pens of Puritans such as Increase Mather, which resonate through American history—that Native Americans were different, inferior, and savage. Whereas Massasoit had celebrated with the pilgrims at their first thanksgiving in 1621, his son Philip met a different fate. On August 17, 1676, after John Cotton's thanksgiving day sermon in Plymouth, Philip's severed head was carried into town by military hero Benjamin Church and staked to a pole where it stayed for decades. Though the aftermath of war was a dark and dangerous time for New England's Indians, historians have begun to outline the myriad ways in which Native Americans remained a part of New England's social landscape, with an evolving sense of Indian identity, in communities such as Natick, Mashpee, and Stockbridge. But King Philip's War further restricted the choices available to New England's native peoples, especially those left behind a westward-moving frontier.

Michael Gunther

FURTHER READING:
Drake, James. *King Philip's War: Civil War in New England, 1675–1676.* Amherst: University of Massachusetts Press, 1999.

Kawashima, Yasuhide. *Igniting King Philip's War: The John Sassamon Murder Trial.* Lawrence: University Press of Kansas, 2001.

Lepore, Jill. *The Name of War: King Philip's War and the Origins of American Identity.* New York: Knopf, 1999.

1676 ◆ BACON'S REBELLION

On June 23, 1676, Nathaniel Bacon and a rebel army of 500 colonists stormed Jamestown, the capital of Virginia. Under the threat of loaded muskets, Governor William Berkeley and the House of Burgesses conceded to Bacon's populist demands. The legislative assembly passed a series of acts, granting Bacon full authority to battle Native Americans, extending voting rights, and dismantling monopoly on trade. Governor Berkeley branded the newly appointed General Bacon a rebel and ordered his capture. Bacon then issued a "Declaration of the People," which reflected farmers' cries of economic corruption and neglect within the Berkeley governorship. He later burned Jamestown. Berkeley could not amass sufficient military support to suppress the rebellion until the arrival of the English navy. With Bacon's death in October, Berkeley finally regained control over Virginia in January 1677 and hanged 23 of the rebels. Though short-lived, Bacon's rebellion showed the extent to which impoverished colonists, mainly black and white farmers, servants, and slaves, were willing to challenge a government they deemed oppressive.

Virginia's economy stagnated in the 1670s. As Berkeley noted in 1676, "six parts of seaven at least are Poore Endebted Discontented and Armed." Berkeley and the wealthy elite, known as the Tidewater gentry, owned the best farmland in the tidewater areas, leaving commoners to farm less prosperous land on the frontier. The majority of the population—small farmers, indentured servants, and slaves—lived in poverty. Dry summers, hurricanes, and hail led to low production of tobacco—the colony's cash crop—which in turn made it difficult for colonists to pay the numerous taxes required by the colonial government; competing colonial markets in Maryland and the Carolinas lowered the selling price of tobacco, while England's mercantile economy raised the price of goods sent to Virginia.

FACTBOX

PLACE Jamestown, Virginia

DATE June 23, 1676–January 16, 1677

TYPE Rebellion

DESCRIPTION Thousands of impoverished farmers, servants, and slaves supported Nathaniel Bacon's calls for rebellion against the Virginia government. Bacon invaded Jamestown to force Governor William Berkeley and the House of Burgesses to address colonists' grievances. After Bacon died suddenly, Berkeley ended the popular rebellion, with help sent from England, six months after it began.

CAUSE The lack of protection offered by the colonial government against frontier Native Americans, coupled with rampant poverty throughout Virginia

CASUALTIES 23 rebels hanged

IMPACT The popular rebellion galvanized future government support of western expansion against Native Americans and of an increase in slaves to alleviate economic woes of poor white settlers.

The influx of colonial farmers along the frontier, and the harsh economic conditions they faced, strained relations with Native Americans on whose lands they were encroaching. Colonists shared the perception that Berkeley's policies with the Native Americans focused not on the safety of the frontier populace but on balancing relations in order to preserve the Tidewater gentry's monopoly on beaver trade. Consequently, frontiersmen typically ignored Berkeley's nonaggression policies, and Natives retaliated in equal or greater force.

In July 1675, a clash between the Doeg Indians and Thomas Mathew, a plantation owner in the Northern Neck region of Virginia, started a chain of reciprocal raids. Thirty militiamen went after a Doeg war party, killing 24 Natives from both the Doeg and Susquehannock tribes. A surge of violence followed, killing 300 colonists, including men, women, and children, by the spring of 1676.

In March, Berkeley ordered the construction of 10 forts to defend the frontier. Berkeley and the legislative assembly understood the concerns of the colonists, but they also wanted peace with the Susquehannock. This policy did nothing to allay fears on the frontier; rather, it enraged farmers, who viewed the forts as expensive and useless.

Nathaniel Bacon, an educated Englishman who had arrived in Henrico County, Virginia, in 1674, shared the fear and frustration of his frontier neighbors. Bacon vowed to lead them against the Natives, with or without Berkeley's consent. Bacon quickly became a chosen leader of the common people, and by May, hundreds enlisted to join his campaigns against the Pamunkey and Occaneechee tribes. By June 1, Bacon was elected a burgess by Henrico County.

Berkeley declared Bacon a rebel, and on June 10, Bacon was brought to Jamestown as a prisoner. Upon hearing of his capture, nearly 2,000 supporters gathered in Jamestown; however, they dispersed after hearing that Berkeley had pardoned Bacon and promised a commission to battle natives. Bacon never received his commission, and on June 23, he entered Jamestown with a volunteer rebel army of 400 infantry and more than 100 cavalry.

With Bacon's army outside the statehouse, the House of Burgesses passed a series of acts addressing the economic oppression and general neglect of Berkeley's governorship. These acts set out the means for fighting Natives with an army instead of forts, led by newly appointed General Bacon, and funded, in part, by the spoils of war with Natives; the right of all free men to vote; limitations on trade with Natives; and term limitations on county executives, mainly sheriffs.

With newly granted authority, Bacon left Jamestown to continue war against the Native Americans, gathering nearly 1,300 men by August. Berkeley simultaneously raised a small army to capture Bacon, again proclaiming him a rebel, but

Bacon responded by issuing a "Declaration of the People." He declared Berkeley and several others as enemies and gave a list of reasons for rebellion. In late August, Bacon headed back to Jamestown, plundering the Tidewater areas along the way. He found that Berkeley had fortified Jamestown. After a five-day siege, Berkeley and his men retreated, and on the night of September 19, Bacon burned Jamestown.

By October, Bacon had the upper hand: He had support from the assembly and the majority of Virginians. The rebellion abruptly changed, however, when Bacon died of dysentery in late October. With help from the English navy, Berkeley ended the rebellion by January. In the following months, the remaining Bacon followers were captured, slaves and servants were returned to their owners, and 23 rebels were hanged.

With Jamestown in ruins, Virginia made Williamsburg its new, temporary capital. But Bacon's rebellion had a far wider impact on colonial America. No factor was more catalytic than the violent relations between settlers and Native Americans, but economic and political oppression fueled Bacon's rebellion. The popular uprising demonstrated to England and the colonies that rebellion could facilitate change. Colonists ignored government policy, forced new elections, and, after invading the capital, forced legislation to address grievances. Their example galvanized future government support of western expansion and increased the influx of slaves. Slave labor would alleviate the economic woes of poor white settlers but at the expense of blacks. Poor whites, situated above slaves and allied to the government in pursuing western expansion, were now less likely to rebel. A hundred years would pass before another uprising, the American Revolution, echoed the spirit of Bacon's rebellion.

Richard A. Fournier

FURTHER READING:

Carson, Jane. *Bacon's Rebellion, 1676–1976.* Virginia: Jamestown Foundation, 1976.

Washburn, Wilcomb. *The Governor and the Rebel: A History of Bacon's Rebellion in Virginia.* Chapel Hill: University of North Carolina Press, 1957.

Webb, Stephen Saunders. *1676: The End of American Independence* New York: Knopf, 1984.

1692 ◆ SALEM WITCHCRAFT TRIALS

The Salem hysteria far surpassed earlier episodes of New England witchcraft. Prior to the events of 1692, records document less than 100 cases of New England witchcraft. They typically involved one or two accused witches who were often brought to trial. Most were acquitted. From 1638, when the first New Englander was put to death for witchcraft, to 1692, Puritans executed a total of 16 convicted witches (11 in Connecticut and five in Massachusetts). During the Salem hysteria, 185 individuals were accused of witchcraft. The web of accusations spread from Salem to neighboring Essex County towns in northeastern Massachusetts. Before the hysteria ran its course, 19 convicted witches were hanged, one accused witch died from the weight of stones placed on his chest to force him to testify, and four adults and several children perished while in custody. The unprecedented outburst of 1692 persists as the most infamous event in New England colonial history.

The key events that exploded into fears of a demonic conspiracy against Massachusetts unfolded over the first 10 months of 1692. Several young girls who had experimented with fortune-telling began to behave as if they were tormented. They fell into fits and complained that they were being choked, pinched, and pricked. The odd behavior originated in the home of Reverend Samuel Parris, minister of Salem Village. His nine-year-old daughter and her 11-year old cousin were the first to be afflicted. The local doctor concluded that the girls were bewitched. They were not directly possessed by Satan, he claimed, but the victims of his agents—human witches. Parris relied on traditional Puritan remedies for bewitchment: prayer and fasting. Yet Parris, a former businessman from Barbados in the West Indies, was not a skilled pastor but a divisive figure whose actions contributed to what soon became a witch hunt.

The minister and other local authorities pressed the girls to identify their tormenters. In February 1692, the girls named three women, including Parris's West Indian slave Tituba. She was beaten by the minister for involvement in occult activities—namely, fortune-telling—that had occurred in his home. At a preliminary public hearing in March, Tituba, fearful

of the minister's wrath, confessed. More important, she led an enthralled audience in the Salem Village meetinghouse through the byways and back alleys of the town's diabolical underground. Clandestine meetings and dark rituals flourished side by side with pious worship. Strange apparitions threatened to harm Tituba if she did not serve as Satan's agent or reward her if she did. She confirmed that her two codefendants were practicing witches and claimed that the circle of black magic extended well beyond them.

This preliminary hearing marked a turning point toward hysteria. Tituba's testimony and the girls' public display of their torment—they would writhe and twitch incoherently—during the inquiry suggested that Salem and Massachusetts confronted a demonic conspiracy. The three accused witches were packed off to jail. Still, a widening ring of girls, mostly between 12 and 19 years of age, became afflicted with the symptoms of bewitchment. Accusations and arrests in Salem surged throughout the spring. The hysteria then spread to the nearby Essex

---

FACTBOX

PLACE Salem, Massachusetts, and nearby Essex County towns of Andover and Gloucester

DATE January–October 1692

TYPE Witchcraft hysteria

DESCRIPTION A hysterical fear led several communities to accuse 185 individuals of witchcraft, many of whom were tortured, tried, and killed.

CAUSE Amid local conflict, political instability in Massachusetts, and threatening Indian warfare, girls' accusations of witchcraft spread quickly and led to trials and executions.

CASUALTIES 185 accused; 19 executed; 1 crushed to death; 4 adults and several children died in prison; and others accused fled from Massachusetts.

IMPACT Last major outbreak of witchcraft accusations in American history

During the Salem witchcraft trials in 1692, 19 people were found guilty and executed. *(Library of Congress)*

County towns of Andover and Gloucester. Afflicted Salem girls visited Andover in July to assist in the detection of witches. Forty accusations emerged from Andover alone. The traditional focus on Salem, some historians believe, may obscure how the hysteria acquired the dimensions of a much broader Essex County witchcraft crisis.

The trial and execution of witches began in June and extended into September. Some accused witches confessed to avoid the gallows (those who admitted to being witches were not executed). Such confessions buttressed popular belief in a satanic conspiracy. But many accused witches proclaimed their innocence in front of the court convened by the colony to hear the cases and were found guilty. The final and largest group of executions occurred in September, when eight convicted witches were put to death.

Jails remained full of accused witches. The net of accusation reached into the ranks of merchants and ministers. Even the governor's wife was identified as a witch. As summer shaded into fall, some civic and religious leaders began to assert their doubts about accusations and executions. Alarmed by the continuing empowerment of young girls and the execution of pious individuals, ministers raised questions about the use of so-called spectral evidence: Under affliction, witchcraft victims identified the image, or specter, of their tormenters. Ministers had always cautioned that Satan, to sow havoc among godly people, could use the specter of an innocent person. In his *Cases of Conscience Concerning Evil Spirits Personating Men* (1693), a sermon first delivered to fellow ministers in October 1692, prominent clergyman Increase Mather stressed, "It were better that ten suspected witches should escape than that one innocent person should be condemned." The governor then halted further arrests and dissolved the court.

A new, more cautious court convened in January 1693. Forty-nine accused witches were acquitted. The jury convicted only three women, but the governor reprieved them. The hysteria had receded well before April when the governor released the last of the accused from jail. Though belief in witchcraft persisted, no one was ever again executed for the crime in New England.

Though we know much about the witchcraft hysteria of 1692, it remains a complex event that, in many respects, has resisted satisfactory explanation. The behavior of individuals fueled the outburst: Reverend Parris, Tituba, and the afflicted girls. Some historians have viewed the hysterical or fraudulent accusations of the girls against older females as evidence of generational divisions and stress in Salem and nearby communities. Yet in 17th-century New England and Europe, women consistently occupied the center of witch hunts. Of the 185 accused witches in the 1692 hysteria, more than three-quarters were women. Courts tried more than seven females for every male. The gender gap among the executed (14 women and 5 men) would have been wider if accused and convicted women had not confessed to avoid the hangman, died in custody, or been reprieved. Witchcraft accusations had long been used to stigmatize women who deviated from the Puritan idea of a good wife, women who were quarrelsome, single, or widows who failed to remarry. Yet Puritan-Christian belief held that women were "weak vessels"; this understanding of female nature meant that all women were susceptible to Satan's intrigues.

The accusations against women—and men who were often related to them—originated in a community that claimed more than its share of common local strife. Salem was divided between the "Town," the commercial maritime settlement on the coast, and the "Village," the heavily agricultural backcountry five miles to the west. Longstanding conflict festered in Salem, particularly in the Village where the hysteria gained momentum before it spread to other Essex County towns. Historians have noted that accusations followed an east-west geography that outlined the distress within Salem. Many accusers clustered around the Village in the west. Alleged witches often resided in the east, within Salem Town and especially in the section of the Village closest to it.

Other tensions have often been cited as contributing to the rise and spread of the hysteria. The upheaval occurred during a period of political and military turmoil. England revoked Massachusetts's charter in 1684, and the Crown appointed a royal governor to oversee all of New England. This political arrangement collapsed in 1689, and Massachusetts was left without a new charter, which did not arrive until May 1692. Uncertainty over Massachusetts's political future added to the smoldering local strife in Salem. Then, too, a Native American uprising in northern New England, starting in 1688, further unnerved the inhabitants of Essex County. Refugees from frontier warfare fled south to Salem and other Essex County towns, inflaming fears of a Satanic conspiracy against New England. References to links between Indian warfare and witchcraft recur in the records of the hysteria. After all, Puritans viewed Natives and their powwows, or holy men, as New England's original devil worshippers.

The hysteria had one lasting historical consequence for New England. The notorious episode has often led people to view Puritan New England through the exceptional events of 1692, branding the region as a distinctive blend of superstition, intolerance, and persecution. However, it also signaled the end of an era: While scattered accusations of witchcraft continued throughout the 18th century, no major outbreak ever again convulsed the colonies.

Joseph Conforti

FURTHER READING:

Boyer, Paul, and Stephen Nissenbaum. *Salem Possessed: The Social Origins of Witchcraft.* Cambridge, Mass.: Harvard University Press, 1974.

Hoffer, Peter Charles. *The Devil's Disciples: Makers of the Salem Witchcraft Trials.* Baltimore: Johns Hopkins University Press, 1996.

Norton, Mary Beth. *In the Devil's Snare: The Salem Witchcraft Crisis of 1692.* New York: Knopf, 2002.

1704 ◆ DEERFIELD MASSACRE

In the early morning hours of February 29, 1704, French and Indian raiders launched a surprise attack on the English settlement of Deerfield, Massachusetts. The attackers burned the village, killed several dozen inhabitants, and captured 112 men, women, and children whom they led on a forced march through the wilderness to New France (present-day Canada). While the raid on Deerfield was one of the most devastating assaults on a colonial village in all of New England, New York, and New France, it was one small episode in a global contest between Britain and France and one event in the violent struggle between Native peoples in the Northeast and European colonists.

For the French, the 1704 Deerfield raid was an opportunity to impede the expansion of the British empire in North America and to confirm alliances with Native peoples who helped them control the fur trade and supported them in their conflicts with the vastly more populous British colonies. For certain Native peoples, such as the Abenaki, an assault on Deerfield offered an opportunity to strike back at the British invaders of their homeland who were intent on acquiring more land to expand their empire. Each Native group also had its own economic and political goals and individual motives for the raid, including conflicts over specific lands, desires for captives, and the chance to acquire plunder.

Located on the western edge of New England and situated at the crossroads of major Native trails, the frontier town of Deerfield was a convenient target for Native and French hostilities with the British. Deerfield and many nearby towns had been attacked before, and in the fall of 1703, there were fresh rumors of an allied French-Native assault on Deerfield. A few days before the raid, the village repaired the 10-foot-high palisade that protected its

FACTBOX

PLACE Deerfield, Massachusetts

DATE February 29, 1704

TYPE Raid on a British village by a coalition of French and Native American forces

DESCRIPTION A surprise attack by French and Native American raiders who killed 41 Deerfield inhabitants, plundered and set fire to homes, and forced more than a hundred captives on a 300-mile trek to New France (Canada)

CAUSE One battle in the global contest between French and British empires and an attack by Native Americans who had been forced from their homeland by British settlers

CASUALTIES As many as 73 died: 41 Deerfield defenders and six raiders in the attack; 23 to 26 captives died on the forced march to New France (Canada).

IMPACT Intensified the violent struggle between European colonists and Native peoples in the Northeast

275 inhabitants and welcomed garrison soldiers to help them defend the town, if necessary.

A French lieutenant named Jean Baptiste Hertel de Rouville (who viewed expeditions such as this as a route to promotion) led the raiding party of 48 French soldiers and militiamen and 200 to 250 Native warriors from five independent nations: Abenaki of Odanak/St. Francis; Huron of Lorette; Mohawk of Kahnawake; Pennacook; and Iroquois of the Mountain. Two hours before dawn on February 29, 1704, Rouville, who had participated in similar raids under his father's leadership, led the attackers as they advanced quietly on snowshoes toward the town across snow-covered meadows. They evaded the sleeping watchman, climbed up snowdrifts banked against the palisade, and dropped silently onto snowbanks on the inside. The allies planned to surround all 20 houses and then attack, but they lost the advantage of surprise when discipline broke down among the large and diverse raiding party and a shot rang out—no one knows who fired it—that awoke villagers. With axes and hatchets, the raiders broke open doors and windows; Deerfield men grabbed armaments and fired from their windows.

Some escaped, running to nearby towns for help, and a few armed inhabitants battled for hours. In the end, 41 English and six raiders lay dead.

Raiders ransacked homes and rounded up families to claim captives. After killing those who resisted or were too young to survive the grueling trip north, they seized 112 of the village's men, women, and children. They killed livestock and set fire to the village center, destroying half the town. Alerted by the glow of the fires, a relief party of British militiamen from nearby towns arrived and battled the retreating attackers to little effect.

Captive-taking had deep cultural roots in Native cultures and was often a tradition of warfare. Natives sought captives to adopt as an act of mourning their own dead, to use as slaves, to kill in a ritual, or for monetary ransom. Since captive-taking was the primary reason that some Natives participated in the raid, they made every effort to keep them alive. For New Englanders on the frontier, the threat of captivity was a fact of life.

The captives were marched 20 miles each day over snow-covered wooded hills and along icy rivers. Those who could not keep up, particularly young children and pregnant women or those who had just given birth, were killed. Between 23 and 26 of the captives perished and 86 to 89 survived the punishing 300-mile trek to Native and French communities in New France (present-day Canada), where the French and Natives competed for them. Eventually, two-thirds returned to New England, many after intense negotiations by officials in Boston and in New France. Of the one-third of captives who remained permanently in New France, most converted from Protestantism to Catholicism and approximately 16 stayed with the French. Only seven captives are known to have remained in Native villages.

In the short term, the raid was a success for New France, a small victory in a European war—the War of the Spanish Succession (1701–13)—that had spread across the Atlantic to the French and British colonies where it eventually became known as Queen Anne's War. In addition, the raid reinforced France's alliances with Native groups, sharpened the conflict between the British and Native peoples, and created widespread fear among the British of similar attacks. That fear drove the British to embrace their empire more intensely and to begin counterattacks, which in turn put their French enemies on the defensive.

One hundred years after the Deerfield raid, the event became a symbol of Native savagery and aggression. To justify 19th-century westward expansion and Indian removal, Americans recalled times when white settlers were the victims of brutal Indian and French attacks. Thus, the 1704 raid that New Englanders had called the "destruction of Deerfield" (emphasis on the physical devastation of the village) for a century was termed a massacre, and the barbarous killing and capture of Deerfield's innocents became the focus. The name "Deerfield massacre" was fixed in the early 1900s as preservers and pro-moters of "Old Deerfield" sought to commemorate and revive a colonial past in which their ancestors, despite great adversity, "civilized" New England.

See also 1622 MASSACRE AT JAMESTOWN.

Elizabeth M. Sharpe

FURTHER READING:

Demos, John. *The Unredeemed Captive: A Family Story from Early America.* New York: Knopf, 1994.

Haefeli, Evan, and Kevin Sweeney. *Captors and Captives: The 1704 French and Indian Raid on Deerfield.* Amherst: University of Massachusetts Press, 2003.

1721 ◆ SMALLPOX EPIDEMIC

The Boston smallpox epidemic of 1721–22 was the most severe health crisis that city experienced during the 18th century. Out of a population of 10,700, more than 900 fled the disease, 5,889 came down with smallpox, and 844 died. The epidemic accounted for three-fourths of all deaths in Boston for 1721. However, the epidemic has earned a place in medical history not for its severity but rather for being the first large-scale demonstration of the effectiveness of smallpox inoculation in the Western world. The procedure consisted of inserting a small amount of smallpox matter into the body to induce immunity. Inoculation reduced the average death rate for smallpox from 10 to 25 percent to about 2 percent, but it was a highly dangerous procedure because it employed the live virus which could start or intensify an epidemic.

On April 22, 1721, the British naval vessel HMS *Seahorse* arrived in Boston with one of its crew suffering from smallpox and another about to come down with it. By June, the city was confronted with a full-blown epidemic. On June 6, the influential but controversial Congregational minister Cotton Mather, who had taken a strong interest in smallpox inoculation, wrote a circular letter to Boston's 10 doctors "requesting" that they meet for a "consultation" as to whether they should conduct a "tryl" of inoculation. At this time, Boston had the best educated and most professionalized clergy of the major colonial urban centers and the least professionally conscious

---

FACTBOX

PLACE Boston and neighboring towns

DATE June 1721–February 1722

TYPE Smallpox epidemic

DESCRIPTION A devastating smallpox epidemic in Boston

CAUSE The epidemic was triggered by the arrival of infected seamen on a British naval vessel.

CASUALTIES 844 deaths

IMPACT The epidemic helped convince doctors and others of the efficacy of smallpox vaccination and saw the first large-scale use of inoculation (287 inoculees with six deaths) in the Western world.

---

doctors. Only the recently arrived Scottish-born and European-educated William Douglass had earned a medical degree, and it was he who led the opposition to the use of inoculation during this epidemic.

The city's doctors ignored Mather's letter. Persisting in his quest, Mather wrote to the physician and surgeon Zabdiel Boylston on June 24, asking him to give "mature deliberation" to whether or not he should test the procedure on his own. Both Mather and Boylston were highly apprehensive that their children would contract smallpox at this time. Two days later, Boylston, who had already had smallpox, successfully inoculated his six-year-old son, Thomas, and two of his slaves. He performed these and his other inoculations in Boston at his home in crowded Dock Square in the heart of the city. While fully aware of the highly contagious nature of smallpox, he did little or nothing to isolate his patients.

Boylston's actions caused an uproar. On July 21, the city's selectmen ordered him to cease inoculating immediately. This injunction had the full support of the city's other doctors and the majority of its citizens. However, on August 5, backed by Boston's Congregational clergy and many of the city's elite, Boylston defied the selectmen and renewed inoculating. Boston's Congregational ministers were convinced of the efficacy of inoculation and genuinely felt that it was their Christian duty to promote it even if it meant defying the selectmen. However, they were also trying to reassert their traditional role as community leaders, which had been weakening for the past half-century. At the same time, the city's doctors were feeling the first stirrings of professional identity.

The uproar caused by the actions of Boylston and his supporters centered around mobs and Boston's three newspapers. The mobs, which appeared sporadically, were frightening, threatening, and sometimes violent. However, their excesses were often exaggerated by contemporaries and some later writers for dramatic and partisan purposes.

The debate, which appeared in the newspapers, was more important. The chief arguments of those who opposed inoculation were that all the city's doctors but Boylston were opposed to it and that it was the meddlesome clergy that championed it; that the use of inoculation would prolong the epidemic and cause more deaths; that Boylston took no effective measures to prevent his inoculees from spreading the disease; and that the public was being arbitrarily put upon without their consent. Two effective arguments of those who supported inoculation were that there was enough evidence in favor of the procedure to at least try it, and that the epidemic was out of control and it was the duty of people to protect themselves and their loved ones as best they could. However, the most compelling argument in favor of inoculation came from the statistics compiled by the order of the selectmen near the end of the epidemic. These data clearly demonstrated that the death rate among those who were inoculated was six out of 287, or 2.1 percent, while the rate for those without inoculation was 842 of 5,759, or 14.6 percent. Nonetheless, the danger associated with this procedure and its cost, including the loss of several weeks' time in preparing the material to be injected, slowed the broad acceptance of inoculation. It would take another half-century of improvement in the procedure, the adoption of more effective measures to reduce the chances of spreading the disease, and an increase in the availability of the vaccine before inoculation won general acceptance in America.

See also 1775 SMALLPOX EPIDEMIC IN THE AMERICAN REVOLUTION.

Philip Cash

FURTHER READING:

Blake, John B. *Public Health in the Town of Boston, 1630–1822.* Cambridge, Mass.: Harvard University Press, 1959.

Winslow, Ola Elizabeth. *A Destroying Angel. The Conquest of Smallpox in Colonial Boston.* Boston: Houghton Mifflin, 1974.

1739 ◆ STONO REBELLION

Despite its small size compared with slave rebellions in the Caribbean and South America, the Stono Rebellion of 1739 ranks among the largest in American history. Sixty to 100 slaves killed about 25 whites in St. Paul Parish, South Carolina. In all, perhaps 35 slaves lost their lives. Even though the uprising did not last long, its effects were felt for many years.

Because documentation is sparse, historians do not know all of the facts about the Stono Rebellion, though the basic narrative as first related by historian Peter Wood still stands. On Sunday, September

9, 1739, a large group of slaves led by a man named Jemmy met before sunrise at the Stono River some 20 miles from Charleston. They raided a local store for weapons, killing the owner and several others. After attacking a tavern and killing several more whites, the rebels moved south, probably aiming for Spanish Florida, where they would be free. Their numbers swelled with new recruits to somewhere between 60 and 100. Along the way, they selectively murdered white colonists and burned property.

By chance, Lt. Gov. William Bull and four companions came upon the rebels later that morning. Unnoticed by the rebels, Bull managed to alert the militia who met the insurgents near the Edisto River, about 10 miles from their original starting point. While a core group of the slaves fought well, the militia prevailed in the battle that followed. Some 30 slaves escaped individually. It took a month before all of them were hunted down. The planters shot or decapitated those they believed responsible for the uprising on the spot, without a trial. The rest were released to their masters. A group of another 30 rebels had taken flight together. This group was defeated a week later in a second battle. One of the rebel leaders remained at large for three years.

Limited documentation leaves historians not only to speculate about the facts of the rebellion but also about their meaning. We do not know, for instance, why the slaves rebelled or what exactly they aimed for. We do know that they rose up at a time of increasing tensions in the colony. Smallpox, yellow fever, poor harvests, and a marked increase in the number of black runaways put white South Carolinians on edge. News of hostilities between Britain and Spain increased white anxieties and may have made Spanish St. Augustine a likely destination for the rebels. It appears that the core of the rebellion consisted of a group of Africans from martial societies in West Central Africa, especially the kingdom of Kongo, referred to in the records as "Angolans," whose familiarity with military techniques would have made them confident of success. Their experiences in their homeland as soldiers, historian John Thornton has suggested, likely influenced their actions and tactics in the uprising.

The Stono rebellion marked the end of the more fluid social conditions that had characterized South Carolina slavery in its first 80 years. With the passage of the "Negro Act" in 1740, enslaved people in

---

FACTBOX

PLACE Stono River, St. Paul's Parish, South Carolina

DATE September 9, 1739

TYPE Slave rebellion

DESCRIPTION A short-lived South Carolina slave rebellion, but one of the largest in American history

CAUSE Immediate cause is unclear, but slave rebels were likely influenced by rising tensions in the surrounding community and by the African military culture shared by core members of the rebel group.

CASUALTIES Approximately 60 people were murdered, an estimated 25 whites and 35 blacks.

IMPACT Passage of the "Negro Act" of 1740, which led to greater restrictions on and closer surveillance of slaves; new duties on slave imports

---

South Carolina lost many of the liberties they had informally enjoyed, such as limited freedom to move about the colony or to congregate, to raise livestock or to grow food for sale, or to learn how to read and write. At the same time, the authorities forced masters to pay an import duty on new slaves, hoping to rectify uneven black-white ratios by slowing down importation. In short, South Carolina became a more repressive slave society after Stono.

See also 1741 New York City fires and slave "conspiracy"; 1822 Denmark Vesey slave plot; 1831 Nat Turner slave rebellion.

Marjoleine Kars

FURTHER READING:

Smith, Mark M. *Stono: Documenting and Interpreting a Southern Slave Revolt.* Columbia: University of South Carolina Press, 2005.

Thornton, John K. "African Dimensions of the Stono Rebellion." *American Historical Review* 96 (October 1991): 1,101–1,113.

Wood, Peter H. *Black Majority: Negroes in Colonial South Carolina from 1670 through the Stono Rebellion.* New York: Knopf, 1974.

1741 ◆ NEW YORK CITY FIRES AND SLAVE "CONSPIRACY"

In 1741, 10 mysterious fires broke out in New York City. Panicked whites quickly suspected they had been set by slaves. A grand jury investigation led to a trial in New York's Supreme Court. The judges concluded that the fires were indeed part of a larger plot to destroy the city and end slavery. Thirty-four people were executed in punishment and many others sold to the Caribbean. It is unclear, however, whether any "conspiracy" actually took place.

In the spring of 1741, New Yorkers grew increasingly alarmed as mysterious fires destroyed Fort George, the governor's mansion, and eight other buildings. At first, these fires aroused no suspicion because in a city built of wood, fires were common. But 10 fires in three weeks were too many to chalk up to chance; suspicions turned to the slaves who made up a fifth of the city's 10,000 inhabitants.

As it happened, the Supreme Court was simultaneously investigating a burglary committed by two enslaved black men. The slaves had sold their loot to a white couple who owned a tavern frequented by both black and white New Yorkers. The testimony of the 16-year-old female servant employed at the tavern suggested that the robbery was linked to the fires, and so the justices launched an in-depth investigation. They impaneled a grand jury which started asking questions.

As fearful suspects realized that fingering others might save their lives, the jail filled up. Close to 200 people were examined. From their depositions, the eager court concluded that the fires were part of a vast interracial conspiracy to burn New York City to the ground and murder its white inhabitants. Based on this "evidence," the courts began to execute slaves. After several months, suspects began to name highly placed whites. This brought the investigations to a halt. By then, however, 30 black men had died—13 of them burned at the stake. The other 17 were hanged on the gallows; two white men and two white women had swung with them. One black prisoner had killed himself in jail. Eighty-four men and women were sold into slavery in the Caribbean as punishment, and seven white men were banned from New York forever.

It is hard to tell from the available documents what exactly happened in New York City in 1741. Did a coalition of slaves and poor whites really try to overthrow the social order, or did the so-called "conspiracy" only exist in the minds of fearful whites who misinterpreted the disgruntled talk of their enslaved workers? We may never know, but the records generated by this "conspiracy" allow some intriguing glimpses into the world of urban slaves in a northern colony. Such slaves, especially males, had a fair degree of freedom to move about the city. The court papers also reveal the extensive interracial socializing of blacks and whites at the bottom of colonial society. More than anything, the events in 1741 reveal the depth of white fears of their slaves, and the vulnerability of enslaved people to the whims of white society.

See also 1739 STONO REBELLION; 1822 DENMARK VESEY SLAVE PLOT; 1831 NAT TURNER SLAVE REBELLION.

Marjoleine Kars

FACTBOX

PLACE New York City

DATE Spring 1741

TYPE Urban fire and possible slave conspiracy

DESCRIPTION The mysterious burning of 10 buildings in New York City led to the execution of 34 men and women, mostly of African descent.

CAUSE Injustice of slavery; white fears in a slave society

CASUALTIES 35 deaths

IMPACT Increased white fear and black despair

FURTHER READING:

Davis, Thomas. J. *A Rumor of Revolt: The "Great Negro Plot" in Colonial New York.* New York: Free Press, 1985.

Lepore, Jill. *New York Burning: Liberty, Slavery, and Conspiracy in Eighteenth-Century Manhattan.* New York: Knopf, 2005.

Zabin, Serena. *The New York Conspiracy Trials of 1741: Daniel Horsmanden's Journal of the Proceedings, with Related Documents.* Boston: Bedford/St. Martin's, 2004.

1752 ◆ GREAT SOUTH CAROLINA HURRICANE

Hurricanes were a new phenomenon for British colonists who settled in America during the 17th and 18th centuries—the word itself comes from the Native word *hurakán*—but they quickly became one of the most feared elements of nature in the plantation colonies of the Lower South. Planters and merchants soon learned that no crop was safe until the hurricane season had passed. Although storms were frequent events, the hurricane that came ashore south of Charleston, South Carolina, in the early morning hours of September 15, 1752, was perhaps the worst to strike the region until the 1890s. The storm killed upwards of a hundred people and caused tremendous physical and economic damage. It also helped spark a political struggle between the royally appointed governor and the locally elected assembly concerning the relative powers of their respective branches.

The great hurricane began on the night of September 14. The winds blew hard from the northeast, and the sky appeared "wild and threatening," according to the *South Carolina Gazette.* The storm intensified throughout the early morning hours of September 15. By 9 o'clock, the storm surge had flooded Charleston with water 10 feet above the high-water mark of spring tides, and residents scrambled to upper stories to escape the floodwaters. As winds and water battered the city, many began to worry about the onset of high tide, which would completely overwhelm Charleston. But just after 11 A.M., in what the *Gazette* called "as signal an instance of the immediate interposition of Divine Providence, as ever appeared," the wind shifted to the southeast and southwest, and the waters receded five feet in 10 minutes. Strong winds continued for several hours, but by late afternoon the hurricane had passed.

The storm claimed numerous lives, although the exact number is unclear. One account reported that 95 people were killed. The *Gazette* stated only that "many people" drowned and that others were "much hurt by the fall of houses." Most buildings in Charleston suffered considerable damage. Ships were swept out of the harbor and driven ashore. Wharves were washed away, along with the goods in warehouses awaiting shipment. The city's fortifications were also demol-

FACTBOX
PLACE South Carolina
DATE September 14–15, 1752
TYPE Hurricane
DESCRIPTION Perhaps the worst hurricane to strike South Carolina until the 1890s
CASUALTIES As many as 95 deaths
IMPACT Damaged or destroyed much of Charleston and surrounding low country, cut rice production in half, disrupted tar and pitch production. Precipitated a dispute between the royally appointed governor and locally elected legislature, foreshadowing the conflict to come between the colonies and Britain

ished, their brick walls "torn to pieces, as if Mines had been sprung," according to Governor James Glen. The storm also caused tremendous physical damage throughout the surrounding low country. Few plantations within 30 miles of the city had any outbuildings left standing. The large number of trees thrown down in the storm rendered roads impassable. Large numbers of cows, hogs, and sheep also perished. Provisions became scarce, and local officials prohibited the export of food crops and sought outside aid from northern neighbors. And just as colonists were beginning recovery efforts, a second hurricane swept across the region on September 30. Although less intense, the storm added to colonists' misery.

The destruction caused by the hurricanes had major economic consequences. Exports of rice—the colony's principal crop—plummeted from 82,000 barrels to 37,000 barrels in the year following the hurricanes. By 1754, however, rice exports exceeded their prehurricane levels by more than 10,000 barrels. Such a quick turnaround testifies to the labor of the region's African-American slaves, who managed both to rebuild the plantations and continue a regular planting schedule, despite food shortages and often the loss of their own houses. In addition, the widespread damage to pine trees disrupted the production of tar and pitch in the region. One planter near Charleston estimated the damage to his trees at £10,000.

Political conflict emerged in the wake of the storm as Governor Glen and the assembly squared off about how to rebuild Charleston's forts and about who should pay. The assembly argued that the Fortifications Commission should control the rebuilding and that the British government should pay for it. They drafted a petition to London requesting such aid, but Glen delayed forwarding the petition. Governor Glen, an appointee of the king, viewed the commission as an infringement of the royal prerogative. Believing he should control the process, he appointed William de Brahm, a German engineer, to draft a new comprehensive plan for the fortifications. The assembly refused to go along. They blocked payment to Brahm for his plans and threatened to petition the king directly about Glen's actions. Worried about any criticism reaching London, Glen backed down. The political debate highlights the growing assertiveness of colonial legislatures and foreshadows some of the means by which local elites would challenge royal authority in the ensuing decades. Charleston's fortifications were eventually rebuilt, but not until 1755–56 when war with France loomed. The new defensive lines were four feet higher than the previous ones, an effort in part to keep the surge of future storms at bay.

Matthew Mulcahy

FURTHER READING:

Fraser, Walter. *Charleston! Charleston! The History of a Southern City.* Columbia: University of South Carolina Press, 1989.

Mercantini, Jonathan. "The Great Carolina Hurricane of 1752." *South Carolina Historical Magazine* 103 (October 2002): 351–365.

Mulcahy, Matthew. *Hurricanes and Society in the British Greater Caribbean, 1624–1783.* Baltimore, Md.: Johns Hopkins University Press, 2006.

1755 ◆ EXILE OF THE ACADIANS

In the afternoon of September 5, 1755, several hundred Acadians gathered in a church in Grande-Pré, Acadia—known today as Nova Scotia—to hear a British proclamation from Colonel John Winslow, in charge of removing them from the region. Winslow's words were translated from English to French: ". . . your Lands & Tennements, Cattle of all Kinds, and Live Stock of all Sortes are Forfitted to the Crown with all other [of] your Effects Saving your money and Household Goods and you your Selves are to be removed from this Province." After generations of relative peace, the Acadians, a self-sufficient, agrarian society, were forced to leave their possessions and homes. Between 1755 and 1763, more than 10,000 Acadians were deported, sent throughout the colonies between Massachusetts and Georgia. The Acadian expulsion, known to Acadians as Le Grand Dérangement, was a consequence of the French and Indian War—Britain and France's fight for dominance in North America—and one of the first instances of "ethnic cleansing" in North America.

As early as 1604, a century and a half prior, French explorers had noted the potential for permanent fur-trade settlements. They to began trade in areas around Nova Scotia, which they named *l'Acadie*, and established major trading posts such as Port Royal. High profits led quickly to coastal settlements along the shore of the Bay of Fundy, where distinct farming techniques consisted of turning marshes into fertile lands through networks of dikes and dams. The new settlers shared the land with local native inhabitants, mainly the Mikmaq. Strong ties developed with the Mikmaq out of trade dependency and admiration for each other's culture, perpetuated by intermarriages and Mikmaq assimilation to Catholicism.

French colonization had begun; yet, a new people, the Acadians, emerged from these early settlements, their society and culture derived from French language and customs, a strong Mikmaq influence, and distinct farming techniques. Between 1650 and 1755, the population grew to an estimated 15,000. The Acadians developed into a self-sufficient, agrarian society; however, an additional distinction would

FACTBOX

PLACE Nova Scotia, Canada

DATE 1755–63

TYPE Forced deportation, ethnic cleansing

DESCRIPTION Between 1755 and 1763, British and colonial militias forced more than 10,000 Acadian men, women, and children from their homes in Nova Scotia. They spread mainly through the colonies between Massachusetts and Georgia, as well as to France, Quebec, and Louisiana.

CAUSE The refusal of Acadians to fight for or against their French relatives or British rulers encouraged the British to expel the Acadians to eliminate any risk of rebellion and to secure completely their dominance of the Nova Scotia territory in colonial North America.

CASUALTIES At least 5,000 died during the deportation.

IMPACT The Acadian expulsion was one of the first instances of ethnic cleansing in North America, an episode that nearly exterminated an entire culture. But Acadians survived, even flourishing in their new homes in North America, particularly in Louisiana, where the Cajun culture developed.

come to define their culture and, eventually, their fate: political neutrality.

By 1713, Britain had overtaken Port Royal and controlled the rest of Acadia, authorized by the Treaty of Utrecht. Under British rule, the Acadians were free to maintain their religious, social, and political infrastructure. As tensions grew between France and Britain for colonial supremacy in North America, however, so did British suspicions of the Acadians, whom they dubbed the "French Neutrals," despite the Acadians' oath of allegiance to the British in 1730. Acadian allegiance, however, was on the condition of neutrality, even amid war, ensuring that they would never have to raise arms against the French. The British remained cautious of an Acadian rebellion, and debate of their removal heightened during the 1740s.

In 1755, the British found a reason to remove the Acadians. In an attack on Fort Beausejour, France's northernmost fort, located in New Brunswick, British regulars and New England militia met resistance

from a small number of Acadians. This outraged the royal governor, Colonel Charles Lawrence, who demanded that his council seek a renewed oath of allegiance of complete loyalty from the Acadians. The Acadians refused to sign another oath, noting the conditional oath they had already pledged. Governor Lawrence and his council resolved to expel the Acadians, viewed as rebels, and disperse them throughout the colonies. In the first year of deportation, British and New England troops forced more than 6,000 Acadians from their homes.

The Acadians, who had tried desperately to avoid the conditions of war, watched their homes and land, including hundreds of houses and barns, set ablaze. As word of forced exile spread, hundreds of Acadians fled to the woods. Some survived with the help of the Mikmaq, reaching Quebec; others perished from lack of food or dysentery. The majority, however, boarded ships for deportation and, in some cases, were separated from family members in the process—never to be reunited. Acadians were forced onto cargo vessels in great numbers where they experienced all the risks of sailing in the 18th century and more. The overcrowded ships provided inadequate food and bad water and faced dreadful weather conditions. On ships such as the *Cornwallis,* smallpox spread among the 417 Acadians, and 210 died before reaching their destination. Overall, at least 5,000 Acadians died during their deportation ordeal.

Ships delivered the Acadians to France and Britain and to colonies between Massachusetts and Georgia, to such cities as Boston and Philadelphia, into a world far different from their agrarian society in Nova Scotia. In subsequent years, city governments struggled to deal with the influx of poor Acadians, while Acadians struggled to adapt to new cultures. The highest number of Acadians ended up in Quebec, France, and Massachusetts, and in each place, the Acadians survived. In some cases, they were able to maintain aspects of their distinct culture; this is most evident in Louisiana, where many Acadians—ultimately known as Cajuns—settled. Generations of intermarriages between Acadians, Spanish, German, and French settlers in southern Louisiana created a new Cajun culture, distinct in its food, language, religion, and music—with strong Acadian influence. Cajun culture remains prevalent in Louisiana today and exemplifies the perseverance of the Acadians.

The Acadians, like Native American cultures that thrived on the frontier, could not avoid the

This 19th-century French illustration conveys the agony of the Acadians in the village of Grand-Pré, forced at gunpoint to leave their homes and settle elsewhere in North America. *(Getty Images)*

repercussions of entangling alliances between the French and British. Acadian culture had no ulterior motives in its progress; that is, Acadians did not look to conquer other lands or cultures but to live simply among their extended families of French, Mikmaq, and British influence. Ironically, their attempt to avoid conflict provoked a devastating response from British officials who could not accept their neutrality in what was considered wartime. Thousands of Acadians perished as a result, but thousands persevered just as they had done in their undeveloped lands in Nova Scotia in the early 17th century. Today, nearly 3 million descendants around the world trace their ancestry to the Acadians.

See also 1838 TRAIL OF TEARS.

Richard A. Fournier

FURTHER READING:

Faragher, John Mack. *A Great and Noble Scheme: The Tragic Story of the Expulsion of the French Acadians from Their American Homeland.* New York: W. W. Norton, 2005.

Jobb, Dean. *The Cajuns: A People's Story of Exile and Triumph.* New York: Wiley, 2005.

1755 ◆ NEW ENGLAND EARTHQUAKE

At four o'clock in the morning on November 18, 1755, New England suffered the most severe earthquake in its history. Colonists in the Boston area felt the quake—which seismologists have estimated would have registered a 5.8 on the Richter scale—most strongly, but newspapers reported that the tremors reached all the way from western New York to Nova Scotia to Annapolis, Maryland. Because most people were in bed at such an early hour in the morning, falling bricks and shingles did not hurt or kill passersby, and the only casualties were shattering china in the houses of the wealthy and a large number of damaged brick chimneys and roofs. Despite the lack of a death toll, the larger significance of this disaster should be considered within its historical context. The bleakest year of the French and Indian War was 1755, with staggering colonial losses and the complete breakdown of backcountry government. In addition, the New England tremor occurred amid a peak in transatlantic earthquake activity. In February 1750, the residents of London had experienced two substantial but not life-threatening quakes, and on November 1, 1755, only 17 days before the New England quake, the city of Lisbon, Portugal, was completely destroyed by a massive earthquake. In this tense atmosphere of international disaster and war between France, Britain, and their colonies, the New England earthquake appeared both an ominous portent of worse to come and a rare opportunity for comparative scientific study.

The principal description of the earthquake, which was reprinted in multiple colonial newspapers, including the *Boston Gazette* and the *Pennsylvania Journal,* was written by an educated Boston gentleman who provided his narration so that "people at a distance may possibly have a juster idea of the earthquake, by comparing several accounts of it together." The writer's stated purpose suggests an enlightened attempt to gather facts about "remarkable phenomena" that, when combined with other accounts, would create a coherent and scientific explanation. The tone of his description was very rational, focusing on measuring the exact duration of the quake and damage caused. Not once did he mention his emotional response. In addition, he dismissed out of hand the more supernatural elements that others had reported, such as a "great noise" and "glimmering lights." In his method, this unnamed Boston writer reflected the attitude that many educated elite adopted toward the earthquakes in various parts of the world. Just as Benjamin Franklin had harnessed the power of electricity earlier in the decade, this international community of Enlightenment-era thinkers hoped to fully understand the causes and functions of earthquakes.

The goals of the educated, however, stood in stark contrast to the popular response, which was near unanimous fear and awakening awe. According to an anonymous diarist in Boston, "upon the first shock of the earthquake, many persons jumped out of their beds, and ran immediately into the streets

FACTBOX

PLACE New England, most strongly in the Boston region

DATE November 18, 1755

TYPE Earthquake

DESCRIPTION An earthquake, registering an estimated 5.8 on the Richter scale, struck New England early in the morning, resulting in damage to chimneys, roofs, and breakable objects, but caused no fatalities.

IMPACT The rarity of the event and the historical context, including other transatlantic earthquakes and war between France, Britain, and their colonies, led to significant religious and scientific speculation over the causes and consequences of the earthquake.

. . . shriek[ing] with the apprehension of its being the day of judgment." A Sudbury, Massachusetts, resident named Experience Wight Richardson hoped that the response to the earthquake would be a "great reformation in our land." Farther north, a New Hampshire man recorded that "the older people had not forgotten the earthquake of 1727, and now, as on that occasion, they recognized the hand of God in the occurrence." Amid all of this religious speculation, the editors of the *Boston Gazette* requested that the ministers "whose particular province it is, will not fail . . . to declare the whole counsel of God."

The Reverend Jonathan Mayhew of Boston answered this call for spiritual counsel. His sermon, reprinted in the *Gazette,* placed the earthquake within the contexts of national war and sin rather than scientific earthquake theory. After a paragraph in which he voiced his fear of a French invasion, Mayhew concluded, "such is the present critical situation of our [political] affairs, such the aspects of providence towards us [in reference to the earthquake], so numerous our sins against heaven, that all who value their lives, liberties, and estates, not to say their souls, [need to] secure God's favor and protection." Mayhew thus combined his audience's religious concern for their souls with their political anxieties in his interpretation of this unusual and portentous phenomenon.

While earthquakes were not unknown during the colonial era—smaller ones had occurred in the 1680s and as recently as 1727—the relative rarity of this natural event led to intense religious and scientific speculation. In addition, the historical context of international earthquakes and war added greater significance to the interpretation of the New England quake, despite the fact that no fatalities resulted. Today, if such a tremor were to strike the Boston area, seismologists have estimated that it would result in billions of dollars of damage as well as considerable loss of life. Religious-minded colonists therefore had not only God to thank for sparing their lives, but their smaller population and dwelling structures made the quake less of a disaster in colonial times than it would be today.

Lauri Bauer Coleman

FURTHER READING:

Brigham, William Tufts. *Historical Notes on the Earthquakes of New England.* Boston, 1871.

1765 ◆ STAMP ACT CRISIS

Burdened by heavy debts from the French and Indian War (1754–63), the government of British prime minister George Grenville passed a series of measures aimed at raising revenue in the thirteen colonies that included the Sugar Act, Quartering Act, Currency Act, and the Duties in American Colonies Act of 1765, commonly called the Stamp Act. Passed by the House of Commons on February 27 and House of Lords on March 8, 1765, the Stamp Act required the purchase of stamps and their placement by colonists on all legal documents, licenses, insurance policies, school and college diplomas, playing cards, newspapers, pamphlets, and almanacs. The £60,000 in revenues expected from the act, which was to take effect November 1, 1765, were to be used to defray the costs of defending the colonies. The Stamp Act initiated the first of several political crises that over the next 10 years propelled Americans to resist British authority and declare independence.

American opposition to the Grenville program and King George III focused on the Stamp Act because it was the one measure to directly affect the greatest number of Americans spread across the largest area in the colonies. Opponents denounced its novelty as the first direct tax levied by Parliament on America and condemned it as unconstitutional because suspected violators would be tried in vice-admiralty courts, which had no juries. Virginia lawmaker Patrick Henry delivered his famous "treason" speech likening King George to Caesar and Charles I, spurring

---

FACTBOX

PLACE Thirteen Colonies; most pronounced in cities such as Charleston, New York, and Boston

DATE 1765

TYPE Political crisis; riots

DESCRIPTION Tax passed by Parliament provoked widespread opposition throughout the thirteen colonies.

CAUSE Enactment by Parliament of legislation designed to raise revenue in British colonies

IMPACT Precipitated debate over the legal structure of the British Empire, led to the most widely attended intercolonial meeting to date, and set in motion forces that would lead to the American Revolution.

---

the House of Burgesses to pass the Virginia Resolutions protesting the Stamp Act. Groups often called the Sons of Liberty formed in every colony, and their members destroyed stamps, forced agents charged with sale of the stamps to resign their commissions, and enforced boycotts of British goods. Mobs rioted against its enforcement in Charleston, South Carolina, New York City, and Boston where a crowd broke into Lieutenant Governor Thomas Hutchinson's house, threw furniture out the window, and destroyed most of its contents. The mob also hung stamp collectors in effigy in hopes of intimidating British officials from collecting the hated tax.

In the most widely attended intercolonial meeting to date, 27 delegates from nine of the 13 colonies (Virginia, Georgia, North Carolina, and New Hampshire excepted) gathered at the Stamp Act Congress in New York City on October 7–25, 1765. The delegates adopted an address to the king, petitions to Parliament, and a "Declaration of Rights and Grievances" in which they asserted that Americans could only be taxed by their own legislatures and that the terms for enforcing the Stamp Act violated Americans' right to trial by jury. Agreements were widely adopted to ban the importation and consumption of British goods until the Stamp Act was repealed. In defiance of the law, most courts closed on November 1 before reopening and then operated without stamps.

From Georgia to New Hampshire, colonists rich and poor united to oppose British policy. Further violence and a constitutional crisis were only averted when Parliament—pressured by British merchants who saw their sales to North America fall more than 13 percent from £2,249,710 in 1764 to £1,944,108 in 1765—repealed the act on March 18, 1766. At the same time, British lawmakers also passed the Declaratory Act asserting that Parliament had the right to legislate for the colonies in all matters whatsoever.

Yet Americans still claimed victory in the confrontation and ignored the Declaratory Act.

Grenville was surprised by the vehemence of the American reaction. That response, the first widespread American resistance to British authority in the 18th century, should have warned his successors, particularly Chancellor of the Exchecquer Charles Townshend whose duties on tea, lead, paint, and paper led to a similar crisis in 1767–68, that Americans would resist any infringements on what they considered to be their constitutional rights.

See also 1770 BOSTON MASSACRE; 1774 COERCIVE ACTS.

James C. Bradford

FURTHER READING:

Bailyn, Bernard. *The Ordeal of Thomas Hutchinson.* Cambridge, Mass.: Belknap Press of Harvard University Press, 1974.

Bullion, J. L. *A Great and Necessary Measure: George Grenville and the Genesis of the Stamp Act, 1763–1765.* Columbia: University of Missouri Press, 1982.

Morgan, Edmund S., and Helen M. Morgan *The Stamp Act Crisis: Prologue to Revolution.* 3rd ed. Chapel Hill: University of North Carolina Press, 1995.

Thomas, P. D. G. *British Politics and the Stamp Act Crisis: The First Phase of the American Revolution, 1763–1767.* New York: Clarendon Press, 1975.

1770 ◆ BOSTON MASSACRE

On March 5, 1770, Bostonians and British soldiers clashed in what colonists quickly labeled the "bloody massacre on King Street." Now known as the Boston Massacre, the incident was the culmination of five years of violence that had been occurring in Boston and other major colonial towns since the enactment of the Stamp Act in 1765. The crisis that surrounded the enactment of both the Stamp Act and Townshend Duties pressured the British government to send soldiers to the American colonies to preserve order. The colonists saw the troops as threats to their lifestyle and jobs. The presence of British "redcoats" not only sparked

violence in the streets of Boston but also shifted colonial determination to resist Britain's imperial policy toward its American possessions.

The days leading up to the massacre were tense for Bostonians. On March 2, 1770, Patrick Walker, a British soldier, was patrolling the ropewalks, a shop where rope was manufactured. William Green, one of the ropewalk workers, approached Walker and asked him if he was interested in cleaning his latrine. It was common for colonists to offer work to the soldiers so that they could earn extra money, which they either sent home to their families or spent where they were stationed. Walker took offense at the offer, a fight ensued, and the redcoat lost. The soldier went back to his barrack and gathered fellow troops, who returned to the ropewalk, where the fight resumed. Scuffles broke out around Boston for the next few days. Snow fell in Boston on March 4, confining residents to their homes and dampening the week's tensions.

On March 5, 1770, people emerged from their homes and went about their business. One of the busiest areas in Boston was the square in front of the Town House, a government building located at the top of King Street (today 15 State Street). Fanueil Hall, Boston's meetinghouse and public market, was to the east. The British guardhouse was to the west. Bostonians shopped and milled about the square at all hours of the day. This area was the site of an altercation between a young barber's apprentice, Sam Maverick, and Captain John Goldfinch, a British sol-

A brilliant piece of colonial propaganda, Paul Revere's engraving of the Boston Massacre helped rally Americans against the British. It includes many inaccuracies, such as the colonists standing unarmed, the British soldiers organized in a line, and the captain ordering them to fire. *(Library of Congress)*

FACTBOX

PLACE King Street (today 15 State Street), Boston

DATE March 5, 1770

TYPE Civil disturbance

DESCRIPTION Altercation between British soldiers and Bostonians led soldiers to fire on an unruly crowd.

CAUSE Tensions between Bostonians and British soldiers

CASUALTIES 5 killed, 11 wounded

IMPACT By depicting the "massacre" as an unprovoked attack on an innocent crowd, Boston radicals led many colonists to be more critical of Britain, ultimately contributing to the cause of American independence.

dier who was having work done at the barbershop. As Goldfinch exited the shop, Maverick followed him into the busy square shouting that he did not pay his bill. The allegation was not true, but it embarrassed Goldfinch, who ordered Maverick to return to his shop. When the youngster refused, Goldfinch ordered Private Hugh White, the sentry guarding the Custom House, to enforce the command. The sentry had been pelted with snow, ice, spit, and curses by Bostonians throughout the day. Exasperated and impatient, White butted Maverick in the side of his head with his musket and then hit him again, knocking him to the ground. Maverick ran down King Street with blood dripping from his head.

It was early evening, and the pubs along King Street were full of men who had finished their day's work. Some were members of violent street gangs that roamed the streets of Boston and terrorized upper-class Bostonians. Seeing the bloodied Maverick, pub patrons poured into the street and gathered at the Town House. The bells of the Old South Meeting House were rung, signaling an emergency and drawing additional people into the square. As confusion grew, Goldfinch panicked and summoned reinforcements from the guard house to protect the beleaguered sentry. Seven soldiers emerged from the guard house, led by Captain Thomas Preston. As they made their way through the crowd, they were pushed, provoked, and threatened. When Preston's instructions to the mob to return home went unheeded, he ordered his troops to load their muskets, hoping this action would scare the crowd. It did not. The soldiers had almost reached the sentry's post when Crispus Attucks, a runaway slave, pushed Private John Montgomery to the ground. As the private rose, he pointed his musket at Attucks and yelled, "Damn you, fire!" The other soldiers heard what they believed was the order to shoot and fired their muskets also. The gunshots killed five people and wounded 11.

Governor Thomas Hutchinson, a Crown loyalist already unpopular with many Bostonians, realized the way to keep peace in Boston was to quickly and fairly bring the soldiers to trial. One of the city's respected young attorneys, John Adams—the future president—represented them, and at the trial that fall, the jury acquitted six of the eight soldiers of all charges. Two privates, including Montgomery, were convicted of manslaughter.

But well before the trial began, local radicals and the Sons of Liberty used the "bloody massacre" for propaganda that informed citizens in the countryside, other colonies, and even London that British occupation in Boston could not be successful and that the colonists should resist British tyranny. Paul Revere produced drawings of the brawl, drawn from the American point of view, and his engraving of the Boston massacre was distributed throughout the colonies and around the world. The picture inaccurately depicted the "redcoats" as well organized and lined up against unarmed, harmless Bostonians, with the captain giving the order to fire. Copies of the engraving circulated faster than the results of the trial, influencing negative views of the British occupation. The Boston massacre proved to be a decisive set back for the British and an example of successful propaganda for the American cause of independence.

See also 1765 STAMP ACT CRISIS; 1774 COERCIVE ACTS.

Julie Arrison

FURTHER READING:
Zobel, Hiller. *The Boston Massacre*. New York: Norton Library, 1970.

1771 ◆ NORTH CAROLINA REGULATOR MOVEMENT

The North Carolina Regulation was a farmers' reform movement in the Piedmont region of the colony. For a period of five years, farmers who called themselves Regulators tried to create a more just and democratic society. They were defeated by the army led by the governor of North Carolina in May 1771, the largest such battle in colonial America. The movement's bloody repression disillusioned many backcountry farmers and made them reluctant to risk committing themselves to one side or another in the subsequent American Revolution.

The Piedmont of North Carolina, the area west of what is now Raleigh, then known as the "backcountry," was first settled by whites in the 1740s. Most of the newcomers hailed from colonies to the north; others came directly from Europe. Many of them did not belong to the established church (Church of England, now Anglican); rather, they were dissenters eager to follow their own religious principles. They had come to obtain sufficient land to ensure family independence, but it proved harder than they had expected to obtain farms at reasonable prices. Corrupt backcountry officials used their control of the land market to keep the best lands for themselves, and large land speculators drove up prices. Farmers were also outraged at the high court costs they were assessed. Because county courts served as the only local government institution in the southern colonies, no one could avoid coming to court sooner or later to authorize contracts, to register deeds, or to settle debts. High fees made such routine transactions prohibitively expensive. Farmers also resented high taxes and the fact that local sheriffs regularly embezzled such

FACTBOX

PLACE Alamance and the Piedmont, North Carolina

DATE Battle of Alamance on May 16, 1771; Regulator movement spanned 1766–71

TYPE Rural uprising

DESCRIPTION A farmers' movement aimed at agrarian democracy was suppressed with military force.

CAUSE Government corruption and unreasonably high land prices resulted in anger and disillusionment among immigrant farmers, leading them to take justice into their own hands.

CASUALTIES 33 to 36 fatalities

IMPACT Influenced support for the American Revolution in the state; precursor to future agrarian movements

hard-earned monies. They also objected to debt laws that favored creditors over debtors.

The protest movement began in 1766 when farmers in Orange County organized the Sandy Creek Association, led by Herman Husband, a deeply religious and prosperous farmer from Maryland, who had first come to the Piedmont in the mid-1750s. Husband quickly became the main spokesman for the farmers' movement. His ideas about the duty of Christians to help bring about social justice were tremendously influential among Piedmont farmers. Within two years of its organization, the members of the Sandy Creek Association joined with other reform-minded farmers under the name of *Regulators*, a term used in Britain for people appointed to reform government abuse.

At first, Regulators pursued traditional legal means to stop corruption. They petitioned the governor and the assembly for relief, tried to talk with local authorities, and took extortionate officials to court. When such legal measures did not work, they resorted to extralegal action: They refused to pay taxes, repossessed property seized for public sale to satisfy debts and taxes, and disrupted court proceedings. In 1770, they disrupted a superior court meeting in Hillsborough, attacked some local officials and shopkeepers, and destroyed the house of Assemblyman Edmund Fanning, the most hated official in the area.

The authorities retaliated forcefully. They jailed Herman Husband, who had been elected a legislator for Orange County in 1769, on a pretext. Next, the assembly passed a sweeping Riot Act that gave Governor William Tryon the authority and funds he needed to raise a militia to march against the Regulators. On May 16, 1771, about 1,100 militiamen confronted some 2,000 farmers near Alamance Creek about 20 miles west of Hillsborough. Two hours after the first shot was fired, 17 to 20 farmers lay dead, along with nine militiamen; more than 150 men on both sides were wounded. One Regulator was hanged on the spot without benefit of trial; six others were hanged in Hillsborough on June 19 after a hasty trial. At least 6,000 Regulators and sympathizers were forced to take an oath of allegiance to the king as the victorious troops terrorized backcountry settlements, burning farms and requisitioning foodstuffs. Some of the best-known Regulators, including Herman Husband, fled the province. By summer, the Regulators had been suppressed.

Five years later, the men who had suppressed the Regulators in the assembly and on the battlefield in North Carolina led their colony into the Revolutionary War. Not surprisingly, many former Regulators displayed a noncommittal attitude toward the struggle with England, nor did the Revolution bring about the kind of independent society that Regulators had envisioned during their struggle with colonial officials. Yet aspirations for agrarian social justice lived on, finding expression in social movements such as populism a century later.

See also 1786 SHAYS'S REBELLION.

Marjoleine Kars

FURTHER READING:

Kars, Marjoleine. *Breaking Loose Together: The Regulator Rebellion in Pre-Revolutionary North Carolina.* Chapel Hill: University of North Carolina Press, 2002.

Powell, William S., James K. Huhta, and Thomas J. Farnham, eds. *The Regulators in North Carolina: A Documentary History, 1759–1776.* Raleigh, N.C.: State Department of Archives and History, 1971.

1774 ◆ COERCIVE ACTS

The British prime minister, Lord North, and the members of the English Parliament were furious when they first heard that Boston inhabitants had thrown 90,000 pounds of tea belonging to the East India Company into the city's harbor on the night of December 16, 1773. This "tea party" was the last straw. British leaders had engaged in a long-running quarrel with the colonists in general and Bostonians in particular for slightly more than a decade. From their perspective, they had bent over backward to satisfy provincials who insisted that they could not be taxed by a government in which they were not represented. Appeasement had not worked. Hence, in the spring of 1774, Parliament passed four punitive laws—the Port Act, the Massachusetts Government Act, the Administration of Justice Act, and the Quartering Act—designed to strengthen English authority in Massachusetts and to send a signal to the other colonies that further resistance would be futile. Called collectively the Coercive Acts in Britain, the colonists dubbed the offending legislation the Intolerable Acts. Instead of quelling incipient rebellion, the acts actually intensified hostilities, uniting the colonies and leading ultimately to American independence.

The Coercive Acts were broad in scope. The Port Act closed Boston's harbor until the colonists paid for the tea they had destroyed. The Massachusetts Government Act replaced a Governor's Council, which had been elected by the lower house of the colony's legislature, with a body appointed by the king. It also expanded the king's authority to appoint judges and other officials. Perhaps most galling, it curtailed the authority of town meetings—undermining a New England institution that had existed for more than a century. The Administration of Justice Act allowed governors to move trials of revenue officials to a neutral province, thus circumventing biased Boston juries. Finally, the Quartering Act allowed governors from all the colonies to house troops in vacant buildings without seeking legal permission.

The English government had been trying to rein in its mainland possessions in North America since the end of the Seven Years' War in 1763. It had attempted, without success, to tax the colonies. It had also sought to make English officials—especially governors and

FACTBOX	
PLACE	London and Boston
DATE	Spring 1774
TYPE	Political crisis
DESCRIPTION	Confronted with Boston's destruction of tea belonging to the East India Company, Parliament passed the Coercive Acts, designed to punish Massachusetts, to gain control of the colony, and to warn other colonies not to imitate Boston's example.
IMPACT	The colonists united behind Boston, setting themselves on the road to revolution and independence.

customs regulators—independent of colonial interference. It had been met at each turn by stubborn locals who resisted their every effort, repeatedly forcing Parliament to back down. When word of the "tea party" arrived in London, Parliament decided that conciliation was not the best way to deal with the colonies. A no-nonsense, get-tough policy was the only way to bring the Americans back in line.

The colonists saw things differently. Many believed that the British government was engaged in a deep-laid plot to destroy their liberty. They valued their "rights of Englishmen," which included property, self-government, and trials by juries—all of which the Coercive Acts threatened. They saw each effort to tax them or to undercut their "rights" as evidence of this conspiracy. The Intolerable Acts were proof positive that their liberties were in danger and that if they did not defend themselves, they would soon be little more than slaves. When colonial leaders met in Philadelphia in September 1774, in what became known as the First Continental Congress, they had no desire for independence from Britain. They wanted only to force the British government to reconsider its harsh legislation. They had no way of knowing that this time the British would not back down. Thus the Coercive Acts of 1774 set the colonists and Britain on a collision course, creating the conditions that would lead to the American Revolution and independence. In its efforts to save the empire, Parliament had ended in destroying it.

See also 1765 STAMP ACT CRISIS; 1770 BOSTON MASSACRE.

Sheila L. Skemp

FURTHER READING:

Bailyn, Bernard. *The Ideological Origins of the American Revolution.* Cambridge, Mass.: Belknap Press, 1967.

Bonwick, Colin. *The American Revolution.* Charlottesville: University Press of Virginia, 1991.

1775 ◆ BATTLES OF LEXINGTON AND CONCORD

"From these movements," Paul Revere recollected, "we expected something serious was to be transacted." The famed silversmith did not act alone in alerting the countryside west of Boston, Massachusetts, that the British were coming. Still, the image of Revere's midnight ride, conducted at great risk, and contributing to the readiness of the local minuteman companies and the safety of patriot leaders Samuel Adams and John Hancock, remains iconic. It reminds us that the Revolution arose after years of evolving resistance and months of detailed preparations in Massachusetts. Yet preparedness is not synonymous with the courage to stand with one's fellow townspeople and countrymen and take a round of fire from trained British soldiers. And to fire back. Therein lies the drama of the Battles of Lexington and Concord, fought on April 19, 1775, the beginning of America's Revolutionary War.

The imperial crisis that produced the Revolution had its roots deep in the colonial period, but tensions escalated after the French and Indian War ended in 1763. Over the next dozen years, controversies surrounding the Stamp Act, the Townshend Duties (including the impost on tea), and the quartering of British troops in Massachusetts and New York provoked rioting, propagandizing, and organized resistance. The British parliament, led by Lord North, determined to suppress colonial resistance in Massachusetts after the Boston Tea Party of December 1773. The so-called COERCIVE ACTS of 1774 mandated the temporary closure of the port of Boston, the annulment of the colony's charter, and the installation of martial law under the governorship of General Thomas Gage. Gage dissolved the colonial

FACTBOX

PLACE Eastern Massachusetts

DATE April 19, 1775

TYPE The first battles of the America Revolution

DESCRIPTION A series of small engagements between armed Massachusetts militiamen and British soldiers in Lexington and along the road from Concord to Boston

CAUSE Massachusetts governor Thomas Gage, also commander in chief of Britain's military establishment in North America, was given orders in early 1775 to seize the arms and military stores of rebel militia units and arrest principal leaders. Gage's decision to send a detachment of light infantry from Boston west to Lexington and Concord, and the preparations of the Massachusetts Provincial Congress and local minutemen companies, assured some manner of confrontation. Who fired the "shot heard 'round the world," however, remains unknown.

CASUALTIES The British lost 73 dead and 200 wounded or missing. Massachusetts militia forces suffered 49 dead and 39 wounded.

IMPACT Lexington and Concord were among the smaller battles of the Revolutionary War, but because the war itself began on Lexington Common, their importance cannot be exaggerated. The British offensive and the local minutemen's stout resistance resulted in a quick mobilization of militia from all parts of New England to the Boston area, where they would lay siege to General Gage's occupying force.

The Battle of Lexington marked the beginning of the American Revolution. *(Library of Congress)*

Assembly but could exercise no practical authority outside of Boston. Indeed, the elected assembly, now calling itself the Massachusetts Provincial Congress, took over practical governance in most of the colony. The Provincial Congress put into motion measures of economic retaliation passed by the First Continental Congress, which met in Philadelphia in the fall of 1774. It was in Massachusetts where patriots first, in the words of historian Robert Gross, "dismantled royal authority." In most localities, agreements were made whereby companies of townsmen would "stand at a minute's warning in case of an alarm." Tax revenues were diverted to the illegal Provincial Congress. Local committees of safety also stockpiled arms and began to ostracize community members who refused to sign on to these acts of organized resistance. When General Gage reported what he saw to his superiors in London, the colonists' actions were interpreted as rebellion. As King George III himself said, "the dye is now cast, the Colonies must either submit or triumph." Lord North likewise could see that "it must come to violence."

Though war may have seemed inevitable to key actors in the unfolding drama, shots had not yet been exchanged. Lord Dartmouth, Britain's colonial secretary, ordered Gage to suppress the resistance with the numbers he then had, roughly 3,500 soldiers. Dartmouth's letter, received by Gage on April

14, 1775, more than any other event, precipitated the outbreak of war. Dartmouth advised Gage to "arrest and imprison the principal actors & abettors"; if the colonists persisted, then "force should be repelled by force." Open hostilities, the British government felt, would be better risked now than when the colonists were in "a riper state of Rebellion." Four days later, Gage prepared a column of light infantry under the command of Lt. Col. Francis Smith to attempt to capture Adams and Hancock in Lexington, 13 miles west of Boston, and to proceed to nearby Concord to capture a stockpile of arms and powder. Gage's attempts to maintain secrecy notwithstanding, the Patriots succeeded in hustling Adams and Hancock out of Lexington and most of their stores out of Concord by the morning of April 19. As Smith's column proceeded late on the night of April 18, Dr. Joseph Warren, a patriot leader still living in Boston, having gained knowledge of British movements, dispatched Paul Revere and William Dawes to warn the countryside. Amid the darkness, Revere, Dawes, and a third rider, Dr. Samuel Prescott, raced on horseback to alert patriots that the redcoats were advancing. On April 19, just before five in the morning, Major John Pitcairn's advance column reached Lexington where, thanks to the warnings of Revere, Dawes, and Prescott, the local militia led by Captain John Parker anxiously guarded the town green.

What next transpired—and who fired the "shot heard 'round the world"—will forever be lost to history. Participants on the American side would write that the first shot came from a British musket, whereas the British would claim that the Americans fired first. Patriot leaders such as Samuel Adams felt that strategically, in order to retain the support of the other colonies, local militia would have to act defensively, drawing the British to act as the aggressors. Captain Parker assembled roughly 70 minutemen, some of them more than 60 years old, as Pitcairn approached. Both Parker and Pitcairn gave prior orders to hold fire until fired upon. As Parker ordered a withdrawal, Pitcairn or some other officer ordered Parker's men to lay down their arms, which they refused to do. Pitcairn maintained that, while turning toward his men, he saw a musket fire from behind a stone wall; only then did his men fire a volley and actually charge the patriots with bayonets. Eight minutemen died and 10 were wounded at Lexington, and after the battle Parker was forced to withdraw. Only one of Pitcairn's men was injured, and the British marched onward to Concord. The American Revolution had begun.

In Concord, town leaders decided to withdraw to the heights northwest of town, across the North Bridge, to await reinforcements, which would file in throughout the day. The British, meanwhile, searched with little success for military stores and accidentally set afire the town courthouse and blacksmith shop, which prompted Concord's townsmen to take action. Colonel James Barrett ordered his company forward to the North Bridge, where they exchanged rounds of fire with three British companies and drove them back. Realizing the impending danger and satisfied with his search, Smith ordered his column to march back to Boston. At Meriam's Corner, between Concord and Lexington, minutemen poured fire on the British column as it crossed a narrow bridge. This engagement foretold what was in store for the British as the woods and farms surrounding the road to Boston filled with rebels who fought in an unorthodox manner, from behind trees and fences, without coordination, but with frightening success. Fortunately for the British, Smith had earlier in the day requested reinforcements from Gage, and it was Earl Percy and his roughly 1,000 men who saved Smith's column from annihilation. For the day of April 19 taken whole, the British suffered 73 deaths and 200 wounded or missing (a fairly high 20 percent casualty rate). The Americans lost 49 dead and 39 wounded.

Immediately after the British retreat to Boston, militia from all over New England gathered on the heights outside of town to lay siege to the city. The battles of Lexington and Concord demonstrated the patriots' willingness to fight for their principles and for their property, though it has been said the successes of the day gave undue weight in American strategic thought to the potential of militia fighting regulars. If there had been more coordination, the minutemen might have destroyed the British column even after Percy's reinforcements. It would, in the end, require a disciplined regular army to confront the British over the long haul.

Michael Gunther

FURTHER READING:

Fischer, David Hackett. *Paul Revere's Ride.* New York: Oxford University Press, 1994.

Gross, Robert A. *The Minutemen and Their World.* New York: Hill and Wang, 1976.

1775 ◆ SMALLPOX EPIDEMIC IN THE AMERICAN REVOLUTION

From the return of British troops to Boston in October 1774 until the adoption of a policy of general inoculation in eastern Massachusetts during the last half of 1776, Boston was plagued by the recurrence of smallpox. Straddling the beginning of the American Revolution, these outbreaks constituted serious threats to Continental and British troops, Boston's civilians, and residents in adjacent towns. Despite receiving uneven support from lesser British officers, Boston's selectmen, aided by the solid cooperation of

FACTBOX

PLACE Boston

DATE 1775–76

TYPE Smallpox epidemic

DESCRIPTION Smallpox was present in Boston for more than two years with periodic surges of intensity.

CASUALTIES 68 deaths (28 from inoculations)

IMPACT George Washington and the Massachusetts government were able to keep the epidemic from spreading to the American troops, thus avoiding a military disaster at the outbreak of the revolution. The large-scale inoculation in Boston in 1776 was the most successful one during the 18th century.

British general Thomas Gage, were able to keep smallpox in check until the outbreak of hostilities at Lexington and Concord on April 19, 1775. Throughout the siege of Boston from June 1775 to March 1776, smallpox was always present. In November and December 1775, the British army was hard hit by the disease. In late November, British general William Howe adopted the effective but dangerous program of isolating and inoculating all soldiers who had not had this contagious disorder and were willing to be inoculated. Civilians were also allowed to undergo this procedure, a perilous undertaking at the time. However, in a besieged city in which the disease was highly active, the decision was probably a wise one.

Between late November 1775 and the middle of January 1776, Howe permitted some 500 men, women, and children, most of them poor, to leave Boston to escape the disease. These refugees were sent to Winthrop, not far from the Cambridge wing of the Continental army lines. At this time, General George Washington and the Massachusetts government were alarmed by rumors and reports that Howe was deliberately sending out newly inoculated civilians in order to spread smallpox among the Continental army and the inhabitants of eastern Massachusetts. This accusation seemed vindicated when three of the early refugees came down with smallpox. However, it is also possible that Howe simply allowed the Boston civilians to come out indiscriminately and let the Patriots worry about any difficulties that they might present. Whatever the case, Washington and the Massachusetts government handled the challenge successfully.

When Howe evacuated Boston on March 17, 1776, Washington moved cautiously to secure the city, mindful that smallpox was still present in it. Both the Cambridge and Roxbury wings of the army sent small detachments made up of troops who had had smallpox into Boston. However, on March 20, with Howe still lying off Nantasket Road, Washington ordered the bulk of his army into the city. Both Washington and the city selectmen were now faced with the problem of controlling the smallpox that was present there. On March 22, apprehensive state officials ordered the Boston selectmen to "use the utmost vigilance and industry" in locating all persons infected with smallpox and to isolate them in several houses in the westernmost part of the city. All places known to have been exposed to smallpox were to be fumigated and cleansed. Lastly, the selectmen were to make periodic reports on the progress of the disease within the city. To complement this program, Washington instructed all regimental surgeons on March 25 to carefully examine their sick. Any person who showed the slightest symptom of smallpox was sent immediately to the army's smallpox hospital on Fresh Pond in Cambridge.

The rapid increase in social and economic activity between town and country, the steady, if forbidden, fraternizing of the military with the civilian population, plus the secret use of inoculation by soldiers and private citizens kept the smallpox virus alive and dangerous in Boston throughout the rest of the spring. Fortunately, by early April, most of the Continental troops had left for New York. By July, however, it was clear that the official policy of isolation had failed. Both the remaining Continental soldiers and the Boston civilians were allowed to undergo inoculation, a step agreed to by the Massachusetts legislature. Large-scale inoculation continued in eastern Massachusetts for the rest of the year. In Boston in 1776, 304 persons contracted smallpox naturally and 40 died; 4,988 had been inoculated, with 28 deaths. This was the most successful large-scale inoculation against smallpox in Boston during the 18th century.

The smallpox outbreaks that struck Boston at the outbreak of the American Revolution in 1775–76 were of greater importance for what did not happen than for what did. Had the American troops who besieged Boston and then occupied it come down with smallpox in large numbers, the course of the Revolution might well have been far different. This outcome takes on significance in relation to the other major American campaign at this time, the attempt to seize Quebec, which ended in disaster. The success in keeping the American troops around Boston largely free from smallpox was due in large measure to the efforts of General Washington and officials of the government of Massachusetts. Thus, a threatening outbreak of smallpox was prevented from becoming a major health disaster at a critical time in the nation's history.

See also 1721 SMALLPOX EPIDEMIC.

Philip Cash

FURTHER READING:

Blake, John B. *Public Health in the Town of Boston, 1630–1822.* Cambridge, Mass.: Harvard University Press, 1959.

Cash, Philip. *Medical Men at the Siege of Boston, April, 1775–April, 1776: Problems of the Massachusetts and Continental Armies.* Philadelphia: American Philosophical Society, 1973.

1777 ◆ DEPRIVATION AT VALLEY FORGE

It is preserved as a national historical park, yet a battle was not fought there, nor was a declaration signed or enacted. Valley Forge, located where Valley Creek empties into the Schuylkill River in southeastern Pennsylvania, was the site of General George Washington's Continental army encampment in the winter of 1777–78. The experiences of the soldiers and officers and the accounts they produced have given Valley Forge a special place in American history. It was both the nadir of America's revolutionary hopes and the turning point in the evolution of the Continental army into a formidable force. Washington himself gives us the barest picture of suffering transformed into strength: "To see Men without Cloathes . . . , without Blankets to lay on, without Shoes, by which their Marches might be traced by the Blood from their feet . . . is a mark of Patience and obedience which in my opinion can scarce be parallel'd."

Washington's army of 11,000 men entered Valley Forge on December 19, 1777, heartened by news of the recent victory at Saratoga in upstate New York but dispirited by their own recent failures at Brandywine and Germantown. Sir William Howe's British army, by the result of the 1777 campaign, could enjoy the winter of 1777–78 in the relative comfort of the finest colonial city, Philadelphia. Washington chose Valley Forge, 23 miles away, for its defensible position on the west side of the Schuylkill, but also to watch the

---

FACTBOX

PLACE Valley Forge, Pennsylvania

DATE December 1777–May 1778

TYPE Starvation and exposure

DESCRIPTION Shortages of shoes, clothing, medicines, bread, meat, and rum caused severe malnutrition, disease, and low morale, while at the ebb points of winter, many soldiers deserted and officers engaged in infighting.

CAUSE A constellation of factors, including the choice of Valley Forge as the site of camp, severe winter weather, administrative incompetence, and the disaffection of many civilian farmers and merchants in the environs of Valley Forge

CASUALTIES Roughly 2,000 died, primarily from disease and malnutrition.

IMPACT The British were not able nor did their commander intend to take advantage of the Continental army's weakened position in the winter of 1777–78. By most accounts, the Valley Forge experience strengthened Washington's army in the long run, contributing to their ultimate victory at Yorktown in 1781.

movements of Howe. The site had its disadvantages, however. The men immediately had to construct their own rude huts and struggled through harsh blasts of cold and snow in so doing. More important, in choosing to shadow Howe for the winter and to protect (as best he could) the Philadelphia hinterland, Washington put his army in competition with the British for food and other essential supplies.

The suffering of Washington's men was caused in large part by critical supply problems, exacerbated by frigid winter conditions that made travel with wagons difficult. There were at various times shortages of shoes, clothing, meat, bread, medicines, and rum. In February 1778, in the time of greatest misfortune, approximately 4,000 soldiers were reported as unfit for duty. Hay shortages helped account for the deaths of about 500 horses. On three occasions, the men went completely without provisions, turning the battle-hardened veterans into, by Congressman Gouverneur Morris's observation, "an army of skeletons." Out of 11,000 men who entered camp on December 19, 1777, roughly 2,000 died, primarily from disease and malnutrition. Some of the problems stemmed from disarray in the commissary and quartermaster departments, whose head staff officers had recently resigned, and the Continental Congress took an excessive length of time considering the departments' reorganization and the appointment of new chiefs. Corruption and ineptitude were allowed to fester in the chain of supply, and middlemen charged exorbitant rates, forcing a cash-strapped Congress to reject some contracts that would have brought needed supplies to camp. Valley Forge also raised the discomfiting quandary of civilian farmers and merchants in southeastern Pennsylvania choosing to sell their produce to the enemy. This "widespread indifference of patriot civilians toward an army so desperately in need of help," argue historians James K. Martin and Mark E. Lender, marked the particularly "gruesome" nature of Valley Forge.

Despite the dire conditions and the apparent inability of Washington, his officers, and Congress to solve the short-term supply crises, the army survived the winter more confident and disciplined. Desertion did occur; some historians estimate that as many as 2,000—close to 20 percent—left the ragged camp that winter. There was also a wave of officer resignations taking place amid a troubling climate of factionalism. A small group of officers and members of Congress even plotted Washington's ouster. Unrest was partly abated by congressional approval of seven-year pensions for officers and extra bonuses to soldiers who agreed to enlist for the war's duration. Three new appointments, made during the Valley Forge ordeal, combined to strengthen Washington's army by the late spring of 1778. Friedrich von Steuben, Prussian émigré, self-styled baron, and volunteer, earned promotion to the post of inspector general after demonstrating with a model company a systematic discipline of drill. His instructions in how to march in formations and properly handle weapons were particularly useful. What is more, the enlisted men admired his gruff demeanor and salty, if broken, language skills, and their morale seemed to rise with greater discipline. All was predicated on improvements in supply. The appointments of Nathanael Greene as quartermaster general and Jeremiah Wadsworth as commissary general, by all accounts, brought supplies into camp at a more acceptable level for most of the spring of 1778. By most accounts, the Valley Forge experience strengthened the character, skills, and commitment of the soldiers and officers who survived and stayed with Washington's army. In later years, this contributed to victory at Yorktown and an increasing sense of nationalism and of veneration toward Washington among veterans.

There were other harsh winters for Washington's army, with similar supply problems and more difficult weather conditions, such as the winter of 1779–80 in Morristown, New Jersey. But it was Valley Forge that came, symbolically, to stand for the sacrifice of all orders of Americans, including men from the lower classes who increasingly came to fill the ranks of the Continental army. Washington and his men, from their perspective, overcame environmental difficulties and inefficient, bickering politicians to learn how to stand together, in the words of Private Joseph Martin, in a "band of brotherhood."

Michael Gunther

FURTHER READING:

Bodle, Wayne. *The Valley Forge Winter: Civilians and Soldiers in War.* University Park: Pennsylvania State University Press, 2002.

Carp, E. Wayne. *To Starve the Army at Pleasure: Continental Army Administration and American Political Culture, 1775–1783.* Chapel Hill: University of North Carolina Press, 1984.

Fleming, Thomas. *Washington's Secret War: The Hidden History of Valley Forge.* New York: Smithsonian Books/Collins, 2005.

Lender, Mark, and James Kirby Martin. *A Respectable Army: The Military Origins of the Republic, 1763–1789.* Arlington Heights, Ill.: H. Davidson, 1982.

1780 ◆ THE "DARK DAY" FOREST FIRES

On Friday, May 19, 1780, total darkness prevailed at high noon over much of New England. Most prominent in Connecticut and Massachusetts, the darkness lasted all afternoon and into the evening. No casualties resulted from the blackened skies, but the "dark day" still stands as one of the most fascinating and frightening meteorological events to occur in New England in the 18th century. Foremost in everyone's mind was determining the meaning of this ill-timed darkness that occurred amid the trying years of the American Revolution. Was it a supernatural message from God portending the end of the world or a natural occurrence that could be explained scientifically? The responses of New Englanders to this remarkable event demonstrate the diversity of beliefs about the natural world that coexisted in America in 1780. In addition, discussion of the dark day calls attention to the expansion of public debate. Common people now joined elite spokesmen in determining the meaning of uncommon nature in forums such as newspapers and broadsides.

During the early morning hours of this extraordinary day, the sun appeared deep red, and all of nature took on an unusually brassy hue. These sights, alarming enough in themselves, were followed by a deepening pall of sooty blackness that covered the skies by early afternoon. The almost complete lack of light forced women to carry out their work by candlelight in the middle of the day, brought farmers in from their fields in bewilderment, and kept students from their studies. In addition to disrupting the routines of New England residents, the darkness threw the animal kingdom into such confusion that frogs peeped as if night had come early, and daytime birds returned to their roosts. When night did come, the darkness was nearly palpable and forced travelers to find immediate lodging or to

FACTBOX

PLACE New England, with the most pronounced darkness in Connecticut and Massachusetts

DATE May 19, 1780

TYPE Forest fires and ecological crisis

DESCRIPTION Total darkness in daytime

CAUSE Forest fires and an unusual wind pattern caused skies to blacken at midday and through the evening.

IMPACT Debate over the cause of darkness demonstrated the range of opinions about the natural world and new participation of nonelites in public discourse during and after the American Revolution.

risk becoming lost even on familiar routes. Many horses refused to leave their stalls for those riders brave enough to take on the blackened roads. The following morning did not dawn brightly, but the overwhelming darkness had passed, leading many to sigh in relief that the unusual weather had not portended a devastating storm or, worse yet, the end of the world.

In hindsight, historians attribute the remarkable darkness to a combination of backcountry forest fires and a highly unusual wind pattern that suspended the soot-filled air over New England for a longer amount of time than normal. While the atmospheric conditions were rare, the burning of forests was a common practice that occurred every year as part of the process of clearing and fertilizing new farmland. Because they were so common, most New Englanders did not consider forest fires an adequate explanation for the intense darkness and instead searched for other reasons to account for the dark day. The most striking features of this public debate were the diversity of opinions and the range of participants.

Many educated gentlemen were convinced that the darkness could be explained rationally despite biblical references to the darkening of the sun at the crucifixion and the end times. In anonymous letters submitted to newspapers, these writers debated scientific causes of the darkness ranging from the rapid evaporation of heavy winter snows to burning leaves suspended in the atmosphere. Ironically, this last explanation, which was closest to the truth, received the most contemporary criticism. While these newspaper editorials demonstrate a lack of consensus in regard to scientific knowledge, the elite contributors did agree that the darkness should be "accounted for by the laws of nature, without having recourse to any thing miraculous or ominous."

Other less-educated participants in the public debate were unwilling to rely on human knowledge to account for what they considered the supernatural darkness. In a published broadside, a "Farmer from Massachusetts" turned to scriptural prophesies that linked the dark day to Christ's second coming following five years of tribulation. This period of tribulation, he suggested, referred to the current revolutionary war. The anonymous writer of a popular pamphlet on the dark day also warned against a rational rather than religious explanation. In verse he queried: "Can mortal man this wonder scan? Or tell a second cause? Did not our God, then shake his rod,

and alter nature's laws?" These contributors sought to understand God's will in the remarkable darkness while their more educated counterparts were interested in identifying its natural causes. However, not all of the learned dismissed the religious significance of the dark day. The president of Brown College in Rhode Island was reported to have considered the unusual darkness "a prelude to that great and important day when the final consummation of all things is to take place."

Once it had safely passed, the dark day of 1780 became the fodder of local histories and entertaining anecdotes. In one of these, an alarmed Boston resident sent her servant in the midst of the darkness to ask the local minister whether he thought the blackened skies portended some coming evil. The minister glibly responded, "Give my respectful compliments to your mistress, and tell her I am as much in the dark as she is." Yet, in the midst of this event, the ominous darkness was far from humorous, inspiring both religious fear and scientific awe among all classes of people at the unusual workings of the natural world.

Lauri Bauer Coleman

FURTHER READING:

Errington, Sara. "Wonders and the Creation of Evangelical Culture in New England, 1720–1820." Ph.D. diss., Brown University, 2000.
Perley, Sidney. *Historic Storms of New England.* 1891. Reprint, Beverly, Mass.: Memoirs Unlimited, 2001.

1785 ◆ ECONOMIC CRISIS

Americans' exuberance for achieving independence in 1783 dissolved into gloom and frustration by 1785 as the economy of the new nation sank into depression. During the middle years of the 1780s, slumping exports, falling prices for agricultural products, lower wages, and stagnant industries caused widespread hardship, indebtedness, and, eventually, armed protests. In his classic portrait, *The Critical Period of American History 1783–1789* (published in 1888), covering the years between the Treaty of Paris and the commencement of the new federal government under the Constitution, historian John Fiske wrote that "the whole country was in some measure pauperized." By 1786, "all trade had well-nigh stopped." These economic problems were accentuated by public debt that had accumulated during the war against Britain. Resistance to tax levies designed to pay these obligations deeply

FACTBOX

PLACE United States

DATE 1785–88

TYPE Economic depression and tax revolt

DESCRIPTION A prolonged slump in the economy and a crisis over public debt and the payment of taxes

CAUSE Unknown, but likely influenced by the total public debt of the United States and state governments, approximately $40 million

IMPACT The writing and ratification of the Constitution of the United States, 1787–88

troubled elites, such as James Madison and George Washington. Worries about this fiscal crisis triggered the movement to write the United States Constitution, which created a stronger central government.

The Treaty of Paris, ratified in 1783, signaled the reopening of trade with Britain. American merchants scrambled to purchase imports from abroad, bought largely on credit, and resell these goods to retailers around the country. Payments from buyer to seller, including British exporters, drained specie ("hard" money, in the form of gold and silver) from the United States. This outflow of currency slowed the initial flurry of commercial activity and contributed to a downward spiral of business. Prices began to fall in 1784 and continued downward for several years. Surveying his native Virginia, James Madison observed in mid-1785 that "the trade of the country is in a deplorable condition," with prices for tobacco—a major export—slipping 50 percent. Wholesale prices for farm products in Philadelphia in 1786 had dropped by nearly two-thirds from their 1784 levels, and they stayed depressed through 1790. Charleston, South Carolina, experienced equally glum conditions. Merchant firms on both sides of the Atlantic went bankrupt. One recent estimate calculated that the economy declined by 41 percent between 1774 and 1790.

The southern states and New England suffered more than the middle states, such as Pennsylvania and New York. Tobacco prices in Virginia and Maryland dropped in 1785 and remained low in 1786.

The South Carolina indigo market dried up, crippling the state's economy during the middle years of the decade. The level of prices for both agricultural and manufactured goods in Maryland fell until 1790. Conditions in New England followed an analogous course: Prices for farm products plummeted between 1783 and 1786 and remained low for the remainder of the decade. With reduced demand for commodities, "apples and pears rotted on the trees." Shipbuilding in New Hampshire virtually halted between 1783 and 1787; the state's lumber industry was distressed as well. Suits against debtors in New Hampshire increased by a factor of five from 1781 to 1785. The number of debtor suits during the decade nearly equaled the number of families in the Granite State, signifying the widespread financial hardship.

What caused this economic crisis? Historians are perplexed by the postwar malaise, in part because they lack adequate data. But five key factors appear to explain primary reasons for the hard times. The first problem was that after eight years of war, which had interrupted trade, a glut of British goods flooded the nation once peace had returned. This inflow of foreign products hurt American manufacturers, some of whom had benefited from the closed market during the Revolution. Furthermore, payments to British firms transferred specie overseas, leaving the new nation starved for currency. A second factor was the weather. The winters of 1783–84 and 1784–85 were among the coldest on record in the United States. Much of the Chesapeake Bay froze in early 1784, closing busy ports such as Baltimore for several months and contributing to great floods in the Tidewater region in the spring. Further south, huge ice floes passed New Orleans in 1784, a once-in-a-century event. In Virginia, 1785 was exceptionally dry, stunting crops. George Washington, whose Mount Vernon plantation was located in upper Virginia, had no surplus corn to sell in 1785 and 1786, and his income suffered in consequence. New Hampshire had been plagued by an early frost in 1783, followed by large floods in 1784. Similar meteorological afflictions ravaged harvests in western Europe.

A third factor behind the economic crisis was the restrictions Britain placed on American commerce with the British West Indies. This policy removed an important market for American products, especially from New England, and stimulated the search for new opportunities. The American trade with China was born in this commercial crisis, with the first ship, the *Empress of China,* sailing between the two nations in 1784. State governments countered Britain's trade policy by enacting tariff laws, which offered some protection from foreign competition and raised revenue. Eight of the nation's 13 states adopted these retaliatory laws. New York imposed duties on both imports and reimports (goods imported and sent to other states). These laws impeded the free flow of commerce.

Tariffs also helped to prevent the outflow of specie, the fourth cause of America's economic dilemma. The export of coinage from the United States stirred efforts to get the states to print paper money. The search for solutions to the economic gloom prompted residents in every county of Massachusetts to hold conventions in 1786. Many of these assemblies petitioned the legislature with requests for paper money acts, as well as "tender laws" that allowed the payment of taxes and debts "in kind" (with products rather than money). Merchants and economic elites in Massachusetts and elsewhere bitterly denounced such measures, in part because paper money lessened the value of their loans. Seven states eventually passed various forms of paper money laws (Georgia, North Carolina, South Carolina, Pennsylvania, New Jersey, New York, and Rhode Island). A demonstration of aggrieved New Hampshire residents at the state capital in Exeter pressured their legislature to adopt paper money, only to see the measure repealed by a close vote in town meetings. Spirited political struggles in Maryland, Virginia, and Massachusetts saw conservatives narrowly triumph over advocates of currency inflation. James Madison rallied lawmakers in Virginia to avert this "mischief."

The battle over paper currency was linked to disputes over taxation. Bitter and often violent, these fights deepened a fiscal crisis, the fifth factor that handicapped the economy. The heart of the tax issue derived from the debts left over from the American Revolution. The states owed money to creditors, whose loans had helped fund the war against Britain; the remaining debt had been contracted by the Continental Congress and Congress under the Articles of Confederation. Most economic elites such as George Washington and Thomas Jefferson saw the honor of the nation fused with timely payment of these fiscal obligations. As the national government had no power to tax and hence no independent source of revenue, it was obliged to requisition (essentially, beg for) financial payments from the states—and national officials wanted the money in specie. The prospect that Virginia lawmakers might defer collection of part of their state's tax levy, in Thomas Jefferson's opinion, would "stamp us with ignominy." State lawmakers, many of whom shared Washington and Jefferson's outlook on the public debts, complied with congressional requests by levying direct taxes (taxes on the ownership of property, mainly land and real estate). They reinforced these acts with stiff enforcement provisions that threatened delinquent citizens and tax collectors with the loss of their property and debtor's prison.

The mass of the citizenry, however, labored under a staggering financial burden. A large portion of the population lacked the ability to pay the new levies. Private and public debt in New Hampshire equaled half a year's salary for all its adult men in 1787; debtor cases in western Massachusetts counties numbered nearly one-third of the adult male population. Alexander Hamilton estimated that the value of land had fallen between 25 and 50 percent during the price deflation of the depression years. And payment of the new taxes removed specie from circulation that otherwise could have been used for private transactions.

Communities throughout New England and other regions petitioned legislators for relief, recommending the issuance of paper money, stay laws that delayed tax collections, and other remedies such as tender acts. The intransigence of conservatives who controlled most state governments provoked numerous protests, which evolved from petitions and county conventions into tax boycotts, armed attacks on court proceedings against debtors, and arson. Civil disorders erupted in most states in 1785 and 1786, as aggrieved, armed citizens physically halted the sales of debtors' property or court proceedings against debtors. SHAYS'S REBELLION in Massachusetts in the winter of 1786–87 was the most serious of these uprisings. The national government was powerless to put down the armed insurrection, pushing the country to the brink of anarchy.

The Massachusetts militia crushed the Shaysite challenge to state authority. Yet lawmakers acted in 1786 and 1787 to ameliorate some of the fiscal crisis. Virginia, for instance, allowed residents to pay the state tax in 1786 in tobacco. The governor of

Maryland halted auction sales for nonpayment of taxes. In addition to paper money laws, most states adopted an assortment of tax reductions or deferments and debtor statutes. Massachusetts residents replaced a vindictive state government with more accommodating leaders in 1787. All states gave up on the goal of collecting taxes in specie, leaving conservatives to fret about the poverty of the national treasury and armed protests against authority.

Nationalists such as George Washington had long lamented the weakness of the central government created under the Articles of Confederation and viewed the semiautonomy of state governments as threatening "our downfall as a nation." Madison reflected these views in his famed 10th Federalist Paper that indicted the "wickedness . . . in the conduct of the states." Shays's Rebellion was the critical catalyst to remedy the defects in the Articles of Confederation. The delegates who convened in Philadelphia in May 1787—just three months after the rebellion was crushed—bypassed the existing compact and wrote a wholly new constitution by September. Conventions of elected delegates in the states ratified the document in 1788, and George Washington was elected the nation's first president. The Constitution can be read as a litany of provisions that grew out of the economic and fiscal malaise of the 1784–87 depression years. First and foremost, Congress received authority to levy taxes and imposts, as well as to coin money, which spoke to the fiscal incapacity of the Articles of Confederation. By allowing Congress to create an army and a navy, as well as to call out the militia and to guarantee the states a "republican government," the Constitution granted to the central government critical powers to enforce its financial will. Limits were imposed on the states, such as prohibition against levying tariffs and emitting bills of credit (in essence, paper money). Debts contracted before 1788 remained valid. The Constitution's preamble, which charged the new government with insuring "domestic tranquility," reflected apprehension over the civil turmoil still fresh on the minds of the delegates at the Constitutional Convention. Without much exaggeration, historians can claim that the building of a powerful national government was triggered by the economic crisis of the 1780s.

See also 1819 FINANCIAL PANIC AND DEPRESSION.

Ballard C. Campbell

FURTHER READING:

Brown, Roger. *Redeeming the Republic: Federalists, Taxation, and the Origins of the Constitution.* Baltimore: Johns Hopkins University Press, 1993.

Fiske, John. *The Critical Period of American History, 1783–1789.* 1888. Whitefish, Mont.: Kessinger Publishing, 2004.

Flexner, James. *George Washington and the New Nation, 1783–1793.* Boston: Little, Brown, 1970.

Morris, Richard B. *The Forging of the Union, 1781–1789.* New York: Harper and Row, 1987.

Nettels, Curtis. *The Emergence of a National Economy, 1775–1815.* New York: Harper and Row, 1962.

Nevins, Allan. *The American States during and after the Revolution, 1775–1789.* New York: Macmillan, 1924.

1786 ◆ SHAYS'S REBELLION

A citizen uprising occurred in central and western Massachusetts during the winter of 1786–87 that shocked elites throughout the new nation. Expressing their bitterness toward taxation and the lack of representation, the dissidents demanded fundamental changes in state government and its financial policies. Initially this challenge to authority took the form of resolutions and petitions. But when the state chose coercion over compliance with citizen grievances, some hinterland residents led by destitute farmer Daniel Shays, backed their protests with muskets and sabers. This uprising of "regulators," named Shays's Rebellion, unnerved many conservatives. Elites in Massachusetts raised an army, paid largely through private donations, to restore order. Martial force scattered the upstarts yet the "rebellion" fed a movement to replace the Articles of Confederation with the Constitution of the

FACTBOX

PLACE Springfield, Boston, and places in interior Massachusetts

DATE September 1786–February 1787

TYPE Armed insurrection against state government and county courts in Massachusetts

DESCRIPTION Led by destitute farmer Daniel Shays, rural citizens rebelled against the government.

CAUSE Anger of residents in central and western counties over taxation, debt, and elite control of the state government

CASUALTIES 10 deaths

IMPACT The uprising hastened the movement to hold a constitutional convention in Philadelphia in 1787 to revise the Articles of Confederation. The resulting Constitution contained provisions designed to contain disorders such as Shays's Rebellion.

United States. Adoption of the new compact fulfilled George Washington's hope of creating an "energetic" national government.

The roots of Shays's Rebellion lay in economic depression and a tax crisis. After the peace treaty with Britain concluded the American Revolution in 1783, the new nation slipped into a severe and prolonged economic slump. By 1785 farmers in most parts of the nation faced declining prices for their products and a scarcity of specie (money in the form of coins) to pay for manufactured products and taxes. Paper money issued during the Revolution had dropped to a fraction of its original value. American payments for imported British goods after the war further drained specie from the country. Purchases based on credit were common, borrowing was widespread, and indebtedness was endemic, as were lawsuits to collect debt. During the middle years of the 1780s, 30 percent of the males in Worcester and Hampshire counties, Massachusetts, became parties to debt cases, and many debtors were sentenced to jail. As courts heard a growing docket of private debtor cases in 1785 and 1786, resentments against the mercantile elite, judges, and lawyers increased.

A second fiscal burden weighed on the backs of Massachusetts residents. Both the state and national governments emerged from the Revolution with a large debt. This borrowing had financed much of the war against Britain, which possessed one of the world's most powerful armies. Because Congress lacked the power to tax under the Articles of Confederation, the national government had to requisition—essentially plead with—the states for funds. Furthermore, Congress demanded that these obligations be paid in specie rather than paper money. Creditors wanted to be paid, of course, preferably in specie, but equally important, elites believed that the moral foundation of the new nation hinged on honoring government's fiscal promises.

Economic elites opposed adoption of paper-money schemes, which seven states had enacted in the 1780s, to relieve the stress of private debt and state taxation. The Massachusetts legislature, known as the General Court, however, rejected paper-money bills in November 1785 and again in May 1786. The General Court also turned down a "tender law," which would have allowed the payment of taxes in goods, not money. Debt and tax aversion in the Massachusetts hinterland, the legislature concluded, stemmed from "habits of luxury." The state lawmakers prescribed "industry, sobriety, economy, and fidelity to contracts" to instill compliance with the law. Instead of tax relief, lawmakers sided with Governor James Bowdoin, a tough conservative who successfully advocated new levies, earmarked for paying off the state debt. The new tax law made sheriffs personally responsible for obtaining collections and authorized them to auction off homes if necessary to obtain the levy.

Conventions of citizens in central and western Massachusetts protested this action in August and September 1786. They demanded financial relief, a new state constitution, and regulation of lawyers who were perceived to prey on debtors. Some petitions requested the relocation of the state capital from Boston to an interior site and thus distanced from the commercial elite that lived in and around the coastal city. Forming themselves into groups styled "regulators," the dissidents blocked court proceedings in numerous central Massachusetts counties during early fall 1786. Some residents went further by arming themselves under the command of Daniel Shays, a Revolutionary War veteran and resident of Pelham, a town near Springfield. During the days when Shays's band was drilling, the Massachusetts legislature adopted a set of coercive measures that made it illegal to join a "mutiny" or for groups of armed persons to gather in public. Governor Bowdoin took a more dramatic step. He called for the formation of an army of 4,400 soldiers, under the leadership of General Benjamin Lincoln. Most of Lincoln's recruits for the militia came from coastal counties, not the interior where insurrection brewed. Wealthy eastern elites funded the army through private subscriptions.

Following militia attacks on the homes of three regulators, the insurgents advanced on the federal arsenal in Springfield, intent on securing weapons and ammunition. On January 25, 1787, Shays's poorly armed and badly coordinated regiments were met by a militia force, outnumbered but possessing artillery. A cannon blast killed four regulators and sent the others scurrying toward the town of Petersham in north-central Massachusetts. On Sunday morning, February 4, General Lincoln, who had conducted a 20-mile overnight march in a blinding snowstorm, surprised the Shaysites while they were having breakfast. Some insurgents were captured and the remainder fled, including Daniel Shays. A final encounter between the "regulators" and state troops occurred in the town of Sheffield in late February; this clash signaled the effective end of armed resistance in Massachusetts.

Governor Bowdoin thus defeated the Shaysites, but his hard-line policy did not impress most Bay State voters, who elected John Hancock and a new legislature in April 1787. The Hancock administration enacted a set of concessions, including a suspension of the state tax and a plan of clemency for some insurgents. In 1788, the legislature adopted a tender law, established a mint, and granted pardons to most regulators. Encouraged by Samuel Adams, former hero of revolutionary Massachusetts and currently its Senate president, prosecutors secured 17 death sentences against alleged regulators. Only one condemned prisoner, John Bly, was hung. Daniel Shays escaped Massachusetts and eventually settled in New York, where he died in 1825 at the age of 78.

Massachusetts's legislative concessions on taxes and specie payments paralleled actions in other states to the consternation of elites such as James Madison and George Washington. Madison snarled at "the mischiefs of various experiments" of relief legislation, such as paper-money schemes, which "excited the disgust of all the respectable in America." The "anarchy and confusion" in Massachusetts disturbed George Washington. The timing of Shays's Rebellion was opportune for advocates of a stronger national government. Out of a meeting in Annapolis, Maryland, of delegates from several states in September 1786 came a recommendation to hold a national convention in Philadelphia to suggest revisions to the Articles of Confederation. Delegates were appointed to this convention during the months that the Shays affair unfolded. The civil turmoil in Massachusetts was on the minds of the delegates in Philadelphia who decided to scrap the articles and draft an entirely new plan of government—the Constitution—during the summer of 1787.

The Constitution addressed the "disorders" that had troubled Massachusetts in 1786 and 1787. As its preamble states, the purpose of the Constitution, ratified in 1788, was to "insure domestic tranquility." Article I, section 8, allowed the federal government to call up the militia to "suppress insurrections," a reference to the insurgencies in Massachusetts and elsewhere. States were forbidden from keeping troops without the consent of Congress and from issuing paper money. Section 4 guaranteed each state a republican form of government, which the United States pledged to protect against "domestic violence." And of critical importance, given the debt that hung over most states, Congress under the Constitution gained the power to tax and to coin money. To insure compliance with these policies as well as to assert its independence in the world, Congress was authorized to raise an army and a navy. Daniel Shays and the Massachusetts regulators had fought for tax relief and state government reform, never intending to influence national policy. Their actions, however, helped transform the U.S. government by prodding delegates to abandon the Articles of Confederation and draft a new Constitution.

See also 1771 North Carolina regulator movement; 1785 economic crisis.

Ballard C. Campbell

FURTHER READING:

Feer, Robert A. *Shay's Rebellion.* New York: Garland Press, 1988.

Richards, Leonard R. *Shays's Rebellion: The American Revolution's Final Battle.* Philadelphia: University of Pennsylvania Press, 2002.

Szatmary, David P. *Shays' Rebellion: The Making of an Agrarian Insurrection.* Amherst: University of Massachusetts Press, 1980.

1793 ◆ YELLOW FEVER EPIDEMIC

The 1793 yellow fever epidemic in Philadelphia, which lasted from August to the frosts of November, was a severe one, resulting in nearly 5,000 deaths, about 10 percent of the city's population. Nearby towns and cities in Pennsylvania and New Jersey warned residents to keep away and that "all unnecessary intercourse be avoided with Philadelphia." The outbreak was particularly dramatic and conflict ridden, due in part to the nature of yellow fever but also because of Philadelphia's importance at this time in the nation's history. It was the capital of the new nation as well as of the state of Pennsylvania. With 51,000 residents, it was also the country's largest and wealthiest city as well as its busiest port and chief point of entry for immigrants. In addition, Philadelphia was the country's leading intellectual, scientific, and medical center.

Urban yellow fever is an acute, infectious viral disease that is transferred from an infected person to an uninfected one by the bite of the female *Aëdes agypti* mosquito. The virus attacks a person's internal organs, especially the liver and kidneys. Its most dramatic symptoms are the yellowing of the skin and eyes, bleeding from the nose and mouth, purple hemorrhages into the skin, and black vomit. The true nature of infectious disease was unknown in 1793. Hence, physicians did not understand how the disease was transmitted. Moreover, the primitive condition of medical knowledge and practice at the time limited the ability of doctors to cure patients. Doctors were forced to treat symptoms rather than the true cause. Most of their therapies were ineffectual or harmful. The best treatment was rest, attentive nursing, and reliance on the body's impressive ability to heal itself.

The majority of the members of government and a third of Philadelphia's residents fled the disease-infested city. Most of Philadelphia's 80 doctors, however, dutifully remained in the city during the epidemic, and several died. In late August, Mayor Matthew Clarkson turned to the prestigious College of Physicians of Philadelphia for advice and recommendations, but its members provided little help. The city's medical community became mired in bitter quarreling about the source and method of transmission of yellow fever and how to treat it. One group maintained that the disease was imported and

> ## FACTBOX
>
> **PLACE** Philadelphia, Pennsylvania
>
> **DATE** August–November 1793
>
> **TYPE** Yellow fever epidemic
>
> **DESCRIPTION** A severe yellow fever epidemic wiped out about 10 percent of the city's population.
>
> **CASUALTIES** Nearly 5,000 deaths
>
> **IMPACT** The epidemic increased concern about the conditions and dangers of large urban areas in the United States and stimulated the early public health movement.

contagious, arguing that there was no known case of an outbreak of yellow fever originating in the United States. All cases were imported, most often from the West Indies. Members of this group also stressed that all of Philadelphia's yellow fever epidemics first appeared near the city's waterfront. Some observers suggested that the most likely source of the new outbreak was the recent arrival of more than 2,000 refugees from the slave revolt in Haiti. A second group argued that the source of the epidemic was local (an unpopular contention), citing the city's size, its location adjacent to marshes and swamps, which exuded foul air, and poor sanitation as causes. At the time, Philadelphia lacked a sewage system, fresh water supply, and an effective system for removing filth and decaying matter. These conditions, members of this group contended, resulted in the release of poisons called miasma or effluvia into the air from which they attacked the body.

There were two competing schools of thought about treatment of the disease. The more traditional school sought to strengthen the body through the use of quinine, wine, and cold baths. In strong contrast to this school, Benjamin Rush, one of the nation's most prominent physicians, contended that the problem was excessive excitement of the cardiovascular system, which was to be relieved by copious bleeding and strong purgatives.

The most important organization in the fight against yellow fever was a broad-based ad hoc

> AT a MEETING of the Corporation of the city of Burlington, August 30th, 1793, the following recommendations to the citizens was unanimously agreed to.
>
> WHEREAS there is great reason for caution against the malignant Fever or contagious disorder, which prevails in Philadelphia, and it is our duty to use every probable means to prevent the same in the city of Burlington; the Corporation of Burlington after collecting every advice which could be obtained,
>
> RECOMMEND to the Citizens of Burlington,
>
> 1. That all unnecessary intercourse be avoided with Philadelphia, that no dry goods, woollen cloths, woollens, cottons or linens, or any packages where Raw, hay or shavings are used, be imported within twenty days.
>
> 2. That the masters of the boats which ply to and from Burlington to Philadelphia, be very careful that they do not receive on board their vessels, or bring to this city within twenty days, any person or persons but those who appear in good health.
>
> 3. That no animal or vegetable substances be thrown or permitted to lay in the streets or alleys, but that all offals, water-melon rinds and substances that putrefy be thrown into the delaware or buried.
>
> 4. That no water be permitted to stagnate about the pumps, in the streets or near any houses; but that the wharves, streets, alleys and gutters, ditches, house, and barnyards, be kept as clean as possible.
>
> 5. The Physicians in Burlington are requested to make report to the Mayor or Recorder as soon as possible, after they shall have been called to and visited any person or persons, who shall have the said malignant Fever.
>
> Signed by order of the Corporation,
>
> BOWES REED, Mayor.
>
> ———————————
>
> The following means to prevent the contagion is recommended by the College of Physicians in Philadelphia.
>
> " To avoid all fatigue of body and mind."
>
> " To avoid standing or setting in the sun, also in a current of air, or in the evening air."
>
> " To accommodate the dress to the weather, and to exceed rather in warm than in cool cloathing."
>
> " To avoid intemperance, but to use fermented liquors, such as wine, beer and cyder with moderation."
>
> " The burning of gunpowder, the use of vinegar and camphor upon handkerchiefs or in smelling bottels, particularly by persons whose duty calls them to visit or attend the sick."
>
> Published by order of the Corporation,
>
> ABRAHAM GARDINER, Clerk.

As the yellow fever epidemic raged in Philadelphia, nearby towns issued warnings to prevent the "malignant Fever" from spreading. (New York Public Library, Academy of Medicine, New York)

body known as the Committee on Malignant Fever (sometimes referred to as "the Committee"). It took a wretched temporary hospital known as Bush Hill and turned it into a well-run and effective institu-

tion. Committee members also founded homes for children left orphaned by the epidemic. They worked to clean up the city and minister to the needs of the poor. Another organization that rendered valuable service was the Free African Society. Because blacks were considered to be less susceptible to yellow fever than whites, several civic leaders, including Rush, implored the society to mobilize the city's free blacks in the struggle against the disease. With a few exceptions, blacks responded admirably as nurses, transporters of the dead, gravediggers, housecleaners, and watchmen. However, their hopes that their efforts would lead to more equitable treatment by the white community proved illusory.

The Philadelphia yellow fever epidemic of 1793 heightened the nation's concern about the conditions of large urban areas and the threat that they posed to the country's well-being. The episode also energized the nation's infant public health movement, which sought to supply these areas with fresh water, effective sewage control, and cleaner streets.

See also 1878 YELLOW FEVER EPIDEMIC.

Philip Cash

FURTHER READING:

Estes, J. Worth, and Billy G. Smith, eds. *A Melancholy Scene of Devastation: The Public Response to the 1793 Philadelphia Yellow Fever Epidemic.* Canton, Mass.: Science History Publications/USA, 1997.

Murphy, Jim. *An American Plague: The True and Terrifying Story of the Yellow Fever Epidemic of 1793.* New York: Scholastic, 2004.

Powell, John H. *Bring Out Your Dead: The Great Plague of Yellow Fever in Philadelphia in 1793.* 1949. Reprint, Philadelphia: University of Pennsylvania Press, 1993.

1800–1801 ◆ PRESIDENTIAL ELECTION CRISIS

The 1800 presidential election, which culminated in an electoral college tie and narrow tiebreaking vote in the House of Representatives, was the most significant constitutional and political crisis the young American republic had faced in its brief history. Before the election was decided in favor of Virginia Democratic-Republican Thomas Jefferson, threats of political usurpation and military violence swirled around the new national capital, Washington, D.C. While the election is now remembered primarily as the first transfer of national power between opposing political groups in U.S. history, this result's tranquility belied the political tumult and very real sense of crisis felt by Americans as the election's outcome remained stalemated into the spring of 1801. Shortly after the resolution of this electoral crisis, the Twelfth Amendment to the Constitution was ratified (in the fall of 1804). This amendment stipulated that the electoral college would henceforth cast separate votes for president and vice president, thus removing the potential for maneuver and confusion that had produced the 1800 deadlock.

The political climate of the early U.S. republic was a combustible one even without disputed elections to add to the volatility. The elites who participated in and controlled the apparatus of politics believed that the emergence of rival, organized political factions was a sign that something had gone seriously wrong with their revolutionary "republican experiment"; yet the reality of fiercely partisan party politics was everywhere around them. Two factions had emerged out of the multifaceted debates of the 1790s—the Democratic-Republicans and Federalists. The Democratic-Republicans, often just called the Republicans, led by Virginians Jefferson and James Madison, had gained significant strength by 1800, due to the backlash from several unpopular measures emanating from the Federalist-controlled executive and Congress. The United States was involved in an undeclared naval war with France—the "quasi-war," as it was called—and anti-French hysteria had spawned both a significant expansion of the nation's military (funded by higher taxes) and a series of draconian laws known as the Alien and Sedition Acts, which were essentially a Federalist effort to legislate the Republican opposition out of existence. To the Republicans, these laws were palpable violations of the Constitution, and their antiforeign provisions pointed toward an ugly nativist streak within the Federalists, who were already stereotyped as a patrician and elitist party.

The election of 1800 took place against this backdrop of crises, foreign and domestic. The Federalist congressional caucus nominated incumbent president John Adams for reelection, with South Carolinian Charles Cotesworth Pinckney as the designated

FACTBOX

PLACE United States

DATE Fall 1800–February 1801

TYPE Disputed election and political crisis

DESCRIPTION A tie in the electoral college vote produced a temporary stalemate in the presidential election and triggered a political and constitutional crisis that was narrowly resolved in 1801.

CAUSE Flaws in the electoral college system permitted circumstances in the balloting that could produce a tie.

IMPACT Thomas Jefferson became president, consummating a significant political realignment; the Twelfth Amendment to the Constitution was ratified in 1804 to prevent another such deadlock in the electoral college.

vice presidential choice. But profound schisms existed among the Federalists; moderates within the party preferred Adams, while archly conservative "High Federalists" (prominent among them was the politically powerful Alexander Hamilton) favored abandoning Adams in favor of Pinckney. The motivations underlying these machinations were complex, but the essential complaint of the "Hamiltonians" was that Adams was too "independent" in that he catered to no man, regardless of political affiliation. His 1800 diplomatic overtures to France ended the "quasi-war" crisis but were strenuously opposed by many Francophobe Federalists who saw them as a surrender to the greatest threat to international order.

Republican-controlled state legislatures in the South, seeing an opportunity in the Federalist schism, put forth Thomas Jefferson (currently vice president under Adams) as their presidential nominee. The vice presidential spot remained contested among several likely candidates until New York went Republican (somewhat surprisingly) in its state elections of 1800. In an era where members of the electoral college were chosen by state legislatures rather than the voters at large, New York's entry into the Republican column was a huge development, and the Republican leadership rewarded the architect of this victory, Aaron Burr, with their vice presidential nomination.

Voting by various states for members of the electoral college, who would in turn actually elect the president and vice president, went on throughout the fall of 1800. By the time the college met in December in each state, it was clear that the balloting would be close. With a few exceptions, northern states tended to vote Federalist and southern states Republican. While some Federalist electors did indeed abandon Adams (with some prodding by Hamilton and others), the Republicans to a man stuck to their "ticket." This was a problem, though, because there was no distinction made in the balloting between president and vice president; each elector cast two ballots, and, as the Constitution stated, the candidate with "the greatest Number of Votes" (provided it was a majority) was elected president, while the recipient of the next-highest total became vice president. In 1800, Jefferson and Burr received the two ballots of every Republican elector, giving them each 73 electoral votes. Adams received 65, and Pinckney 64.

According to the Constitution, in the event of a tie, the election moves to the House of Representatives, with each state delegation granted one vote, and a majority of states was necessary for election. The House at the time was composed of 16 state delegations, and thus nine votes were needed for victory. The old Federalist-controlled Congress (the new Republican majority would not take its seats until after the election) began its balloting on February 11, 1801. On ballot after ballot, Jefferson carried eight state delegations, Burr six, and two remained divided, preventing anyone from winning the presidency. For the next week, the House voted 34 more times, with each ballot inconclusive, as no candidate could win a majority. With Inauguration Day just more than two weeks off, tension and anxiety prevailed across the country, as the possibility of *no* president being elected became increasingly real. The governors of Pennsylvania and Virginia hinted to Jefferson that they would march their states' militias into Washington should the Federalists attempt to take advantage of the impasse by keeping Adams in the presidency.

Prominent Federalists, for their part, argued that Jefferson as president (with his perceived support of the French Revolution) would menace the republic's political order. Back and forth, the rumors, veiled threats, and dire predictions flew until the crisis was resolved—ironically—by Alexander Hamilton. Hamilton used his influence with James Bayard, a Federalist and the lone congressman from Delaware (and thus the sole holder of a crucial state vote), to shift his vote from Burr to Jefferson, giving him the decisive ninth vote for a majority of the state delegations. While Hamilton was opposed to everything Jefferson stood for politically, he despised the ambitious Burr, his longtime political nemesis in New York who he characterized as "an embryo Caesar."

Thus the electoral deadlock was resolved, and the severest test of the Constitution to date had been passed. Before the next election, the Twelfth Amendment to the Constitution was ratified, which mandated that presidential electors would cast separate ballots for president and vice president, in order to prevent another crisis from occurring. While a general sense of relief and conciliation prevailed in the aftermath of the election, the fault lines it revealed—particularly those between North and South—remained marked features of the country's political landscape in the coming years. The United States would have a handful of disputed elections in its future but none quite so agonizing and dangerous as that of 1800. Both its process and outcome revealed how potent the divisions were among Americans committed to a republic and the Constitution but agreeing on little else.

See also 1824–1825 PRESIDENTIAL ELECTION DEADLOCK; 1876–1877 CONTESTED PRESIDENTIAL ELECTION; 2000 PRESIDENTIAL ELECTION STALEMATE.

Kevin M. Gannon

FURTHER READING:
Elkins, Stanley, and Eric McKitrick. *The Age of Federalism: The Early American Republic, 1788–1800.* New York: Oxford University Press, 1993.

Sharp, James Roger. *American Politics in the Early Republic: The New Nation in Crisis.* New Haven, Conn.: Yale University Press, 1993.

1807 ◆ IMPRESSMENT CRISIS

This diplomatic crisis resulted from the British navy's forcible recruiting of sailors from American merchant ships in the 1790s and early 1800s. The issue of impressment, to use its formal name, led to the virtual collapse of Anglo-American diplomatic relations by 1807. Conflict over the practice provoked two bloody naval incidents that created considerable prowar sentiment in the two nations. By 1812, the impressment crisis helped to initiate the second war between Britain and the United States.

Impressment itself was a product of Great Britain's frequent wars in the 18th and 19th centuries, during which the Royal Navy often found itself short-handed. Conditions on naval vessels were notoriously bad, making it difficult to recruit volunteers. Deaths from disease, accidents, and combat ran quite high—an average of 5,000 British sailors and marines died each year between 1793 and 1815. The British navy thus resorted to impressment, or the drafting of civilian sailors, to keep its ships manned.

British naval officers impressed sailors not only from British ports and vessels but also from American merchant ships as well, for at least 30 percent of the sailors on American vessels were British nationals. Few of them had ever become American citizens. Armed impressment squads, known as "press gangs," forcibly took about 3,000 sailors from American merchant ships in the 1790s and another 7,000 between 1803 and 1812. This practice left civilian ships dangerously short of crewmen, and it deprived sailors of their freedom—usually for years at a time. Sometimes it cost them their lives.

Most American merchants and captains accepted impressment as part of the price of doing business. American officials and congressmen, however, found it obnoxious because British naval ships frequently lurked within American territorial waters waiting to stop American merchant ships as they left port. In 1806, President Thomas Jefferson rejected the Monroe-Pinckney Treaty, a commercial pact with Britain, because the British government refused to include a ban on the impressment of American sailors.

The next year, an impressment-related crisis nearly ignited war between the two nations: On June 22, 1807, HMS *Leopard* fired on the American frigate

> ## FACTBOX
>
> **PLACE** Atlantic Ocean, near the East Coast of the United States
>
> **DATE** 1807–12
>
> **TYPE** Diplomatic crisis over the kidnapping of seamen
>
> **DESCRIPTION** The British practice of impressment led to a breakdown in Anglo-American diplomatic relations, two deadly naval incidents, and ultimately to war. As many as 10,000 sailors were taken from U.S. merchant ships from the 1790s through 1812.
>
> **CAUSE** British "press gangs" forcibly seized sailors from American ships.
>
> **CASUALTIES** Three American sailors killed and 18 wounded in an impressment-related naval skirmish in 1807; 10 British sailors killed and 22 wounded in 1811.
>
> **IMPACT** Impressment was a principal cause of the War of 1812, sometimes called America's second war of independence from Britain.

Chesapeake, killing three and wounding 18 crewmen, then boarded the stricken ship, and apprehended four British deserters serving in its crew. The incident provoked anti-British riots in the United States, but instead of treating the attack as an act of war, Congress imposed an embargo on American foreign trade. The embargo was supposed to clear American ships from the seas and put economic pressure on Britain, but it proved so unpopular with voters that Congress lifted it in 1809. Thereafter American trade with Europe resumed, as did British impressments of American sailors for several years.

In 1811, the U.S. Navy Department ordered the frigate *President* to patrol the Atlantic coast to deter impressments. On the night of May 16, the frigate exchanged fire with a British warship, the *Little Belt,* killing 10 British crewmen and injuring 22. The incident led to demands for war in the British press, but the royal government remained unwilling to fight the United States. Indeed, the British government adopted a friendlier attitude toward the Americans later that year, returning the surviving sailors taken from the *Chesapeake* four years earlier and stopping naval patrols along the American coast.

The past practice of impressment, however, had poisoned the political atmosphere between the United States and Britain. In June 1812, President James Madison sent a message to Congress that listed impressment as one of several American grievances that bolstered his case for war. Congress agreed and declared war on June 18 against Great Britain. Some-

times referred to as the United States's second war of independence, the War of 1812 lasted three years and ultimately ended most British interference with American affairs. Meanwhile, the Royal Navy abandoned the practice of impressment after 1815.

David A. Nichols

FURTHER READING:

Hickey, Donald. *Don't Give Up the Ship! Myths of the War of 1812.* Urbana and Chicago: University of Illinois Press, 2006.

———. *The War of 1812: A Forgotten Conflict.* Urbana and Chicago: University of Illinois Press, 1989.

1811 ◆ NEW MADRID EARTHQUAKES

A sequence of intense earthquakes during the winter of 1811–12 that shook the nation from southeastern Missouri to Boston in the northeast and to New Orleans in south remain today the strongest known seismic events in North America east of the Rocky Mountains. These earthquakes were centered in the Mississippi River valley of western Kentucky and Tennessee, southeastern Missouri, and northeastern Arkansas, and they are known today as the New Madrid earthquakes due to their devastating effects on the small town of New Madrid, Missouri. Even today, the seismic hazard for cities such as Memphis, Tennessee, St. Louis, Missouri, and Louisville, Kentucky, is based on the possible recurrence of future strong earthquakes in the New Madrid seismic zone.

The New Madrid earthquake sequence began with a major shock at about 2 A.M. on the morning of December 16, 1811. The ground shook and heaved like waves on the ocean, damaging many chimneys and causing objects be thrown about in dwellings in settlements along the Mississippi River. Landslides were common along the bluffs of the Mississippi and other rivers in the area, and in numerous places, sand and water were thrown onto the surface of the land in earthquake-induced liquefaction features called sand blows. The seismic waves from the earthquakes spread with decreasing intensity throughout eastern

North America, being reported along the Gulf and Atlantic coasts and in southern Ontario in Canada, more than a thousand miles away. The citizens of the towns within about 200 miles of New Madrid reported frequent earthquakes during the night, including a particularly strong shock at dawn.

Thousands of minor shocks and occasional stronger earthquakes were experienced during the following days and weeks. On January 23, 1812, at about 9 A.M., an earthquake comparable to the one on December 16 took place. This event was reportedly felt as far away as Boston. The strongest earthquake of the sequence shook the area on February 7, 1812. This event caused waterfalls to form at two places on the Mississippi River near New Madrid, and for a short while, the river ran backward until the mighty force of the water eroded the falls. A broad area of land near New Madrid was uplifted by perhaps a few feet and changed the course of the Mississippi River, while an area of land sank in Tennessee, causing the formation of Reelfoot Lake. Some buildings at New Madrid collapsed due to this earthquake. After the February 7 earthquake, only weaker aftershocks took place.

No one was reported killed during the earthquakes of 1811–12, but many towns and cities experienced damage from the shaking ground. Cracked chimneys and plaster were reported at St. Louis, Louisville, Cincinnati, Vincennes, Indiana, Wheel-

FACTBOX

PLACE Centered in the Mississippi Valley near New Madrid, Missouri, and felt throughout much of the eastern United States

DATE December 16, 1811–February 12, 1812, with strongest shocks on February 7, 1812

TYPE Earthquake

DESCRIPTION A series of strong earthquakes, with several above magnitude 7, were centered in the Mississippi Valley area near New Madrid, Missouri, in 1811–12. These earthquakes caused major damage and land deformations near the active faults in western Kentucky and Tennessee, southeastern Missouri, and northeastern Arkansas. They caused minor damage or were felt along the Gulf and Atlantic coasts from New Orleans to Boston and north to southern Ontario.

IMPACT These are the largest earthquakes known to have taken place in North America east of the Rocky Mountains. Continuing modern earthquake activity in this region and evidence of other strong earthquakes within the past two millennia indicate that there continues to be a hazard from strong earthquakes to cities such as Memphis, Louisville, and St. Louis.

Analyses of the felt effects of the 1811–12 earthquakes combined with information from modern seismic monitoring in the region have provided a new understanding of this earthquake sequence. Recent studies have estimated the magnitudes (according to "modern movement magnitudes," related to the Richter scale) of the December 16, January 23, and February 12 events as 7.3–7.6, 7.0–7.5, and 7.5–7.8, respectively. The December 16 earthquake probably took place on a fault that extends from about Caruthersville, Missouri to Blytheville, Arkansas. The January 23 earthquake probably occurred on one that stretches from the southeast to the northwest of New Madrid. The February 7 earthquake probably took place on a fault from New Madrid to about Dyersburg, Tennessee. Even today, small earthquakes are detected on one or more of these faults on almost a daily basis.

Geological investigations of sand blows and other surface deformation features caused by the 1811–12 earthquakes show that this area has experienced strong earthquakes in the past. These studies further show that earthquakes with magnitudes of probably 7.0 or greater took place in the New Madrid seismic zone around A.D. 300, A.D. 900, and A.D. 1450. There is also evidence for a strong earthquake in about 2350 B.C.

John E. Ebel

FURTHER READING:

Fuller, Myron L. "The New Madrid Earthquakes." 1912. Reprint, Cape Girardeau, Mo.: Ampere Press.

Hough, Susan E. *Earthshaking Science: What We Know (and Don't Know) about Earthquakes.* Princeton, N.J.: Princeton University Press, 2002.

Johnston, Arch C. "A Major Earthquake Zone on the Mississippi." *Scientific American* 246, no. 4 (April 1982): 60–68.

ing, West Virginia, and Charleston, South Carolina. Most of the damage at cities away from the New Madrid seismic zone appears to have taken place on soft river-bottom land, which apparently amplified the ground-shaking relative to nearby settlements on hard rock.

1814 ◆ BURNING OF WASHINGTON, D.C.

On August 24, 1814, the War of 1812 came to the U.S. capital. After routing a token American force at Bladensburg, Maryland, a British force commanded by General Robert Ross and Admiral George Cockburn marched into Washington, D.C., and burned most of its public buildings to the ground. The military significance of the British victory was minimal, but the political effects on the United States were devastating; the war had gone poorly thus far, and the burning of Washington

FACTBOX

PLACE Washington, D.C., and outlying environs in Maryland

DATE August 24, 1814

TYPE Invasion of national capital, destruction of much of the city

DESCRIPTION British forces, after routing inexperienced and ineffective American militia, entered Washington, D.C., burning many public buildings and inflicting a humiliating defeat on the United States.

CAUSE Ineffective American war effort, British strategic targeting of Chesapeake region (Washington-Baltimore corridor)

CASUALTIES Fewer than 250 deaths; significant physical destruction and effects on morale

IMPACT Underscored serious problems faced by the United States during the War of 1812, increased opposition to both the war and the Madison administration, lowered American morale significantly as Washington was taken and burned with minimal resistance, and was a major element contributing to the crisis facing the U.S. government by the end of 1814

signaled the nadir of President James Madison's war efforts. By the end of the year, the United States was virtually bankrupt, facing the very real threat of New England's secession from the Union and anticipating a British invasion of the southern Gulf coast that seemed quite likely to seize New Orleans and dismember the republic along the Mississippi River.

The War of 1812 was, in the words of historian Samuel Eliot Morison, "America's most unpopular war." The United States had declared war on Great Britain in June 1812 in response to British restrictions on American trade and impressment of American seamen into the Royal Navy (at this time, the Napoleonic Wars were reaching their climax in Europe). Not all Americans, however, supported the war; in particular, the Federalist majority in the New England states was almost unanimously against the declaration of war, arguing that Madi-

son and the Republicans sought to undermine Great Britain—which was the only defense against Napoleon's conquest of the Atlantic world in their eyes. Furthermore, New Englanders believed, the war was the culmination of Republican efforts, which had begun under President Jefferson, to destroy their section and its commercial basis of wealth. How else to explain what seemed to them a wrongheaded foreign policy that favored Napoleon and a spectacularly inept prosecution of the war on the part of the Madison administration? This internal dissent would be one of the most significant problems confronted by the Republican-led war effort.

Of even more immediate concern to the administration, however, was the constant tide of defeat and reversal emanating from the battlefields throughout 1812 and 1813. The 1812 campaign, an attempted three-pronged invasion of British Canada, was marred by a lack of coordination and was a conspicuous failure. While Oliver Hazard Perry's victories on the Great Lakes and William Henry Harrison's defeat of a Shawnee Indian force at the Battle of the Thames seemed to augur improving fortunes in 1813, British victories along the Niagara front ensured that American fortunes at the end of 1813 looked no brighter than they had a year earlier. By 1814, then, Madison's war effort was in serious trouble. Efforts to finance the war by floating government loans, already unpopular, proved mostly fruitless at this juncture, and the national treasury was nearly empty by the summer. The British extended their naval blockade to cover the New England coast, thus placing the entire Atlantic seaboard behind this nautical cordon. New England's state governments refused to release their militia units to fight outside their home states, thus exacerbating an already critical manpower shortage for American forces. By the summer of 1814, many Americans, including a significant element of the political leadership, characterized the war effort as one of incompetence, ineptitude, poor leadership, and defeat.

All of these assessments, accurate or exaggerated, appeared confirmed by the British Chesapeake campaign of 1814. A British flotilla of approximately 20 transport ships made its way up the Chesapeake Bay to the mouth of the Patuxent River. There, General Ross landed a force of some 4,500 troops (many of them hardened and skilled veterans of the European war) at Benedict, Maryland, on August 19 and 20,

1814. By August 22, the force was at Upper Marlboro, a scant 16 miles from Washington, D.C., and was joined by Admiral Cockburn and additional men. Amazingly, the Madison administration had made no provision for the capital city's defense. Secretary of War John Armstrong believed the real target for the British was Baltimore, and the move toward Washington was thus a feint; he persisted in this belief even as it became evident that a sizable British force threatened the capital. The general in charge of the city's defenses had not been appointed until July 1, and he held his office more from political connections than military ability. As the British closed on Washington and the reality of the situation hit, the evacuation of the city was thus chaotic and poorly conducted.

The British approach was made all the easier by the lack of coordinated resistance to their maneuvers. The American forces, mostly militia scraped together to defend the outskirts of Washington, were deployed on the east branch of the Potomac River, northeast of Washington at the town of Bladensburg, Maryland, where the British encountered them in the early afternoon of August 24. The American lines were deployed so as to be unable to support one another, and thus their effort was uncoordinated and largely ineffective during the battle, and—despite inflicting more casualties on the British than they suffered themselves—the defenders were routed. With the last organized resistance swept aside, the British entered Washington and burned most of the public buildings—including the White House, the Capitol building, the Treasury building, the offices of the State and War departments, and the Washington Navy Yard (the best-equipped facility of its kind in the United States).

The sack of the city began, according to British soldiers, as a response to an advance unit being fired on from a private residence at the edge of town. After destroying the house and killing the residents, the British vanguard continued into Washington, where they continued to wreak havoc on government buildings. At the navy yard, the British destroyed the ropewalks, as well as an almost-completed 60-gun frigate in the dry docks. The destruction of several gunpowder magazines near the navy yard only added to the damage, as their explosions leveled the homes and other buildings in the immediate vicinity. Most gratifying to the British, though, was the discovery in the White House of a formal dinner laid out for some 40 guests—who had been forced to evacuate rather quickly. The hungry troopers quickly consumed the fare and drank liberally from the wine cellar before torching the building. The entire British army was in Washington by late evening; the rear elements of the force were able to see quite well in the twilight because of the glow from the burning residences and magazines. Newly arriving soldiers beheld nothing but smoldering ruins in the capital city, with scarcely a building standing, and none undamaged. Effects of this destruction on American morale are difficult to overstate: What was already a disastrous war effort had now produced the humiliating spectacle of government officials fleeing the capital city while enemy forces were able to march in virtually unopposed and burn the symbols of American sovereignty to the ground.

By the end of August, the British had moved on to Baltimore, where they were eventually turned back after failing to take Ft. McHenry in Baltimore Harbor. But things still looked bleak—calls for resistance and secession emanated from New England with increasing frequency, culminating in the HARTFORD CONVENTION of December 1814. The dreaded British invasion of New Orleans seemed as if it would be the final blow in an American defeat, but contrary to almost everyone's expectations, a ragged American force commanded by Andrew Jackson

In this composite view of the burning of Washington, D.C., by the British on August 24, 1814, huge flames billow skyward from the White House. *(Library of Congress)*

was able to defeat the British south of New Orleans in January 1815. A peace treaty had already been proposed a few weeks earlier, and a war-weary Britain, exhausted from the efforts to defeat Napoleon in Europe, showed little inclination to continue the conflict with the United States. Thus, the Treaty of Ghent, ending the War of 1812, essentially mandated a return to the situation that had existed prior to the war's outbreak. In the aftermath of Jackson's stunning triumph at New Orleans, however, Americans celebrated the war as a signal victory over the hated British, and the crisis and humiliation of the previous summer's destruction of Washington was all but forgotten. Despite the nationalist gloss that arose after New Orleans, however, the British destruction

of Washington, D.C., was a significant example of how poorly conceived and executed the American war effort was during almost the entire conflict with Britain. It would not be until 1941, at Pearl Harbor, that a comparable amount of destruction—both real and symbolic—would be visited upon the United States within its borders.

Kevin M. Gannon

FURTHER READING:

Hickey, Donald. *The War of 1812: A Forgotten Conflict.* Urbana: University of Illinois Press, 1989.

Pitch, Anthony S. *The Burning of Washington: The British Invasion of 1814.* Washington, D.C.: Naval Institute Press, 1998.

1814 ◆ HARTFORD CONVENTION

In December 1814, in response to a call from the Massachusetts legislature, a group of New England's political leaders assembled in the city of Hartford, Connecticut, to discuss the means by which their region could more effectively respond to the War of 1812. "Mr. Madison's War," as it was often called in New England, had been unpopular there from the very start. The Hartford Convention was the culmination of many years of Yankee frustration, beginning with their opposition to President Jefferson's Embargo Act of 1807, which had devastated New England's international trade. All the delegates were members of the Federalist Party, which, as a result of its opposition to the war, appeared to be taking on a new life, at least in New England, after losing four presidential elections in a row from 1800 through 1812. Some delegates contemplated secession from the Union if the war did not end, but most were moderates, seeking ways to arrest what they correctly perceived as the declining influence of their region and the Federalist Party.

Since its commencement in June 1812, the war had not gone well. The American fort in Detroit had surrendered almost immediately after the war

FACTBOX
PLACE Hartford, Connecticut
DATE December 15, 1814–January 5, 1815
TYPE Political crisis
DESCRIPTION Angered by the War of 1812, delegates from the New England states met in Hartford to consider political grievances, sparking rumors of secession.
IMPACT The Hartford Convention's report, published just as the news of Andrew Jackson's victory at New Orleans broke, is perhaps the all-time example of poor political timing. It tainted the careers of the participants and contributed to the ultimate disintegration of the Federalist Party.

began, and in spite of a few spectacular victories at sea, the tiny American navy had been manhandled by the much larger Royal Navy. A few months before the delegates met in Hartford, the British had sailed up the Potomac and sacked the nation's capital, burning the executive mansion and chasing President Madison and his wife across the river to Virginia. Rumor had it that a large British armada was heading toward New Orleans with the intent of wresting it from the Americans. This, combined with the destruction of Washington, would bring an end to the war on humiliating terms.

On the surface, it seemed that the convention was remarkably well timed if the goal was to solidify and expand opposition to the War of 1812. As it turned out, however, disaster awaited, not for the American war effort but for the Hartford Convention itself. The armada sailing for New Orleans was real enough, but Major General (and future president) Andrew Jackson was able to rally the citizens of New Orleans. At the same time an American delegation headed by New Englander (and also future president) John Quincy Adams, was in Belgium negotiating the Treaty of Ghent, which ended the war on terms that avoided all of the issues that had allegedly started the war in the first place. Due to slow communications of the time, however, delegates knew of neither event when they gathered behind closed doors in Hartford from December 15, 1814, to January 5, 1815. No record of their deliberations exists. George Cabot, scion of one of the oldest Massachusetts families, presided. Among those in attendance were Harrison Gray Otis and Representative Timothy Pickering of Massachusetts and Theodore Dwight of Connecticut. A former secretary of state and U.S. senator, Pickering was one of the few delegates who actually contemplated secession from the Union; indeed, he had been contemplating it ever since 1804. But Cabot, Otis, and Dwight were representative of the "moderates" who opposed secession but favored instead a bold assertion of state authority over defense matters and the financing thereof, as well as a series of constitutional amendments. Otis wrote the final report and was appointed as part of a committee of three to deliver the report to Congress.

Most of the constitutional amendments in the convention's report reflected New England's concerns or those of the Federalist Party—which often meant the same thing. Examples included requiring a two-thirds vote in both the Senate and House of Representatives for the admission of new states, and the elimination of the provision counting three-fifths of the slave population in southern states as part of their congressional allotment (and therefore in the electoral college as well, without which Thomas Jefferson would not have been elected president in 1800). Others would have required a two-thirds vote in both houses of Congress for a declaration of war and limited a president to one term. Contrary to the accusations flung at it in later years, the convention's report never mentioned or even hinted at secession.

The report's timing, however, proved disastrous. Three days after it was issued on January 5, 1815, Andrew Jackson's forces decisively defeated the British at New Orleans. Six weeks later, news of the Treaty of Ghent arrived. As a result, the Hartford Convention quickly became an object of ridicule and derision, its members stigmatized as examples of selfish sectionalism at best and seditious treason at worst. Most of the delegates spent a good part of their remaining careers explaining their actions and denying any unpatriotic intent. The Federalist Party never recovered from its association with the convention. While it is easy to dismiss the Hartford conventioneers as misguided reactionaries out of touch with the destiny of the young republic, their standing in the annals of American history might have been quite different had the negotiations failed at Ghent and the British captured New Orleans.

Lynn Hudson Parsons

FURTHER READING:

Banner, James M. *To the Hartford Convention: The Federalists and the Origins of Party Politics in Massachusetts, 1789–1815.* New York: Knopf, 1970.

Dwight, Theodore. *History of the Hartford Convention: With a Review of the Policy of the United States Government Which Led to the War of 1812.* 1833. Reprint, Freeport, N.Y.: Da Capo Press, 1970.

Morison, Samuel Eliot. *Harrison Gray Otis, 1765–1848: The Urbane Federalist.* Boston: Houghton Mifflin, 1969.

1816 ◆ THE YEAR WITHOUT A SUMMER

A rare June snowstorm and hard frosts in every month of the year in New England earned 1816 the contemporary moniker "the year without a summer." The agricultural damage done by these cold spells was increased by a lack of rain in the early summer months, corresponding forest fires, and severe late summer storms. In October 1816, one Massachusetts reporter appropriately summed up the state of the season in *The Farmer's Cabinet*: "we have before us twenty different paragraphs from every quarter reiterating similar complaints of drought, frost and snow—of gale and flood—of short crops, and melancholy prospects." Overall, the price of wheat, a fair indicator of economic stability, was higher in 1816 than in any other year in the first half of the 19th century. Farmers were hard pressed to feed their cattle in cold, parched fields, they feared a shortage of winter provisions, and some of the more remote even experienced shortages of foodstuffs for human consumption, though no one died as a result. Even animals seemed aware of this weather-related disaster. One writer for the *Connecticut Courant* reported that a "great number of squirrels . . . appeared to be moving south [and] our old men say, when the squirrels move south, it prognosticates a severe winter."

But unusual weather was only part of the problem in this agricultural crisis. Speculators hoarded and sold farm goods to Canada, and parts of Europe also suffering crop shortages, further driving up the prices of necessary commodities in local markets. As a result, many New Englanders migrated to the Midwest, which was spared from the brunt of the cold and drought. In fact, historians contend that the intensification of agriculture in the Midwest in response to 1816 was at least partly responsible for the panic of 1819, when the weather and the price of wheat returned to normal and boom turned to bust. The "year without a summer" is, therefore, not only significant as a widespread catastrophic weather event but also provides important insight into the state of the market economy in the early 19th century and the human role played in seemingly natural disasters.

While many Americans blamed extraordinary dark spots visible on the sun for the cold summer weather, the true cause of this climatic disturbance

---

FACTBOX

PLACE Eastern United States, with harshest conditions experienced in New England

DATE 1816

TYPE Weather-related natural disaster

DESCRIPTION Climate-cooling volcanic ash in the atmosphere led to summer frosts and snows that combined with drought conditions to create an agricultural crisis in the eastern United States as well as western Europe.

IMPACT The "year without a summer" demonstrates the impact that a volcano can have halfway around the world and the human role played in natural disasters: A weather-related agricultural crisis—caused by Mount Tambora erupting in Indonesia—was intensified by speculation and alarmist news reporting in the United States. In addition, the decisions of midwestern farmers to increase their agricultural output to supply markets in Europe, Canada, and New England ultimately led to the panic of 1819 when production outstripped demand.

---

was related to a volcanic eruption halfway around the world. On April 10, 1815, Mount Tambora, located on the island of Sumbawa in Indonesia, spewed forth an immense amount of volcanic ash into the atmosphere, where it remained for several years, effectively blocking the sun's rays. Some contemporary writers did recognize the unusual atmospheric conditions, commenting on the haze that blanketed the sky and the deep red hue of the setting sun, but they were unaware of any connection between the debris from volcanic eruptions and a cooling trend in the weather. Between 1780 and 1820, the weather turned particularly chilly due to an unprecedented level of volcanic explosions of which Tambora was the most spectacular. This 40-year span was in fact the climax of what historians have labeled "The Little Ice Age" that stretched for 300 years, from approximately 1550 to 1850. The effects of the extreme four-decade climatic cold spell were felt most strongly in the eastern United States and western Europe, leading to what historian John D. Post has called "the last great subsistence crisis in the Western world" between 1816 and 1819.

In the United States, the human causes that intensified this weather-induced agricultural crisis were related to the expanding market economy and newspaper industry; by 1816, neither news nor goods was strictly a local commodity. Newspapers had grown exponentially since the revolutionary era, from just 20 in 1780 to more than 100 in 1820. At the same time, the amount of agricultural products sold by merchants to distant markets had far surpassed goods exchanged locally. Widespread alarmist reporting on the weather and merchant sales to the profitable Canadian market reinforced each other to create a scarcity of agricultural goods at home. Unembarrassed by their own role in the process, many newspaper reporters complained that the "high price of bread excites general alarm and is owing to *artificial causes.*"

Ironically, the "year without a summer" occurred during the period identified by political historians as the "Era of Good Feelings," when partisanship on the national level briefly declined. Despite this lack of political contention, most rural residents who struggled through the summer and winter of 1816 were likely short on good feelings. Contemporary community leaders and even the president of the United States also addressed the impact of the disastrous weather on their society. Many wealthy farmers attempted agricultural experiments to extend the meager harvest, like planting the previously neglected potato, and passed their advice on to others through the newspapers. Seeking a more religious solution, the governor of New Hampshire admonished residents to "be mindful that in the course of the present year, the earth has not yielded her usual supply for our returning wants, and it is our duty, when God's judgments are in the earth, to humble ourselves for our transgressions." And finally, the unusual weather was important enough to James Madison that he began his yearly presidential address in 1816 with the following quote: "In reviewing the present state of our country, our attention cannot be withheld from the effect produced by peculiar seasons, which have very generally impaired the annual gifts of the earth."

Lauri Bauer Coleman

FURTHER READING:

Post, John D. *The Last Great Subsistence Crisis in the Western World.* Baltimore: Johns Hopkins University Press, 1977.

Stommel, Henry, and Elizabeth Stommel. *Volcano Weather: The Story of 1816, the Year Without a Summer.* Newport, R.I.: Seven Seas Press, 1983.

1819 ◆ FINANCIAL PANIC AND DEPRESSION

The panic of 1819, the first major financial crisis of the 19th century, triggered a serious commercial slowdown whose roots can be traced to political antecedents arising from the War of 1812. Because the federal government had enormous difficulties in raising money during the war, the Madison administration resorted to the issuance of Treasury notes, certificates given by the government promising to pay the amount printed on the bill plus interest within a year. The Madison administration expected such notes to serve as a paper money but instead, state banks—private local banks authorized by state legislatures—began to use them as monetary reserves. Based on the amount of reserves a bank held, the bank could extend credit in the form of bank notes. Because the federal government issued so many Treasury notes, the nation witnessed a considerable expansion of the money supply. Also, during the war, which lasted until 1815, and for three years thereafter, the banks suspended payment in specie (gold and silver coin) and relied on bank notes for currency needs. Thus, the seeds for the nation's most serious economic crisis to date had been sown.

Coincident with the expansion of the money supply in the 1810s was an expansion of the number of banks. Outside of New England, the number of

FACTBOX

PLACE United States

DATE 1819–22

TYPE Banking panic and economic depression

DESCRIPTION The recession lasted three years, but its effects were limited due to the noncommercial quality of American economic life.

CAUSE An economic downturn resulting from readjustment of international trade to peacetime conditions, plus a failed banking system that reduced the money supply

IMPACT Temporarily slowed the westward movement and spurred the creation of a new party system consisting of Whigs and Democrats

banks swelled from 88 in 1811 to 392 in 1818. Some of these banks were related to the westward expansion of cotton farmers to Alabama, Mississippi, and other new southern states; some of it arose from the migration of small farmers to the Great Lakes area. But basically the increased number of banks reflected a growing commerce between the United States and Europe. The end of the war released much pent-up demand for European goods; imports soared from $113 million in 1815 to $147 million in 1816, though they declined to $122 million by 1818. At the same time, exports rose as well, from $53 million in 1815 to $93 million in 1818. This trade imbalance would contribute to the Panic of 1819.

A further political complication originated in the determination of many congressmen not to endure international embarrassment again because of a faulty financial system. In 1816, Congress passed, and President Madison approved, a Second Bank of the United States. This institution had branches spread throughout the country. With its authority to require state banks to redeem their notes in specie or to allow them to circulate freely as currency, the Second Bank of the United States had the power to expand or contract the money supply. In short, it had some of the hallmarks of a modern central bank.

By the late 1810s the U.S. economy was on the verge of faltering and in need of adjustment. Europe was beginning to recover from the Napoleonic Wars and demand for American products lessened. Americans were engaged in heavy speculation in western

lands, and the trade imbalance only added to existing dramatic deficits in the U.S. balance of payments—which would have to be repaid by the transference of gold overseas. Finally, the United States had experienced considerable inflation during the War of 1812 because of the issuance of Treasury notes.

At the root of most of the economic problems of the United States during the 19th century was the lack of a central bank run by knowledgeable officials. All the European powers had central banks; the United States was the great anomaly. Central banks in the 20th century would undertake two major functions: (1) Through their manipulation of available credit and the money supply, they would engage in countercyclical activity and smooth out the extreme bumps of the business cycle; and (2) they would stabilize the banking establishment by being the lender of last resort to solvent banks that faced a "liquidity crisis," that is, lacked gold and silver coin to satisfy a horde of agitated note-holders and depositors. In the 19th century, however, no agency in the United States supplied these two crucial central banking functions. This omission set the stage for banking "panics," which unfolded more or less in the following fashion during the 1800s. The economy drifted downward or rumors of a banking insolvency spread among the public; banks suddenly had difficulty meeting the demands of note-holders and depositors; the public swarmed the banks demanding their funds; the banks lost most of their specie; the banks suspended specie payment; and finally, banks dramatically curtailed loans and credit to the business community, thereby signaling the onset of a depression. The so-called panics of the 19th century were really depressions but were called panics because the public "panicked" when banks went bankrupt and depositors lost their money. (It is worth noting that in the 20th century, the central bank policies of the Federal Reserve have eliminated most panics, with the Great Depression of the 1930s an important exception. In addition, the Federal Reserve has greatly softened the heights and depths of the bust-and-boom cycle that terrorized American citizens in the prior century.)

In 1819 the economic crisis was triggered by the Second Bank of the United States (BUS) and Secretary of the Treasury William Crawford. The first president of the bank was William Jones, an incompetent leader who allowed BUS branches to engage in unsound financial practices. Jones brought the bank close to insolvency, and he did not curtail the expansion of state bank notes. Secretary Crawford wanted the nation to return to the gold standard and specie payment; to do so required elimination of the Treasury notes issued during the war. Jones was eased out of his position as president of the bank in 1818 and replaced with Langdon Cheves of South Carolina. Cheves read the situation correctly and demanded that state banks redeem their notes by returning the Treasury notes in payment. In doing so, he was curtailing the money supply and in fact eliminating the reserves of state banks. It is estimated that the amount of bank notes in circulation fell from $68 million in 1816 to $45 million in 1820. As this domestic contraction of the money supply occurred, European harvests returned to normal and prices of agricultural products dropped. In short, European demand for American goods evaporated. The combined pressure of monetary contraction and falling European demand led to widespread bankruptcies in 1819. Although New York City and New England banks did not suspend specie payment, banks elsewhere did, bringing on the panic. Credit then failed, and the nation slipped into recession, which lasted for two years, with prices falling as much as 20 percent. Imports and exports hits their lows in 1821, but by 1822 recovery had begun.

Economic information and statistics in this period of American history are scarce, so the dimensions of the Panic of 1819 are difficult to determine with certainty. What is known is that unemployment shot up in some cities and many manufacturers closed their doors. Speculators in western lands suffered severe losses, and importers and exporters experienced reverses. But beyond these groups, the impact of the depression is unclear. The American economy had not yet been stitched together by canals and railroads into an integrated market economy; many regions of the nation were still in a semisubsistent, agricultural condition. The nation was still overwhelmingly rural, with only 8 percent of the population living in urban communities.

If the panic of 1819 had limited economic effects, it had strong political ones. The downturn occurred when the crisis of Missouri's admittance to the nation as a slave state shook the halls of Congress. The westward movement was thwarted by the depression, and many eager cotton planters blamed the state of affairs on the federal government. Out of the economic concerns of the West and the South, plus worries about a too powerful national government among southern slaveholders, a new political party system, consisting of the Whigs and the Democrats, emerged during the 1820s. By introducing economic discontent at the same time that political unrest over slavery roiled the land, the panic of 1819 induced national effects far beyond its limited impact on economic growth.

See also 1785 ECONOMIC CRISIS; 1837 FINANCIAL PANIC AND DEPRESSION.

James L. Huston

FURTHER READING:

Rothbard, Murray N. *The Panic of 1819: Reactions and Policies*. New York: Columbia University Press, 1962.

Taylor, George Rogers. *The Transportation Revolution, 1815–1860*. New York: Holt, Rinehart, and Winston, 1951.

Timberlake, Richard H., Jr. *The Origins of Central Banking in the United States*. Cambridge, Mass.: Harvard University Press, 1978.

1822 ◆ DENMARK VESEY SLAVE PLOT

In the summer of 1822, 35 men were hanged in Charleston, South Carolina, for planning the Denmark Vesey plot to launch a slave uprising. Had the scheme been implemented, it could have become the most deadly act of black resistance in antebellum history. Possibly 9,000 African Americans could have joined instigator Denmark Vesey in the torching of Charleston. The terrifying implications of the plot were evident in the large number of blacks that white authorities executed for participating in the conspiracy.

Denmark Vesey's origins are obscure. Born in about 1767, he spent his teenage years as a slave in the Danish Virgin Islands (today the U.S. Virgin

Islands). It is not certain whether he was born there or had recently been brought over from West Africa. In 1781, slave trader Joseph Vesey purchased the 14-year-old boy and resold him to the hot and harrowing sugar plantations on St. Domingue (present-day Haiti). Vesey's crew named the young man "Telemaque," after the son of Odysseus, who in the ancient Greek epic traveled the Mediterranean in search of his father. The name proved a fitting omen for a youth spent at sea. Vesey bought Telemaque back a year later and put him to work as a sailor in his slave-trading business. Before master and slave settled down in Charleston, their frequent journeys along the Atlantic coast sensitized Telemaque to the fate that African slaves shared in the Americas. He developed an avid interest in politics and religion and learned to speak several languages. News of the successful Haitian slave revolt of 1792 strengthened him in his belief that African Americans could and should unite against their oppressors.

Telemaque's luck changed in 1799 when he won the jackpot of $1,500 in the Charleston lottery. He spent $600 to secure his freedom and used the rest of his winnings to establish himself as a carpenter. In honor of his former master, he changed his name to "Denmark Vesey." His loyalties, however, remained with the oppressed.

Although the United States had won independence from Britain in the 1780s, circumstances for most African Americans had not improved. During the revolutionary period, blacks had sought the same freedom and equality that whites demanded for themselves. Their hopes fell short, however, and slavery remained entrenched throughout the South, sanctioned by the U.S. Constitution ratified in 1788. Nor was life much easier for southern blacks who had managed to gain their freedom. On entering economic competition with white workers, African Americans were perceived as a threat and encountered hatred and discrimination. Some blacks responded by calling for violence. Others found solace in the evangelical faith that regained its strength during the Second Great Awakening of the 1820s and 1830s. Denmark Vesey combined both trends.

Preaching and reading to fellow blacks, Vesey gained influence in Charleston's African-American community. In sermons he delivered at the African Methodist Episcopal (AME) Church, he portrayed himself as a "Black Moses" and would at times travel

FACTBOX

PLACE Charleston, South Carolina

DATE Summer 1822

TYPE Attempted slave revolt

DESCRIPTION Led by Denmark Vesey, African Americans planned an attack on Charleston's white population.

CAUSE Slavery and oppression of African Americans

CASUALTIES 35 blacks implicated in the conspiracy were hanged, and 43 were deported from South Carolina.

IMPACT Growing will to resist among enslaved blacks, stronger slave codes and laws restricting black freedom, rising fears among plantation owners

up to 80 miles on foot up and down the coast of South Carolina to garner support for his plot. Among Vesey's recruits, who later described him as an inspiring, yet sometimes despotic leader, were free black craftsmen as well as enslaved plantation workers and apparently even some whites. The group planned to strike on Sunday, July 14, 1822. Blacksmith Tom Russell was to handcraft pikes as makeshift weapons, and a barber agreed to provide wigs as disguises after the attack. Come midnight, the rebels wanted to raid weapons arsenals in and around Charleston. They then would have burned down the entire city and slaughtered its 10,000 white citizens as they fled from their homes. Afterward, the culprits planned to flee to Haiti.

Authorities learned of the scheme on May 30, 1822, when a confidant of the conspirators, a slave, told his master about the plot. Under pressure, more participants betrayed the plan, and all attempts to conceal or to immediately begin the uprising failed. From June 17 to August 3, 131 black suspects were put on trial. Fifty-three were acquitted, 43 were deported from South Carolina, and 35 were hanged. The AME church was ordered burnt down. Vesey himself was apprehended on June 22, sentenced to death six days later, and executed on July 2. He left seven wives and two sons in several coastal towns.

In 2001, historian Michael Johnson suggested that the entire Vesey trial may have been based on fabricated evidence. South Carolina governor Thomas Bennett had questioned the gravity of the threat early on. After analyzing the original court records, Johnson concluded that Charleston's mayor James Hamilton had framed Vesey for a mere rumor in the black community in order to advance his political career (he later served as a U.S. congressman and governor of South Carolina). Scholarly opinions differ about the veracity of Johnson's claim. Whether valid or not, the plot's significance lies in the very real hopes and fears it raised among contemporaries. False accusations merely added to Vesey's notoriety, and rumors of impending rebellion prompted three distinct responses. First, Vesey's example encouraged many imitators, the most prominent of which was Nat Turner, who led a bloody slave uprising in Virginia nine years later. Second, authorities tried to curb potential uprisings by tightening slave codes. Because of Vesey's past as a mariner, South Carolina legislators passed the Negro Seaman Act of 1823, calling for black sailors to be imprisoned while at harbor to keep them from conspiring. Lawmakers also restricted African Americans' access to churches since the Old Testament's salvation language of Moses leading his people out of bondage had been one of Vesey's major inspirations. Last, some white southerners started to doubt their ability to permanently suppress rebellions, with a few considering options such as manumission and compensated abolition. These conflicting sentiments about the institution of slavery evolved into intractable positions in the years preceding the Civil War.

See also 1739 STONO REBELLION; 1741 NEW YORK CITY FIRES AND SLAVE "CONSPIRACY"; 1831 NAT TURNER SLAVE REBELLION.

Mathias Hanses

FURTHER READING:

Egerton, Douglas R. *He Shall Go Out Free: The Lives of Denmark Vesey.* Madison, Wis.: Madison House, 1999.

Johnson, Michael P. "Denmark Vesey and His Co-Conspirators." *William and Mary Quarterly* 58 (October 2001): 915–976.

Paquette, Robert L. "From Rebellion to Revisionism: The Continuing Debate about the Denmark Vesey Affair." *Journal of the Historical Society* 4, no. 3 (Fall 2004): 291–334.

1824–1825 ◆ PRESIDENTIAL ELECTION DEADLOCK

The presidential election of 1824 remains the only election to date in which the House of Representatives exercised its power to choose the president when no candidate received a majority of the electoral votes, as provided for in the Twelfth Amendment to the Constitution. The election also remains as the only contested one in American political history in which there were no organized political parties. The quest for the presidency initially pitted an unusual group of five highly ambitious men against one another: John Quincy Adams, Henry Clay, John C. Calhoun, William H. Crawford, and Andrew Jackson.

Although there were no organized political parties in the modern sense of the term, the election was not without conflict or issues. Every president up to then had either been from Virginia or named Adams, and there was an increasing number of Americans who had come to regard the presidency as the province of elite members of society closed off from the public. Fear of "corruption," which in the early 19th century meant the use of patronage and appointment power to in effect exclude the masses from any significant role in the outcome, was expressed in various editorials and pamphlets. Then too, personal issues intruded into the race. Jackson had a profound dislike for Crawford and Clay; Adams and Clay had a history of disagreement over foreign policy.

Secretary of State John Quincy Adams had the most impressive résumé. His public services had begun as a teenager in the 1780s, accompanying his father, John Adams, the future second president, in Paris. His New England background made him a logical choice as President Monroe's secretary of state,

FACTBOX

PLACE United States

DATE November 1824–March 1825

TYPE Political crisis

DESCRIPTION As no candidate in the election of 1824 received a majority of electoral votes, the House of Representatives had to determine the president. Although Andrew Jackson had received the largest number of electoral and popular votes, the House selected John Quincy Adams as president. Adams then picked Henry Clay, Speaker of the House and an unsuccessful presidential candidate, as secretary of state, opening up charges of a "corrupt bargain."

IMPACT Adams's presidency was seriously crippled as a result of charges of a "corrupt bargain," and Clay would be tainted by the charges for the rest of his career. The charges also aided Andrew Jackson's quest for the presidency, achieved in 1828.

from 1817 through 1825. Contrasted with the dour Adams was the magnetic Henry Clay, representative from Kentucky. As Speaker of the House of Representatives in 1820, Clay helped arrange the various measures to be known later as the Missouri Compromise which concerned the future of slavery in the West. South Carolina's John C. Calhoun was a former congressman and at age 42 was the youngest of the five candidates. In 1817, President Monroe appointed him to his cabinet as secretary of war. Treasury Secretary William H. Crawford of Georgia had served in the U.S. Senate and as U.S. minister to France. In September 1823, he suffered a crippling stroke from which he never fully recovered, but he remained in the race.

General Andrew Jackson was the only contender who had not compiled an extensive record in politics. Although he had briefly represented his state of Tennessee in Congress in the 1790s, his reputation was built more on his military career, specifically his victory over the British at New Orleans in 1815. Lacking a formal education, he was not taken seriously until late in the campaign. But the very qualities that caused some to dismiss him were those that appealed to thousands of voters. To Americans who had been schooled in the virtues of republicanism—suspicion of power, distrust of elites, and belief in the potential for "corruption"—Jackson's potential strength was enormous. To a nation no longer embroiled in the wars of Europe, Jackson's western frontier background was an asset, not a liability.

The young Calhoun recognized Jackson's popular appeal. After a disappointing effort in a Pennsylvania convention where the Jackson men routed his supporters, Calhoun withdrew from the race and announced his willingness to accept the vice presidency, which indeed is what occurred. Crawford's illness meant in reality that there were only three candidates remaining: Adams, Clay, and Jackson. Congress had yet to enact legislation requiring a single day for choosing electors—hence there was no national "election day" as we know it today—and in several states electors were chosen not by popular vote but by state legislatures. By December 1824, it was clear that no candidate could claim a majority of either the popular or electoral votes. Jackson led in the popular vote with 152,901 (42 percent) to Adams's 114,023 (32 percent), Crawford's 46,979 (13 percent), and Clay's 47,217 (13%). Jackson also led in the electoral vote with 99 (38 percent) to Adams's 84 (32 percent), Crawford's 41 (16 percent), and Clay's 37 (14 percent).

Although Jackson received the most electoral votes, he did not receive a majority, which is necessary to be elected president. The Twelfth Amendment to the Constitution, ratified in 1804, provides that when no candidate receives a majority of the electoral vote in the general election, the House of Representatives determines the winner by choosing from among the top three vote-getters—in this case, Jackson, Adams, and Crawford. House members vote by state delegations, with each state casting one vote, regardless of size. A majority of the states was needed (13 in 1824) to select a victor. Had a majority not been obtained, the vice president–elect, John C. Calhoun, would have become president.

Although Henry Clay's hopes of being the third candidate from which the House could choose were dashed, he still had the power as Speaker to influence the House vote on the remaining three. As the day of the House's selection drew near, backdoor maneuvering and negotiations began. Approached by friends of all three finalists, Clay listened courteously, but in fact he had already made his decision. On January 8, 1825, he met with Adams and announced his intention to support him. The news was met with some disbelief because Clay had been one of Adams's severest critics and Clay's own state, Kentucky, clearly favored the westerner Jackson over the New Englander Adams. Rumors that Adams had "bargained" with Clay for the presidency began to circulate.

On February 9, the House met to count the electoral ballots and make its choice. Clay's influence was felt as Kentucky, Missouri, Louisiana, Ohio, and Illinois supported Adams, giving him the required 13 states on the first ballot, with Jackson obtaining seven states, and Crawford four. Following the result, Adams announced his nomination of Henry Clay to be his secretary of state, thus opening his presidency to the charge by the Jacksonians that the wishes of the people had been illegitimately defied by a nefarious "corrupt bargain." It was a colossal error on Adams's part to make the offer and an even greater one for Clay to accept it. Although most historians in later years have discredited the notion of "bargain and sale," it wounded, perhaps fatally, the presidency of the second Adams from the very beginning. For Clay, it was like a tin can tied to a dog's tail, attached to him for the rest of his political career. Jackson would challenge Adams again in 1828, soundly defeating him.

See also 1800–1801 PRESIDENTIAL ELECTION CRISIS; 1876–1877 CONTESTED PRESIDENTIAL ELECTION; 2000 PRESIDENTIAL ELECTION STALEMATE.

Lynn Hudson Parsons

FURTHER READING:

Hopkins, James F. "The Presidential Election of 1824." In *History of American Presidential Elections.* Edited by Arthur J. Schlesinger Jr. and Fred L. Israel. Vol. 1. 349–409. New York, Chelsea House, 1971.

Parsons, Lynn Hudson. "The Election of 1824." In *American Presidential Campaigns and Elections.* Edited by William G. Shade and Ballard C. Campbell, 214–231. Armonk, N.Y.: M.E. Sharpe, 2003.

1831 ◆ NAT TURNER SLAVE REBELLION

The Nat Turner rebellion of 1831 was the most devastating slave revolt in the history of the United States. In less than two days, 70 black insurgents killed 59 white Virginians, and whites slaughtered more than 100 blacks in retaliation. One of several uprisings in the early 19th century, the Turner rebellion produced more casualties than even the Louisiana slave revolt of 1811 with its 500 participants.

This willingness to resort to violence can be linked to the broken promises of the American Revolution. Public discussions about independence from the British Empire during the late 18th century had sensitized black as well as white Americans to Enlightenment ideas of freedom and equality. African Americans tried to take advantage of the new intellectual climate by adopting the rhetoric of the Revolution for their own cause. Despite their contributions to the War for Independence and the numerous petitions filed to secure their freedom, blacks were disappointed by northern politicians, who chose to make concessions

FACTBOX

PLACE Southampton County, Virginia

DATE August 21–22, 1831

TYPE Slave uprising

DESCRIPTION Approximately 70 rebellious slaves led by Nat Turner killed 59 white southerners. In retaliation, whites killed more than 100 blacks.

CAUSE The institution of slavery in the South

CASUALTIES More than 160 deaths

IMPACT Blacks' access to churches was restricted. The uprising amplified fears of slave revolt among white southerners and sparked increased debate about the future of slavery nationwide.

to southern slave owners. American independence left slavery intact throughout the South, and it became more entrenched in the opening decades of the 19th

This contemporary woodcut from *An authentic and impartial narrative of the tragical scene which was witnessed in Southampton County* (New York, 1831) portrays the hand-to-hand combat of the Nat Turner slave rebellion and the militia's pursuit of black insurgents. *(Library of Congress)*

century. In the Second Great Awakening of the 1820s and 1830s, many African Americans sought relief in religious revival and the evangelical faith. In spite or rather because of prior disappointments, influential blacks like David Walker in his 1829 *Appeal to the Colored Citizens of the World* called for violent resistance to slavery and racial injustice. Both the futile efforts to fight the system with legal means and the salvation language of the Old Testament had provided the African-American community with the necessary vocabulary—and perhaps, the inspiration—to further their own fight for freedom.

Nat Turner was born on October 2, 1800, in Southampton County, Virginia. He was deeply religious and, although a plantation slave, literate since his childhood. Very early in his life, his parents strengthened him in his belief that he would grow up to be a prophet and a liberator of his people. In the tradition of the plots of fellow Virginian Gabriel Prosser (1800) and the South Carolinian Denmark Vesey (1822), both of which failed before they could be put into practice, Turner started to prepare his own revolt in February 1831. When he interpreted an eclipse of the sun as the omen for which he had been waiting, he implemented his plan.

On Monday, August 21, 1831, shortly after midnight, Turner and his followers killed slave owner

Joseph Travis, his family, and all other whites on the Travis plantation. The rebellious slaves then kept moving from household to household across Southampton County, gathering weapons, freeing every black, and killing every white man, woman, and child they encountered. On Monday morning, the rebels repulsed local militia troops who tried to halt the marauders. By nightfall of that same day, the number of insurgents had risen to almost 70.

On Tuesday, August 22, Turner and his group decided to head to Jerusalem, the county seat, which housed an arsenal. After marching 20 miles, the Turner band was ambushed by the heavily reinforced militia three miles outside of the town. Outnumbered and overpowered, the rebels scattered and the uprising collapsed. Yet within little more than 24 hours, Turner and his collaborators had killed 59 whites: 10 men, 14 women, and 35 children. Retaliation came swiftly. That same day, whites killed more than 100 members of the black community. They cut off their heads and fixed them on poles to serve as a deterrent for anyone who might be harboring similar ideas. Nineteen rebels were tried quickly and executed. Turner himself managed to escape and eluded capture for nine weeks. Virginian militiamen apprehended him on October 30 and put him on trial in

November. During this time, a young lawyer named Thomas Ruffin Gray interviewed Turner in his jail cell and transcribed a statement, known as Turner's *Confessions.* Most historical knowledge about Turner's motivations and actions is based on this short account. Nat Turner was hanged on November 11, 1831.

As the bloodiest slave uprising the nation had ever seen, the Nat Turner Rebellion raised anxiety among white southerners about the security of their society. More than ever, they were aware of the mortal threat lurking on their doorstep. Some plantation owners immediately tightened slave codes. They restricted blacks' access to churches, which were perceived as sources of revolt, and especially tried to keep slaves from becoming preachers. Conversely, however, the Turner Rebellion planted seeds of doubt among some planters concerning their ability to maintain the slave system indefinitely. Further repression, after all, could intensify threats to personal safety rather than lessen the danger. These conflicting approaches helped kindle the increasingly emotional debate about the future of slavery in the mid-19th-century United States.

See also 1739 Stono rebellion; 1741 New York City fires and slave "conspiracy"; 1822 Denmark Vesey slave plot.

Mathias Hanses

FURTHER READING:

Greenberg, Kenneth S. *Nat Turner: A Slave Rebellion in History and Memory.* New York: Oxford University Press, 2003.

Tragle, Henry Irving. *The Southampton Slave Revolt of 1831: A Compilation of Source Material, Including the Full Text of* The Confessions of Nat Turner. Amherst: University of Massachusetts Press, 1971.

1832 ◆ CHOLERA EPIDEMIC

On June 26, 1832, a poor Irish immigrant father in New York City came home ill with painful stomach cramps and severe diarrhea. By morning he recovered, but his two children fell ill and were soon dead. With these three cases, all attending physicians agreed: Cholera had finally come to New York City. By the end of the fall, the disease claimed the lives of more than 3,500 mostly poor New Yorkers. Spread west via the recently completed Erie Canal and south by land and sea, the 1832 epidemic claimed between 50,000 and 150,000 lives in the United States.

Cholera is caused by the bacterium *Vibrio cholera* and is exclusively a human disease. With little or no warning, it causes cramps, massive diarrhea, and spasmodic vomiting resulting in dehydration, which leads to rapidly falling blood pressure. The skin becomes shriveled and takes on a bluish tinge. Death can occur within a day of the onset of symptoms. Although unknown at the time, cholera is transmitted mainly through sewage-contaminated water supplies.

The 1832 cholera epidemic appears to have begun in Russia in 1830. New Yorkers read almost daily about its spread across Europe. By the fall of 1831, even the most optimistic knew that New York would not be spared. The mayor declared a quarantine against almost all European and Asian ships. Cholera came instead via Canada.

The city reacted quickly to news of the breach of the Canadian quarantine. By mid-June, New York City reorganized its sanitation system, appropriated funds to set up hospitals, and sent observers to Canada. It reconvened the Board of Health, which included the mayor and some members of the city council. The New York Medical Society recommended that the city keep the streets clean and that streets, yards and cesspools be disinfected with chloride of lime or quicklime. The public was advised to stay calm and be moderate in their eating and drinking.

The flurry of municipal activity dissipated as quickly as it began. By the time the first cases appeared, all street cleaning had ceased. By the end of June, several cases of cholera were reported to the Board of Health, but the board refused to make these reports public. The Medical Society, acting on its own, publicly announced on July 2 that nine cases were known and that only one person survived. The society was criticized by the political and business leadership who

FACTBOX

PLACE New York City and the eastern United States

DATE June–August 1832 in New York City; summer 1832–fall 1834 in the rest of the United States

TYPE Epidemic

DESCRIPTION The 1832 epidemic was the first of three major cholera outbreaks in the United States during the 19th century.

CAUSE Cholera is an infectious disease spread through sewage-contaminated water supplies.

CASUALTIES More than 3,500 died in New York City, with estimates of 50,000 to 150,000 nationally.

IMPACT New York City and other cities across the country slowly began to construct municipally provided water and sewer systems.

feared that the announcement was premature and would have a negative effect on business.

By this time, however, New York City was empty except for the poorest. Those who could afford to leave the city had done so or were planning to leave. Residents who stayed stocked up on cayenne pepper, laudanum (extract of opium), and calomel (mercury chloride)—remedies suggested by the Medical Society. Prisoners confined to the almshouse on misdemeanors were discharged. Felons were sent to a temporary shelter. By the second week of July, the entire city was eerily silent. There was no business activity. Even many of the churches closed their doors.

In the week that it took the Board of Health to open the cholera hospitals, the epidemic raged. The disease spread as people came in contact with contaminated water. Water distribution was the responsibility of the privately owned Manhattan Water Company. The company entirely ignored the poorer sections of the city, forcing those residents to rely on wells contaminated by privies and cesspools, which explains why the vast majority of victims were among the poorer classes.

Days after appearing in New York City, the epidemic spread to Philadelphia, Baltimore, and other cities along the Atlantic Coast and the Gulf of Mexico. Throughout the summer and for the next two years, the epidemic raged in almost every state in the country, hitting the poor in New York City and New Orleans the hardest. Local authorities set up makeshift hospitals but were woefully unprepared. The poor were the overwhelming majority of patients in the cholera hospitals and were often admitted against their will. Many of the poorer residents believed that the doctors were taking them to the hospital to experiment on them. In some neighborhoods, residents organized their own defense and refused to allow city officials, nurses, and physicians in under the threat of violence.

Physicians did not believe that cholera was contagious. According to the Medical Society, intemperance, excessiveness, imprudence, and filth made people vulnerable. This view coincided neatly with the generally held notion that cholera was God's punishment for sinners. Both physicians and the lay public blamed the poor, especially the Irish immigrants, for predisposing themselves through their "sinful" behavior. Respectable people were confident that their virtuousness made them immune to cholera. Death from cholera among the higher classes was disquieting but was usually quickly explained by revelations of secret vices.

The epidemic peaked at the end of July. On August 20, the Board of Health began to close the cholera hospitals. By Christmas the scourge had passed. Milder outbreaks recurred in the summer of 1833 and 1834, and then it disappeared. Epidemic cholera returned in 1849, killing even more people.

The 1832 epidemic began to motivate city leaders to overcome their historic indifference to public health problems. After the 1832 epidemic subsided, New York City leaders took control of the water distribution system, highlighted by the completion of the Croton aqueduct in 1842. The fear of cholera heralded the awakening of a stronger public health consciousness and the importance of sanitation to the public's health in many urban communities.

Neenah Estrella-Luna

FURTHER READING:

Bollet, Alfred Jay. *Plagues and Poxes: The Impact of Human History on Epidemic Disease.* New York: Demos, 2004.

Duffy, John. *A History of Public Health in New York City: 1625–1866.* New York: Russell Sage Foundation, 1968.

Koeppel, Gerard R. *Water for Gotham: A History.* Princeton, N.J.: Princeton University Press, 2000.

Rosenberg, Charles E. *The Cholera Years: The United States in 1832, 1849, and 1866.* Chicago: University of Chicago Press, 1962.

1833 ◆ NULLIFICATION CRISIS

During the waning months of his administration in 1828, President John Quincy Adams signed a bill that its critics called the Tariff of Abominations. The controversy that followed led to the most serious constitutional confrontation between states and the central government since the Alien and Sedition Acts of the late 1790s. Equally ominous, the dispute foreshadowed the crisis that led to the secession of southern states and the beginning of the Civil War in 1860–61. The impasse over the tariff in 1832–33 raised fundamental issues concerning who holds supreme power—the federal or the state governments—and about the nature and permanence of the federal union.

In an age in which there was no income tax, the main source of federal revenue was the tariff, also known as duties or customs, imposed on goods imported from abroad. But some duties were levied with the intent less of raising revenue than of increasing the price of the import so that domestic producers of the good would be "protected" from lower-priced foreign competition. The Constitution authorized Congress to impose duties, but it was silent about the matter of "protection" as one of the purposes of tariffs. Indeed, in the four decades following the adoption of the Constitution, "strict constructionists" maintained that a protective tariff was unconstitutional. Prior to 1828, these concerns had been either swept aside or mollified by nationalists such as South Carolina representative John C. Calhoun, who was one of the key sponsors of a highly protective tariff law passed in 1816.

But by the late 1820s, economic conditions in the United States had changed drastically. Commitment to what came to be called King Cotton had grown almost exponentially in southern states in the intervening years. So had the region's reliance on the slave system, which helped to make cotton production profitable—so

FACTBOX
PLACE Washington, D.C., and South Carolina
DATE 1828–33
TYPE Political controversy over interpretation of the Constitution
DESCRIPTION After Congress passed a tariff in 1828, lawmakers in South Carolina declared it null and void, thereby generating a constitutional crisis and a political showdown with President Andrew Jackson.
IMPACT South Carolina's nullification of a federal law, which threatened the authority of the U.S. government and the unity of the nation, reopened a political dispute that remained unresolved until the Civil War.

profitable that as the factory system and new industries began to emerge in the North, the South continued to specialize in agriculture. In 1828, Congress narrowly passed a new tariff that raised duties on woolens, iron, hemp, and molasses. Southerners saw the action as a tax on everyday goods that would yield them little benefit. Facing the prospect of higher prices for materials with which to clothe and house their slaves, many southern cotton growers denounced tariff protection, which they saw as serving the interest of northern manufacturers. The conflict spurred southerners to renew their interest in strict construction of the Constitution. John C. Calhoun was prominent among this group of southern critics. He abandoned his former constitutional nationalism and went on to become the South's leading advocate of both strict construction and slavery. Calhoun led the protest against the so-called Tariff of Abominations.

Calhoun launched his attack in 1828 in a pamphlet entitled *South Carolina Exposition and Protest*, published anonymously because he was vice president of the United States at the time under John Quincy Adams. Calhoun's denunciation of the tariff revived the so-called compact interpretation of the Constitution, originally publicized in the Virginia and Kentucky Resolutions in 1798 in denunciation of the Alien and Sedition Acts. The *Exposition* maintained that the Constitution was the creation of the states, which had merely delegated certain powers to Congress but which otherwise retained their basic sovereignty. Consequently, the states, not the federal government or its courts, should have the final say on the constitutionality of disputed questions, such as a protective tariff.

Calhoun's position on the constitutionality of congressional actions ran afoul of Andrew Jackson, who replaced Adams in the presidency following the election of 1828. Although he continued as vice president, Calhoun continued to insist that states—like his own South Carolina—could nullify (that is, reject) acts of Congress they considered unconstitutional. But more ominous, Calhoun and the other "nullifiers" argued that states had the right to secede from the Union if Congress insisted on enforcing an "unconstitutional" law.

President Jackson was not a man to take lightly a challenge to his authority or that of the federal government. If states had the right to reject national laws, Jackson and his supporters argued, then the federal government would bow in subservience to the states and have scant power. The top two elected officials in the U.S. government—the president and the vice president—clashed dramatically over this issue at a dinner in 1830 honoring Thomas Jefferson's birthday. To Jackson's toast "The Federal Union: It Must Be Preserved," Calhoun responded "To The Union: Next to Our Liberty, The Most Dear." Eventually Calhoun resigned as vice president but was promptly elected senator from South Carolina. With the two antagonists' positions broadcast so publicly, the battle lines were plainly drawn.

Although some attempts were made to soften the terms of the 1828 tariff, the principle enunciated by Calhoun and his followers in South Carolina kept the issue of nullification alive, even after Jackson was reelected president in 1832. In November of that year, a special convention in South Carolina declared that the 1828 tariff and future protective tariffs were "unauthorized by the constitution of the United States, and violate the true meaning and intent thereof and are null, void, and no law, nor binding on this State."

President Jackson was quick to respond to a refusal to obey a statute of the United States. Privately, he said he would hang the first person who shed blood in defiance of federal law. Publicly, he used his power as commander in chief of the military to send seven small naval vessels and a man-of-war to Charleston, South Carolina. He followed this show of force with a declaration that rejected the compact theory of the Constitution, arguing that it was a product of the whole people, not of the individual states. "The Constitution of the United States . . . forms a government, not a league," he said. Jackson charged that the real object of Calhoun and his allies was disunion, and "disunion, by armed force, is TREASON." Congress assented to his request for a Force Bill early in 1833, giving the president power to enforce compliance with the tariff laws. Behind the scenes, a deal was in the works. Henry Clay, a leader in the House of Representatives, worked with his old ally Calhoun to produce a Compromise Tariff in 1833 that gradually reduced import duties. South Carolinians accepted the new arrangement, but to be consistent, they also nullified the Force Bill.

President Jackson and his allies could rightfully claim victory over Calhoun and his challenge to the integrity of the Union. Historians, however, as well as Jackson's critics at the time, point out that South Carolina in fact had attained its long-range goal of significantly reducing tariff protection and emerged as the most consistent advocate of the state sovereignty position. The controversy was a stepping-stone along the path toward the secession of the South in 1860–61, led, not coincidentally, by South Carolina.

See also 1860 SECESSION CRISIS.

Lynn Hudson Parsons

FURTHER READING:

Ellis, Richard E. *The Union at Risk: Jacksonian Democracy, States Rights and the Nullification Crisis.* New York: Oxford University Press, 1987.

Freehling, William W. *Prelude to Civil War: The Nullification Controversy in South Carolina, 1819–1836.* New York: Harper and Row, 1965.

1834 ◆ URSULINE CONVENT RIOT AND FIRE

The Ursuline Convent was a Roman Catholic boarding school for upper-class girls in the Charlestown section of Boston, Massachusetts. Opened in 1826 by the Ursuline Sisters, an elite order of nuns, the school enrolled the young daughters of wealthy families from several states and Canada. The sisters' reputation as experienced teachers of young girls attracted many non-Catholic students to the new academy. It was located on a 24-acre Charlestown farm (now in Somerville) at a hill the sisters named Mount Benedict in honor of their patron, the Boston bishop Benedict J. Fenwick.

In the summer of 1834, Charlestown Yankee Protestants became suspicious of the fashionable school, incited by deeply rooted anti-Catholic prejudice and lurid rumors that young women were being debauched in the convent "dungeons" under the shadow of the revered Bunker Hill. Earlier that year Rebecca Reed, a former student, lectured and published a sensational book, *Six Months in a Convent* (1834), with harrowing tales of her "escape" from the alleged immorality of this convent, and one mentally disturbed Ursuline nun was found wandering away from the convent. When the town selectmen inquired about the incident, the sister superior refused to permit any investigation. In addition to these hysterical rumors, incendiary sermons by the popular Protestant minister Lyman Beecher prompted 50 Yankee and Scotch-Irish laborers to surround the convent school on the night of Monday, August 11, 1834. Despite the sister superior's warning that Bishop Fenwick and thousands of Irish Bostonians would defend the school, the mob broke into the buildings, evicted the 10 nuns and 50 students, and vandalized the three-story brick building, garden, mortuary chapel, and graves. With the building consumed by flames, the sisters and the girls fled the marauders as 1,000 spectators and members of nearby fire companies jeered or joined the rioters and looters. Neighboring families in Charlestown and Somerville sheltered the nuns and the girls. By morning, the school building, valued at $50,000, lay in smoldering ruins.

Newspapers and public meetings at Faneuil Hall in Boston and in Cambridge and Charlestown decried

FACTBOX

PLACE Charlestown, Massachusetts

DATE August 11, 1834

TYPE Fire, mob attack on a Catholic convent

DESCRIPTION Anti-Catholic arsonists destroyed a Catholic convent school.

CAUSE Arson by a nativist mob, inflamed by religious bigotry

COST $50,000

IMPACT Closed the school and demonstrated rising anti-Catholicism in United States

the riot and expressed sympathy for the unfortunate victims. Massachusetts governor John Davis offered a $500 reward for information. Although 13 rioters were arrested for arson and burglary, none were convicted. City, state, and prominent community leaders deplored the violence and religious bigotry, but the state legislature refused to indemnify the Ursuline Sisters or the bishop of Boston for their property losses. Later attempts and threats of arson at Catholic churches and the 1835 celebration by some Yankee bigots of the anniversary of the Charlestown attack proved that anti-Catholicism was endemic in Massachusetts.

This notorious riot developed into a national controversy, serving for many years as an argument in propaganda campaigns for and against Catholicism. It demonstrated the profound religious prejudice rooted in antebellum America, a Puritan legacy exacerbated by the nativist reaction to increasing Irish Catholic immigration. Tensions released by the burning of the convent foreshadowed the rise of the nativist Know-Nothing Party in the 1840s and 1850s. This mob attack remains a symbol of religious prejudice and violence in Boston, the city known as the Athens of America. All that remains of the Ursuline Convent today are some bricks taken from the ruins and used in the vestibule of the new Cathedral of the Holy Cross in

Boston's South End. The archdiocese of Boston has never been compensated for the losses.

See also 1844 PHILADELPHIA RIOTS.

Peter C. Holloran

FURTHER READING:

Cohen, Daniel. "Passing the Torch: Boston Firemen, 'Tea Party' Patriots, and the Burning of the Charlestown Convent." *Journal of the Early Republic* 24, no. 4 (Winter 2004).

O'Connor, Thomas H. *Boston Catholics: A History of the Church and Its People.* Boston: Northeastern University Press, 1998.

Schultz, Nancy Lusignan. *Fires and Roses: The Burning of the Charlestown Convent, 1834.* New York: Free Press, 2000.

1836 ◆ BATTLE OF THE ALAMO

The Battle of the Alamo on March 6, 1836, was the pivotal event of the Texas revolution. Over time, the Alamo has become one of the most heavily mythologized events in both Texas and United States history. This battle was an utter defeat of the Texan defenders of the Alamo fortress in San Antonio de Béxar (known today as San Antonio) by a large Mexican army under President Antonio López de Santa Anna. The significance of the battle, however, has transcended this defeat. The defenders were anointed as martyrs to the cause of Texas independence and almost immediately elevated into the pantheon of heroes during the subsequent revolution. The outsized legacy of the Battle of the Alamo and the physical site itself have since become symbolic of Texas and have served to transform this battle into a cherished if complex myth of heroism and defiance.

The smoldering Texas independence revolution formed the crucial context for the siege and Battle of the Alamo. Texas, then a part of Mexico, saw increasing conflict between independent-minded American settlers and a Mexican government bent on squashing challenges to its authority north of the Rio Grande. Small, sporadic, and unorganized revolts against Mexican authority occurred in 1826 and 1832 and finally coalesced into full revolt in the fall of 1835. The sources of the revolt were many. Mexico suspected that American settlers in Texas (called Texians) served as opportunistic cover for broader United States expansionist ambitions. Texians chafed at Mexican restrictions on their actions and mobility,

FACTBOX

PLACE San Antonio de Béxar, Texas (today San Antonio)

DATE March 6, 1836

TYPE Battle

DESCRIPTION After a 12-day siege, a large Mexican army under President Antonio López de Santa Anna killed the defenders of the Alamo in San Antonio de Béxar, including such legendary figures as William B. Travis, James Bowie, and Davy Crockett.

CAUSE The nascent Texas revolutionary movement successes in the fall of 1835 triggered an invasion by Santa Anna. The Texian occupation of the symbolically significant Alamo led to Santa Anna's call for unconditional surrender and to the final assault with no quarter given.

CASUALTIES At least 189 Texan defenders were killed, and approximately 600 Mexican soldiers died during the final assault.

IMPACT This siege and defeat served to galvanize the Texas independence movement at a critical time, provided the opportunity for political independence to be declared, and supplied a rallying battle cry and thirst for revenge that aided Texans in their successful bid for independence. The memory and myth of the Alamo have become potent symbols of heroism and defiance in American culture.

including the Law of April 6, 1830, which restricted their area of settlement. Texians also sought greater autonomy within Mexico, preferential tariff treatment, and the establishment of a separate state government. In settling Texas, many Texians had brought their slaves with them, and some harbored a strong desire to expand slavery, which was illegal in Mexico. American settlers became particularly alarmed by Santa Anna's abrogation of the Constitution of 1824 when he consolidated his presidency into a dictatorship. At first, many Texians did not seek independence from Mexico but rather a return to the old order, clearer autonomy within the country, and a limitation on Santa Anna's consolidated power. This position began to evaporate when Stephen F. Austin, a Texas pioneer who had successfully petitioned to end the Law of April 6 but also was imprisoned briefly in Mexico City, returned to Texas determined to create an independent state. "WAR is our only resource," he wrote in September 1835.

By October, war had indeed broken out in Texas, with Texian successes at Gonzales, Goliad, Mission Concepción, and San Patricio. Alongside Austin, the leaders of this early phase of the revolt became the central figures in the drama soon to unfold at the Alamo, including Colonel James Bowie, namesake of the famous knife, and Lieutenant Colonel William B. Travis. A Texian siege of Mexican forces under General Martin Perfecto de Cos, Santa Anna's son-in-law, had also settled in at the Mission San Antonio de Valero—also known as the Alamo—in San Antonio de Béxar. The mission was a three-acre complex named after either cottonwood trees (*alamo* in Spanish) growing nearby or after the Mexican Alamo cavalry company that once had been stationed there. The Alamo was robustly built, the compound surrounded by walls between eight and 12 feet high (the sources vary) and two feet thick. The church, which is most familiar to modern visitors as the indelible image of the Alamo, was actually an unfinished component in the southeastern section of the whole complex.

The rebellious Texians attacked San Antonio, rallied by Benjamin R. Milam's famous cry "Who will go to San Antonio with old Ben Milam?" After three days of battle, during which Milam was shot in the head, Cos surrendered at the Alamo and took his defeated troops back to Mexico. For a time, it

Some 600 Mexican soldiers and at least 189 Texans died at the Battle of the Alamo on March 6, 1836. (© *Friends of the Governor's Museum*)

seemed that Texas independence was imminent and easily won until news that General Santa Anna, the self-styled "Napoleon of the West," had crossed the Rio Grande with a powerful if undisciplined force of thousands, determined to put down the revolt.

The general Texian defense, although unorganized, was built around two major fortresses, at the Presidio La Bahía at Goliad under James W. Fannin, Jr., and at the Alamo under Colonel James C. Neill. The latter was not the most strategic of the two, but it had already gained symbolic significance for Santa Anna because of his son-in-law Cos's defeat. General Sam Houston, now in overall command of the independence forces, had initially decided that the Alamo was indefensible and had ordered Neill to abandon it. Bowie, eager to make a stand, convinced Houston otherwise, and Neill was permitted to fortify the Alamo with the 100 or so soldiers in his command. On February 2, Bowie wrote that "we will rather die in these ditches than surrender." The next day, Travis arrived with approximately 30 additional men and thereafter announced that the Alamo was "the key to Texas." Unexpectedly and remarkably, famed frontiersman, bear hunter, former congressman, and living legend Davy Crockett soon arrived with a group of Tennesseans, ready to fight for Texas independence. When Neill left because of an illness in his family at home, Travis and Bowie eventually split command of the approximately 150 fighting men. However, Bowie soon became ill and incapacitated.

Thus did the situation at the Alamo stand when it was surrounded by Santa Anna's enormous forces in late February. The Mexican army demanded immediate surrender and ran up a red flag indicating no quarter would be given. A defiant Travis fired a cannon in response and sent out word "to the People of Texas and All Americans in the World . . . I shall never surrender or retreat." The stage was set for, as Travis put it most famously, "victory or death," although there are indications that he would have surrendered if it had seemed possible to save the lives of his men. A few dozen additional Texans crept into the Alamo to help defend it, bringing word that no more troops would be forthcoming. One of the most powerful stories in the Alamo myth, which remains unknowable, was Travis drawing a line in the sand and asking each man to step over it. The legend has it that only one man was unwilling to stand and fight.

Given the size and disposition of Santa Anna's army, victory or even survival for the Texans was not likely. After a 12-day siege, Santa Anna launched a massive and bloody assault on March 6. The defenders of the Alamo did not collapse without first inflicting heavy casualties on the Mexican army. However, the final fate of the Texians was sealed. Travis died early in the fighting, and Bowie was killed sick in his bed. The others were overwhelmed and driven back to a final defense in the barracks and the chapel. Crockett's death was shrouded in controversy and mystery, although it seems most likely he was captured and brutally executed along with all of the other survivors. The exact details are unknown. In the end, at least 189 Texas defenders and approximately 600 Mexican soldiers were killed.

The siege and defeat of the Alamo galvanized Texans and Americans and clarified the fight for independence. The Texian political leadership formally declared independence on March 2 at Washington-on-the-Brazos. The defeat at the Alamo energized the revolution, but the military campaign took time. After a period of retreat and no little dissension in the ranks, General Houston finally drew his own line in the sand by attacking Santa Anna at the Battle of San Jacinto on April 21, 1836. With the battle cry of "Remember the Alamo!" rippling through the line, the energized Texans killed 630 Mexican soldiers and captured 730 at the loss of only two killed and six wounded. Among the captured in this great victory was General Santa Anna himself, a major coup that guaranteed the independence of Texas. The final victory helped the memory of the Alamo glow brightly as a symbol of bravery and independence.

Daniel S. Margolies

FURTHER READING:

Davis, William C. *Three Roads to the Alamo: The Lives and Fortunes of David Crockett, James Bowie, and William Barret Travis.* New York: HarperCollins, 1998.

Hardin, Stephen L. *Texian Iliad: A Military History of the Texas Revolution.* Austin: University of Texas Press, 1994.

Roberts, Randy, and James S. Olson. *A Line in the Sand: The Alamo in Blood and Memory.* New York: Free Press, 2001.

1837 ◆ FINANCIAL PANIC AND DEPRESSION

The debate in America over banks resumed in the mid-1830s. Central banking came under attack during the presidency of President Andrew Jackson (1829–37), whose administration was followed by the first major financial collapse in American history. Thus was born a belief that political parties could greatly disturb the functioning of the economic system. That version of history has changed, as the financial crisis is now seen as the result of the international movement of the precious metals, gold and silver (called specie by contemporaries). However, the panic of 1837 had consequences of great significance beyond its immediate causes. Far more than the panic of 1819, the panic of 1837 introduced Americans to the reality of the business cycle in a profound way. From that moment onward, Americans

FACTBOX

PLACE United States

DATE May 1837–1843

TYPE Banking crisis, leading to depression

DESCRIPTION Following an economic boom from 1831 to 1837, the Bank of England raised its interest rate, thus draining specie from the United States. As a consequence, the banks in the United States contracted their loans, producing a general economic depression that lasted until 1843.

IMPACT The panic of 1837 generated much ill will against banks, leading to the creation of free-banking laws in the states, and stymied the creation of a central bank for the rest of the century. State governments withdrew from financing and building major internal improvements and many other economic activities, inaugurating the age of economic laissez-faire.

became aware of a business cycle and sought to tame it—an effort that would prove unsuccessful until the late 20th century. Moreover, the panic of 1837 brought public investment into disrepute, especially in regard to transportation services. Because state finances were so deranged from the effects of the depression, states foreswore building internal improvements and allowed private enterprise to take over the task. In a very real sense, the panic of 1837 produced an important result in political economy: the establishment of laissez-faire practices in the states.

The political side of the panic of 1837 was connected to the Second Bank of the United States, a surge in land sales, and the actions of President Jackson. In 1823, Nicholas Biddle became president of the Second Bank of the United States (BUS). He evidently followed countercyclical policies—knowingly or not is an unresolved question—which was good for the economy overall but frustrated many southerners and westerners, who demanded easier credit. By the middle 1820s, prosperity had returned to the United States, cotton was being crowned king in international trade, and Americans were flooding into the Great Lakes states due to the Erie Canal and other transportation improvements. Southerners

wanted cotton land, while northerners wanted wheat land, and both wanted easy credit. The federal government, which owned massive tracts of western territory, sold 1.2 million acres of public land in 1829, 3.9 million acres in 1833, 4.7 million acres in 1834, and 20 million acres in 1836.

As this boom in western land sales proceeded, the nation experienced general price inflation. Prices rose from an index of 90 in 1834 to a level of 115 in 1837. People were upset with the inflation and the wild speculation in western lands. They thought they knew the culprit: improper banking policies. Many economists (called political economists or moral philosophers at the time) referred to banking practices as wildcat banking: that is, banks that extended loans and credit without sufficient reserves to redeem their bank notes. The amount of money (specie, or "hard money") needed to redeem loans and bank notes ("paper" money at the time) was called the reserve ratio. Contemporaries were uncertain as to what the proper ratio between specie and paper money should have been, guessing anywhere from 10 to 33 percent, but they believed a number of banks were operating under a 1 percent ratio, which was wholly inadequate.

At the same time, the newly elected Democratic president, Andrew Jackson, was hostile to banks in general and to the BUS in particular. Biddle had used his power earlier to both contract and later expand the money supply; Jackson hated the power an unelected official had over the entire economy. Somehow the bank's power had to be curbed and brought under the process of elective government. Moreover, Biddle had used bank funds to finance campaign literature against Jackson in the presidential race of 1828. Therefore, Jackson had decided the BUS needed reforming—but Biddle refused to be reformed. In 1832, in an effort to coerce Jackson to approve the bank before its existing charter expired four years later, Biddle's supporters in Congress drafted a bill to give the BUS an additional 20 years of life. The probank crowd figured that the president would accept the proposal because 1832 was an election year, and Jackson was running for a second term. He would not want to threaten his chances of reelection by attacking an institution that was popular in the Atlantic states and New England. But Jackson defied them. He vetoed the legislation, issuing a memorable veto message to validate his action. Winning reelection, the president then turned on the bank. First, he removed government deposits in the BUS in an effort to cripple it (the proceeds were given to certain state banks, called "pet banks"). To stop land speculation, he issued the "Specie Circular" in 1836, which specified that purchases of public land had to be paid with specie, not bank notes. In the spring of 1837, after he left office, panic struck financial agencies, and a general suspension of specie payment occurred in May. New York City banks, the bellwether institutions of American finance, suspended specie payment on May 10, 1837.

Jackson's program may have had some effect on note issue and banking practices, but other factors better explain the boom and bust of the business cycle in the 1830s. American banks extended credit freely not because they permitted their reserve ratio to fall but because they had a large increase in their specie holdings. This circumstance came about for several reasons. First, Chinese merchants dropped their demand for gold and silver coins in trade and accepted bills of exchange. Thus, Americans had less need for the precious metals in the China trade and could keep specie in bank vaults. Second, Mexico had discovered silver deposits and began to flood the world market with silver. Americans earned some of that silver through trade with Mexico. The upshot was that bank holdings of specie nearly tripled from $31 million in 1832 to $88 million in 1837. Because of their increased amount of specie, banks could extend more loans, and this was the circumstance that made credit easy. Easy credit then fueled the surge in land speculation.

What ended the boom was not Jackson's war on the BUS but a decision by the governing board of the Bank of England to stop a gold outflow from their land. Terms of trade had become unfavorable to England, and so the nation was paying its international debt in specie. That lowered England's specie reserve and threatened its economy. So the Bank of England raised the interest rate it charged on loans to other banks (the rediscount rate), making it more profitable for specie holders to invest within England than purchase goods overseas.

The rise in the English interest rate led to a movement of silver and gold toward England and depleted the United States's reserves. When that started, banks in the United States had to contract their loans. Individuals found that easy credit had disappeared, and many discovered that their dreams of instant riches

from land sales were never to be realized. As some banks announced difficulties resulting from defaults in loan repayments, the public panicked (this is why, in the 19th century, economic troubles were called "panics"). Thousands of people jammed the streets of the banking districts of New York, Philadelphia, and Boston demanding redemption of their notes in specie. That further drained the banks of their specie reserves. To protect themselves from complete bankruptcy, the banks in mid-May 1837 suspended specie payment—an admission that they were insolvent and unable to live up to their obligations as specified in law. It also meant that people were left with paper money that was rapidly dropping in value. This financial crisis became known as the panic of 1837.

The economic instability that followed the panic lasted for six years and had two distinct components. The first part was the initial panic in 1837, which lasted only a year. Then the banks resumed specie payment, and the economy began to recover from the financial collapse. However, the Bank of England in 1839 raised its rediscount rate again, inducing another banking panic, sometimes referred to as the panic of 1839. In the latter banking crisis, a general specie suspension did not occur (banks in New York and New England did not suspend, but banks elsewhere did), and the nation settled into disjointed economic times. About 1843, the economy began to revive, and a new economic boom commenced, this time fed by enhanced international trade in cotton and foodstuffs and abetted by the decision of England to drop its protective duties on imports in 1846.

In terms of the American economy, the panic of 1837 had some sharp results that unsettled people, but in other ways it did not afflict the nation for long. By 1837, the nation had become more commercial, with a larger urban core; financial crises therefore had more power to affect the lives of people than they had in 1819, and thus a stronger political reaction emerged. Banks became the subject of bitter disputes for the next 20 years, and political success depended frequently on which party was in office when these depressions occurred. On the other hand, neither unemployment nor output was greatly affected. In 1838, unemployment probably rose to 8 percent (on average, the economy hummed along at 4 to 5 percent unemployment). Protests against the lack of jobs spread among urban centers. However, prices adjusted themselves quickly to the new depressed conditions, and so the excess unemployment disappeared within one year. Moreover, national output grew by 16 percent during the years 1837 to 1843—not exactly the result one would expect from a depressed economy. Much of the grumbling in the country apparently arose from people readjusting to prices that had dropped from hoped-for levels.

The panic of 1837 did not significantly alter the path of the American economy, but it had important political results. First, the demonstrations against unemployment in the cities revealed that financial panics evoked crises in the social structure, crises that in some way had to be met to relieve dangerous political challenges to the free market (and a free government). This would be a continuing problem throughout the 19th century, growing especially acute after 1873.

Perhaps more profoundly, the panic of 1837 changed the course of American political economy. First, and probably most profoundly, the United States failed to develop a central bank. The popular anger at banks led to the demise of the Second BUS in 1836. The United States did not authorize a central bank again until 1913. The lack of a central bank impeded government intervention in the economy and helped doom Americans to a devilish business cycle that later in the century inspired mob revolts. Instead of a central national bank, the states resorted to free-banking laws that enabled anyone to operate a bank as long as certain reports were filed with state agencies.

The second consequence in political economy involved state policies toward the economy. Prior to the crisis of 1837, state governments undertook many projects to build infrastructure, primarily in transportation. State governments owned and operated canal systems and turnpikes, improvements that spurred a "revolution" in American transportation. Northern states had grandiose visions about creating canal systems and went deeply into debt to do so in the early and middle 1830s. The panic of 1837 caught state officials by surprise and crushed their dreams of development. Plunged into a debt crisis—indeed, the states of Indiana and Illinois virtually declared bankruptcy in 1842—states started to sell off their internal improvement projects and foreswore future government activity in the economy, often through amendments to their state constitutions. As railroads came into prominence in the 1840s, governments did not try to set up state-owned railroad systems (as became common in Europe) but relegated the enterprise entirely to the private sector. Thus the nation witnessed a retreat from government investment in the economy. The United States entered a period of official laissez-faire that would last, with some exceptions, until the 20th century. The panic of 1837 acted as a midwife to that development.

See also 1819 FINANCIAL PANIC AND DEPRESSION; 1857 FINANCIAL PANIC AND DEPRESSION.

James L. Huston

FURTHER READING:

Hammond, Bray. *Banks and Politics in America from the Revolution to the Civil War.* Princeton, N.J.: Princeton University Press, 1957.

Taylor, George Rogers. *The Transportation Revolution, 1815–1860.* New York: Holt, Rinehart, and Winston, 1951.

Temin, Peter. *The Jacksonian Economy.* New York: W. W. Norton, 1969.

Timberlake, Richard H., Jr. *The Origins of Central Banking in the United States.* Cambridge, Mass.: Harvard University Press, 1978.

1838 ◆ EXPLOSION OF THE *MOSELLE*

One of the most destructive steamboat accidents in American history occurred on April 25, 1838, when the vessel *Moselle* exploded on the Ohio River just outside of Cincinnati. Deadly steamboat explosions were the scourge of 19th-century transportation. Steamboats were the dominant form of transportation in the United States from the 1830s through the 1860s, but this new convenience also presented new hazards as frequent, spectacular explosions, collisions, and fires caused dozens of casualties each year and made headlines across the country.

Isaac Perrin, the proud captain and co-owner of the new, 150-ton *Moselle,* was eager to show off his acquisition. While not especially large by the standards of the day, the *Moselle* had muscle. Perrin had already set a steamboat speed record on the voyage from St. Louis, demonstrating his willingness to test the boundaries of safety in the process. One strategy for maximum speed was to keep the boiler safety valve closed during stops—that way, no steam would be lost and pressure would build up in the engine. Although this was obviously dangerous, the excitement of speed and competition was contagious; Perrin had been cheered by *Moselle* passengers coming from St. Louis, who on disembarking, congratulated him for his skill and daring.

On the day of the disaster, Perrin again sought to impress onlookers. The *Moselle* left port in Cincinnati in the afternoon and stopped to pick up passengers about a mile upstream. This distance was adequate to stoke the fire to a roar and heat up the boilers. When Perrin stopped, as previously, he built up steam in the engine. Presumably, he hoped to race

With its paddle wheel visible, the 150-ton steamboat *Moselle* explodes on the Ohio River. *(Cincinnati Public Library)*

back to the city and show off his vessel's impressive speed. The *Moselle* pulled away from the dock with approximately 280 passengers. Just moments later, the enormous pressure overwhelmed three of its four boilers, resulting in an ear-splitting explosion of steam, smoke, and flame. Fragments of timber, iron, steel, and copper cascaded in every direction. A cloud mushroomed several hundred feet into the air.

Steamboat explosions were notorious for their gory, horrific human casualties, and this incident was the worst yet. Along with debris from the splintered ship, bodies and body parts flew in every direction and came down yards away on shore and in the water. Perrin and several of the ship's officers were among the casualties. Survivors still on board what was left of the *Moselle* panicked as it became clear that its remains were sinking fast. Many leapt into the strong current of the river and drowned; others were trapped in the wreckage and pulled under to meet their fate. Within 15 minutes, only the smokestacks and the very top of the vessel were visible above the water. Rescue efforts were feeble, with just a few boats available nearby—many bodies were never recovered. The deaths resulting from the incident can only be estimated, but historians agree that at least 150 people perished that day, and dozens more suffered serious injury.

The *Moselle* incident made headlines around the country. While it remained the deadliest steamboat disaster until the explosion of the *Saluda* in 1852,

FACTBOX

PLACE Ohio River, just outside of Cincinnati

DATE April 25, 1838

TYPE Explosion

DESCRIPTION After picking up passengers near Cincinnati, Ohio, the boilers of the *Moselle* exploded, killing more than half of the people on board.

CAUSE Reckless piloting, overheating, boiler failure under steam pressure, inadequate safety precautions

CASUALTIES At least 150 deaths and dozens of serious injuries

IMPACT As one in a long series of deadly steamboat incidents, the explosion generated support for federal legislation to improve steamboat safety. Although initial regulations were largely ineffective, they were an important step in expanding the capacity of the federal government to regulate private industry in the mid-19th century.

in many respects it was typical of steamboat accidents of the time. Masculine bravado contributed significantly to the safety problem as ambitious and competitive steamboat captains vied for status and celebrity. The danger of the job added to its appeal for many reckless operators. Often, explosions took place just as a voyage began; boilers were stoked up in order to embark with a flourish. One analyst estimated in an 1848 report to Congress that more than 2,500 Americans had been killed and almost as many injured in at least 233 steamboat explosions since 1816. Property losses topped $3 million in the currency of the day.

The *Moselle* disaster of 1838 was just one of many fatal explosions and fires in the 1830s that fueled public outrage and ultimately inspired federal legislation. Within weeks, both the *Oronoko* and the *Pulaski* exploded as well, each killing about 100 people. These widely reported incidents added momentum to federal legislation to create a federal Steamboat Inspection Service. Later that year, the agency began operations, but its officials had little authority. It was not until the Supreme Court verified the authority of the federal government to impose safety regulations on industry that effective laws were implemented. In 1852, Congress passed new regulations, including construction guidelines for boats and boilers, requirements for safety and monitoring equipment on board, and river traffic guidelines to prevent collisions. Stricter licensing requirements for pilots and engineers were accompanied by annual exams and inspections. New laws also significantly increased the authority and powers of federal inspectors, allowing them to act and to impose sanctions without court rulings.

Conditions during the Civil War heightened violations and increased annual casualties, leading to the most deadly steamboat explosion in U.S. history, the EXPLOSION OF THE *SULTANA*, which took more than 1,500 lives in 1865. Railroads, which were safer, faster, and cheaper, largely displaced steamboats for inland freight and passenger transportation after the Civil War.

Louise Nelson Dyble

FURTHER READING:

Brockmann, R. John. *Exploding Steamboats, Senate Debates, and Technical Reports: The Convergence of Technology, Politics and Rhetoric in the Steamboat Bill of 1838.* Amityville, N.Y.: Baywood Publishing Company, 2002.

Brown, John Kennedy. *Limbs on the Levee: Steamboat Explosions and the Origins of Federal Public Welfare Regulation, 1817–1852.* Middlebourne, W.Va.: International Steamboat Society, 1988.

Burke, John C. "Bursting Boilers and the Federal Power." *Technology and Culture* 7 (1966): 1–23.

Hunter, Louis C. *Steamboats on the Western Rivers: An Economic and Technical History.* Cambridge, Mass.: Harvard University Press, 1949.

1838 ◆ TRAIL OF TEARS

On June 22, 1839, a Cherokee Indian named Elias Boudinot was working in his yard in Indian Territory, Oklahoma, when three Cherokee men approached him soliciting medicine. As he turned toward them, the men attacked him, hacking him to death. Thus did these survivors of the Trail of Tears punish one of the men who signed the 1835 Treaty of New Echota, which had led to the forced removal of the Cherokee Nation from their homes in the southern Appalachian Mountains in 1838 and 1839. Boudinot's execution could not restore the thousands of people who died on that disastrous 1,200-mile march, but it provided justice according to Cherokee law. Back in 1827, in an attempt to stop the loss of their territory to white settlers, the Cherokee had constructed a representative government modeled on that of the United States and had decreed the selling of Cherokee lands a capital offense. Indeed, in 1832, the Supreme Court had upheld the right of the Cherokee people to hold political sovereignty over their homelands. How, then, had the Cherokee's lands been taken and the majority of their people forcibly removed west of the Mississippi River? The answer to this question suggests that the tragedy of Indian removal went beyond the 4,000 to 6,000 people who perished during the journey. A deeper tragedy lies in the delusion of misguided policymakers who argued that removal was for the Cherokee's own good and in the Indians' naïve belief that the acceptance of white culture could prevent their dispossession.

The Cherokee had lived in their aboriginal homelands in what eventually became Georgia, North Carolina, and Tennessee for thousands of years when European settlers began to encroach on their territory in the 18th century. Some of the outsiders came as traders, marrying Cherokee women, introducing manufactured goods, and establishing plantation agriculture. The children of these unions were bicultural, and they often rose to positions of economic and political prominence. More often, however, encroachment provoked conflict, as settlers depleted game resources and took agricultural lands. Moreover, in the 19th century, missionaries and government agents began to pressure the Cherokee to assimilate to white culture and to cede the lands that they held in common.

The Cherokee wrestled with a solution to these demands, but many decided that limited assimilation was their best chance at survival. Led by the

FACTBOX

PLACE Georgia, North Carolina, Tennessee, and Oklahoma

DATE 1835–39

TYPE Social crisis for the Cherokee

DESCRIPTION The illegal dispossession and forced relocation of Native Americans led to thousands of deaths.

CAUSE Anglo-European desire for land and racist attitudes toward native peoples

CASUALTIES Estimated 4,000–6,000 Cherokee deaths

IMPACT One of the most egregious instances of forcible removal of American Indians from lands in the eastern United States and resettlement in Indian Territory

wealthiest trader families, the Cherokee National Council created a republic, with a constitution that defined the boundaries of the nation, declared sovereignty over it, and outlawed land cessions. The state of Georgia, however, opposed this action and, in 1829, extended state law over Cherokee territory. The Cherokee resisted the usurpation of their political autonomy by legal challenges. These cases eventually landed before the Supreme Court, which affirmed the rights of the Cherokee to their lands and to political control over them. The Cherokee were jubilant, but their joy was short-lived.

Meanwhile, Congress—emboldened by the 1828 election of a pro-removal president, Andrew Jackson—passed legislation in 1830 mandating Indian removal beyond the Mississippi River. Not only the Cherokee were ultimately forced to move west but also the Choctaw and Chickasaw from Mississippi, the Creek from Alabama, and the Seminole from Florida. In earlier treaties with southern tribes, Congress had set aside lands for the purpose of relocating native peoples; these lands gradually came to be called Indian Territory. While some pro-removal promoters cited the need of land occupied by the "savages," most removal advocates framed their arguments in humanitarian terms—unscrupulous whiskey traders and frontier ruffians were hurting the Indians and preventing their assimilation. This line of reasoning recommended that the Indians move west for their own good. Champions of the Cherokee countered that the Indians were indeed "civilizing" and called for justice. The majority of Cherokee agreed.

A handful of Cherokee, however, sought removal either because they despaired of justice or because they saw opportunity for financial and political gains in the new territory. In 1835, they signed the Treaty of New Echota, surrendering Cherokee lands. Most Cherokee protested the treaty and refused preparations to move, confident that justice would prevail. In the summer of 1838, however, soldiers entered Cherokee territory and began to drive the Indians from their homes, often at the point of bayonets. Settlers then seized and plundered the possessions that the Cherokee were forced to abandon. Soldiers herded the Cherokee into stockades to await removal, where many died because of inadequate provisions, bad water, and disease.

By mid-June, the majority of Cherokee had been detained, and the first contingent began the tortuous

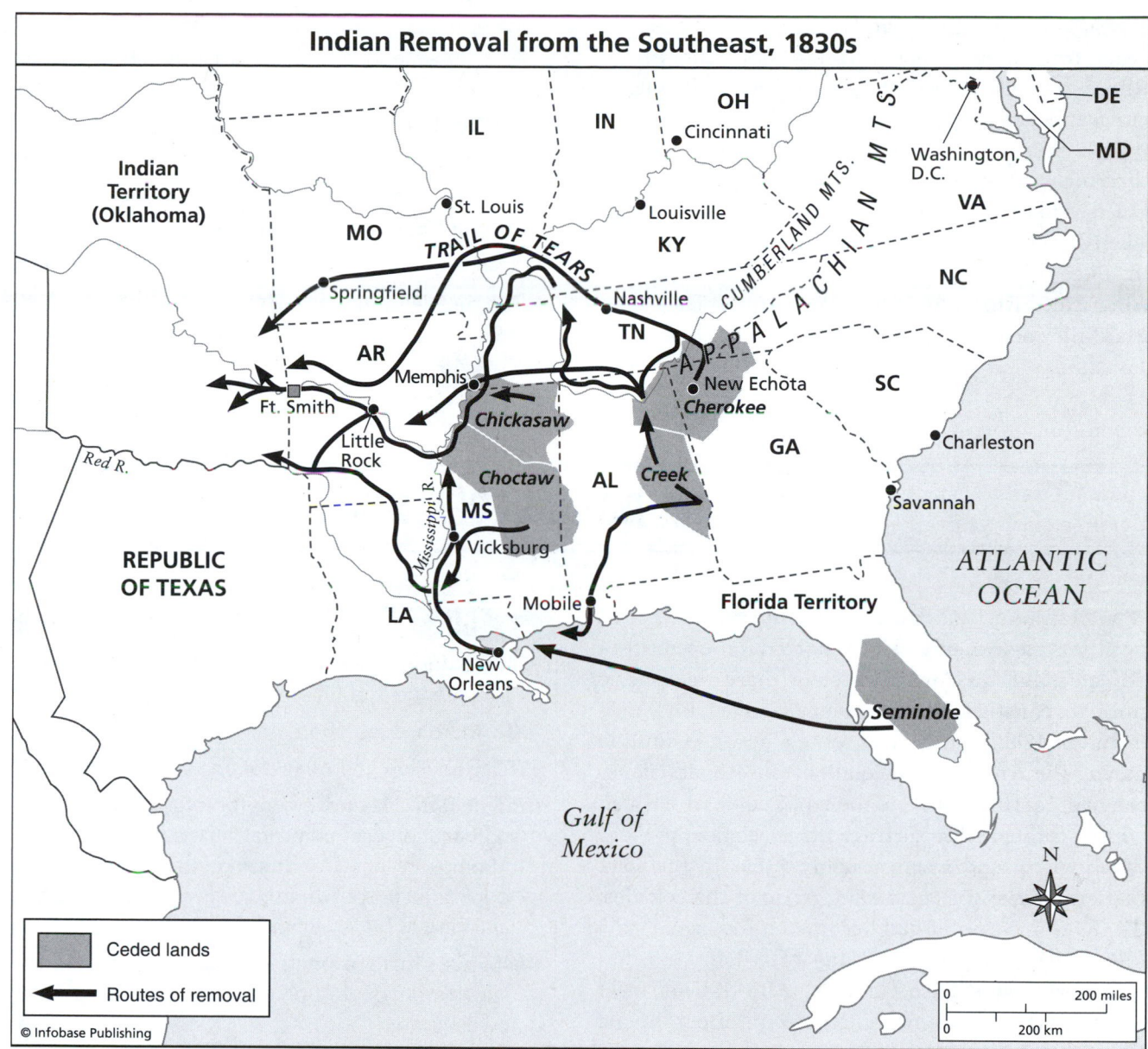

Indian Removal from the Southeast, 1830s

The Cherokee followed the "Trail of Tears" from New Echota, Georgia, to Indian Territory in present-day Oklahoma. The Choctaw, Chickasaw, Creek, and Seminole were forced to follow similar trails west in the 1830s.

five-month march to Oklahoma, walking through suffocating summer heat during a prolonged drought. Reports of great suffering filtering back from this first group led General Winfield Scott, who oversaw removal, to allow the remainder of the Cherokee to leave in the fall. The last detachment left in November, enduring deadly winter storms that often forced the groups to camp for several days waiting for a break in the weather. The majority of Cherokee had not had time to pack sufficient food, tents, and blankets for the journey, and congressional appropriations were not adequate to make up the gap, often because the men who contracted to provision the Cherokee along the way charged exorbitant prices, sometimes for shoddy goods. While some Cherokee had wagons and horses, many walked barefoot, carrying what little they could salvage of their possessions. Sympathetic settlers along the route sometimes donated provisions, but it was never enough. Exhaustion and exposure encouraged diseases such as measles and whooping cough that claimed many lives, mostly the elderly and children. The Cherokee followed two routes—one went across Tennessee, up through the Cumberland Mountains into Kentucky, across southern Illinois, and into Missouri, while the other dropped down across Arkansas Territory from Illinois. By late March of 1839, the last remnants of emigrants straggled into Indian Territory. In the west, the Cherokee slowly rebuilt their lives and created a thriving revitalized culture, but the Trail Where We Cried remains central to their identity as Indians. Their uprooting stands as one of the most egregious instances of forcible removal of American Indians in American history. As former principal chief Wilma Mankiller noted, "It was indeed our holocaust."

See also 1755 EXILE OF THE ACADIANS.

Katherine M. B. Osburn

FURTHER READING:

Perdue, Theda, and Michael D. Green. *The Cherokee Removal: A Brief History with Documents.* 2nd ed. Boston: Bedford/St. Martin's Press, 2005.

Wallace, Anthony F. C. *The Long, Bitter Trail: Andrew Jackson and the Indians.* New York: Hill and Wang, 1993.

1842 ◆ DORR REBELLION

The only time in the early history of the United States when violence marred a movement to make an American state more democratic through constitutional revision occurred in Rhode Island in 1842. Rather than write a new constitution during the American Revolution, the Rhode Islanders had continued under their old colonial charter, which limited the suffrage to freeholders—those who owned land worth roughly $150. In the colonial era, it was the most democratic of the colonies. By 1840, however, it had become an industrial state filled with workingmen, many of whom were foreign born, often Irish Catholic, who did not meet the property requirements to vote. In effect, Rhode Island had become a sort of patrician oligarchy, out of step with political developments in other northern states, which had abolished property requirements for voting. A movement for reform led by Thomas Wilson Dorr brought the acceptance of universal manhood suffrage to Rhode Island but only after armed confrontation.

The story of the Dorr Rebellion involves several competing constitutions and a contest between two elected governments. Dorr's political career provides a thread that knit these elements together. Dorr was born in 1805 into a quite respectable family. His father Sullivan Dorr had made a fortune in the China trade and was an influential factory owner, as well as a trustee of Brown University. He provided his sons

FACTBOX
PLACE Rhode Island, with armed confrontations in Providence and Chepachet
DATE March–June 1842
TYPE Rebellion and constitutional crisis
DESCRIPTION The movement for reform of the state constitution with universal male suffrage, led by Thomas Wilson Dorr, turned into a brief armed confrontation between two governments, each claiming to be legitimate.
CAUSE Desire to expand suffrage, which Rhode Island's antiquated charter limited to property-owning men
CASUALTIES 1 death
IMPACT After a brief armed conflict, the Rhode Island government abolished property requirements for voting (although it retained limits on the rights of naturalized citizens). The conflict also led to a Supreme Court ruling in *Luther v. Borden* (1849).

with the best education. Thomas attended Exeter Academy and Harvard University before reading law with Chancellor Kent in New York. Dorr settled in as a gentleman/lawyer in Providence, both Rhode

Island's largest city and the center of early American industrialization. Rhode Island faced two political challenges in the 1830s: First, perhaps as many as half of the adult males could not vote because of the property requirements, and second, representation in the state's legislature favored the rural areas.

Dorr entered politics as a very young man in 1833, running for the state legislature as an opponent of the Jacksonian Democrats and an advocate of both school reform and abolition of slavery. A year later he helped establish the Rhode Island Constitutional Party devoted to writing a new constitution that would expand the suffrage. While both workers and Whigs in the urban areas wanted to change the constitution, the Democrats, who were strong in the rural areas, opposed any change that would weaken their influence. The Constitutional Party received a mere 10 percent of the vote. In 1838 Dorr, who had been affiliated with the Whigs, shifted to the Democrats but could not get the local party to back constitutional reform.

In 1841, the new Whig state government proposed to change the constitution to provide for a broader suffrage and fairer representation in the legislature. But Dorr and his followers, who had organized the Rhode Island Suffrage Association, had already called their own constitutional convention, which aimed to write a new constitution and create an entirely new government. The Dorrites reasoned that since the people were sovereign, they could act outside of the framework of an unjust government. The convention of the Rhode Island Suffrage Association met in November 1841 and wrote a new constitution that provided for white manhood suffrage, but, against Dorr's personal wishes, disfranchised blacks (a small African-American community lived in Rhode Island). In a referendum in December, not sanctioned by the sitting government, the "People's Constitution," as the Dorrites' new plan of government was called, passed, although the vote probably involved fraud.

Amid these dramatic events, the traditionally elected government under the old charter, led by Governor James Fenner and calling themselves the Law and Order Party, held their own Landholders Convention to draft a new constitution. In a referendum in March 1842, this new constitution, which included black suffrage along with that for white

adult male citizens, was narrowly defeated. A month later, in an election not sanctioned by the Fenner government, voters elected Dorr governor. Thus Rhode Island in 1842 had the old charter and a government elected under it and the new and extralegal People's Constitution with a government elected under it. The Fenner Law and Order government then passed a law that ordered the arrest of individuals who took part in Dorr's renegade People's government.

Against the advice of some of his Democratic supporters, Dorr decided that the movement must resort to force to assert the legitimacy of the People's government. Two modest military encounters resulted from this decision. The first occurred at the arsenal in Providence in May and the second a month later at Acote's Hill in Chepachet, west of Providence. In both cases Dorr's troops were turned away by more powerful charter government forces, and in the latter, one Dorrite was killed. Dorr's decision to turn to force probably cost the People's movement its advantage. The regular government passed a new constitution that came close to providing universal manhood suffrage but contained limitations on the rights of naturalized citizens. Dorr was ultimately jailed in 1844 and pardoned in 1845, but he refused to swear allegiance to the Law and Order government. Ironically, Dorr thus remained one of the few adult males in Rhode Island without the right to vote. After a new Democratic government took control of the state in 1851, they reversed Dorr's conviction. Dorr died three years later at the age of 49.

While Dorr was a decent man who tried to obtain broad outside support for his efforts to modernize the Rhode Island government, his name has become synonymous with the only violent attempt to democratize American state politics in the pre–Civil War era. The Dorr Rebellion gave rise to an important legal precedent in American history. The case of *Luther v. Borden* (1849) arose from the imposition of martial law, which allowed a member of the militia, Luther Borden, to search the home of a Dorrite, Martin Luther. The question at stake was whether a group of Americans, even if they comprised the majority in a state, could rise up and unseat the existing government in the name of democracy. The Supreme Court avoided this issue by declaring it was up to Congress and not the courts to resolve the matter. By keeping the Court from ruling directly on what had happened in Rhode Island, Chief Justice Roger. B. Taney in effect upheld the actions of the established state government. In the process, he articulated a principle long observed by the Court—that it should refrain from involvement in political controversies.

William G. Shade

FURTHER READING:

Dennison, George M. *The Dorr War: Republicanism on Trial, 1831–1861.* Lexington: University of Kentucky Press, 1976.

Gettleman, Marvin E. *The Dorr Rebellion: A Study in American Radicalism.* New York: Random House, 1973.

1844 ◆ PHILADELPHIA RIOTS

Like racism and other forms of prejudice, anti-Catholic sentiment pervaded many parts of the country in the mid-19th century. The confluence of the Second Great Awakening—a Protestant religious movement in the 1820s and 1830s—and the rising immigration of Irish Catholics spawned an increase in anti-Catholicism, which led to the Philadelphia riots of 1844, the most serious urban disorder in early American history. This clash between mobs of native-born residents and Irish Catholic immigrants occurred in two neighborhoods and required state troops to suppress the violence. The riots forced a reorganization of the government of Philadelphia and the creation of a city police department. Nativism—the hostility to immigrants—briefly abated in Philadelphia after the riots, but it returned a decade later in the Know-Nothing movement of the 1850s.

Several factors underlay the clash in Philadelphia. The population of the city was increasing dramatically in the 1840s, a situation that forced newcomers toward the fringes of the old city. In addition to the Irish, black migrants from the South joined a sizable free black population in the city, which was growing as well from white Protestant migrants from rural areas. The rapid rise in population produced fierce competition between the Irish, most of whom were Catholic, and other groups for scarce jobs and living space. Thus Philadelphia in the 1840s contained a volatile mix of racial, ethnic, religious, class and economic tensions, particularly among workers. Moreover, in 1844 the city was still reeling from the hard times caused by the FINANCIAL PANIC AND DEPRESSION of 1837. Given this frenetic pace of social and economic change, one historian has written, "Any

FACTBOX
PLACE Philadelphia, Pennsylvania
DATE May 3–July 7, 1844
TYPE Riot
DESCRIPTION A sequence of brawls between Irish immigrants and native Protestants occurred in Philadelphia
CAUSE Industrialization, depression, racial, ethnic, and religious rivalries, and absence of adequate policing
CASUALTIES At least 15 but probably more deaths and an unknown number of injured
IMPACT Creation of modern Philadelphia by integrating many outlying areas under a single municipal government and the formation of a modern police force for the entire city

year in the early 1840's could have been the year of prolonged rioting."

Philadelphia's ineffective municipal government contributed to these explosive conditions. A fragmentation of governments existed, beginning with the old city, which was surrounded by nine incorporated districts, six boroughs, and 13 townships with no centralized authority encompassing all of them. The city was beset by rowdy volunteer fire companies that critics charged set more fires than they put out, and by street gangs with such names as the Killers, the Rats, the Skinners, and the Blood-Tubs, who controlled their own turf. Because of his limited jurisdiction and scant power, the sheriff had little influence. The local militias were more like ethnic clubs, similar to the fire companies. And because the city had no police department, disorder was the order of the day in Philadelphia.

While racial and ethnic riots were endemic in the United States in the Jacksonian era, the Philadelphia riots moved these conflicts to a new level. The origin of the 1844 riots lay in events two years earlier when the depression was at its deepest point. In 1842, a major race riot had erupted that featured Irish hostility to blacks, with African Americans defending their community with rifles and shotguns. The situation was further complicated by a conflict between Irish workers and the Reading Railroad, as well as a strike of Anglo-American weavers who were angered both by wage cuts and the hiring of Irish workers to replace them. On top of this, the question of Bible reading in the public schools ignited passions.

Catholics had complained for a decade that the public schools forced their children to read the Protestant King James translation of the Bible, denying them the right to use the Douay version approved by the Catholic Church. In November 1842, the bishop of Philadelphia, James Kenrick, asked the school controllers of Philadelphia to allow Catholic children to read the Douay version or to let them out of class when the King James Bible was read. The Philadelphia school directors accepted this compromise, but in February 1844, Hugh Clark, an Irish member of the suburban Southwark School Controllers, advised a teacher to cease all Bible reading—a move some viewed as an assault on Protestant Christianity.

The nativists in Philadelphia responded by organizing the American Protestant Association. On May 3, 1844, they held a meeting in Kensington, a northern suburb of the old city that contained a heavily Irish ward and some of the area's most Protestant wards. Their first attempt to gather was thwarted by an Irish mob. The Protestants returned in large numbers on May 6 to hold an outdoor meeting. The local nativist leaders, including congressional candidate Lewis Levin, were addressing the crowd when rain began to fall, driving listeners into the nearby Nanny Goat Market. Violence between local Irish Catholics and nativist Protestants erupted almost immediately in the market. Most of the rioting at this time involved blunt instruments and soft tomatoes, but during the chaos, Protestants came under fire from Irish Catholic riflemen in the nearby Hibernia Hose

House, a local fire station. The gunmen wounded several nativists and killed 19-year-old George Shiffler who became a martyr to the Protestant cause (and after whom a nativist gang, the Shifflers, was named). The arrival of heavily armed fellow Protestants triggered a two-hour battle.

The Kensington phase of the Philadelphia riots of 1844 went on for two more days. Nativist mobs burned St. Michaels Church, the Sisters of Charity convent, and St. Augustine's Church. Although no one in the mobs, the Catholic Church, or the local governments had acted responsibly, the violence had subsided by May 9 with peace continuing through June. A grand jury, made up of Protestants, concluded that the Irish Catholics had initiated the riots in Kensington.

On July 4, the nativists staged a celebration that included a parade that went off without incident. The next day, nativists noticed that arms were being delivered to the Catholic Church of St. Philip de Neri in Southwark, a heavily Protestant suburb south of the old city. A mob formed. Two aldermen and the sheriff tried to defuse the situation by searching the church and impounding 12 muskets. Militia under General John Cadwalader took control of the church and found many more guns. In the midst of this tense situation, Charles Naylor, a Protestant Whig politician who had attempted to restore order, was arrested by General Cadwalader for disobeying his command. Naylor was held in a Catholic church under the control of the state militia. In order to remove a source of tension on the scene, General Cadwalader had ordered the Hibernian Greens, an Irish Catholic militia, to leave. But hostilities resumed that night when some of the worst fighting and greatest destruction took place. Groups of young men from both sides roamed the streets, clashing, fighting, and setting fires. At least 14 men were killed, an unknown number were wounded, and several buildings were burned. During the melee, the militia ended up fighting the nativist mob, which was made up of Protestants. The riots finally ended on July 7.

When tempers cooled, the responsible citizens of Philadelphia responded to the riots and some of the conditions that had sparked them. The most conspicuous reforms included the integration of many of the outlying areas of Philadelphia into a single municipal government and the establishment of a citywide police force.

See also 1834 URSULINE CONVENT RIOT AND FIRE.
William G. Shade

FURTHER READING:
Billington, Ray Allen. *The Protestant Crusade, 1800–1860.* Chicago: Quadrangle Books, 1964.

Feldberg, Michael. *The Turbulent Era: Riot and Disorder in Jacksonian America.* New York: Oxford University Press, 1980.
Warner, Sam Bass, Jr. *The Private City: Philadelphia in Three Periods of Its Growth.* Philadelphia: University of Pennsylvania Press, 1968.

1844 ◆ MILLERITES AND THE END OF THE WORLD

For the followers of William Miller, known as the Millerites, October 22, 1844, marked the end of the world and the second coming of Jesus Christ. Born in 1782, Miller was a farmer who lived in Poultney, Vermont. In 1830, he began to study the Bible, eventually creating a 14-point interpretation of the Scripture. The verses of Daniel 8:14 were the most prophetic to him. This section proclaimed, "Then I heard a holy one speaking, and another holy one said to the one that spoke, 'For how long is the vision concerning the continual burnt offering, the transgression that makes desolate, and the giving over of the sanctuary and host to be trampled under foot?' And he said to him, 'Two thousand and three hundred evenings and mornings; then the sanctuary shall be restored to its rightful state.'" Based on the dating of the first Jewish sanctuary, Miller calculated that these 2,300 days pointed to the year 1844. The first "sanctuary" was the creation of the Jewish nation, which dated from the time of Moses to the destruction of the last temple of Jerusalem in A.D. 70. Miller viewed the Earth as a sanctuary and believed that a massive fire would cleanse it for the return visit of Christ.

Many Millerites belonged to the Baptist and Methodist faiths. These denominations had grown tremendously during the Second Great Awakening, a time of religious revival in the United States in the early 19th century. This era of religious enthusiasm produced a renewed belief in Christ and a desire to spread the Christian faith into the American frontier. The Awakening was centered in the "burned-over" district of upstate New York (so-called because of the frenzied religious activity that had gripped the region), western Vermont, and western Massachu-

FACTBOX

PLACE Northern and midwestern United States

DATE 1844, with October 22 as the date of the most famous prediction

TYPE Religious upheaval

DESCRIPTION According to William Miller's biblical interpretations, especially of Daniel 8:14, the second coming of Jesus Christ would mark the end of the world, and many followers stopped work in preparation.

CAUSE The Millerite phenomenon was influenced by the preaching of William Miller and a religious revival known as the Second Great Awakening.

CASUALTIES Some individuals were institutionalized as a result of the hysteria leading up to 1844.

IMPACT Creation of the Seventh-Day Adventist Church

setts. Out of this fervor emerged a variety of new religious groups, including the Mormons, the Shakers, and the Spiritualists. The burned-over district was also known for its incubation of social reforms, such as the antislavery movement, health reform, and temperance. Miller's teaching appealed to many of the rural folk of the region. Miller believed that prophecies of the Bible usually were fulfilled. Daniel 8:14, he thought, signaled the future cleansing of the world and the second coming of Christ. Fearful of how others would react to this news, Miller kept his vision private until he was invited to talk about it publicly in 1831. Then he launched a frenetic speaking schedule, giving an estimated 4,500 lectures to more than 500,000 people during the course of his career.

Joshua Hines, a follower of Miller and an entrepreneur from Exeter, New Hampshire, recognized that Miller would never be able to preach to all that were willing to listen. Inviting Miller to Boston in 1840, Hines was responsible for expanding the appeal of Millerism in the cities. Hines crafted the phrase "for at the appointed time, the end shall be" as a device to reach out to all who believed in the coming of Christ. The catchphrase was imprinted on seals, maps, and newspapers and became the motto for thousands of lectures, conferences, and retreat camps attended by Millerites. Hines spearheaded the founding of the two important Millerite publications, *Sign of the Times* (1840) and *The Midnight Cry* (1842). He also assisted in creating the Bearean Society that sponsored reading rooms dedicated to Miller's prophecy in larger cities.

In 1843, Hines's entrepreneurialism and Miller's preaching ignited a hysteria among an estimated 500,000 adherents of Miller, most of whom lived in the eastern United States. Miller preached that salvation would come only by preparing for the end of the world through prayer and heeding the word of preachers. The conviction that Christ would reappear was so strong among some individuals that they developed a condition known as "Millerite insanity." Symptoms of this malady included violent tremors and melancholy, which reputedly could cause violent behavior and even murder. Some of the afflicted were sent to asylums from Boston to Chicago.

Millerites believed the end was near in January 1844. As the year proceeded, Millerite fervor grew. More people joined the movement and prayed for the cleansing of the sanctuary. But new deadlines for the estimated end of the world in May and July came and went without the anticipated cataclysm. Samuel Snow, a Millerite preacher from New York, told his followers to expect Christ's appearance on the 10th day of the seventh month on the Hebrew calendar—October 22, 1844. Many Millerites took the prediction seriously and stopped work in order to prepare for the anticipated miracle. But nothing happened, and the revised deadline passed without evidence of the great event. As the year closed without a sighting of the savior, a "Great Disappointment" spread among Miller adherents.

While rebuffed, many Millerites did not lose all faith in a second coming of Christ. Some believers returned to their Baptist or Methodist faiths. An uncounted number abandoned formal religion, apparently too embarrassed to admit their false hopes. But others helped to form a new denomination, the Seventh-Day Adventist Church, which was based on the teachings of William Miller, who died in 1849. Adventists viewed October 22, 1844, as the test that the nonbelievers failed. To believe in the coming of Christ meant accepting Miller's mistakes in mathematical calculations and preparing for the end of the world. Between 1844 and 1852, the Adventists grew in numbers, preached their beliefs, and established missions in the American frontier.

Julie Arrison

FURTHER READING:

Butler, Jonathan, and Ronald Numbers, eds. *The Disappointed: Millerism and Millenarianism in the Nineteenth Century.* Bloomington: Indiana University Press, 1987.

Clark, Jerome. *1844: Intellectual, Social, and Religious Movements.* Nashville, Tenn.: Southern Publishing Association, 1968.

1845 ◆ IRISH FAMINE AND IMMIGRATION

In July 1845, Irish farmers noticed that some of the potatoes harvested from their fields had turned black, as if they had rotted. Other potatoes that initially had appeared normal later rotted as well. The potato blight that affected Ireland in 1845 appeared suddenly and spread rapidly, destroying about a third of the crop throughout the country. The disease returned with greater force in 1846, wiping out virtually the entire planting. The consequences of the blight were catastrophic because a large percentage of Ireland's inhabitants depended primarily on potatoes for subsistence. They supplemented this staple with milk or butter and sometimes pork, which came from pigs that had also been fattened on potatoes. While mindful of the frequent harvest failures in the past, most farmers kept only enough food to survive a year of famine until the next growing season. But in 1846, when the crop again rotted in the ground, the misfortune proved devastating. Known as the Great Famine, the potato blight of the mid-19th century in Ireland caused massive starvation that led to the nation's largest emigration in its history. Most of these emigrants ended up in the United States, a process that transformed the character of American cities.

The blight was caused by a fungal plant disease, officially known as *Phytophthora infestans,* that afflicted potato yields throughout Europe, but its impact was felt most keenly in Ireland for two reasons. First, the boggy and wet Irish soil was poorly suited for most crops, potatoes excepted. This was a particular problem for poor peasant and tenant farmers, who had been pushed into very marginal land, and often were saddled with exorbitant rents. In addition, Irish farmers still practiced a form of partible inheritance, called subdividing, which meant that existing farms were continuously partitioned among a farmer's male heirs. As a result, some farms had been reduced to one or two acres, a size too minuscule to support a sustainable horticulture—except with potatoes.

The potato did have some attractive features. Its calorie-per-acre yield is higher than that of almost any other crop. One acre sown with potatoes normally was sufficient to sustain a family of four for a year, whereas dependence on wheat required at least twice the acreage. In addition, potatoes eaten with buttermilk supply sufficient dietary nutrients when eaten in large quantities (an astonishing 12–14 pounds a day per adult laborer). Potatoes are so nutritious, in fact, that when not rotten, they enabled Irish families to subsist on tiny plots of land. Despite the predominance of small farms in Ireland, the rural population density of the island in the early 19th century was probably the highest in Europe. Potatoes had enabled the Irish population to increase to roughly 9 million people, a level

FACTBOX	
PLACE Ireland and the United States	
DATE July 1845–1854	
TYPE Famine	
DESCRIPTION Potato famine caused widespread starvation and death and forced millions of Irish people to emigrate, 85 percent of whom came to the United States.	
CAUSE Fungal infestation of the potato crop	
CASUALTIES As many as 1 million deaths	
IMPACT Emigration reduced Irish population permanently by 50 percent. Extensive Irish population and influence in North America	

sustainable only with a healthy potato harvest. Irish peasants subsisted almost wholly on potatoes, unlike other European peasant populations, with the exception of the Scottish Highlanders, and in Ireland there was no alternate food source in times of dearth. Whole villages of small farmers starved to death in the great famine of 1846.

Although the crop of 1847 was not blighted, bringing momentary hope, the famine was far from over. The blight returned in 1848 and continued with lesser virulence for six more years. Even in 1847, hunger persisted because disheartened farmers had planted only about 10 percent of the usual crop. The British government, overlord of its Irish possession, was slow, inefficient, and, some argued, insensitive in its response to the catastrophe, which contributed to the number of deaths. Nonetheless, government aid as well as religious and private charities probably saved millions of lives.

As many as 1 million Irish died during the famine. The blight also induced a million and a half Irish to leave Ireland by 1854. Irish people had emigrated before 1846, but the famine transformed a trickle of emigrants into a tidal wave. Substantial outflows of Irish emigrants continued through the latter half of the 19th century, when the population of Ireland contracted to about 4.5 million. By the end of the 20th century—some 150 years later—Ireland still sustained only about 5 million people, roughly half its pre-famine population.

The famine was a principal cause of a massive emigration of Irish men and women. Four million fled their island homes during the second half of the 19th century, relocating to the United States, Canada, Australia, and England. Because of cheaper fares, greater opportunities, and the desire to join a burgeoning Irish community, approximately 85 percent came to the United States. Many Irish who initially settled in Canada later relocated south across the border.

Starving Irish peasants rarely could muster the money to finance their journey overseas. British government agencies, charities, American relatives, and sometimes landlords provided the funds for the passage. Famine immigrants who crossed the Atlantic often rode in "coffin ships" that were overcrowded, disease-ridden, and unseaworthy. As many as 30 percent of the immigrants reputedly died on these voyages. Conditions in their new home were better than those they had left behind, but famine immigrants were forced to take the worst-paid jobs. Native residents shunned the motley newcomers.

The famine shaped the pattern of Irish immigration. Irish immigrants during the famine years and after included lower numbers of skilled workers than other immigrant groups. Irish men looked for work as low-paid, unskilled, day laborers in jobs such as construction and railroad or dock work, while women tended to seek employment as maids, cooks, or unskilled factory hands. The famine also ended the practice of subdividing farmland in Ireland. This change allowed the eldest son to inherit the family farm, creating conditions that helped induce his siblings to emigrate. During the nine years of famine (1846–54), Irish people of all ages traveled across the ocean. By the late 1850s, however, the outflow had become overwhelmingly young men and women, who went in search of better opportunities in America.

Eventually, Irish refugees became ensconced in urban America. Prejudice against the Irish— virulent in mid-century—began to diminish by the 1860s. As Irish men and women sank roots into their new homes, they encouraged family members or friends to emigrate or to send money back across the ocean to support family members in Ireland. The exodus from Ireland had a marked impact on the urban population of the United States. By the late 1800s, Irish immigrants made up a quarter of the population of some of the large coastal cities, such as New York and Boston. Their contributions to American society were many and varied. Thousands of recent Irish arrivals fought on the side of the Union in the Civil War. They also formed a majority of the laborers who built the eastern half of the first transcontinental railroad in the 1860s. They dominated many occupations, such as building contractors and schoolteachers, and trades such as plumbing, steamfitting, roofing, and painting. Irish Americans were prominent in labor unions and became key constituents, as well as leaders, of the Democratic Party. They were a critical component to the growth of the American Catholic Church. By the beginning of the 20th century, the Irish had established a permanent presence in American life—a presence that can be traced directly to the horrors of the great famine.

Anna Suranyi

FURTHER READING:

Miller, Kerby. *Emigrants and Exiles: Ireland and the Irish Exodus to North America.* Oxford: Oxford University Press, 1985.

Mokyr, Joel. *Why Ireland Starved: A Quantitative and Analytical History of the Irish Economy, 1800–1850.* London: George Allen & Unwin, 1983.

Ó Gráda, Cormac. *The Great Irish Famine.* New York: Cambridge University Press, 2000.

Schrier, Arnold. *Ireland and the American Emigration 1850–1900.* Chester Springs, Pa.: Dufour Editions, 1997.

Woodham-Smith, Cecil. *The Great Hunger: Ireland 1845–1849.* London: Penguin, 1991.

1846 ◆ THE DONNER PARTY

In mid-April 1846, George Donner, his family, relatives, and friends left Illinois to start new lives in California. Their nearly yearlong journey became the most infamous trek across the American West. Symbolizing the dangers of crossing the western two-thirds of the North American continent by foot and wagon, the Donner party trip endured one of the most grisly migrant experiences along the Overland Trail. Bad planning, bad weather, and bad luck dogged the band of migrants, who became trapped by snow in the Sierra Nevada of western California. Only half of the 87 members of the Donner party survived the ordeal and then only by resorting to cannibalism.

After traveling to Independence, Missouri, the famed launching point for the Oregon Trail, Donner and his group of 33 individuals departed on May 12. Crossing the vast prairie, they met another 54 migrants in Wyoming in late June and headed for Fort Bridger. Along the route, they elected Donner captain of the party. The Donner group decided to follow the Hasting Cutoff, a trail touted by Lansford W. Hasting in his well-known 1845 *Emigrants' Guide to Oregon and California,* which claimed a new, speedier route to the Sierra Nevada. But the advice cost them precious time, as the party had to hack a new wagon trail through Weber Canyon in the Wasatch Range in Utah, traveling only 36 miles in 21 days. Once over the Wasatch, the emigrants still had to cross Nevada's Great Basin desert. This grueling six-day trek in early September left both humans and animals thin and exhausted. With food running low, desperation turned to fear, and the company decided to send two men ahead to Sutter's Fort in California in hopes that they could bring back relief supplies to the party. Now in mid-September, the group faced possible starvation. They began to wonder if their expedition, started with such optimism, might end in failure and death.

The bad situation deteriorated further. First, tensions rose between the families, leading to an altercation on October 5 that left one man dead. The group banished the killer, James Reed, who went ahead to Sutter's Fort, leaving his wife and children behind. After another month, the scraggly bunch reached

FACTBOX

PLACE Sierra Nevada, California

DATE Winter 1846–47

TYPE Starvation and cannibalism

DESCRIPTION Members of the Donner party turned to cannibalism after becoming stranded in the mountains en route to California.

CAUSE Severe winter storms and deep snow

CASUALTIES 40 of the 87 Donner party members perished.

IMPACT Californians planned relief measures for future migrants.

their final challenge, the Sierra Nevada. Here Charles T. Stanton, one of the men sent ahead, met the weary travelers with seven mules loaded with supplies. They rested for five days and then continued upward into the mountains along the Truckee River (which passes through Reno, Nevada) in mid-October. The first snows had already fallen and blown into drifts as high as 10 feet. The group pressed on, but fierce storms trapped them at Truckee Lake (now Donner Lake, in California, along Interstate 80), below the pass. The emigrants settled into a cabin that had been built several years before and built two more shelters, one nearby, the other about half a mile distant.

Meanwhile, James Reed arrived at Sutter's Fort in early November and began to assemble a relief party. He generated enough local support to gather a rescue team, but it met with total failure after leaving the fort. The rescuers' pack animals could not get through the deep snow, and the men barely could. It seemed unlikely that any aid would reach the party until at least February, when the winter storms were supposed to abate.

High in the mountains, one member of the Donner party, Patrick Breen, wrote a journal of the harrowing days that followed the group's entrapment. Day after day, it snowed. Two attempts to send groups over the mountains failed. By December 1, the snow lay five to six feet deep, and Breen found it nearly impossible to get out of the cabin to chop wood. They had killed all the cattle, and food ran low. The work of clearing snow off the shelters and chopping wood for warmth and cooking wore out the trapped group. Their rations were reduced to boiled oxen hides. One by one, members of the group died, leaving survivors who were sickly and weak.

On December 16, 15 of the desperate members finally made it over the pass on improvised snowshoes. Thirty-three days later, seven in this group emerged on the western side of the mountains. They explained to residents of Johnson's Ranch, the first settlement they reached, that, in desperate circumstances, they had eaten the individuals who had died along the way.

On February 17, 1847, seven men from California arrived at Truckee Lake with provisions for the trapped party. The rescuers left a few days later, taking a few of the strongest emigrants along. The failure of the rescuers to bring in many supplies, however, forced those left behind to subsist on hides for food. Recording this situation, Patrick Breen wrote that Lavina Murphy had confessed to him that she "thought [she] would Commence on Milt. [Milford Elliott] & eat him," which, he found "distressing." The equally desperate Donners, he penned, had claimed they too would begin to eat their dead.

A second relief party, led by James Reed, made it through to the miserable survivors on March 1, 1847. Over the next few weeks, several more rescue parties reached people still stranded. By the middle of March only five Donner party travelers remained at the lake. A final group of rescuers turned back, discouraged by slushy snow, an oncoming storm, and the belief that those still at the lake were probably dead. In April, a salvage party went to gather the goods left behind at the camp. Only Lewis Keseberg remained alive, surrounded by the half-eaten remains of his comrades.

By the end of the winter of 1846–47, only 47 of the original 87 members of the Donner party remained alive. Five had died along the trail and 35 succumbed to the harrowing conditions in the mountains. In subsequent years, California residents organized more effective relief efforts to help migrants cross the mountains before winter set in. This was a welcome development for later western pioneers, as the Donner party served as a gruesome reminder of the hazards of the Overland Trail.

Diana Di Stefano

FURTHER READING:

Stewart, George R. *Ordeal by Hunger: The Story of the Donner Party.* Lincoln: University of Nebraska Press, 1986.

Unruh, John D. *The Plains Across: The Overland Immigrants and the Trans-Mississippi West, 1840–1860.* Urbana: University of Illinois Press, 1979.

1850 ◆ COMPROMISE OF 1850

On January 29, 1850, the aged Kentucky Whig senator Henry Clay introduced resolutions designed to solve problems that threatened to tear the United States asunder. These resolutions, which aimed to eliminate issues dividing the free states from the slave states, called for (1) California to be admitted to the Union as a free state; (2) New Mexico and Utah territories to be permitted to have slavery if desired; (3) Texas to relinquish land claims to a portion of the New Mexico Territory in exchange for national assumption of its unpaid debts; (4) the enactment of a stronger Fugitive Slave Act with strict enforcement provisions; and (5) the abolition of the slave trade in the District of Columbia but not the abolition of slavery. After a bitter debate that occupied much of the Senate's time, and that of the public, until July, the Senate rejected the proposed legislation and the nation teetered on the brink of dissolution. With the failure of Clay's compromise resolutions, Illinois senator Stephen A. Douglas took the lead in averting the crisis by introducing separate bills on each of the issues. These measures ultimately passed with differing majorities in September 1850, delaying secession for 10 years until the election of Abraham Lincoln, who opposed the extension of slavery into the territories and whose victory prompted southern leaders to attempt to secede, thus bringing on the long-threatened Civil War.

As early as the writing of the Constitution by the founding fathers in 1787, the nation had skirted the issue of slavery. Over the next 70 years, while northern states abolished slavery, the institution became more firmly entrenched in the southern states. By the early 19th century, an equilibrium had been established, resulting in an equal number of free and slave states in the Union. Southern leaders relied on this balance because it enabled them to maintain political equality in the Senate, while the House, based on population, was dominated by representatives from the North whose population was increasing faster than that of the South. In the meantime, however, a growing number of religious and northern leaders began to question the morality of slavery and to call for its gradual or immediate abolition. As a result of these demands, southern slaveholders and their allies searched for ways to protect the institution, which was becoming increasingly important economically. In addition, as the population of enslaved African Americans grew in the South, leaders became increasingly concerned about the possibility of a bloody race war. For these reasons the region became defensive. Its leaders developed a rationale

that justified slavery as an economic necessity and as a positive factor in the American republic.

For a time, Americans believed that the conflict over slavery had been definitively settled by the Missouri Compromise of 1820, which had admitted Missouri as a slave state, Maine as a free state, and divided the Louisiana Territory along the extended line of Missouri's southern border. Slavery was prohibited in the territory north of 36°30 but allowed south of that line. This agreement began to break down, however, as antislavery and abolition sentiment gathered adherents in the northern free states. Finally, the proposed admission of Texas in 1836, and the acquisition of New Mexico and California territories after the Mexican War (1846–48), rekindled the debate over slavery. During the war, Congressman David Wilmot of Pennsylvania had introduced an amendment to a military appropriation bill providing that "neither slavery nor involuntary servitude shall ever exist in any part" of territory that might be acquired from Mexico. Although the Wilmot Proviso passed in the House several times, the Senate never approved it.

On the heels of victory in Mexico, the United States teetered on the edge of disunion as a result of bitter disagreement over the western territories won from the war. The root of the controversy lay in slavery. Leaders from the slave states demanded that slavery be allowed to expand into the new territories; many northern leaders, opposed to slavery and its expansion, wished to reserve the states for free labor. Southern leaders such as South Carolina senator John C. Calhoun and "fire-eater" William Lowndes Yancey of Alabama, among others, threatened to take their states out of the Union unless slavery was protected and allowed into the new territories.

The battle over the compromise of 1850 ignited a memorable debate, often called the greatest in the history of the U.S. Senate. It began with the introduction of the Compromise Resolutions by Henry Clay in January. Those resolutions led to an omnibus compromise bill on which every leading senator would speak during the next several months. It was the aging giants of the senate—Clay, aged 73, John C. Calhoun, 68, and Daniel Webster of Massachusetts, 68—who took the spotlight. Clay and Webster delivered powerful speeches in favor of the compromise with the latter senator even dampening his antislavery rhetoric in favor of maintaining the Union by compromise. On the other hand, Senator

John M. Mason of Virginia read the blistering attack prepared by the dying Calhoun. The South Carolinian declared that the only way for the Union to avert a break-up was for the North to provide permanent protection to the South's "inalienable right" to slavery. Days later, William H. Seward, a young antislavery senator from New York, was equally uncompromising as he denounced the proposed compromise measures as immoral. The Constitution, he proclaimed, was subject to a "higher law."

The omnibus compromise bill failed in the Senate because southern senators would not support any restrictions on slavery, while northern senators would not support the expansion of slavery. The outcome left many Americans fearing that the union of states could not survive. At this point, Illinois's young Democratic senator Stephen A. Douglas, chairman of the Committee on Territories, proposed a plan to save the compromise. He submitted five bills, one for each element of the compromise, in hopes that each separate piece of legislation would gain a majority to enact it. Perhaps the most notable portion of the resulting compromise was the way slavery was handled in the creation of the Utah and New Mexico territories. The act was silent about the legality of slavery. Instead, the law allowed each territory to apply for admission to the Union "with or without slavery as [its] constitution may prescribe." Slaves were recognized as property and "all cases involving title to slaves" were to be, upon appeal from the territorial courts, sent directly to the U.S. Supreme Court. Undoubtedly the most controversial measure of the compromise was the amendment of the Fugitive Slave Act of 1793 that provided for return of "fugitives from labor" without a trial in the state where they were apprehended. Instead, a commissioner, upon presentation of an affidavit that the accused was a fugitive slave, was to return the fugitive to the alleged owner, and the matter was to be decided in the state from which he or she had escaped. Further, northern citizens could be compelled to participate in the capture of alleged runaways. The final bill, to be signed by President Millard Fillmore on September 20, 1850, was "An Act to suppress the Slave Trade in the District of Columbia." The compromise was accomplished.

In a real sense, the compromise of 1850 was not a genuine compromise. Rather, in most cases, the acts confirmed what was likely to happen. California would have been admitted as a free state; few people believed that the territories of Utah and New Mexico would sustain slavery. The law strengthening the Fugitive Slave Act served primarily to increase northern opposition to slavery. The measure did little to assist the South because few slaves were successful in escaping to the North. In the end, the compromise only delayed what in retrospect appeared inevitable, the Civil War.

Roger D. Bridges

FURTHER READING:

Hamilton, Holman. "Democratic Senate Leadership and the Compromise of 1850." *Mississippi Valley Historical Review* 41 (December 1954): 403–418.

——. *Prologue to Conflict: The Crisis and Compromise of 1850.* Lexington: University of Kentucky Press, 1964.

Hodder, Frank H. "The Authorship of the Compromise of 1850." *Mississippi Valley Historical Review* 22 (March 1936): 525–536.

Russell, Robert R. "What Was the Compromise of 1850?" *Journal of Southern History* 22 (August 1956): 292–309.

1853 ◆ SINKING OF THE *SAN FRANCISCO*

On December 22, 1853, the steamship *San Francisco* left New York City on its maiden voyage, bound for San Francisco, California, with 718 passengers and crew aboard. The ship was chartered by the U.S. government for $75,000 to transport eight companies of the U.S. Army's 3rd Artillery Regiment and other officers to the West Coast of the United States. Less than 36 hours out of port, the ship encountered strong gales as it headed south. The first officer, Edward Mellus, later testified that in his 20 years at sea, it was the heaviest storm he had ever seen. By Christmas morning, the seas were strong enough to sweep the superstructure containing the main saloon and 160 soldiers over the side.

The *San Francisco* was designed by William H. Webb for the firm of Aspinwall & Co. One of America's foremost naval architects and builders, Webb designed clipper ships, warships, and steamships and founded what later became the Webb Institute for naval architecture and marine engineering in Glen Cove, New York. Businessman William Henry Aspinwall owned the Pacific Mail Steamship Company, which received government contracts to deliver mail to the West Coast of the United States. He also founded the Panama Railroad in Central America, the aim of which was to cut traveling time between New York and California by eliminating the need to sail around South America. Ships would journey southward along the Atlantic coast to Panama, transfer the mail and passengers by rail to the Pacific side, and then ferry their cargos northward by ship up the west coast to California. The *San Francisco* was built with the intention of serving the west coast leg of the trip after its maiden voyage around Cape Horn at the tip of South America.

The *San Francisco* was 280 feet long, displaced 2,200 tons, and had three decks, including a superstructure above the hull that housed a main saloon. The ship's propulsion consisted of two oscillating steam engines that turned two 28-foot-diameter paddle wheels, each capable of producing 1,000 horsepower. It also had two sailing masts. A massive ship, the *San Francisco* had stateroom accommodations for 350 people and steerage berths for an additional 1,000.

A major design innovation fortified the ship's hull. According to a *New York Times* report during the *San Francisco's* construction: "The bottom is solid, and there are double diagonal braces as an additional security for the frame. Another method of strengthening has been introduced into this vessel never before adopted. This consists in having two bulkheads, running fore and aft, one on each side of the engine and boilers, and secured to the bottom and the middle deck beams, and diagonally braced with iron the whole length." The use of diagonal braces significantly strengthened the hull, much like the diagonal beams on the USS *Constitution* (completed

in 1797), allowing it to carry a full main gun deck of heavy 32-pounders.

Under the command of Captain James Watkins, the *San Francisco* steamed from New York Harbor on Thursday, December 22, with 718 crew and passengers, mostly army personnel. Although the ship could accommodate nearly twice that many passengers, military equipment and supplies for 12 months reduced the available passenger space. By Friday afternoon, the seas were already rough. By 3 A.M. on December 25, the mainmast was lost and the rudder chain was broken. Thirty minutes later, the engines failed and the foremast was lost, causing the ship to swing broadside to the seas. Because of the extra army cargo stored below deck, soldiers were forced out of the berthing area to the saloon on the upper deck. At 9 A.M., a wave crashed onto the saloon and swept it into the ocean, taking with it 160 soldiers and all the lifeboats.

The *San Francisco* floundered for three days, during which time more than 60 passengers succumbed to fever and an outbreak of cholera. Its approximate location was 38°20' N/69°30' W, about 400 miles east of Cape Hatteras, North Carolina. On December 28, the *Kilby,* a commercial ship, arrived and rescued 100 survivors but had no room for more as it was a much smaller ship. A week later, on January 5, two more ships arrived—the *Three Bells* and the *Antarctic*—and rescued the remaining 398 passengers, after which the *San Francisco* sank. The ship's fate was relayed by telegraph on January 6, the first time news of a maritime disaster had been transmitted by wire in the United States. At least three other ships were lost, crippled, or abandoned in the same storm.

Among the survivors of the *San Francisco* disaster was navy Lieutenant Francis Key Murray, who was familiar with maritime mishaps. While he commanded the coastal survey steamship *Jefferson* in 1851, a storm had toppled both masts off Montevideo, Uruguay. Another survivor was army Lieutenant Lucien Loeser, who had delivered the dispatch in December 1848 from California to Washington, D.C., that gold had been discovered, sparking the gold rush of 1849.

Despite the loss of the ship, naval architects concluded that the *San Francisco* had remained seaworthy for several days during the severe conditions. This favorable verdict about the ship's construction influenced the design of later vessels.

Claude G. Berube

FURTHER READING:

Cutler, Carl C. *Queens of the Western Ocean: The Story of America's Mail and Passenger Sailing Lines.* Annapolis, Md.: U.S. Naval Institute, 1961.

Stackpole, Edouard A. *The Wreck of the Steamer* San Francisco. Mystic, Conn.: Marine Historical Association, 1954.

1854 ◆ WRECK OF THE *ARCTIC*

The steamship *Arctic* was one of four Collins Line ships that operated between New York City and Liverpool, England, between 1850 and 1858. In heavy fog off the coast of Newfoundland on September 27, 1854, during a westbound crossing, the *Arctic* collided at high speed with the French fishing ship *Vesta.* Nearly 300 passengers and crew members, all from the *Arctic,* perished in the collision. The accident was one of the worst maritime tragedies involving commercial vessels during the 19th century. The mishap caused the adoption of reforms designed to make transatlantic sailing safer. The loss of the *Arctic,* as well as a sister ship two years later, contributed to the demise of the Collins Line, which removed the United States from transatlantic passenger shipping.

The Collins Line, incorporated as the U.S. Mail Steamship Company, had been founded by Edward Knight Collins in 1848 to challenge the preeminence of the British merchant marine, specifically the Cunard Line. Collins Line steamers could cross the Atlantic in nine or 10 days. Under contract with the U.S. government to transport mail, the line was required to make 20 round trips per year. The company benefited from the outbreak of the Crimean War in 1854 because Cunard Line ships were requisitioned by Britain for military uses.

The *Arctic* disaster helped to eclipse this temporary advantage.

The *Arctic* had a length of 284 feet and displaced 2,856 tons. It was designed by the famed naval architect George Steers who had designed the racing yacht *America,* for which the racing cup is named. Launched in 1850, the *Arctic* was constructed at the Novelty Iron Works in New York City, which later built the turret for the first ironclad, the USS *Monitor.* The *Arctic* possessed two 35-foot paddle wheels powered by 1,000-horsepower

After a head-on collision with a French fishing vessel, the steamship *Arctic* sank in the frigid waters of the North Atlantic. *(Library of Congress)*

FACTBOX

PLACE Atlantic Ocean, 60 miles off Cape Race, Newfoundland

DATE September 27, 1854

TYPE Maritime disaster

DESCRIPTION Steamship *Arctic* on a westward-bound voyage to New York collided with the eastbound fishing vessel *Vesta*.

CAUSE Heavy fog resulted in low visibility; high speed by both ships

CASUALTIES Approximately 296 deaths

COST Ship insured for $300,000

IMPACT The accident helped cause the demise of the Collins Line, which removed the United States from the transatlantic passenger trade. Future ship construction incorporated subdivisions within the hull to mitigate damage; navigational safety rules were reformed, including establishment of parallel shipping lanes and the use of horns and bells in poor weather.

engines, although it also retained two masts for sails.

The *Arctic* weighed anchor from Liverpool, England, September 21, 1854, with 150 crew members and 233 passengers. On board was the manager of the line, Edward Knight Collins, his wife, and one son. On September 27, 60 miles off Cape Race, Newfoundland, it encountered heavy fog conditions. Visibility was only about one-half to three-quarters of a mile, according to testimony of her captain, James Luce. Despite the poor conditions, Luce ordered the *Arctic* to continue at her top cruising speed of 13 knots. His decision followed company orders that high speed be maintained in order to keep trip time to a minimum and to clear fog conditions as quickly as possible.

At noon on September 27, the lookout on the *Arctic* sighted an oncoming ship. It was the *Vesta*, a French fishing vessel from the Island of St. Pierre with 147 fishermen and 50 crew members aboard and all sails set. At 152 feet long and 250 tons and built only the year before, the *Vesta* threatened the *Arctic* since the former was constructed with an iron hull and water-

tight bulkheads, while the latter had a wooden hull. Due to the high rate of speed of both vessels, the limited visibility, and their head-on course—the *Arctic* westbound and the *Vesta* eastbound—a collision became unavoidable. The impact ripped off a section of the *Vesta*'s bow and tore a five-foot hole in the *Arctic*'s bow below the waterline, as well as inflicting two additional punctures above the waterline. When it became clear that the damage would doom the *Arctic*, Captain Luce ordered the vessel to make best speed toward shore. This decision ran contrary to an unwritten rule of the sea to aid other ships in distress. Leaving the *Vesta* to its own fate, the *Arctic* proceeded at 15 knots toward land. Two hours later, however, with water rising in the engine rooms, the boilers' fires died, the paddle wheels stopped, and the ship began to sink. The last lifeboat was launched by 4 P.M., as the *Arctic* slipped beneath the surface of the ocean. A year later, the hull of the *Arctic* was located on the western edge of the Grand Banks.

The *Arctic*'s five lifeboats were inadequate to handle the large number of passengers on board. A few rafts had been hastily constructed, but they proved largely ineffective. Life preservers, save those made from tin, proved serviceable, although many drowned in the frigid water. The next day, two nearby ships, the *Huron* and the *Lebanon*, rescued the *Arctic*'s survivors. Estimates of the number of passengers and crew vary; according to Captain Luce's later testimony, the *Arctic* had 383 on board, of whom only 87 were rescued. No women or children survived, including Edward Collins's own family (although Collins himself survived). Luce was saved by the *Cambria* on September 29. He never went to sea again. The *Vesta*'s design was more seaworthy: The internal subdivisions of its hull trapped the water in certain compartments and kept the ship afloat. All of the *Vesta*'s crew members and fishermen survived. But the *Arctic*, which had no internal bulkheads, flooded after the collision. This fact led to the subsequent construction of ships with subdivisions in the hulls, as a protective safeguard.

A grand jury of the U.S. Circuit Court investigated the accident in 1855. The jury determined that the *Arctic* had too few lifeboats for its passengers. The observation was accurate, but the *Arctic* had been in compliance with maritime requirements in place at the time for ships of more than 1,500 tons, but the regulations were hopelessly outdated for large ships.

The grand jury also found that the *Arctic* carried too few crew members skilled in handling lifeboats. Reforms to improve the safety of transatlantic crossings followed in the wake of the disaster. To prevent possible future head-on collisions, U.S. Navy Lieutenant Matthew Fontaine Maury recommended that Atlantic traffic follow largely parallel westbound and eastbound shipping lanes, each 20 to 25 miles wide; at some points the shipping lanes were 300 miles apart. First adopted by the U.S. Navy, the shipping lanes were implemented by the larger steamship lines at the recommendation of insurance companies. Fixed routes for steamships in the Atlantic were finally accepted by the principal maritime powers in 1898. In addition, new safety regulations, such as the use of horns or bells at intermittent intervals to warn other nearby ships in conditions of limited visibility, were imposed.

Cunard ships returned to the transatlantic passenger trade at the conclusion of the Crimean War in 1856. The renewed competition from the British line, coupled with the loss of the *Arctic* as well as

the *Pacific,* a second Collins Line ship, which disappeared in the North Atlantic in 1856, pushed the firm into bankruptcy in 1857. The United States was left without a shipping firm engaged in trans-Atlantic passenger transportation.

The *Arctic* disaster received wide notice, inspiring poet Walt Whitman to pen "Thought," one of his lesser-known poems. "A huge sob—A few bubbles—the white foam spirting up," he wrote, "And then the women gone, Sinking there, while the passionless wet flows on. . . ."

Claude G. Berube

FURTHER READING:

Bennett, William Edward [Warren Armstrong, pseud.]. *The Collins Story.* London: R. Hale, 1957.

Brown, Alexander Crosby. *Women and Children Last: The Loss of the Steamship* Arctic. New York: Putnam, 1961.

Shaw, David W. *The Sea Shall Embrace Them: The Tragic Story of the Steamship* Arctic. New York: Free Press, 2002.

1857 ◆ FINANCIAL PANIC AND DEPRESSION

A sharp banking panic and subsequent economic downturn disrupted the United States just prior to the Civil War. In the ups and downs of the economy in the 19th century, the panic of 1857 was a comparatively tame affair with limited impact on commercial activity. Yet the recession did bring labor difficulties to the fore, as demonstrations by the unemployed troubled the nation for several months, a harbinger of more serious outbursts during the 1837 FINANCIAL PANIC AND DEPRESSION. The financial problems of 1857 did not deflect the debate concerning slavery but in fact reinforced sectional cleavages. Southerners grew more suspicious of northern banking practices and more confident in the ability of the cotton crop to weather any storm. Northerners increasingly came to believe that a slave power worked conspiratorially to block legislation favorable to their region.

The economy had roared back to life after the 1837 financial panic and depression, as railroad investment, new business connections, and overseas trade expanded. By the mid-1850s, a national transportation network was taking shape, farmers became increasingly commercial and abandoned subsistence agriculture, and cotton became king of

The panic of 1857 set off bank runs in which many depositors lost their savings. *(Library of Congress)*

FACTBOX

PLACE United States

DATE August 1857–mid-1860

TYPE Financial collapse, resulting in suspension of specie payments by banks

DESCRIPTION The failure of the Ohio Life Insurance and Trust Company produced a run on the banks, leading to specie suspension on October 13, 1857. The panic produced a mild recession that lasted until the middle of 1859.

CAUSE Banks had overextended loans, induced by an inflation originating in the gold discoveries of California and trade buoyed by the Crimean War. The end of the war in 1856 cut foreign demand for goods. Defaults on loans resulted, pushing banks into liquidity problems, which in turn triggered panic among depositors.

IMPACT The panic highlighted the growing problems of industrial society manifested by unemployment demonstrations and emboldened the South, which weathered the panic unscathed, to contemplate secession from the Union. The ensuing depression injected economic issues into political discussions, helping the Republican Party win the election of 1860.

international commerce. However, no national bank controlled the nation's money supply; instead, each state government adopted its own banking system. A key development during the period was the discovery of gold in California in 1848. Shipments of the precious metal to the East increased bank reserves and underwrote an expansion of credit, a situation that grew inflationary. Prices rose 32 percent in the United States from 1848 to 1854. The expansion of the money supply led to speculation in cotton, western lands, and railroads. A correction seemed probable.

The reversal might have occurred in 1854, when banks experienced a sharp contraction, but these pressures soon passed and the future seemed prosperous. An international dispute had given the economy a helpful boost. France and Great Britain went to war against Russia in the Crimea, spurring a rise in American food exports. The enhanced demand for American goods buoyed agricultural development in the Great Lakes states and stimulated railroad construction. The conclusion of the Crimean War in 1856, however, reduced this demand for American products, setting the stage for the panic of 1857.

Prospects for a prosperous 1857 seemed good. Yet demand from Europe slumped in the spring, alarming bankers, who foresaw problems for debt repayment. As this worry grew, a large and reputedly trustworthy bank, the Ohio Life Insurance and Trust Company, failed on August 24, 1857. Company officials blamed the collapse on excessive speculation in currency in the west. The bankruptcy alarmed bankers, who began to call in notes and pile up specie, or hard money, in their vaults. Doubts spread that banks would be able to pay specie to depositors and note holders. These concerns were magnified by other events, such as the floundering of a clipper ship off the coast of South America. The vessel had been bound for New York City with a cargo of gold, which was lost. This mishap denied an injection of gold into New York banks, a step that might have eased the fears of note holders. In late September, a panic developed as depositors stormed banks to get their money in specie. The drain was so intense that bankers announced suspension of specie payment on October 13. The remedy worked; banks resumed specie payment by December 12. "It was a *fast* panic," a North Carolina editor remarked, "and therefore in entire keeping with this fast age."

The immediate impact of the panic was negligible. Most banks did not fail, partly because stronger state banks aided the weaker ones. The nation had suffered a liquidity crisis (insufficient specie reserves to cover customer demands), a situation exacerbated by a rampant distrust of banks generally. When a financial institution went bankrupt in the 19th century, individual depositors could lose all their money. There were no guarantees for the security of depositors' holdings when a bank fell into insolvency. This financial risk induced a "dog-eat-dog" mentality when rumors spread about troubles in the banks.

The broader economy experienced greater trouble than the financial sector as a recession developed, lasting until the middle of 1859. Unemployment perhaps reached 10 percent in 1858, with some industries hurt more than others. Land sales in the western states plummeted, railroad construction in the North stalled for two years, iron-making suffered, and Great Lakes farmers endured depressed prices because of the lack of foreign demand. The cotton-rich South escaped most of these effects, as demand soared; King Cotton had entered its glory years. Railroad construction in the South charts the region's good fortune. In 1858 and 1859, the South led the country in the construction of track mileage for the first time. By the middle of 1859, the worst of the recession has passed. Spring crop failures in Europe produced an enhanced demand for American grains in 1860, regenerating growth. But as the expansion was taking shape, the secession of southern states at the end of 1860 plunged the nation back into recession.

The immediate effects of the panic of 1857 were limited. It produced no great change in banking legislation, and it did not induce any changes in productive activity. The unemployment demonstrations caused some concern, but they were not severe enough to trigger policy remedies from state or federal governments. But the panic did fan the looming sectional crisis: Because cotton had fared so well during the financial downturn, southern leaders were convinced that a secession movement could succeed. In the North, the panic revived concerns about the economy. The financial crisis of the 1837–42 had favored the Democrats, who sharply criticized banks. In 1857 and 1858, however, cures for the depression were found in Republican nostrums, which centered around a higher tariff, lowered land prices, and federal spending on internal improvements. These ideas helped Republicans to win Pennsylvania and New Jersey, key states in the presidential race of 1860. Thus the panic of 1857 abetted the rise of the Republican Party and contributed to the coming of the Civil War.

See also 1873 FINANCIAL PANIC AND DEPRESSION.

James L. Huston

FURTHER READING:

Huston, James L. *The Panic of 1857 and the Coming of the Civil War.* Baton Rouge: Louisiana State University Press, 1987.

Van Vieck, George W. *The Panic of 1857: An Analytical Study.* New York: Columbia University Press, 1943.

1859 ◆ JOHN BROWN'S RAID

In an early case of political terrorism within the United States, abolitionist John Brown led a raid into the slaveholding South in 1859 with the intention of sparking a slave rebellion. Although Brown's raid failed to free a single slave, it greatly intensified the sectional conflict between the North and South and brought the nation closer to Civil War.

John Brown, born in Connecticut in 1800, embraced the abolitionist cause with an almost mystical fervor. A devout Calvinist who believed in a wrathful God, Brown saw himself as an Old Testament warrior battling the evil of slavery. As early as the 1850s, he accepted violence as a necessary means to end slavery in America. One of his favorite biblical passages was: "Without the shedding of blood there is no remission of sins." Brown went to Kansas to join the free-state fight against the forces of slavery. On the night of May 24–25, 1856, Brown and six followers executed five proslavery colonists at Pottawatamie Creek. Although his contemporaries and some later historians have questioned his mental stability, Brown clearly had a charismatic if domineering and self-righteous personality that attracted a loyal band of abolitionist followers wherever he went.

Between 1856 and 1859, Brown devised a daring plan to free the slaves and set up a provisional freedman's republic in the Appalachian South. He traveled throughout the North gathering recruits, money, and arms and secured support from a group of white abolitionists known as the "Secret Six." Brown's target was the federal arsenal at Harper's Ferry, a small village at the confluence of the Potomac and Shenandoah Rivers in Virginia (today West Virginia). He collected arms and ammunition at a farm in nearby Maryland and waited.

A fervent abolitionist, John Brown organized the Harper's Ferry raid in the hopes of igniting a mass slave uprising across the South. His actions, capture, and subsequent execution electrified both sections of the country. *(Historic Photo Collection, Harpers Ferry NHP)*

On the night of October 16, 1859, Brown led a force of 18 men (which included three of his sons and five free blacks) into the quiet west Virginian town. The invading abolitionists succeeded in capturing the arsenal and taking a few hostages from the town. The fatal flaws in Brown's tactical plans, however, soon became clear. He and his men carried no supplies or rations. They had failed to plan an escape route and had no defensive lines against a counterattack. Most significantly, no slaves joined Brown in his planned uprising. The next day, local militias from Virginia captured the bridges across the two rivers, cutting off any avenues of escape. After two days, a group of U.S. Marines commanded by future Confederate general Robert E. Lee stormed the arsenal where Brown and his men were cornered. Brown was wounded and two of his men were killed. Brown surrendered and was immediately tried and convicted of treason on

October 31 in a Virginia court. On December 2, 1859, John Brown was hanged at Charlestown. Before his execution, he told the court:

> Now, if it is deemed necessary that I should forfeit my life for the furtherance of the ends of justice, and mingle my blood further with the blood of my children and with the blood of millions in this slave country whose rights are disregarded by wicked, cruel, and unjust enactments, I say, let it be done.

Six of Brown's followers were later executed.

The shock of the Harper's Ferry raid reverberated throughout the nation. In the North, abolitionists claimed him as a martyr to their cause and compared him with Christ. Brown himself recognized that he was "worth inconceivably more to *hang* than for any other purpose." Ralph Waldo Emerson predicted that Brown would "make the gallows as glorious as the cross." In the South, Harper's Ferry dramatized the worst fears of southern whites that the new northern "Black Republican" Party was bent on destroying slavery and increased secessionist strength in the slaveholding states. "The day of compromise has passed," the radical *Charleston Mercury* astutely

FACTBOX

PLACE Harper's Ferry, Virginia (today West Virginia)

DATE October 16–18, 1859

TYPE Abolitionist raid on a federal arsenal

DESCRIPTION With a force of 18 men, abolitionist John Brown raided the federal arsenal at Harper's Ferry with the aim of seizing weapons and instigating a slave rebellion. His capture, trial, and execution electrified the nation.

CAUSE John Brown's vision of launching a slave uprising in the South

CASUALTIES Nine deaths. Two of John Brown's accomplices were killed during the raid; Brown and six of his followers were tried for treason and executed.

IMPACT John Brown's raid reinforced southern apprehensions of northern efforts to overturn slavery and thus contributed to the tensions that sparked the Civil War.

noted. John Brown's raid is rightly considered an important final step in the coming of the Civil War.

Mitchell Snay

FURTHER READING:

Boyer, Paul. *The Legend of John Brown.* New York: Knopf, 1973.

Oates, Stephen. *To Purge This Land with Blood: A Biography of John Brown.* New York: Harper & Row, 1970.

Reynolds, David S. *John Brown, Abolitionist: The Man Who Killed Slavery, Sparked the Civil War, and Seeded Civil Rights.* New York: Knopf, 2005.

1860 ◈ WRECK OF THE *LADY ELGIN*

On September 8, 1860, the steamer *Lady Elgin* was struck by the lumber schooner *Augusta* in Lake Michigan while bringing a large group of Milwaukee Irish militiamen back from a political rally. A double-decked wooden side-wheel steamer built in Buffalo, New York, in 1851 and named for the wife of Lord Elgin, the governor-general of Canada, the *Lady Elgin* was one of the largest and most opulent passenger steamers on the Great Lakes, but it quickly broke apart, casting passengers into the storm-tossed waters. Although many passengers made it to the shallows on makeshift rafts, hundreds died in the towering breakers just offshore. The *Lady Elgin* was the *Titanic* of her day and forever changed the social fabric of Milwaukee.

The *Lady Elgin* disaster occurred during a time of unprecedented tension in America, with a decisive presidential campaign under way and the Civil War fast approaching. Wisconsin was known as a militantly abolitionist state and had threatened to secede from the Union if the federal government did not abolish slavery. Milwaukee's Irish Union Guards were caught in the middle of the political tug of war when they refused to pledge their support to the state in the event of Wisconsin secession. Governor Alexander Randall promptly revoked the militia's commission and disarmed them, but the Union Guards responded by chartering the steamer *Lady Elgin* for an overnight excursion to Chicago to hear a speech by Democratic candidate Stephen Douglas and to raise money to rearm their proud unit.

The excursion left Milwaukee in the early morning hours of September 7, 1860, and arrived at Chicago by dawn, where they went on parade and attended the debate. At about 11 P.M., the *Lady Elgin* departed Chicago Harbor with 500 to 600 passengers. It left with little warning, reportedly departing before a number of unticketed visitors on the steamer had had a chance to disembark. Within a few hours, the winds had increased to gale force and the waves grew larger, but the *Lady Elgin* was weathering the storm well.

By 2:30 A.M. on September 8, the *Lady Elgin* was about seven miles off Winnetka, Illinois, when passengers reported seeing the lights of a vessel rapidly approaching. When the oncoming vessel struck the *Lady Elgin,* a tremendous jar was felt throughout the ship, and it suddenly lurched onto its port side. The impact doused most of the *Lady Elgin*'s oil lamps, creating an air of confusion on board. Captain Jack Wilson went hurriedly below and found a massive amount of water entering the engine room, while First Mate George Davis ran to the pilothouse and ordered the *Lady Elgin* turned toward shore. When Captain Wilson returned to the pilothouse, he privately told the mate that the *Lady Elgin* was doomed.

The vessel that had inflicted the damage was the lumber schooner *Augusta,* bound for Chicago. Despite the gale, it was still flying most of its canvas and sailing out of control. As it shot through the water, its deckload had shifted, and it was nearly sailing on its side. Although the *Augusta* saw the *Lady Elgin* from a distance, Captain Darius Malott did not take evasive action until it was too late. He gave the command "Hard Up! For God's sakes, man! Hard Up!" as the *Augusta* plunged into the side of the *Lady Elgin* just aft of its port paddle wheel.

The *Augusta* was pulled along with the *Lady Elgin* for a short distance and pried the *Elgin*'s sidewheel

FACTBOX

PLACE Lake Michigan, off Winnetka, Illinois

DATE September 8, 1860

TYPE Passenger ship sank following collision

DESCRIPTION Sailing out of control amid a raging storm, the schooner *Augusta* struck the side-wheel steamer *Lady Elgin*, which carried more than 500 passengers. The *Lady Elgin* sank, disintegrating and exploding in the process, forcing passengers to cling to any debris they could find.

CAUSE Storm conditions and the poor lighting configuration of the *Lady Elgin* made it difficult to discern its heading.

CASUALTIES About 400 deaths

IMPACT Escalation of pre–Civil War abolitionist fervor and a major change of Milwaukee's population demographics.

and hull planking out as it swung around. Captain Malott and his crew were immediately concerned for their vessel and feared they had sustained extensive damage below the waterline. Believing they had struck the *Lady Elgin* only a glancing blow and fearing they might founder, the *Augusta* continued on for Chicago immediately.

Meanwhile, onboard the *Lady Elgin,* all was pandemonium. Fifty head of cattle that had been in pens below deck were driven overboard in an attempt to lighten the vessel, and a cargo of iron stoves was moved to the starboard side in order to raise the gaping hole in the *Elgin's* side. An attempt was made to launch one of the lifeboats, but it drifted free with no oars. Another lifeboat leaked so badly that it could not be used. As the *Lady Elgin* sank, it began to disintegrate, and a split in its hull cut most passengers off from the life preservers. A crew of Irish Milwaukee firemen began to chop the hurricane deck off with axes to create a raft, and people grabbed anything that would float. The *Lady Elgin* sank stern first, and the air rushing forward caused its upper works to explode. As the scene unfolded, a thunderstorm gathered and poured rain on the survivors, with occasional flashes of lightning illuminating the horrific scene.

About 150 to 250 of the ship's passengers drowned that night, and when the light of dawn appeared over the horizon, it revealed about 350 survivors floating on various pieces of debris and decking. Two large hull sections with more than 100 passengers on each remained afloat for nearly five hours until they neared land. When the first mate's lifeboat reached shore, he immediately telegraphed news of the disaster, and by 8 A.M., many student volunteers from Northwestern University were on the scene as the wreckage approached the shore.

The heavy seas, however, had generated a massive surf with a powerful undertow just off shore. When the frail rafts reached the breakers, they immediately disintegrated, pounding their human cargo into the water mercilessly. Perhaps as many as 300 survivors reached the shallows, but only 160 were saved, the remainder drowning in the churning wreckage and surf. One of the several distinguished people lost in the disaster was Herbert Ingraham, a member of the British Parliament and owner of the *London Illustrated News.* Among the best-known heroes of the *Lady Elgin* disaster is Northwestern University student Edward Spencer. He repeatedly charged back into the roiling surf to rescue 18 people despite numerous injuries from floating wreckage. His deeds were the impetus for the establishment of the Evanston, Illinois, U.S. Lifesaving Station which was henceforth run by Northwestern students.

When the *Augusta,* which had survived the collision, reached port, it was leaking badly, and its bow was stove in. Captain Malott was horrified to learn that the *Lady Elgin* had gone down. He stated to shipping officials that the lighting configuration on the *Lady Elgin* was incorrect, causing him to misjudge its distance, and that he thought his own vessel was in peril. Public outcry against Captain Malott, a Canadian, was severe. The popular press attacked him as a secessionist agitator and a southern sympathizer. Many felt that the ramming was deliberately planned to do away with the Union Guards.

The exact death toll will never be known, but of the 400 or so confirmed lost, less than half were ever found. Many were returned to Milwaukee, where numerous headstones still bear the inscription "Lost on the *Lady Elgin.*" The disaster was said to have orphaned more than 1,000 Milwaukee children, and the entire city went into mourning because of the tragedy. Most of the Union Guards were members of the Catholic St. John Cathedral in Milwaukee which continues to hold a memorial service for the *Lady Elgin* victims every September 8. The disaster prompted popular songwriter Henry C. Work to pen the song "Lost on the *Lady Elgin*" which became one of the most enduring pieces of Civil War–era music. An official inquest into the disaster exonerated both captains, finding the rules of Great Lakes navigation in effect at the time to be at fault. Milwaukee's Irish Third Ward was decimated by the tragedy, permanently changing the city's demographic composition. More than a hundred years later in 1989, Chicago salvager Harry Zych discovered the *Lady Elgin*'s remains in 60 feet of water. The wreck became the subject of a protracted legal battle with the state of Illinois, which Zych eventually won. The *Lady Elgin* is now the only privately owned historic wreck site on the Great Lakes and has been the subject of ongoing archaeological survey work.

See also 1915 CAPSIZING OF THE *EASTLAND*.

Brendon Baillod

FURTHER READING:

Barry, James P. *Ships of the Great Lakes*. Holt, Mich.: Thunder Bay Press, 1996.

Boyer, Dwight. *True Tales of the Great Lakes*. New York: Dodd, Mead, 1971.

Braun, Mark S. *Chicago's North Shore Shipwrecks*. Polo, Ill.: Transportation Trails, 1992.

Scanlan, Charles M. *The* Lady Elgin *Disaster*. Milwaukee, Wis.: Charles M. Scanlan, 1928.

1860 ◆ SECESSION CRISIS

On November 8, 1860, the day after Republican Abraham Lincoln was elected 16th president of the United States, the *Charleston Mercury* declared that "the tea has been thrown overboard; the revolution of 1860 has been initiated." Exactly six weeks later on December 20, a state convention in South Carolina unanimously resolved to reverse the state's ratification of the U.S. Constitution in 1788 and declared the old federal union at an end. That decision went far deeper than the outcome of a presidential election and carried grave consequences far beyond those envisioned by its authors. Secession confronted outgoing President James Buchanan with an unprecedented crisis of federal authority. It also presented the newly independent state and its growing circle of allies among the Deep South states of Texas, Louisiana, Georgia, Florida, Mississippi, and Alabama with an unforeseen set of crises that headed the country to civil war and its slaveholding economy toward extinction.

Secession was a familiar term in American political life, but the precise nature of its operation had only been discussed in detail for the decade immediately preceding the Civil War. Although not specifically mentioned in the Virginia and Kentucky Resolutions of 1798 and 1799 that were the manifesto of the states' rights creed, those declarations' emphasis on the right of a state to judge the constitutionality of federal acts was seen as a theoretical justification for the ultimate remedy of secession. The Tenth Amendment to the Constitution also offered support for secessionist thinking in its provision for rights "reserved to the states respectively, or to the people" that were not already "delegated" to the federal government "nor prohibited" by the Constitution "to the States." New Englanders opposed to the War of 1812 with Britain had toyed with secession at the HARTFORD CONVENTION in 1814, but secession became firmly grounded in geographical distinctions that emerged with the rise of the Cotton South early in the 19th century. During sectional crises in 1819, 1833, and 1850, southerners fearful of a full-scale northern assault on slavery frequently invoked the term. In June 1850, when the country hotly debated the federal government's jurisdiction over slavery in the territories acquired from Mexico, delegates met at a Southern Convention in Nashville, Tennessee, to contemplate it as the entr'acte to the birth of a new southern confederacy.

Throughout the 1850s, southern politicians drew on writings by St. George Tucker, John C.

FACTBOX

PLACE South Carolina, Mississippi, Florida, Alabama, Georgia, Louisiana, Texas, Virginia, Arkansas, Tennessee, and North Carolina

DATE December 20, 1860–May 20, 1861

TYPE Political crisis about the departure of 11 states from the federal union

DESCRIPTION Beginning with South Carolina, southern states withdrew from the United States and formed a new nation, the Confederate States of America.

CAUSE Refusal to accept the election of an anti-slavery president; resistance to a presidential call to arms to suppress insurrection and to force seceded states to return to the union

IMPACT Four years of civil war between the armies of seceded states and those of the federal government. The ensuing war cost approximately 650,000 lives, formally ended slavery in the United States, and permanently reestablished national authority over the rebellious states.

Calhoun, Spencer Roane, and Abel Upshur to expound a "compact theory" of the Constitution that recognized the power of any state to reclaim the sovereignty it had temporarily delegated to the federal government in ratifying the Constitution in the late 1780s or later. Against this tide of opinion, nationalists from all regions of the country, including Supreme Court Justices Joseph Story and John Marshall, Daniel Webster, Edward Livingston, Andrew Jackson, James Madison, John Quincy Adams, and Abraham Lincoln, posited a perpetual Union founded in sovereign acts of the people (such as declaring independence from Britain, the Articles of Confederation, and ratification of the Constitution). Some argued that secession was revolution and could be rightly resisted by the federal government. In all such cases, the government could still defend itself against disunion. By 1860, however, these legal arguments were of much less importance than the emerging sense in both sections of the country that the question of American nationality would be resolved not in the courts but by a contest of power, either of majorities in the ballot box or of armies on the battlefield.

The country's response to South Carolina would determine whether the latter rather than the former would resolve this debate. The secession crisis followed three overlapping phases: the formal decision to secede in response to Lincoln's election; the federal government's (and the remaining loyal states') response to that decision—including last-minute efforts at sectional compromise and the showdown over Fort Sumter in Charleston Harbor; and the final decision by the remaining slave states to secede, remain loyal, or try to remain neutral. The dynamic of these decisions revealed a public deeply troubled about this crisis of authority; in many places the frustration from years of unresolved sectional conflict evolved into a hardened determination to settle the matters of slavery and nationality once and for all. The pace and pattern of the secession crisis also was framed by the decentralized structure of American national politics, which lacked a concrete center of power to focus public opinion and to develop federal policy. Also, a lame-duck president and Congress had every incentive to pass the crisis over to their successors in March 1861.

The formal decision to secede was not made in a direct democratic process. In most states, voters selected delegates to special state conventions. Only three states held referenda on the question—after the state government had already committed itself to secession. Voting for the state conventions in the Lower South was disorganized and lacked party alignments, but a division of opinion did emerge between radicals who demanded immediate secession regardless of other states' decisions and "cooperationists" who counseled delay until an "overt act" by the North (such as a call-up of troops to force a seceding state to remain in the Union) signaled the need for action either together or individually. Considering that narrow range of perspectives, the popular voting was close; perhaps 50–60 percent of voters in these elections supported immediate secession. In the subsequent conventions, however, radicals drawn especially from slave-heavy districts seized the initiative. Armed with a program, emboldened by the region's fear of slave insurrections after John Brown's abortive Harpers Ferry raid in October 1859, and strengthened by the South's near-unanimity on the legality of secession, the seceders triumphed by overwhelming majorities in conventions across the Gulf states, and South Carolina, Mississippi, Florida, Alabama, Georgia, Louisiana, and Texas sent delegates to Montgomery, Alabama, where, on February 7, 1861, they adopted a provisional constitution for their Confederate States of America. The Confederacy's new president, former Mississippi senator Jefferson Davis, promptly demanded the removal of federal troops from his new nation and the surrender to the new government of all federal property in the Confederacy.

But the movement spent itself as quickly as it had emerged. A sizable minority of slave-state Unionists in the Upper South blocked or delayed secession in North Carolina, Tennessee, Delaware, Maryland, Kentucky, Missouri, Virginia, and Arkansas. Vibrant two-party competition in those states offered an alternative to secession and real leverage in any peace deal; here the commitment to slavery was weaker than in the black belt near the Gulf, and fears of a civil war in their own backyards prompted caution. Comprising more than two-fifths of the Confederacy's future manpower, more than half of its industrial and agricultural resources, and control of vital waterways for transport of troops and materiel, the Upper South claimed the attention of both sides in the ensuing struggle over the Union.

Northerners responded to the early tide of secession with a mixture of indifference and alarm seasoned by long experience with southern bluster. Some abolitionists expressed their happiness with the departure of slave states. The Buchanan administration groped its way through the crisis. On December 4, the president blamed abolitionists for the crisis, denied the constitutional right of secession as "wholly inconsistent with the history as well as the character of the Federal Constitution," reaffirmed his duty to enforce federal laws against armed resistance but carefully disclaimed authority to force a seceded state back into the Union and referred the issue "in all its bearings" to Congress and his successor. Buchanan's message failed to unite the North or to check the progress of secession; his cabinet began to crumble as disaffected members from both sections withdrew.

Republican leaders believed that the secession movement comprised a small slaveholding elite against whom the silent majority of patriotic southerners would eventually turn if left unprovoked by the federal government. In Springfield, Illinois, closeted with advisers and inundated with office seekers, president-elect Lincoln kept a low profile. Mixing conciliation with firmness, Lincoln signaled that his administration would leave slavery alone where it was already established, enforce the Fugitive Slave Law, and even accept the addition of slave state New Mexico but would not back down on the primary Republican principle of no slavery in the territories.

Northern conservatives with extensive contacts in the South took secession very seriously. National politicians such as Senators John J. Crittenden of Kentucky and Stephen A. Douglas of Illinois mounted a peace offensive to negotiate a new sectional compromise. Crittenden proposed in December that protections for slavery be locked into unamendable amendments to the Constitution to be voted on in a national referendum. The Crittenden compromise went down to defeat in January from Senate Republicans determined to prevent a backdoor surrender of their victorious platform. Similar proposals by a peace convention in Washington in February 1861, chaired by former president John Tyler of Virginia, met the same fate.

By mid-February, with the new Confederacy in place, the president unwilling to go beyond occasional reinforcements for federal posts in the South, and Congress unable to agree upon any plan of compromise, northern efforts focused on avoiding a collision between federal and Confederate troops that could precipitate another wave of secession. In his inaugural address on March 4, Lincoln firmly rejected secession as "the essence of anarchy," proclaimed his belief in a perpetual union, argued that southerners had no just cause to leave the Union or to fear the North, and reaffirmed his duty to "hold, occupy and possess" all federal property. For the following six weeks, Lincoln and William Seward, his new secretary of state, engaged in a delicate and often inconsistent diplomatic dance with representatives of the Confederacy and the border states in order to give Unionist sentiment a chance to recover and regroup in the South.

However, eventually President Lincoln and Confederate President Davis were forced to act. Wavering between evacuating and resupplying Fort Sumter, a federal garrison in Charleston Harbor, South Carolina, Lincoln finally opted in late March for "humanitarian aid"—food, blankets, and supplies, but no weaponry or reinforcements—for the beleaguered soldiers facing a host of angry and tense South Carolina troops around Charleston Harbor. A shaky truce had been in place since January when South Carolina forces had repelled a relief expedition sent by President Buchanan, but now the federal soldiers were running out of food and time. Warned by Lincoln of the forthcoming relief expedition and facing a government-building challenge of his own, Davis and his new cabinet on April 9 authorized Confederate general P. G. T. Beauregard to take the fort before the expedition arrived. On April 11, after a flurry of last-minute negotiations in Washington and Charleston, Beauregard demanded, and the next day the federal garrison refused, the surrender of the fort. Commanding his troops to open fire, Beauregard's forces attacked on the morning of April 12; in the one-sided contest, the Confederates captured the fort and set off the American Civil War.

In response on April 15, 1861, Lincoln formally proclaimed that insurrection had begun, summoned Congress into special session, and called for 75,000 90-day militiamen to meet the threat. The effect in the North was electric as officials throughout the region telegraphed their willingness to mobilize troops to preserve the Union. But Virginia (April 17), Arkansas (May 6), and North Carolina (May 20) denounced Lincoln's "coercion" of seceded states and now formally seceded; Tennessee declared its independence and formed a league with the Confederacy on May 7. Missouri, Kentucky, and Maryland remained deeply and bloodily divided, contributing almost equal numbers of soldiers to both sides of the conflict. Kentucky declared "neutrality" but joined the other border states as a bloody battleground in the oncoming civil war. Secession also produced another irony: the secession of West Virginia from Confederate Virginia and its accession to the Union in 1863.

In the end, secession meant something more personal and emotional to Americans than the dry legal punditry of the debaters. To northerners, secession meant treason, an affront to the mystical historical unity of the nation bought dearly with the blood and treasure of generations and reaffirmed by peaceful majorities at every election. The seceders' defiance

of the will of the majority therefore appeared to be defiance of the law and an invitation to anarchy. To southerners, secession expressed the region's collective code of honor in the face of insult and "degradation into inferiority" whereby historic institutions were to be protected from the whims of northern radicals far removed from the responsibilities and risks of maintaining a large slave population.

The Civil War, lasting until 1865, eventually killed 650,000 people, ended slavery, overthrew the Confederacy, and finally settled the question of secession. Almost as an afterthought, the Supreme Court declared in 1869 in *Texas v. White* that "The Constitution, in all its provisions, looks to an indestructible Union, composed of indestructible States."

See also 1833 NULLIFICATION CRISIS.

Peter Knupfer

FURTHER READING:

Channing, Steven A. *Crisis of Fear: Secession in South Carolina.* New York: W. W. Norton, 1974.

Craven, Avery Odelle. *The Growth of Southern Nationalism, 1848–1861.* Baton Rouge: Louisiana State University Press, 1953.

Dumond, Dwight Lowell. *The Secession Movement, 1860–1861.* New York: Negro Universities Press, 1968.

Freehling, William W. *The Road to Disunion: Secessionists Triumphant, 1854–1861.* New York: Oxford University Press, 1990.

McCardell, John. *The Idea of a Southern Nation: Southern Nationalists and Southern Nationalism, 1830–1860.* New York: W. W. Norton, 1979.

Stampp, Kenneth M. *And the War Came: The North and the Secession Crisis, 1860–1861.* Baton Rouge: Louisiana State University Press, 1950.

1861 ◆ BATTLE OF BULL RUN

The Battle of Bull Run, fought on July 21, 1861, was the first major battle of the Civil War and a humiliating and bloody defeat of the approximately 35,000-man Union army under General Irvin McDowell. The battle ended with a Union

retreat that, as McDowell later described it, "became a rout, and this soon degenerated still further into a panic." Bull Run was the first in a dismaying series of Union battlefield losses in the eastern theater as the Lincoln administration sought a leader capable of

FACTBOX

PLACE Manassas, Virginia

DATE July 21, 1861

TYPE First major battle of the Civil War, ending in the defeat and disorderly retreat of the Union army under General Irvin McDowell

DESCRIPTION After a day of close, confusing, and heavy fighting in intense heat, Confederate troops under Generals Joseph E. Johnston and P. G. T. Beauregard defeated General Irvin McDowell's Union forces, which retreated in confusion and disorder to Washington, D.C. Although victorious, Confederate forces were unable to pursue.

CAUSE The Union army's delay in positioning itself before the battle allowed Johnston's troops to arrive by railroad from the Shenandoah Valley to reinforce Beauregard's forces. These troops, including Stonewall Jackson's brigade, held Henry House Hill and successfully forced a rapid and humiliating Union retreat.

CASUALTIES Confederates: 387 killed, 1,582 wounded, 12 missing; Union: 481 killed, 1,011 wounded, 1,216 missing

IMPACT The Battle of Bull Run revealed that the Civil War was going to be long, costly, and difficult. The Confederate victory helped to create a long-lasting legend of Southern superiority on the battlefield, while the hard Union fighting proved that the North was a formidable and committed opponent. General McDowell was replaced with George McClellan.

defeating the Confederacy. Fought hard by inexperienced troops on both sides during a hot and humid day on the banks of Bull Run Creek near Manassas, Virginia, and observed by civilians including six senators, 10 representatives, and dozens of festive picnickers, the battle demolished the fanciful idea (held on both sides) that the war would be easily and quickly won without high losses. The Battle of Bull Run demonstrated the value of defensive positions and the unforeseen challenges of fighting this scale of war. The battle also witnessed the emergence of new battlefield uses of the telegraph and the railroad and the rise of a group of famous and effective American warriors who embraced the concept of hard war after their involvement in this battle, including William Tecumseh Sherman and Thomas "Stonewall" Jackson.

Only months after the Civil War started when the Confederates fired on Fort Sumter on April 12, 1861, and shortly after Richmond, Virginia, was named the Confederate capital in May, the Union leadership under President Lincoln and Winfield Scott, commanding general of the Union army, sought a strategy for defeating the new Southern nation. Scott urged a broad and methodical strategy of naval blockade and division along the Mississippi River known as the Anaconda Plan and wished to postpone major action until the fall. Lincoln, however, sought a more immediate approach to defeating the South and to meeting the danger of a large army in northern Virginia under the leadership of General P. G. T. Beauregard. These Confederate forces were 30 miles southwest of Washington, D.C., at the strategic Manassas Junction where the Manassas Gap Railroad (which ran to the Shenandoah Valley) and Orange & Alexandria Railroad (which ran to Richmond) met.

In desiring action, Lincoln was responding to several imperatives, including the looming end of three-month stints for Union volunteer soldiers and the strong public pressure for Union military action in the northern press and among politicians. There were strident calls for action in such newspapers as the influential *New York Tribune,* with headlines crying "Forward to Richmond! Forward to Richmond!" The opportunities for rapidly defeating the Confederates seemed good just as the desire intensified in the North to defeat the Confederates decisively in battle.

Brigadier General McDowell, elevated to command despite Scott's concerns, developed a plan to attack what he thought were Beauregard's 35,000 troops at Manassas (in fact he had 22,000), and this plan was accepted by Lincoln with little additional analysis. To concerns that Union troops were untested in battle, Lincoln famously responded "You are green, it is true; but they are green also."

Beauregard in turn had planned to attack and defeat the Union army in a decisive battle. Ironically, each general decided to focus the attack on his enemy's left flank. McDowell attacked first but slowly. In the end, his lethargy in starting the battle, combined with confusion and insufficient vigor during the battle itself, proved to be a fatal flaw. The Confederates managed to overcome Beauregard's initially unclear orders to gain the commanding position and carry the day.

McDowell's approximately 35,000 soldiers, a mix of volunteers and regular army, inexperienced troops and new officers, formed the largest fighting force ever assembled in North America up to that time. They marched onto the battlefield wearing a bewildering array of uniforms in a variety of colors from standard blue to gray to the outlandish red trousers and fezzes of the Zouaves units who fought on each side, including the Eleventh New York and the Louisiana Tigers. The diversity of uniforms at this early point in the war, as well as the similarity of each side's battle flags, deepened confusion on the battlefield and proved to be a problem during the fighting.

The Union army marched through a difficult terrain that intensified and complicated the battle, including a bewildering array of roads, scattered farms broken by thick woods, hills, and ravines. Through it all ran winding Bull Run Creek, broken with a number of fords and a few important bridges. The battle was shaped by the landscape and particularly by the dominance of the major hills, but the outcome was decided by the actions and mistakes of leaders and soldiers on the day of battle.

A major reason for the Union loss was that McDowell's forces moved slowly and fitfully toward the Southern armies and did not rapidly get in position to attack Beauregard. It was this tentative movement and delay, as well as the intelligence provided by Confederate spies that surrounded the Union armies, that allowed Confederate forces the time to be reinforced by the 11,000 troops of General Joseph E. Johnston from the Shenandoah Valley. Deftly avoiding being pinned in place by indecisive Union major general Robert Patterson, as called for in the North's plan, Johnston moved east and sent his infantry by train through the Manassas Gap and his artillery and cavalry by road. This bold and innovative move marked the first time troops had been moved by rail in a battle, and it had a major impact on the outcome of the battle as large numbers of much-needed troops appeared on the Confederate left, the primary focus of the Union assault.

The Battle of Bull Run centered on two successive hills of strategic importance, Matthews Hill and Henry House Hill. In the morning, the Union army pushed the Confederates off Matthews Hill and seemed to be besting Beauregard's forces by 11:30 A.M. Union troops shouted "Victory! Victory! The day is ours!" but the celebration was premature.

By noon, Confederate general Thomas Jackson's troops reached and fortified Henry House Hill as McDowell's men rested and reorganized, squandering precious time. As the struggle for Henry House Hill reached its peak, General Barnard Bee rallied Confederates with his famous cry "Yonder stands Jackson like a stone wall; let's go to his assistance." Although Bee would soon be killed, he created the nickname for "Stonewall" Jackson, one of the South's most fearsome generals and enduring icons.

The struggle for Henry House Hill involved approximately 15,000 soldiers on both sides, of whom 500 were killed. Confusion reigned in the violence. Two Union batteries were overrun by the 33rd Virginia Infantry, which were blue, causing fatal hesitation on the part of McDowell's chief of artillery, William Barry. McDowell never committed more than two of his regiments at a single time, which negated his numerical superiority. Shortly after 4 P.M., Arnold Elzey and Jubal Early's Confederate brigades appeared, forcing Union soldiers to begin to retreat. What started as an orderly withdrawal soon descended into a chaotic fleeing. Civilian teamsters attempting to cross Bull Run lost their nerve, abandoned equipment, and began a mad and fitful rush. Civilian observers, who had blithely anticipated an entertaining day picnicking and watching the battle, promptly panicked and fled. Some politicians among them attempted to calm the growing disorder, but the chaos and hysteria soon spread to the defeated troops. Confederate shelling helped spur a mad dash to Washington.

The battle established two themes of the war: Although the Confederates won the battle and garnered a reputation for fearsome military skill, they were not able to capitalize on the victory; in addition, casualties were high on both sides. As General Sherman wrote in his memoirs, "Our men had been told so often at home that all they had to do was to make a bold appearance, and the rebels would run; and nearly all of us for the first time then heard the sound of cannon and muskets in anger, and saw the bloody scenes common to all battles with which we were soon to be familiar. We had good organization, good men, but no cohesion, no real discipline, no respect for authority, no real knowledge of war. . . . Though the North was overwhelmed with mortification and shame, the South really had not much to boast of, for in the three or four hours of fighting their organization was so broken up that they did not and could not follow our army, when it was known to be in a state of disgraceful and causeless flight."

The Battle of Bull Run was the bloodiest battle in American history up to this point, which provided an indication of the much greater bloodletting that would soon follow. The Confederates had 387 killed, 1,582 wounded and 12 missing while the Union had 481 killed, 1,011 wounded, 1,216 missing. Despite this defeat, Union troops soon regained their morale as Lincoln dismissed McDowell and brought in the popular general, George B. McClellan, to lead the Army of the Potomac. Lincoln remained steadfast in his determination to continue fighting the war to preserve the union. The two armies would meet again at the same spot one year later in the even more decisive Confederate victory at the Second Battle of Bull Run on August 30, 1862.

Daniel S. Margolies

FURTHER READING:

Davis, William C. *Battle at Bull Run: A History of the First Major Campaign of the Civil War.* Mechanicsburg, Pa.: Stackpole, 1995.

Detzer, David. *Donnybrook: The Battle of Bull Run, 1861.* Orlando, Fla.: Harcourt, 2004.

Weigley, Russell F. *A Great Civil War: A Military and Political History, 1861–1865.* Bloomington: Indiana University Press, 2000.

1863 ◆ NEW YORK CITY DRAFT RIOTS

In the midst of the Civil War in 1863, attempts to implement the Union draft led to four days of bloody rioting in New York City, the worst rioting Americans had ever witnessed. "Unparalleled in atrocities by anything in American history," wrote Anna Elizabeth Dickinson, a prominent abolitionist and women's rights activist who witnessed the event, the outbreak was "equaled only by the horrors of the worst days of the French Revolution." The draft riots resulted from an explosive mixture of simmering ethnic tensions in New York, white working-class hostility to African Americans, and opposition to the emancipationist aims of the Civil War. The New York City draft riots vividly exposed the fault lines in Northern society during the Civil War.

Disturbances against the Union draft erupted throughout the North, in rural areas like Holmes County, Ohio, and cities like Troy, New York, and Newark, New Jersey. Yet draft resistance was most explosive in New York City, the nation's largest metropolis. New York in the 1860s was fertile ground for race, class, and ethnic violence. The cost

FACTBOX
PLACE New York City
DATE July 13–16, 1863
TYPE Urban riot
DESCRIPTION Irish immigrants and others in New York City rioted for four days, attacking and lynching African Americans.
CAUSE The Conscription Act of 1863, which sparked long-simmering racial and ethnic tensions
CASUALTIES More than 100 fatalities
IMPACT Resistance to conscription demonstrated deeper opposition to the Lincoln administration's prosecution of the Civil War.

of waging war had produced a high rate of inflation that struck unskilled laborers particularly hard. Many of these workers were Irish immigrants who had previously developed strong ties to a Democratic Party hostile to racial equality. Many white immigrant workers opposed emancipation, fearing it would send thousands of freed slaves into an already crowded job market in the urban northeast. New York City itself harbored a strong element of sympathy with the South. Major newspapers, such as the *New York World* and the *Journal of Commerce,* in addition to Governor Horatio Seymour, stood in firm opposition to the Republican administration of Abraham Lincoln.

A highly unpopular military draft by the federal government provided the spark that fused these elements into violent conflict. The Conscription Act of March 1863 contained a loophole that allowed any man who could pay a commutation fee of $300 (a sum close to the yearly wage of a worker) to avoid the draft. This loophole enabled many rich and middle-class men to get out of fighting, fueling resentment among the poor and working classes. On Saturday, July 11, 1863, one week after the Battle of

Opposition to the draft during the Civil War sparked four days of rioting in New York City, the deadliest civil disturbance in American history. *(Corbis)*

Gettysburg, the draft authorities in New York began to draw names. On Monday, July 13, rioting erupted when mobs composed mainly of skilled workers in the building trades, "including myriads of wretched, drunken women, and the half-grown, vagabond boys of the pavements," according to Anna Dickinson, began their assault on the Republican-run conscription organization. They attacked the provost marshal's office, cut telegraph lines across the city, and tried unsuccessfully to destroy the offices of the pro-administration *New York Tribune.* By Tuesday, mobs of largely unskilled Irish workingmen and women took to the streets. Crowds estimated at 12,000 spread to affluent neighborhoods, where they looted the homes of the wealthy. The main target of these rioters was New York's black population. Chanting such phrases as "kill the naygers," these mobs lynched 12 African Americans, mutilated bodies, and burned the Colored Orphan Asylum. According to Anna Dickinson, children were "assailed and beaten; all,—orphans and caretakers,—exposed to every indignity and every danger, driven on to the street." Scores of frightened blacks fled the city. The draft riots ended when five Union regiments from Gettysburg arrived in New York and restored order.

The New York City draft riots took the lives of more than 100 people—mostly rioters—in what remains as the highest loss of life in a civil disturbance in American history. They seriously marred the image of Irish Americans throughout the North and contributed to a general wave of revulsion against Peace Democrats, who sought conciliation with Southerners. The draft riots remain a striking reminder of the ethnic, class, and racial hostility that lay beneath the surface of Northern society during the Civil War.

Mitchell Snay

FURTHER READING:

Bernstein, Iver. *The New York City Draft Riots.* New York: Oxford University Press, 1990.

Cook, Adrian. *The Armies of the Street: The New York City Draft Riots of 1863.* Lexington: University Press of Kentucky, 1974.

Schechter, Bernard. *The Devil's Own Work: The Civil War Draft Riots and the Fight to Reconstruct America.* New York: Walker, 2005.

1864 ◆ SAND CREEK MASSACRE

The Sand Creek massacre of November 29, 1864, was one of the bloodiest, most significant Indian massacres to take place during the 19th century. Once erroneously known as the "Battle of Sand Creek," it is now recognized as a one-sided slaughter of noncombatants during the smoldering Indian War of 1864 in southeastern Colorado. The massacre is also known as the "Chivington massacre" after Colonel John M. Chivington, the officer principally responsible for it. A tall, fiery Methodist minister of fearsome renown who gained the nickname "fighting parson" for his Civil War heroics, Colonel Chivington led the volunteer 3rd Colorado Cavalry on a surprise morning assault on the peaceful Cheyenne and Arapaho encampment on trickling Sand Creek. Approximately 725 U.S. soldiers attacked 500 Indians camped in 100 lodges spread over about a mile. The soldiers killed at least 150 people with rifle fire and exploding howitzer shells and then horribly mutilated the dead, including cutting off pieces of their bodies for souvenirs. The majority of the victims were women and children, many of whom were killed as they attempted to flee or dig protective holes in the sandy banks of the creek. The events at Sand Creek immediately created a political firestorm in Colorado and Washington, D.C., galvanized the Indians, and led to intensified and prolonged warfare on the southern plains.

The Sand Creek massacre occurred during an anxious and tragic period on the western frontier. American relations with such Indian tribes as the Southern Cheyenne were already strained by intermittent Indian attacks and cattle thefts as well as settler pressure on treaty-secured lands and strong anti-Indian sentiment. These conflicts, combined with fear, ambition, and poor leadership in the Colorado Territory, exploded into genocidal war. During the tense fourth year of the Civil War, the West also experienced heightened fear of Indians, following the surprise Sioux uprising in Minnesota in 1863 which led to the deaths of hundreds of whites. The boisterous Colorado territory witnessed a continued press of settlers, gold seekers, and politicians who were not interested in accommodating Indians.

Situated at the end of a long and tenuous supply chain from the East, Colorado residents lived in an environment of hostility, uncertainty, and real and imagined fear of Indian attacks. Ambitious leaders in the territory, led by the territorial governor and ex officio superintendent of Indian affairs, John Evans, sought statehood and the power and opportunity that came with it. Evans was eager to grab what proved to be a winning political issue, and the destruction or total removal of the Indians from the territory seemed irresistible. Chivington, the commanding hero of the Battle of Glorieta Pass (March 26–28, 1862), where the Union had stopped the Confederacy in the southwest, also harbored strong anti-Indian feelings and political ambition. He sought another victory to help his political prospects and to

---

FACTBOX

PLACE Sand Creek, Colorado (Kiowa County, southeastern Colorado)

DATE November 29, 1864

TYPE Massacre of Cheyenne and Arapaho Indians by the volunteer 3rd Colorado Calvary

DESCRIPTION One of the bloodiest Indian massacres in American history, in which Colorado soldiers led by Colonel John M. Chivington attacked and destroyed a Cheyenne and Arapaho encampment of 500 at Sand Creek

CASUALTIES Approximately 150 Cheyenne and Arapaho killed, of whom at least 90 were women and children. Nine Colorado Volunteers were killed and 38 wounded.

IMPACT The massacre intensified and prolonged warfare between the United States and Indians on the southern plains in the 1860s and 1870s.

vanquish a people that he saw as an implacable foe of "civilization."

This was the complex situation in the spring of 1864 when a few aggressive bands of Indians, resentful of white encroachment, launched a series of events that culminated in the massacre later that fall. Although the vast majority of the Southern Cheyenne were at peace with the United States, small bands of independent "Dog Soldiers" did engage in cattle and mule theft and in small skirmishes with troops that chased them. Chivington ordered the troops pursuing these Indians to "make sure you have the right ones and then kill them." There were killings on both sides, which fueled the crisis. In May, troops killed 25 Cheyenne warriors as well as Chief Lean Bear as he tried to talk peace while displaying a medallion recently given to him by President Lincoln. Fighting now spread quickly across the Colorado landscape, including reprisal killings. One of the most notorious instances was the Cheyenne killing of the Hungate family 30 miles from Denver on June 11. Denver authorities publicly displayed the mutilated bodies of Nathan W. Hungate, shot more than 80 times, his ravaged wife, and two children (with heads almost severed). The incident whipped up fears of future massacres and whetted a strong desire for revenge.

Following this event, Governor Evans released the first of two proclamations that helped provoke the Sand Creek massacre. The first, on June 27, directed "all friendly Indians [to] keep away from those who are at war, and go to places of safety." This proclamation convinced Cheyenne led by Black Kettle to seek accommodations with the authorities and to live in peace. After some unclear negotiations with Evans at Camp Weld, Black Kettle's people and a related group of Arapaho under Left Hand camped near Fort Lyon on Sand Creek with what they thought was a guarantee of peace. Unbeknownst to them, Evans released a second proclamation on August 11 claiming that "most of the Indian tribes of the plains are at war" and authorizing all citizens of Colorado "to kill and destroy, as enemies of the country, wherever they may be found, all such hostile Indians." Evans also sought and received permission from the federal government to form a volunteer 3rd Colorado Cavalry. These volunteers,

led by Chivington, felt shamed when they were given the nickname "Bloodless Third" since they killed no Indians during almost all of their 100-day term of service. They finally found the blood they sought at Sand Creek.

Evans sought to subdue the Indians in the territory and justify his calls for volunteer soldiers. Chivington adopted an approach based on "kill and scalp all, little and big." On the morning of November 29, the cavalry surrounded and abruptly attacked the Indians at Sand Creek, even as Black Kettle raised both an American flag and the white flag of truce over his lodge. Chivington ordered his troops to take no prisoners, and the killings at the creek continued until midafternoon. The surviving Indians fled while soldiers picked off stragglers and then destroyed the encampment.

Colonel Chivington and the 3rd Colorado reported a great battle victory and enjoyed broad support in the territory immediately after the massacre. For a time, hundreds of Indian scalps were displayed in Denver, along with other trophies. But as details of the massacre became widely known, the support turned to disgust and outrage. A series of military commissions and congressional committees strongly criticized Chivington's conduct and castigated him for the unwarranted slaughter of nonhostile Indians. Chivington's once-distinguished military reputation and once-promising political career were finished, Evans lost his appointment as governor, and the plains witnessed many subsequent years of vicious fighting with the embittered Cheyenne.

Daniel S. Margolies

FURTHER READING:

Greene, Jerome A., and Douglas D. Scott. *Finding Sand Creek: History, Archeology, and the 1864 Massacre Site.* Norman: University of Oklahoma Press, 2004.

Hatch, Thom. *Black Kettle: The Cheyenne Chief Who Sought Peace but Found War.* Hoboken, N.J.: Wiley, 2004.

Hoig, Stan. *The Sand Creek Massacre.* Norman: University of Oklahoma Press, 1961.

Schultz, Duane. *Month of the Freezing Moon: The Sand Creek Massacre, November 1864.* New York: St. Martin's Press, 1990.

1865 ◆ ASSASSINATION OF PRESIDENT LINCOLN

On Good Friday, April 14, 1865, President Abraham Lincoln and his wife, Mary Todd Lincoln, attended a showing of the comedy *Our American Cousin* at Ford's Theater in Washington, D.C., with their guests Major Henry R. Rathbone and his fiancée, Clara Harris. The latter had joined the party at Mrs. Lincoln's invitation after Lieutenant General Ulysses S. Grant and his wife, Julia, changed their plans to attend and left Washington on a train for New Jersey. Just after 10 P.M., early in the second act, an assassin gained entry to the president's box, fired one pistol shot into Lincoln's head, struggled briefly with Major Rathbone, leaped to the stage with the shout *"Sic Semper Tyrannis!"* ("Thus always to tyrants!" the motto of the State of Virginia), and escaped on a horse waiting in the alley behind the theater. Lincoln was rushed across the street to the William Petersen house, where he died the next morning at 7:22 A.M., April 15, surrounded by his distraught wife and most of the cabinet. At 11 A.M. Vice President Andrew Johnson of Tennessee took the oath of office as the 17th president of the United States.

The story of the assassination inspired a multitude of conspiracy theories that are as durable as they are inaccurate, but the preponderance of evidence has established that the assassin was indeed 26-year-old John Wilkes Booth, a successful actor from a family of noted actors, a deep-dyed Confederate sympathizer and drug runner who circulated among Washington's shady street culture of rebel spies, sympathizers, and informants. Embittered by the Confederacy's continued misfortunes and determined to join its heroes, Booth had over the previous six months concocted several plots to kidnap Lincoln and other Union leaders and exchange them for Confederate prisoners. There is some reliable circumstantial evidence that the Confederate government knew of some of these plans but probably not of the assassination itself. Barely three weeks before the assassination, a last-minute change in the president's plans had foiled the latest of these attempts. The surrender of General Robert E. Lee's Confederate army on April 9 intensified Booth's desperation. On April 11, hearing Lincoln speak in favor of limited civil rights for freed slaves

FACTBOX

PLACE Ford's Theater, Washington, D.C.

DATE April 14, 1865

TYPE Presidential assassination and the attempted assassination of several members of his cabinet

DESCRIPTION Embittered by the South's loss of the Civil War, assassin John Wilkes Booth murdered President Lincoln while he was watching a play.

CAUSE Assassin's ire over defeat of the Confederacy in the Civil War and the possibility of civil rights for freed slaves

CASUALTIES Death of President Lincoln, three wounded at the scene, one more wounded at another location; assassin and four accomplices were later executed, including one woman, the first executed under federal law

IMPACT The assassination replaced a highly successful war president with an untried leader at the onset of postwar national reconstruction and thereby set a markedly different course for federal policy on race relations, economic development, and the treatment of ex-Confederates in the conquered South.

and hint that an announcement on postwar policy was forthcoming, Booth unsuccessfully urged his accomplice Lewis Paine to shoot Lincoln right there, declaring "that means nigger citizenship. Now by God I'll put him through. That is the last speech he will ever make." The plan to kill the president came to him around noon the day of the assassination, when Booth learned that Lincoln and Grant would be together at Ford's Theater that night. To cripple the government further, he added Johnson, Secretary of State William Henry Seward, and possibly Secretary of War Edwin M. Stanton to his target list.

Booth recruited various veterans of his previous plots to help him. George A. Atzerodt, a German

Five days after the South surrendered, President Abraham Lincoln was assassinated in Washington, D.C. He was the first president to be murdered. *(Library of Congress)*

carriage painter; David E. Herold, a druggist's clerk in Washington; Lewis Paine (actually Lewis Powell), Michael O'Laughlin, and Samuel Arnold, all rebel veterans; and Mary Surratt and her son John, owners of a local boardinghouse where members of the group occasionally met, all certainly knew of Booth's intentions, if not the details of his plans. The night of the assassination Booth dispatched Paine to Seward's house, where the secretary lay bedridden from a serious carriage accident. Paine seriously wounded Seward and others with a large knife and escaped with Herold's assistance. Atzerodt's assignment to kill Johnson never got started; an attempt on Grant possibly occurred on his train, but the would-be assassin escaped after train officials caught him pounding on the general's door and tried to restrain him.

After firing the fatal shot, Booth fled into northern Virginia, accompanied by Herold. Suffering from a leg broken in the jump to the stage, Booth received medical attention from an acquaintance, Dr. Samuel Mudd. On April 26, federal cavalry caught up with them at their hideout in a barn at Garrett's Farm near Port Royal; the troops captured Herold, set the barn afire to flush out Booth, and shot him dead when he emerged. Mudd was arrested along with the remaining conspirators snared in a sweep organized by Stanton who, with customary efficiency, briefly sealed off the capital. From May 9 to June 30, 1865, the conspirators were tried by a military commission of dubious legal authority (the civilian courts were still operating) under extraordinary procedures that prevented them from mounting more than a

simple defense. On July 7, 1865, Paine, Atzerodt, Herold, and Mary Surratt went to the gallows (the latter as the first female to be executed by the federal government). Mudd, Arnold, and O'Laughlin were sentenced to life at hard labor; Edman Spangler, a stagehand at Ford's, got six years' hard labor for holding Booth's horse outside the theater. O'Laughlin died in prison, and the rest were pardoned and released in 1869. John Surratt escaped abroad, was extradited, and charges against him were dropped after a hung jury failed to convict in 1867. The debate over Mrs. Surratt's and Dr. Mudd's guilt continues, but the latest research suggests that they were involved at least in Booth's kidnap plots and knew more than they claimed concerning the assassination.

This was the first successful assassination attempt in American history. Considering the remarkable accessibility of public figures in those days as well as the depth of hatred for Lincoln in and near Civil War Washington, it is remarkable that no one had succeeded before Booth. Just 10 days before Lincoln's death, the president had visited wartorn, lawless Richmond on the heels of the fleeing Confederate government and accompanied by a small complement of sailors. He also frequently received death threats and recounted premonitions of death in his dreams, even on the last day of his life.

Coming amid celebrations of Lee's surrender, the assassination plunged the North into an unprecedented period of public grief especially among blacks, who viewed him as their liberator. Mary Lincoln never recovered from the event and suffered from severe depression and mental illness the rest of her life. Lincoln's body lay in state until the funeral in the East Room of the White House on April 19. The next evening it was placed upon a funeral train for a long and sad journey across the North to his resting place in Springfield, Illinois, on May 4.

The assassination of Abraham Lincoln is notable in part for what did *not* occur in its aftermath. There was no crisis in the transition of power—Vice President Johnson ascended to the presidency and enjoyed a brief honeymoon with Congress and the electorate. There also was no crisis in federal authority, no coup d'etat or even the hint of one, and the North already had been under some form of martial law since 1862. After a flurry of arrests of supposed Confederate sympathizers, reprisal was limited to the effort to convict the conspirators themselves.

But the assassination inflicted a deep wound on the republic just as its bloody civil war was ending and the arduous struggle for reconstruction was beginning. The Confederate leadership was still at large, and several of its armies were still active. The president's murder also left serious policy issues unresolved and deprived African Americans of a friend in the White House at the most critical moment in their history. Engaged in a divisive debate with radical Republicans over the shape and severity of wartime reconstruction, Lincoln had not specified his postwar plans beyond a Proclamation of Amnesty and Reconstruction in December 1863 that clearly was intended as a war measure. With the war's end, pressing matters of restoring loyal governments to the seceded states, of securing the future of 4 million freed slaves, of determining the fate of ex-Confederate soldiers and politicians, and of repairing the economic devastation of four years' unrelenting civil war demanded far-sighted presidential leadership.

Into this vacuum stepped Andrew Johnson of Tennessee, a Democrat nominated to balance the national ticket in 1864 and known for his unflinching loyalty, hard-bitten racism, and deep commitment to states' rights. Although historians continue to debate the extent to which Johnson understood or intended to carry out Lincoln's wishes concerning reconstruction and black civil rights, the new president's deteriorating relations with Congress by December 1865 demonstrated that the assassination had set the country on a far different path from the one marked out, albeit dimly, by the martyred president. It is hard to imagine Lincoln's presidency sliding into impeachment as Johnson's did in 1868 when some congressmen were even trying unsuccessfully to implicate him in Lincoln's death.

It is sometimes erroneously asserted that the creation of the Secret Service on July 5, 1865, was a response to Lincoln's assassination. The service's mission from the start was to stop counterfeiters; it did not assume responsibility for presidential protection until 1902, after the assassinations of presidents James Garfield in 1881 and William McKinley in 1901.

See also 1881 ASSASSINATION OF PRESIDENT GARFIELD; 1901 ASSASSINATION OF PRESIDENT MCKINLEY; 1963 ASSASSINATION OF PRESIDENT KENNEDY.

Peter Knupfer

FURTHER READING:

Donald, David Herbert. *Lincoln*. New York: Simon and Schuster, 1996.

Hanchett, William. *The Lincoln Murder Conspiracies*. Urbana: University of Illinois Press, 1983.

Kauffman, Michael W. *American Brutus: John Wilkes Booth and the Lincoln Conspiracies*. New York: Random House, 2004.

Rhodehamel, John, and Louise Taper, eds. *"Right or Wrong, God Judge Me": The Writings of John Wilkes Booth*. Urbana: University of Illinois Press, 1997.

Tidwell, William A., James O. Hall, and David Winfred Gaddy. *Come Retribution: The Confederate Secret Service and the Assassination of Lincoln*. Jackson: University Press of Mississippi, 1988.

1865 ◆ EXPLOSION OF THE *SULTANA*

After the surrender of General Robert E. Lee at Appomattox on April 9, 1865, thousands of captured Union soldiers from the prison camps at Andersonville, Georgia, and Cahaba, Alabama, were scheduled to return north from Vicksburg, Mississippi, via steamship on the Mississippi River. Rival steamship companies competed for these special passengers because ships were paid $5 per enlisted man and $10 per officer. Captain J. Cass Mason of the *Sultana*, owned by the Merchants' and Peoples' Line, had received assurances from the army that his ship would receive plenty of freed prisoners, amid growing rumors that the rival Atlantic and Mississippi Steamboat Line (A&M) was bribing lower-level army officials to load soldiers onto their boats.

On April 21, the *Sultana*, which had accommodations for 376 passengers, left New Orleans for Vicksburg with 100 people, 100 hogs, 60 mules, 100 hogsheads of sugar, and a leaking boiler. In Vicksburg, boilermaker R. G. Taylor told Captain Mason that two metal sheets on one of the ship's four boilers had to be replaced, but Mason opted to simply patch the boiler in order to save time. Mason demanded a full load of soldiers even though the rosters for each group were not yet prepared. Army officials then agreed that the rosters could be worked out after the soldiers boarded, making it difficult to keep track of how many were being loaded. Two nearby steamships, owned by A&M, received no prisoners. Rumors of A&M's bribery attempts may have spurred the army to snub them, though those rumors were never substantiated.

The *Sultana* left Vicksburg on April 24 with about 2,100 troops, 200 civilians, and a full cargo of sugar—more than six times its legal carrying capacity. Soldiers were jammed onto every deck "like sheep for the slaughter," according to survivor Isaac van Nuys. They spilled out onto the main stairs, with some even sleeping in the coal bin.

On the evening of April 26, the *Sultana* reached Memphis, unloaded cargo, and then crossed the river to buy coal, despite a strong current caused by the flooded Mississippi, swollen from spring rains and war-damaged levees. At about 2 A.M., as the *Sultana* moved through Paddy's Hen and Chick Islands, seven to eight miles north of Memphis, at least one boiler exploded. The explosion hurled pieces of iron and wood into the soldiers on the main deck, while escaping steam scalded those near the boilers. Passengers on the boiler and hurricane decks were tossed into the air and then fell back onto the boat or into the cold water. A smokestack fell, breaking through the upper deck and pinning men on the lower decks, where they roasted to death in the ensuing fire.

Survivors of the initial explosion jumped into the river, though many could not swim. Those who could maneuver in the water faced other life-threatening situations, including being pulled down by drowning victims or sucked into whirlpools created by the sinking ship. Survivor A. C. Brown recalled, "The water seemed to be one solid mass of human beings struggling with the waves."

Most of the soldiers—sick or malnourished from spending months as prisoners of war—could not swim in the cold water for any length of time. They crawled on flimsy wreckage, clung to dead mules, floated with the current, or hung from tree branches along the banks. One group stuck in a grove of trees as the river raged below them sang "The Star-Spangled Banner." Survivors would later recall this odd sight and sound because they felt it a futile act.

Ninety minutes after the explosion, the *Bostonia II,* heading south toward Memphis, began to pick up survivors. As word of the disaster spread, any vessel available—from homemade rafts to river boats—joined in the rescue effort. Estimates of the rescued vary from 590 to 760, though 200 to 300 of them would die from their injuries. By midafternoon on April 27, the boats were recovering more corpses than survivors. Hundreds of bodies were never recovered, including that of Captain Mason. The final death toll, never determined precisely, has been estimated at 1,700 to 1,800.

On April 30, Secretary of War Edwin Stanton created a board of inquiry to investigate the explosion and sinking of the *Sultana.* Surviving passengers, including senator-elect William Snow, boilermaker R. G. Taylor, and army officers pointed the finger at each other, resulting in little conclusive evidence after a year of testimony. Ultimately, no individual was officially blamed for the overcrowding, and no exact cause was determined for the boiler explosion. Despite the lack of consequences for those involved, there was no public outcry.

The explosion and sinking of the *Sultana*—considered the deadliest marine disaster in U.S. history, with a higher death total than the *Titanic*—remains largely overlooked primarily because of

FACTBOX

PLACE Mississippi River, seven to eight miles north of Memphis at Paddy's Hen and Chick Islands

DATE April 27, 1865

TYPE Ship explosion and sinking

DESCRIPTION A steamship carrying Union soldiers exploded on the Mississippi River.

CAUSE Boiler explosion

CASUALTIES Estimated 1,700 to 1,800 dead, though exact number is impossible to determine

COST Loss of the *Sultana* steamship, built in 1863 for $60,000

IMPACT Despite an investigation, no one was found responsible, and no changes or reforms were instituted.

In the deadliest nautical disaster in American history, flames engulf the steamship *Sultana* on the Mississippi River. *(Library of Congress)*

another tragedy that occurred at the same time. The aftermath of the ASSASSINATION OF PRESIDENT LINCOLN, the search for assassin John Wilkes Booth (killed on April 26, the day before the *Sultana* exploded), and news of Lincoln's funeral train knocked the *Sultana* off the front pages of the newspapers and out of the chapters of the history books.

Susan Doll

FURTHER READING:

Berry, Chester D., ed. *Loss of the* Sultana *and Reminiscences of Survivors.* Rev. ed. Knoxville: University of Tennessee Press, 2005.

Potter, Jerry O. *The* Sultana *Tragedy: America's Greatest Maritime Disaster.* Gretna, La.: Pelican Publishing, 1992.

1868 ◆ IMPEACHMENT OF PRESIDENT JOHNSON

The impeachment of President Andrew Johnson in 1868 was the culmination of the great crisis over restoring the Union after the Civil War. Johnson, who succeeded the assassinated Abraham Lincoln to the presidency in April 1865, was a Tennessee unionist and former Democrat concerned primarily with reviving loyalty in the South. He was not much concerned about the status of former slaves. Johnson established a mild reconstruction program during Congress's recess during the summer and early fall of 1865. By the time Congress reconvened in late November, most southern states had reestablished governments and elected new senators and representatives.

In contrast to President Johnson, the Republican majority in Congress was determined to secure racial equality in basic civil rights. But Johnson broke with Republicans, opposed civil rights legislation—which

Congress passed over his veto—and then urged southern states to reject a proposed Fourteenth Amendment to the Constitution that would define citizenship and guarantee basic rights.

Johnson's course fomented such strong resistance in the North that Republicans in Congress passed new Reconstruction Acts in 1867. These acts placed the southern states under military control until they ratified both the Fourteenth Amendment and new state constitutions, which secured equal civil and political rights for all citizens. To reduce Johnson's political clout, Congress also passed the Tenure of Office Act, which forbade the president from removing important government officers until the Senate confirmed their replacements. Under the law, the president could suspend an official while Congress was recessed, but the Senate could reject the suspension when it reconvened. Significantly for future events, the Senate and House of Representatives used ambiguous language to paper over a disagreement on whether the law covered the president's cabinet.

Congress's radical reconstruction program enraged white southerners, who bitterly resisted it with President Johnson's support. Johnson subverted the operation of the Reconstruction Acts by interpreting their provisions narrowly and by replacing military officers who enforced it vigorously. Finally, he suspended Secretary of War Edwin M. Stanton, who had come to sympathize with the Republicans, replacing him temporarily with General Ulysses S. Grant.

As early as January 1867, radical Republican congressmen had urged Johnson's impeachment. In November, the House Judiciary Committee reported in favor of bringing impeachment articles by a 5-4 vote. But it became clear that few specific charges could be sustained. The real question was how far the president could use his powers to oppose a congressional program that had been enacted over his vetoes. On December 7, the House refused to impeach the president, with every Democrat opposed, as well as even a majority of Republicans.

Spectators packed the Senate galleries to witness the impeachment trial of President Andrew Johnson. *(Library of Congress)*

As President Johnson became even more resistant to the Republican Congress, emboldened white southerners redoubled their efforts to fight Reconstruction and worked to prevent the ratification of the new state constitutions being framed under the Reconstruction Acts. Johnson also determined to keep control of the army. Although the president had conformed to the Tenure of Office Act when he suspended Secretary of War Stanton, he intended to defy an adverse decision by the Senate reinstating him. But when the Senate did reject the suspension, Grant confounded the president by returning the office to Stanton. A month later, on February 21, 1868, Johnson ordered Stanton's removal despite the law. The House voted to impeach him the following day. It was the first time a U.S. president had been impeached.

On March 4, the House of Representatives presented 11 articles of impeachment to the Senate. Most were legalistic, based on Johnson's effort to replace Stanton without regard to the Tenure of Office Act. Only the 11th made clear the serious political context in which Johnson's offenses took place. With an overwhelming Republican majority in the Senate, most observers thought that Johnson's conviction was certain. But a number of Republican senators joined Democrats to slow the process and insist on a measure of fairness and decorum. Chief Justice Salmon P. Chase, whom the Constitution designated to preside over the trial, supported their efforts. His rulings, sustained by a majority of senators, slowed the pace of the trial, gave the president's lawyers wider leeway in presenting evidence, and turned the trial into a legal rather than political proceeding.

The courtlike atmosphere in the Senate created the impression that all charges against the president had to be conclusively proved and that political considerations should not affect the verdict. This severely weakened the position of the House's prosecutors because the essence of Johnson's offense was political—a defiance of Congress that threatened to undermine the law and the constitutional system itself.

In this environment, the president's counsel, who were among the leading lawyers in the country, shone. They argued that the Tenure of Office Act was unconstitutional and that Johnson had removed Stanton only to test its validity in court. Furthermore, they argued that the law did not cover Stanton, pointing to the vagueness of its language. Meanwhile, the politically charged arguments of the

---

FACTBOX

PLACE U.S. Congress, Washington, D. C.

DATE February 22–May 26, 1868

TYPE Political crisis

DESCRIPTION Trial of the president of the United States on charges of violating the Tenure of Office Act

CAUSE Disagreement between President Andrew Johnson and Congress over Reconstruction policy after the Civil War

IMPACT Allowed Reconstruction to proceed according to Congress's program but in the long run discredited impeachment as mode of restraining presidential misconduct

---

House prosecutors seemed strident and out of place in a legal trial.

The change in tone of the proceedings fostered a backlash against impeachment. The president ceased his attacks on Congress and his interference in the South. People began to worry that a conviction would fatally weaken the presidency. As the trial dragged on throughout the spring, most of the southern states met the Reconstruction Act's requirements and were restored to the Union. The sense of crisis faded.

When the Senate finally voted on the three strongest articles on May 16 and 26, 1868, seven Republicans joined with the Democrats to prevent the president's removal. The tally was 35 in favor, 19 opposed—just one vote shy of the two-thirds necessary for conviction. Knowing that other articles had less support, the Senate adjourned the trial on May 26, bringing the confrontation to an end. Johnson completed his term as president.

Despite the failure to secure a conviction, impeachment ended presidential obstruction of Congress's reconstruction policy. But it was too late to counteract the damage Johnson had done to hopes for a reconstruction based on equal rights for African Americans. The persistent intransigence Johnson had fostered ultimately led to the collapse of the state governments established during Reconstruction. Most historians have regarded the Johnson impeachment as an ill-advised, politically motivated effort to establish congressional supremacy. The consequence has been to weaken the utility of impeachment as a deterrent to presidential misconduct.

Michael Les Benedict

FURTHER READING:

Benedict, Michael Les. *The Impeachment and Trial of Andrew Johnson.* 1973. Reprint, New York: Norton, 1999.

Rehnquist, William H. *Grand Inquests: The Historic Impeachments of Justice Samuel Chase and President Andrew Johnson.* New York: Morrow, 1992.

Trefousse, Hans L. *Impeachment of a President: Andrew Johnson, the Blacks, and Reconstruction.* 1975. Reprint, New York: Fordham University Press, 1999.

1869 ◆ AVONDALE MINE DISASTER

The greatest mine disaster in the United States to that point in the nation's history occurred in Avondale, Pennsylvania, on September 9, 1869. About 10 A.M. on a Monday, fire broke out in a shaft more than 300 feet below ground in the Avondale Mine, which was owned by Delaware, Lackawanna & Western Railroad. It was quickly ascertained the 108 men trapped underground had died in the accident. Two miners subsequently perished in a rescue attempt. Adding to the tragedy was the fact that five of the victims were between 12 and 17 years old. Studies released in 1916 and 1946 by the Bureau of Mines of the United States Interior Department claimed that 179 miners perished in the accident, but the figure of 110 is more commonly accepted.

Avondale is located in Luzerne County in northeastern Pennsylvania. The mine itself lay one mile south of Plymouth, a mining town in the Wilkes-Barre area, which is situated in the heart of Pennsylvania's anthracite, or "hard," coal fields. Anthracite coal was extremely valued in home heating at the time when virtually all hard coal in the United States was mined in a relatively small area of Pennsylvania that stretched roughly 65 miles from Scranton, the city known as the King of Anthracite, to Pottsville, the city known as the Queen of Anthracite.

The tragedy was accentuated because a three-month strike had ended the Friday before the fire. Tensions had been running high all summer long between Welsh and Irish miners. The largely Protestant Welsh tended to be the skilled "miners" and favored the ending of the strike, while the Irish, predominantly Catholic, were overwhelmingly "laborers" and were less enthusiastic about settling

---

FACTBOX

PLACE Steuben Shaft of the Avondale Mine, located in Plymouth, Pennsylvania

DATE September 9, 1869

TYPE Mine fire and explosion

DESCRIPTION Three hundred feet below the earth's surface, a fire broke out in the Avondale Mine, trapping and asphyxiating more than 100 miners.

CAUSE A ventilating furnace ignited a wooden breaker, causing asphyxiation from sulfuric and other lethal gases in a mine that lacked an escape exit.

CASUALTIES 110 fatalities

IMPACT Prodded Pennsylvania to adopt mine safety laws; gave more power to company men termed "fire bosses," causing miners to lose control over their work

---

quickly. At the official inquest—begun just two days after the accident—some Welsh miners claimed the Irish had sabotaged the mine because of this ethnic feud. Only six of the 110 men killed were Irish, a fact that fueled the conspiracy claims. Many of the Irish miners did not report for work that fatal day because of the funeral of a prominent Irish civic leader. No credible evidence has ever emerged to prove the conspiracy claims. However, the already volatile ethnic-religious tensions that ran through the industry certainly were exacerbated.

The official inquest and virtually every subsequent study of the disaster concluded that all deaths were caused by asphyxia. In the words of the inquest, death was due to "the exhaustion of atmospheric air or a prevalence of sulfuric and carbonic acid gases caused by fire." The fire in Avondale's Steuben Shaft, which ran down 327 feet, started when a ventilating furnace ignited a wooden coal breaker. (Coal breakers broke chunks of coal into various sizes and eliminated slate. Coal was sold in sizes such as pea, nut, and stove. Furnaces required specific types of coal. Hence, breakers were an integral part of every mining operation.) The miners had no way to escape. Contemporary and later investigators concluded that had a second or exit shaft existed, nearly all deaths could have been avoided.

The conspiracy theories were given impetus by the belief that a secret Irish order called the Molly Maguires was operating in the area. The "Mollies" had been blamed for causing much labor unrest during the Civil War. However, the Mollies' primary area of strength was in Schuylkill County, which lay to the south of Luzerne County. Pennsylvania governor John Geary blamed "grossly negligent operators" for the disaster. The inquest strongly supported Geary's beliefs.

A mass outpouring of support for the families of the victims materialized immediately. Thousands of people flocked to the shaft within hours. Their arrival added to the confusion and hampered the delivery of rescue equipment. More than $155,000 was raised to support the families of the deceased. Papers throughout the country, including *Harper's Weekly* and *Frank Leslie's Illustrated Newspaper,* covered the tragedy.

Efforts were made to improve mine safety in the aftermath of the accident. The Pennsylvania legislature passed a Mine Safety Act in 1870 that required mine inspections and two outlets in all mines and placed safety concerns in the hands of operators. The death rate in America's anthracite mines ran three times higher than in Great Britain, an imbalance that contributed to the adoption of safety legislation. But the "reforms" also cost coal miners much of their autonomy. Companies now relied on "inside bosses" or company men to police mines. These supervisors were commonly called fire bosses because their main job was to prevent Avondale-type fires. The disaster temporarily increased membership in the Workingmen's Benevolent Association (WBA), a union led by John Siney. The WBA claimed that safety, not wages, was its primary concern. Siney had spoken eloquently at Avondale shortly after the fire, boosting the popularity of the union. The WBA, however, went out of existence in 1875, a development that gave the companies and their fire bosses supreme control of mining operations until the emergence of the United Mine Workers years later. The Avondale incident marked the beginning of the end of miners as "independent contractors." They were on their way to becoming simply employees. Fire bosses remained the rulers of inside mining operations in the anthracite fields for the next century until strip or machine mining replaced inside mining.

William Gudelunas

FURTHER READING:

Kenny, Kevin. *Making Sense of the Molly Maguires.* New York: Oxford University Press, 1998.
Pinkowski, Edward. *John Siney: The Miners' Martyr.* Philadelphia: Sunshine Press, 1963.
Wallace, Anthony F. C. *St. Clair: A Nineteenth-Century Coal Town's Experience with a Disaster-Prone Industry.* New York: Knopf, 1987.

1871 ◆ REVERE RAILROAD ACCIDENT

On August 26, 1871, an express train bound for Portland, Maine, slammed into the rear of a passenger train in Revere, Massachusetts. The force of the collision plus the release of scalding steam and a subsequent fire in the passenger train killed 29 people. Adding injury to insult in this horrible accident, the collision probably was preventable had the Eastern Railroad Company, owner and operator of both trains, installed modern equipment. The mishap prompted the Eastern and

FACTBOX

PLACE Revere, Massachusetts

DATE August 26, 1871

TYPE Railroad accident

DESCRIPTION A Portland express train rear-ended a parked passenger train at a station in Revere.

CAUSE Delays in the scheduling of north- and southbound trains, and the failure to install available communication technologies

CASUALTIES 29 deaths and 57 injuries

COST $510,000 personal liability and damage to property

IMPACT The Massachusetts Board of Railroad Commissioners persuaded rail lines in the state to endorse numerous safety reforms, including telegraphic communications, sturdier passenger cars, and electric block signals.

other railroads to invest in new safety devices. Nevertheless, rear-end collisions remained a common occurrence on the nation's railroads for the next 50 years.

A variety of factors led to the accident in Revere. The summer of 1871 was a busy one for the Eastern Railroad Company, which ran an extra "accommodation" train on Saturday evening, August 26, to handle the demand. Four trains had been scheduled to depart from Boston between 6:30 P.M. and 8 P.M. Three trains were headed for Lynn, 11 miles north, while a fourth express train was bound for Portland. But the 6:30 train and the two that followed it, including the accommodation train, left the station behind schedule. The Portland express set out a few minutes after its scheduled 8 P.M. departure. Already behind schedule, the accommodation train lost more time on account of the delay of a southbound train from Lynn. This snag halted traffic at the Everett Junction, which lay between Boston and Revere, until the track cleared. Normally, a flagman kept traffic flowing by directing waiting trains to unused rails. On August 26, however, the experienced flagman was ill. His substitute held the accommodation train in place rather than coordinate a maneuver to allow it to continue northward. The delay allowed the Portland express to draw closer to the lagging accommodation train.

Telegraphic communications could have warned the engineers of the narrowing distance between the trains. Automatic block signals could have provided further information of the interval between them. But the Eastern had failed to invest in these new technologies. Nor did the accommodation train, which had stopped at the Revere station, have effective rear illumination, which might have helped the engineer of the Portland express see the obstruction ahead. It was dark by 8:30 P.M. (the United States had not yet adopted daylight savings time), and a mist that drifted in from the ocean further obscured vision. Moreover, the engineer of the Portland train had averted his gaze upward to check on a signal-pole that controlled the switch to a siding just as his train rounded a curve in the approach to Revere station. Eight hundred feet away from the accommodation train, the engineer of the Portland express sounded the whistle that instructed trainmen to set the brakes—manually. Moist from the mist, the rails were slippery, a condition that reduced the ability to stop the train, which had been traveling at about 30 miles per hour. It slammed into the rear of the accommodation train at about 10 or 15 miles per hour. The engine of the express train penetrated two-thirds of the way into the rear passenger car, which was packed with people. The force of the collision ruptured the locomotive's steam valves, releasing scorching hot vapors. All of the cars of the accommodation caught fire, fueled by the kerosene lamps that illuminated each car. "Crushing, scalding and burning did their work together," wrote Charles Francis Adams, the member of the Massachusetts Board of Railroad Commissioners, who reported on the accident. In addition to the 29 fatalities, 57 people received serious injuries.

Charles Francis Adams, grandson of President John Quincy Adams, converted the Revere disaster into an object lesson on behalf of safety improvement. Adams converted the Massachusetts Board of Railroad Commissioners, established in 1869, into a pioneer for rail improvements. Focusing especially on rear-end collisions, the most common form of railroad accident, he convinced rail managers in Massachusetts to endorse a variety of reforms, such as the use of telegraphic communications, the adoption of sturdier passenger cars (the "Miller" platform design), and the installation of automatic (electric) block signals. Adams also urged the introduction of the Westinghouse air brake, which allowed the train engineer to set the brakes for the entire train, rather than continue with the old method whereby brakemen reacted to the locomotive's whistle and manually set individual car brakes. Federal legislation in 1893 required all trains to install the system. By 1887, rail companies began to illuminate cars electrically, which reduced the fire hazard from kerosene fueled lamps.

The Eastern Railroad Company adopted some of these improvements, but the cost of the reforms added to its growing debt, a financial burden acquired in part from the $510,000 cost of the accident in property losses and liability settlements. Its financial solvency also suffered from competition with the Boston and Maine railroad and reduced revenues caused by the severe FINANCIAL PANIC AND DEPRESSION of 1873. The Eastern barely dodged bankruptcy in 1876 through financial reorganization. In 1882, the Boston and Maine leased the Eastern and absorbed it in 1890.

Ballard C. Campbell

FURTHER READING:

Adams, Charles Francis. *Notes on Railroad Accidents.* New York: G. P. Putnam's Sons, 1879.

McCraw, Thomas K. *Prophets of Regulation.* Cambridge, Mass.: Harvard University Press, 1984.

1871 ◆ PESHTIGO FIRE

October 8, 1871, was the date of the single most destructive fire in American history. The Peshtigo fire, which swept through northeastern Wisconsin, destroyed 2,400 square miles of forest (1.5 million acres)—an area about the size of Delaware—and took between 1,200 and 2,400 lives. Because the fire occurred on the same day as the GREAT CHICAGO FIRE, it is perhaps the least known of all major natural disasters in the United States. Despite the seriousness of the blaze, it failed to capture the public's imagination in the way that the Chicago fire did.

The cause of the disaster lay in the convergence of several factors. Perhaps most important, the summer and fall of 1871 were extremely dry. The upper Midwest was experiencing a period of severe drought and very high temperatures. Almost no rain fell between July and the beginning of October. Wisconsin's forests were ready to burn. Other factors such as logging and milling in the area increased the probability of a serious fire. Loggers had left large piles of timber in the woods, and the lumber mills were surrounded with logs, milled products, and piles of sawdust. Railroad building was also under way, and railroad crews simply stacked felled trees along the tracks, leaving a potential forest fire hazard. The

> ## FACTBOX
>
> **PLACE** Northeastern Wisconsin
>
> **DATE** October 8, 1871
>
> **TYPE** Forest fire
>
> **DESCRIPTION** A massive forest fire destroyed 2,400 square miles of forest and most of the farms, homes, and businesses within it.
>
> **CAUSE** Drought conditions, high winds, availability of combustible materials
>
> **CASUALTIES** 1,200 to 2,400 deaths
>
> **COST** Millions of dollars in lumber, railroad, and business losses
>
> **IMPACT** Information about the fire was used to develop fire policies and procedures in the early 20th century. During World War II, it was studied by the army as a model for creating firestorms by bombing.

towns, too, were prone to fire, since builders had used the most abundant local product, wood, in constructing homes and businesses. Farmers pursuing slash and burn agriculture had recently cleared acre upon acre of timbered land, leaving more piles of flammable debris. Farm homes, barns, and fields had been baked by the drought and were tinder dry.

Although the reasons why the fire was so severe are obvious, the exact origins of the fire remain a mystery. It could have been started by a careless farmer or logger or by stray sparks from a locomotive. At the time of the fire, individuals were also deliberately setting fires to clear farmland of unwanted timber and train tracks of fallen debris. One of these fires could have gotten out of control. Whatever their origins, the flames were whipped into a conflagration by the winds from a cold front advancing from the west. The fire spread rapidly through the area, destroying homes, farms, and towns. It swept into the area with an enormous roar, entirely consuming some towns, such as Peshtigo and Williamsonville, and burning much of the farming community surrounding them, known as the Sugar Bush. The air became so hot that some houses and people simply burst into flame. Others died from suffocation, as the fire burned the oxygen out of the air. Some of those who survived did so by standing in the Peshtigo River until the flames had passed. Even they had to continually duck their heads into the water because hot air and embers caused their hair to catch fire.

The speed with which the fire moved and the thoroughness of the destruction indicate that although surface winds were moderate to high, the super-heated air was moving at a considerably faster speed, estimated at 80 miles an hour or greater. The conflagration achieved firestorm proportions, burning out of control until the wind dropped and the rain began to fall. In fact, the origin of the word *firestorm* may be found in the newspaper coverage of the Peshtigo fire.

It is impossible to know how many people died in the fire. The bodies could not even be counted and identified because many victims of the fire were burned beyond recognition and others reduced to ashes. No one even knew how many people were living in the area. Northern Wisconsin was in a period of rapid development, and many new settlers had arrived since the previous year's census. Additionally, workers were arriving daily to take jobs in logging and in iron mines nearby. A group of 50 Italian immigrant railroad workers were supposed to have arrived the day before the fire. After the fire, none of them were to be found. Many individuals and families, believed to have been in the area before the fire, vanished, their relatives and friends unable to locate them.

News of the firestorm was slow to get out, given the overwhelming public interest in the Chicago fire. Newspapers appended descriptions of the Peshtigo fire to their coverage of the Chicago blaze. In the aftermath of the firestorm, public and private aid was delivered to the survivors. Many sought refuge in Green Bay, the largest city in the area. Nearly 10,000 people received some sort of aid in the months following the fire. Those who remained began to rebuild their towns and farms almost immediately, but Peshtigo would never fully recover. A woodenware factory that had been one of the most important employers in the town would not be rebuilt after the fire. New farmers, however, would come into the area in large numbers. The newspapers and other boosters advertised that the fire had improved the area's agricultural prospects by removing all excess timber in the farmers' path.

Peshtigo and its firestorm would remain a historical footnote, to be consulted when circumstances required. There would be regular, large forest fires throughout the north woods over the next half-century, as farmers, loggers, and railroads developed the area. The Peshtigo fire, thankfully, would be the largest; those that followed would be lesser, although destructive and deadly, events. When firestorms ravaged much of the West in 1910, information from the Peshtigo fire would be unearthed to help the Forest Service understand firestorms and how they were produced. During World War II, the army would turn to information about Peshtigo as it contemplated the use of firestorms as a weapon. The public, however, has remained generally unaware of the disaster because of where it took place and the relative lack of publicity surrounding the event. Despite the large numbers of people killed and enormous property loss, interest would remain lower than for the far less devastating Chicago fire, 250 miles to the south. Nevertheless, in modern history, the destructiveness of the Peshtigo fire stands third only to World War II's deliberately created firestorms that destroyed Dresden and Tokyo.

Pamela Riney-Kehrberg

FURTHER READING:

Brown, D. Alexander. "The Great Peshtigo Fire." *American History Illustrated,* 3, no. 10 (1969): 26–32.

Gess, Denise, and William Lutz. *Firestorm at Peshtigo: A Town, Its People, and the Deadliest Fire in American History.* New York: Henry Holt, 2002.

Pernin, Peter. "The Great Peshtigo Fire: An Eyewitness Account." *Wisconsin Magazine of History* 54, no. 4 (1971): 246–272.

Pyne, Stephen J. *Fire in America: A Cultural History of Wildland and Rural Fire.* Seattle: University of Washington Press, 1997.

Wells, Robert W. *Fire at Peshtigo.* Englewood Cliffs, N.J.: Prentice Hall, 1968.

1871 ◆ GREAT CHICAGO FIRE

On the night of October 8, 1871, fire broke out in a busy neighborhood of Chicago in a cattle barn owned by Patrick and Catherine O'Leary at 137 West Dekoven Street. Fanned by strong winds and fed by structures left tinder-dry in the wake of a four-month drought, the fire marched uncontrollably through the "Queen of the West," as the city was known. Fire posed a potentially disastrous threat to most major American cities in the mid-19th century, but Chicago was uniquely susceptible to this danger. Embracing its role as a transportation and manufacturing nexus joining the East to the ever-expanding West, the city had experienced a hasty 40-year boom in which numerous wooden structures were thrown up in close proximity and haphazard order as the city rapidly grew from a prairie outpost of roughly 100 people in 1830 to the fourth-largest urban center in the United States, with almost 300,000 inhabitants in 1870. Indeed, Chicago had already suffered through 20 major fires in the eight days prior to October 8, including a 17-hour multialarm blaze that had been extinguished only hours earlier, exhausting the understaffed fire department and using up precious fuel and equipment. Still, the beleaguered firefighters of Maxwell Street Firehouse Engine 6 responded quickly, and within five minutes of the first alarm, they were battling the fire of the century.

Folklore maintains that Catherine O'Leary's finicky cow kicked over a kerosene lantern, which set ablaze the barn, the neighborhood, and then the city, but the bulk of this tale is the concoction of an unscrupulous reporter who was capitalizing on anti-Irish sentiment of the day. Though an exact cause may never be determined, Chicago historians speculate that a party at the McLaughlins—the O'Learys'

FACTBOX

PLACE Chicago, Illinois

DATE October 8–10, 1871

TYPE Fire

DESCRIPTION A fire that began in a barn burned through downtown Chicago for 30 hours, destroying a 2,000-acre area of the city, leveling 18,000 buildings, and rendering 90,000 residents homeless.

CAUSE Accidentally dropped match or other lit object

CASUALTIES Approximately 300 deaths

COST Estimated property damage of $200 million

IMPACT Some building reforms were enacted that banned wooden structures in the heart of the city, but more important, Chicago rebuilt itself with a more coherent design and infrastructure, making it among the most modern and influential of American cities.

neighbors—may have led to the blaze. On the evening of October 8, two neighbors who were determined to get into the party thought an offering of fresh milk might do the trick. After they entered the O'Leary barn, one of them accidentally dropped a lit match or other incendiary object into the hay, which immediately sparked a fire.

After the arrival of Maxwell Street Firehouse Engine 6, other firehouses raced to the scene despite the failure of several alarms in the immediate vicinity. Added misfortune came in the guise of a fierce south wind that fanned the blaze. Out-of-control flames raced toward the central business, financial, and mercantile districts. When the pumping engine stationed on the northern edge of the fire ran out of fuel, crews frantically stoked its boiler with boards from nearby sidewalks and fences but were unable to maintain adequate pressure. Within minutes, the last chance of containing the blaze was lost. The flames spread through the downtown area throughout the following day, destroying homes, churches, factories, warehouses, and municipal buildings and driving terrified residents before it. Horrific stories of residents being trampled to death as they fled, women giving birth on the run, panicked fire victims jumping into Lake Michigan, and desperate souls seeking refuge in the city's graveyards paint a picture of devastation that dollar amounts cannot measure. As one eyewitness later declared, "It was a chapter of horrors that can only be written as it was, with a pen of fire."

The fire eventually reached the Chicago River, but even that natural barrier proved inadequate to stem the destruction as the winds carried a rain of smoldering embers to the other side and started the conflagration anew. For 30 hours, the blaze consumed nearly everything in its path, flickering out only after reaching the city limits and thus running out of fuel by the early morning of October 10. With an estimated 300 dead, 90,000 homeless, and some 18,000 destroyed buildings across 2,000 acres, the Queen of the West lay in ruins, save for the Chicago

When Chicagoans woke up on October 10, 1871, most of the city lay in ruins, destroyed by the great fire. *(New York Public Library)*

Water Tower and Waterworks and a few other stone structures. Although property damage was estimated at $200 million, some losses were impossible to calculate, including that of the original Emancipation Proclamation signed by Lincoln eight years earlier, which was destroyed when the Historical Society burned to the ground.

In the wake of the disaster, Mayor Roswell Mason declared martial law, and federal troops led by General Philip Sheridan arrived to maintain order, assisted by private police including agents of the Pinkerton Detective Agency. The story made national headlines, and relief in the form of food, supplies, and donations poured in from around the country. Chicago proved itself a remarkably resilient community. Within hours of the fire's end, a massive rebuilding effort was under way. A year later, $40 million worth of new buildings had already been erected, and the city had extended its boundaries into Lake Michigan by using refuse from the disaster as landfill. Reforms were enacted that included a ban on wooden buildings in the central downtown area. Drawing opportunity from the chaos, city planners created a new, greatly improved vision for Chicago, designing an open lakefront dotted with public recreation areas and laying out a systematic grid pattern for the streets. The rebuilding effort drew the ambitious and the innovative to the city. Within a generation Chicago had become a leader in the modernism movement as the home to radical new styles of architecture, the birthplace of a new genre of realistic fiction, and a center for the scientific study of society. The fire also proved to be a defining moment for the city's image, giving it an identity as the first truly modern urban center and characterizing its citizens as a combination of hearty, hardscrabble pioneers and innovative, forward-thinking cosmopolitans.

See also 1872 GREAT BOSTON FIRE.

Susan Doll and David Morrow

FURTHER READING:

"Chicago as It Was," *Harper's Weekly,* October 21, 1871.

Cowan, David. *Great Chicago Fires: Historic Blazes That Shaped a City.* Chicago: Lake Claremont Press, 2001.

Miller, Ross. *American Apocalypse: The Great Fire and the Myth of Chicago.* Chicago: University of Chicago Press, 1990.

1872 ◆ CREDIT MOBILIER SCANDAL

The Credit Mobilier scandal, along with Tammany Hall and the Whiskey Ring, has long epitomized the corruption of the Gilded Age. Compared to the other two, however, Credit Mobilier, although less blatantly illegal, was more novel and disturbing. Whereas the first two involved political corruption of a traditional sort, Credit Mobilier highlighted the changing political and business ethics of the new industrial order. Americans were shocked by the financial mismanagement of the Union Pacific Railroad, the company hired to build the eastern portion of the transcontinental railway, and by the selfish behavior of public figures affiliated with the project. Promoters of the railroad had organized a construction company called the Credit Mobilier to divert to themselves the profits from building the line. According to historian Richard White, the construction of the transcontinental railroads ushered in a new era of corruption in American history. Because the scope of the project was national, it necessitated unprecedented amounts of capital and federal government subsidies. This combination created a new formula for corruption in which a limited number of inside investors controlled information and influenced legislation to manipulate the huge capital investments for personal advantage. This joining of financial and political corruption defined Gilded Age corporate corruption. Credit Mobilier was its first and greatest instance.

The scandal erupted on September 4, 1872, when the *New York Sun*'s front page trumpeted headlines including "The King of Frauds" and "Congressmen who Have Robbed the People, and who now Support the National Robber." In the accompanying exposé, the *Sun* accused 11 members of Congress of each accepting 2,000 to 3,000 shares of Credit Mobilier stock from Representative Oakes Ames (R-Mass.). Those named included Vice President Schuyler Colfax, Senator (and vice presidential candidate) Henry Wilson (R-Mass.), Speaker of the House James G. Blaine (R-Me.), and Representative and future president James Garfield (R-Ohio). In addition to his congressional seat, Ames was a successful businessman and a major investor in the Union Pacific and Credit Mobilier. He had served as a director of the

FACTBOX

PLACE Washington, D.C.

DATE 1872–73

TYPE Political scandal

DESCRIPTION Members of Congress became involved in distributing and receiving shares of stock in a railroad enterprise associated with the building of the transcontinental railroad.

CAUSE Greed, and an article in the *New York Sun* exposing the distribution of shares

IMPACT The scandal inflamed public opinion, leading to the disgrace of several politicians, inspired fictional accounts of the Gilded Age, and continues to epitomize the corruption of the period.

Union Pacific since 1870, and his brother and business partner Oliver Ames, Jr., had been president of the railroad from 1866 until 1871. The Ameses and their associates were opposed by Thomas C. Durant, one of the railroad's original investors, and his allies. The *Sun* based its information on the lawsuit of Henry McComb, a Durant crony and Credit Mobilier investor, who had sued the company in 1868 to recover shares of stock he believed were rightfully his. Among the evidence McComb submitted in court papers was correspondence from Representative Ames, in which the latter described his efforts to place Credit Mobilier stock with members of Congress in late 1867. The correspondence included, according to the *Sun*, a list of congressmen and senators with stock amounts jotted next to each name and Ames's assurance that he had placed the shares "where they will do the most good for us."

How the *Sun* obtained the documents from Philadelphia's Chancery Court remains unknown. The timing, however, confirms the story's political intentions. It appeared in the midst of the 1872 presidential campaign in which incumbent Ulysses Grant was opposed by famed *New York Tribune* editor Horace Greeley. Running as a Liberal Republican and Democratic candidate, Greeley defected from the Republican Party concerning the issues of the Grant administration's corruption and Reconstruction policies. As a Democratic paper, the *Sun* supported Greeley in the campaign. The motivation of the Greeleyites, as they were called, was to discredit regular Republican candidates in the upcoming elections. The story hit the week before the Maine state election (Maine held one of the earliest state contests), and Representative Blaine's opponents circulated handbill reprints of the *Sun* article forcing the Speaker to defend his innocence. Senator Wilson and Representative Garfield issued statements denying that they ever received or purchased shares of the company, and Vice President Colfax gave a speech exonerating himself. On September 17, Ames issued a circular letter to his constituents rebutting the *Sun*'s "infamous charges." He insinuated the real causes behind the malicious squib: McComb's attempts to blackmail Ames into a settlement in the stock case. Furthermore, Ames asserted that the list of names had been written by McComb—not Ames—a fact McComb had admitted in his 1868 legal deposition. Ames denied ever giving any member of Congress shares of the stock, pointing out that the legislation affecting the Union Pacific had all been passed years before the alleged transactions took place. Finally, Ames defended his promotional activities—without detailing their extent—by appealing to the national interest: "I may have done wrong in my efforts to aid this great national enterprise. If so, I am unconscious of it. I have always regarded it as among the most creditable and patriotic acts of my life."

Despite the scandal's prominence, it had little impact on the election. Blaine and Garfield won reelection, as did Grant and his vice presidential choice, Senator Wilson. The scandal, however, did not go away. When Congress reconvened in December, Blaine stepped down from the Speaker's chair to call for an investigation of the Credit Mobilier affair. The result was the establishment of two committees: The first, chaired by Luke Poland (R-Vt.) and known as the Poland Committee, examined the specific issue of bribery; and the second, chaired by Jeremiah M. Wilson (R-Ind.) and known as the Wilson Committee, took up the broader issue of whether the Union Pacific Railroad and Credit Mobilier had engaged in illegal activities or had violated the public trust.

Hearings lasted into February 1873. Testimony by 23 current or former members of Congress, including Oakes Ames, and assorted figures from the Union

Pacific and Credit Mobilier revealed that while no outright bribery took place and no shares of stock were *given*, Ames had in fact sold Credit Mobilier stock at par to 11 members of Congress, including Garfield and Henry Wilson. In some cases he sold the shares on credit, guaranteed the investment against loss, and acted as trustee. Other members, including Blaine, had been approached by Ames but declined his offer. The average number of shares involved in each case was 15, not the thousands alleged by the *Sun*. However, as Credit Mobilier declared its only substantial dividends in December 1867, Ames's offer to his colleagues amounted to a sure thing. Furthermore, it was revealed that Representative James Brooks (D-N.Y.), a government director for the Union Pacific, had purchased 150 shares from Durant just after the dividend was declared. As a government director, Brooks was expressly forbidden from owning any stock in the venture. Thus, while the *Sun* erred in the details and wrongfully accused some people, it had uncovered a good measure of the truth. The Poland Committee concluded that while Ames had never requested special favors, he "feared the interests of the road might suffer from adverse legislation, and what he desired to accomplish was to enlist strength and friends in Congress." As for the members of Congress, there was no evidence of inappropriate behavior resulting from their ownership of the stock. They had, however, exercised poor judgment in accepting it.

The committee recommended no punishment for most of those involved but did recommend that Brooks and Ames be expelled from the House. Following the final debates on the report, Blaine managed to have the move to expel reduced to censure. Brooks and Ames, both elderly and broken by the ordeal, died within a few months.

The Wilson Committee's deliberations centered on whether the Union Pacific and Credit Mobilier violated the Pacific Railway Acts of 1862 and 1864. These acts provided federal subsidies to facilitate the construction of the transcontinental railroad in the form of Treasury bonds and grants of land. The laws held the Union Pacific to certain conditions, including cash payment in full for all shares of stock issued, and the application of 5 percent of the railroad's net revenues to pay off the bonds. The Wilson Committee found that Ames and his associates had violated the acts on two counts. First, they had not paid cash in full for their stock, thus hampering the railroad's capitalization. Second, in creating Credit Mobilier, the investors had established an inside company to siphon off the railroad's assets by overcharging for the construction of the line, manipulating the railroad's bonds and stocks to their personal benefit, and engaging in other side transactions detrimental to the Union Pacific's financial health. Most alarming, the committee found that although the actual cost of construction was $51 million, Credit Mobilier had charged the Union Pacific $94 million, resulting—depending on how the stocks and bonds were valued—in a profit of as much as $43 million. Instead of safeguarding the public interest, Credit Mobilier had operated for the sole benefit of the railroad's principal investors. The Wilson Committee recommended legislation directing the attorney general to institute a lawsuit to recover the ill-gotten gains.

Congress passed the legislation, and the government's lawsuit made its way to the Supreme Court in 1878. The Court ruled for the Union Pacific, holding that while the railroad's principal investors may have engaged in dubious finances, the government trust had not been endangered since the railroad remained solvent and had not defaulted on its obligations. The scandal damaged several political reputations, particularly those of Brooks, Ames, and Colfax. Credit Mobilier became an issue in the presidential campaign of 1876, in which Blaine failed to gain the Republican nomination, and in the succeeding two contests, in which both Garfield (1880) and Blaine (1884) were candidates. The scandal also contributed to the general investor mistrust toward railroad stocks and bonds, which in turn helped precipitate a major financial panic in September 1873. In the end, however, the scandal's most lasting impact has been the ways in which it has served to symbolize the tawdry business and political ethics of the new industrial era. Aside from its appearance in numerous history textbooks, Credit Mobilier lives on in American literature. It served as inspiration for Henry Adams's novel *Democracy,* Walt Whitman's *Democratic Vistas,* and for portions of Mark Twain and Charles Dudley Warner's satirical novel *The Gilded Age.*

C. Wyatt Evans

FURTHER READING:

Ambrose, Stephen J. *Nothing Like It in the World: The Men Who Built the Transcontinental Railroad, 1863–1869.* New York: Simon and Schuster, 2000.

Bain, David Haward. *Empire Express: Building the First Transcontinental Railroad.* New York: Viking, 1999.

Fogel, Robert W. *The Union Pacific Railroad: A Case of Premature Enterprise.* Baltimore: Johns Hopkins University Press, 1960.

Klein, Maury. *The Union Pacific: Birth of a Railroad, 1862–1893.* New York: Doubleday, 1987.

White, Richard. "Information, Markets, and Corruption: Transcontinental Railroads in the Gilded Age." *Journal of American History* 90, no. 1 (June 2003): 19–43.

1872 ◆ GREAT EPIZOOTIC

In November 1872 an epizootic—the animal equivalent of an epidemic—spread rapidly southward from Ontario, Canada, laying low thousands of urban horses with flulike symptoms in the United States. In an age before automobiles, subways, and electricity, horses played a vital role in American cities. They provided transportation for people and goods and supplied power for some manufacturing. They were also essential for police and fire protection and other public services. Municipalities needed about one horse for every 20 people. Every city housed thousands of horses. Manhattan alone had close to 130,000 in 1900, and as late as 1926, the *New York Times* declared that the horse was indispensable to the city's functioning.

The epizootic that raced across the Northeast in 1872 represented an energy crisis of the first order, causing significant disruption to everyday life. With horses ailing and unable to move, people used wheelbarrows to haul groceries along city streets. Gangs

FACTBOX

PLACE New York, Boston, Philadelphia, and other eastern cities

DATE September–December 1872

TYPE Horse epidemic

DESCRIPTION Epidemic with flulike symptoms that spread from city to city infecting horses, thereby shutting down transportation, shipping, and manufacturing

CAUSE Influenza affecting horses, originating in Canada

CASUALTIES More than 2,000 horses died

IMPACT Transportation and other activities in many eastern cities were slowed or stopped during the epidemic.

of unemployed men pulled some street railway cars, but virtually all transit came to a standstill. The epizootic also affected trade between cities, much of which still relied on horses. New York City, for example, received much of its coal from Pennsylvania via the horse-powered Delaware and Hudson Canal and much of its food from upstate New York and the Great Lakes region via the horse-powered Erie Canal. Prices of both commodities spiked as the city faced winter shortages. Fortunately, the horses recovered in time to resume deliveries.

Boston experienced the worst problem. Just as the epizootic was reaching its peak, a blaze erupted in a warehouse on November 9. Because the fire department's horses were too ill to pull engines, men had to haul them on foot, which took hours instead of minutes. As a result, the fire spread unchecked for 15 hours, destroying 776 buildings worth more than $75 million. The city finally resorted to blowing up buildings to stop the conflagration. For want of horses, much of the city was lost.

Public health officials tracked the movement of the epizootic, which began in York, Ontario, and then moved steadily south and west over the next year, eventually migrating more than 2,000 miles to Managua, Nicaragua. Their data on the spread of the disease showed a clear pattern of contagion, a finding that provided support for the emerging

germ theory of disease. A close look at New York City public health records for humans during the epizootic of 1872 showed no elevation of human mortality, so the health crisis was not a zoonose, that is, a disease that spread between species (from horses to humans). New York data suggest a mortality rate of less than 3 percent for horses, so most of the problem came from the inability of horses to work, not from deaths. Nonetheless, more than 2,000 horses perished in New York, Philadelphia, and Boston, and hundreds, perhaps thousands, more across the country. One estimate claimed that 36 horses a day died in Manhattan. Disposal of their carcasses posed a major public health problem. One fairly successful solution seems to have been found in rendering plants that processed the dead animals into a number of useful by-products, including furniture stuffing, leather, animal food, and a fertilizer additive.

The entire episode highlighted the risks of relying on living sources for power. Not only was animal power prone to interruptions from diseases, but it was also dangerous: Horse-operated wagons and carriages had more accidents per vehicle than automobiles would later. Stables posed fire risks; the most notable instance was the 1871 GREAT CHICAGO FIRE that had started in a stable. These establishments were full of flammable materials such as hay, oats, and varnish for vehicles, as well as animals that might kick over lanterns. Stable manure also provided a breeding place for disease-bearing insects. The removal of horse manure on streets was an ongoing problem in 19th-century cities. The rapid spread of electric trolleys after their invention in 1886 can be attributed in good measure to the problems of horse-power.

Clay McShane

FURTHER READING:

Jones, Susan. *Valuing Animals: Veterinarians and Their Patients in Modern America.* Baltimore: Johns Hopkins University Press, 2003.

McShane, Clay. "Gelded Age Boston." *New England Quarterly* 74 (August 2001): 274–301.

——, and Joel A. Tarr. "The Centrality of the Horse to the Nineteenth-Century American City." In *The Making of Urban America,* edited by Raymond Mohl, 103–130. Rev. ed. Wilmington, Del.: Scholarly Resources, 1997.

1872 ◆ GREAT BOSTON FIRE

The great Boston fire on November 9, 1872, the largest conflagration in the city's history, changed the face of the Massachusetts capital. The fire was one of the nation's most costly disasters in property losses up to that time. Despite the efforts of firefighters from five New England states, the inferno raged for 15 hours and destroyed 65 acres of downtown Boston, including 776 buildings. It caused $75 million in property damage, killed 30 people, and left thousands of Bostonians jobless and homeless. Far more extensive than earlier Boston fires in 1653, 1676, 1711, 1747, 1761, 1787, and 1794, this disaster earned the name the great Boston fire of 1872. It occurred only one year after the GREAT CHICAGO FIRE of 1871.

The conflagration began in the basement of Tebbetts, Baldwin & Davis, a five-story wholesale dry-goods firm at the corner of Kingston and Summer Streets, probably triggered by sparks from a coal-fired steam boiler on Saturday night at about 7:20. Although Boston boasted the nation's oldest fire department, founded in 1678, it was ill-prepared to cope with this disaster. Within minutes of the first sparks, spotted by a Boston policeman patrolling on Lincoln Street, Boston Fire Chief John Stanhope Damrell (1829–1905) and his men responded. Racing to the scene, they were frustrated by the absence of fire horses who were suffering from the GREAT EPIZOOTIC flu that had weakened or incapacitated horses across the Northeast. Volunteers were forced to haul the steam fire engines on foot, causing firefighters to lose valuable time in arriving at the blazing commercial district. Additional problems were caused by obsolete hydrants, low water pressure, and fire hoses punctured by cart wheels and falling chunks of granite. The narrow streets were crowded by as many as 100,000 spectators, anxious property owners, looters, and debris, which further impeded efforts to put out the fire. The steam-engine pumpers and ladders could not reach many tall buildings, and gas pipelines, which carried fuel to light street lamps and commercial buildings, exploded and fed the flames.

Mayor William Gaston (1820–94) permitted concerned citizens to use gunpowder to demolish buildings in the path of the fire until Chief Damrell objected. Many of the five-to-seven-story ornate granite and brick buildings, assumed to be fireproof, had combustible mansard roofs made of wood, copper, and slate that spread the fire. It raged overnight, before 1,700 firefighters got the conflagration under control by 10 on Sunday morning, November 10. Despite destroying hundreds of buildings, the great Boston fire stopped short of the historic Old State House, Faneuil Hall, and Old South Meeting House, some of the city's oldest and most treasured landmarks. The ruins smoldered and smoked for days, and the intense heat of the flames had reduced granite facades to grotesque ruins surrounded by immense piles of bricks across the commercial district.

As a result of this enormous destruction, depicted in a Currier and Ives lithograph, *Boston in Flames,* and on the cover of *Harper's Weekly* magazine, a new commercial district was built from Washington Street to the harbor. Urban development spread toward Copley Square and the elite Back Bay district. The city introduced the first steam fireboat and aerial ladders and founded new fire companies fully staffed by permanent professional firefighters with a new telegraph communication

FACTBOX

PLACE Boston, Massachusetts

DATE November 9, 1872

TYPE Fire

DESCRIPTION Fire raged through the commercial district of downtown Boston for 15 hours, destroying 65 acres and 776 buildings.

CAUSE Probably triggered by sparks from a coal-fired steam boiler

CASUALTIES 30 deaths

COST $75 million

IMPACT Led to construction of a new commercial district, professionalization of the fire department, modernization of equipment, and adoption of a model building code system to City Hall. With the appointment of a new board of fire commissioners and permanent district fire chiefs, the city led a national movement to modernize urban firefighting techniques. In 1874, the respected architect George A. Clough was elected the nation's first city architect to oversee the rebuilding of Boston's burnt downtown district.

Even before the fire, Chief Damrell had reported on inadequacies in Boston's fire prevention plans in 1867 and campaigned with the Massachusetts State Firemen's Association to improve American fire prevention methods. The great Boston fire spurred his efforts, and in 1873 Damrell organized the National Association of Fire Engineers to establish universal building safety standards. Four years later, he became the city building inspector. As founder and first president of the National Association of Commissioners and Inspectors of Public Buildings, organized in 1891, Damrell drafted the nation's first model building code, which the association adopted in 1905. This code vastly improved fire safety and was perhaps the most important consequence of the great Boston fire of 1872.

Peter C. Holloran

FURTHER READING:

Sammarco, Anthony M. *The Great Boston Fire of 1872.* Dover, N.H.: Arcadia, 1997.

Schorow, Stephanie. *Boston on Fire: A History of Fires and Firefighting in Boston.* Beverly, Mass.: Commonwealth Editions, 2003.

1873 ◆ FINANCIAL PANIC AND DEPRESSION

The financial panic of 1873 triggered five years of economic depression in the United States. By 1876, more than half of the nation's railroads faced bankruptcy, hundreds of banks had failed, and thousands of factories had shut down. Unemployment approached 30 percent in some cities, and desperate workers roamed from town to town in search of work, creating a "tramp" problem nationwide. Governor John A. Dix of New York called this commercial breakdown "a destructive pestilence" that "desolated hundreds of households." His successor, Governor Lucius Robinson, referred to the crisis as "the great depression in every branch of business." The famed steelmaker Andrew Carnegie described these years as "fearful times." The slump in American business was part of a global slowdown that produced the world's most severe industrial depression to date. Affecting attitudes about taxation, business, banking, and labor in the United States, the panic of 1873 and the economic crisis that followed testified vividly to the growing pains of industrialization.

The panic began during the week of September 13 when the value of stocks and bonds dropped sharply. The slide escalated into a rapid financial meltdown on September 17. The financial collapse forced Jay Cooke and Company, one of the nation's most venerable securities firms, and the First National Bank of Washington into bankruptcy. The shock of these failures threw the stock market into turmoil. The New York Stock Exchange closed for 10 days, while financiers sought to stem the carnage. The secretary of the U.S. Treasury sought to bring New York banks back to solvency by buying $26 million worth of bonds in gold. But the magnitude of the financial downdraft overwhelmed these efforts and sent shock waves throughout the nation, leaving a trail of failed banks and brokerages in its wake. A web of contracting credit, falling prices, and closed factories brought commerce almost to standstill during the winter of 1873–74.

Governor Robinson of New York blamed the depression on the use of paper money, which he said promoted inflation and "reckless business schemes." Certainly the prosperity of 1869–73 helped to set up the fall. Credit was easy in the post–Civil War years. Business flourished, railroads expanded by leaps and bounds, and completion of the first transcontinental railroad in 1869 helped create a national economy. Jay Cooke joined the boom in the early 1870s by marketing bonds for the North Pacific Railroad, the

FACTBOX

PLACE Wall Street (New York City), Washington, D.C., and the United States.

DATE September 17, 1873 (financial crash); 1873–78 (depression)

TYPE Financial panic and depression

DESCRIPTION A five-year depression precipitated bankruptcies, bank failures, and factory shutdowns, causing unemployment to approach 30 percent in some cities.

CAUSE Financial crises in the stock market, triggered by an economic slump in Europe and the collapse of Jay Cooke and Company in the United States

IMPACT Produced widespread business failures, mass unemployment, a national rail strike, a tax revolt, construction of armories, and a general sense that industrialization and class divisions had arrived

nation's second transcontinental line. Cooke had difficulty finding buyers for North Pacific securities, in part because the feverish commercial activity had made American investors cautious. Further damping the investment climate were the devastating fires in Chicago (1871) and Boston (1872), which placed demands on capital markets to finance rebuilding. The Credit Mobilier railroad scandal in Congress, which unfolded in the spring of 1873, added to the gloomy outlook for railroads. The nation had an unfavorable balance of trade with Europe, causing an outflow of gold. Further, uncertainties in Europe foiled Cooke's intention of selling rail bonds abroad. French war reparations to Germany following the Franco-Prussian War of 1870–71 and railroad over-expansion triggered a financial crisis in Austria and Germany in May 1873. The contagion spread to the United States by September and then recrossed the Atlantic to roil markets in England, France, and Russia. The economic shakeout from these events caused a depression that circled the globe.

The financial crisis caused more than 400 American banks to fail between 1873 and 1878. Savings banks, which granted mortgages on homes and busi-

ness properties, watched their assets plummet in value. A banking panic swept through San Francisco in 1875 and Chicago in 1877. The decline in stock and bond prices hurt commercial banks. An index of leading stock prices hit a low point in 1877 after losing 40 percent of its value since 1873. Railroad stocks dropped 60 percent. More than 47,000 businesses closed their doors between 1873 and 1878, a decline exceeded only in the Great Depression of the 1930s.

Railroad revenue dropped annually between 1873 and 1877. Construction of new track mileage fell from 5,217 miles laid in 1873 to only 1,606 miles in 1875. Having borrowed heavily to expand, the railroads were vulnerable to a sharp downturn in the economy. By 1874, a quarter of railroad debt was in default, and numerous companies slid into bankruptcy. Securities brokers, including the famed financier J. P. Morgan, moved to protect their investors by reorganizing failed lines into new companies. Thereafter, the railroads were closely linked to the securities industry and to northern investors. Lines that survived the crisis experimented with pooling agreements as a way of avoiding devastating rate wars. The Interstate Commerce Act of 1887, which grew out of these railroad problems, made pooling illegal.

Troubles for railroads meant hardship for thousands of workers. The *New York Labor Standard,* a working-class newspaper, observed in 1877 that "in every State of the Union men are out of employment by thousands. The poorhouses and prisons are full to overflowing; . . . an army of tramps, homeless and desperate, wander back and forth through all the land, while our cities swarm with the destitute and starving." No accurate count of unemployment in the 1870s exists, but contemporary accounts indicate widespread layoffs. Joblessness perhaps reached 16 percent of all industrial workers during the winter of 1873–74. This rate probably was double in major cities such as New York and Chicago. This mass of jobless individuals motivated Carroll Wright, chief of the Massachusetts Bureau of the Statistics of Labor, to launch a pioneering survey of unemployment. But several additional depressions and 60 years passed before the federal government continuously monitored the level of joblessness. Besides unemployment, wage cuts swept through most industries. A congressional investigation in 1879 reported declines of 8 to 50 percent in workers' pay.

Smaller paychecks and widespread layoffs put a burden on local government and private organizations to assist the newly poor. Many of the unemployed turned to "tramping" from town to town to find work or, at the least, a meal. Although no modern welfare programs were in place, some communities did provide assistance, such as soup kitchens to provide transients with a meal. Metropolitan police opened their stations for homeless men and women during the winter. Numerous cities expanded or established public projects to help the jobless. Overwhelmed by the crush of the needy, charity leaders pushed to discriminate between the truly needy, often called the "deserving poor," and so-called freeloaders, or "undeserving poor." Local officials demanded tougher laws against vagrancy, which made begging illegal and allowed communities to arrest individuals who had no visible means of support. Massachusetts could sentence vagrants to two years in the state workhouse. Ohio enacted a three-year jail sentence for kindling a fire on a public thoroughfare.

Workers staged rallies in cities around the country, demanding that government offer help. In Scranton, Pennsylvania, hungry workers marched in a snowstorm in 1877 demanding "bread or blood, relief or riot." A protest meeting in New York City had ended in a "riot" in 1874. On January 13, some 7,000 workers assembled in Manhattan at Tompkins Square to urge the city to create public works jobs. After several speeches in the brutal cold, police forcibly dispersed the crowd, injuring many. New York mayor William F. Havemeyer refused to talk to this "body of crazy men" and called a public works program something that "belonged to other countries, not ours." In New York and throughout the nation many viewed labor demonstrations as un-American, alien, and advancing "communism."

Panic erupts on Wall Street in front of the office of Jay Cooke and Company. *(Library of Congress)*

In the coal fields of Pennsylvania, hit hard by the depression, miners organized a secret society known as the Molly Maguires to protest wage cuts. Operatives of the Pinkerton Detective Agency infiltrated the group, which led to the conviction and execution of 20 miners on trumped-up charges. In California, Denis Kearney, an Irish immigrant who ran a trucking business, led worker protests against railroad monopolies and Chinese immigrants. Anti-Chinese riots erupted in San Francisco in 1877. Strikes broke out at numerous locations, including in the coal mines of Ohio, where owners replaced striking white miners with African Americans. Anger and frustration erupted into widespread violence during the Great Strike of 1877. The conflict began as a walkout of workers on the Baltimore and Ohio Railroad, which had slashed wages. The strike spread to other cities in the East and Midwest, where random violence destroyed considerable railroad property. State militias called out to maintain order killed scores of demonstrators.

The uncertain outcome of strikes and demonstrations persuaded some workers to seek redress through politics. A variety of new minor parties, including Socialists, appeared in the wake of the Great Strike. In 1878, a coalition of the Socialistic Labor Party and the Greenback Party netted a million votes and elected 14 members to Congress. In 1880, the National Greenback Labor Party platform advocated an income tax (with higher rates on the wealthy), a bureau of labor statistics, and programs to assist workers. Despite this political activism, workers got little from government. Middle-class voters and business leaders tended to see the organization of workers as radical and dangerous, rather than efforts to help families weather the economic storm.

Farmers suffered too during the depression. Demand for agricultural commodities in the United States fell at a time when American farmers were experiencing new competition in international markets. When prices for agricultural goods fell, land values also declined. When farmers could not meet mortgage payments, foreclosures stripped them of their homes. Some states enacted "stay" laws that delayed bank repossession of property. In the South, the depression drove many farmers into cotton production, the region's primary cash crop, a shift that contributed to the acceleration of farm tenancy.

President Ulysses S. Grant was personally caught up in the agricultural depression. He had invested in a farm near St. Louis, which he had hoped to develop into a country estate. Declining prices for cattle and farm products forced him to auction off this stock and rent the land in 1875. Many farmers turned to the Grange as a place to air their grievances. Founded in 1867 to promote agricultural interests, the organization pressured state lawmakers for relief, such as the regulation of railroads. Numerous states placed limits on railroad rates during the mid-1870s.

Farmers, however, suffered less than did industrial workers. Moreover, agriculture led the way out of the depression. Poor yields in Europe increased orders for American agricultural commodities late in the decade. By 1878, the United States had a large export balance, which brought gold streaming back across the Atlantic. Foreign investment in American properties accelerated as well. The economy picked up speed in 1879, stocks advanced to new highs in 1880, and prosperity continued until the recession of 1884.

The panic and depression had a jarring impact on finances of local government. Because cities, towns, and counties paid for the largest share of public services (such as schools, police, and public health), their treasuries were at risk when the economy slumped. Besides carrying large debts incurred from public improvements, such as roads and water works, many municipalities increased spending to assist the unemployed during the hard times. Yet the economic slowdown lowered the value of property, which shrank the local tax base and shriveled revenue inflows. Faced with mounting deficits, municipalities practiced rigorous "retrenchment" by cutting expenditures. State governments experienced similar stringency, despite raising taxes on business. Faced with taxpayers' demands for "strict economy," officials reduced state spending.

The financial crisis sparked a tax revolt among property owners, who complained about unnecessary expenditures and loans. They demanded that caps be placed on the finances of local government. Lawmakers responded by amending the constitutions of 21 states between 1873 and 1879 with provisions that restricted the amount of debt that cities could assume. Some states also limited property taxes and prohibited certain municipal investments, such as in private rail companies. Northern states imposed restrictions on state government taxation and borrowing. In addition, lawmakers gave mayors and governors more power over the administration of financial accounts.

Federal revenues fell 31 percent between 1872 and 1879, a drop due mainly to slumping tariff collections, a sign of the decline in business. Only a substantial reduction of spending kept the U.S. Treasury solvent. Congress increased tariff rates 10 percent on manufacturing items in 1875. Calling tariffs a tax on consumers, Democrats attempted to lower custom duties in 1876 and 1878 but could not overcome Republican support of "protectionism." Republicans argued that high tariffs would speed economic recovery and that a reduction of revenue jeopardized the exchange of paper currency (or "greenbacks") for gold via the Resumption Act of 1875. Preserving the gold standard, or "sound money" as supporters called it—was a high priority to conservatives. Nonetheless, Congress passed the Bland-Allison bill in 1878, which added silver to the monetary base. Two hours after President Rutherford B. Hayes rejected the measure, Congress overrode his veto. Hayes later vetoed a bill to restrict Chinese immigration, legislation born of economic frustrations as well as ethnic prejudice and political opportunism.

The struggles over these economic issues are traceable to problems caused by the panic of 1873 and the ensuing depression. The hard times also helped the Democrats win a majority of the House of Representatives in 1874 and to capture the majority of popular (though not electoral) votes in the presidential election of 1876, which resulted in the election of Rutherford B. Hayes. Longer-lasting repercussions of the economic crisis of the 1870s are visible in popular attitudes. Historians have detected a shift among the middle and upper classes toward conservatism during the 1870s. Once, these groups had seen blue-collar workers as partners in a harmonious economy. By the end of the 1870s, class differences had become more pronounced, as workers came to be viewed as a distinct and sometimes dangerous entity called labor. Propertied citizens demanded stronger militias and fortified armories to protect against future worker uprisings. Some sought to restrict voting only to property owners. Surveying the conflicts and transformation of these years, observers thought that the crisis of the 1870s heralded the arrival of America's industrial age.

See also 1857 FINANCIAL PANIC AND DEPRESSION; 1872 CREDIT MOBILIER SCANDAL; 1877 GREAT RAILROAD STRIKE; 1893 FINANCIAL PANIC AND DEPRESSION.

Ballard C. Campbell

FURTHER READING:

Foner, Eric. *Reconstruction: America's Unfinished Revolution.* New York: Harper and Row, 1988.

Kindleberger, Charles. *Historical Economics: Art or Science?* New York: Harvester/Wheatsheaf, 1990.

Nevins, Allan. *The Emergence of Modern America, 1865–1878.* New York: Macmillan, 1927.

Re/ Rezneck, Samuel. "Distress, Relief, and Discontent in the United States During the Depression of 1873–78." *Journal of Political Economy* 58 (1950): 494–512.

1873 ◆ LOCUST INVASIONS ACROSS THE GREAT PLAINS

The locust invasions of the 1870s had a devastating impact on farmers in the Midwest, the Great Plains, and the West. The plague of Rocky Mountain locusts began in 1873 and continued through 1878, although its impact and extent varied by location. The locusts, or grasshoppers, were found as far east as Missouri and Minnesota and as far west as Utah and Nevada. The voracious pests ate everything in their path, including field crops, gardens, and orchards. Before leaving an area, the locusts generally laid their eggs, guaranteeing that unless weather conditions changed, the infestation would continue in the following year. Hot, dry conditions usually invited locust infestations.

FACTBOX

PLACE The Midwest, Great Plains, and West

DATE 1873–78

TYPE Plague of Rocky Mountain locusts

DESCRIPTION An insect invasion caused destruction of crops across a large area of the country, resulting in widespread despair and poverty.

CAUSE A periodic event caused by insects seeking the proper conditions to feed and to lay their eggs

COST Loss of agricultural production in many states; dollar value of crop loss estimated at $56 million for 1874 alone

IMPACT Farmers were forced to consider diversification into new crops and livestock. The invasions may have contributed to agrarian unrest in the late 19th century.

The arrival of the locusts was usually a dramatic event, remembered long after by area residents, many of whom were homesteaders who had recently settled the land. Farmers scanning the skies for rain clouds would notice a large dark cloud on the horizon. As they watched its approach, they might notice that the cloud glittered. Before long, the fields would be pelted by locusts, rather than raindrops, with hundreds, thousands, and tens of thousands descending at once. The insects would soon be eating the crops, as well as items of wood and cloth that they found in their paths. Infestations were capricious. The locusts arrived on the wind, and while some communities suffered terribly, others were spared. Those who suffered infestations saw dramatic crop losses. In affected counties in Minnesota, for example, the wheat yield fell by as much as 60 percent. The U.S. government estimated crop losses for 1874 alone at more than $56 million.

For farm families dependent on crops for both a cash income and their subsistence, the results were devastating. Families found themselves without food or clothing or the means to purchase them. Hunger and starvation spread through communities, forcing families to appeal for aid. Some received help through local charities, and state governments allocated some funds to assist the destitute. The federal government allowed homesteaders to take leave of their claims in order to find work without endangering their rights to the land. The government also allocated $30,000 for the purchase of seed wheat for affected farmers, but that seed wheat had to be spread across needy farm families in five states and territories. Unable to gain adequate aid, many coped by simply moving to areas that they hoped were uninfested.

Although experts suggested a number of solutions to the locust problem, such as the planting of forests, the use of irrigation, oiling the ditches and canals across which the locusts traveled, and collecting their eggs, none of the measures had much effect. The locusts consistently reappeared during drought periods such as the 1890s and 1930s. It would only be with the development of more effective pesticides during and after World War II that farmers would gain some measure of control over locusts and other insect pests.

The locust invasions, like other natural disasters, forced farmers to reevaluate their operations. Many diversified their crops and began to raise more livestock in response to the problems of these years. The experience of the locust invasions may very well have contributed to the rise of farm protest in the 1890s, when the Great Plains and West experienced yet another round of drought and locusts, and farmers demanded greater aid and attention than they had received in the 1870s.

Pamela Riney-Kehrberg

FURTHER READING:

Atkins, Annette. *Harvest of Grief: Grasshopper Plagues and Public Assistance in Minnesota, 1873–1878*. St. Paul: Minnesota Historical Society Press, 1984.

Ise, John. *Sod and Stubble: The Story of a Kansas Farm*. Lawrence: University Press of Kansas, 1996.

Packard, A. S., Jr. *Report on the Rocky Mountain Locust and Other Insects Now Injuring or Likely to Injure Field and Garden Crops in the United States*. Washington, D.C.: United States Geological Survey, Department of the Interior, 1877.

Schlebecker, John T. "Grasshoppers in American Agricultural History." *Agricultural History* 27 (July 1953): 85–93.

1874 ◆ MILL RIVER DAM COLLAPSE

The Mill River flood in western Massachusetts was the first major dam disaster in the United States and one of the greatest calamities of the 19th century. It happened early one May morning in 1874, in the hills above the Berkshire towns of Williamsburg and Northampton, when a reservoir dam used for water power suddenly burst, sending an avalanche of water down a narrow valley lined with factories and farms. Within an hour, 139 people were dead, and four mill villages were washed away. The Mill River flood instantly became one of the nation's big news stories. Newspapers and magazines recounted survivors' daring escapes from the floodwaters and described the horrors of the weeklong search for the dead among acres of debris. Investigations showed that the dam had collapsed because it was poorly and negligently constructed, but like many other disasters of the 19th century, no one was held accountable. The flood's legacy was that it prompted Massachusetts and nearby states to grasp the hazards of unregulated reservoirs and to pass landmark dam safety laws.

The Mill River is a slim, rocky stream, just 15 miles long, that tumbles down the foothills of the Berkshires into the Connecticut River. By the mid-19th century, it powered small-scale industries that made brass goods, grinding wheels, silk thread, buttons, and cotton and woolen fabrics. As the century wore on, the Mill River manufacturers, like their counterparts around New England, required more water to sustain profits. Increased flow allowed them to scale up production to stay competitive in the nationwide marketplace created by railroads. It also enabled them to counteract the effects of upstream deforestation as eroding soil washed downriver and silted in mill ponds, thereby reducing water storage capacity at the mills. The solution was to build an upstream storage reservoir that could be tapped as needed to provide a steady flow to the factories downstream. Thus, in 1864, 11 manufacturers formed the Williamsburg Reservoir Company to dam the upper reaches of the Mill River in Williamsburg. Completed in 1866,

FACTBOX

PLACE Williamsburg and Northampton, Massachusetts

DATE May 16, 1874

TYPE Flood caused by dam failure

DESCRIPTION Sudden break in reservoir dam sent 600 million gallons of water down Mill Valley, destroying factories and farms.

CAUSE Inadequate design and faulty construction of earthen reservoir dam

CASUALTIES 139 deaths, 740 made homeless

COST $1 million in property lost

IMPACT Massachusetts and nearby states passed dam safety measures.

the earthen embankment dam consisted of a stone wall—meant to keep the dam watertight—supported by massive banks of packed earth. It stretched 600 feet between hillsides and rose 43 feet above the river. The reservoir covered 100 acres.

In the absence of state regulation on dam construction, the reservoir company was free to design and build the dam as it pleased. Frustrated with the $100,000 cost of a design prepared by professional civil engineers, the company opted to dictate its own design to an incautious local engineer who wrote general specifications. The company then hired careless contractors for $24,000 who made the inadequate design worse. Despite repairs, the dam leaked and slumped for eight years. Anxious valley residents who questioned the dam's safety were reassured by the manufacturers that the dam would hold.

At seven o'clock on Saturday morning, May 16, 1874, when the reservoir was full, the damkeeper spied a 40-foot-wide slab of earth slide off the downstream face of the dam. Within minutes, dozens of streams spurted through the bank as it began to crumble. The damkeeper jumped on his bareback horse and raced three miles downriver to Williamsburg village. While he was warning the inhabitants there, the dam burst open. Reservoir water had found its way through the base of the poorly grouted stone wall and into the downstream bank which, once saturated, could no longer hold. Unsupported, the stone wall gave way to the pressure of the reservoir water. A convulsive boom roared through the hills that farmers miles away described as louder than the biggest clap of thunder they had ever heard. The breach quickly enlarged to nearly half the width of the dam, and 600 million gallons of water poured out, forming a flood wave 20 to 40 feet high that roared down the valley, picking up everything in its path. One observer said the wave looked like a hayroll, but instead of strands of hay, the roll was composed of timber, roofs, boulders, mill wheels, furniture, animals, and people, with no water visible.

Villagers had no warning except for the shouts of four brave men (the first was alerted by the damkeeper) who relayed the message down the valley by racing ahead of the flood in wagons and on horseback to alarm the factories first and then villagers at home. Most of the factory workers escaped, and the majority of the dead were women, children, and older people at home eating breakfast or doing morning chores. Half of the victims were immigrants, mostly from Canada and Ireland. Within an hour of the dam break, 139 were dead, 740 were homeless, and the villages of Williamsburg, Skinnerville, and Haydenville (in the town of Williamsburg) and Leeds (in the town of Northampton) were washed away. One million dollars in property was destroyed, most of it the value of the factories owned by reservoir company members, all uninsured.

Minutes after the flood passed, survivors began to search for the dead by culling through wreckage so dense and snarled that mattresses and quilts were knotted with belting and machinery, and hanks of raw silk were lodged with toys and potatoes. With no federal and state disaster relief programs, cleanup and relief were managed by local committees who organized thousands of volunteers and pleaded for Americans to send money to help the sufferers. When $100,000 was raised, it was called the largest outpouring of charity since the GREAT CHICAGO FIRE three years earlier.

Members of the Williamsburg Reservoir Company and Northampton bankers took charge of the valley's economic recovery. Although they rebuilt all the villages except Skinnerville, the valley never returned to its former prosperity. The heavy business losses had occurred as the era of profitable manufacturing on small New England rivers was ending, and so the flood hastened the decline of industry on the Mill River.

A coroner's inquest thoroughly investigated the disaster's cause. The verdict named five parties at fault: the reservoir company that owned the dam; the contractors who built it; the engineer who provided an inadequate design; the county commissioners who inspected and approved it; and the Massachusetts legislature that chartered the reservoir company without requiring any assurance that it was safe. There were no indictments, no fines, and no subsequent lawsuits. A year after the flood, in 1875, Massachusetts passed its first legislation regarding reservoir dam design, construction, and liability. Considered weak by today's standards, the law was, nevertheless, a first step toward safer dams.

Americans in 1874 saw the Mill River flood as a terrible calamity and as one example out of hundreds of disasters—including steamboat explosions, railroad bridge collapses, and mill fires—caused by the carelessness and dishonesty of self-interested manufacturers and businessmen. It took disasters such as the Mill River flood to expose such negligent practices and to serve as a catalyst for legislation to ensure public safety.

See also 1928 ST. FRANCIS DAM COLLAPSE.

Elizabeth M. Sharpe

FURTHER READING:

Sharpe, Elizabeth M. *In the Shadow of the Dam: The Aftermath of the Mill River Flood of 1874.* New York: Free Press, 2004.

1876 ◆ BATTLE OF LITTLE BIGHORN

The Battle of Little Bighorn of June 25–27, 1876, also known as "Custer's Last Stand," was the most famous battle of the American Indian Wars in the late 19th century and arguably the one with the greatest long-term cultural legacy. It was a three-part battle, although the most important and well-known part ended with the annihilation of five companies of the U.S. 7th Cavalry and the death of its famous and complicated commander, Lieutenant Colonel George Armstrong Custer.

The causes of the events leading to this great Indian victory are better known than the details of the battle itself, which still attract controversy. The Battle of Little Bighorn occurred as part of a broader campaign by the U.S. government to subdue the Plains Indians and force them onto the Great Sioux Reservation in South Dakota. The desire of the federal government to force the Indians to submit reached a crescendo after an expedition led by Custer discovered gold in the Black Hills in 1874. Covetousness on the part of the Americans was complicated by the fact that the U.S. government had granted the hills to the Lakota Sioux in the Treaty of 1868. Independent-minded Sioux and Northern Cheyenne Indians from different tribes under Gall, Sitting Bull, Crazy Horse, and other tribal leaders refused the government attempt to buy back the hills from them, and also thereafter the requirement to return to the reservation by January 1, 1876.

Soon the largest grouping ever of Indians hostile to the U.S. government gathered on the plains, approximately 8,000 people with upward of 2,500 warriors, including Hunkpapa, Oglala, Minneconjou, Brule, Blackfoot, Two Kettle, Sans Arc, and Northern Cheyenne. The U.S. Army, not entirely clear on the number and disposition of the people involved, resolved to defeat the Indians and force their compliance with the government's demands. General Philip Henry Sheridan devised a plan for a three-pronged assault on the Indians, with General George Crook to march north from Wyoming, General John Gibbon to march east from Fort Ellis in Montana, and General Alfred Howe Terry to attack west from Fort Abraham Lincoln in the Dakota

FACTBOX

PLACE Little Bighorn River, Montana

DATE June 25–27, 1876

TYPE Battle between the U.S. 7th Cavalry and Sioux and Northern Cheyenne tribes on the frontier during the United States's effort to subdue the Indians of the northern plains

DESCRIPTION Custer's midafternoon attack on June 25 on the largest gathering of Indians ever in the northern plains resulted in the destruction of his men in one of the most complete Indian victories in the Indian wars. "Custer's Last Stand," as it came to be known, became the most famous event of the Indian wars in the late 19th century.

CAUSE The battle resulted from concerted Indian resistance to the broader campaign of the United States to force the Plains Indian tribes to yield the Black Hills and return to the Great Sioux reservation in South Dakota. The immediate cause of the defeat was Custer's attack on a much larger Indian force.

CASUALTIES 263 American soldiers and approximately 60 Native Americans killed

IMPACT This great Indian victory blunted the U.S. Army's campaign to subdue the northern Plains Indians. The battle elevated Custer's exploits into the realm of myth.

territory. Custer, head of the 7th Cavalry, was the spearhead of Terry's movement.

An aggressive and headstrong commander, Custer was celebrated as the greatest of Indian fighters because of his victory over Black Kettle and the Southern Cheyenne at Washita in 1868, despite the killing of noncombatants and the controversial loss of some of his men. Custer was not above controversy and commonly ignored his orders, but he was skilled at warfare and self-promotion, and he remained a respected fighter and leader. As he moved toward the

Little Bighorn River in 1876, Custer was unaware of the number of warriors that awaited him and of the fact that a large Indian force had defeated Crook's troops on June 17 in the Battle of the Rosebud River. Custer did not anticipate that these Indians had moved to the large Little Bighorn camp and were strong, confident, and protective of the women and children in their village.

Custer was told to find the Indians and await further instruction. Terry had included a statement in his orders allowing a change of plans if "you shall see sufficient reasons for departing from them." This language was vague enough for Custer to act. Custer's Crow scouts had discovered a large Indian village on the morning of June 25, and a few of these Indians had happened on some lost supplies and triggered a response from the troops. Having lost the element of surprise, and not wanting to wait in case the Indians slipped out of his grasp, Custer determined to attack immediately without full reconnaissance. The scouts were released from duty and survived. One, named Curly, observed the battle and became a major source for information about Custer's fate, although his testimony was considered suspect by some at the time and is debated to this day.

The daytime assault was unorthodox since most army attacks on Indian villages occurred as surprises at dawn. Custer was nonplussed and confident. He was used to attacking superior numbers of Indians and considered American organization and tactics superior. He ordered Captain Frederick Benteen to move southwest with a battalion and, if the Indians appeared, to "pitch in." Custer then sent Major Marcus Reno across the Little Bighorn River to attack the village. Custer took five companies and marched parallel to Reno, although they could not see each other.

Major Reno's men soon encountered Indians and experienced very heavy fighting along what was later known as Reno Creek. Custer called for Captain Benteen with a note (written by an adjutant reading "Come on. Big Village. Be quick. Bring packs."). Meanwhile, Reno's men were quickly overmatched and retreated in panic. Reno himself lost nerve when he was splattered in blood after his scout was shot in the head.

Custer rushed his men toward the village in a split movement that rapidly became overwhelmed by Indian warriors from all sides. Historians disagree about what precisely happened, but in short order Custer and his men were totally wiped out. Testimony

of Indian participants and archaeologists who have studied the battlefield have helped to reconstruct a picture of the 7th Cavalry surrounded and pushed up what is now known as Custer Hill, and then destroyed. Brave Wolf, a Northern Cheyenne, recalled that "They were all drawn up in line of battle, shooting well and fighting hard, but there were so many people around them, that they could not help being killed." Young Two Men, another Northern Cheyenne, recalled that each soldier had to fight perhaps 40 warriors. The 210 dead included two of Colonel Custer's brothers, Tom Custer and Boston Custer; his nephew Armstrong Reed; and his brother-in-law Lieutenant James Calhoun. Tom Custer's heart was cut out, his body mutilated, and his head smashed. He was identified only by his tattoo. Nobody knows exactly when in the battle Custer died. He was shot in the left temple and the left breast, but for some reason, unlike most of his soldiers', his body was not scalped or mutilated. Although Custer's Last Stand is the best known part of the battle, the warriors proceeded to attack Benteen's and Reno's men strongly, and they were not relieved until the morning of June 27. All told, 263 American soldiers were killed; approximately 60 Native Americans were killed in these engagements.

In finding death, Custer also found immortality. His exploits, life, and "Last Stand" have been condemned, celebrated, and otherwise disputed virtually since the moment the battle ended. Custer's character, perceived heroism, and actions soon became larger than life. Custer's Last Stand became iconic in the mythology of the "Winning of the West" even though it was an uncommon total defeat of the U.S. Army. The substantial Indian victory at the Little Bighorn slowed but ultimately did not prevent their final subjugation by the United States.

Daniel S. Margolies

FURTHER READING:

Greene, Jerome A., ed. *Lakota and Cheyenne: Indian Views of the Great Sioux War, 1876–1877.* Norman: University of Oklahoma Press, 1994.

Utley, Robert M. *Cavalier in Buckskin: George Armstrong Custer and the Western Military Frontier.* Rev. ed. Norman: University of Oklahoma Press, 2001.

Welch, James, and Paul Stekler. *Killing Custer: The Battle of the Little Bighorn and the Fate of the Plains Indians.* New York: Norton, 1994.

1876 ◆ ASHTABULA BRIDGE COLLAPSE

At about 7:30 P.M. on Friday, December 29, 1876, Daniel McGuire, engineer of the Lake Shore & Michigan Southern Railway train, the *Pacific Express,* traveling west between Erie, Pennsylvania, and Cleveland—with Chicago as its destination—heard an ominous crack and felt a sagging as he eased his train over a 165-foot iron truss bridge spanning Ashtabula Creek in northeast Ohio. Opening his throttle wide, McGuire managed to bring his engine to the west abutment when the bridge gave way. Amid heavy snow, stiff winds, and freezing temperatures, all the remaining train—11 cars and a second engine—fell 72 feet into the creek. About 160 people, including 15 crew members, were aboard. As cars fell, perpendicular or at angles, and crashed on top of one another, stoves and lamps lit the cars on fire. Within minutes, flames engulfed trapped survivors, who screamed in agony and desperation from within the pile of cars. A volunteer fire crew from the nearby town of Ashtabula struggled to the crushed and burning cars, but the station agent organizing the rescue made a potentially fatal decision to try to pull survivors from the wreckage rather than to fight the flames. In a chaotic, ghastly scene of blinding snow, debris, fire, injured and shocked passengers, and charred bodies, rescuers attempted to locate trapped people only to give up toward midnight and leave the fires to burn themselves out.

An estimated 92 people died from the crash, fire, or drowning in the Ashtabula Creek bed or later from injuries sustained in the disaster. About 50 people were burned unrecognizably. Sixty-four people survived the country's worst railroad accident to that time. The dead included Philip Paul Bliss, the composer of hymns. According to witnesses, Bliss was one of a number of survivors of the crash who subsequently perished attempting to pull family members from the burning wreck.

An investigation in 1877 by the Ohio state legislature revealed that back in 1863–65, when the Ashtabula Creek Bridge was built, engineers had warned Cleveland railroad builder and philanthropist Amasa Stone, promoter of the patented Howe

truss design, that such a lengthy iron truss span might not be safe. Having overseen numerous similar bridges, usually with shorter spans or made of wooden trusses, Stone ignored these warnings, satisfied by a test involving six locomotives shortly after completion. Subsequent inspections had been cursory; at the time, the dangers of metal fatigue were not well understood. Some in the press implied that the legendary stinginess of the railroad's owner, Cornelius Vanderbilt, who died of old age a few weeks later, was to blame for the "Ashtabula Horror." But the railroad's chief engineer, Charles Collins, blamed himself and committed suicide shortly after testifying to Ohio investigators. In 1883, Stone also shot himself to death, though the bridge collapse was only one of a number of setbacks that sent him into fatal despair.

The Lake Shore Railroad paid some $500,000 in damage claims. The railroad soon erected a standard, wooden truss bridge in place of the collapsed iron one. Engineers took from the disaster the lessons that iron in bridges required continual scrutiny and that bridge builders should follow standard design specifications. The engineering profession began to publish such standards in the 1880s.

Alan Lessoff

FURTHER READING:

Gasparini, D. A., and Melissa Fields. "Collapse of the Ashtabula Bridge on December 29, 1876." *Journal of Performance of Constructed Materials* 7 (May 1993): 109–125.

Peet, Stephen D. *The Ashtabula Disaster.* Chicago: J. S. Goodman, 1877.

1876–1877 ◆ CONTESTED PRESIDENTIAL ELECTION

The disputed presidential election of 1876 was the culmination of the election disputes that arose from Reconstruction after the Civil War. During the late 1860s and 1870s, a large majority of southern whites denied the legitimacy of Republican state governments elected by black votes under constitutions ratified according to the Reconstruction Acts. When southern Democrats—almost all of whom were white—resorted to fraud, violence, and terror to suppress black voting, Republican election boards rejected or changed returns, often relying on the simple conviction that black voters were Republicans rather than on hard evidence of wrongdoing. During the 1876 election, the impact of this power struggle threw the nation into a dangerous political crisis.

In the South during Reconstruction, rival candidates often claimed to have won the same local and state offices. Sometimes, unsuccessful candidates turned to the local courts to resolve these disputes. At other times, they threatened force, leading one side or another or both to appeal to President Ulysses S. Grant to carry out the federal government's constitutional obligation to guarantee each state a republican form of government. Democrats won the control of several southern states through such violence, which persisted through the 1870s. In other states, Republicans hung on to power with the aid of federal troops, which the president authorized. By 1875, however, Grant expressed impatience with the repeated requests for federal intervention.

The 1876 presidential election pitted Republican Rutherford B. Hayes against Democrat Samuel J.

FACTBOX

PLACE U.S. Congress, Washington, D.C.

DATE November 1876–March 1877

TYPE Disputed election and political crisis

DESCRIPTION Disputed electoral votes from southern states threatened to disrupt the election of the president.

CAUSE Persistent violence and fraud in southern elections during the Reconstruction era

IMPACT The compromise led national Republicans to abandon support for southern Republicans, allowing the erosion of rights secured for African Americans during Reconstruction.

Tilden. The contest took place in an atmosphere of violence and intimidation, especially in South Carolina (with seven electoral votes), Louisiana (eight electoral votes), and Florida (four electoral votes). In each of these three states, a majority of voters were African American and presumably Republican. In South Carolina and Louisiana, especially, Democrats campaigned in armed, uniformed groups, broke up Republican meetings by force, and threatened Republican candidates and voters. Republicans alleged similar conduct in parts of Florida. Although the raw returns from the election on November 7 gave all three states and their 19 electoral votes to Tilden, Republican election boards had the power to counteract the fraud and violence. This emerging dispute took on immense importance because the presidential election was close.

Nationwide, Tilden appeared to have won a majority of the popular canvas by roughly a quarter-million votes, but the electoral vote was extremely tight, with Tilden leading 184 to 166. If the three disputed southern states cast all their 19 electoral votes for Hayes, the Republicans would win the presidency by a single vote. Therefore, national Republican leaders, many of whom had been distancing themselves from southern Republicans, encouraged the election boards to act firmly to counteract fraud. Each party claimed that the other was attempting to steal the election. Both sent observers south, especially to Louisiana, to monitor the actions of the election boards. Meanwhile, President Grant ordered federal troops to maintain the status quo to prevent Democrats, who were better organized and led by Confederate veterans, from seizing power by force.

In November and December, state Republican election officials in each of the three disputed states rejected voting returns from counties where they found evidence of violence, based on personal testimonies and voting results that were at odds with the counties' racial makeup. These officials awarded the election to the Republican candidates. The Republican governors of South Carolina, Louisiana, and Florida certified the votes of the Republican electors to Congress. Charging fraud, Democratic state officers certified the votes of the Democratic electors. Thus each of the three southern states had two sets of conflicting electoral votes.

Under the U.S. Constitution, the presiding officer of the Senate, usually the vice president, is required to count the electoral votes in the presence of both houses of Congress. But it is silent on how to proceed if the results are disputed. If the disputed electoral votes were not counted at all, no candidate would have received a majority. In that case, the election would have been turned over to the House of Representatives, as the Constitution mandates. The Democratic congressional majority would certainly have elected Tilden. However, Republicans, who held a majority in the Senate, insisted that the presiding officer, a Republican senator who stood in for the deceased vice president, was obligated to count the votes that came from the governors. Angry Democrats blasted what they saw as a virtual coup d'état. Some threatened violent resistance. President Grant

controlled the army, but a number of state militias were responsible to Democratic governors. People worried about the prospect of another civil war. Most Democrats, however, believed it would be suicidal to be identified with rebellion again. By the same token, public pressure induced Republicans to seek a peaceful solution to the impasse.

In January 1877, over the objections of Hayes's closest allies, a coalition of Republicans and Democrats created a special electoral commission of 15 members. If the two houses of Congress could not agree which electoral votes to count from a state, both sets would be referred to the commission, which would consider the case and report to Congress. The electoral commission would consist of five Republican congressmen, five Democratic congressmen, and five justices of the Supreme Court. Four justices, two Republicans and two Democrats, would name the fifth Supreme Court member. The plan seemed to be a victory for Democrats because everyone expected the four Supreme Court justices to choose Justice David Davis, an independent who leaned toward the Democrats, as the fifth court member. But when the Illinois state legislature suddenly elected Davis to the U.S. Senate, the justices settled on Joseph P. Bradley, a Republican, who seemed unsympathetic to his party's Reconstruction policy.

On February 1, the two houses of Congress met to count the electoral vote, as the Constitution prescribed. Democratic congressmen objected to counting Florida's votes, which went to Hayes, and they appealed to the commission. To Democrats' dismay, the commissioners decided by a strict 8-7 party-line vote that they were not authorized to verify the certificates sent by the various state officers to see whether they accurately reflected the actual vote. The Republican Senate voted to accept the report, while the Democratic House voted to reject it. So Florida's electoral votes went to Hayes. The result foretold the decision in the succeeding cases. The commission reported similarly on Louisiana on February 23 and South Carolina on February 27, the votes going to Hayes after the Senate accepted the commission's reports.

Some angry Democrats determined to use delaying tactics to prevent the House from accepting the remaining electoral ballots before its term expired on March 3—just hours before Grant's term as president would end, potentially leaving the country without a leader. But Speaker of the House Samuel J. Randall, a Democrat backed by most Democrats as well as Republicans, ruled all dilatory motions out of order. He was encouraged to do so by secret negotiations between Hayes's advisers and southern Democrats. Hayes believed Republican Reconstruction policy had become outdated. Moreover, he sought to support southern Republicans by stressing economic issues rather than interfering in local elections. Informing southern Democrats of his intentions, he promised not to intervene militarily in their states. Thus in the so-called Compromise of 1877, Republicans agreed to end Reconstruction efforts if the South and Democrats agreed to accept Hayes's victory as president. Hayes was declared president on March 2, with 185 electoral votes to Tilden's 184. Inaugurated three days later, Hayes proved true to his word, rejecting southern Republican pleas to intervene in local elections. In Florida, the courts recognized the Democratic claimants for state offices. But in South Carolina and Louisiana, the Republicans relinquished their claims to state office rather than fight Democratic militias.

The election crisis of 1876–77 made clear to Americans the danger posed by political instability and the sometimes deadly struggle for power that raged in the South. To avoid similar crises, it was necessary either to use force to secure fair and peaceful elections and protect the constitutional rights of African Americans or to abandon the effort. Hayes concluded that there was not enough political support for the former course. Only by winning white support in the South could Republicans hope to secure fair and peaceful elections, and this required the elevation of economic issues and the subordination of issues of racial justice. However, this program proved futile as well. Hayes's decision began the process by which white southerners reversed the gains African Americans had won in Reconstruction and ushered in a long era of segregation and discrimination. Some 80 years would pass before Americans made a second, more successful, but still incomplete, effort at establishing racial justice.

See also 1800–1801 PRESIDENTIAL ELECTION CRISIS; 1824–1825 PRESIDENTIAL ELECTION DEADLOCK; 2000 PRESIDENTIAL ELECTION STALEMATE.

Michael Les Benedict

FURTHER READING:

Benedict, Michael Les. "Southern Democrats in the Crisis of 1876–1877: A Reconsideration of *Reunion and Reaction.*" *Journal of Southern History* 46 (November 1980): 489–524.

Polakoff, Keith Ian. *The Politics of Inertia: The Election of 1876 and the End of Reconstruction.* Baton Rouge: Louisiana State University Press, 1973.

Rehnquist, William H. *Centennial Crisis: The Disputed Election of 1876.* New York: Knopf, 2004.

Woodward, C. Vann. *Reunion and Reaction: The Compromise of 1877 and the End of Reconstruction.* 1951. Reprint with new preface, New York: Oxford University Press, 1999.

1877 ◆ GREAT RAILROAD STRIKE

On the morning of July 16, 1877, only miles outside of Baltimore, Maryland, a railroad worker on Engine 32 of the Baltimore & Ohio Railroad (B&O) walked off his post as the train's fireman and convinced others to join him. Within two weeks of this spontaneous action, workers from St. Louis to Syracuse and from Galveston to Chicago had left their jobs, demanding higher wages and improved working conditions. In total, by the first week of August, more than 100,000 workers, many unconnected with railroad labor, had joined the first nationwide general strike in U.S. history.

The strike also marked the first widespread use of federal and state troops to suppress labor unrest.

No central leadership directed this outpouring of working-class discontent, yet all participants struck in the context of both their seemingly permanent dependence on industrial wage labor and the more immediate deprivation of a severe economic crisis. In the wake of the Civil War (1861–65), the pace of industrialization in the United States had increased rapidly, and a critical component of this expansion was the railroad industry, which between 1869 and 1879 had seen workers forge the iron, lay the rails,

FACTBOX

PLACE Many cities and small towns, mostly in the northern and midwestern United States, but also in the South and Far West

DATE July 16–August 1, 1877

TYPE Labor strikes, community riots, and violent military repression

DESCRIPTION Railroad workers, with no central leadership, struck across the country. In some places the discontent of the railroad workers pushed other workers to strike as well. In large cities, such as Baltimore, Pittsburgh, and Chicago, the strikes were put down with the first widespread use of state and federal troops to quell labor unrest among industrial workers.

CAUSE Expansion of industrial capitalism, economic depression, and wage cuts

CASUALTIES More than 100 deaths, with many other injuries

IMPACT More than a decade of vigorous political and union organizing among workers, increasing hostility of business owners toward strikes, construction of armories in many towns and cities, and a public consciousness of the "labor question"

and run the trains on 50,000 miles of new track. Since the fall of 1873, however, the American economy had been reeling from the effects of a financial panic and industrial depression. Yet between 1873 and 1876 the Pennsylvania (PRR) and B&O Railroads each paid 10 percent cash dividends to their stockholders, while workers on these lines and in other industries bore the worst costs of the decline in production. Through 1877, average wages among workers had declined by as much as 45 percent from their 1873 levels, and 3 million Americans could not find jobs.

The more specific grievances of the strikers that sparked the fuel of unemployment and low wages came from decisions by the largest eastern railroad companies: the PRR, the New York Central & Hudson, the Erie, and the B&O. These companies had recently met in Chicago to collude over shipping rates and also to reduce all employees' wages by 10 percent. By early July most eastern rail workers had been forced to stomach the cut.

On the B&O, where the strike wave began, its outcome marked an ill omen for the conflicts developing elsewhere in the country. After workers succeeded in bringing the entire length of the line to a halt and local militia refused to disperse workers, President Rutherford Hayes called in federal troops to break the strike. In Baltimore, militia killed 11 civilians before rioters burned railroad property and more troops arrived to restore order.

Coming only days after news of the struggle on the B&O, the railroad strike on the PRR in Pittsburgh, Pennsylvania, shocked the nation. For three days, workers prevented freight trains from leaving the city. As the sympathetic Pittsburgh militia was unwilling to break up the strike, Governor John Hartranft called in 600 men from the First Division of the Pennsylvania Militia based in Philadelphia. On July 21, these troops fired into a crowd of workers and community members assembled at a railroad crossing in the city, killing at least 20 citizens.

That evening, Pittsburghers rioted, destroying 39 buildings and more than 1,200 freight cars owned by the PRR. Most of the rioters were not workers but community members reacting to the "invasion" of the Philadelphia militia. The following day, the Philadelphia militiamen escaped the city but not before killing 20 more citizens as they fled. Until July 28, when more state troops arrived after breaking strikes in Reading, Harrisburg, and Altoona, workers in Pittsburgh controlled tracks usually commanded by the largest corporation in the United States.

In other cities, the extent of the labor unrest (and its violent repression) spread far beyond rail lines. In St. Louis, a citywide "Workingman's Party" formed and demanded an eight-hour workday and an end to child labor. Declaring a general strike on the city's industries on July 24, workers nearly completely shut down the city's business for two days before police and federal troops arrived and arrested its leaders. Fears of tumult spread across the country as newspapers talked of revolution, working-class uprisings, and, as a *New York Times* headline put it, "The Reign of Mob Law." In Chicago on July 26, workers and police clashed, leaving 18 laborers dead. In San Francisco, a gathering of more than 8,000 white workingmen, assembled in support of the strikers in the East, took on a nativist tone as these workers lashed out violently against Chinese immigrants.

July 1877 was also a formative moment for workers in the smaller railroad towns and market centers across the United States. In tiny Terre Haute, Indiana, the strikers on the Vandalia Railroad stressed the unity of interests between themselves and the line's owners. The emphasis by strikers on "class harmony" may have helped avoid the deadly violence experienced in Pittsburgh, but it did not prevent the strike's leaders from being jailed or the workers from returning to their jobs without achieving their demands.

All told, by the end of July, more than 100 Americans had been killed as many strikes were brutally repressed by state and federal troops. Most workers returned to their jobs without gaining any material benefits for their efforts—wages remained at subsistence levels for many, while others were blacklisted from entire industries. Despite the short-term failure of the largest strikes, however, this experience marked the emergence of a decade of vigorous union and third-party political organizing by workers.

For middle-class and elite citizens, unfamiliar with the privations and struggles of the working class, the strikes and riots of 1877 also marked the emergence of a public consciousness on the "labor question." In general, these Americans responded to the strikes and riots with a new apprehension toward the potential (but very real) power of the working class. Elites also took concrete steps to ensure their physical and military dominance over workers. Industrialists in New York City, for example, immediately began to build armories to house national guard troops as a measure for quelling any future worker violence. Similar steps were taken in other large cities. Through the rest of the 19th century and into the 20th century, the use of overt physical violence on strikers, whether through the deployment of militia or the hiring of private security forces, would color many labor disputes.

In the 1880s, even as elites drew the line in the sand and staked out their militarized opposition to working-class organizing and autonomy, the development of working-class institutions increased dramatically. In Pittsburgh for example, workers, beaten badly in the disorganization and rage in 1877, formed the Greenback-Labor Party of Allegheny County. The party fared well in the fall of 1877 in working-class wards and grew dramatically over the next three years. Additionally, the Knights of Labor, an underground organization in the city during the 1870s, and the American Federation of Labor,

Wielding swords, soldiers on horseback attack a crowd of workers during the great railroad strike of 1877. *(Library of Congress)*

founded in 1886, both emerged to organize segments of the working class.

The 1877 strike, then, represented a critical turning point in the history of American class relations. In its wake, industrialists and other elites sought to defend their property through physically dominating workers and repressing strikes. For many workers, the strike's suppression laid bare the illusions of both an impartial government and the "unified interests" of capital and labor while catalyzing further working-class organization.

Kevin C. Brown

FURTHER READING:

Bruce, Robert V. *1877: Year of Violence.* New York: Bobbs-Merrill, 1959.

Foner, Philip S. *The Great Labor Uprising of 1877.* New York: Monad Press, 1977.

Stowell, David O. *Streets, Railroads, and the Great Strike of 1877.* Chicago: University of Chicago Press, 1999.

Stromquist, Shelton. *A Generation of Boomers: The Pattern of Railroad Labor Conflict in Nineteenth-Century America.* Urbana: University of Illinois Press, 1987.

1878 ◆ YELLOW FEVER EPIDEMIC

In the summer of 1878, the *Aedes Aegypti* mosquito made its presence felt in New Orleans, where a virulent reoccurrence of yellow fever broke out. With its proximity to the sea, New Orleans provided the entry point for the dangerous insect, and the city's public wells provided a breeding paradise for the mosquito. The tendency for crowds to gather near these cisterns made it possible for a mosquito, which is unable to fly very far, to easily feed on human blood. The death toll from the epidemic in New Orleans and from its journey up the Mississippi, Ohio, and Tennessee Rivers over the next four months is estimated at 20,000 individuals.

Yellow fever is a viral disease that derives its name from the jaundiced appearance of the infected person. Yellow fever symptoms unfold over distinct phases. There is the incubation period where the virus lays dormant for three to six days, followed by an acute phase involving fever, muscle pain, headache, shivers, and vomiting. While most people may recover after the acute phase, some continue on to the toxic phase, which involves jaundice, black vomit, and kidney failure, and sometimes death.

In 1878, Americans had already experienced this exotic disease. Its reoccurrence brought back memories of its visitation to New Orleans in 1853. In the intervening years, the cause of the ailment remained unknown, and no cure existed, filling people with dread about contracting the disease. When word reached American officials that yellow fever had appeared abroad, President Rutherford B. Hayes signed the Quarantine Act of 1878, which granted the Marine Hospital Service the power to prevent sailors afflicted with the disease from disembarking from incoming ships. Lawmakers assumed that barring entry to infected persons would be adequate protection to the population on land.

In spite of the preventive measure, two ships slipped through the embargo in New Orleans during 1878. The *Emily B. Souder* arrived in late May 1878 and was allowed to dock after a sailor believed to be afflicted with malaria was removed from the ship. Yellow fever is hard to recognize in its early stages and has similar symptoms to such other tropical diseases as malaria. The misdiagnosis of what

FACTBOX

PLACE New Orleans, Louisiana; Memphis, Tennessee; Vicksburg, Mississippi; and towns along the Mississippi, Ohio, and Tennessee Rivers

DATE May–November 1878

TYPE Epidemic

DESCRIPTION Yellow fever, a viral disease that causes jaundice due to kidney failure, struck the South.

CAUSE *Aedes aegypti* mosquito

CASUALTIES Approximately 20,000 deaths

COST $100 million in trade losses and relief efforts

IMPACT Passage of the Quarantine Act of 1878; formation of permanent National Board of Health in 1879; New Orleans and numerous other cities improved sanitary conditions by building sewer and drainage systems; and increased attention to finding the cause and means of prevention of yellow fever

was probably yellow fever was discovered only after another crew member fell sick, while yet another perished that same night. Soon after the ship left New Orleans, the *Charles B. Wood* docked; within weeks, all members of the captain's family had fallen ill. The disease, and likely the vector had arrived in New Orleans, but the foundation had already been set for an epidemic. The previous winter had been mild, the spring long, and the summer hot—all aiding in producing the optimum environment for the *Aedes Aegypti* mosquito to breed.

The "yellow jack," as the scourge was called, struck rich and poor alike. Because doctors were at a loss to cure the disease, they treated its symptoms. In this environment of misinformation, people employed well-meaning and essentially dangerous methods such as bleeding and sweating to cure the fever. The city of New Orleans declared an epidemic in late July, but it was already too late. Those who could afford it had already fled. Quarantines were imposed in Shreveport, Memphis, and Galveston, with Mississippi and Texas officials threatening to destroy railroad tracks and shoot at boats attempting to dock at their ports. These so-called "shotgun" roadblocks turned out to be the only effective deterrent to afflicted individuals migrating with the disease. Yet many had already infiltrated these and other areas, carrying the disease with them.

A mass exodus of people from New Orleans and from Memphis aided in spreading the disease. In just four months, the disease spread throughout the Mississippi and Ohio River valleys, and along parts of the Tennessee River. The population that remained in these areas tended to be poor. Their only assistance came from volunteer and relief organizations, such as the Ocean Springs Relief Society, the Howard Association of New Orleans, the citizens of Galveston, Texas, and the Moss Point Relief Committee. But only the onset of a particularly cold winter in late November 1878 had the power to stem the epidemic.

The epidemic caused huge economic and human losses. In New Orleans, more than 4,000 people died from the fever; approximately 7,000 more perished in Memphis and Vicksburg. In addition to fatalities, New Orleans lost one-fifth of its population due to the migration of its citizens. The epidemic cost the nation about $100 million in lost trade and relief efforts for the victims.

In the aftermath of the tragedy, the federal government took steps to prevent further outbreaks of yellow fever. A federal commission investigated the disease and created the National Board of Health in 1879. In the New Orleans area, the local governments improved drainage and sewage systems, which reduced breeding grounds for mosquitoes. After the epidemic of 1878, there was increased attention given to the cause and prevention of yellow fever. In 1881, Carlos Finley identified mosquitoes as the vector, and 19 years later, Walter Reed discovered that the carrier of the virus was the *Aedes aegypti* mosquito.

See also 1793 YELLOW FEVER EPIDEMIC.

Mayumi Grigsby and Diana S. Grigsby

FURTHER READING:

Ellis, John Hubert. *Yellow Fever and Public Health in the New South.* Lexington: University of Kentucky Press, 1992.

Humphreys, Margaret. *Yellow Fever and the South.* Rutgers, N.J.: Rutgers University Press, 1992.

Reeves, J. E. "The Eminent Domain of Sanitary Science and the Usefulness of Boards of Health in Guarding the Public Welfare." *Journal of the American Medical Association* 1, no. 21 (1883): 61.

1881 ◆ ASSASSINATION OF PRESIDENT GARFIELD

On July 2, 1881, James A. Garfield, not yet four months in office, became the second U.S. president to be shot fatally by an assassin. The attack occurred in Washington's Baltimore and Potomac railroad station, where the president had gone to board a northbound train. He was headed to Massachusetts to deliver a commencement address at Williams College, his alma mater. As Garfield and Secretary of State James Blaine walked toward the waiting room, two shots came from behind. One grazed the victim's arm. The other struck his back. "My God, what is this?" said Garfield as he collapsed. The fleeing gunman reached the Sixth Street entrance to the station, where policeman Patrick Kearney (whom the president only moments earlier had asked for the time) seized him. The shooter, a slightly built man with dark hair, remarked to Kearney and a fellow officer, "I did it. I will go to jail for it. I am a Stalwart and Arthur is President." In the depot, doctors organized care for Garfield, lying conscious in a pool of blood and vomit. After a futile search for the bullet in the president's back, the doctors had the wounded man moved to the White House.

The assailant was Charles Guiteau, 39 years old, a failed lawyer and bill collector who suffered delusions that a later age would probably label schizophrenic. He had spent months in 1880 hanging around campaign offices in New York City and upstate New York offering to speak on behalf of the Republican presidential ticket—an offer accepted on only one occasion. After Garfield's narrow victory in November 1880, Guiteau became convinced that the new administration owed him a prestigious federal job. Soon after the president's inauguration on March 4, 1881, Guiteau joined the crowd of job seekers who pestered White House and State Department staff. Guiteau sent notes to the president suggesting himself for diplomatic posts in Vienna and Paris. In late May, after the White House staff finally began to refuse entry to Guiteau, he conceived the idea of "removing" Garfield. He bought a high-caliber British Bull Dog revolver and wrote justifications for his action, which he left at the station newsstand on the day of the shooting. In an era before extensive security surrounded the president, Guiteau was able to stalk Garfield, even to church. Once before, in mid-June, he had gone to the railway station to shoot Garfield as the president saw off his wife, Lucretia. The farewell scene between the first couple persuaded him to desist for the moment.

A former Union general and competent veteran congressman before his unexpected nomination broke a deadlock at the Republican convention in

FACTBOX

PLACE Baltimore and Potomac Railroad Station, Washington, D.C.

DATE July 2, 1881

TYPE Presidential assassination

DESCRIPTION Embittered by being passed over for federal appointments to which he imagined himself entitled, attorney Charles Guiteau shot President James A. Garfield twice, with one bullet grazing Garfield's arm while the other lodged in his back. Garfield suffered for more than two months before dying on September 19, probably because doctors spread infection while hunting for the bullet.

CASUALTIES Death of President Garfield

IMPACT Elevation of Vice President Chester Arthur to the presidency and passage of the Pendleton Civil Service Act in 1883

June 1880, Garfield hardly seemed worth Guiteau's obsession. But Guiteau had taken to heart the overblown, at times violent rhetoric generated by a bitter faction fight during the spring of 1881 between "Half-Breed" Republicans, led by Blaine, and "Stalwart" Republicans, identified with New York senator Roscoe Conkling and his associate, Vice President Chester Alan Arthur. This factional quarrel had roots in Republican differences over the failed policy of Reconstruction in the post–Civil War South. But by 1881, the intraparty dispute had degenerated into a nasty struggle for control of patronage, in keeping with the "spoils system" that then determined government jobs at the federal as well as state and local levels. As president, Garfield pushed the nomination of a supporter, William H. Robertson, to the post of customs collector for the Port of New York, a lucrative position that Conkling claimed to control through the custom of "senatorial courtesy," according to which senators could veto presidential appointments in their state. Through its oversight of tariffs on imports, the main source of federal revenue at the time, the New York customhouse was indispensable to the web of patronage and financial contributions that sustained Conkling's New York political "machine." After a lengthy deadlock, the Senate con-

As a shocked Secretary of State James Blaine looks on, President James Garfield lies mortally wounded, victim of an assassin's gunshots. *(Library of Congress)*

firmed Robertson in May. Stung by this assault on his power base, Conkling resigned his U.S. Senate seat at about the same time Guiteau formed his plan to murder the president. Garfield, in Guiteau's view, had thrown in his lot with the Half-Breeds. The Stalwart Arthur could save the party from corruption— but only if Garfield was killed.

Convalescing at the White House through a miserably humid Washington summer, Garfield several times seemed to rally, only to begin again to waste away. Reports of his condition appeared in newspapers across the country, enabling Americans to follow the president's health on a daily basis for the first time. Critics of Garfield's medical treatment have speculated that his wounds would not have been fatal except for infections spread by doctors using unsterilized instruments to search for the bullet lodged near his pancreas. Antisepsis, an idea newly imported from Louis Pasteur's France, was not yet practiced by established doctors such as those treating the president. Moved by train to the seashore town of Elberon, New Jersey, in early September, Garfield died on September 19, 1881, the anniversary of the 1863 Civil War Battle of Chickamauga, in which as a Union general, Garfield had won recognition for his bravery.

At his trial, which lasted more than two months and generated 2,600 pages of testimony, Guiteau claimed that the doctors killed Garfield: "I simply shot at him." Guiteau's courtroom outbursts and his long history of disturbed behavior seemed to support his lawyers' innovative use of the insanity defense. The voluble Guiteau, however, undercut his lawyers with statements suggesting that his strangeness might be an act. On January 25, 1882, the jury convicted him after brief deliberation. He was hanged on June 30 of that year. The assassination had a sobering effect on querulous politicians, given copious evidence that the insults and tensions of spring 1881 had fed Guiteau's murderous state of mind. After succeeding the slain Garfield, President Arthur distanced himself from the blatant patronage politics with which his career to that time had been identified. Arthur supported the bipartisan effort to pass the Pendleton Civil Service Act of 1883. This bill set in motion the gradual ending of the spoils system in the federal government in favor of a civil service system based on qualifications and examinations.

See also 1865 ASSASSINATION OF PRESIDENT LINCOLN; 1901 ASSASSINATION OF PRESIDENT MCKINLEY; 1963 ASSASSINATION OF PRESIDENT KENNEDY.

Alan Lessoff

FURTHER READING:

Ackerman, Kenneth D. *Dark Horse: The Surprise Election and Political Murder of President James A. Garfield.* New York: Carroll & Graf, 2003.

Leech, Margaret, and Harry J. Brown. *The Garfield Orbit.* New York: Harper & Row, 1978.

Peskin, Allan. *Garfield: A Biography.* Kent, Ohio: Kent State University Press, 1978.

Rosenberg, Charles E. *The Trial of the Assassin Guiteau: Psychiatry and the Law in the Gilded Age.* Chicago: University of Chicago Press, 1968.

1886 ◆ HAYMARKET SQUARE INCIDENT

On the evening of May 4, 1886, a crowd of workers and social activists gathered in Chicago's Haymarket Square to protest the police brutality at the McCormick Reaper Works the previous day, which had resulted in the deaths of six strikers. At about 10:30 P.M., after the arrival of police, an anonymous assailant threw a bomb into the crowd, killing patrolman Mathias Degan. Six other police officers and at least three civilians died in the riot that followed the explosion. In the days following the attack, the police rounded up prominent activists believed to be anarchists, who were charged with the murder of Officer Degan. Following a trial that critics called unfair, four of the accused were hanged. Louis Lingg, one of the accused, committed suicide in the county jail the day before his scheduled execution. The swift legal response to the Haymarket violence calmed the fears of members of Chicago' s middle and upper classes who were alarmed about workers' violence. To the more

FACTBOX

PLACE Desplaines and Randolph Streets (Haymarket Square), Chicago, Illinois

DATE May 4, 1886

TYPE Industrial strike and riot

DESCRIPTION At the McCormick Reaper Works, an unknown assailant threw a bomb into the crowd at a rally where workers had protested police brutality the previous day at a demonstration. The police responded with indiscriminate shooting.

CAUSE The proximate cause was the detonation of a bomb, which killed one police officer. More generally, a long-running strike and workers' demand for an eight-hour day created a tense situation between labor and law enforcement officials in Chicago.

CASUALTIES At least 15 deaths: Seven police officers and at least three civilians died in the Haymarket altercation; four anarchists were subsequently convicted of murder and hanged; and a fifth convicted anarchist committed suicide in jail.

IMPACT The Haymarket riot and the deaths of the five martyred anarchists remained a memorable event in labor's struggles for decades, as well as a reminder to the middle and upper classes that industrial America had produced social divisions that could explode into violence.

radical workers in Europe and the United States, the fallen anarchists served as martyrs for the causes of labor and free speech in the years following their execution.

The riot in Haymarket Square was one of several catastrophes that upset the social structure in Chicago in the latter half of the 19th century. The GREAT CHICAGO FIRE swept through the city in 1871, and once the metropolis had recovered, the GREAT RAILROAD STRIKE upset the social balance in 1877. In the 1880s, labor activists fought for the eight-hour workday, a campaign that challenged prevailing norms among manufacturers and employers, who often required workers to labor nine, 10, and sometimes more hours per day. Anarchism gained popularity

among the radical sects of disgruntled workers in the United States and Europe, where labor unionization proliferated in the 1880s.

Chicago's industrial workers had been restless during the spring of 1886. For more than two decades, unions and workers across the country had been demanding a shorter workday, and in 1884 the Federation of Organized Trades and Labor Unions (the forerunner of the American Federation of Labor) had targeted May 1, 1886, for a nationwide strike for an eight-hour day. In February 1886 workers at the McCormick Reaper Works in Chicago had gone on strike, and the company had hired scabs to replace them. The combination of these two events—the local strike and broader demand for the eight-hour day—united both conservative and radical workers' groups in Chicago and led to a tense but peaceful march on May 1. Two days later, August Spies, a journalist for the German-language anarchist newspaper *Arbeiter-Zeitung,* spoke at a rally for the eight-hour day at the McCormick Reaper Works, which ended when approximately 200 police officers broke up fighting between strikers and strikebreakers. The police shot and killed six strikers.

In response to the riot at the McCormick plant, about 1,500 people gathered on Desplaines Street in Chicago, near the intersection with Randolph Street, at 7:30 P.M. on the night of May 4. Carter Harrison, Chicago's mayor, observed the earlier part of this rally in Haymarket Square to ensure that the previous day's violence would not be repeated. Deciding that the gathering posed no threats, he left early. When English activist and anarchist Samuel Fielden began to speak after 10 P.M., only 600 people remained in the square. Fielden addressed the protesters with evocative language, encouraging workers to "throttle" and "kill" the law that enslaved them and "impede its progress." Six companies of city police had been positioned in the vicinity of Haymarket in anticipation of trouble at the start of the rally but had left when Mayor Harrison deemed the event peaceful. An undercover police officer in the square reported on Fielden's remarks, which led 175 police officers to return from the Desplaines Street Police Station. Leading the officers into the square, police Captain William Ward ordered: "I command you in the name of the people of the state of Illinois to immediately and peaceably disperse." Fielden assured Ward the group was peaceful. When Ward repeated his command, Fielden relented. He jumped off the wagon that

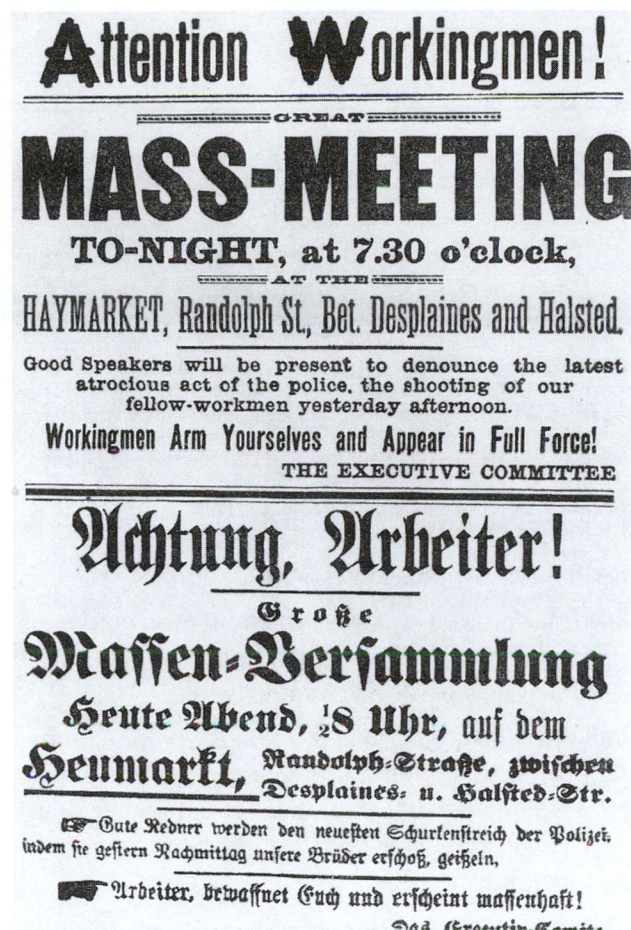

In both English and German, a placard issued on May 4, 1886, urges workers in Chicago to gather at Haymarket Square to condemn police brutality. At the meeting that night, a bomb would explode, setting off fears of anarchism nationwide. *(Library of Congress)*

had served as his platform. At that moment, someone flung a bomb into the crowd of police.

Chaos ensued. The police started to shoot indiscriminately, often injuring their fellow officers. Nineteen-year-old S. T. Ingram, a worker at the rally, later testified that the shooting came from the policemen in the center of the street, not from the wagon where Fielden stood. Ingram did not see any civilians carrying guns. Inspector John Bonfield from the Desplaines Street Station insisted in his statement to the press that the bombing was a deliberate conspiracy by the anarchists.

The police rounded up suspected anarchists in the days and weeks after the Haymarket incident. "Suspicious" houses were ransacked without search warrants. Civil liberties were discarded. On June 5, barely a month after the bombing, eight men, including Fielden, were arraigned for Degan's murder: August Spies, Albert Parsons, Eugene Schwab, Adolph Fischer, George Engel, Louis Lingg, and Oscar Neebe. The jury chosen for the trial at the Cook County Courthouse included white-collar workers who had admitted their belief in the defendants' guilt. Although none of the eight was linked directly to the throwing of the bomb, the jury found their past advocacy of violence and endorsement of anarchism sufficient to convict them. All eight were found guilty, and seven were sentenced to death. Neebe received a sentence of 15 years at hard labor. Fielden and Schwab's death sentences were commuted to life imprisonment, and they were later pardoned. Lingg committed suicide in jail. Spies, Parsons, Fischer, and Engel were hanged on November 11, 1887. The identity of the bomb thrower was never determined and remains a mystery to this day.

Workers and immigrants in the United States were disheartened by the executions. To them, the injustice performed in Chicago contradicted the ideals for which America stood, the principles of freedom and liberty that had inspired many of the workers to emigrate from Europe. The executions stunned some members of Chicago's middle and upper classes. Yet many Chicagoans were relieved to have order restored after weeks of upheaval. Like the national railroad strike of 1877, the Haymarket incident exposed the growing class divisions in the United States and exacerbated their prejudices against immigrant workers and political dissenters. Although the labor movement was temporarily weakened by the fury surrounding Haymarket, those who died for the causes of free speech and equality were remembered in future May Day festivals. In spite of the violent consequences suffered by the convicted anarchists, union workers and anarchists alike continued to fight for fair treatment in the workplace.

Jennifer A. Jovin

FURTHER READING:

Green, James. *Death in the Haymarket: A Story of Chicago, the First Labor Movement, and the Bombing that Divided Gilded Age America.* New York: Pantheon Books, 2006.

Smith, Carl. *Urban Disorder and the Shape of Belief: The Great Chicago Fire, the Haymarket Bomb, and the Model Town of Pullman.* Chicago: University of Chicago Press, 1995.

1888 ◆ BLIZZARD OF '88

Perhaps the most famous snowstorm in American history, the blizzard of 1888 is sometimes referred to as the "Great White Hurricane." The storm deposited as much as 50 inches of snow from northern Virginia to Maine. In all, 400 deaths were attributed to the blizzard of '88 and almost 200 ships were lost. There are no adequate figures to reflect the monetary losses, but the entire Northeast was immobilized for a week. Buildings, rail lines, and telephone and telegraph lines sustained heavy damage.

The blizzard began as an inauspicious low-pressure system off the coast of North Carolina. When the system drifted eastward on Sunday, March 11, the National Weather Service (NWS) estimated it would continue its path out to sea. As a result, the NWS predicted moderate rain and winds for the Atlantic coastal region from Virginia north to Maine. The NWS lacked oceanic monitoring facilities and had no way of knowing that, instead of following its predicted course, the storm had moved due north.

FACTBOX

PLACE East Coast of the United States from northern Virginia to Maine, reaching as far inland as Buffalo, New York, and Pittsburgh, Pennsylvania

DATE March 11–13, 1888

TYPE Blizzard

DESCRIPTION Most devastating blizzard in U.S. history, which dumped up to 50 inches of snow on the Northeast

CASUALTIES Approximately 400 deaths

COST 200 ships. No real attempt was made to assess the financial impact, but the entire East Coast was paralyzed for one week.

IMPACT New York City began to plan a subway system, telegraph and telephone lines were moved underground, and the National Weather Service constructed oceanic monitoring stations.

New Yorkers spent days digging out from the great blizzard of 1888. (© Bettmann/CORBIS)

Furthermore the storm gained power on the open Atlantic and the barometric pressure dropped dramatically. The storm had turned into a cyclone.

Sunday, March 11, 1888, was a mild day on land with springlike temperatures in the mid-50s. Ships at sea were the first to feel the effects of the storm. Captains piloted their ships as best they could to the most accessible safe haven. At Lewes, Delaware, a port hub of the Pennsylvania Railroad, ships started to arrive in the harbor at nightfall just as the storm did, creating chaotic and dangerous conditions. In all, 35 ships were destroyed in the harbor. In the late afternoon, rain started to fall in Washington, D.C., and by evening, the downpour was torrential. During the night, the rain turned to snow. Rain also began to fall in New Jersey, New York, Pennsylvania, and across New England. No one sensed that a major blizzard was imminent.

When the Northeast awoke on Monday morning, March 12, they were startled to see a blizzard. Strong, bitterly cold winds blew frozen shards of snow horizontally, reducing visibility, and making it nearly impossible for man or beast to walk in the conditions. The snow downed telegraph and telephone wires, cutting off the East Coast, including Washington, D.C., from the rest of the nation as well as from each other. Trains could not pass through accumulations of almost 50 inches of snow or drifts, which could be as high as 10 or 12 feet. Up and down the Eastern Seaboard, commuters were stranded, including the New York City elevated trains, which were stuck on the tracks with passengers helplessly trapped inside. New York City, Philadelphia, Boston, Washington, D.C., and New Haven, Connecticut, were all incapacitated by the blizzard, which reached as far inland as Pittsburgh and Buffalo. Business virtually halted, and essential goods and services, such as daily coal or milk deliveries, could not be made. Rural homes were equally affected, with the occupants locked in by the snow unable to tend to their animals. Cases of extreme kindness, such as residents helping stranded commuters, were mixed with incidents of extreme greed, as in the case of carriages giving rides in New York City for 50 dollars.

For most areas affected by the blizzard, snow fell continuously for about 24 hours, and once it stopped, repair crews were dispatched to fix the downed telegraph lines and get the railroads running again. It would be another 48 hours before the trains were moving, even on a limited basis. The storm continued across the Atlantic. Although the system, which the Europeans referred to as "the American Blizzard," hit England and Germany, its energy had dissipated, and it caused only losses of livestock.

The blizzard of '88 was one of the most important natural disasters in U.S. history, and there were several significant outcomes. First, telegraph lines in New York and other cities were moved underground to prevent another national breakdown in communication. Second, urban leaders realized that New York City's elevated train lines were too vulnerable to the weather to meet the demands of the nation's commercial and financial center, and the city soon began the process of constructing a subway system. Finally, the NWS realized that it needed better oceanic and atmospheric monitoring in the Atlantic region and placed stations from Nassau, the Bahamas, and Bermuda in the south to New Hampshire and Newfoundland in the north.

See also 1978 BLIZZARD OF '78.

Gregory J. Dehler

FURTHER READING:

Cable, Mary. *The Blizzard of '88.* New York: Atheneum, 1988.

Werstein, Irving. *The Blizzard of '88.* New York: Crowell, 1960.

1889 ◆ JOHNSTOWN FLOOD

At a time when Americans were coming to terms with the tragedy of the Civil War, a devastating flood occurred in Johnstown, Pennsylvania, that claimed thousands of lives within moments. The failure of a dam located on a sporting resort owned by a group of wealthy Pittsburgh industrialists triggered the disaster. Occurring on May 31, 1889, the Johnstown flood became the second biggest news story of the second half of the 19th century, following only the assassination of President Abraham Lincoln in 1865. The catastrophe proved to be a defining moment for the Red Cross and Clara Barton, who led relief efforts. Reporting about the flood and its aftermath also raised important questions concerning class differences and fed a string of accusations about an incident that many believed was caused by negligence among the rich and prominent.

Located 78 miles east of the steel center of Pittsburgh in the Allegheny Mountains, Johnstown was a thriving mill town of about 30,000 residents, many of them poor immigrant laborers who worked in the Cambria Iron Works. In the mountains high above Johnstown lay the South Fork Hunting and Fishing Club, an exclusive vacation resort established in 1879 by an elite coterie of Pittsburgh business executives, including banker Andrew Mellon and steel producer Andrew Carnegie. A focal point of the club's 160-acre property was the South Fork Lake. Club members

FACTBOX

PLACE Johnstown, Pennsylvania

DATE May 31, 1889

TYPE Flood and fire

DESCRIPTION A rush of water as high as 36 feet and approximating the velocity of Niagara Falls slammed into Johnstown, dislodging houses and railroad cars and drowning thousands of residents. Debris traveling down the Conemaugh River caught fire, causing more deaths.

CAUSE Unusually heavy rains that caused a dam improperly maintained by the South Fork Hunting and Fishing Club to give way

CASUALTIES 2,209 deaths officially counted, not including individuals whose remains were not recovered and people who succumbed to typhus months later

COST Damages totaled $17 million. Many lawsuits were filed charging the South Fork Fishing and Hunting Club with negligence, but no damages were paid.

IMPACT A defining moment for the Red Cross, which aided victims of a disaster for the first time; provided intensive journalistic training on the practicalities of disaster reporting

made major improvements to the property for recreational purposes, including enlarging the lake and lowering the wall of its dam to form a road wide enough so that two carriages could pass along side-by-side. But they did little to maintain and fortify the dam itself. When the heaviest rains ever recorded in the Conemaugh region of western Pennsylvania hit on Memorial Day in 1889, water began to spill over the South Fork Lake's flood wall.

Club engineer John Parke, fearing that the dam might break, rode into the town of South Fork to tell the telegraph operator to warn the residents of Johnstown, less than 15 miles away. However, the wires had been damaged in the heavy rains the night before, so the message never arrived. When Parke returned to the lake, he watched in horror as the dam gave way. Twenty million tons of water traveling 60 miles per hour rushed through the villages of Mineral Point,

East Conemaugh, and Woodvale, cascading to the end of the valley at Johnstown, which was already flooded due to excessive rain. The huge wave of water, estimated to be at least 36 feet high and flowing with the intensity of Niagara Falls, scooped up everything in its path: trees, houses, people, horses, cows, a locomotive, railway cars, boulders, barbed wire, and a large stone viaduct. It took roughly 10 minutes for the mass of water and debris to race through Johnstown until it reached the Stone Bridge, where it formed a new lake. Later that evening, the debris caught fire, probably caused by oil that had leaked from a derailed tank car that had collided with a coal stover.

The Johnstown flood resulted in the greatest loss of life ever caused by a dam break in the United States. The official death count of 2,209 makes it one of the deadliest catastrophes in American history. The exact number of fatalities, however, will never be known. More than 600 bodies were listed as unknown or were incinerated, dismembered, or carried hundreds of miles away in flood waters. Many entire families were wiped out, leaving no survivors to file insurance claims. Throughout the summer, even more residents of Johnstown died of typhus, making the total loss of life even greater. All told, the flood destroyed 1,500 homes, and property damage totaled $17 million.

Because the flood occurred during the era of "yellow journalism" in American newspapers, press coverage was sensational and extensive. Reporters and photographers from all over the country rushed to the scene, attempting to capture the gruesome reality. They learned to work quickly under difficult conditions, filing emotional stories that described the devastation. Newspaper sales skyrocketed as initial accounts, both lurid and sentimental, reported "hands of the dead stuck out of ruins," bodies "roasted and charred," and tearful parents lamenting, "My God, my babies are gone." A photograph, which proved to be the signature image of the disaster, depicted the house of John Schultz and his family, which was lifted from its foundation before being impaled by a huge tree; all six family members survived. Other survival stories, such as 16-year-old Victor Heiser's wild ride down the river atop the roof of his family's barn, contrasted with the grim roll call of the dead.

After the initial shock of the flood, attention turned to the intensive relief effort and plans to rebuild. Coverage of the flood resulted in an outpouring of

American Red Cross

On May 21, 1881, Clara Barton, a former teacher and volunteer nurse during the Civil War, established the American Red Cross. After years of lobbying Congress, she was successful on June 6, 1900, in securing a congressional charter that mandated that the organization observe the provisions of the Geneva Convention (signed in 1863). Although the charter was amended in 1905, the broad purpose of the organization continues today more than a century later. This mission includes rendering aid to members of the U.S. military and providing communication services for their families, as well as administering relief to individuals affected by national and international disasters. Despite its national authorization, the American Red Cross does not receive federal funds. Rather, it operates as an independent, volunteer-led organization that receives financial support from public contributions and cost-reimbursement charges. The organization is led by a 50-member, voluntary board of governors with the president of the United States serving as the honorary chairman. The president appoints eight governors, including the chairman of the board, who nominates the president of the Red Cross, who is then formally elected by the board. In 2006, the American Red Cross reported total revenues of approximately $5.8 billion.

Clara Barton was the pivotal figure in the establishment of the American Red Cross. Her commitment to helping the weak and the wounded originated at the time of the Civil War, during which she earned the nickname "Angel of the Battlefield" for attention to the needs of wounded soldiers. She was appointed superintendent of union nurses in 1864. After the war, she traveled to Europe, where she observed the work of the International Commission of the Red Cross, established as part of the Geneva Convention of 1863. While abroad, Barton, served as a volunteer with the organization during the Franco-Prussian War (1870–71), an experience that convinced her that the United States needed a similar organization. In the decades since its formation, the American Red Cross has remained committed to the original tenets of the International Federation of Red Cross and Red Crescent Societies, which is to promote humanity, impartiality, neutrality, independence, voluntary service, unity, and universality. Less than a decade after its founding, the American Red Cross played a central role in helping victims recover from the devastating JOHNSTOWN FLOOD of 1889 and soon became a fixture in disaster relief nationwide. After the 1909 CHERRY MINE FIRE, which killed 259 coal miners in Illinois, the American Red Cross insisted on establishing a pension fund for the widows and orphans, and in 1927, the organization fed some 700,000 victims rendered homeless by the MISSISSIPPI RIVER FLOOD. During the 1940s, the Red Cross became one of the first major organizations in the United States to end segregation policies by hiring African Americans to contribute to the efforts of the organization. Of particular significance was the appointment of Dr. Charles Drew, an African-American physician who created a model for the current blood collection system of the American Red Cross that continues to save many lives today.

With 1.2 million volunteers, the American Red Cross currently addresses needs in blood collection, disaster relief, aid to soldiers and victims of war, HIV/AIDS education, and childhood diseases. In addition, the organization partners with the U.S. government to develop strategies for addressing potential acts of terrorism. The American Red Cross has been in existence since 1881 and continues to receive the support of the public. In response to the coastal earthquakes and tsunami in Southeast Asia and East Africa in December 2004, the organization received $575 million in donations and another $2.6 billion in the wake of HURRICANES KATRINA, Rita, and Wilma in 2005—more than was collected by any other relief body in the United States. This financial generosity is testimony that the American Red Cross remains a respected organization that is expected to help people in times of tragedy.

Diana S. Grigsby
and Mayumi Grigsby

Reaching 36 feet in height and traveling at 60 miles per hour, the roaring surge of water destroyed virtually everything in its path during the Johnstown flood. *(Library of Congress)*

support. Food, workers, money, and supplies came from neighboring communities, every state in the country, and 14 foreign nations. Five days after the flood, the new and relatively unknown American Red Cross, headed by 67-year-old former Civil War nurse Clara Barton, who had founded the agency in 1881, set up tents in Johnstown and began to help the victims by offering food, shelter, clothing, and hope. The Red Cross erected a field hospital, built three hotels for the homeless, and sent relief workers to people's homes. Barton stayed in Johnstown for nearly five months, spending $25,000 and assisting 25,000 victims. It was the first time that the Red Cross ever aided victims of a disaster.

Immediately after the flood, people speculated whether the cause of the great disaster was an act of God or negligence on the part of the South Fork Fishing and Hunting Club. On June 4, the *New York Times* reported, "There is no question who is responsible. . . . Justice is inevitable even though the horror is attributable to men of wealth and station, and the majority of the victims the most downtrodden in any industry in the country." Many lawsuits were filed charging the South Fork Fishing and Hunting Club with negligence. Yet the club was able to avoid damage payments, in part because the cases were tried in Pittsburgh rather than Johnstown, and its powerful members had access to skilled lawyers, who argued that the catastrophe was the result of unusually heavy rains. Under present-day legal standards, the club may have lost.

The Johnstown flood provided American journalists with intensive training in disaster reporting and solidified the sensational style of reporting that characterized yellow journalism. It brought recognition to Clara Barton and the American Red Cross, which more than a century later remains one of the county's most prominent relief agencies. The organization's relief activities in Johnstown showed how a town practically obliterated by catastrophe could rebuild. Finally, the disaster highlighted the dynamics of blame, power, and victimization that continue to stand at the center of high-profile lawsuits in America.

Kathy Merlock Jackson

FURTHER READING:

Guggenheim, Charles. "The Scene of the Crime." *American Heritage* (November 1992): 120–127.

McCullough, David. *The Johnstown Flood: The Incredible Story Behind One of the Most Devastating "Natural" Disasters America Has Ever Known.* New York: Simon and Schuster, 1968.

Munson, Howard. *The Triumph of the American Spirit: Johnstown, Pennsylvania.* Lanham, Md.: Johnstown Flood Museum and American Association for State and Local History Library, 1989.

1892 ◆ LYNCHING TRAGEDY

While lynching was a phenomenon of the sparsely settled frontier that reached back to the American Revolution, this deadly vigilantism took on a peculiar racial tint between the 1880s and the 1960s. Prior to the 1850s, "lynch-law" was associated with extralegal corporal punishment, such as flogging, but did not usually lead to death. Then, during the 1850s, as the nation began to rupture in the sectional conflict over slavery and territorial expansion, southern vigilantes began routinely to kill outlaws and persons suspected of fomenting slave insurrections, especially in Texas and Louisiana. During the Civil War and Reconstruction, lynching in the South accelerated, but its magnitude is obscured because no systematic records were kept until 1882. The availability of data after 1882 clearly demonstrates the racial bias in lynching: Almost 80 percent of all American lynch victims were black males. The deadliest year for lynching in U.S. history was 1892, when 230 people were executed, of whom 162, or 70 percent, were African-American. During the entire decade of the 1890s, an average of 104 blacks were lynched annually—or an average of two every week for 10 years. Death was usually inflicted by hanging or burning and sometimes both.

The extralegal killing of African Americans was often a tool to subjugate blacks and keep them in subordinate positions. The Department of Research and Records at Booker T. Washington's Tuskegee Institute in Alabama began to systematically document lynching in 1882. Historian Philip Dray has characterized the Tuskegee tabulations, published annually until 1962, as "a kind of Dow Jones ticker

of the nation's most vicious form of intolerance." Between 1882 and 1964, more than 4,700 people were lynched in the United States. For the years 1882–85, the Tuskegee records show that more whites than blacks were lynched. In 1886, however, 74 blacks and 64 whites were lynched, marking the first year since Tuskegee had been compiling lynching statistics that more blacks than whites were lynched. From that point forward, the number of black lynch victims has always exceeded the number of whites. According to data in the *Negro Year Book: 1937–38,* between 1882 and 1936, 3,383 blacks were lynched.

As the sociologist Allen Grimshaw has demonstrated, racial violence in the United States has a long history. Notorious instances include the virtual pogrom of blacks in Cincinnati, Ohio, during the 1820s, the "Nig hunts" in Philadelphia and other northern cities during the 1840s, and the rampant antiblack violence in the South during the Reconstruction era. Race riots in New Orleans, Louisiana, and Memphis, Tennessee, in 1866, were among the factors that convinced many Republicans in Congress that southern state governments installed under President Andrew Johnson's lenient plan of Reconstruction failed to protect the life and limb of the freed people. During the Colfax massacre of 1873, white mobs killed more than 100 blacks in Grant Parish, Louisiana.

An upsurge of lynching during the early 1890s prompted antilynching efforts by such crusading journalists as Ida B. Wells-Barnett and activist Mary Church Terrell. Wells-Barnett (1862–1931), born a slave in Holly Springs, Mississippi, became half-owner of the weekly *Memphis Free Speech and Headlight* newspaper in 1892. The lynching of three of her personal acquaintances—Thomas Moss, Calvin McDowell, and Henry Stewart—intensified her antilynching activism. In an article in her newspaper, Wells-Barnett rebutted the allegation that the three had raped three white women, calling the claim a subterfuge. The real offense, she argued, was that these three partners in the new People's Grocery were competing too vigorously with W. R. Barrett, a white grocer. In May 1892, a white mob destroyed the offices of the *Memphis Free Speech.* Wells-Barnett left Memphis permanently and settled in Chicago. In 1895 she published a pamphlet, *A Red Record: Tabulated Statistics and Alleged Causes of Lynchings in the United States, 1892–1893–1894* (with a preface by

Frederick Douglass) in which she also urged such organizations as churches, the YMCA, and the Women's Christian Temperance Union to join the antilynching crusade.

During the early 20th century, other individuals and organizations joined the crusade against lynching. One of the main thrusts of the National Association for the Advancement of Colored People (NAACP), formed in the aftermath of the SPRINGFIELD RACE RIOT of 1908, was to push for federal antilynching legislation. Taking up where Wells-Barnett left off, the organization published compilations of statistics on lynching such as *Thirty Years of Lynching* (1919). Other antilynching activists linked with the NAACP included W. E. B. DuBois, James Weldon Johnson, and Walter White, and in 1932, under the leadership of Jessie Daniel Ames, the Association of Southern Women for the Prevention of Lynching was formed.

Advocates of lynching justified it as a defense of white womanhood against black rapists or, as

Georgia governor Allen D. Candler asserted, a general deterrent against black crime. However, Wells-Barnett pointed out in the 19th century that rape or attempted rape were not even the alleged offense in a majority of instances—claims corroborated by later generations of historians and social scientists. Less than one-third of all lynch victims were alleged to have committed rape or attempted rape. The alleged offenses of the remaining two-thirds of the lynch victims included chronic "impudence," chicken-stealing, slapping or otherwise disrespecting a white person, arson, refusal to pay debts, and murder or attempted murder, with murder or attempted murder topping the list.

Hooded night riders—members of the Ku Klux Klan or some other secret terrorist organization—perpetrated some lynching, but many more took place in broad daylight with hundreds of bystanders. There are instances in which lynchings were advertised in advance in newspapers, whose readers were urged to pack picnic baskets, board trains,

In this grisly scene of a lynching—repeated in town after town for decades in the late 19th and 20th centuries—a crowd of white onlookers poses for the camera in front of the mutilated bodies of two murdered African Americans. *(© Bettmann/CORBIS)*

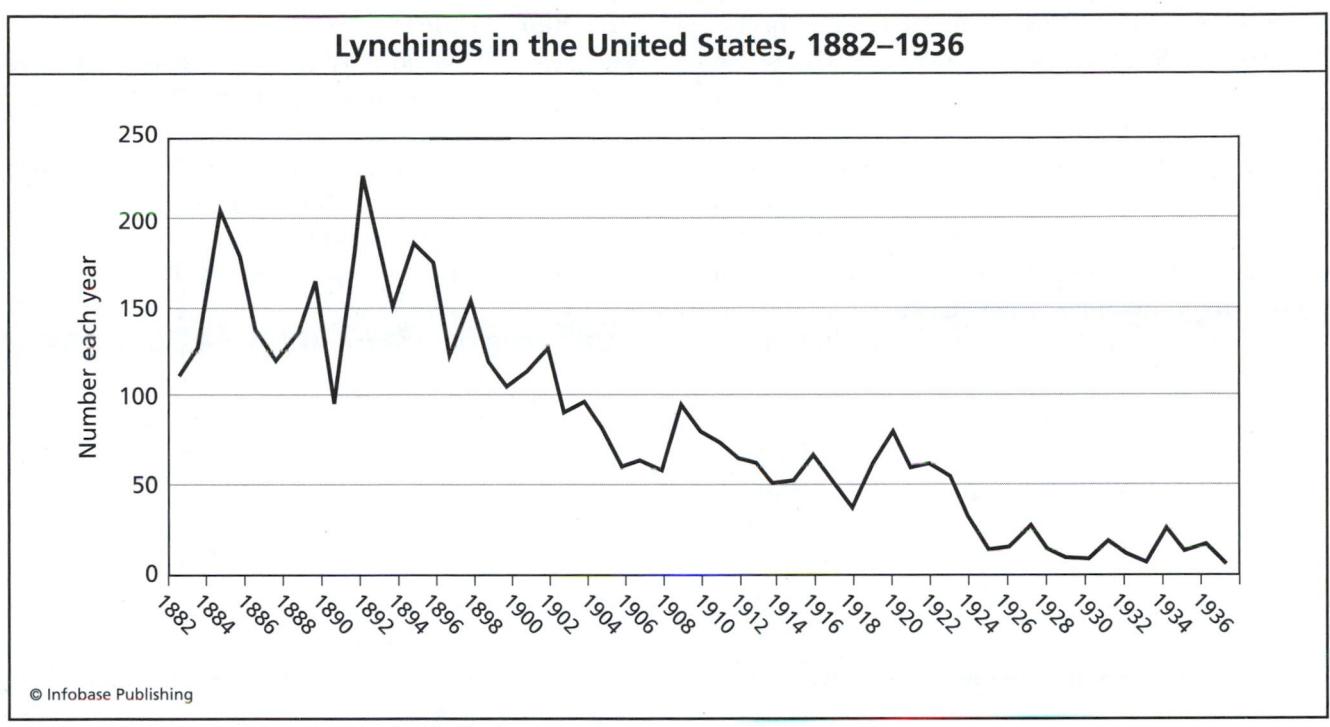

Lynchings in the United States, 1882–1936

In the half-century from the 1880s to the 1930s, not a year passed in the United States without multiple lynchings. For most of this period, the United States averaged more than one lynching per week. Source: Susan B. Carter et al., eds. *Historical Statistics of the United States Millennial Edition Online.* New York: Cambridge University Press, 2006, Table Ec251.

and bring their entire families to the gruesome festivities. These were bold public rituals of white supremacy. Often, the leaders of the lynch mobs not only were known to the community, but they also posed for "before" and "after" photographs that were subsequently published in local newspapers or sold as postcards.

Although most lynching occurred in the 11 former Confederate states, such killings were not confined to the South; of the 3,383 blacks lynched from 1882 to 1936, 108 were killed outside the region. Two of the most notorious northern lynchings happened in Springfield, Illinois, in 1908, and Coatesville, Pennsylvania, in 1911. Within the South, the frequency of lynching varied among the states, reflecting the region's demographic, ecological, and economic diversity. They were especially prevalent in the upland counties of Georgia and in the borderlands of the Mississippi River between Memphis and New Orleans, especially the majority-black areas of the Delta. Historian W. Fitzhugh Brundage pointed out that more lynchings occurred in Georgia in 1919 than happened in Virginia throughout the entire 20th century. The states with the largest total number of lynchings between 1882 and 1989 were Mis-

sissippi with 581 deaths (92.7 percent black), Georgia with 530 (92.9 percent black), Texas with 493 (71.4 percent black), and Louisiana with 391 (85.7 percent black). More common in rural areas and small towns but not absent from cities, lynchings also manifested a certain seasonal pattern, tending to take place more often during the hottest months of the year in June, July, and August.

When did lynching stop? There is no mutually agreed-upon date when the history of lynching could be said to have come to an end. Clearly, the available statistics indicate that the main era of lynching in the United States was from 1890 to the infamous Red Summer of 1919 (see CHICAGO RACE RIOT). The frequency of extralegal executions then began to decline, yet no year passed between 1882 and 1951 without a black person being lynched in the United States. By the mid-1930s, the annual number of black lynch victims had dropped below 10 and the so-called spectacle lynchings with advanced publicity and crowds of onlookers had virtually died out. The first year since records had been kept when no blacks were lynched was 1952. Those who thought that this signaled the dawn of a new day in race relations were soon disabused of the notion when teenager Emmett Till was brutally lynched in Mississippi in 1955, a year after the U.S. Supreme Court's decision in *Brown v. Board of Education,* which declared racial segregation in public schools unconstitutional. Mack Parker was lynched in 1959 in Mississippi, and three civil rights workers (James Chaney, James Goodman, and Michael Schwerner), two of whom were white, were killed in 1964, also in Mississippi. These more recent tragedies were instrumental in motivating the civil rights movement of the mid-20th century.

See also 1844 PHILADELPHIA RIOTS; 1863 NEW YORK CITY DRAFT RIOTS; 1964 FREEDOM SUMMER MURDERS.

Robert L. Hall

FURTHER READING:

Allen, James, et al. *Without Sanctuary: Lynching Photography in America.* Santa Fe, N.Mex.: Twin Palms, 2000.

Brundage, W. Fitzhugh. *Lynching in the New South: Georgia and Virginia, 1880–1930.* Urbana: University of Illinois Press, 1993.

Dray, Philip. *At the Hands of Persons Unknown: The Lynching of Black America.* New York: Random House, 2002.

Raper, Arthur F. *The Tragedy of Lynching.* Chapel Hill: University of North Carolina Press, 1933.

Zangrando, Robert. *The NAACP Crusade against Lynching, 1909–1950.* Philadelphia: Temple University Press, 1980.

1892 ◆ HOMESTEAD STRIKE

In 1892, the factory town of Homestead, Pennsylvania, was the scene of a violent strike that came to symbolize the bitter conflict between craft workers proud of their skills and industrialists determined to replace skilled workers with new technologies. Since acquiring the plant from a rival firm in 1883, steel magnate Andrew Carnegie and his partners had invested millions of dollars in giant open-hearth furnaces and other new technologies. The relentless drive for cost-cutting through technological and organizational innovation enabled Carnegie Steel to expand into the world's largest steel manufacturer. One of Carnegie's numerous factories in the Pittsburgh area, the Homestead plant covered 110 acres and employed 3,800 men in producing structural beams and girders, bridge steel, and armor plate for the U.S. Navy during the early 1890s. The plant's 16 open-hearth furnaces and two 10-ton Bessemer converters could produce around half a million tons of steel ingots per year.

Carnegie's innovations made the plant and town prosper. Even so, they threatened the livelihood of the town's highest-paid workers, the skilled craftsmen who controlled the Amalgamated Association of Iron and Steel Workers (AAISW), an affiliate of the

FACTBOX

PLACE Homestead, Pennsylvania

DATE July–November 1892

TYPE A strike that turned violent

DESCRIPTION After maneuvering the Amalgamated Association of Iron and Steel Workers into a lockout, Carnegie Steel partner Henry Clay Frick arranged for 300 Pinkerton agents to secure the plant and break the strike; an armed clash ensued between the Pinkertons and workers and supportive townspeople. Frick was later able to reopen the plant with strikebreakers, forcing the union to concede defeat.

CAUSE Use of armed, ill-trained Pinkertons to break a strike

CASUALTIES An estimated 10 deaths, with dozens seriously injured

IMPACT Unions were driven from steel industry for four decades, 26 states passed anti-Pinkerton laws.

American Federation of Labor. This union claimed to favor technological progress, even when innovations enabled companies to replace skilled workers with semiskilled or unskilled ones. In practice, however, the union exacted what a Carnegie official labeled "a tax on improvements." It did this by insisting on work rules that slowed the displacement of union members and piece rates that channeled to labor a portion of the extra profits attributable to new, more productive machinery. At Homestead and other plants where industrialists installed labor-saving technologies, workers feared for their social and political status, as well as their income. According to the artisan republican tradition that was widespread in the 19th-century United States, skilled workers such as those in the Homestead union counted as fully respectable citizens, while unskilled workers occupied a vulnerable, precarious social position. Andrew Carnegie made statements at times concerning the stability and well-being of towns in which his firm operated. When weighed against innovations that could increase productivity, however, these values mattered not at all to the industrialist and his partners. The gulf between a company famously obsessed with change and workers demanding respect for their position and traditions set up a dramatic confrontation.

Carnegie executives looked forward eagerly to July 1, 1892, when a three-year contract with the Homestead union would expire. In 1889, plant managers had settled a brief strike on terms that Carnegie and his partners viewed as far too favorable to the union. The company now hoped to force the AAISW into concessions or, better still, to break the Homestead union altogether. In preparation for a confrontation, the partners put Henry Clay Frick, a colleague with a reputation for toughness, in charge. They encouraged Carnegie, who had a record of pro-labor pronouncements and a penchant for unguarded statements to the press, to take a lengthy vacation in the Scottish highlands. Carnegie later insisted that he had only authorized a lockout, not the use of force to break the strike, but before leaving for Scotland, he assured Frick that he would "approve of anything you do."

Frick's strategy was to make proposals that he expected the union to refuse. Key items in the negotiations included the expiration date of the next contract, along with adjustments both to piece rates (which could lead to reduced weekly wages) and to a "sliding scale" that was to be used to protect workers against excessive fluctuations in the market price for steel. The important thing to understand about such issues is that for Frick they were largely pretexts; the point was to pressure the union into making embarrassing concessions or to maneuver it into a prolonged work stoppage that it would have difficulty sustaining.

The union, meanwhile, had accumulated a $146,000 strike fund. Since 1889, membership had grown, though the AAISW branch at Homestead still represented only 800 skilled workers, mainly of British-American, Irish, and German ethnic backgrounds. Despite the eastern European origins and unskilled or semiskilled status of a large segment of the 3,000 nonunion workers, the union counted on their support if it came to a strike. Throughout the steel industry, not just at Carnegie's plants, the trend was toward union-busting and deteriorating pay and working conditions. Despite their lower pay and status compared with unionized craftsmen, Homestead's unskilled workers understood that their situation would worsen if the union disappeared.

As the company compiled inventory and built a 12-foot fence around its plant, Frick presented the union with an obviously unacceptable "ultimatum" on the contested issues. If the union did not accede, it faced a lockout when its current contract expired on July 1. Several days before that deadline, nonunion workers met to offer overwhelming support to the union, which immediately began to set up a strike organization. By the evening of June 29, work at the plant had already ground to a halt. Technically, the company had locked out the workers, although the confrontation quickly became known as the Homestead strike.

Fearing an attempt to reopen the factory with strikebreakers, union leaders stationed lookouts at strategic points near the plant. Frick indeed planned to bring in armed guards, who would secure the factory and protect the anticipated strikebreakers from angry workers. He arranged with the Pinkerton National Detective Agency for 300 agents, mainly untrained recruits hired in New York, Philadelphia, and Chicago. On the night of

This array of scenes illustrates the Homestead strike of 1892, highlighting the confrontation between workers and Pinkertons. (© CORBIS)

July 5–6, the Pinkertons were sent on barges up the Monongahela River toward the Homestead plant. Warned by their lookouts, the strikers, along with thousands of supportive townspeople, hurried to the factory. Ignoring requests for calm from union leaders, the crowd tore through the new fence surrounding the steel plant and rushed to the river's edge. The crowd was intent on preventing the Pinkertons from landing. At about 4:30 A.M., as the Pinkertons attempted to land the barges, fighting broke out between the hired guards and the townspeople. In the confusion, shots were fired, leaving dead and wounded on both sides. Trapped on the barges, the Pinkertons attempted to land again at about 8 A.M., which resulted in another gun battle and more dead and wounded. Amid intermittent gunfire, strikers attempted repeatedly but without success to set the barges on fire with burning oil and explosives.

After a harrowing 12 hours, the Pinkertons surrendered at 5 P.M. Strike leaders guaranteed their safe conduct. Yet as the Pinkertons scrambled up the riverbank, the angry crowed formed a gauntlet 600 yards long. While lines of people taunted, beat, and kicked the agents, others from the crowd, mainly women and boys, dismantled and burned the barges. A crowd attacked the terrified Pinkertons again as they marched under guard into a makeshift jail in the town opera house. Shortly after midnight on July 7, local officials and strikers put the Pinkertons on a train back to Pittsburgh. The press estimated that seven townspeople and three Pinkertons died at the scene or shortly thereafter, with dozens seriously wounded.

The failed Pinkerton operation left the strikers in physical control of the plant. The battle with the Pinkertons increased worries among union leaders that the public would perceive the strikers as a mob of violent lawbreakers. On July 12, therefore, strike leaders agreed to turn the factory over to Pennsylvania state militiamen, 8,000 of whom the governor sent to Homestead to restore order. In this way, the union sought to demonstrate that workers distinguished between soldiers lawfully authorized by the government and mercenaries hired by the company. With workers and townspeople cleared from the factory, Frick gradually resumed operations with strikebreakers. The union now found itself trapped in a prolonged strike that the company could endure but that unpaid workers could not.

During the fierce labor conflicts of the late 1800s, middle-class Americans exhibited limited sympathy for unions, which seemed to violate American traditions of individualism and respect for property. Carnegie Steel's provocative use of Pinkertons seemed to push the middle-class public about as far toward the union side as it would go. This tenuous sympathy for labor dissipated after July 23, however, when Alexander Berkman, a Lithuanian-born anarchist closely associated with Emma Goldman but with no connection to the strikers, forced his way into Frick's office, shot the steel executive twice, and stabbed him three times as Frick and a company vice president wrestled the assailant to the ground. A deputy sheriff then arrived on the scene and pulled an explosive capsule from Berkman's mouth. Frick sat at his desk, let a doctor yank the bullets from him, dictated telegrams to his mother and Carnegie, and finished the day's work. Few Americans were willing to express support for a cause now associated with anarchist terrorism. When a private in the Pennsylvania militia shouted, "Three cheers for the man who shot Frick," his colonel ordered him hung by the thumbs.

In late July, Republican Party leaders, who feared that the strike would drive away labor voters in that fall's presidential election, attempted to mediate between the company and the union. Frick refused, insisting, "I will never recognize the Union, never, never!" The strike dragged on for nearly four more months. On November 21, with workers destitute, the strike fund exhausted, and union leaders jailed or blacklisted, the remaining members of the Homestead AAISW voted 101-91 to give up. More than 160 steelworkers faced charges ranging from riot and murder to treason against Pennsylvania. When juries acquitted the first three strikers brought to trial, the company gave up its prosecution attempts. The union then dropped its countercharges of murder against company officials.

The bloody encounter at Homestead induced 26 states, beginning with Pennsylvania, to enact laws that prohibited the use of private armed guards to break strikes. Yet Carnegie Steel's victory at Homestead sent a signal to the steel industry, which strengthened its stand against labor unions. By 1903, unions had disappeared from the country's steel plants, a situation that endured until the 1930s, when New Deal legislation gave support to union-organizing efforts in heavy industry. By the early 20th century, semiskilled and unskilled labor, often working 12-hour shifts seven days per week, prevailed in the American steel industry.

Alan Lessoff

FURTHER READING:

Brody, David. *Steelworkers in America: The Nonunion Era.* Cambridge, Mass.: Harvard University Press, 1960.

Demarest, David P., Jr., ed. *"The River Ran Red": Homestead 1892.* Pittsburgh: University of Pittsburgh Press, 1992.

Krause. Paul. *The Battle for Homestead, 1880–1892.* Pittsburgh: University of Pittsburgh Press, 1992.

Nasaw, David. *Andrew Carnegie.* New York: Penguin, 2006.

Standiford, Les. *Meet You in Hell: Andrew Carnegie, Henry Clay Frick, and the Bitter Partnership That Transformed America.* New York: Crown, 2005.

1893 ◆ FINANCIAL PANIC AND DEPRESSION

The financial panic of 1893 triggered a deep and prolonged economic depression. The ensuing crisis in business and agriculture fueled tumultuous upheavals that sent shockwaves through politics, society, and international relations. Famed steel manufacturer Andrew Carnegie doubted "if a more disastrous financial cyclone ever blasted a country to such an extent." President Grover Cleveland, elected for the second time in 1892, called the depression the "luckless years." As the financial panic deepened into a massive depression, thousands of businesses failed, roughly a fourth of all railroads went bankrupt, and unemployment spiked to nearly a fifth of the industrial workforce at the worst of the crisis. The economic difficulties of the middle 1890s are considered by many historians to have been the severest industrial depression of the 19th century. The hard times had an enormous impact on the direction of American society at the turn of the century.

The crisis began when the National Cordage Company, a twine-making firm, fell into bankruptcy on May 4, 1893. This misfortune was triggered by a sagging stock market, which unraveled into panic selling on the news of the company's collapse. By July 26, the Dow Jones average of stock prices for 20 industrial companies, a leading indicator of business health, had fallen nearly 39 percent over the index's high in January. Economic troubles in Europe in the early 1890s had left finances in the United States vulnerable to a meltdown. Foreign investors, especially in Britain, responded to a depression in Europe by liquidating investments in the United States. These sales contributed to the outflow of gold from the United States to Europe. British confidence in American securities was also weakened by the demands of inflationists who sought to increase the money supply by basing it on silver as well as gold. A spike of American imports in the wake of lowered prices in Europe also caused concerns.

Fears gripped business leaders that the United States might abandon the gold standard, the holy grail of financial stability to the moneyed classes. They saw the payment of debts in silver-based money or paper "greenbacks" as reducing the value of wealth.

FACTBOX

PLACE Wall Street (New York City), Washington, D.C., and the United States

DATE May 4, 1893 (stock panic); 1893–98 (depression)

TYPE Financial panic and depression

DESCRIPTION Depression led to hundreds of bank failures and thousands of factory closings, causing unemployment to soar to 35 percent and higher in some parts of the country.

CAUSE Rapid decline in the value of stocks and bonds following the bankruptcy of the National Cordage Company on May 4, 1893.

IMPACT The panic triggered economic depression in the United States, 1893–98, which was the nation's severest commercial downturn to date, and contributed to the Republican Party's ascendancy, the Spanish-American War, and a wave of giant business mergers.

Andrew Carnegie saw the cause of the panic linked to efforts to add silver to the foundation of American currency. But labor leader Eugene Debs, president of the American Railway Union, called the financial crisis a premeditated "bankers' panic." Attorney General Richard Olney viewed the crash as the result of "over-trading, of reckless speculation . . . of the mad rush to be quickly rich." Thomas Reed, the powerful Republican leader in the House of Representatives, put the blame on the Democrats, whose pledge to eliminate protective tariffs, he charged, unnerved business operators.

Whatever its causes, the panic sent the economy into a tailspin. The meltdown on Wall Street sliced millions of dollars off the value of businesses and property. Worried depositors rushed to pull their holdings out of banks, which reduced their financial reserves and initiated the cancellation of loans. Some 642 banks failed nationwide by the end of 1893. One-fifth of Wisconsin's banks closed their doors during the year. Tight credit and higher interest rates, in addition to lower consumer demand and vicious price competition among firms fighting to stay solvent, produced a swath of bankruptcies. More than 15,000 businesses went under in 1893.

The rise in bankruptcies reflected a steep decline in commerce and agriculture. Manufacturers of consumer and industrial products slumped sharply in 1894. Iron production dropped, coal tonnage sagged, and the market for railroad equipment, such as locomotives and rails, largely evaporated. The Burlington Railroad, a major midwestern carrier, purchased no new equipment in 1895 and little in 1897 and 1898. The construction of new railroad mileage, a mark of economic prosperity, declined 60 percent from 1892 to 1895 and then fell further in 1897. Housing construction followed a similar pattern.

The economic decline hurt farmers, too. Although declining prices had troubled agriculture before the 1893 crisis, the depression further undercut demand for cotton, corn, wheat, and tobacco, pushing down prices and thus farmers' incomes. A drought in the West during the summer of 1894 added to the turmoil in the countryside, where farm tenancy and debt rose. The gross national product declined 5 percent in 1893 and 3 percent more in 1894.

Reduced farm prices and fewer manufactured goods meant less traffic for railroads. Like many large companies, Burlington's net income declined between 1893 and 1897. The firm survived the hard times, but the rail industry as a whole, burdened with overcapacity and debt, was not so lucky. More than 100 lines failed in 1893. Bankruptcies included well-known companies such as the Northern Pacific, the Union Pacific, and the Santa Fe. By mid-1894 the number of financially wrecked lines rose to 156, and the total mounted during the decade. This carnage provided an opportunity for investment firms such as J.P. Morgan and Company to salvage the industry. Morgan and other financial leaders built new companies out of failed ones, reorganizing nearly two-thirds of all rail mileage into seven lines by 1906. Similarly, manufacturers initiated a "merger wave" between 1897 and 1904, as firms sought to gain greater control over their markets by acquiring or joining their rivals.

Workers probably suffered more from the depression than did business owners. The decline of production, construction, and railroad traffic meant layoffs and wage cuts. Unemployment rose rapidly

in the latter half of 1893. Estimates place the rate of joblessness at 13 to 18 percent in 1894, but national averages understate the crisis. Unemployment may have exceeded 35 percent of the workforce in Milwaukee during the winter of 1893–94. Estimates place joblessness at 43 percent in Michigan and 35 percent in New York during these months. Jobs were particularly scarce in the coalmines, on the railroads, in the textile mills, and in construction. In an age before federal unemployment insurance and other "safety net" programs, unemployment meant evictions, hunger, and poverty for hundreds of thousands of workers.

Many jobless individuals went "tramping" from city to city in search of work and a meal, straining the resources of local communities to offer assistance, however limited. Police stations became overcrowded with homeless men during the winter months. Private donations funded temporary jobs in some cities, such as New York and Milwaukee, and state governments enacted "stay" laws that delayed foreclosures on loans for homes and farms. But more often local officials pressured state lawmakers to pass vagrancy laws in an effort to keep tramps out of town.

The hard times prodded some Americans to take desperate measures, including hijacking trains and organizing mass demonstrations. Jacob Coxey, a retired industrialist, proposed that Congress borrow half a billion dollars to finance public works, such as road construction, as a way to create jobs and put people back to work. In spring 1894, he led a small, ragtag "army" of unemployed men from Ohio to Washington, D.C., where he planned to read his petition on the steps of the Capitol. Alarmed city police arrested Coxey for walking on the grass, foiling his plan. "Coxey's Army," as it was called, rapidly melted away.

Workers who managed to keep their jobs usually experienced cuts in their wages. Besides tightening their belts, workers had few options in these circumstances except to strike for higher wages, but such moves posed risks amid an ever-growing pool of unemployed workers. Major job actions occurred in the coal, textile, and railroad industries. Because of its huge scale and violence, the PULLMAN STRIKE epitomized the volatility of the depression years. The seeds of the conflict lay in the reduction of wages at George Pullman's factory, which manufactured railroad sleeping cars at the industrialist's model town south of Chicago. What began as a walkout in early summer 1894 at the Pullman factory spread to Chicago, the nation's rail hub, halting rail traffic for days and to much of the country. Siding with railroad owners, President Cleveland authorized federal troops to assist state militia and railroad detectives in breaking the strike. Fourteen strikers were killed in Chicago and more elsewhere.

The economy was emerging from its doldrums in 1895 when a second panic on December 20 blunted the recovery. The immediate cause of alarm on Wall Street was President Cleveland's ultimatum that Britain settle a dispute with Venezuela over its boundary with the colony of British Guiana. Several financial houses collapsed and gold exports again poured out of the United States. The presidential campaign of 1896, in which the Democratic and Populist parties both championed "free silver," may have also slowed recovery by worrying business owners and investors. The election of Republicans reassured entrepreneurs that the federal government would remain on the gold standard. Other factors contributed to the recovery in 1897 and 1898. Wheat shortages in Europe and India, plus a bumper crop in the United States, boosted agricultural exports. A gold rush in the Yukon helped to increase gold output, which expanded the money supply. The depression induced some corporations, such as steelmakers, to adopt cost efficiencies, which made their products more competitive overseas. Manufacturing exports rose in the latter half of 1897, although some industries remained depressed through 1899.

Local governments struggled with the effects of the depression. Because private funds were inadequate to handle the spiraling caseload of indigent and jobless families during the hard times, local government became the last bastion of help. Municipalities substantially increased their funding of public assistance (an early form of welfare), either by cash stipends or by initiating new public works, such as constructing waterworks, parks, and public buildings. Some cities, such as Milwaukee, Cleveland, and Jacksonville, borrowed to pay for these projects. Most localities and many states watched their revenues fall during the lean years. Taxpayers demanded that local authorities retrench by cutting back on city services and by eliminating extraneous expenditures, which included relief for the jobless in the minds of some

critics. Simultaneously, pressures built to acquire additional revenues. The city of Birmingham, Alabama, raised taxes on tradesmen and charged tuition for its public schools. State governments filled part of the fiscal breech by enacting new taxes, especially on businesses and railroads, and by raising the amount of debt that localities could carry. Over the long run, the depression contributed to a growing realization that state government would have to pay a larger share of the cost of providing public services.

National finances also suffered, as the U.S. Treasury ran deficits between 1894 and 1898. President Cleveland advocated the elimination of "extravagance in governmental appropriations" as the solution for "a depleted public Treasury." He also recommended tariff reform, one of his pet objectives, and suggested that the federal government should levy an income tax on corporations. The Wilson-Gorman Tariff of 1894 failed to achieve the downward revision of custom duties that Cleveland desired, but the act did impose an income tax on individuals and businesses. The Supreme Court declared the tax unconstitutional in the *Pollack* cases in 1895.

The depression sparked a spirited fight in Washington over the nation's monetary standard. Southern and western members of Congress pressed to add silver to the nation's money supply. The availability of more currency, they argued, would cure the depression. President Cleveland, other conservative Democrats, and Republicans adamantly stood by gold as the sole standard on which to base the currency. Over the opposition of his party, Cleveland persuaded Congress in 1893 to repeal the 1890 Silver Purchase Act. Faced with dwindling stocks of gold in the Treasury vault, Cleveland authorized four loans for the purchase of additional gold. The president's defense of the gold standard cost him the support of his own party and contributed to the Democrats' devastating defeats in the congressional elections of 1894. This setback offered silver inflationists an opportunity to capture the leadership of the Democratic Party. In 1896, Democrats nominated William Jennings Bryan as the party's candidate for president. Bryan enthusiastically embraced the monetarization of silver, a position that induced the Populist Party also to select him as their presidential candidate.

Bryan's decisive loss to William McKinley in 1896 had significant implications for national politics. The election established Republicans as the nation's majority party, a position they retained until 1932, with the exception of an interlude during Woodrow Wilson's presidency (1913–21). President McKinley opposed the "free silver" movement and reaffirmed that the monetary system would be based solely on gold. Republicans also raised custom duties in the Dingley Tariff Act of 1897, crafted partially to stop the "continuing deficit" in federal accounts. In addition, Republicans argued that a higher tariff would protect American products from foreign competition and therefore boost the nation's economy.

America's declaration of war against Spain in 1898 had links to the depression. A rebellion had broken out in Cuba in 1895 against Spanish colonial rule, an event provoked by the Tariff of 1894, which had placed new duties on sugar imported from the island. By 1897, when Cleveland left office, the Spanish had launched a brutal campaign to quell the dissidents. Congress pressured McKinley to intervene and approved a declaration of war in 1898. Although brief, the Spanish-American War had lasting repercussions, as the nation demonstrated its new military capability to the world. The peace settlement also transferred territories in the Caribbean and the Pacific to the United States.

The effects of the depression reverberated widely within business, society, and politics. In the South, the hard times had boosted the attractiveness of the Populist Party, which appealed for support from African-American voters. The backlash against black support for Populists added fuel to the movement that stripped the right to vote from African Ameri-cans. The economic crises of the 1890s and its impact on the business community also contributed to the emergence of the Progressive Movement in the early 20th century. The economic uncertainty brought on by the depression motivated many business managers to reduce competition through mergers and acquisition of rival firms or, in essence, to grow larger. Giant corporations such as U.S. Steel, International Harvester, and American Tobacco came into existence in the wake of the depression. The desire to rein in the power of these economic goliaths was one of the major goals of Progressive reformers.

See also 1873 FINANCIAL PANIC AND DEPRESSION; 1898 EXPLOSION OF THE USS *MAINE*; 1907 FINANCIAL PANIC AND DEPRESSION.

Ballard C. Campbell

FURTHER READING:

Carter, Susan B., and Richard Sutch. "Great Depression of 1890s: New Suggestive Estimates of the Unemployment Rate, 1890–1905." *Research in Economic History* 14 (1992): 347–376.

Hoffman, Charles. *The Depression of the Nineties: An Economic History.* Westport, Conn.: Greenwood, 1970.

Rezneck, Samuel. "Unemployment, Unrest, and Relief in the United States during the Depression of 1893–1897." *Journal of Political Economy* 61 (1953): 324–345.

Steeples, Douglas, and David O. Whitten. *Democracy in Desperation: The Depression of 1893.* Westport, Conn.: Greenwood, 1998.

1893 ◆ EXTERMINATING THE BUFFALO

North American buffalo, otherwise known as bison, had thrived on the continent for millennia. In the early 1800s, more than 30 million buffalo roamed the United States and Canada. Although human settlement in the east had pushed them west of the Mississippi River by 1833, vast numbers of buffalo remained in the midsection of North America. Herds of these majestic beasts ranged from the Canadian plains in the north to the border of Mexico in the south, and from the Rocky Mountains in the west to the Mississippi River in the east. Once wolves, fire, and harsh winters had been the buffalo's only threats. Later, European intrusion brought new and more menacing threats in the form of agriculture, commerce—and hunters. With farmers came domesticated grazing animals, notably cattle, which competed with buffalo for foraging grounds. The western penetration of the railroads in the 19th century hastened the migration of vast numbers of people. This juggernaut of "progress" nearly drove the bison to extinction.

The bison had long fit comfortably into the Great Plains ecosystem. Although many species of North American mammals had perished at the end of the last ice age, about 10,000 years ago, the bison survived. Their rapid rates of reproduction, their resiliency in relation to native hunters, and their adaptability to the arid conditions that followed the Ice Age explain this persistence. Impressive in size, the average male animal stood seven feet tall and weighed more than 1,500 pounds. The bison's relatively long lifespan of 25 years helped the species to flourish. Although Plains Indians hunted the bison and relied on the animal for food, clothing, and shelter, they did not overhunt the buffalo or threaten its survival before whites and a commercialized economy arrived on the Plains.

European migration to the Americas upset this ecological balance. Fur traders, who first arrived in the 1600s, constituted the first threat. After trappers had exhausted the beaver populations in the Great Lakes region and the Ohio River Valley, they turned their attention to the bison. Trade in buffalo robes and tongues increased dramatically by the early 19th century, resulting in more than 200,000 killings annually. Slaughter of the bison became more systematic between 1830 and 1860, when wagonloads of robes, tongues, and bison meat flowed to eastern markets. Enterprising businesses even ground up bison bones for fertilizer.

From atop a train crossing the prairie, passengers indiscriminately shoot buffalo. *(Getty Images)*

FACTBOX

PLACE Much of North America, especially the grasslands of the western Great Plains

DATE Late 19th century; by 1893 only 300 bison remained in North America

TYPE Mass animal slaughter by hunters

DESCRIPTION From roughly 30 million in the early 18th century, the bison population was nearly hunted to extinction by 1893.

CAUSE Excessive hunting, driven by the expansion of the eastern market and robe trade, western settlement, changes in Native American lifestyles, and the building of transcontinental railroads

CASUALTIES Some 30 million buffalo

IMPACT Decimation of the buffalo deprived Plains Indians of food and essential supplies and came close to eradicating a symbol of the original West.

The completion of the first transcontinental railroad in 1869 accelerated pressure on the buffalo, facilitating excesses such as the slaughter of the "southern herd" in 1877–78. The scale of this mass kill is suggested by the fact that one outpost alone—Fort Griffin in Shackelford County, Texas—sent out 1,500 hunting parties armed with .50 caliber and larger rifles. Hunters claimed more than 100,000 hides from the southern herd in December and January. This pattern of carnage was replicated throughout the 1880s and early 1890s. One man, Orlando Brown, killed 5,700 buffalo by himself, firing his .50 caliber so often that he lost hearing in one ear. Private companies such as the American Fur Company partnered with Native Americans to hunt bison. The U.S. Army approved of the collaboration because elimination of the bison helped to reduce the Indian population, which the army deemed dangerous.

Native Americans themselves contributed to the demise of the buffalo. Pressure from Europeans drove Indians from the eastern grasslands to the Great Plains between 1730 and 1880. European pathogens played a significant role in provoking this migration. Diseases such as measles and smallpox decimated Native American societies, fragmenting village economies that practiced both hunting and farming. Once dispersed across the plains, Native Americans adopted a nomadic lifestyle based primarily on hunting bison. The availability of guns and horses facilitated the transition. But heavy dependence on the bison for their livelihood put plains-dwellers in a vulnerable position. The demands of the market economy drove hunters toward a single objective: kill more bison in order to supply the East with hides, tongues, and meat.

By 1893, nearly all the buffalo had been killed. Only 300 beasts remained in the wild, threatening the extinction of the species. Yellowstone National Park, created in 1872, contained the only surviving herd. With the bison's existence hanging by a thread, Congress took action in May 1894 by giving the national government authority to rejuvenate buffalo populations. The act outlawed "killing, wounding, or capturing any bird or wild animal" in Yellowstone National Park and imposed penalties for violating the regulations. Conservationists founded the American Bison Society in 1905 and selected President Theodore Roosevelt its honorary president. Roosevelt persuaded Congress to establish several wildlife preserves, which the society helped to stock with bison. The scheme worked. By 1929, the number of bison had rebounded to 3,385 animals. The society's role in the rejuvenation of the buffalo became less important after 1930 as ranchers and breeders began to raise them.

As the United States industrialized, fanciful visions of the frontier entered the American memory. William "Buffalo Bill" Cody's show—Buffalo Bill's Wild West, which featured trick riding, horse-racing, stagecoach robberies, and Indian warfare—thrived a century ago by capitalizing on this nostalgia. The bison has remained an important element of the romanticized image of the American West. This relationship between free, roaming animals and America's frontier heritage is probably more effective in insuring the bison's survival than conservation policy or the commercialization of meat production. Perhaps because of its emergence as a symbol of the western frontier, the bison not only avoided extinction but is now thriving. The National Bison Association estimates that more than 200,000 bison now populate North America.

See also 1492 DECIMATION OF NATIVE AMERICANS BY EUROPEAN DISEASES.

David G. O'Donnell

FURTHER READING:

Crosby, Alfred. *Ecological Imperialism: The Biological Expansion of Europe, 900–1900.* New York: Cambridge University Press, 1986.

Haines, Francis. *The Buffalo: The Story of American Bison and Their Hunters from Prehistoric Times to the Present.* 1970. Reprint, Norman: University of Oklahoma Press, 1995.

Isenberg, Andrew. *The Destruction of the Bison.* Cambridge: Cambridge University Press, 2000.

1894 ◆ PULLMAN STRIKE

The Pullman strike hit the United States with an electrifying jolt in the summer of 1894 when violence between workers and authorities erupted in Chicago and at other points in the country. Fear and apprehensions rippled throughout the nation, as some observers warned of impending revolution. The strike, its violence, and predictions of social catastrophe arose out of a confluence of developments, beginning with a severe economic depression that started in May 1893 following a financial panic in the New York stock market. The economic slowdown deepened during the winter of the 1893–94, resulting in mounting unemployment and the bankruptcy of numerous businesses. Railroads in particular fell victim to the depression, with one-fourth of the industry in receivership by mid-1894. In addition to layoffs of workers, many businesses cut wages in an effort to weather the hard times.

George Pullman (1831–97) was one of the industrialists forced to retrench. Pullman manufactured

FACTBOX

PLACE Chicago, the Midwest, and the West.

DATE June 21–mid-July 1894

TYPE Railroad strike

DESCRIPTION A major railroad strike shut down commerce in Chicago and other cities, prompting violence and the summoning of militia who shot demonstrators.

CAUSE George Pullman cut wages for his workers during a severe economic depression. The newly formed American Railway Union refused to handle trains that pulled Pullman sleeping and dining cars.

CASUALTIES 34 deaths

IMPACT Near-national stoppage of railroad traffic and fears of a revolutionary upheaval resulted in federal injunctions against strike leaders.

sleeping and dining cars and leased them to railroad companies. His operation was centered in the town of Pullman, a self-contained community south of Chicago that the businessman had built as a company town in an effort to keep his workers "clean, contented, sober, educated, and happy." Declining orders for his cars prompted Pullman to cut wages, but he did not reduce the rents that he charged to his workers, nor did he allow representatives of the America Railway Union (ARU), organized in June 1893, to enter his town. These grievances and Pullman's refusal to negotiate with his employees stirred Pullman workers to vote for a strike on May 10, 1894. George Pullman responded by closing his plant.

The ARU voted on June 21 1894, to support the Pullman workers. The decision was a bold step for the new union, which its president, Eugene Debs (1855–1926), and other labor leaders had formed in an effort to bring solidarity to a fragmented labor group. Prior to the ARU, rail workers had been organized into separate craft unions, such as engineers, firemen, and conductors. Debs had no fondness for George Pullman, calling him "a rich plunderer" and "an oppressor of labor." Yet he had counseled against a strike, realizing that depression conditions created a large pool of unemployed workers who could

be hired as strikebreakers. Debs also realized that the railroads would exert their power against a unified rail union. Nonetheless, ARU leaders resolved on June 21 not to handle trains that pulled Pullman cars, a decision that made the work stoppage a "secondary boycott," or sympathy strike. Debs stood by the decision of his union. He worked tirelessly encouraging rail workers to honor the boycott but also urged them not to resort to violence. By June 28, as many as 125,000 workers had joined the boycott which had virtually shut down rail traffic in and out of Chicago and throughout much of the western United States. Eventually, all but one transcontinental railroad stopped running.

The railroads were ready to meet the union challenge. The executives of railroads that converged on Chicago, the hub of rail activity in the Midwest, had organized the General Managers Association (GMA) in 1886. Besides crushing the boycott, the GMA's primary goal was to resist unionization among rail workers. Plotting their strategy in collaboration with George Pullman, the rail managers agreed to attach U.S. postal mail cars to trains that pulled Pullman cars. By so doing, interference with Pullmans would constitute an illegal impediment to a federal activity, subjecting participants to arrest. Trainmen who refused to handle Pullman cars were fired. The rail managers took an even bolder step by requesting that Richard Olney, the attorney general of the United States, seek an injunction, or court order, that proclaimed the boycott illegal. Olney quickly complied. Federal marshals hired several thousand deputies, many of whom were loyal railroad employees, to enforce the antiboycott order.

Richard Olney (1855–1917) was a willing accomplice in the rail company effort to crush the strike and the American Railway Union. Olney had been an attorney for the railroads prior to his cabinet appointment by President Grover Cleveland. The attorney general considered strikes illegal and actively collaborated with the General Managers Association to squash the Pullman boycott. He appointed Edwin Walker, an attorney for the rail managers, as a special Justice Department agent for Chicago, and instructed him to request federal injunctions against Debs and the ARU. The order issued on July 2 declared the boycott illegal and forbade practically every ARU official in Chicago from advocating or participating in the work stoppage. Over the next several days, Olney had similar orders issued at other rail centers in the west. He doubted the ability of federal marshals to enforce the court's orders and—despite opposition from state governors—persuaded President Cleveland to authorize the mobilization of federal troops. On July 4, 1894, U.S. soldiers took up positions in the Windy City.

Chicago became the focal point of the crisis. The boycott virtually shut down commerce in the Windy City, causing the prices of produce and dairy products to spike upward. Shortages of coal were reported in eastern cities. Slackening business reportedly caused the layoff of half a million workers. Some unions engaged in sympathy strikes for the trainmen. As Debs wired telegrams to colleagues throughout the country urging solidarity in maintaining the boycott, mainstream newspapers labeled the labor leader a "dictator" who was inciting mob action and violence. The *New York Times* called Debs "an enemy of the human race." On July 2, the *Chicago Tribune* head-lined "Strike is Now War."

Debs urged nonviolence, but ARU officials could not control all the individuals that took to the streets in the heat of the conflict. On July 6, a mob in Chicago destroyed hundreds of millions of dollars of railroad property. The next day, Illinois militiamen fired into demonstrators, killing four. During the next several days, 13 individuals were fatally wounded in confrontations with authorities in the Chicago area. At the peak of the conflict, Chicago was turned into an armed camp, with 14,000 police officers, militiamen, federal soldiers and federal deputies patrolling the streets and rail yards. Up to 34 demonstrators, none strikers, were killed across the country.

Debs called the confrontation between workers and their opponents "a contest between the producing classes and the money power of the country." Many major newspapers expressed a different viewpoint, issuing hysterical warnings of an impending revolution. The *Chicago Tribune* described the unfolding events as an "insurrection." *Harper's Weekly* called the situation a "rebellion." The *Washington Post* reported that "Chicago is at the mercy of the Incendiary's Torch" and was under the spell of "anarchists and socialists." Jane Addams, founder of Hull House, a center formed to help immigrants and workers in Chicago, recalled that the city "became divided into two cheering sides." Because of the "class bitterness" that resulted, Hull House lost numerous sponsors.

On July 10, Debs and other ARU officials were arrested for violating the federal injunction. With the boycott leaders in jail and unable to coordinate the work stoppage, resistance to the railroads deflated quickly. By August 2, the Pullman works reopened, although it did not rehire former strikers. Thousands of striking trainmen were "blacklisted" for their participation in the boycott. Debs was convicted in federal court for violating the injunction and was sentenced to six months in the McHenry County jail. Debs's legal battle wound up in the Supreme Court. Attorney Clarence Darrow (1857–1938), who gained fame representing numerous social justice cases, argued that Debs had been the victim of a conspiracy organized by Chicago railroads in an effort to smash the trainmen's unions. But the Supreme Court agreed with Olney that the federal intervention into the strike was justified because the railroads assisted in the delivery of the mail, which was plainly a responsibility of the government. The attorney general called the railroads "national highways" that were critical to the functioning of national life. Justice David J. Brewer, who wrote the court's unanimous opinion *In re Debs* (1895) agreed. "If the emergency arises," he wrote, "the army of the nation and all its militia are at the service of the nation to compel obedience to its laws." The Pullman strike not only provoked a new level of federal protection of business, but it also produced a legal rationale for an expansion of presidential authority. The Supreme Court did not reprimand federal officials for deliberately ignoring protests from state governors for the use of federal troops to quell the strike.

Debs emerged from jail in July 1895 to a hero's welcome from his supporters and with a changed outlook. Doubting the capacity of unions to overcome the power of big business, he abandoned labor activity for politics. In 1900, he ran the first of his five campaigns for president as the nominee of the Socialist Party. Whereas Grover Cleveland's use of federal resources to break the ARU was successful, the president's resolve backfired politically. His snub of workingmen in favor of railroad owners contributed to the disastrous Democratic defeat in the congressional elections of 1894. Coupled with the lingering depression and its associated controversy over the gold standard, the Pullman strike left Cleveland isolated from his party. Democrats turned to reformer William Jennings Bryan as their presidential nominee in 1896. Bryan lost, but politicians trod more carefully with labor-business disputes in subsequent years, as President Theodore Roosevelt's handling of the 1902 anthracite coal strike demonstrated. The prospect of a national rail strike in 1916 persuaded President Woodrow Wilson that it was politically prudent to compromise worker demands rather than run the risk of allowing the nation to repeat the tragedy of the Pullman strike.

See also 1893 FINANCIAL PANIC AND DEPRESSION.

Ballard C. Campbell

FURTHER READING:

Eggert, Gerald G. *Richard Olney: Evolution of a Statesman.* University Park: Pennsylvania State University Press, 1974.

Lindsey, Almont. *The Pullman Strike: The Story of a Unique Experiment and of a Great Labor Upheaval.* Chicago: University of Chicago Press, 1942.

Salvatore, Nick. *Eugene V. Debs: Citizen and Socialist.* Urbana: University of Illinois Press, 1982.

1898 ◆ EXPLOSION OF THE USS *MAINE*

The USS *Maine* was an American battleship on a peaceful visit to Havana, Cuba, when it suddenly exploded at 9:45 P.M. on February 15, 1898, killing all 274 American sailors aboard. The ship was at anchor at the place assigned by port authorities. The exact cause of the disaster was never determined, but most speculation at the time and subsequent investigations pointed to the explosion of an external mine that set off five tons of gunpowder in the ship's magazines. The explosion came during escalating tensions between the United States and Spain regarding Spain's maladministration of Cuba, one of its last colonial possessions, and harsh suppression of the island's independence movement. Two months after the event and largely because of it, the United States declared war on Spain.

Immediately after the explosion, Spain offered its regrets and helped the survivors. The *Maine's* captain said he could not explain what had happened. While newspapers, such as William Randolph Hearst's *New York Morning Journal* and Joseph Pulitzer's *New York World,* printed sensationalistic stories blaming Spain for the explosion, President William McKinley and most American opinion leaders called for a suspension of judgment until the navy reported on its inquiry a month later. The U.S. Naval Court of Inquiry interrogated survivors and eyewitnesses, and several navy divers explored the sunken wreck. The explosion of the forward ammunition magazines, they determined, obviously had caused the sinking. Divers said the ship's bottom plates were all

FACTBOX

PLACE Havana Harbor, Cuba

DATE February 15, 1898

TYPE Ship explosion and sinking

DESCRIPTION The USS *Maine* was sunk by an explosion.

CAUSE An external explosion, probably from a mine, but of unknown origin

CASUALTIES 274 American sailors killed

IMPACT The ship's explosion and the battle cry "Remember the *Maine*" proved instrumental in prodding the United States to declare war against Spain in 1898. The Spanish-American War led to U.S. expansionism and the nation's emergence as a world power.

bent inward, consistent with an external mine. (If an internal accidental explosion had occurred, the bottom plates would have been bent outward.) On the floor of the harbor, a large cavity was seen, presumably from the explosion. The official report on March 28 indicated that the explosion was probably not an accident inside the ship but was deliberately set by an outside mine. On hearing the report, many groups demanded war.

Public opinion in the United States had been hostile to Spain for several years as that country tried to suppress growing rebellions in Cuba and other colonies. The *Maine* was sent to Havana to protect American citizens in case of rioting and to show the intense American interest in resolving the crisis. The *Maine* explosion so dominated headlines and public attention that quiet diplomacy became extremely difficult. Although opposed to war, McKinley demanded that Spain immediately end the chaos. Madrid repeatedly stalled for time, making promises that never took effect, hoping perhaps to gain diplomatic support from European powers that never came. Cuban insurgents advised McKinley that their insurrection would fall apart if Spain granted an armistice. The American business community, although opposed to war, warned that further months of uncertainty were intolerable. Finally, McKinley told Congress to make the decision, knowing that the war hawks dominated Congress. On April 25, 1898, Congress declared war on Spain. "Remember the *Maine*" became a popular rallying cry and song.

The United States quickly won the Spanish-American War, and Cuba gained its independence from Spain. But the mystery of what caused the *Maine* to explode continued. A thorough investigation in 1911 by the navy pointed to an outside mine as the source of the initial explosion. Sixty-five years later, U.S. Admiral Hyman Rickover reanalyzed the data and concluded it might have been an accident. The latest inquiry, completed in 1999, was sponsored by the *National Geographic Magazine*. It commissioned an analysis by Advanced Marine Enterprises (AME), using computer modeling that was not available for previous investigations. The AME analysis concluded that "it appears more probable than was previously concluded that a mine caused the inward bent bottom structure and the detonation of the magazines."

Multiple theories have circulated as to what happened. The first theory is that it was an accident, caused by spontaneous ignition of the bituminous coal in the coal bunkers, located near the powder room, that could have heated the gunpowder to 450°F and set it off. There was no direct evidence for this hypothesis. The blast effects on the hull seem to show the causal force was outside, not inside; the coal bunkers were inspected daily, had never shown problems before, and the coal used was not known to spontaneously ignite. The alternative theory held that an external mine was detonated underwater on the port side by experts who knew what they were doing. Spain had recently purchased mines that could easily have done the job. One could have been seized by Cuban insurgents and set off to incite Americans into declaring war, or a mine could have been detonated by rogue Spanish officers angry at the intervention of the Americans. Perhaps Spanish authorities had ordered the mine placement, or one could even have been placed by American authorities seeking to escalate the conflict. Historians agree that it is highly unlikely that the Spanish government or the American government ordered the sabotage. The most likely suspect, for most historians, are the insurgents or rogue Spanish officers, but there is no direct evidence to implicate either group.

Spain's reluctance to negotiate in 1898 was caused by its own internal crisis. Spain was itself on the verge of civil war, but simply withdrawing from Cuba would have worsened its crisis. One honorable solution was to lose a short war to a much more powerful country, which is what happened. A new generation came to influence in Spain (the "Generation of 98"), and civil war was averted for another 35 years.

Historians have debated whether American public opinion was deliberately inflamed by the sensationalistic "yellow journalism" of newspaper publishers William Randolph Hearst and Joseph Pulitzer in New York City. Early 20th-century historian James Ford Rhodes concluded that the press "had manipulated the real news, spread unfounded reports, putting all before their readers with scare headlines." By contrast historian John Offner has insisted, "there is no evidence" to indicate that the "sensational press" influenced McKinley's policy, suggesting that "its impact on changing public opinion may have been limited." When the war came—"a splendid little war," one official called it—it lasted only six months and drew Americans together, especially the southerners whose patriotism had been in doubt since the Civil War a generation earlier. The Spanish-American War represented a significant turning point in America's position in the world. Besides acquiring Puerto Rico in the Caribbean and the Philippine Islands in the Pacific, territorial possessions that created new defensive responsibilities, the United States demonstrated that it had built up its naval capacity sufficiently to defeat an established European power.

Richard Jensen

FURTHER READING:

May, Ernest R. *Imperial Democracy: The Emergence of America as a Great Power.* New York: Harper and Row, 1973.

Offner, John L. "McKinley and the Spanish-American War." *Presidential Studies Quarterly* 34, no. 1 (2004): 50–61.

Perez, Louis A., Jr. "The Meaning of the *Maine*: Causation and Historiography of the Spanish-American War." *Pacific Historical Review* 58, no. 3 (1989): 293–322.

Samuels, Peggy, and Harold Samuels. *Remembering the* Maine. Washington, D.C.: Smithsonian Institute Press, 1995.

1898 ◆ SINKING OF THE *PORTLAND*

Late in the morning of November 27, 1898, the paddle-wheel steamship *Portland* foundered at sea off the northern tip of Cape Cod in Massachusetts Bay. The vessel sank, carrying 192 individuals to their deaths. They were among the 500 or so victims of the "Portland Gale," an epic blizzard that packed winds of hurricane force, a storm of greater ferocity than the famed blow of 1841. Why the ship's captain did not return to port in face of the fierce blizzard and how the ship succumbed to the elements remain a mystery. So did the wreck's location, until underwater photography more than a century later confirmed its resting place. In a region that has recorded hundreds of ship disasters, notes renowned maritime historian Edward Rowe Snow, the loss the *Portland* was "the worst marine tragedy of the 19th Century in New England waters."

Commissioned in 1890, the *Portland* was a sleek wooden side-wheel steamship, 281 feet in length and 62 feet wide, displacing 2,282 tons. The ship had 168 staterooms and could carry 800 passengers. Drawing only 11 feet of water, the *Portland's* design facilitated navigation in shallow harbors and rivers but made the craft less stable on the open sea. Its 1500-horsepower engine powered the vessel at 12–13 knots, allowing the ship to make its regular run between Boston and Portland, Maine, in nine hours. One newspaper described the craft as "the finest vessel that will travel eastern waters."

At 7 P.M. Saturday evening on November 26, the *Portland* left India Wharf in Boston destined for Portland, carrying 127 passengers and 65 crew members. The ship was under the command of Captain Hollis Blanchard, who had worked for the Portland Steamship Company, the vessel's owner, for nine

FACTBOX
PLACE Massachusetts Bay
DATE November 27, 1898
TYPE Shipwreck
DESCRIPTION The paddle-wheel steamship *Portland* sank off Cape Cod en route from Boston to Portland.
CAUSE The "Portland Gale," an epic blizzard
CASUALTIES 192 individuals lost at sea
IMPACT The accident stimulated shippers to leave passenger lists on shore and to substitute propeller-driven ships for steam paddle wheelers.

years as a first pilot but only recently had become the *Portland's* master. Captain Blanchard had seen the noon weather report that predicted snow during Saturday night but warned of no unusually dangerous conditions. The steamship company's manager indicated that the line received its normal 3 P.M. weather report from New York by wire, which was compared with conditions in Boston and Portland. Snow was reported to the south, but the reports failed to foresee the convergence of two powerful weather systems. One low-pressure system formed over the Great Lakes and brought cold air as it swept into New England. A second and larger front originated in the Gulf of Mexico and gained energy and moisture as it moved into the Gulf of Maine. While the midday weather was pleasant, the dual fronts combined into a raging "nor'easter" blizzard by evening,

Almost as long as a football field, the steamship *Portland* sank amid a raging blizzard off the coast of New England with 192 people aboard. There were no survivors. *(Portland Steamship Historical Society)*

with wind gusts reaching hurricane force. Observers on the U.S. Weather Station on Block Island (off the coast of Rhode Island) recorded wind speeds of 90 miles per hour before their instrument blew away and estimated that gusts topped 110 miles per hour.

Snow began to fall as the *Portland* pushed out into Boston harbor. The steamship *Kennebec,* which had headed out earlier, sounded four warning blasts on its horn as it passed the *Portland* on its return to port. Blanchard acknowledged the signal but kept his ship's bow pointed seaward. Once caught in the storm's fury, with waves as high as 40 feet, the *Portland* was severely handicapped. Reversing direction put the ship in peril because if it turned broadside into the mountainous waves, it could capsize. The *Portland* was observed close to Thasher's Island off Cape Ann at 9:30 P.M. but was later sighted a dozen miles southeast of this location. Blanchard apparently adopted this new heading in hope of riding out the gale in the open sea rather than attempt to put in at Gloucester harbor, as other vessels had. A later sighting, believed to be the *Portland,* put the vessel off the coast of North Truro on Cape Cod on Sunday morning. Pocket watches on the bodies of victims that later washed up on Cape Cod had stopped between 9 and 10 P.M., suggesting the time when the vessel went down. How the ship met its end is

unknown, but one conjecture is that the furious seas swept away the upper decks of the vessel, leaving the hull exposed to seawater.

The "Portland Gale" inflicted terrible damage on New England, sinking upward of 400 vessels and taking perhaps 500 or more lives. Some ships simply disappeared without a trace. Coastal communities from New York to Maine were ravaged. Snow drifts higher than 15 feet were reported. Downed telegraph wires kept Cape Codders isolated from the mainland for days, hindering the effort to determine the fate of the *Portland.* Even the cable between the United States and Britain had broken. As no passenger manifest had been left at port, weeks elapsed before the identity of all passengers and crew were established. There were no survivors. The tragedy spurred shipping companies to leave a list of passengers on shore and to substitute screw propeller vessels for older paddle wheelers. Screw propulsion not only was more efficient, but it also eliminated enclosures for the paddle wheels, which increased the stability of vessels in heavy seas.

The final resting place of the *Portland* remained a mystery for nearly a century, despite numerous attempts to locate the wreck. In 1989, John Fish, a marine historian, located the ship 20 miles north of Provincetown on Cape Cod. In 2002, a research team working in collaboration with the Stellwagen Bank National Marine Sanctuary used sonar devices and an underwater remotely operated vehicle to pinpoint the ship's coordinates and photograph its remains. The find solved one chapter of what Snow considered "New England's greatest sea mystery."

Ballard C. Campbell

FURTHER READING:

Backelder, Peter Dow. *Four Short Blasts: The Gale of 1898 and the Loss of the Steamer* Portland. Portland, Me.: Provincial Press, 2003.

Snow, Edward Rowe. *Great Storms and Famous Shipwrecks of the New England Coast.* 3rd ed. Boston: Yankee Publishing, 1946.

1899 ◆ AUTOMOBILE FATALITIES

On September 13, 1899, H. H. Bliss disembarked from a trolley car at the corner of 74th Street and Central Park West in New York City. As he stepped onto the street, Bliss was struck and killed by a taxicab, whose driver was attempting to pass another vehicle on the right. The fatal accident was the first traffic death recorded in the United States. Seven years later, future U.S. president Woodrow Wilson, then president of Princeton University, noted: "Of all the menaces of today, the worst is the reckless driving of automobiles." Wilson's observation held true for the remainder of the century. Between 1899 and 1999, more than 3 million Americans lost their lives to motor vehicle accidents, far more than perished in combat from all of the nation's wars. Unlike the other leading causes of death, wars excepted, fatalities from traffic accidents have their greatest incidence among relatively young people.

Technical issues complicate the measurement of this modern plague. Should only the total number of deaths be counted, or should it be based on ratios, such as deaths per 100,000 miles traveled or deaths per 100,000 population (in keeping with other public health statistics)? Also, should auto fatalities be broken down by region, gender, or age? Actually, all of these considerations are useful in answering various questions about the history of traffic fatalities. Although these statistics paint a changing picture over the years, some trends are evident.

Before 1925, most automotive fatalities occurred in urban locations. Most victims in this early period were killed on streets and not in vehicles, as thoroughfares were commonly used as playgrounds and for peddling, as well as for travel. There were many

---

FACTBOX

PLACE United States

DATE 1899–present

TYPE Fatal motor vehicle accidents

DESCRIPTION Drivers, passengers, and pedestrians struck by motor vehicles

CASUALTIES More than 3 million fatalities

COST Hundreds of billions of dollars in lost wages, medical expenses, property damage, and litigation costs

IMPACT Skyrocketing traffic fatalities led to greater federal regulation of safety features in automobiles, including installation of seat belts and air bags.

---

inexperienced drivers during this early era of automobility, a factor that also elevated the risk of collision. This period also saw car ownership concentrated among upper-income families who tended to live in urban areas. Car ownership grew during the early 20th century, as automobiles began to replace horse-drawn vehicles. In 1912, New York City recorded for the first time more fatalities caused by accidents from automobiles than by horses.

In 1923, the United States recorded its 100,000th traffic death. Three years later, traffic fatalities reached their peak on the basis of miles driven and represented the fifth leading cause of death in America. Rates of traffic fatalities declined after 1926, and increasingly the victims were car occupants, not people in the street. Urban fatalities began to decline relative to accidents in rural areas, partly because pedestrians, especially children, became more savvy about the dangers from vehicular traffic. The emergence of traffic signals and playgrounds reduced risk in the streets. Urban traffic was slowing, down to 3 miles per hour in rush hour in New York City during the 1930s. Auto fatalities also dipped during this decade when hard times caused by the Great Depression forced some people to give up their cars. Gasoline rationing during World War II (1941–45) took many cars off the road, further lowering auto fatalities.

After the war, traffic fatalities began to soar again, despite the increased number of women drivers, whose safety record has always been better than that of men. One reason for the upward spike was that American automakers built bigger and faster cars. In the quarter-century following World War II, when gasoline was remarkably cheap (under 25 cents per gallon and sometimes considerably lower), drivers logged more miles, increasing their exposure to accidents. American cars were overpowered and underbraked, and neither consumers nor manufacturers paid much attention to design safety. Almost no cars had seat belts, and few had padded dashboards. The tendency for automakers to emphasize styling over safety features was the theme of *Unsafe at Any Speed: The Designed-In Danger of the American Automobile* (1965), Ralph Nader's exposé of the car industry that highlighted the deadly flaws of General Motors' Chevrolet Corvair. Another contribution to the mounting volume of traffic accidents was the spread of cars to rural areas, where auto fatality rates have consistently been higher than in cities— probably because people drove faster on country roads. The growth of suburbs and massive construction of new roads in the postwar era played a similar role. In 1951, the United States recorded its 1 millionth traffic fatality. Traffic mortality increased to its highest level in the 1960s, peaking at nearly 56,000 deaths in 1969 as baby boomers came of driving age, putting more inexperienced young drivers on the roads. In 1973, the United States recorded its 2 millionth traffic fatality.

Since 1980, deaths in motor vehicle accidents (both total numbers and rates) have declined, in good part due to the use of seat belts, the installation of which became mandatory in the 1960s, and air bags, which became standard equipment in the 1980s and 1990s. Higher gasoline prices have reduced travel, which in

Since the first automobile fatality in 1899, accidents like this one in the Catskill Mountains of New York have killed more than 3 million Americans. *(New York Public Library)*

turn lessened the exposure to accidents. However, considerable resistance to use of seat-belt laws grew in the 1980s, when conservatives argued that mandatory seat-belt use intruded on individual choice and symbolized a police state. Drivers turned increasingly to sports utility vehicles (SUVs) and pick-up trucks, which consumers believed afford afforded greater safety for their occupants—although not for the people in smaller cars that collide with them. But SUVs, which are essentially trucks with autolike bodies, have a high risk of a rollover due to their high center of gravity and can pose dangers to passengers and occupants. Another factor influencing contemporary fatality rates is the increased number of Americans of more than 80 years old, a population group with a high rate of auto accidents. While the risk of driving a motor vehicle has lessened in recent decades, the roads remain—as H. H. Bliss learned in 1899—a dangerous zone for both passengers and pedestrians.

Clay McShane

FURTHER READING:

Bradsher, Keith. *High and Mighty: SUVs, The World's Most Dangerous Vehicles and How They Got That Way.* New York: PublicAffairs, 2002.

Eastman, Joel W. *Styling vs. Safety: The American Automobile Industry and the Development of Automotive Safety, 1900–1966.* Lanham, Md.: University Press of America, 1984.

Mashaw, Jerry L., and David L. Harfst. *The Struggle for Auto Safety*. Cambridge, Mass.: Harvard University Press, 1990.

Nader, Ralph. *Unsafe at Any Speed: The Designed-In Danger of the American Automobile*. New York: Grossman, 1965.

1900 ◆ OUTBREAK OF BUBONIC PLAGUE

The first outbreak of bubonic plague in the continental United States took place in San Francisco in March 1900. There, plague erupted in two separate phases: The first phase, from 1900 to 1904, centered on Chinatown, claiming mostly Chinese-American victims; the second phase followed the 1906 earthquake and fire and lasted until 1908, claiming largely Caucasian victims. In all, there were 281 cases and 191 deaths from bubonic plague. Discriminatory measures applied to Chinese living in San Francisco sparked protests and legal appeals. Jurisdictional disputes between federal authorities and state and local authorities, coupled with an uncertain knowledge of the disease, made for a muddled and ineffective response to the first, more serious, phase of the epidemic.

Chinese in the United States had long been subjected to discriminatory legislation, none more odious than the Chinese Exclusion Act of 1882 and its successors, which had severely restricted the entry of Chinese and barred them from obtaining citizenship. The exclusion acts embodied the prejudices and fears of many Americans, particularly Caucasian inhabitants of West Coast states, against the Chinese and other Asians. Fears conflating "Chinese" with "disease" and "contagion" were intensified by the arrival of bubonic plague.

Bubonic plague is believed to have a historic reservoir in southwestern China, and periodically this disease crosses over from animals to humans and spreads rapidly. One such eruption occurred in the late 19th century, when mass migrations enabled this rat-borne disease to travel around the world rapidly by steamship. In the 1890s, bubonic plague spread throughout southern China and on to India, killing millions of people in both places. It spread to Japan, Australia, South Africa, Europe, and Hawaii. In January 1900, the Honolulu board of health believed it could eradicate the plague by burning

FACTBOX

PLACE San Francisco

DATE March 1900–February 1908

TYPE Epidemic

DESCRIPTION Two eruptions of bubonic plague in San Francisco claimed 191 lives. Racially motivated quarantine measures against residents of San Francisco's Chinatown sparked resistance to health authorities. By the time of the second eruption, in the wake of the 1906 earthquake and fire, advances in knowledge of the disease and a more partnership-building approach to the Chinese community by the Public Health Service made for a more successful response to the plague.

CAUSE Infected travelers arriving from China, Japan, or Hawaii

CASUALTIES 191 deaths

COST In addition to the human costs, many businesses suffered from a quarantine of Chinatown, and shipping companies and railroads suffered losses through fumigation and avoidance of San Francisco by travelers and shippers of goods.

IMPACT The San Francisco plague demonstrated that, because rats and their fleas were the agents of transmission, killing rats was the most effective means of controlling plague. It also helped establish federal primacy over state and local governments in coordinating responses to major threats to public health.

the houses of infected people, most of whom were Chinese; the fire became out of control and burned most of Chinatown.

Public Health Service

The U.S. Public Health Service (PHS), a division of the U.S. Department of Health and Human Services, is responsible for promoting the protection and advancement of the nation's physical and mental health. The PHS traces its roots to 1798 when President John Adams signed into law an act "for the relief of sick and disabled seamen," which authorized the creation of hospitals to care for American merchant sailors. In 1870, a reorganization converted the loose network of locally controlled hospitals into a centrally controlled Marine Hospital Service. By the end of the 19th century, the scope of activities of the Marine Hospital Service had expanded well beyond the care of merchant seamen and included the control of plague and infectious disease. Until the early 20th century, one of the major responsibilities of the service was the coordination of quarantine at sea ports and medical inspection of immigrants arriving at sites such as Ellis Island in New York.

Because of the broadening responsibilities of the PHS, Congress changed its name in 1902 to the Public Health and Marine Hospital Service and again in 1912 to just the Public Health Service. Throughout the 20th century, the PHS continued to expand its public health activities. The Public Health Service Act of 1944 provided the PHS with its broadest mandate and provided much of its modern structure.

Today, the PHS accomplishes its goals through numerous agencies and programs. The eight agencies that constitute the PHS are the major health arm of the federal government and the world's leading health organizations. These include the Agency for Health Care and Research Policy, the Agency for Toxic Substances and Disease Registry, the Centers for Disease Control and Prevention, the Food and Drug Administration, the Health Resources and Services Administration, the Indian Health Service, the National Institutes of Health, and the Sub-

stance Abuse and Mental Health Services Administration. These entities coordinate and implement national health policy on the state and local levels, conduct medical and biomedical research, and enforce laws to ensure the safety of drugs and medical devices and to protect the public against impure foods and cosmetics. In addition, the PHS administers hundreds of grant-in-aid programs, ranging from grants to support basic laboratory research by investigators in university departments to block grants to states for support of maternal and child health services. Approximately 6,100 commissioned corps officers and 50,000 civil service employees carry out the work of the PHS. Commissioned officers are assigned to all of the PHS agencies and to several agencies outside of the PHS, including the Bureau of Prisons, U.S. Coast Guard, Environmental Protection Agency, Health Care Financing Administration, and the Commission on Mental Health of the District of Columbia.

Marcos Luna

San Franciscans were aware of the events in Honolulu, associating them with the fearsome Black Death of the 14th century and other bubonic plague epidemics of the past. Scientific knowledge of bubonic plague itself was growing, but still incomplete. The plague bacillus (*yersinia pestis*) had been identified in 1894, although it was difficult to distinguish visually from other bacilli. Beyond a vague association with rats, little was known about how it spread. Potential remedies depended on whether one thought plague was a disease infecting a particular place or race of people or, following the emerging "germ theory"

of disease, the product of "germs" transmitted by some unknown agent.

Plague may have first come to San Francisco in June 1899 aboard the Japanese ship *Nippon Maru*, although that case is in dispute. One author identifies the American passenger liner *Australia* as bringing the plague in January 1900 but that, too, remains unproven. The first confirmed case of plague in San Francisco was Wing Chung Ging (known by a different transliteration as Wong Chut King, or by the nickname Chick Gin), a resident of Chinatown who died on March 6, 1900. City health authorities immediately decided on a quarantine of the Chinese in Chinatown. This Chinese-only quarantine paralyzed Chinese businesses, and its patent unfairness led to protests and threats of legal action; within several days, the first quarantine was lifted.

Even as deaths mounted among the Chinese and began to include Caucasian victims, many state and local authorities refused to acknowledge the presence of plague. Caucasian businessmen and politicians feared that doing so would harm the reputation of San Francisco and California, while Chinese suspected an attempt to remove them from prime downtown real estate. One official who did diagnose the deaths as plague-related and called for vigorous action to keep the plague from spreading was Dr. Joseph Kinyoun, the senior Marine Hospital Service (forerunner of the U.S. Public Health Service) officer on the scene. However, Kinyoun's anti-Chinese attitudes and aggressive tactics greatly antagonized the Chinese. He tried to have Chinese and Japanese residents inoculated with the unproven and highly toxic Haffkine vaccine; railroads and ferries leaving the city were persuaded not to carry any Chinese who did not have a health certificate. The Chinese successfully resisted the vaccination campaign and sued in federal court to stop the second quarantine program. In agreeing with the Chinese and their Caucasian lawyers, the court ruled in *Jew Ho v. Williamson* that the quarantine was being applied "with an evil eye and an unequal hand."

In April 1901, the Marine Hospital Service transferred Kinyoun to Detroit and replaced him with Dr. Rupert Blue. Blue's superior diplomatic skills and emphasis on killing rats either led to or coincided with a decrease in the number of new cases. The 113th and last victim of the first plague outbreak died on February 29, 1904.

Two years later, in the wake of the April 18, 1906, earthquake and fire, San Francisco's sewage and sanitation services crumbled, along with buildings and other infrastructure, providing ample opportunity for the rat population to explode. In May 1907 came a new outbreak of bubonic plague, and this time most of the 78 deaths were Caucasians. By then, however, scientists had confirmed that rat fleas were the actual agents spreading the disease. Dr. Blue was again sent out to work with San Franciscans, and he was able to win the confidence of both the city's Caucasian and Asian inhabitants for basic public health measures to combat the plague. Avoidance of racial scapegoating led to prompt reporting of new cases, destruction of rat populations became the centerpiece of an energetic public campaign, and "rat-proofing" the city and its waterfront cut down the arrival of new, infected rats. The last new case was reported in February 1908.

Fatalities from the San Francisco plague were relatively few compared to other diseases of the day. The principal impacts were in definitively establishing that the federal government, rather than state or local entities, would take charge of major threats to public health and in establishing the effectiveness of rat-control measures in preventing and controlling the spread of plague. By using the courts and popular resistance to vaccination, the Chinese marked an important step in the long process of going from a group viewed as a source of contagion to being a group perceived as meriting preventive and remedial measures that might benefit the entire population.

Robert Barde

FURTHER READING:

Chase, Marilyn. *The Barbary Plague: The Black Death in Victorian San Francisco.* New York: Random House, 2003.

McClain, Charles. *In Search of Equality: The Chinese Struggle against Discrimination in Nineteenth-Century America.* Berkeley: University of California Press, 1994.

Risse, Guenter B. "The Politics of Fear: Bubonic Plague in San Francisco, California, 1900." In *New Countries and Old Medicine: Proceedings of an International Conference on the History of Medicine and Health,* edited by Linda Bryder and Derek Dow, 1–19. Auckland, New Zealand: Pyramid Press, 1995.

1900 ◆ GALVESTON HURRICANE

Water had been rising since early morning in the streets and yards of the island city of Galveston, Texas, along the coast of the Gulf of Mexico. By midafternoon on Saturday, September 8, 1900, water and debris made movement through the streets hazardous. People gathered in the houses near them that seemed highest and sturdiest. Those delayed in leaving work took shelter in City Hall, the Tremont Hotel, the Union Passenger Station, or downtown office buildings and warehouses. A thousand people took shelter in the Ursuline Convent, including four women who went into labor and gave birth amid the stress. Stragglers determined to reach home waded through water, waist-deep and rising, holding on to fence posts while dodging roof slates and timber that became missiles in the wind. No wind gauges endured to record the entire storm, but estimates placed maximum sustained winds at around 120 miles per hour, perhaps greater. One of the worst storms in American history was unfolding.

As the afternoon became evening, violent waves battered buildings into debris farther and farther inland. The waves peaked shortly after 6 P.M. when a storm surge—later estimated at 15.7 feet—sent a shudder across the island and tore buildings from their foundations. Houses disintegrated around terrified people, who watched spouses, parents, siblings, and friends disappear into the flood. Survivors drifted clinging to wreckage until the waters receded and the winds weakened after 10 P.M.

Those who survived until the next morning, a Sunday with a clear, blue sky, found a 30-block-long barricade deposited by the storm. This ocean-made rampart consisted of building debris, ruined furniture and possessions, branches and sand, and human and animal corpses deposited by the storm. The city had flooded from two sides, the Gulf of Mexico and Galveston Bay. Corrosive salt water soaked every object not above eight feet. About 3,600 houses were destroyed. Of the city's 42,210 residents, probably about 6,000 had died—almost 15 percent of the population—although only about 4,260 casualties were identified during the first month of cleanup and recovery. When casualties caused as the storm lumbered 4,000 miles through the United States and

FACTBOX

PLACE Galveston and the Texas Gulf Coast

DATE September 8, 1900

TYPE Major hurricane with storm surge and flood

DESCRIPTION Hurricane with sustained winds estimated conservatively at 120 miles per hour pushed 15.7-foot storm surge across the port city of Galveston, which was built on a low-lying barrier island along the Gulf of Mexico. The surge inundated the city. Debris carried by wind and water battered down houses where people had taken shelter, causing damage and casualties unprecedented in the United States.

CASUALTIES 6,000 deaths estimated for Galveston, 10,000 deaths estimated for storm's entire path

COST $30 million (estimated)

IMPACT To protect the city from future storms, Galveston constructed a 17-foot-high seawall (which ultimately reached 10.4 miles in length), deposited landfill to raise 500 city blocks, built a two-mile concrete causeway across Galveston Bay, and made numerous wharf and harbor improvements. The Texas legislature authorized a new commission-style municipal government that became a model for Progressive Era reform.

Canada are added, probably more than 10,000 people died. More than a century has passed, yet the unnamed hurricane of September 1900 remains the deadliest natural disaster in American history.

Although by 1900, Houston, Dallas, and San Antonio had surpassed Galveston in population, the island port remained by consensus the most sophisticated city in Texas. With nearly 500 saloons and about 50 brothels, it vied with New Orleans for notoriety as the most risqué city on the Gulf of Mexico. Dredging and railroad projects during the 1890s secured Galveston's position as a deep-water port, ranking second in the country in cotton exports and third in wheat. Merchants and bankers poured their profits into magnificent Victorian mansions along Broadway, which at nine feet in elevation was the city's highest street. (About as protected as buildings could be in Galveston, these mansions would survive the storm relatively unscathed and in the late 20th century become a focus of the city's acclaimed historic preservation movement.) Built on one of the chain of narrow, sand-and-silt barrier islands along the Texas coast, Galveston had experienced periodic "overflows" wrought by tropical storms. At most, residents accommodated this vulnerable geography by building some houses on stilts. The Gulf of Mexico made Galveston wealthy and special—a distinctive place cherished by residents and visitors. Occasional flooding and wind was the price for living in such a splendid city.

Responsibility for warning residents and tourists of danger from the sea fell to Isaac and Joseph Cline, brothers who ran the Galveston office of the U.S. Weather Bureau. For a week, reports had arrived of a severe hurricane that had moved through the Caribbean, passed over Cuba, and threatened west Florida before turning into the Gulf of Mexico. But as yet no reliable method existed for tracking storms over water. As late as Friday evening, September 7, the typical indications suggested at worst a mild blow. By Saturday morning, however, the falling barometer, the swirling northeast winds, the unusually high tide and fast waves, and the pouring rain portended something severe. Isaac Cline warned residents within three blocks of the beach to evacuate. Even this was not enough; by the next day, every building within six blocks of the beach would disappear. Until the phone went dead at midafternoon, Joseph Cline took calls from anxious residents and sent reports to Washington. That dreadful evening, Isaac Cline's pregnant wife was among a crowd of people who, having taken refuge in the Cline house, drowned when a loosened streetcar trestle rammed into the building, which was then "torn to pieces" by floodwater, as Cline remembered. Searchers found her body two weeks later beneath the house's wreckage.

Even with earlier, more emphatic warnings, it is doubtful that the city could have evacuated effectively over the one wagon bridge and three railroad bridges that stretched across Galveston Bay. The storm took out all bridges and indeed all communications and infrastructure connections to the mainland except an undersea freshwater main whose pumping station needed repair. Of 16 ships in the harbor, the storm jarred all but two loose from their moorings.

One British ship came to rest 22 miles from where it had anchored, while another British ship plowed into a freighter and then through three bridges. Most brick buildings were repairable, although the large roofs of sturdy buildings such as churches generally gave way before the winds and flying debris. Perhaps the most wrenching tragedy of that horrible night took place at St. Mary's Orphan Asylum near the beach west of the city. Ninety children and 10 nuns died when the roof collapsed onto the second floor where they had taken refuge from the flood. Three boys survived by lashing themselves to an uprooted tree that floated into the gulf in the storm and back onshore.

On Sunday morning, a delegation of residents used one of the few undamaged boats to cross Galveston Bay, which swirled with debris in the storm's aftermath. The men made their way north in a handcar until a train appeared that took them to Houston, where they were able to spread the awful news by telegraph. Sensing the extent of damage to their southeast, Houston civic leaders had already begun to organize volunteers, the advance guard of a national relief effort that eventually included the U.S. Army, the Salvation Army, and the Red Cross, whose aging president, Clara Barton, with financial backing from Joseph Pulitzer's *New York World*, set up headquarters in the Tremont Hotel. In response to Barton's vivid appeals, Americans donated money, food, clothing, and supplies. A central relief committee of local business and civic leaders coordinated recovery and cleanup. This committee's effectiveness, in contrast to the alleged mismanagement and incapacity of elected officials, prompted a proposal to consolidate Galveston's municipal government in the hands of a five-member commission. Authorized by the Texas legislature in July 1901, the Galveston city commission became an archetype for the Progressive Era movement for revamping city government, which by World War I had yielded commission and council/manager governments in hundreds of localities across the United States.

The most gruesome task facing relief workers was the disposal of thousands of drowned and mangled bodies, which quickly decomposed in the Texas summer heat. Authorities assigned this work to gangs of African-American survivors, at times forced to work at gunpoint. The recovery crews resorted to burning bodies after corpses dumped at sea came loose from their weights and washed up on the beach. Sensationalized reports of African-American "ghouls" looting corpses underscored the extent that shared disaster did not wipe away entrenched racial divisions during this era of Jim Crow and increasing segregation.

By November, outside agencies such as the Red Cross withdrew their relief teams. By March 1901, six months after the hurricane, the central relief committee ended its operations after having overseen—in addition to the mass distribution of food, clothing, and money—the construction of hundreds of serviceable, clapboard houses and the repair of several thousand damaged homes. By January 1902, the new city commission presented a $3.5 million plan to raise the level of the city with soil drawn from the bay and to fortify Galveston behind a 17-foot concrete seawall. During the next decade, enormous pipes stretched through the city depositing 16.3 million cubic yards of dredged soil under 2,156 raised buildings spread over 500 city blocks. Meanwhile, 10,000 residents came out to celebrate completion of the first segment of seawall in 1904. Extended in stages through decades, the Galveston Seawall reached 10.4 miles by 1962. During the 20th century, this storm-protection system proved its worth repeatedly, beginning in 1915, when a hurricane comparable to the 1900 storm resulted in just eight deaths in Galveston and only a fraction of the damage suffered in the earlier storm. Even the two-mile, concrete causeway constructed to replace the city's vulnerable bridges held in 1915, although its approaches were washed away.

One durable myth about the 1900 hurricane is that it caused Houston to surpass Galveston as Texas's leading port. In fact, with an inland site more suitable for railroad traffic and manufacturing, Houston was already asserting regional supremacy before the storm, a trend accelerated by improvements in port construction technology that enabled the opening of Houston's Buffalo Bayou to ocean traffic in 1914 and especially by the shift of Texas toward petroleum production and processing during the early 20th century. Galveston recovered in population, with only 808 fewer residents counted in the 1910 census than in 1900. By 1912, Galveston's rebuilt wharves and modern cotton compresses handled 4.3 million bales of cotton, making the city the world's leading cotton port. Only gradually did Galveston shift to its later function as a picturesque ocean resort.

See also 1938 NEW ENGLAND HURRICANE; 1992 HURRICANE ANDREW; 2005 HURRICANE KATRINA.

Alan Lessoff

FURTHER READING:

Bixel, Patricia Bellis, and Elizabeth Hayes Turner. *Galveston and the 1900 Storm.* Austin: University of Texas Press, 2000.

Greene, Casey Edward, and Shelly Henley Kelly. *Through a Night of Horrors: Voices from the 1900 Galveston Storm.* College Station: Texas A&M University Press, 2000.

Larson, Erik. *Isaac's Storm: A Man, a Time, and the Deadliest Hurricane in History.* New York: Crown, 1999.

McComb, David. *Galveston: A History.* Austin: University of Texas Press, 1986.

Weems, John Edward. *A Weekend in September.* 1957. Reprint, College Station: Texas A&M University Press, 1989.

1901 ◆ ASSASSINATION OF PRESIDENT McKINLEY

On September 6, 1901, President William McKinley was shot while attending the Pan-American Exposition at Buffalo, New York. He died eight days later, the third president in 36 years to fall victim to an assassin's attack. The previous day, the president had made a major policy speech at the exposition, and on September 6, he followed a full round of public events. Late in the afternoon, McKinley, accompanied by his secretary George Cortelyou, attended a public reception at the exposition's Temple of Music, where he was to stand in a receiving line for 10 minutes. After seven or eight minutes, an unknown man approached, and although his right hand was wrapped in a handkerchief, the president offered his own for a shake. The man returned the gesture by firing two bullets from a gun swathed in his hand. Guards immediately pounced on the assailant, and McKinley urged them

FACTBOX

PLACE Pan-American Exposition, Buffalo, New York

DATE September 6, 1901

TYPE Presidential assassination

DESCRIPTION Leon Czolgosz, who claimed to be an anarchist and was probably insane, shot President William McKinley, who died eight days later of infection.

CASUALTIES Death of President McKinley

IMPACT Elevation to the presidency of Vice President Theodore Roosevelt, who continued and accelerated McKinley's expansion of presidential power and activism. Law enforcement suppressed activities of anarchists and radicals, and Congress enacted laws prohibiting the immigration of anarchists to the United States.

not to hurt him. Fearful of how the news would affect his wife, who was in fragile health, the president also cried, "be careful, Cortelyou, how you tell her—oh, be careful!"

A button in front of McKinley's sternum deflected one of the bullets, but the other pierced the president's stomach and pancreas and passed through to his back, never to be found. In the exposition's makeshift hospital, physicians performed emergency surgery to repair the stomach walls and clean the peritoneal cavity. Transported to a private home, the 58-year-old McKinley at first seemed on the road to recovery. Although an X-ray machine was available at the exposition, the doctors did not consider its use necessary to find the bullet, which they thought had reached McKinley's back muscles without damage to organs other than the stomach. Confidence in the president's survival was such that Vice President Theodore Roosevelt, who had rushed to Buffalo, resumed a vacation in the Adirondacks. Within a week, however, the physicians had concluded that gangrene, which had begun at the imperfectly cleaned wound and spread along the bullet's path, had bred general infection. On Friday the 13th, McKinley collapsed. He died early the next morning. Roosevelt sped back to Buffalo and took the oath of office as the 26th president.

The assassin was Leon Czolgosz, an American citizen born of Polish immigrant parents in Detroit in 1873. Although reasonably well-educated in Catholic parochial and public schools, he made his living by manual labor in factories and on his family's small farm. Religious as a youth, he experienced a crisis of faith in the mid-1890s after his employer fired him for participating in a strike. Although he got his job back by using an alias, the prevailing 1893 FINANCIAL PANIC AND DEPRESSION and its impact on workers and the poor convinced Czolgosz that the nation's capitalist system was not only a failure but fundamentally exploitative, benefiting only the rich and powerful at the expense of ordinary Americans. Still, his political ideas remained inchoate. He dabbled in socialist organizations and became enamored of the utopian notions set forth in Edward Bellamy's 1888 novel, *Looking Backward.* Relatively late, he came to a vague espousal of anarchism, which intensified after he heard a speech by Emma Goldman in the spring of 1901.

After his arrest, Czolgosz claimed that he was an anarchist who saw killing McKinley as doing his "duty." Ten days after the president's death, a jury convicted him of murder. His lawyers' insanity defense was lame, although a team of psychologists who later studied his background concluded that he had been insane, perhaps suffering from what would later be called paranoid schizophrenia. Yet Czolgosz himself saw his act as rational and went to the electric chair proclaiming that he had "killed the President because he was the enemy of the good people—the good working people." Politicians and the nation at large accepted Czolgosz's avowed anarchism as the true explanation for his heinous crime. In the aftermath, law-enforcement officials suppressed the activities of anarchists and other radicals. New York enacted an antianarchist statute in 1902, and Congress prohibited the immigration of anarchists in 1903. McKinley's assassination led the Secret Service in 1902 to provide full-time protection of the president, a function that Congress affirmed and expanded in 1907 and 1913.

Conventional wisdom used to portray the presidential succession occasioned by Czolgosz's act as a profound turning point in American history, when the conservative, humdrum, business-dominated stodginess of William McKinley gave way to the progressive, exciting, reformist energy of Theodore Roosevelt. More judicious accounts now regard the changes between the two administrations as more nuanced. After a triumphant reelection in 1900, McKinley stood at the height of his power and popularity in 1901. In foreign affairs, he had defeated the Spanish in a brief but far-flung war, launched the Open Door policy in East Asia, and acquired an overseas empire. McKinley, not Theodore Roosevelt, first took the country onto the world stage. Domestically, McKinley presided over a prosperous and rapidly expanding economy. Once the avatar of the protective tariff, McKinley used his last speech at the exposition to highlight his new drive for reciprocity negotiations, a program to expand trade that Roosevelt failed to carry forward. On the monopoly question, McKinley denounced trusts as "dangerous conspiracies against the public good." An investigative commission he appointed generated information that aroused public opinion and laid the groundwork for Roosevelt's later antitrust court actions.

McKinley set a pattern for Roosevelt and his successors in developing various presidential leadership tools, including employing expert commissions, cultivating smooth relations with Congress, shaping public opinion through the "bully pulpit" and broadening the application of the president's war powers. Still, the two men had contrasting styles. Whereas McKinley was methodical and circumspect, Roosevelt was robust and vigorous and sometimes impetuous. Roosevelt seized upon McKinley's innovations and expanded them immensely. Roosevelt's reputation as an energetic president reflected his belief that the national government should move beyond standard concerns such as taxation, the currency, and defense and give greater attention to business regulation, conservation, and other new issues affecting citizens' well-being. Although Roosevelt

Carrying a revolver concealed in a handkerchief, an assassin fires at President William McKinley at the Pan-American Exhibition in Buffalo, New York. The president died eight days later. *(Library of Congress)*

built on McKinley's techniques, the quantum leap in his administration's activity and accomplishments earned him the traditional designation as the nation's first modern president.

See also 1865 ASSASSINATION OF PRESIDENT LINCOLN; 1881 ASSASSINATION OF PRESIDENT GARFIELD; 1963 ASSASSINATION OF PRESIDENT KENNEDY.

Charles W. Calhoun

FURTHER READING:

Gould, Lewis L. *The Presidency of William McKinley.* Lawrence: University Press of Kansas, 1980.
Morgan, H. Wayne. *William McKinley and His America.* Kent, Ohio: Kent State University Press, 2003.
Rauchway, Eric. *Murdering McKinley: The Making of Theodore Roosevelt's America.* New York: Hill and Wang, 2003.

1903 ◆ IROQUOIS THEATER FIRE

The nation's most disastrous theater fire occurred on the afternoon of December 30, 1903, in Chicago, Illinois, when 602 people, mostly women and children, died shortly after the state-of-the art Iroquois Theater opened. The theater in downtown Chicago was not quite finished on November 23, 1903, when it opened its doors to *Mr. Bluebird* starring Eddie Foy. Although the theater was advertised as "absolutely fireproof," less than six weeks later, with more than 1,900 patrons in its audience for a holiday matinee performance, a fire broke out at the beginning of the second act. In less than 15 minutes the interior was in flames, leaving many people dead or dying and hundreds of other panic-stricken patrons suffering burns, cuts, and bruises as they exited. Although subsequent investigations revealed numerous safety and building violations, no one connected with the theater was ever convicted or officially cited for dereliction of duty. Nevertheless, as a result of the disaster, governments around the world, including Chicago's, reviewed and strengthened safety regulations and enforcement of them. In the immediate aftermath, numerous theaters and even other public buildings were closed for inspection and in some cases structural changes. In addition, fire departments across the nation were enhanced, and in at least one case, Kenosha, Wisconsin, a professional paid department replaced a volunteer department.

At the turn of the 20th century, the theater business in Chicago was booming. Believing there was room for additional playhouses in Chicago, two Chicago theater owners—William Davis and Harry J. Powers—united with two out-of-town companies to build a large new theater in downtown Chicago. They engaged a young architect known for designing playhouses—Benjamin H. Marshall—to design the new theater. The theater syndicate purchased land surrounding a building at the corner of Randolph and Dearborn. Although initial plans were completed in mid-1902, the final drawings and a building permit were not available until mid-December. The George H. Fuller Company was chosen to erect the building. The company did not break ground for the 1,724-seat theater until midsummer 1903 with plans to open for the 1903 holiday season. When the plans for the building were filed, its costs were listed at $300,000. Later information indicated that the actual cost would be between $500,000 and $1.1 million, and because of delays in beginning construction and numerous changes, the contractors took many shortcuts in order to hurry the building along.

In this era of rapid construction in Chicago, corruption and payoffs of Chicago officials were rampant. By the time the theater was ready to open in early November, considerable finishing work remained to be done, and the building abounded in fire code violations. There were no exit signs, the exits were not visible because the walls were covered with heavy curtains, the exit doors had locks that were virtually impossible to open, the stage ceiling vents were wired shut, there were no sprinklers and only a few tubes of Kilfyre (a bicarbonate of soda anti-inflammatory chemical mixture), and the supposedly asbestos curtain to prevent a stage fire from reaching the audience was apparently made of canvas instead.

The playhouse opened on November 23, 1903. The play, *Mr. Bluebird,* starring the well-known actor and comedian Eddie Foy, had traveled from New York to Chicago and was extremely popular. During the Christmas holiday season, the play offered matinees and attracted large numbers of women, children, and people from out of town. On December 30, 1903, the play (with a cast and production crew of 500) opened to a standing-room-only crowd of 1,900 people. As a double mixed octet was performing after the first intermission, a bit of the painted canvas scenery brushed against a calcium arc spotlight and caught fire. The only fireman present tried to put out the flame with his hands but could not extinguish it. He tried the tubes of Kilfyre, again without success. When the audience spotted the fire spreading, it panicked and

FACTBOX

PLACE Chicago, Illinois

DATE December 30, 1903

TYPE Theater fire

DESCRIPTION With 1,900 spectators in the audience and 500 cast and crew members, the new Iroquois Theater burst into flames and burned, killing 602 people, mostly women and children.

CAUSE A piece of scenery brushed against a spotlight and caught fire.

CASUALTIES 602 deaths

IMPACT The incident created local, national, and international awareness of the danger of fires and the necessity for adequate escape routes and plans. Fire codes were strengthened, sprinklers were installed in some buildings, and fire companies were upgraded and professionalized.

headed for safety. Unfortunately, the fire exits were not visible and, even when located, only a few of the doors could be opened. Moreover, closed and locked accordion gates blocked stairs leading from the balconies. Without trained ushers available, fear quickly turned to panic. As people tried to get out of the theater, bodies of people, some stacked as high as 10 feet, piled up at the gates and the fire exit doors. Eddie Foy returned to the stage attempting to calm people, urging them to stay in their seats, that the fire would be quickly suppressed. But that was false hope.

Whatever could go wrong did. The alleged asbestos canvas curtain that was to drop and keep a stage fire from the audience caught on a stage light and never reached the floor. Moreover, fire inspectors later raised doubts that the existing curtain was even made of asbestos. Because the vents above the stage would not open, the fire accelerated, and as people opened the doors at the back of the audience, the fire roared through the theater killing many immediately and suffocating those who were not trampled in the effort to escape. Because there was no direct alarm to the closest fire station, by the time the fire department arrived, almost 20 minutes after the fire commenced, the worst of the fire was over. While the interior was gutted, the building walls and ceiling withstood the firestorm and, following renovation, were used for another 20 years.

Although there were numerous investigations, and it was clear that both public officials and theater owners were guilty of malfeasance, corruption, and neglect, no one was convicted in the disaster that left more than 600 people dead. In the immediate aftermath, fire laws in Chicago were strengthened, existing laws were enforced more strictly, and theaters and public spaces were closed until corrections could be made. In the long run, however, Chicago returned to its lax enforcement. But across the nation and around the world, governments enacted stricter building and fire codes, including requiring sprinklers in many buildings where they had not been required before. Cities improved or created professional fire departments where none had existed before. In large measure, then, the devastation and destruction wrought by the Iroquois fire served to improve public safety around the world.

See also 1942 Cocoanut Grove fire; 1944 Hartford Circus fire.

Roger D. Bridges

FURTHER READING:

Brandt, Nat. *Chicago Death Trap: The Iroquois Theatre Fire of 1903*. Carbondale: Southern Illinois University Press, 2003.

Everett, Marshall. *The Great Chicago Theater Disaster*. Chicago: Publishers Union of America, 1904.

1904 ◆ *GENERAL SLOCUM* DISASTER

The deadliest of America's numerous passenger steamboat fires occurred on New York City's East River on the morning of June 15, 1904. The stately, 264-foot *General Slocum* was carrying an estimated 1,331 passengers, most of them immigrant or second-generation Germans setting off on an excursion to celebrate the end of the Sunday School year at St. Mark's Lutheran Church on East Sixth Street in lower Manhattan. The passengers included many families and small children. Minutes after the *General Slocum* embarked from the Third Street pier on Manhattan's East Side, fire broke out in a lamp room near the bow. The fire spread through the ship when the crew, which had received no fire training, panicked upon failing to extinguish the blaze, largely because an untested, 13-year-old fire hose burst.

The panic spread to the passengers, who, to escape the rushing flames, trampled one another and leaped into the river. Once in the water, even passengers who could swim well and who somehow wriggled out of their heavy clothing were in danger in the crowd of flailing, drowning people. Desperate mothers strapped outdated life preservers on their children and plunged into the water, only to find to their horror that, once wet, the disintegrating cork

had received an award for his hitherto exemplary safety record, served prison time under a federal law that defined fatal negligence in running steamboats as manslaughter. Captain Van Schaick was sentenced to 10 years in Sing Sing Prison. The incident did lead to a strengthening of federal steamship inspections and a housecleaning of inept officials. Because nearly every member of several extended families from the Manhattan neighborhood of Little Germany perished in the fire, the disaster accelerated the decline of German ethnic life in New York City.

Steamboat excursions provided a welcome escape for working-class and lower-middle-class Manhattanites such as the residents of St. Mark's parish. At a rental of $350 per day, chartered steamboats also served as lucrative investments for businessmen such as Frank A. Barnaby, president of the Knickerbocker Steamboat Company, which owned the *General Slocum*. Barnaby, a real estate operator with a dubious reputation, encouraged employees to maintain his boats' luxurious appearance while cutting costs on safety. In the *General Slocum*'s case, this entailed, in addition to rotten fire hoses and an unprepared crew, ill-maintained lifeboats that were painted and wired in place and thousands of defective life preservers. Barnaby counted on the incompetence and corruption of federal inspectors, one of whom had certified the *General Slocum*'s safety devices only six weeks before the disaster.

Some on board, including the church's reverend, George Haas, and two policemen moonlighting as excursion guards, resisted the panic and prevented groups of passengers from leaping into the water until the ship neared the shore. This, along with quick action by seamen and police in the vicinity and personnel at the New York contagious disease hospital on North Brother Island, saved hundreds of lives. The incredible scene of families drowned as a group, along with bodies burned beyond recognition or exposed by the receding tide with useless life preservers strapped on, motivated normally unsentimental New York officials to endeavor to expose the company's malfeasance. Barnaby responded by pressuring surviving crew members to perjure themselves, altering documents to make life preservers seem newer than they were, and issuing press releases that implied that panic among women pas-

acted like a load of dirt, sinking children beneath the waves. Amid tremendous confusion, the steamship captain lost crucial minutes by racing to beach the ship on North Brother Island off the Bronx rather than turning sharply to the nearby Queens or Bronx waterfront, probably out of fear of shoals and currents in that part of the river. As terrified onlookers watched from the shore, tugboat crews and police in commandeered rowboats struggled to pull victims off the burning steamer or from the water, but the fire spread too quickly, and help could not arrive fast enough. An estimated 1,021 people died by trampling, fire, or drowning. The majority of victims were female, and 356 were children under the age of 14.

Despite a brazen cover-up attempt, local and federal investigators learned that gross negligence on the steamship company's part, sanctioned by slipshod inspections by the United States Steamship Inspection Service, certainly multiplied the death toll. In the end, only the captain, 67-year-old William Van Schaick, who two years earlier

Passengers leap from the *General Slocum* as flames engulf the doomed vessel. *(New York Public Library)*

sengers was the main cause of the death toll. The company president finally escaped prosecution after three trials of the federal inspector who had certified the defective life preservers ended in hung juries. With the employer's escape from punishment, Van Schaick's 10-year sentence came to seem unfair, despite the captain's having abided his ship's poor safety preparations and having continued sailing north for a mile beyond the Hell Gate pass when he might have saved lives by beaching the burning ship on exiting the pass. The elderly captain was released in 1911 after serving three and a half years in Sing Sing.

For days, police struggled to control crowds of desperate relatives at the city pier used as a temporary morgue. At least one morgue attendant went insane, while suicide attempts occurred among mothers and fathers who had escaped the wreck or who had cheer-fully sent families on the excursion before going to work. About a half-dozen relatives succeeded in killing themselves. Having lost families of parishioners along with most of its officers, St. Mark's Church, a pivotal institution in Little Germany, continued as a shadow of itself. In 1905, a survivors' group erected a memorial in the Lutheran cemetery in Middle Village, Queens, to unidentified victims of New York's deadliest catastrophe before the attacks of September 11, 2001, almost a century later.

Alan Lessoff

FURTHER READING:

O'Donnell, Edward T. *Ship Ablaze: The Tragedy of the Steamboat* General Slocum. New York: Broadway Books, 2003.

Rust, Claude. *The Burning of the* General Slocum. New York: Elsevier/Nelson Books, 1981.

1904 ◆ AMERICAN CHESTNUT TREE BLIGHT

One of the largest ecological disasters ever to devastate the eastern United States, a blight first reported in 1904 killed billions of American chestnut trees and removed numerous important resources from the vast forests it affected. The American chestnut (*Castanea dentata*) had been a dominant tree in the forest canopy throughout much of eastern North America from Georgia to Maine and west to Mississippi and the Ohio Valley. The species comprised about a quarter of the forest canopy within its range. In parts of the southern Appalachians, the heart of chestnut country, this proportion accounted for half or more. Mature trees often stood 120 feet tall and reached seven feet in diameter. In bloom, the trees were beautiful, "like big, potted flowers," in the words of one Appalachian resident. A naturalist wrote that the creamy blossoms made mountain forests look "like a sea of white combers." Chestnut Streets in cities and towns across the eastern United States recall the grace of these once-flourishing ornamental shade trees.

The chestnut's usefulness matched its beauty. The trees flowered in summer, well after the danger of frost, and thus rarely failed to produce an abundant crop of sweet and nutritious nuts. Wildlife species such as bear, squirrel, grouse, and turkeys fattened on this reliable mast crop, as did domestic animals such as free-ranging hogs. Humans too, from early inhabitants of the eastern woodlands to 20th-century metropolitans, consumed the nuts in a variety of ways. Appalachian residents used chestnuts as food and as a cash crop. Families gathered nuts by the bushel and hauled them on foot and by wagon to neighboring towns, where purchasing merchants often shipped them to buyers in distant cities such as New York and Baltimore. For poor Appalachians, chestnuts seemed like manna from heaven.

Chestnut wood, too, held value for its rot-resistance, light weight, strength, and easy workability. It made its way into fences, buildings, coffins, shingles, railroad ties, pianos, furniture, utility poles, and many other products. In the early 1900s, chestnut lumber brought $10 million each

FACTBOX
PLACE Eastern United States
DATE 1904–present
TYPE Tree blight
DESCRIPTION One of the nation's largest ecological disasters destroyed an estimated 3.5 billion chestnut trees across 20 states.
CAUSE Imported Asian fungus devastated a species with little genetic resistance.
CASUALTIES Estimated 3.5 billion trees killed
IMPACT An equivalent of 9 million acres of chestnut trees were lost. The blight destroyed an important source of lumber, reliable food, and a cash crop; depleted wildlife; increased the hardships of the Great Depression; and obliterated a scenic treasure.

year to the Appalachians, and it made up about 25 percent of New England's annual hardwood timber harvest. In 1925, researchers reported to North Carolina's governor that "chestnut is perhaps the most important [commercial] tree in the forests of western North Carolina."

Finally, chestnut wood and chestnut bark were rich sources of tannic acid and important to the early 20th-century American leather industry. Dozens of extract plants in the Appalachians converted chestnut to tannin and supplied tanneries throughout the eastern United States with this crucial ingredient. Leather was such a critical industry that in 1924, confronted with the devastating blight, the U.S. Department of Commerce worried about dependence on "foreign sources of supply of tanning materials in the event of a national emergency." Demand for tannin enabled many Appalachian families to supplement their incomes by peeling chestnut tanbark, and at least one mountain resident recalled that his family paid off its farm with tanbark money.

For all these reasons, when an imported Asian fungus (*Cryphonectria parasitica*) began to rapidly kill American chestnuts, professional foresters called the result "a National calamity." The fungus invaded tree bark and effectively girdled and killed everything above the infected site. American chestnuts had little resistance to the disease. First discovered in the Bronx, New York, in 1904, the blight almost certainly arrived on nursery stock imported from China or Japan. Traveling via wind, water, bird, squirrel, and human, the pathogen worked its way rapidly and inexorably through North America's chestnut forests.

Within four years, the blight had spread to Massachusetts, Pennsylvania, Connecticut and New Jersey. Alarmed scientists, politicians, foresters, and industry leaders fought the blight with every tool at their disposal. Congress appropriated funds; scientists experimented with sprays, surgery, and fungicide injections; and foresters tried quarantines and tree removals. Nothing worked. No cure emerged, no containment strategy succeeded, and no effort even slowed the pathogen's progress for long. Within two decades, the fungus had infected trees in most of the chestnut range across 20 states, and by the 1940s, nearly all mature chestnuts had been reduced to skeletal remains. Residents of the chestnut belt called the terrible sound a blight-infected forest giant made as it crashed to the ground "clear day thunder." The pandemic eventually killed an estimated 3.5 billion American chestnuts, or about 9 million acres worth of trees, an area larger than the state of Maryland.

It is difficult to calculate fully the impact of the chestnut blight. It removed valuable forest resources just as the Great Depression loomed, and it certainly contributed to the hardships faced by Appalachian residents. The blight also coincided with

With its massive branches and capacious foliage, the majestic American chestnut once covered much of the continent's eastern half. *(The American Chestnut Foundation)*

industrialization in the southern mountains, and the loss of mature chestnut trees may have symbolized for many residents the loss of a way of life dependent on agriculture and use of the forest commons. The pandemic's legislative legacy includes the 1912 Plant Quarantine Act, which aimed to prevent another such catastrophe. Present-day United States plant importation and customs policies continue to reflect the disease's impact.

Devastating as the blight was, American chestnuts did not disappear entirely, though they did cease to be a significant source of nuts, lumber, and tannic acid. Even today, sprouts continue to grow from old tree stumps, but they too succumb eventually to blight infection. Some mature surviving American chestnuts have been identified, and efforts to develop blight resistance in the species are ongoing.

See also 1930 DEMISE OF THE AMERICAN ELM TREE.

Kathryn Newfont

FURTHER READING:

Davis, Donald Edward. *Where There Are Mountains: An Environmental History of the Southern Appalachians.* Athens: University of Georgia Press, 2000.

Lutts, Ralph H. "Like Manna from God: The American Chestnut Trade in Southwestern Virginia." *Environmental History* 9 (July 2004): 497–525.

Youngs, Robert L. "'A Right Smart Little Jolt': Loss of the Chestnut and A Way of Life." *Journal of Forestry* 98 (February 2000): 17–21.

1905 ◆ INSURANCE INDUSTRY SCANDAL

The 1905 insurance industry scandal centered on the improper activities of three of the country's major life insurers: Equitable Life Assurance, Mutual Life, and New York Life. Investigations revealed these companies habitually engaged in a number of questionable or illegal practices, including paying excessive executive compensation, charging excessive commissions, using company assets for personal gain, using premiums for speculative investments, and making payments to politicians to ensure favorable legislation and payments to newspapers to print favorable copy. As the investigations unfolded, the nation's entire life insurance industry was implicated, affecting millions of consumers. Adding to the scandal's impact was the fact that it was one among several spectacular revelations of corporate abuse in 1905 and 1906. Other scandals hit the meatpacking industry, the patent medicine industry, and public utilities.

In the decades following the Civil War, the life insurance industry grew by leaps and bounds. By the end of the 19th century, the leading insurance companies were worth hundreds of millions of dollars originating from policy premiums. Their financial power was unsurpassed in American business. While subjected to some regulatory oversight by the individual states, how companies used their premiums and whether they honored their obligations to policyholders were always in question. Renegade financier Thomas Lawson's articles in *Everybody's*

FACTBOX

PLACE Nationwide but centered in New York State where the major insurance firms were incorporated

DATE 1905

TYPE Business and political scandal

DESCRIPTION Investigation of insurance companies revealed a variety of illegal practices, including bribery of lawmakers.

CAUSE An internal feud at Equitable Life Assurance Company, and "muckraking" journalism, especially Thomas Lawson's articles in *Everybody's Magazine*

IMPACT Resignations of leading insurance executives, legislation aimed at more effective regulation of the industry, and the further investigation of business practices, which became the hallmark of Progressive Era "muckraking" and public regulation

Magazine in 1904 (republished in 1905 as *Frenzied Finance*) provided the first insider revelations of what the companies were up to. Lawson stated his intention of "Giving facts about the life insurance branch of a 'System' which is foully plundering the people." He proceeded to outline the various ways in which insurance companies used premiums to speculate in stocks and other Wall Street schemes. His accusations aroused public opinion, and other muckraking journals picked up the theme. However, Lawson's own previous career as a financial schemer undermined his claims. A lack of hard evidence made it difficult to bring the companies to account.

Ironically, it was a boardroom struggle within Equitable Life that led to the industry's undoing. Early in 1905, Equitable president James Alexander attempted to trim the power of company vice president James Hazen Hyde. An ambitious young socialite, Hyde was accused of lavish living using company funds, including throwing a $12,000 dinner for the French ambassador. He would also turn 30 in 1906 and take full charge of the controlling stock interest bequeathed him by his father. Unable to reconcile their differences, Alexander and Hyde precipitated a crisis in Equitable's management. This in turn led policyholders and officials to worry over the firm's stability. In late May, an internal committee sharply criticized the company's management and recommended personnel changes, which Equitable's board rejected. Along with Alexander's resignation and the sale of Hyde's stock to financier Thomas Fortune Ryan, this provoked a new crisis. The public outcry increased, fueled by the muckraking press and the state's political factions. On July 20, after dragging his feet for several months, New York governor Frank W. Higgins called for the establishment of a joint legislative committee to investigate the major insurance firms based in the state.

This committee, known as the Armstrong Committee after the state senator who chaired it, appointed attorney Charles Evans Hughes as its lead counsel. Hughes had gained a reputation earlier in the year as a progressive, nonpartisan investigator of the pricing abuses involving Consolidated Gas. Beginning on September 6, Hughes called company executives to testify. Under his careful questioning they revealed the details of unreported stock transactions, the establishment of dummy financial firms, unreported loans to themselves and others, influence peddling in Albany, nepotism, and excessive compensation. The most shocking news concerned the role of New York's Republican officials in accepting payments and favors. State Republican chairman Benjamin Odell, U.S. Senator Chauncey Depew, and former Republican boss Thomas Platt were all called to testify.

By the time the hearings ended in December 1905, the insurance industry was discredited, and New York's Republican organization stood in disarray. The political fallout reached to the White House. President Theodore Roosevelt, whose political base was New York, viewed the scandal with concern and as an opportunity to reform the state's GOP ranks. Meanwhile, Hughes and his associate counsels completed their report and proposed legislation aimed at reforming the industry. New York passed a series of measures the following year specifically targeting insurance operations. The new laws limited how much new insurance a company could write annually, controlled where and how companies invested their assets, regulated lobbying, forbade campaign contributions, and opened up the companies' management by requiring new elections for directors and the filing of policyholder lists with the state. By the end of 1907, 29 states had passed some form of revised insurance legislation. The effect on the life insurance business was revolutionary. It marked the first instance when the states successfully investigated and reformed a large, politically influential, interstate industry.

The scandal also boosted Charles Evans Hughes's public career. With Roosevelt's support, he won the Republican gubernatorial nomination in 1906, and narrowly defeated newspaper magnate William Randolph Hearst in the fall election. Hughes ultimately served two terms as governor, two separate terms as a U.S. Supreme Court justice, and as secretary of state under Warren Harding. In retrospect, the insurance scandal, along with the other scandals of the period, is understood as marking the American public's "awakening" to the problem of corporate abuse. The reforms that ensued marked an important transformation in corporate governance—how American society regulates corporate behavior and the relationship between business and government. The need for vigilance, however, did not end there. Almost a full century later, in 2004, New York State's attorney general filed charges against major insurance brokers for bid rigging and similar violations.

C. Wyatt Evans

FURTHER READING:

Beard, Patricia. *After the Ball: Gilded Age Secrets, Boardroom Betrayals, and the Party That Ignited the Great Wall Street Scandal of 1905.* New York: HarperCollins, 2003.

Keller, Morton. *The Life Insurance Enterprise, 1885–1910: A Study in the Limits of Corporate Power.* Cambridge, Mass.: Belknap Press, 1963.

Lawson, Thomas. "Lawson and His Critics." *Everybody's Magazine* 11 (December 1904): 72. Reprinted in *The Muckrakers,* Arthur and Lila Weinberg, eds, 286–296. Urbana: University of Illinois Press, 2001.

Report of the Joint Committee of the Senate and Assembly of the State of New York Appointed to Investigate the Affairs of Life Insurance Companies. Albany: Brandow Printing Co., 1906.

1906 ◆ SAN FRANCISCO EARTHQUAKE AND FIRE

At 5:12 A.M. on April 18, 1906, Californians around San Francisco Bay and for many miles north and south were jolted awake when a monstrous earthquake rumbled along the San Andreas Fault. Shaking could be felt hundreds of miles away in Los Angeles, Oregon, and Nevada. Recent geologists estimate the magnitude of the earthquake as 7.7–7.9, as compared to older estimates of 8.3 on the Richter scale. It was not only one of the largest earthquakes in American history, it was also perhaps the most important in helping scientists to understand earthquakes and how to protect against them.

Geologists have mapped the San Andreas Fault over a distance of 800 miles from Cajon Pass in southeastern California to the Pacific coast near Mendocino. South of Cajon Pass, faultlines extend into the Gulf of California in Mexico. North of Mendocino, faults follow the coast to Alaska. Lying 10 miles or more deep, the San Andreas Fault marks the meeting point of two tectonic plates, the Pacific and the North American. These huge plates of rock are in constant slow motion. Geologists describe the San Andreas Fault as a right-lateral strike-slip, which means that the Pacific side of the fault is creeping horizontally northward, usually at a rate of an inch or two per year. At times, however, stress builds up along the fault, and it may lurch as much as several feet. Such movements deep in the earth produce earthquakes—and movements along the San Andreas Fault and its branches have produced most of the largest earthquakes in American history.

FACTBOX

PLACE San Francisco and adjacent areas in California along the San Andreas Fault

DATE April 18, 1906

TYPE Earthquake and fire

DESCRIPTION An earthquake on the San Andreas Fault of magnitude 7.7–7.9, followed by fires that merged into a firestorm

CASUALTIES 664 deaths officially, though researchers estimate as many as 3,000

COST $400 million

IMPACT In rebuilding San Francisco, many wooden buildings were replaced by high-rise steel-frame buildings, erected in new residential and commercial and industrial districts. The city built a new, earthquake-resistant water system, and engineers and architects improved technologies for withstanding earthquakes.

The San Andreas Fault runs just west of San Francisco. Since its beginnings as an outpost on the northern frontier of New Spain in 1776, its residents have recorded their experience with earthquakes, with the first major ones in June and July 1808. Shortly after the Mexican War made California part of the United States, the discovery of gold in 1848 made San Francisco an "instant city." Devastating fires in the early 1850s led San Franciscans to improve fire protection and to adopt a building code aimed at preventing the spread of fires. Wooden buildings, for example, were prohibited in a "fire district" centered on the central business district. The city consequently experienced no serious conflagration between 1852 and 1906.

Similarly, earthquakes in the 1850s and 1860s alerted San Franciscans to the seismic dangers of life on the Pacific rim. As the architectural historian Stephen Tobriner has demonstrated, some architects and engineers sought to stabilize buildings against seismic stress, even as earthquakes in the 1880s and 1890s provided new evidence of the dangers. During the city's rapid growth between 1849 and 1906, when San Francisco became the largest city in California and ninth-largest in the United States, developers filled in streams, marshes, lakes, and the bay—creating fill land likely to liquefy during an earthquake. Eventually, some builders understood the dangers of fill land and developed methods of stabilizing foundations in those areas. Similarly, some builders knew that the masonry construction required within the fire district carried special risks during earthquakes, so they reinforced masonry walls with iron bands or rods. The Chicago firm of Burnham and Root designed the city's first skyscraper, the 10-story De Young building, completed in 1889; knowing the danger of earthquakes, the architects sought to create the world's first earthquake-resistant steel-frame building. The designers of subsequent steel-frame buildings also integrated seismic protection into their plans.

On April 18, 1906, those efforts were given their most strenuous test when the San Andreas Fault suddenly shifted along a 296-mile line, with the epicenter of the quake near southwest San Francisco. Geologists have recently estimated that the fault moved as fast as 1.7 miles per second. "I could see it actually coming," a policeman in San Francisco said. "The whole street was undulating. It was as if the waves of the ocean were coming toward me." In some places, the earth suddenly opened in huge crevasses, most of which closed just as quickly. The earthquake toppled ancient redwoods, damaged farms, twisted city streets and streetcar tracks, and broke water lines, gas pipes, and electrical power wires. Buildings 40–50 miles south of San Francisco suffered serious damage. Much of downtown Santa Rosa, 55 miles north of San Francisco, was left in shambles.

At Point Reyes Station, 30 miles north of San Francisco, a locomotive was knocked off the tracks and onto its side, and a nearby road was displaced by 20 feet. North of San Francisco, especially, many roads and fences that crossed the fault line were displaced for several feet as the land west of the fault lurched northward.

In San Francisco, new steel-frame buildings held up quite well, as did most other buildings. Photographs taken immediately after the earthquake show most downtown buildings intact, though often with collapsed chimneys or other damage. The fire chief was killed when a chimney collapsed into his bedroom. Structures on fill land suffered the most. Some wood-frame buildings, especially on fill land, were knocked off their foundations, but most wooden structures held up reasonably well. Masonry buildings were also most likely to be damaged, and some lost entire walls.

Fires broke out almost immediately, fed by escaping gas. Broken water mains rendered most fire hydrants useless. For the next three days, city residents struggled to contain what became a firestorm. General Frederick Funston, commander of army troops at the Presidio, directed soldiers to keep order and help fight the fires. Rumors of widespread looting were mostly without basis, but those rumors led Mayor Eugene Schmitz to issue an order of doubtful constitutionality: "The Federal Troops, the members of the Regular Police Force, and all Special Police Officers have been authorized by me to KILL any and all persons found engaged in Looting or in the

Moments after the great earthquake shook San Francisco in 1906, broken gas lines exploded, spreading fire throughout the city. (© *Bettmann/CORBIS*)

Commission of Any Other Crime." Without water, firefighters and federal troops tried to build firebreaks by blasting buildings, first with black powder (which often spread the fire), then with dynamite.

Earthquake, fire, and blasting destroyed the heart of the city, comprising 4.11 square miles and 28,188 buildings, and rendered 225,000 of the city's 400,000 residents homeless. Destruction was almost universal within the fire zone—corporate headquarters and tenement homes of the poor, churches and brothels, and a million books. The official record listed 498 deaths in San Francisco, 102 in and nearby San José, and 64 in Santa Rosa. Historians Gladys Hansen and Emmet Condon, however, concluded in 1989 that the death toll reached 3,000 or more. Total damage in 1906 dollars was estimated at $400 million (equivalent to more than $8.2 billion in the early 21st century), of which $80 million was due directly to the earthquake.

Financial help poured in from individuals, organizations, and governments, some $9 million in all, which provided meals and temporary housing and assistance to reestablishing homes and businesses. Mayor Schmitz, under a cloud of suspicion due to allegations of corruption, appointed a special committee of 50 prominent citizens, led by former mayor James Phelan, to distribute the funds and plan relief and recovery. The army helped to set up 20 refugee camps, which remained for a year or more. Prompt action by army and city public health officials restored sanitation and thereby averted a potential public health disaster.

Throughout the devastated region, Californians rushed to rebuild. For San Franciscans, there was a special urgency—they feared that any delay in reconstruction would endanger their place as economic leader of the West. Daniel Burnham, the nation's preeminent urban planner, had recently prepared an extensive plan for San Francisco, and some civic leaders urged a careful, planned approach to rebuilding including new boulevards, wider streets, and other civic amenities. Others, however, wanted to rebuild quickly, and the central business district was rebuilt with little change in street plans. In some burned areas, two- and three-story wooden residences were replaced by high-rise steel-frame buildings, creating an apartment district west of the central business district and a commercial and industrial district along major thoroughfares south of Market Street, an area that had formerly been the center of working-class San Francisco. Some civic leaders tried to use the devastation as an excuse to remove Chinatown from its location near the central business district, but they failed. The same political fragmentation that prevented a more centralized approach to rebuilding also hindered reconstruction of some of the public sector—not until 1916 did the doors open on a new city hall.

Scientists who studied the disaster significantly improved their understanding of earthquakes. Careful examination of the effect of the earthquake on various types of buildings helped architects and engineers to improve technologies for resisting seismic stress, and the rebuilding of the city showed efforts to strengthen buildings against seismic stress. A new, auxiliary, high-pressure water system for fighting fires, with special hydrants, reservoirs, and cisterns, and water mains designed to withstand an earthquake, was installed throughout the burned district. San Francisco voters approved construction of a huge dam across the Hetch Hetchy Valley, high in the Sierra Nevada, to increase the city's water supply. Still, changes in the city's building code did not reflect the new knowledge of seismic dangers for many years afterward, and many civic boosters argued that the improved fire-protection system had minimized any future danger from earthquakes.

See also 1989 LOMA PRIETA EARTHQUAKE.

Robert W. Cherny

FURTHER READING:

Fradkin, Philip L. *The Great Earthquake and Firestorms of 1906: How San Francisco Nearly Destroyed Itself.* Berkeley: University of California Press, 2005.

Hansen, Gladys C., and Emmet Condon. *Denial of Disaster: The Untold Story and Photographs of the San Francisco Earthquake and Fire of 1906.* Edited by David Fowler. San Francisco: Cameron, 1989.

Kahn, Judd. *Imperial San Francisco: Politics and Planning in an American City, 1897–1906.* Lincoln: University of Nebraska Press, 1979.

Tobriner, Stephen. *Bracing for Disaster: Earthquake-resistant Architecture and Engineering in San Francisco, 1838–1933.* Berkeley, Calif.: Heyday Books, 2006.

1906 ◆ TYPHOID MARY

The year 1906 marked a turning point for public health when the new science of bacteriology was used in the investigation of a typhoid outbreak that helped identify the first known healthy carrier of a disease, Mary Mallon, the woman more commonly known as Typhoid Mary. Struggling to convince Typhoid Mary she had infected the families she worked for, New York City health officials treated Mary harshly by quarantining her—and no one else—for a total of 26 years despite the fact she was eventually identified as one among many other healthy typhoid carriers. Mary's involuntary detention developed into a class war centered on willingness to accept the new paradigm of bacteriology. Typhoid Mary became a metaphor for fear of contamination from contagious disease, and her legacy now symbolizes the struggle to balance the civil liberties of disease-carrying individuals when population health is at risk while also showing the extent to which the germ theory of disease—and reverence for science—now dominates disease-conquering efforts.

Working-class Irish immigrant Mary Mallon was a cook for several wealthy New York City families in the early 20th century. In the summer of 1906, Mary cooked for the Warren family in Oyster Bay, New York, when six of their 11 household members came down with typhoid fever. The Oyster Bay outbreak resulted in an investigation that in 1907 led public health officials to chase after Mary, by then working for another family, whom they believed was spreading typhoid to wealthy families as she worked in their homes as a cook.

Health authorities were relentless in pursuing Mary, insisting that she spread typhoid to families she worked for, despite the fact that Mary repeatedly told them she was a perfectly healthy person who never had typhoid herself and thus could not have given anyone typhoid. But the disease detectives who chased after Mary knew that, in the new science of bacteriology, the possibility existed that Mary could be a healthy disease carrier, a concept that had been announced by Robert Koch in 1902 but had not yet been proven in any living individual—until Mary.

FACTBOX

PLACE New York City

DATE 1906–38

TYPE Quarantine of first healthy typhoid-disease carrier

DESCRIPTION Typhoid infection and deaths caused by the first identified healthy disease carrier whose civil liberties were sacrificed for 26 years in the name of public health

CAUSE Zealous public-health officials quarantined the first known healthy typhoid carrier and never convinced her she was spreading disease.

CASUALTIES 47 cases including 3 deaths

IMPACT Prompted medical tests for food handlers in New York City, and continued societal struggle over whether to restrict civil liberties of diseased and nondiseased healthy carriers in the name of protecting population health, a question continually faced with HIV, SARS, and MDR-TB

When officials caught up with Mary in 1907 she repeatedly resisted their efforts to prove she was a typhoid carrier. Eventually, five police officers were used to detain Mary by force and escort her to Willard Parker Hospital for sampling. Laboratory results showed that Mary indeed carried typhoid bacilli, making her a typhoid carrier.

As the first healthy typhoid carrier identified in New York City, Mary was made an example of by public health officials and was punished for her resistance to their authority. Officials promptly detained and quarantined Mary on North Brother Island, which housed hundreds of individuals infected with highly contagious tuberculosis and other conditions. The otherwise healthy, typhoid-carrying Mary was confined in a cottage on the island, making newspaper headlines that eventually resulted in Mary's legendary title as Typhoid Mary.

Mary initially remained captive for two years, during which time she wrote letters and filed a legal suit pleading for her freedom and release from the island. In 1909, Mary argued to the Supreme Court that she was never sick and was never given due process before her confinement. The court ruled against Mary, setting a precedent for courts to rule in favor of public health when individual liberties are at stake.

In 1910, New York City's new health commissioner released Mary with the stipulation that she report regularly to the health department and promise not to work as a cook since it was likely that that occupation put her at the greatest risk of spreading typhoid. Though cooking was not the only activity through which typhoid could be spread, health officials knew it was more likely for typhoid to spread through a profession such as cooking where bacteria-laden hands often handled and served raw foods that could then become a vector to transmit the disease. In hopes of identifying healthy carriers, New York City eventually instituted a program requiring annual medical examinations for food handlers, but this resulted in identification of less than 5 percent of disease carriers.

The program to medically test food handlers was prompted in part when the health department lost track of Typhoid Mary in 1914 and rediscovered her in 1915 at the Sloane Maternity Hospital in Manhattan where an outbreak of 25 new typhoid cases occurred while she had been cooking there under a false name. Despite the fact that health officials by then recognized that at least 3 percent of people who recover from typhoid become carriers, they again responded uniquely and harshly to Mary's disobedience, sending her back to the island for captivity. Mary lived there in isolation for the remainder of her life until she died in 1938. In total, Mary is believed to have transmitted typhoid to 47 people, including three that died as a result of their disease, though Mary herself never believed she was responsible for spreading typhoid.

Just 10 years after Mary's death, health officials began to use antibiotics to treat disease and healthy disease carriers. To this day, society continues to struggle with fears of disease contagion, questioning how much individual liberties should be restricted to protect population health—as was the case for Typhoid Mary—now in the face of modern diseases including HIV, SARS, and multidrug-resistant tuberculosis (MDR-TB).

Elaine A. Hills

FURTHER READING:

Bourdain, Anthony. *Typhoid Mary: An Urban Historical.* New York: Bloomsbury, 2001.

Leavitt, Judith Walzer. *Typhoid Mary: Captive to the Public's Health.* Boston: Beacon Press, 1996.

1907 ◆ FINANCIAL PANIC AND DEPRESSION

The panic of 1907 shocked financial markets in the United States and brought on a sharp depression in 1908. The nation's economy stagnated in and out of recession for the next seven years until World War I (1914–18) rejuvenated business. The sting of these slowdowns in business and industry was compounded by unsettling increases in the cost of living. The combination of persistent inflation (price increases) and reduced commercial activity had broad ramifications for society, the business community, and government. Many of the reforms associated with the Progressive Movement are linked to the panic of 1907 and the economic difficulties it produced.

The immediate provocation of the panic was the collapse of the Knickerbocker Trust Company of New York City on October 22, 1907. Trust companies at the time performed certain banking and brokerage services and were weakly regulated, and some had invested heavily in the stock market. They also lent "margin" loans, used for buying securities, with the stock or bond serving as the collateral. Because individuals borrowed on margin to speculate in stocks and bonds, the practice encouraged risky invest-

FACTBOX

PLACE Wall Street (New York City); Washington, D.C.; and the United States

DATE October 22, 1907 (bank collapse); 1907–15 (economic turmoil)

TYPE Financial crash and depression

DESCRIPTION A financial panic brought on a depression followed by a recession that lasted seven years.

CAUSE Financial panic triggered by the collapse of the Knickerbocker Trust Company of New York City on October 22, 1907

IMPACT The years of economic dislocation, 1908–15, unsettled business and public finance and contributed to the reforms of the Progressive Era, including enactment of both personal income and corporate taxes and stricter regulation of the nation's monetary and banking systems.

ments. The Knickerbocker's portfolio was undermined by a drop in stock values and by the collapse of an unsuccessful attempt to corner the copper market. The failure of the Knickerbocker ignited two weeks of panic selling on Wall Street and a rash of bank closures across the country. America's financial problems quickly spread overseas, causing stock market crises in Britain, France, and Germany.

Observers traded accusations about the cause of the panic. John D. Rockefeller, the retired oil baron and the world's first billionaire, repeated a view popular in commercial circles that blamed President Theodore Roosevelt's attacks on business. Roosevelt countered that "ruthless and determined" businessmen were the source of the problem. He claimed that "malefactors of great wealth" deliberately manipulated financial markets in order to discredit government and to roll back regulations. Regardless of who was at fault, stocks lost nearly one-half of their value by 1909 and did not fully recover until 1916.

The origins of the panic actually predated the Knickerbocker collapse. The firm's demise can be traced to the devastating and costly SAN FRANCISCO EARTHQUAKE AND FIRE in 1906. British firms had issued much of the city's insurance, and their payments to

American claimants produced an outflow of gold from the Bank of England as well as from European financial institutions. Foreign banks responded to the drop in their financial reserves in the spring of 1907 by raising interest rates, a step that reversed the gold flows early in 1907. As gold reserves decreased in the United States, interest rates rose, industrial production slowed, and financial markets became susceptible to a panic.

The timely intervention of the broker J. Pierpont Morgan saved financial markets from a total meltdown. A trusted and revered figure on Wall Street, Morgan had built a worldwide reputation as a brilliant financier. With several trust companies teetering on the brink of bankruptcy, Morgan emerged from retirement and orchestrated a plan that propped up weak institutions with stopgap loans financed in part by the U.S. Treasury. He also organized a pool of funds to keep afloat faltering brokerage firms. On learning of this bailout, traders on the floor of the New York Stock Exchange gave Morgan a rousing cheer, which the 70-year-old patriarch of Wall Street heard in his office across the street. On November 2, he arranged another rescue, this time for several speculative brokerages. The deal entailed the purchase of Tennessee Coal and Iron by U.S. Steel, a corporation in which Morgan was heavily involved. Because the purchase potentially ran afoul of the nation's antimonopoly policies, Morgan instructed U.S. Steel president Elbert Gary to take a Sunday night train to Washington in order to obtain President Roosevelt's consent not to prosecute the steel giant. Roosevelt reluctantly consented, and the stock market rallied on Monday, when relieved traders heard the news.

The panic of 1907 produced a tightening of financial credit and a sense of caution among business people, developments that caused a sharp depression in 1908. Industrial unemployment for the year rose to 16 percent, equally as bad, if not worse, in many cities as the hard times during the winter of 1893–94. In New York City, more than a third of union members were jobless. Key indicators, such as manufacturing production (off nearly 19 percent) and railroad traffic (off 11 percent), registered major slides in 1908. Pittsburgh and the steel industry were hit especially hard. The Westinghouse manufacturing company collapsed, the city's stock exchange closed for 14 weeks, the manufacturing of locomotive engines fell 68 percent, and cash virtually disappeared from circulation. One-half of blast-furnace steel workers were thrown out of work for most of 1908. The decline in manufactured goods between May 1907 and June 1908 nationwide was the most severe of any business cycle between Reconstruction and the Great Depression in the 1930s.

The economy enjoyed a brief recovery in 1909 but slipped into recession again during the latter half of 1910. A downturn in auto sales cost William Durant control of General Motors Corporation, the firm that he had created. (He later regained its control.) Drought and crop failures added to the economic woes of 1911, a depression year. Recovery was under way by 1912, only to slow in the latter months of 1913, as war fears in Europe worried financiers. By 1914, the United States was back in depression, as unemployment reached 15.6 percent nationally. The economy experienced no growth between 1907, the year of the panic, and mid-1911, and again from late 1913 through 1915. The value of capital assets declined during these eight years. Railroad profits dwindled, and hundreds of lines folded. Housing went into a tailspin, and prices farmers received for commodities, especially wheat and cotton, dropped in 1910 and 1911.

America's difficulties radiated throughout the global economy. Most large nations experienced a financial crisis in 1907, a depression in 1908, and another downturn in 1913–14. The reverberation of this turmoil on Mexico's economy sparked a revolution in 1910, causing dictator Porfirio Díaz to flee the country in 1911. World War I, which began in August 1914, wreaked havoc on European economies, but it pulled the United States out of recession by 1916. War orders for food, arms, and supplies from Europe, especially Britain, accelerated U.S. exports, and sparked the recovery of America's economy.

Recession was only one of the economic woes of 1907–15. Steadily rising prices made the crisis worse. The return of prosperity after the depression of the 1890s was accompanied by price increases, which ended decades of deflation (declining prices). Prices did dip during 1908 but turned up again by 1909. The cost of living rose 16 percent between 1907 and 1914; prices jumped 11 percent in 1910–11 alone, led by a spike in food costs, especially for meat and grains. But the cost of manufactured items rose, too. Some large manufacturers cut production runs, not prices, as industrialists had done in previous depressions.

Food boycotts, rent strikes, and assaults on ice wagons (delivering for "iceboxes"—the precursors of electric refrigerators) occurred in several cities. Woodrow Wilson, governor of New Jersey, noted the "extraordinary rise in the prices of food stuffs" and pledged to support a law to regulate cold-storage warehouses. The middle class, which had evolved from a producer to consumer group by the early 20th century, was especially sensitive to inflation. By 1910, the rising cost of living became a leading political issue.

Workers suffered from inflation too, as prices rose faster than wages. Faced with the higher cost of living, the average worker was worse off in 1914 than in 1906. The level of real wages varied with workers' occupation and skills. The iron, steel, and textile mills in particular experienced hard times. Skilled workers such as carpenters, lathe operators, and printers suffered less than unskilled workers, such as manual laborers and factory operatives. A record number of immigrants in 1907—1,285,000, the highest annual influx in American history until the 1990s—contributed to the wage slump. Major industries, including textiles and steel, which relied heavily on foreign workers, cut wages. The depression of 1908 and the subsequent recessions caused immigration to decline. Thousands of foreign-born workers returned home during the difficult years.

The dilemma facing workers in the 1907–15 period is reflected in strike activity. Although job actions occurred throughout the early 1900s, labor conflicts peaked between 1909 and 1912. Unionized workers organized some strikes as a device to bring wages in line with prices and to undo union-busting policies of their companies. The strikes of female garment workers in New York City in 1909, 1910, and 1911 and of steel workers in Bethlehem, Pennsylvania, in 1910 are examples. But immigrant workers, who were heavily concentrated in unskilled and semiskilled positions, tended to launch spontaneous walkouts in response to wage cuts. The 1910 strike among Fall River, Massachusetts, textile workers fit this type. A long and violent strike at textile mills in Lawrence, Massachusetts, in 1912 followed wage cuts. Employers reacted to rising costs and slowed business with antilabor policies, such as opposing unionization and harassing union organizers. Business sought injunctions from courts (legal orders to stop a practice) to break strikes. Small businesses, which lacked the resources and flexibility of big corporations, were especially hostile to unions.

The economic troubles after the panic had wide effects on government. One problem was that many governments faced reduced revenues, a situation that increased pressures to cut spending in order to eliminate deficits (situations where spending exceeded revenues). The U.S. Treasury faced deficits between 1908 and 1910 and again between 1913 and 1915. President William Howard Taft took office as this challenge unfolded. In his inaugural address in 1909, he suggested that "new kinds of taxation" were necessary "to secure an adequate income" for the government, pointing to the prospect of more red ink. Congress concurred, enacting a 1 percent "excise" tax on corporation income as part of the Payne-Aldrich Tariff Act of 1909. Lawmakers also voted for an amendment to the U.S. Constitution that authorized the taxation of individual income. The states ratified the landmark Sixteenth Amendment in 1913, the first formal change to the Constitution in more than 40 years.

Taft also appointed a Commission on Economy and Efficiency charged with examining the federal government's financial practices. After studying reforms implemented in New York, Boston, and other cities, the commission recommended that the lawmakers write a budget—a blueprint for managing finances—something that the federal government did not have. While Congress resisted the idea until 1921, most state governments wrote budgets between 1911 and 1919. Led by Wisconsin in 1911, 12 states adopted income taxes by 1918. Many states created tax commissions after 1907, although a few had begun this trend earlier. State lawmakers imposed financial reporting requirements on local governments, whose accounts were being squeezed during the depression by slumps in revenue and the rising cost of public services. Prodded by the fiscal problems of 1908–15, national and state governments assumed more of the costs formerly paid by the cities, towns, and counties.

The unsettled economy worked to the advantage of the Democratic Party, which had been out of power in Washington since the early 1890s. In 1910, Democrats won a majority in the House of Representatives, gaining 55 seats. Two years later, Democrats broadened their hold over the House, took control of the Senate, and put Woodrow Wilson in the presidency. Democrats also picked up several governorships and substantially reduced Republican numbers in northeastern and midwestern state legislatures. While economic stagnation and the "cost of living" issue hurt Republicans after 1908, the depression of 1914 and industrial unemployment helped them regain 62 House seats from Democrats in that year's congressional races.

The temporary revival of Democratic fortunes helped progressive reform to unfold. In Washington, the Wilson administration tackled three major issues related to the economic turmoil of 1907–15: the shortfall in federal revenue, the lack of a central bank as a bulwark against financial panics, and charges that corporate monopolies forced up the cost of living. In 1913, Congress enacted a tax on individual and corporate incomes. The Wilson administration also created a network of Federal Reserve Banks, which helped to stabilize the monetary system. In 1914, lawmakers adopted the Clayton Act and the Federal Trade Commission Act, measures that sought stricter regulations on corporations and banks. The Highway Act of 1916 and the Vocational Education Act of 1917 provided federal funds to state governments for roads and schools.

The panic of 1907 and its aftermath contributed to the adoption of progressive reform at the state level. Some of these reforms, such as workers' compensation, public utility regulations, limitations on banks and building and loan associations, and maintenance of public employment offices, can be linked to popular dissatisfaction with the economy. Other measures, such as mothers' pensions, stronger housing and factory standards, and teacher retirement plans, had more indirect connections to the economic instability of the era. Frustration with the way government handled the economy probably was instrumental in the adoption of certain political reforms, such as the direct election of U.S. senators (through the addition of the Seventeenth Amendment to the Constitution), election primaries, and voter registration. Some historians maintain that business managers withdrew support for reform after progressives began to emphasize the regulation of commerce and banking. In many ways, the panic of 1907 and the years of depression and inflation that followed left deep imprints on American society.

See also 1893 FINANCIAL PANIC AND DEPRESSION; 1933 THE GREAT DEPRESSION.

Ballard C. Campbell

FURTHER READING:

Chernow, Ron. *The House of Morgan: An American Banking Dynasty and the Rise of Modern Finance.* New York: Atlantic Monthly Press, 1990.

Faulkner, Harold U. *The Decline of Laissez Faire, 1897–1917.* New York: Rinehart and Company, 1951.

Mills, Frederick C. *Economic Tendencies in the United States.* New York: J. J. Little and Ives Co., 1932.

Pope, Daniel. "American Economists and the High Cost of Living: The Progressive Era." *Journal of the History of Behavioral Science* 17 (1981): 75–87.

Sarasohn, David. *The Party of Reform: Democrats in the Progressive Era.* Jackson: University of Mississippi Press, 1989.

1908 ◆ SPRINGFIELD RACE RIOT

On August 14 and 15, 1908, Springfield, Illinois, the state capital, was the scene of a devastating attack on the city's African-American community and property. Two days of rioting in Abraham Lincoln's hometown resulted in six deaths—including two vicious lynchings of black citizens and the shooting of four white citizens—and the destruction by fire of several square blocks of black housing and businesses on Springfield's near east side. This riot was the first of a trilogy in Illinois that occurred over the next dozen years; the others being the East St. Louis race riot of 1917, and the CHICAGO RACE RIOT of 1919. The Springfield riot shocked and surprised the nation. It was also one of the events leading to the creation of the National Association for the Advancement of Colored People (NAACP) in 1909.

The riot was sparked by two events: the murder in July of Clergy Ballard, a white mining engineer, allegedly by a black drifter, and the alleged rape of a young white married woman by a black man. Although Joe James—the black out-of-town drifter—was later found guilty and executed for Ballard's murder, there remains some doubt about his guilt owing to heightened racial tensions engendered by the August 1908 riot. The alleged rape victim—Mabel Hallam—later recanted her accusation against George Richardson when it was discovered she had probably fabricated the story to cover up an affair.

The trouble began on the evening of August 14 when approximately 5,000 white Springfieldians gathered outside the city jail that held the accused killer and rapist. They were intent on taking the alleged assailants from the jail and inflicting vigilante justice by hanging them, thereby relieving the city's law-enforcement agencies of the trouble of convicting and punishing them. Fearing that the mob gathered

FACTBOX

PLACE Springfield, Illinois

DATE August 14–15, 1908

TYPE Race riot

DESCRIPTION White rioters attacked black residents and businesses.

CAUSE White racism, which led to violence when a white mob, seeking to lynch two alleged black criminals, found that the alleged criminals had been removed from the city jail

CASUALTIES 6 deaths

IMPACT Founding of the National Association for the Advancement of Colored People

outside the jail would succeed, the Sangamon County sheriff secretly sent James and Richardson out of town for their safety. When the crowd learned that the two men had been placed beyond its reach, the group turned ugly and began to riot. First, they destroyed a downtown restaurant owned by a wealthy white Springfieldian—Harry Loper—because his automobile had been used to get the accused assailants out of town. Then the crowd destroyed his automobile.

Next, the crowd turned its destructive wrath on the small black businesses in an area known as the Levee, the city's vice district. Gunfire erupted from both the white rioters and the African-Americans who were under attack. As a result of the melee, four white men eventually died. Although Illinois governor Charles Deneen called out the state militia, the crowd pillaged and burned at will. Later that night, they turned their attention on "The Badlands," a poor, largely black neighborhood. Most of the black homes were burned while those of their few white neighbors were spared. Fortunately, most of the residents had fled out of town or to the National Guard Armory and thus were not physically harmed. One African American—barber Scott Burton—chose to defend his home. He was taken captive and hanged, the first victim to lose his life as a result of the rampage.

Although there were sporadic attacks on isolated groups of African Americans on the following day, August 15, the city remained relatively quiet until evening, when the still frustrated white residents gathered at the armory where many African Americans had sought refuge. Finding that the troops called out by Governor Deneen the previous evening were protecting them, and failing to find James and Richardson, the crowd went looking for William Donegan, an 80-year-old black man who had had a passing acquaintance with Abraham Lincoln. Apparently Donegan's only offenses were that he had known Lincoln and that his wife of 32 years was a white woman. The crowd dragged Donegan outside his home and hung him from the nearest tree. The National Guard arrived before Donegan died, cut him down, and took him to the hospital where he died a few hours later. Following this lynching and with the National Guard's determined efforts, the riot finally ended.

During the rioting, hundreds of African Americans escaped the city to nearby towns outside Sangamon County such as Decatur, Lincoln, and Bloomington. Smaller communities within Sangamon County refused to allow them to stop there. Although early accounts indicated that large numbers of African Americans left the town permanently, later studies conclude that most returned in the weeks after the riot ended.

Perhaps the most significant outcome of the Springfield riot, other than the damage inflicted on the city's African-American community, was the founding of the NAACP. Upon reading an account of the racial violence, feminist and civil rights activist Mary Ovington White initiated a series of meetings and correspondence that culminated in a "call upon all the believers in democracy to join in a national conference for the discussion of present evils, the voicing of protests, and the renewal of the struggle for civil and political liberty." This meeting, held in New York on February 12, 1909 (the 100th anniversary of Lincoln's birth), was attended by leading advocates of civil rights. These advocates formed the National Association for the Advancement of Colored People, which quickly became the foremost civil rights organization in the country.

See also 1919 CHICAGO RACE RIOT.

Roger D. Bridges

FURTHER READING:

Crouthamel, James L. "The Springfield Race Riot of 1908." *The Journal of Negro History* 45 (July 1960): 164–181.

Krohe, James, Jr. *Summer of Rage: The Springfield Race Riot of 1908.* Springfield, Ill.: Sangamon County Historical Society, 1973.

Ovington, Mary White. "The National Association for the Advancement of Colored People." *The Journal of Negro History* 9 (April 1924): 107–116.

Senechal, Roberta. *The Sociogenesis of a Race Riot: Springfield, Illinois, in 1908.* Urbana, Ill.: University of Chicago Press, 1990.

1909 ◆ CHERRY MINE FIRE

Cherry, Illinois, was the site of the nation's worst coal mine fire, and the third worst coal mine disaster in American history. On November 13, 1909, the carelessness of mine officials and employees led to the deaths of 259 miners. The only disasters that surpassed the Cherry Mine fire in fatalities were explosions at the Monongah Coal Mines in Monongah, West Virginia, that took the lives of 362 people in 1907, and the explosion in Stag Canon No. 2 Mine, Dawson, New Mexico, where 263 miners died in 1913. The St. Paul Coal Company had opened the Cherry mine in 1905 in order to serve the needs of its only customer, the Chicago, Milwaukee, and St. Paul Railroad. Heralded as modern and safe, the Cherry Mine used electricity to light the interior. The failure of its electrical supply a few days before the fire, however, led company managers to revert to using kerosene lamps and torches, rather than closing the mine until electricity could be restored. On November 13, oil dripping from one of the lamps ignited a cart of hay bales intended for the mules in the mine and started the fire. The Cherry Mine disaster prompted the state of Illinois to establish mine rescue stations at LaSalle, Springfield, and Benton, Illinois. The purpose of these stations was to train workers to use rescue equipment and to assist in the creation of mine rescue teams in every mine in Illinois, the first state in the nation to have them.

The Cherry Mine fire started shortly after noon on Saturday when several bales of hay were lowered in a coal car to feed the mules located in the mine. The car rolled to a stop on the second level of the three-level mine under one of the kerosene lanterns lighting the mine. Some kerosene dropped on the hay which ignited some time later presumably when a spark dropped on the soaked hay. Apparently, such fires were usual, and passing miners ignored the blaze for a time. Then, when mine officials were notified, they attempted to move the burning cart to the bottom of the mine, using the cage—a mining term for the elevator used to move both men and material in and out of the mine. However, the fire was so hot that it ignited some timbers near the cage, leading some miners to push the car into the shaft, where it dropped to the bottom and was extinguished, but unfortunately the fire had ignited timbers bracing the cage opening. The hoses that could have been used to extinguish the timbers had fittings that did not match the pipes. The fire itself burned for 45 minutes before

authorities began to evacuate the mines. While some 200 of the approximately 480 miners in the mines escaped, more than 260 remained underground when the mine elevator ceased working, trapping 12 miners in the cage and leaving the others with no escape route. In an effort to clear the mine of smoke, the large fan over the air vent was reversed, blowing fresh air into the mine, an action that fanned the flames rather than aiding the miners.

Because no one was able to enter the mine, the shaft was sealed that night at 8 P.M. to smother the flames. During the next week, several attempts were made to reenter the mine to look for survivors or to bring out the dead. Each time the mine was unsealed, however, the fire quickly expanded. The blaze was finally extinguished seven days after it had started, allowing rescuers to enter the mine. They assumed that there were no survivors.

They were wrong. Twenty-two miners had retreated to the deep recesses of the mine where they managed to seal off the passage and find a small amount of water. On Saturday, November 20, near death, they tried an escape. As they broke through the wall they had created, they heard the sounds of the rescuers. In the haste to get out, one miner was killed after he struck his head on the opening. The others, however, found their way to rescuers and in the early evening of November 20, one week after the fire had begun, 21 miners were brought out of the mine alive. Of the 21 who escaped, one later died, but 20 miners survived the fire.

As a result of the fire, safety laws for mines and miners in Illinois and the nation were strengthened. Illinois governor Charles Deneen called the Illinois General Assembly into special session where it passed stronger regulations. The new regulations required better firefighting equipment in the mines, and key workers, such as hoist operators, were required to be state-certified for their positions. The General Assembly also appropriated funds for more mine rescue stations, and in 1911 it passed a liability act that became the basis for the Illinois Workmen's Compensation Act.

Roger D. Bridges

FURTHER READING:

Stout, Steve. "Tragedy in November: The Cherry Mine Disaster." *Journal of the Illinois State Historical Society* 72 (February 1979): 57–69.

Tintori, Karen. *Trapped: The 1909 Cherry Mine Disaster.* New York: Atria Books, 2002.

1910 ◆ WELLINGTON AVALANCHE AND RAILWAY DISASTER

Early explorers compared the Cascade Range in Washington to the Sierra Nevada in California in that both were formidable mountains, posing a challenge to settlers and railroad builders. The Great Northern Railway (GN), headed by famed railroad magnate James J. Hill, began construction through Stevens Pass in the Cascades in 1891. A series of switchbacks carried passengers and freight over the mountain route. In 1897, work began on Cascade Tunnel, which would eliminate the switchbacks, reduce avalanche risk, and keep grades below 2.2 percent. The 2.6-mile-long tunnel opened in 1900, although snowslides continued to block the entrances. In addition, the threat of avalanches increased after fires destroyed stands of timber that had afforded some protection to the track. But these problems were just a prelude to the disaster that occurred in the winter of 1910 when an avalanche swept two snowbound trains into a ravine, sending 96 people to their deaths. It was the deadliest snowslide in American history.

On February 24, 1910, Passenger Train 25 and Mail Train 27 passed through the Cascade Tunnel heading west. Trainmen moved Train 25 to the siding near the Wellington Depot to let the mail train pass. But an avalanche west of Wellington kept

Rescue workers stand amid the wreckage caused by the Wellington avalanche, the deadliest snowslide in American history. (*Library of Congress*)

the two trains stopped about 1,500 feet west of the tunnel. As the trains sat waiting for plows to clear the tracks, the snow continued, piling up in five- to eight-foot-deep drifts. The four "rotary plows"—locomotives with rotating blades on the front that cut through the snow and blew it out to the side—sent to clear the tracks ran into difficulty. The first hit a stump on February 25, putting it out of commission. A second plow became stuck, could not make it back to refuel, and quit work on February 27. Snowslides trapped the last two rotaries. Strewn with timber, the slides required shovel gangs to dig out the debris before the rotaries could go back to work. But progress stalled because Mountain Division Superintendent James H. O'Neil had fired the shovelers because of a wage dispute. This flap kept the rotary crews immobilized, while trains 25 and 27 waited at the siding, increasing the agitation of their passengers.

On March 1, 1910, a wall of snow 10 feet high and a quarter of a mile wide hurtled down the mountainside above the siding. The avalanche swept the passenger train and the mail train into a gulch 150 feet below, with all the passengers, mail workers, and GN employees trapped inside. Some were killed instantly, while others suffocated, buried in densely packed snow. Hundreds of volunteers and GN employees converged on the scene to dig out the victims. An inquest that followed the disaster absolved the Great Northern of negligence. Nonetheless, several years later, one of the victim's sons sued the rail company, and won his case in King County Superior Court. The Washington State Supreme Court, however, overturned the verdict, ruling the tragedy was an act of God.

The Great Northern executives had assumed that the construction of the Cascade Tunnel had solved most of the challenges of keeping the line open. As the horror of the Wellington slide demonstrated, winter still posed a threat. In an attempt to erase the memory of the connection between Wellington and the avalanche, the GN changed the depot name to Tye. The line took additional steps to preserve its reputation. President James Hill authorized the construction of 26 new snowsheds at a cost of more than $1.5 million. The railway built a 3,900-foot, double-track, concrete snowshed in the area of the slide and, in later years, built a second tunnel through

Windy Point at the trouble spot, where the slides had occurred. Still, Stevens Pass in the Cascade Mountains posed problems for the line. In 1929, the GN rerouted its tracks through this troublesome section by constructing an eight-mile-long tunnel through the mountains, the longest railroad tunnel in the United States, and 40 miles of new track.

Diana Di Stefano

FURTHER READING:

Beckey, Fred. *Range of Glaciers: The Exploration and Survey of the Northern Cascade Range.* Portland: Oregon Historical Society Press, 2003.

Hult, Ruby El. *Northwest Disaster: Avalanche and Fire.* Portland, Oreg.: Binford and Mort, 1960.

Krist, Gary. *The White Cascade: The Great Northern Railway Disaster and America's Deadliest Avalanche.* New York: Holt, 2007.

1911 ◆ TRIANGLE SHIRTWAIST FACTORY FIRE

On Saturday, March 25, 1911, a fire swept through the Triangle Shirtwaist Company on the top three floors of the Asch Building, a 10-story structure located at the corner of Greene Street and Washington Place in New York City. The fire resulted in the deaths of 146 workers, making the incident one of the worst industrial disasters in U.S. history. The tragedy also caused the highest loss of life at a workplace in New York City until the 9/11 TERRORIST ATTACK at the World Trade Center almost a century later on September 11, 2001. Like most of the 500 employees at the factory, the vast majority of the fire's victims were adolescent girls and young women who were the daughters of newly arrived Jewish and Italian immigrants or were immigrants themselves. News of their deaths reported in newspapers across the country stirred a national public outcry and led to innovative policies that were emblematic of reforms in the Progressive Era and beyond.

The Triangle Shirtwaist Company was founded in 1900 by two Russian-born Jewish immigrants, Max Blanck and Isaac Harris. Like most garment manufacturers, Blanck and Harris relied on young

FACTBOX

PLACE New York City

DATE March 25, 1911

TYPE Fire at a garment factory

DESCRIPTION A fire engulfed the Triangle Shirtwaist Company located on the top three floors of the Asch Building in New York City.

CASUALTIES 146 deaths out of 500 employees in the building at the time of the fire

COST Max Blanck and Isaac Harris paid a week's wages to families of deceased workers and received $200,000 in insurance payments. Joseph Asch paid $75 in compensation to 23 families of workers killed in the fire.

IMPACT The Triangle fire focused public attention on working conditions in the nation's factories. In the five years following the fire, New York's state government held dozens of hearings and passed some of the nation's most progressive workplace-safety legislation.

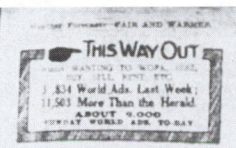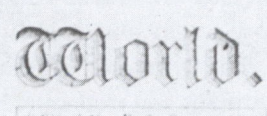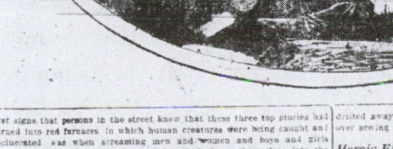

Despite slight inaccuracies—146 died, not 154—this newspaper front page captures the horrors of the Triangle Shirtwaist factory fire. (*Library of Congress*)

females to staff their factory. Also like their competitors, they offered low wages and paid little attention to safety standards. The Triangle Company grew into one of the largest garment factories in New York. The company manufactured shirtwaists, an inexpensive high-necked blouse popularized through Charles Dana Gibson's "Gibson Girl" illustrations and sold through America's expanding ready-to-wear retail market. In 1901, Blanck and Harris moved their operation to the eighth floor of the new Asch Building, a modern high-rise advertised as fireproof. Over the decade, Triangle took over the building's top three floors.

During the same period, labor disputes grew across the industry. In September 1909, Blanck and Harris laid off 150 workers suspected of trying to organize a union. There had been a number of wildcat strikes in the garment industry, and about 100 Triangle workers had taken part in a meeting with union representatives from the International Ladies' Garment Workers' Union (ILGWU). In response to the firings, the ILGWU marked the Triangle Company for a protest. Dissatisfaction with industry owners spread, and on November 23, 20,000–30,000 garment workers in New York, Philadelphia, and Baltimore walked off their jobs. The ILGWU demanded higher wages, a shorter workweek, and elimination of required overtime. In addition, the union complained about locked doors, poorly maintained fire escapes, and other safety hazards. After 13 weeks, factories employing 15,000 garment workers agreed to union contracts that raised wages, limited the six-day workweek to 52 hours, but did not include new safety standards. Despite the compromise, Blanck and Harris refused to sign the union contract, although they raised wages to union scale.

After 10 years at the Asch building location, Triangle had a reputation as a company that exploited its female workers. One consequence of this situation became clear when a fire started at the factory at approximately 4:45 P.M. on March 25, 1911. Workers on the factory's eighth floor spotted smoke coming from piles of fabric scraps. A bookkeeper quickly called the company's executive offices on the 10th floor and told them about the fire. The office employees exited the building at once. On the eighth floor, what started as a small fire was rapidly fueled by tissue-paper patterns, accumulated lint, fabric cuttings discarded under work tables, and other combustible materials. No sprinklers engaged and the fire hose valve was rusted shut. The 125 workers on

the eighth floor ran for their lives down the stairwell, but no one alerted the female workers and their male supervisors on the ninth floor to the danger. To make matters worse, a few minutes before quitting time, a guard had locked the exit door on the ninth floor's Washington Place stairwell. This was a usual practice done to deter theft by employees.

Seeing the flames and smoke rising from the eighth floor, the approximately 250 ninth-floor workers stumbled over cutting tables and sewing machines to reach the exit stairwells. The company had not run fire drills, and the fact that many workers spoke different languages added to the confusion. Suddenly, a barrel of oil used to lubricate the sewing machines exploded and closed the Greene Street stairwell. Panicking workers raced to the Washington Place stairwell only to find the door locked. Others rushed to the fire escapes, which collapsed under their weight and dangled from the building until plummeting 90 feet to the street below. A few workers got out of the building by taking one of the two small elevators, and a handful climbed down the elevator cables to safety. When the fire department arrived, rescuers could not help stranded workers because ladders were not long enough to reach the ninth floor. With no other choice, some of the workers began to leap from the windows. Firefighters tried to catch the jumpers in nets, but the fabric was too weak to support the weight of individuals falling from the building's top floors, and the bodies smashed to the pavement. Fifty-four individuals, some of them on fire, died after jumping or falling from the burning building. Bystanders reported horrific details they would never forget such as seeing firefighters and police using fire hoses to spray smoldering corpses.

A funeral procession on April 5, 1911, held in honor of the victims included more than 80,000 people. New York City charged factory owners Max Blanck and Isaac Harris for the deaths, noting the locked door to the Washington Place stairwell. But a jury concluded in December that there was no way to know if the two factory owners had ordered the door to be locked. A second indictment against the men was thrown out by a judge. Blanck and Harris went free and reopened their business. The ILGWU raised money for survivors and the families of dead workers, distributing $30,000 in relief funds. In addition, Blanck and Harris paid the families of the workers killed in the fire one week's pay in March 1914. The partners received $200,000 in insurance payments. Some 23 families of workers killed also filed civil suits against the building's owner, Joseph J. Asch, and those were settled at the rate of $75 each.

The fire led to much broader public support for the ILGWU. Furthermore, New York City adopted new fire regulations and reenforced existing codes. At the state level, two of New York's leading politicians, Robert F. Wagner and Alfred E. Smith, headed a new factory investigation commission that held 59 hearings and recorded testimony from 472 witnesses during 1911 and 1912. Frances Perkins, who later became the first female cabinet member as secretary of labor under Franklin Roosevelt in 1933, joined the commission's staff. She recalled that witnessing the Triangle fire fueled her interest in labor issues. Between 1912 and 1916, Wagner and Smith guided 36 measures into law that strengthened work safety standards. New York's legislative reforms served as models for the New Deal's labor policies in the 1930s that are still the backbone of federal regulation of workers' protections and rights in the United States.

Kriste Lindenmeyer

FURTHER READING:

Greenwald, Richard. *The Triangle Fire, the Protocols of Peace, and Industrial Democracy in Progressive Era New York.* Philadelphia: Temple University Press, 2005.

The Kheel Center, Catherwood Library, ILR School at Cornell University. *The Triangle Factory Fire.* Available online. URL: http://www.ilr.cornell.edu/trianglefire/. Downloaded April 10, 2007.

McClymer, John F. *The Triangle Strike and Fire.* Fort Worth, Tex.: Harcourt Brace College Publishers, 1998.

Stein, Leon. *The Triangle Fire.* Philadelphia: Lippincott, 1962.

The Triangle Shirtwaist Factory Fire, March 25, 1911: A Memorial Compilation and Testament to the 146 Victims, Their Families and Those Heroic Immigrants Whose Labor and Sacrifice Made America Great. Albany: New York State Senate, 2006.

Von Drehle, David. *Triangle: The Fire That Changed America.* New York: Atlantic Monthly Press, 2003.

1912 ◆ "BREAD AND ROSES" STRIKE

The massive strike began almost spontaneously. Witnesses described it as reminiscent of an electrical spark. Shortly before paychecks were to be handed out at the Washington Mill in Lawrence, Massachusetts, on the frigidly cold morning of Friday, January 12, 1912, workers from a hodgepodge of ethnic backgrounds, speaking dozens of different languages, began to rampage from room to room. Shouting, "Short pay! All out! All out!" they destroyed power looms and other machinery, slashed belts, ran knives through finished cloth, and shattered lights. Angry laborers, upset with both a cut in wages and their living conditions, spread from the Washington and found eager comrades in mills throughout the textile city. The struggle that began that icy day would become one of the American labor movement's defining moments. Never before had so many unskilled immigrant workers banded together so successfully in a labor dispute. The raises they ultimately won would have ramifications for textile workers across New England.

It all started with about 200 Polish women who walked off the job after receiving reduced paychecks at the Everett Mill on the afternoon of Thursday, January 11. Talk of their defiance reverberated throughout Lawrence's tenements that night. The mass uprising began the next morning. From the Washington, the workers marched along the North Canal, crossed the Merrimack River on the trellised Duck Bridge, and headed straight for the Wood Mill, the largest textile factory in the world, housing 6,000 millhands and owned by wool magnate William Madison Wood, the John D. Rockefeller of the textile industry. Wood's American Woolen Co. owned four of the biggest mills in Lawrence and employed half its 28,000 workers. Cajoling and threatening their fellow mill laborers to walk out, the mob rampaged through that monolith as well.

By 2 P.M., nearly 11,000 immigrant laborers from 51 countries, crying "strike" in 30 different languages were on strike or locked out. Thousands more

FACTBOX

PLACE Lawrence, Massachusetts

DATE January 12–March 24, 1912

TYPE Strike

DESCRIPTION More than 20,000 textile workers spent two months on strike, crippling production in one of the nation's largest textile cities. The immigrant workers won substantial wage concessions from mill owners.

CAUSE Dissatisfaction with living and working conditions and a two-hour cut in pay (about 32 cents a week)

CASUALTIES Two deaths and dozens of injuries from skirmishes between strikers and police or Massachusetts state militia

COST $10 million to $12 million in increased wages in the year after the strike and $3.2 million in lost wages, revenues, and reimbursement for the Massachusetts state militia from the strike itself

IMPACT Approximately 300,000 New England textile workers received pay raises from mill owners who wished to avoid similar strikes in the aftermath of the uprising. Workers whose wage hikes failed to match those in Lawrence subsequently went on strike at mills throughout New England.

labored on in mills that remained operational. Thousands went to work on Saturday as well, responding to the morning whistles as if nothing unusual had occurred the day before. But that was soon to change. On Monday morning, January 15, following a quiet Sunday, clashes between strikers and police raged across the city. Most mills did not open at all. Those that started up soon shut down. Strikers had shut down all the factories in Lawrence.

During the strike's next 60 days, the tumultuous situation in Lawrence drew international attention to the plight of textile workers, prompting congressional hearings that shed light on child labor in the mills. Lawrence, a city of 80,000 residents, became an armed camp, with 1,500 soldiers from the Massachusetts state militia and hundreds of police officers patrolling streets and guarding mills during the height of the strike. Two strikers were killed, doz-

ens of people injured in skirmishes between strikers and local police or state militia, and hundreds were arrested. At the standoff's peak, in the week following the fatal January 29 shooting of 33-year-old striker Anna LoPizzo, there were roughly 23,000 workers off the job. John Rami, an 18-year-old Syrian immigrant, died the next day, after being stabbed in the shoulder by a soldier's bayonet.

A major issue in the Lawrence strike was the loss of two hours' pay, which equaled a decrease of about 32 cents a week in wages. The reduction was the result of a new Massachusetts labor law, cutting the workweek from 56 to 54 hours for women and children only, effective January 1, 1912. Mill owners responded by reducing all employees' pay by two hours because everyone's work was interdependent. The strike began when workers received their first paychecks under the new system.

More than wages, however, strikers were driven by the sharp discrepancy between the reality of their brutal existence in the textile city and the ideal they had been lead to expect by recruiting posters in their native countries, from the American Woolen Co. and others, showing mill workers striding from Lawrence's mills carrying bags of gold. Instead, they arrived to find crowded, squalid conditions and watched as diseases killed hundreds every year, most of them children. Although the legal working age was 14, children as young as 12 and 13 could be spotted working in the mills, where many suffered horrible injuries. In fact, industrial accidents, many of them fatal, were common among all mill workers. In a five-year span, the Pacific Mill alone had 1,000 accidents.

Joseph Ettor, a prominent organizer with the militant Industrial Workers of the World union (IWW), crystallized that deep, underlying dissatisfaction. Arriving in Lawrence on Saturday, January 13, Ettor organized the strike in its early days and prevented it from being overwhelmed by the ethnic divisions that had crippled past labor uprisings in the textile industry. Ettor would later be joined by famous IWW strike leaders such as William "Big Bill" Haywood and Elizabeth Gurley Flynn. Ettor was arrested on January 30, along with Arturo Giovannitti, editor of an Italian socialist weekly in New York, who had come to Lawrence at Ettor's request to coordinate striker relief efforts. Both were charged as accessories to LoPizzo's murder, for inciting the crime, even though the men were more than a mile away when it occurred. They were jailed for 10 months until their acquittal in Salem, Massachusetts, on November 26, leaving Haywood to oversee much of the Lawrence strike. Their trial received international news coverage.

American newspapers covered the strike extensively, publishing daily dispatches. Never had there been picketing on the scale seen in Lawrence. Day after day, strikers employed an "endless chain" picket line around the mill district to discourage strikebreakers and keep on the move to avoid being dispersed by the militia and police. The strike also was remarkable for the influential role women played in it as both organizers and participants. Massive parades of singing strikers who marched down the street with interlocked arms took place during the uprising's first two weeks. The colonel in charge of the state militia ordered an end to the parades on January 30 after LoPizzo's death and what became known as the streetcar riot, in which strikers allegedly attacked streetcars carrying "scabs" to work early on January 29. It has been claimed, however, that strikebreakers hired by mill owners were behind the streetcar riot.

The strikers also featured false accusations of a dynamite plot. On January 20, eight days after the strike began, police found dynamite in several locations in the city and arrested a number of strikers and their supporters for scheming to blow up the mills. The allegations quickly unraveled. A week later, all those arrested were exonerated. Police then detained a Lawrence School Committee member named John Breen, a former alderman and son of the city's first Irish mayor, for concocting the alleged scheme to turn public opinion against the strikers. He was convicted in May 1912 and was fined $500. One of William Wood's business associates and his top contractor also were implicated in the plot. Wood himself was indicted in August 1912 but was acquitted in 1913.

IWW organizers and the strike committee put together soup kitchens that fed thousands, as did organizers associated with the much more conservative American Federation of Labor, which was then engaged in a fierce struggle with the IWW for control of the American labor movement. On February 10, in a new IWW tactic, strikers began to send their children by train to temporary shelter with surrogate families. The tactic had not been used in previous strikes in the United States. More than 300 children were sent away

Sent for their own safety from their embattled homes in Lawrence, Massachusetts, strikers' children march in New York City. *(Library of Congress)*

from the embattled city to sympathetic homes in New York City; Philadelphia; Hoboken, New Jersey; Barre, Vermont; and Manchester, New Hampshire.

Massachusetts and Lawrence officials were incensed by the children's exodus. On Saturday, February 24, there was an infamous confrontation between police and a group of mothers, chaperones, and about 46 children at the Lawrence train depot. Refusing to allow the women to send their children away, police began to arrest them. Mothers fought back, and police beat some of them with their nightsticks before throwing them bodily into a waiting military transport truck. Some children reportedly were tossed in the truck as well. The incident was documented by newspaper reporters and drew a firestorm of criticism from across the country, eliciting much sympathy for the strikers. It prompted congressional hearings into the strike, held in early March.

In the end, the mill owners gave in. On March 12, Wood offered raises of 5 to 20 percent, agreed to pay time-and-a-quarter for overtime and curtail an unpopular bonus system, and pledged to refrain from recriminations against strikers at the American Woolen Co. mills. Owners of the Kunhardt and Atlantic mills made the same offers. On March 24, the holdout factories, all cotton mills, caved as well, ending the standoff.

Mill owners throughout New England then gave employees raises to avert similar strikes, though there were copycat uprisings in mill towns throughout New England where the raises were not as large as those in Lawrence. The largest of these was in Lowell, Massachusetts. Ultimately, 300,000 textile workers received pay hikes. A Lawrence newspaper account at the time noted that the raises were

expected to cost $10 million to $12 million in the coming year. The city of Lawrence, meanwhile, estimated that the strike cost $3.2 million in lost wages, revenues, and reimbursement for the militia.

In the strike's aftermath, mill owners reneged on their pledge to refrain from recriminations against strikers. Leaders, activists and anyone continuing to profess allegiance to the IWW found it hard to work in Lawrence's factories. Some were blacklisted. Many were intimidated and ultimately forced to leave the city. From a peak of more than 16,000 members at the height of the strike, the IWW had all but disappeared in Lawrence by the summer of 1913.

Though the great strike in Lawrence has become known as the "Bread and Roses" strike, there is no evidence the slogan was used during the actual uprising. Still, the phrase has become associated with the strike and is widely used by immigrant activists in the labor movement today. As such, it is appropriately connected with one of the country's largest and most successful immigrant worker strikes.

Michael Lafleur

FURTHER READING:

Blewett, Mary H., ed. *Surviving Hard Times: The Working People of Lowell.* Lowell, Mass.: Lowell Museum, 1982.

Cahn, William. *Lawrence 1912: The Bread and Roses Strike.* New York: Pilgrim Press, 1977.

Cameron, Ardis. *Radicals of the Worst Sort: Laboring Women in Lawrence, Massachusetts, 1860–1912.* Chicago: University of Illinois Press, 1993.

Watson, Bruce. *Bread & Roses: Mills, Migrants and the Struggle for the American Dream.* New York: Viking, 2005.

1912 ◆ SINKING OF THE *TITANIC*

A shocked world learned on April 15, 1912, that the RMS *Titanic*, the newest, largest, and most luxurious ship ever built, had struck an iceberg on its maiden voyage en route from Southampton, England, to New York. Late on the cold clear night of Sunday, April 14, 1912, *Titanic* was steaming westward at 21–22 knots. For the previous four days, some of North America's richest people, as well as some of Europe's humblest emigrants, had enjoyed a transatlantic crossing of unprecedented comfort. Suddenly, lookouts spotted an iceberg dead ahead. The first officer ordered the engines reversed

FACTBOX

PLACE North Atlantic Ocean, southeast of Newfoundland

DATE April 14–15, 1912

TYPE Ship accident

DESCRIPTION The White Star liner *Titanic*, considered "practically unsinkable," foundered in the frigid North Atlantic Ocean after colliding with an iceberg, resulting in the loss of two-thirds of its passengers and crew.

CAUSES Overconfidence in technology, lack of communication about ice warnings, errors in judgment about weather conditions and speed, and lack of enough lifeboats to accommodate those on board combined with striking an iceberg

CASUALTIES According to the U.S. Senate Inquiry: 1,517 passengers and crew members; according to the British Board of Trade Inquiry: 1,503 passengers and crew members

COST *Titanic*, fully outfitted, cost about $7.5 million and carried $5 million in insurance; $16,804,112 in claims for loss of life and property were made in the United States against its owners, but after lengthy legal action only $663,000 was paid out to claimants.

IMPACT Major changes in safety regulations for shipping

and tried to steer around the berg, but the ship was too close to avoid it. At about 11:40 P.M., *Titanic* struck what seemed to have been a glancing blow to the iceberg. Most passengers and crew felt no concern about the collision, having faith in their "unsinkable" ship. However, on inspection, it became clear that the ship's first five watertight compartments were rapidly flooding and that the ship would founder.

Captain E. J. Smith ordered the lifeboats uncovered and distress signals sent out by wireless in the hopes of finding a nearby vessel to come to *Titanic*'s aid. He was well aware that there were only enough lifeboats for 1,178 of *Titanic*'s more than 2,200 passengers and crew. Almost half would die in the frigid water if it sank before help arrived. About an hour after striking the iceberg, the first lifeboats were launched, but many were only partially filled. The ship's engineers worked desperately to keep the great vessel afloat as long as possible, but the pumps could not keep up with the volume of water rushing in. At 2:20 A.M. on Monday, April 15, *Titanic* sank, drowning more than two-thirds of its passengers and crew. Several hours later, the Cunard liner *Carpathia* picked up 705 survivors from the lifeboats. A $7.5 million ship had sunk after only four and one-half days in service. Prominent multimillionaires like John Jacob Astor and Benjamin Guggenheim perished alongside working-class immigrants from all over Europe. The Senate investigation that followed failed to find evidence of negligence but recommended that new regulations be introduced governing passenger ship structure, safety equipment, and navigation in order to increase the safety of the transatlantic crossing.

At four city blocks long and 11 stories high, *Titanic* was the biggest ship ever built when it was launched at the Harland and Wolff shipyards in Belfast, Ireland. The White Star Line wanted *Titanic* and its sister ship *Olympic* built to carry passengers between Europe and the United States in unprecedented comfort and safety. *Titanic*, the newer and more luxurious of the two, had a gymnasium, Turkish bath, squash court, and shipboard swimming pool. It also had a hospital and a darkroom for developing shipboard photographs. The opulently decorated staterooms, lounges, and dining areas, as well as the attentive service, reminded first-class passengers of staying in one of the finest hotels. Even third-class accommodations far surpassed those of *Titanic*'s rivals.

White Star ordered Harland and Wolff to build these ships for safety. Theorizing that running aground and collisions were the greatest dangers a ship could encounter, Harland and Wolff engineered *Titanic* to withstand these two types of damage. The craft had a double-bottomed hull and its interior was divided by transverse bulkheads into a series of 16 watertight compartments. According to its designers, in a collision with the bow of the ship, *Titanic* could stay afloat with the first four compartments completely flooded, and in the event of a broadside collision, the ship could stay afloat with any two central compartments completely flooded. It was inconceivable to its owners and builders that *Titanic* would ever encounter a greater threat than this. These features caused *Shipbuilder* magazine to call *Titanic* "practically unsinkable."

SOS

Communication between individuals on shore and ships at sea beyond sight of land or between ships beyond sight of each other became possible with Guglielmo Marconi's patenting of the world's first wireless communication device in England in 1897. Morse Code, developed a half-century earlier for use with inventor Samuel F. B. Morse's telegraph, was the common language of wire and wireless telegraph operators, and the message "SOS" over time became the universally accepted call with which to signal for help. It did not start out that way.

Neal McEwen, in his *The Telegraph Office Magazine,* an online publication on the history of wire and wireless telegraphy, writes that the first wireless call for assistance sent by a vessel at sea came in March 1899. The *East Goodwin* lightship had been struck in the fog during the early morning hours by another ship off the southeastern English coast. The *East Goodwin* issued a distress call to a shore station 12 miles away at South Foreland, and help was dispatched. The transmission "SOS" was contained nowhere in that broadcast. At the time, there was no internationally standardized distress call. McEwen writes that the first wireless call for help by an American ship came in 1905 off the island of Nantucket when the radio operator of *Relief Ship No. 58,* a lightship, sent the message "HELP" in both international and American Morse code.

The first standardized wireless distress signal actually was "CQD." By 1904, according to McEwen, many transatlantic British ships carried wireless equipment operated by men who came from the ranks of English railroad and postal telegraph companies. McEwen writes that in England, a general call to all stations on a landline wire was "CQ." The signal "D" previously had been used internationally to convey urgency. According to McEwen, the Marconi Company in a circular dated Feb. 1, 1904, suggested the use of "CQD" as a maritime distress call after participants in the first international congress of wireless telegraphy in 1903 were unable to come to a consensus on the subject.

It was CQD that was used to convey the first widely reported wireless rescue request on January 23, 1909. The Italian ship *Florida* had struck the British White Star liner *Republic* off Sandy Hook on the northern New Jersey coast during a foggy night, leaving the lives of the two ships' 1,650 passengers dependent on the Marconi apparatus on the *Republic,* which was successfully used to summon assistance. In all, according to *Marconi: The Man and His Wireless* by Orrin E. Dunlap, Jr., four *Florida* crewmen and two *Republic* passengers were lost. The *Republic* sank as it was being escorted back to New York. All crew were rescued. The number of Marconi wireless-equipped ships grew rapidly after the *Republic* disaster.

CQD does not mean "Come Quick Danger," a common misperception. Marconi, testifying during U.S. Senate hearings into the SINKING OF THE *TITANIC,* said the code was introduced to express a state of danger or peril on the ship that sent it. Likewise, SOS is commonly mistaken to mean "Save Our Ship," "Save Our Souls," or "Send Out Succor." In fact, SOS also is a code and its letters have no individual meaning. German regulators adopted its use to indicate distress in 1905. McEwen writes that SOS was selected as an international distress signal during the Berlin Radio-telegraphic Conference of 1906, the successor to the 1903 international congress. SOS was officially ratified as the international standard in 1908, but the use of CQD lingered for several more years, especially in British service. The United States did not officially adopt SOS until 1912. When the White Star liner *Titanic* struck an iceberg on the night of April 14, 1912, its radio officers first used CQD to signal for help, only later interspersing its distress calls with SOS.

The first recorded American use of SOS as a distress signal came in August 1909, McEwen writes. The radio operator on the *SS Arapahoe* used the code to signal for help after his ship lost its screw near Diamond Shoals, off North Carolina. The *Arapahoe* and its radio officer were actually the first in America to receive an SOS signal from another American ship, the *Iroquois,* a few months later.

Michael Lafleur

Overconfidence in this technology led the builders and owners to send *Titanic* into service with only enough lifeboats for about half of those on board. Although in early plans *Titanic* was to have 32 lifeboats for her full capacity of more than 3,000 passengers and crew, they did not consider it necessary to provide lifeboats for all aboard; they believed that in the event of a mishap passengers would be safer staying on the big ship than getting into small lifeboats on the ocean. Additionally, the outdated regulations of the British Board of Trade, the agency that governed safety matters for British ships, required only 16 lifeboats on ships weighing more than 10,000 tons. Although *Titanic* weighed more than 46,000 tons, its total of 20 boats exceeded the board's minimum requirements.

The shortest route between Great Britain and the United States was a "great circle" that took ships far north in the Atlantic Ocean to take advantage of the curvature of the earth. Ice was a well-known navigational hazard on this route. In fact, from January 15 to August 14, ships used the "summer route," which was farther south and longer than the "winter route" but provided protection from the icebergs and field ice that would drift south from late winter to late summer. In April 1912, however, *Titanic*'s use of this summer route was not sufficient to avoid encountering ice. It had been an unusually mild winter and ice had drifted much farther south than usual, into the shipping lanes.

Minor disorganization and occasionally shaky communications, attributable to the unfamiliarity of the crew with each other and the new ship, contributed to the accident. For example, the lookouts stationed high up in the crow's nest had no binoculars. At Southampton, some of the binoculars for the officers of the bridge (the ship's command center) were lost when the senior officers were shuffled at the last minute to bring in more experienced men. The officers kept the remaining pairs on the bridge, leaving the lookouts without any for the duration of the voyage. Binoculars might have enabled the lookouts to spot the iceberg sooner and let the ship avoid it altogether. In addition, although *Titanic* carried a state-of-the-art, long-range Marconi set—an early two-way radio capable of transmitting telegraph communications—two critically important messages, which would have warned *Titanic*'s officers about ice directly in its path that Sunday, did not

reach the bridge at all. During the voyage, *Titanic*'s wireless operators relayed and received several messages from ships encountering ice on the route, but there was no protocol giving priority to picking out messages with navigational information from wireless traffic and delivering them immediately to the bridge. This lack of information led to a key error in judgment. Unaware of how close the dangerous ice field was, *Titanic*'s captain saw no reason to slow down or post extra lookouts on a clear night.

Weather conditions that night added to the danger. Visibility was clear, but there was no moon, and the sea was dead calm. Both these factors made it more difficult than usual to spot icebergs a long way off.

Once *Titanic* hit the iceberg and Captain Smith knew the ship would sink, confusion and lack of communication hampered the evacuation and increased the number of fatalities. Neither the passengers nor all of the officers initially knew the full gravity of the situation, so assembling passengers and readying and loading lifeboats at first went slowly. Many of the boats were lowered half empty by officers who, not having been informed that the boats had been tested fully loaded by Harland and Wolff, did not trust them to hold the stated capacity. The fact that there were no assigned places in the boats and that there had been no boat drill for either passengers or crew during the voyage added to the confusion of the loading and launching process, as did an apparent lack of seamen experienced in lowering and handling small boats. Of a crew of nearly 900, less than 70 were seamen. Most were the stewards, cooks, waiters, bellboys, janitors, and other service workers needed to run a floating five-star hotel. Without a drill and with too few crewmen to help guide them, third-class passengers found it especially difficult to make their way to the lifeboats. As a result, poorer passengers suffered the highest rate of losses. Only a few of the third-class male passengers, and less than half of the third-class female and child passengers survived, despite the officers' emphasis on putting "women and children first" into the lifeboats.

At the beginning, there was little sense of urgency. Passengers, confident of the giant ship's safety, proved reluctant to be lowered some 70 feet down to the surface of the icy water, and the crew did not force them. It was warmer inside the ship and, at least in the first-class lounge, a band played music to

After striking an iceberg in the North Atlantic, the *Titanic* sank on April 15, 1912, killing more than 1,500 people aboard. *(Library of Congress)*

keep spirits up. As the bow sank lower and lower in the water, it finally became clear to all that the ship would sink. By this time, most of the lifeboats were launched. As the final boats were loaded, the officers had to use the threat of firearms to keep order among tense and panicky passengers.

As *Titanic* made its final plunge into the depths, some 1,500 souls were cast into the sea. Survivors remembered that the air was filled with their cries for help. Yet only one of the underfilled boats went back to pick up people in the water. Had a rescue ship arrived before *Titanic* sank, most lives could have been saved. But *Titanic*'s passengers and crew were not that lucky. Although the running lights—the illumination required when a boat was underway at night—of a distant ship were seen roughly

five to 10 miles away, the vessel did not respond to the wireless messages sent or the distress rockets fired by *Titanic*. It remains unclear why this mystery ship, subsequently identified by the British Board of Trade as the *Californian* although its captain denied it, did not assist the *Titanic*. *Carpathia*, the closest ship that did respond, was 58 miles away. It arrived after those in the freezing water had long since succumbed to hypothermia. *Carpathia*'s crew rescued only 705 survivors. Adding to the tragedy was the fact that most of the bodies were carried away by the current and never recovered despite several expeditions sent by the White Star Line to do so.

Fed by inaccurate newspaper reports, all day long on April 15 there was hope that *Titanic* was damaged but under tow and that all passengers and crew would be safe. Finally, a short message to White Star's New York office from the company's managing director, himself a survivor on the *Carpathia,* dashed these hopes.

As the reality set in, waves of grief and anger rolled across the United States. How could the "unsinkable" *Titanic* sink? What negligence or incompetence had cost so many innocent lives? By the time *Carpathia* docked in New York on Thursday, April 18, the U.S. Senate had already formed a subcommittee to investigate the disaster. The hearings began the next morning in New York but soon were transferred to Washington, D.C. The committee's final report, issued six weeks later, noted the misguided assumptions, errors in judgment, and disorganization. However, because of the lax regulations in effect in 1912, these problems did not constitute legal negligence under either U.S. or British law. Thus the Senate report made numerous recommendations to increase regulation to better protect the safety of passengers at sea. From May to July 1912, the British Board of Trade held its own inquiry, chaired by Lord Mersey. Its findings exonerated the owners and crew; it also made recommendations to increase safety on the high seas.

In response to the *Titanic* disaster, the U.S. Congress enacted legislation requiring enough lifeboats for all persons on board ships and 24-hour manning of wireless equipment at sea. In 1915, Congress made lifeboat drills mandatory. Another response was the United States's participation in the International Conference for the Safety of Life at Sea held in London in 1913. It resulted in an international agreement that adopted the requirement of lifeboats for all; mandated moderation of speed and/or alteration of course in the event of ice reports; forbade the use of distress signals for any other purpose; laid down wireless and structural requirements; and provided for the creation of an International Ice Patrol to warn ships of ice and other navigational hazards in the North Atlantic.

Victoria H. Cummins

FURTHER READING:

Eaton, John P., and Charles A. Haas. Titanic: *Destination Disaster.* Rev. and exp. ed. New York: W. W. Norton, 1996.

Kuntz, Tom, ed. *The* Titanic *Disaster Hearings: The Official Transcripts of the 1912 Senate Investigation.* New York: Pocket Books, 1998.

Lord, Walter. *A Night to Remember.* New York: Bantam Books, 1956.

Wade, Wyn Craig. *The* Titanic: *End of a Dream.* Rev. ed. New York: Penguin Books, 1986.

Winocour, Jack, ed. *The Story of the* Titanic *as Told by Its Survivors.* New York: Dover, 1960.

1914 ◆ LUDLOW MASSACRE

On September 23, 1913, some 12,000 coal miners in Ludlow, Colorado, went on strike, commencing the so-called Colorado Coalfield War. As the conflict worsened, miners around Ludlow were driven from their homes and took up residence in a tent city. On April 20, 1914, armed agents of the coal mine owners attacked the encamped strikers and their families, killing 26 people. The Ludlow massacre was the deadliest event of the bloodiest labor conflict in U.S. history.

Life in the coalfields has never been easy, but conditions in the Colorado mines proved more deadly and exhausting than in many other mines. Between 1884 and 1912, more than 1,700 miners died in Colorado's mines, twice the national average. Poor timbering, inadequate equipment, poor communication among the miners of a dozen different nationalities and long hours contributed to the high death rate. The United Mine Workers of America (UMWA), along with the Western Federation of Miners, attempted to organize Colorado miners on numerous occasions, only to be driven from company towns. Miners who joined a union were summarily fired. By mid-September 1913, nonetheless, miners felt strong enough to call a strike in the Trinidad Coalfield of southwestern Colorado, where the town of Ludlow was located. The

FACTBOX

PLACE Ludlow, Colorado

DATE April 20, 1914

TYPE Coal mine strike and massacre

DESCRIPTION A mining strike turned deadly when Colorado militiamen and private detectives hired by mine owners fired on a crowd of miners and their families in a tent city.

CAUSE Antiunion posture of coal company operators in response to strikers' demands

CASUALTIES 26 fatalities in the Ludlow massacre; an estimated 69 to 199 in the Colorado Coalfield War

IMPACT Ultimately led to improved conditions in the mines and prompted hearings in Congress that recommended an eight-hour workday and a ban on child labor

firms affected by the walkout—the Rocky Mountain Fuel Company, the Victor-American Fuel Company, and the Rockefeller-owned Colorado Fuel and Iron Company—essentially controlled the industry in the region. They rejected miners' demands for safer working conditions, recognition of their union, a raise in wages, an eight-hour workday, a fellow miner to check for accuracy in weighing coal (on which pay was based), pay for noncoal-producing work (such as timbering and laying rail), and the freedom to buy supplies where they pleased (many were forced to purchase at company stores).

Sensing an opportunity for unionization, the UMWA entered the fray. Members of the union quickly found themselves without jobs, forced from their homes by company officials, beaten, tarred, feathered, and threatened. The miners, predominantly immigrants from southern and eastern Europe, moved to tent cities on land leased by the UMWA and settled in, while picketing the mines and their scab replacements.

As the strike continued through the fall and winter and coal production fell, Colorado governor Elias Ammons summoned the state militia; mine owners brought in their own armed contingent. Under the guidance of the Colorado Fuel and Iron Company,

the mine owners hired the Baldwin-Felts Detective Agency, an antilabor firm known for its hostility toward striking workers. These mercenaries arrived with Gatling guns and rifles, the cost financed by the Rockefeller family. Throughout the course of the strike, Baldwin-Felts agents raided the tent village in the dead of night. The agents focused bright spotlights on strikers' tents and then shot randomly into them. Men, women, and children died in the gunfire and under the hooves of horses stampeding into the camp. The "Death Special" was especially terrifying. Built in Pueblo by the Colorado Fuel and Iron Company, this steel-plated large automobile could travel with impunity through the makeshift city, firing into tents. Many fathers fearful of their families' lives dug pits to provide some semblance of protection.

On Monday morning, April 20, 1914, Lou Tikas, leader of the striking miners, ventured to the Ludlow train station at the call of the commander of the militia to explain the rumored presence of a man being held against his will. While Tikas met with three militiamen, two companies of the militia took up positions on the surrounding hillsides. Fearing the militiamen and their Baldwin-Felts associates, members of the UMWA took positions in a railroad cut, where they could hide behind a small rise created by the tracks. Other miners attempted to flank the militiamen. Tikas's attempt to flee prompted a gunfight. The gunfire continued throughout the day, ending only when a freight train rolled into camp, shielding miners from further attack. Miners seized this opportunity to flee into the hills surrounding Ludlow. Their attackers then torched the tents. As the smoke cleared on the morning of April 21, strikers and their families returned to the tent city to make a grisly discovery. Concealed by an iron cot, a pit was revealed holding the suffocated bodies of 11 children and two women. The littlest victim, Frank Petrucci, was four months old. The brutality of these deaths led observers to call the murders at Ludlow a massacre.

The carnage at Ludlow triggered virtual open warfare between striking miners and agents of the coal companies throughout the mining camps of Colorado for the next eight months. At the behest of Governor Ammons, President Woodrow Wilson sent federal troops to patrol the area. On December 10, 1914, the UMWA, its funds nearly exhausted, called the strike over. The Colorado state government estimated the number of fatalities in the Colorado Coalfield War at 69 deaths, though a special study commissioned by John D. Rockefeller, Jr., placed the number at 199.

The Ludlow massacre and Colorado Coalfield War spurred numerous events that altered life for the coal miners and other laborers. Rockefeller hired a labor specialist—future Canadian prime minister Mackenzie King—who recommended improved working conditions for miners, construction of recreational facilities, and miners' input on enhancing safety, health and other matters. No miner was to suffer repercussions for his membership in a union, and a

company union came into existence. On the national level, hearings conducted in Congress, resulted in a 1,200-page report supporting an eight-hour workday and an end to child labor.

Kimberly K. Porter

FURTHER READING:

Papanikolas, Zeese. *Buried Unsung: Louis Tikas and the Ludlow Massacre.* Salt Lake City: University of Utah Press, 1982.
Zinn, Howard. *The Twentieth Century: A People's History.* New York: Harper and Row, 1984.

1915 ◆ SINKING OF THE *LUSITANIA*

On May 7, 1915, nine months after World War I broke out in Europe, the British passenger liner *Lusitania* was torpedoed by a German submarine off the southern coast of Ireland near Galley Head. Of the 1,962 people aboard the vessel, 1,198 perished as a result of the attack. Although 10 times as many soldiers were dying every day on the battlefields in western Europe, the sinking of the *Lusitania* seized international attention. The sinking set in motion a train of events that eventually dragged the United States into the war and led to Germany's defeat. The infamous attack has remained as one of the great dilemmas in military ethics in which the rights of noncombatants must be balanced against actions of belligerents.

In 1915, Germany had declared unrestricted submarine warfare against all ships, military or civilian, in the waters surrounding Britain. Since the British navy controlled the ocean's surface and had blockaded its enemy's coast, the Germans resorted to submarines (*Unterseeboot,* undersea boat, commonly called a "U-boat" in the United States) as a countermeasure. Submarines of the era were slow, unarmored boats that a large ship could easily sink by ramming or shelling it. But the submarine had one key advantage—stealth. It was invisible to the eye (and to the ear, for sonar had not yet been invented). Submarines carried a powerful five-inch gun on deck that could destroy

---

FACTBOX

PLACE Atlantic Ocean, off the southern coast of Ireland

DATE May 7, 1915

TYPE Sinking of a passenger ship

DESCRIPTION A German submarine torpedoed the ocean liner *Lusitania*, causing it to sink.

CAUSE German policy of attacking ships in the war zone around the British Isles during World War I

CASUALTIES 1,198 deaths, including 128 Americans

IMPACT Increased anti-German sentiment in the United States led President Wilson to issue an ultimatum to Germany demanding strict observance of neutrality, and contributed to U.S. entry into World War I.

---

a small, unarmed ship, and their torpedoes could sink any ship.

Germany initially conceived of its submarines as weapons for attacking enemy naval vessels, not merchant ships. But faced with a disadvantage on the high seas, German officials revised their policy. The traditional rules of maritime warfare under international law required that an attacker warn a merchant ship and allow its crew to transfer to lifeboats. But Britain had armed some of its merchant ships with deck guns, making it too risky for the frail submarines to surface near their prey. Germany therefore proclaimed a new doctrine, which instructed submarines to destroy merchant ships without warning or guaranteeing the safety of the crew. Passenger ships were then added to the protocol, as were the ships of neutral nations, which included the United States. The United States denounced the German revision of traditional warfare as undermining "the fundamental rights of humanity" and of long-standing neutral rights. President Woodrow Wilson warned that Germany would be held "strictly accountable" for violation of customary international law. Arguing that traditional international law favored Britain, German naval officials appealed to Kaiser Wilhelm II, the German monarch, who consented to unrestricted submarine warfare.

At 790 feet in length and displacing more than 44,000 tons (weighing 31,000 gross tons), the *Lusitania* was the world's largest and fastest passenger ship. Palatial in bearing, the vessel made regularly scheduled trips between New York and Britain. In addition to transporting civilian passengers on its May return from New York to Liverpool, England, the vessel carried Canadian manufactured ammunition, although the commander of the attacking U-boat did not know this fact. Passengers knew it was dangerous to enter a war zone where Germany was sinking ships regularly, although passenger ships had not been attacked. An official German warning had appeared in New York newspapers the day of the sailing, but few people canceled their reservations. William Turner, captain of the *Lusitania,* was confident that his ship's high speed of 22 knots would allow it to outrun the U-boats, whose top speed was 12 knots. As a ruse, Turner flew the American flag, which the submarine crew probably did not see.

The encounter of the two vessels was fortuitous. Neither the liner nor the U-boat was following its prescribed course. Captain Walter Schwieger of the German submarine *U-20* was running low on fuel and therefore was plying in a location off the southern coast of Ireland where he normally would not have been. The *Lusitania* pursued a straight course rather than its prescribed zigzagging maneuver. Schwieger reported in his war diary: "Ahead to starboard four funnels and two masts of a steamer. . . . Ship is made out to be large passenger steamer."

Schwieger was not in range, but suddenly the liner changed course, allowing a clear shot. One torpedo was fired at 2,300-foot range at 2:10 in the afternoon and hit the *Lusitania*'s starboard side. The vessel sank quickly—in just 18 minutes—because the torpedo struck it just below the bridge, causing catastrophic structural failure and a huge secondary explosion.

Most of the ship's 48 lifeboats became entangled or capsized. Only six were launched safely. Schwieger recorded the scene he witnessed through the sub's periscope: "Great confusion on board; boats are cleared away and some are lowered into the water. Apparently considerable panic; several boats, fully laden, are hurriedly lowered, bow or stern first and are swamped at once. Because of the list fewer boats can be cleared away on the port side." About a third of the passengers and crew were rescued from the cold (52°F) waters by fishing boats that rushed from Queenstown (Cobh) harbor, 20 miles away. Of 1,257 registered passengers, 785, including 128 Americans, died, as did 413 members of the 702-member crew and three stowaways. Of 129 children on board, 94 lost their lives, including 35 of 39 infants.

The disaster stunned the world. London made the tragedy the centerpiece of its anti-German propaganda, but it hardly needed to fan public passions. Across Britain, spontaneous riots denounced Germany and attacked German aliens living in Britain. Germany at first denied that the U-boat commander knew that he had targeted a passenger ship but later argued that the *Lusitania* was armed (it was not), that it carried Canadian troops (it did not), and that it carried munitions in the cargo (it did have small arms ammunition, but this cargo did not make the vessel a combatant warship).

Americans were outraged, especially those living on the East Coast where pro-British sentiments were strong. Anglophile spokesmen and intellectuals, led by former president Theodore Roosevelt, called for war and ridiculed Wilson as a coward. The president was assailed both by pro-German groups and ardent pacifists. The former believed that the British blockade justified Germany's submarine warfare; the latter were afraid that strong language in diplomatic notes would lead to war. Wilson's initial response to the emotion over the sinking was that "There is such a thing as a man being too proud to fight. There is such a thing as a nation being so right that it does not need to convince others by force that it is right."

Wilson announced that the "rights of neutrals are based upon principle, not upon expediency, and the principles are immutable. Illegal and inhuman acts are manifestly indefensible when they deprive neutrals of their acknowledged rights, particularly when they violate the right to life itself." The president issued an ultimatum to Germany that insisted on scrupulous observance of neutral rights or "suffer the consequences"—a term left undefined. A committed pacifist, U.S. Secretary of State William Jennings Bryan resigned over the president's peremptory tone, but Germany accepted Wilson's terms in September 1915, agreeing to restricted use of its submarines.

The fallout from the *Lusitania* disaster moved the United States psychologically closer toward war. After 1915, key decision makers such as Wilson, Secretary of State Robert Lansing (Bryan's replacement), and influential Republican leader Elihu Root came to view the German government as autocratic and to see America's destiny bound up with the defense of democracy. Wilson supported a naval buildup. As the war dragged on in Europe, with its mounting toll on

lives and citizen support, Germany's admirals argued that victory was possible if submarines were permitted to interdict supplies destined for Britain. In January 1917, Germany resumed unrestricted submarine warfare, realizing its decision likely meant war with the United States. Three months later, President Wilson delivered a war message to the U.S. Congress, which lawmakers overwhelmingly accepted. The sinking of the *Lusitania* turned out to be a deadly and terrible mistake, for the action allowed critics to brand Germany as a nation of "Huns" driven by ruthless militarists who were callous toward human life.

Richard Jensen

FURTHER READING:

Bailey, Thomas A., and Paul B. Ryan. *The* Lusitania *Disaster: An Episode in Modern Warfare and Diplomacy.* New York: Free Press, 1975.

Preston, Diana. Lusitania: *An Epic Tragedy.* New York: Berkley, 2002.

Ramsay, David. Lusitania: *Saga and Myth.* New York: W. W. Norton, 2001.

1915 ◆ CAPSIZING OF THE *EASTLAND*

On July 24, 1915, the steamer *Eastland*—docked on a wharf in the Chicago River, in downtown Chicago—suddenly capsized, killing 844 passengers, crew members, and rescuers. The accident was Chicago's worst disaster, claiming more lives than both the deadly 1903 Iroquois Theater fire in the city and the great Chicago fire 44 years earlier, and the sixth-worst marine disaster in American history. The *Eastland* was an iron-hull steamer that had plied Lake Michigan for years. How could a ship of this size and record capsize while stationary at its berth? Why did so many people perish? Who was responsible for this dreadful calamity? These are some of the questions that continue to baffle historians about the *Eastland* disaster.

The background of the story begins with the Hawthorne Works, a massive factory complex maintained by Western Electric, the manufacturer of equipment for the Bell Telephone Company. Located

FACTBOX

PLACE Chicago River, Chicago, Illinois

DATE July 24, 1915

TYPE Passenger ship capsized while at berth

DESCRIPTION The Great Lakes steamer *Eastland*, loaded with 2,500 summer picnickers, overturned before casting off from a wharf, drowning hundreds of victims.

CAUSE An inherently unstable design, coupled with the addition of lifeboats and rafts to the upper decks following the sinking of the *Titanic* in 1912

CASUALTIES 844 deaths

IMPACT A closer inspection of Great Lakes ships

in Cicero, Illinois, just west of Chicago's city limits, the Hawthorne Works had expanded since 1904 into a "city within a city," offering a diverse array of athletic, educational, and social activities. Many of the plant's employees were recent immigrants from the present-day Czech Republic, Poland, and Hungary. Since 1912, the factory's entertainment committee had sponsored a daylong picnic at Michigan City, Indiana, located on Lake Michigan's southern shore. Although privately organized and sponsored, the management at Hawthorne Works saw the picnic as a morale booster and encouraged attendance. Employees, who normally worked a six-day week, were given the Saturday off so that they and their families could attend the festivities. A flotilla of five excursion steamers rested at berths in the Chicago River on the morning of July 24, as the crew made preparations to carry some 7,000 picnickers 36 miles east on Lake Michigan to their holiday destination.

People began to gather by 7 A.M. at the gangway of the *Eastland,* the first steamer scheduled to depart. Constructed in 1903, the *Eastland* was 269 feet long, with a beam of 36 feet and four decks above water. The ship was driven by two screw propellers and drew 14 feet of water, which gave it at least 5 feet of clearance over the muddy bottom of the Chicago River which opened onto Lake Michigan. The vessel was sleek, rose higher above the water than older lake steamers, and was outfitted with dining rooms and salons. The ship's licensed capacity, a figure that had fluctuated over the years, was 2,500 in 1915.

Inspectors survey the damage of the *Eastland*, which capsized beside a dock in Chicago with some 2,500 summer picnickers aboard. *(Chicago Historical Society)*

However, no one counted or recorded passengers as they boarded the *Eastland* on this fateful Saturday morning.

Hundreds of passengers packed the ship's decks, taking in the views of the city and the warm, summer air. As the scheduled departure at 7:30 drew close, some observers noticed a listing to port, the side of the ship facing away from the wharf. The leaning alarmed the harbormaster, who hailed Harry Pedersen, the vessel's captain, on the bridge to "trim" the ship. Instructions were relayed to Chief Engineer Joseph Ericksen in the engine room to fill the appropriate ballast tanks, which were designed to stabilize the steamer and keep it upright in the water. For reasons that remain a mystery, several of the tanks failed to fill. Meanwhile, the ship continued its list, shifting from a vertical position to a diagonal position as it tipped more and more into the river. At 7:31 A.M., the *Eastland* capsized, spilling passengers on the upper promenades into the murky, polluted water. Hundreds more were trapped below decks in the salons and dining rooms. A few lucky souls who had held onto the starboard rails—which remained above water—were able to scramble onto the overturned hull.

Pandemonium erupted as bodies were hurled in the turgid Chicago River. A nurse from the Hawthorne Works assigned to duty at the picnic described the scene as it unfolded:

> I shall never be able to forget what I saw. People were struggling in the water, clustered so thickly they literally covered the surface of the river. A few were swimming; the rest were floundering about, some clinging to the life raft that had floated free, others clutching at anything they could reach at bits of wood, at each other, grabbing each other, pulling each other down, and screaming! The screaming was the most horrible of all.

Courageous individuals dove into the water time and again to rescue victims and then to retrieve bodies. Welders cut sections from the hull to extricate victims trapped inside. Tugs and smaller boats converged on the stricken vessel, while thousands of spectators who lined the streets, wharf, and decks of several sister ships watched the horror unfold. Crews worked through the day and all night under arc lights searching for bodies. Of the 844 who perished in the accident, 600 were employees at the Hawthorne Works. Many neighborhoods around the factory complex held scores of funerals. Twenty-two entire families were wiped out. Women had been especially vulnerable. The custom of the outing for both men and women was to dress to the hilt, donning fancy attire. But the elaborate skirts and other finery that women wore acted like weights when they became wet, impeding their ability to stay above water.

Why had it happened? Since no conclusive explanation has surfaced to this day, speculation must suffice to account for the accident. Some marine engineers deemed the vessel's design to be inherently unstable; the ship had experienced unexplained listings in the past. Some marine inspectors asserted the passenger capacity assigned to the vessel was too high. A mystery surrounds the failure of two ballast tanks to fill. One popular theory, that passengers had dangerously assembled on the port side, tipping the ship, has not been confirmed by experts. George Hilton, an economist and marine historian, has theorized that safety measures instituted after the SINKING OF THE *TITANIC* may have proved fatal for the *Eastland*. Reaction to the *Titanic* disaster of 1912 led ship owners to add more lifeboats, rafts, and life preservers to vessels, including the *Eastland*. The new equipment was placed on the *Eastland*'s upper ("hurricane") deck in July 1915, a change that Hilton believes increased the ship's instability. Moreover, the licensed passenger capacity of the vessel was increased in early July

1915 by more than 300 people. The outing of July 24 was the first time since the addition of the new lifeboats that the vessel was loaded to capacity.

Investigation of the mishap began even before the last victim was located. But after 20 years of prosecution and lawsuits, little was resolved. Only Chief Engineer Erickson, who was defended at trial by famed Chicago attorney Clarence Darrow, was convicted of wrongdoing, and Erickson died of natural causes before the verdict was reached. The *Eastland* disaster led to increased inspection of Great Lakes vessels but had little effect on Lake Michigan excursion shipping, which had reached its peak in 1912. The day of the automobile and the bus was dawning rapidly, making such mass riverboat excursions less frequent. Oddly, the *Eastland* survived: The ship was salvaged and refitted after it was refloated, and it was recommissioned as the *Wilmette* for the U.S. Navy. The vessel served as a training vessel on the Great Lakes and even carried President Franklin D. Roosevelt on a summer cruise in 1943 during its second life. In 1947, the former *Eastland* was cut up for scrap.

Ballard C. Campbell

FURTHER READING:

Bonansinga, Jay. *The Sinking of the* Eastland: *America's Forgotten Tragedy.* New York: Citadel Press, 2004.

Hilton, George W. Eastland: *Legacy of the* Titanic. Stanford, Calif.: Stanford University Press, 1995.

1918 ◆ INFLUENZA PANDEMIC

The influenza pandemic of 1918 was the most lethal epidemic ever to strike the United States. Infecting people around the world, the disease is estimated to have killed between 50 million and 100 million individuals. The higher estimate represents about 5 percent of all people alive at the time. In the United States, the flu pandemic caused about 675,000 premature deaths, about 0.6 percent of the U.S. population. Ten percent of the population of Guam died from the scourge. The flu took a third of Labrador's inhabitants, 10 percent of the population of Chiapas, Mexico, and an estimated 7 percent of all the residents of Russia and Iran. Twenty million inhabitants in India may have succumbed to the flu. Dwarfing the 8.5 million battlefield deaths during World War I (1914–18), the flu pandemic of 1918 ranks with the bubonic plague in Europe in the 14th century and the decimation of American Indians from European-borne diseases as history's deadliest and most catastrophic health crises.

FACTBOX

PLACE Throughout the United States and the world

DATE January 1918–April 1919 (peak: September–October 1918)

TYPE An influenza epidemic

DESCRIPTION Flu pandemic struck the United States and the world.

CAUSE Influenza virus; various secondary infections

CASUALTIES 675,000 premature deaths in the United States and 50 million to 100 million worldwide

IMPACT Massive upheaval of everyday life in many American cities; spurred biological research

The first outbreak of pandemic occurred in Haskell County, Kansas, in January 1918, nine months after the United States had declared war on Germany and entered World War I. Within weeks it had spread to Camp Funston, located near Manhattan, Kansas. The camp was one of the nation's largest military facilities that the U.S. government had hurriedly thrown together to train soldiers for World War I. Wartime conditions provided an incubator for influenza, as America's entrance into the conflict produced large concentrations of soldiers and sailors in army encampments and naval installations around the country. From these rendezvous locations, troops were transported across the Atlantic Ocean to the war zone in France. Some ships literally became death traps, producing mass burials of flu victims at sea. Freighters and troop ships of the other countries involved in the war served as conduits between the battlefield in Europe and points around the globe.

Within months of the initial outbreak, the flu spread from camp to camp in the United States as troops were shuttled between facilities. By September 1918, when it arrived at Fort Devens, a training camp in Massachusetts, the disease had reached an extremely lethal stage. A fifth of the 45,000 troops at Devens got sick and hundreds died, sometimes within hours of complaining of flu symptoms. A medical observer noted that "dead bodies are stacked about the morgue like cord wood." Army leaders

were unprepared for such a monumental health crisis. Moreover, they largely ignored cautionary warnings about troop movements, as they were more interested in building up strength in Europe for a final thrust against Germany. Nonetheless, military training in the United States practically halted during October 1918. Despite General John J. Pershing's request for more troops, the draft for October was canceled. On the other side of the lines, the flu contributed to German failure to stop the final Allied assault in the fall of 1918. Germany agreed to an armistice on November 11.

The first European outbreak of the flu occurred in April in Brest, France, the principal port of disembarkation for American troops in Europe. From there, the disease spread across the continent of Europe, trekked toward Africa and Asia, and then leapt back across the Atlantic via troop ships and freighters. The global routings of shipping around the world carried the flu from the coast of Africa to port cities in India and China, the Pacific islands, South America, Alaska, and the Gulf of Mexico and cities on the West Coast of the United States.

Ports such as Boston, New York, New Orleans, and San Francisco suffered especially, as did towns along the Mississippi River and the Great Lakes Naval Training Station in Illinois. In Philadelphia, another port city, a massive Liberty Loan parade was held in October 1918, despite the pleas of some medical officials for cancellation. The city paid a horrible price for proceeding with the event, as fatalities soon approached a thousand a week. As the death toll mounted around the country, the social fabric of many communities began to unravel. In San Francisco, schools closed for six weeks; in Philadelphia, bodies piled up uncollected, and the police were instructed to retrieve bodies from homes. Families were forced to dig graves for loved ones, as grave diggers refused to work. Factories slowed due to high absence rates. The influenza epidemic so permeated national consciousness and everyday life that schoolgirls in Massachusetts jumped rope to a new song:

> I had a little bird
> And its name was Enza
> I opened the window
> And in-flew Enza

Much of normal social intercourse, even kissing, stopped.

When people got sick, death could come swiftly, especially to young adults. Normally the healthiest of age groups, individuals in their twenties had the highest rate of mortality from the flu. More than 1 percent of Americans of this age perished in the pandemic—and worldwide the figure for this age group may have reached as high as 10 percent. Some died agonizing deaths, as author John Barry related: "blood poured from noses, ears, eye sockets; some victims lay in agony; delirium took others away while living." Coughing could tear the muscles of the rib cage apart. When the extremities such as lips and cheeks turned black, death was sure to follow. In some instances, people who appeared fine in the morning were dead by the evening. Some individuals who survived the ordeal bore physical scars later, such as blurred vision and damaged livers.

Doctors were baffled by these developments. Medical science had made enormous strides between the 1880s and 1918 when microbiologists had found the bacteriological origins of many diseases. But influenza was caused by a virus—parasites smaller than bacteria—which scientists had not yet isolated under a microscope. Although hypothesized, viruses would not be seen in the laboratory until 1933. The particular RNA (ribonucleic acid) structure of the 1918 influenza virus was not identified until Dr. Jeffrey Taubenberger, chief of the U.S. Division of Molecular Pathology, diagnosed its genetic makeup from scraps of lung tissue taken from two U.S. soldiers who died from the flu and tissue extracted from a flu victim exhumed from the Alaskan permafrost. After a decade of work reconstructing the RNA of the 1918 virus, Taubenberger concluded in 2005 that it was a strain of avian flu (originating in birds).

Taubenberger speculated that the virus may have mutated from a mild strain early in 1918 into an abnormally lethal one in the latter half of the year. This heightened virulence is what caused many adults in their twenties to suffer excruciating deaths. With young, healthy bodies primed to ward off foreign organisms, their immune systems worked overtime to kill the invading virus. This massive counterattack filled their lungs with fluid, and victims suffocated to death. This was the fate of many young men who joined the army and navy. But a larger number of flu deaths were due to "secondary" bacterial infections, particularly pneumonia, that developed among victims whose immune systems had been weakened by influenza. By the same token, mutation may also

have been an important cause of the declining virulence of the flu in 1919. Such changes in the composition of viruses are now commonly recognized. The diminution of the pandemic also appeared to be the result of increased immunity to the virus as it swept through various communities.

Perhaps one-fourth of all Americans caught the flu between the fall of 1918 and the winter of 1918–19. Even if sufficient physicians had been available, doctors could have done little to intercede. No flu vaccine existed at the time. While some antibacteria serums were available, none served to counter influenza virus. Caregivers could do little for victims other than to provide liquids, administer aspirin, and make patients comfortable. But nurses and doctors were scarce, as the war effort had siphoned them into the military and to France. Despite frantic appeals, calls for more nurses went unfilled. Sometimes entire families lay sick, unaided by professional assistance or help from neighbors, who refused to enter homes that had "Influenza" signs nailed to the front door. Some cities required that people wear surgical masks, which were not effective—the cotton mesh was not fine enough to trap the microscopic virus. Because death rates were the highest among young adults, many of whom were parents, the flu produced hundreds of thousands of orphans in the United States and around the world.

The federal government offered scant assistance to flu victims. The U.S. Public Health Service played a minimal role during the pandemic, in part because President Woodrow Wilson did not publicly acknowledge the epidemic. His priorities in 1918 were the defeat of Germany and supervision of

Police officers in Seattle, Washington, wear masks in an effort to protect themselves from the deadly flu pandemic. *(New York Public Library)*

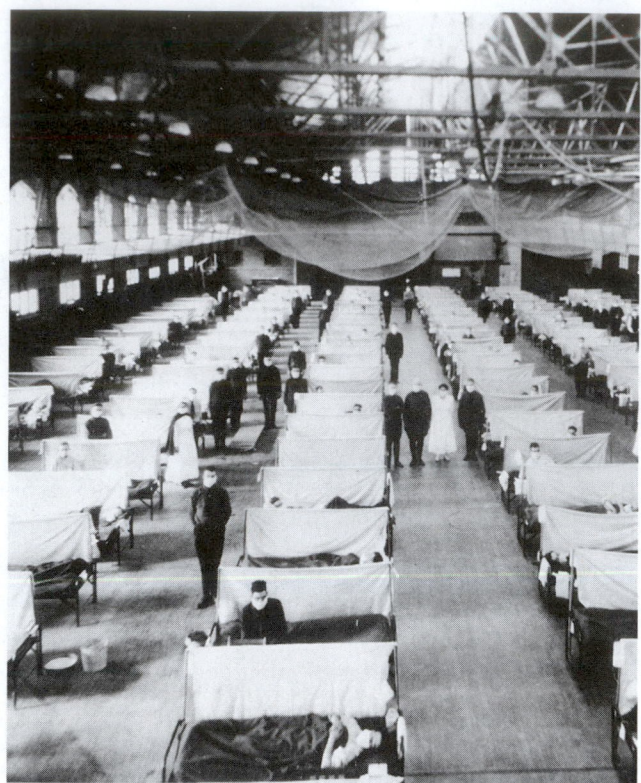

At a makeshift infirmary, flu patients are treated at the Iowa State University gymnasium. *(New York Public Library)*

the peace settlement afterward. Following the president's lead, the nation's newspapers downplayed the pandemic, imploring citizens not to become fearful ("Don't get scared") and pumping up morale for the war effort. Nor did many American writers take note of the pandemic. One of the few exceptions, Katherine Anne Porter, later wrote about her brush with death in "Pale Horse, Pale Rider" in her *Collected Stories* (New York, 1965). The deliberate suppression of bad news during the war helps to explain why the influenza pandemic received so little attention in comparison with the other major catastrophes that struck the United States in the 20th century.

After Germany surrendered, President Wilson went to France as the head of the American delegation to the peace negotiations held at Versailles. In early April 1919, while in France, the president contracted the flu, which came on suddenly. "That night was one of the worst through which I have ever passed," he later recalled. Prior to his illness, Wilson had resisted Allied demands for a punitive approach to Germany, but even before he had fully recovered, Wilson changed course and conceded most of the

Allied position, including the imposition of expensive financial reparations on Germany. Historians are uncertain how much the flu contributed to the president's reversal. The writer John Barry conjectured that Wilson's bout with the flu contributed to his debilitating stroke the following September, an event which clouded his judgment when the Senate considered the ratification of the Versailles Treaty.

Historians must speculate on how the flu pandemic altered the course of world politics. Similarly, social scientists must estimate the scourge's human tally. Few countries had comprehensive death registration systems in place by 1918; the priorities of the war and rapid escalation of deaths late in 1918 also contributed to the underrecording of fatalities. Even in the United States, many deaths went uncounted. In some foreign cities the incidence of illness exceeded 50 percent. The existing data for the United States, however, hold a grim record. More than 6,000 died from the flu in Boston. In New York City, the number was 30,000; in Philadelphia, nearly 16,000; in Chicago, 14,000; and in San Francisco, 3,700. One-half of all deaths occurred among people in their twenties. In the United States more than 1 percent of this age group died, while in Mexico, the figure ranged between 5 and 9 percent of young adults. Partly as a consequence of this age-specific effect, the flu depressed life expectancy for 10 years. The illness and mortality may also have contributed to the economic difficulties that began in 1920 and to popular resentment of American involvement in international affairs that was manifested during the decade. On a more positive note, the pandemic did stimulate medical researchers to dig deeper into the mysteries of human biology.

See also 1492 DECIMATION OF NATIVE AMERICANS BY EUROPEAN DISEASES.

Ballard C. Campbell

FURTHER READING:

Barry, John M. *The Great Influenza: The Epic Story of the Deadliest Plague in History.* New York: Penguin Books, 2004.

Crosby, Alfred W. *America's Forgotten Pandemic: The Influenza of 1918.* New York: Cambridge University Press, 1989.

Kolata, Gina. *Flu: The Story of the Great Influenza Pandemic of 1918 and the Search for the Virus That Caused It.* New York: Farrar, Straus and Giroux, 1999.

1919 ◇ GREAT MOLASSES SPILL

In 1915, the Purity Distilling Company constructed a storage tank in Boston's North End to hold shipments of Caribbean molasses that were to be distilled into rum and industrial alcohol. Located on Commercial Street near Boston harbor, the immense tank—50 feet tall and 280 feet in circumference—towered over the neighboring structures in the mixed residential and commercial neighborhood. For three years after the tank's completion, Purity and its parent company, U.S. Industrial Alcohol (USIA), enjoyed double-digit growth due to the wartime demands for its industrial alcohol, which was used in the production of munitions for World War I. Meanwhile, residents and workers in the neighborhood fronting Boston harbor eyed the new tank warily. The immense structure shuddered and groaned as it was filled with each new shipment, and every day molasses seeped through the seams in the tank's side, running to the ground in thick, sticky rivulets.

During an unseasonably warm afternoon on January 15, 1919, scores of people went about their business on Commercial Street, enjoying the bright sunshine and 45-degree temperature. Just after 12:30, a deep, low rumbling resounded through the street, accompanied by a series of rapid, metallic popping noises reminiscent of machine-gun fire. Many turned toward the sound to see the sides of the huge storage tank slide apart and unleash 2.3 million gallons of roiling, dark molasses in every direction. Powered by its 13,000-ton weight, the dense black wave was estimated to be 30 feet high and moving at 35 miles per hour as it swept outward from the base of the tank. Surging across Commercial Street, the wave crashed against the white stone wall of Copps Hill Terrace and the sides of the neighboring tenements. Molasses quickly poured into the cellars of the buildings and as the wave receded lifted them off their foundations and carried them away. On the north side of the street, the sweet liquid rolled through a freight yard, engulfing hapless workers and splintering flimsy wooden storage sheds and stables. It also uprooted a two-story brick firehouse and carried it to the edge of the harbor.

Rescue workers arriving on the scene found a thick, swirling pool of molasses hundreds of feet

FACTBOX

PLACE Boston, Massachusetts

DATE January 15, 1919

TYPE Industrial accident

DESCRIPTION Collapse of an enormous 50-foot-high tank flooded a section of Boston's North End with molasses.

CAUSE Faulty design of the holding tank and the lack of safety precautions

CASUALTIES 21 deaths, 150 injuries

IMPACT Precipitated the largest and longest civil proceeding in Massachusetts history.

.across and three feet deep stretched before them. The area was littered with debris of every sort—sewing machines sat amid splintered wood and shattered glass, while furniture lay smashed against upended freight cars and automobiles. Around the islands of wreckage, dark, formless shapes of men and horses vainly struggled to free themselves from the thick, clinging ooze. In the end, the great Boston molasses flood led to 21 deaths, 150 injuries, and the destruction of 14 buildings valued at roughly half a million dollars.

Though molasses had been an economic cornerstone of Boston since the colonial era, no precedent existed for the large-scale clean-up of the gooey substance that had completely overtaken this North End neighborhood. Crews worked around the clock for weeks to clear the wreckage. When fresh water from hydrants proved ineffectual on the molasses, fireboats showered the street with salt water, which thinned the syrup enough for it to run into Boston Harbor. Hydraulic siphons slowly pumped the viscous fluid out of cellars and basements in building after building. Spectators came daily to marvel at the unbelievable sight. For weeks after, they and the workers tracked molasses throughout the entire city.

The legal hearing to determine liability in the disaster turned into the largest and longest civil proceeding

With the wreckage of the collapsed Purity Distilling Company storage tank visible in the background, tons of sticky molasses coagulate on the streets of Boston. (*Boston Public Library*)

destroyed by saboteurs. At the time, Boston was recognized as a hotbed for the radical anarchists who had stunned the nation with a series of well-orchestrated bomb attacks on high-profile targets, and USIA was a major military supplier that had previously received anarchist threats. The plaintiffs, on the other hand, showed that company treasurer Arthur P. Jell, who oversaw construction of the tank, never submitted the plans to an architect or engineer for technical review or ordered standard safety tests and that he ignored repeated reports that the tank might be unsound. In a ruling that led to an estimated $600,000 settlement by USIA, the court cited "the absence of every kind of skilled technical supervision and inspection by the defendant" as the root cause of the disaster. The great Boston molasses flood remains one of the most bizarre catastrophes in American history.

Susan Doll and David Morrow

in Massachusetts history, with 119 claimants, three years of argument, and 25,000 pages of transcripts. Capitalizing on the postwar Red Scare that then gripped America, USIA contended that the tank had been

FURTHER READING:

Brust, Beth Wagner. *The Great Molasses Flood.* Mahwah, N.J.: Troll Communications, 1998.

Puleo, Stephen. *Dark Tide: The Great Boston Molasses Flood of 1919.* Boston: Beacon Press, 2004.

1919 ◆ BOMBING OF ATTORNEY GENERAL'S HOUSE

At approximately 11:15 P.M. on June 2, 1919, a bomb composed of an estimated 20 pounds of dynamite exploded in front of U.S. Attorney General A. Mitchell Palmer's house at 2132 R Street in Washington, D.C. The blast killed the bomber and severely damaged the front of the residence. No one was injured, although Palmer himself was hit by shattered glass, and several neighbors were thrown from their beds. Debris from the explosion scattered throughout the neighborhood, causing significant structural damage to surrounding buildings.

The attack was part of a wave of bombings between April and June 1919 orchestrated by a group known as Galleanists, followers of violent anarchist Luigi Galleani. As labor strikes and protests grew during the early months of 1919, many Americans began to fear a growing threat from radicals and communists inspired by the Bolshevik Revolution

in Russia. Most job actions and demonstrations were peaceful; often, violence was perpetrated by opponents of the labor movement. During the last week of April 1919, however, events took a dramatic turn. Galleanists sent package bombs to 30 prominent Americans, including senators, representatives, judges, and public officials at the state and local level. Only one of these bombs exploded, however, injuring a Georgia senator's housekeeper. Most had been mailed with insufficient postage, and a postal inspector alertly intercepted nearly all of the unexploded packages, including one destined for Attorney General Palmer. Then, on June 2, Galleanists planted bombs in eight cities. Between 11 P.M. and 1 A.M. the following morning, blasts rocked one church and eight houses, including the homes of Attorney General Palmer, Cleveland mayor Harry L. Davis, and several judges. Two people were killed in the

FACTBOX

PLACE Residence of Attorney General A. Mitchell Palmer, 2132 R Street, Washington, D.C.

DATE June 2, 1919

TYPE Bombing

DESCRIPTION A bomb composed of roughly 20 pounds of dynamite exploded, shattering windows and causing significant structural damage to surrounding buildings.

CASUALTIES 1 killed

IMPACT This bombing and others at the same time helped provoke a "Red Scare," or fears that Bolshevik-inspired radicals were instigating a revolution in the United States. In response, Attorney General Palmer launched a series of raids on suspected radicals, deporting hundreds and depriving thousands more of civil liberties.

attacks, including the bomber of Palmer's house and an elderly security guard in New York City.

Given the devastation caused by the blast at the attorney general's house in northwest Washington, solving the crime was immensely difficult. The bomber's body was decimated and scattered over more than a block of the fashionable neighborhood, making a positive identification impossible. Some investigators believed that the bomber tripped on Palmer's front walk and accidentally detonated the device; more likely, according to experts in explosives, either the timing mechanism or the fuse malfunctioned, causing the bomb to explode prematurely. Piecing together fragmentary evidence, detectives could trace the bomber's travels from New York City to Palmer's northwest Washington residence. An Italian-English dictionary found in the rubble suggested his nationality. Yet his identity remained a mystery to investigators at the time.

Authorities were more certain about his ties to Galleanists. A leaflet entitled *Plain Words,* found at all the June 2 bomb sites, bore many similarities to known Galleanist screeds. Signed "The American Anarchists" or "The Anarchist Fighters," the leaflets promised a wave of murder and destruction in retaliation for the government's campaign against anarchists and immigrants.

Although the crime was never officially solved, historian Paul Avrich's exhaustive work has identified Carlo Valdinoci, a 24-year-old Galleanist, as the perpetrator. Valdinoci had been implicated in several previous anarchist plots, and he was to be deported if authorities could have found the notoriously elusive man. Avrich suggests that Valdinoci may have helped to plan the June 2 conspiracy from his Newton, Massachusetts, hideout and that he distributed explosives to bombers in New York, Philadelphia, and Patterson, New Jersey, before arriving in Washington to carry out the attack on Palmer.

Although quite shaken by the blast, Palmer was not immediately convinced that the bombing campaign was a sign of an imminent communist revolution. Nevertheless, in the months after the attack, Palmer secured $500,000 from Congress and created the General Intelligence Division within the Justice Department to investigate radicalism. By November 1919, increasingly persuaded of a security threat and under pressure for action from the press and political leaders, the attorney general launched a series of raids against alleged alien subversives. Often acting without warrants, state and federal officials rounded up approximately 10,000 communists, socialists, and radical union members, eventually deporting 591 aliens. These "Palmer Raids," lasting until the spring of 1920, were wildly popular with the press and the public.

By the summer of 1920, however, Palmer's campaign against labor radicals faded. Legal scholars and civil libertarians began to condemn the attorney general's tactics. In addition, a new acting secretary of labor, responsible for authorizing deportations, dismissed thousands of arrest warrants for lack of evidence and freed many aliens who had been incarcerated without charge. When no Bolshevik revolution materialized in 1919 and 1920, as predicted by Palmer and his allies, the American people began to reject the Red Scare's climate of fear and instead looked forward to an era of normalcy and prosperity.

See also 1920 WALL STREET BOMBING.

William J. Nancarrow

FURTHER READING:

Avrich, Paul. *Sacco and Vanzetti: The Anarchist Background.* Princeton, N.J.: Princeton University Press, 1991.

Coben, Stanley. *A. Mitchell Palmer, Politician.* New York: Da Capo Press, 1972.

Murray, Robert K. *Red Scare: A Study in National Hysteria, 1919–1920.* Minneapolis: University of Minnesota Press, 1955.

1919 ◆ CHICAGO RACE RIOT

In late July 1919, a race riot plunged Chicago into a violent crisis that seemingly put the city on the verge of a civil war. The conflict erupted when black residents trespassed into a "white" bathing area on the shores of Lake Michigan. This incursion triggered a brawl with whites who defended "their turf." The fight escalated into four days of citywide violence that left more than 500 Chicagoans injured, countless houses destroyed, and 38 citizens dead. The Chicago race riot was the worst in a wave of interracial clashes that swept the nation from Charleston, South Carolina, to Omaha, Nebraska, and from Longview, Texas, to Washington, D.C., in the "Red Summer" of 1919.

Although slavery had been abolished in 1865, harsh realities compromised African Americans' hopes for freedom and forced them into a new form of economic and political dependence in the late 19th century. Lacking capital to establish themselves as independent farmers, freed slaves gravitated to sharecropping, an agricultural system in which tenants rented a farm, usually from a white landholder, and paid for it with a portion of their crop. This agreement with the former slave owners enmeshed newly freed African Americans in a web of debt and quasi-bondage. Trying to escape the vicious circle, many southern blacks migrated north to industrial cities such as St. Louis and Chicago. Here, white working-class residents widely perceived them as economic competitors. During Chicago's rebuilding following the great fire of 1871, realtors restricted the majority of black newcomers to an area on the city's South Side. Landlords charged residents of this "Black Belt" exorbitant rents, while allowing properties to decay. When World War I exports triggered a military production boom in the 1910s, thousands of rural blacks fled the South and poured into the city. Between 1910 and 1920, the black population on Chicago's South Side tripled from 30,000 to 90,000, with only negligible expansion of the Black Belt's boundaries. Many African Americans embraced the opportunity to leave their crumbling neighborhoods by joining the army when the United States entered the war in 1917. In 1918, the black veterans returned home as confident

FACTBOX

PLACE Chicago, Illinois

DATE July 27–July 30, 1919

TYPE Race riot

DESCRIPTION After the killing of an African-American teenager, a riot raged for four days.

CAUSE Whites' attempts to restrict African Americans' freedom led to increased racial tensions in Chicago and other metropolitan areas.

CASUALTIES 38 people were killed, 537 injured, nearly 1,000 made homeless.

IMPACT The Chicago Commission on Race Relations issued a progressive report that sparked debate about racial desegregation.

"New Negroes," optimistically expecting that service for their country would lead to improvements in their lives at home. Instead, they encountered a series of residential bombings. Black tempers were stretched thin by this blatant intimidation.

On the hot Sunday afternoon of July 27, 1919, four blacks challenged the unwritten laws of segregation by crossing into the "white" section of a Lake Michigan beach between 26th and 29th streets. Whites on the beach drove them back and crowds gathered quickly when both sides started throwing stones. In the general tumult, 17-year-old Eugene Williams swam across the invisible line that separated black from white bathers, who now aimed their rocks at him. Hit on the head, Williams drowned. After a vain rescue attempt, outraged blacks demanded that the policeman on the scene, Officer Daniel Callahan, arrest George Stauber, who allegedly had hurled the fatal rock. Callahan refused and called in reinforcements as the conflict spiraled out of control. When more police officers arrived at the beach, a black rioter fired a gun at them, wounding one. The police shot back and killed him. The exchange caused the combatants to scatter and the fighting to spill into the adjoining neighborhoods south of the city center. By nightfall, four whites had suffered injuries, and by three o'clock the next morning, 38 blacks lay wounded after retaliation by whites.

As the sun rose on Monday, July 28, calm appeared to have returned. Chicago's African-American workers went about their jobs as on any other day. But on their return home on streetcars, whites attacked them with renewed vigor. Disabling the trolleys, they stabbed or shot their victims. Rumors of whites lynching a black man led a furious mob of blacks to the Angelus building on 35th Street and Wabash where a violent clash with the police ensued, killing four African Americans. Notorious white "athletic clubs" like "Ragen's Colts," "Aylwards," and "Our Flag" then drove into the Black Belt, randomly shooting rioters and bystanders from their cars. Black snipers returned the fire. Some black residents used arson to ambush firefighters. At midnight, all streetcar service was discontinued as a labor strike coincided with the raging riot. When Tuesday, July 29, dawned, many black workers had to walk to their jobs, which turned them into easy targets. Later in the day, the bloodshed reached downtown Chicago. White soldiers, seamen, and civilians ventured into the Loop business district, where they terrorized blacks. Violence continued unabated until 10:30 Wednesday morning, July 30, when Mayor William Thompson ordered the National Guard to restore order. Six thousand troops invaded Chicago's South Side. They met little resistance, in part due to a change in the weather. The excessive summer heat that had stoked the violence gave way to rain that helped cool down incendiary tempers. After four days of street fighting and looting, 15 whites and 23 blacks were dead, nearly a thousand people whose residences had been torched were left homeless, and the 537 injured strained the capacity of the city's hospitals to render aid.

On a formal request from 81 distinguished Chicagoans, Illinois governor James Lowden appointed a committee composed of six white and six black prominent citizens to inquire into the roots of the riot. After thorough investigation, the Chicago Commission on Race Relations published *The Negro in Chicago: A Study of Race Relations and a Race Riot* in 1922. The investigators condemned the failure of Chicago's police force to maintain order. Almost two-thirds of the injured had been African Americans, suggesting that whites had been the primary aggressors. Police officers, nonetheless, had arrested twice as many blacks as whites. Not only were city authorities biased in their distribution of justice, but they also fell short of affording protection equally to victims of violence. Although clashes had occurred all over the South Side, more than 90 percent of the city's policemen deployed to the Black Belt to protect the area's non-African-American minority. Here and elsewhere, they frequently sided with white rioters. African Americans who lived outside of the black-majority neighborhoods were left largely unprotected. While the press reports about blacks' cracking down on their neighbors had incited white gangs, it was really African Americans who had to defend themselves from white attackers. The commissioners demanded that city authorities improve housing and access to schools for African Americans and urged police training for riot control. Chicago's racial segregation, they concluded, had intensified the frictions in the city.

The report was a landmark for its progressive insights. Yet in the tense political climate of the early 1920s, the commission's suggestions were never implemented. Attempts to realign national politics after World War I radicalized left- as well as right-wing factions, and when industries cut production to meet peacetime needs, communist ideology became popular in the labor movement. From April to June 1919, anarchist bombings had contributed to the resulting "Red Scare." Once the Red Scare died down, many Americans favored a return to "normalcy" and shied away from demanding change. Consequently, urban race relations remained fragile for decades, with frequent outbreaks of violence. Brutal race riots erupted in Tulsa, Oklahoma, in 1921, in Rosewood, Florida, in 1922, and in Detroit, Michigan, in 1943. Although the emergence of the civil rights movement heralded change after World War II, interracial violence would continue to plague American cities during the remaining half of the 20th century.

See also 1892 LYNCHING TRAGEDY; 1908 SPRINGFIELD RACE RIOT; 1965 WATTS RIOT; 1967 URBAN RIOTS; 1992 LOS ANGELES RIOT.

Mathias Hanses

FURTHER READING:

Chicago Commission on Race Relations. *The Negro in Chicago: A Study of Race Relations and a Race Riot.* Chicago: University of Chicago Press, 1922.

Tuttle, William M., Jr. *Race Riot: Chicago in the Red Summer of 1919.* New York: Atheneum, 1970. Reprint, Chicago: University of Illinois Press, 1996.

Williams, Lee E. *Anatomy of Four Race Riots: Racial Conflict in Knoxville, Elaine (Arkansas), Tulsa, and Chicago, 1919–1921.* Hattiesburg: University and College Press of Mississippi, 1972.

1919 ◆ BLACK SOX BASEBALL SCANDAL

During the World Series between the Chicago White Sox and the Cincinnati Reds, played from October 1 to October 9, 1919, several Chicago baseball players conspired with gamblers to throw games for a reported payment of $100,000. The heavily favored Sox had been a dominant team in professional baseball for years but lost the best-of-nine series five games to three. Rumors of the fix spread before, during, and after the series, and *Chicago Herald-Examiner* journalist Hugh Fullerton and other sports reporters pressed for an investigation for months to no avail. A year later, in September 1920, a Chicago grand jury convened to investigate allegations of another fixed game involving the Chicago Cubs. During the grand jury's tenure, the *Philadelphia North American* newspaper published an interview in which gambler Billy Maharg professed his involvement in the 1919 scheme. Over the next two days, three White Sox players confessed to throwing the series—pitchers Eddie Cicotte and Claude "Lefty" Williams to the grand jury and outfielder Oscar "Happy" Felsch in an interview published in the *Chicago Evening American.* Outfielder "Shoeless" Joe Jackson, one of the most popular and lauded players of all time, also appeared before the grand jury, but the exact nature of his testimony is uncertain because the transcripts disappeared under mysterious circumstances before the end of the year. Ultimately, eight Chicago players and various small-time gamblers were indicted in the scandal. At a 1921 criminal trial, a strong case was presented to establish that some "Black Sox" players—as they became known—had in fact thrown games, but all defendants were found not guilty when prosecutors failed to prove that they had violated any criminal statutes in doing so.

FACTBOX

PLACE Chicago and Cincinnati

DATE October 1–9, 1919

TYPE Sports scandal

DESCRIPTION Several members of the Chicago White Sox baseball team were accused of conspiring with gamblers to throw the 1919 World Series.

CAUSE Greed

IMPACT Nine players were banned from baseball for life for participating in or for having knowledge of the fix. To restore integrity to the Major Leagues, professional baseball's governing national commission was disbanded and replaced with a powerful and independent Office of the Commissioner, headed by Kenesaw Mountain Landis.

Despite the court ruling, the Black Sox scandal greatly undermined the public's trust in organized baseball and so posed a significant financial threat to the Major Leagues. At the time of the scandal, professional baseball was governed by a three-man national commission that operated largely at the behest of the team owners and had long ignored recurring accusations of collusion between players and gamblers. Hoping to restore public confidence in the integrity of the game, the owners replaced this governing body immediately after the Grand Jury hearings of 1920 with an independent commissioner's office headed by retired judge Kenesaw Mountain Landis, who ruled for life. To stamp out any taint of gambling or dishonesty, the new commissioner banned all eight White Sox players from professional baseball for life, as well as a ninth player, St. Louis Browns infielder Joe Gedeon, who had confessed knowledge of the scheme.

Several players, including Jackson and third-baseman George "Buck" Weaver, unsuccessfully lobbied for reinstatement until their deaths, saying they knew of the plot but had played every game to win. Contradictory statements by the players and a lack of hard evidence mean that it will remain uncertain exactly who did and did not hold back performance to throw the games. However, Landis's official decision was meant to encompass any participant in professional baseball who had knowledge of a fix and did not come forward, and on those grounds, all nine players were guilty by their own admission, even though the rule they violated had not been clearly established until after the fact. Some evidence indicates that Sox owner Charles Comiskey and other officials may have known about the fix as the series was being played but attempted to cover it up in order to avoid scandal. If true, Comiskey by the same logic also should

have earned a lifetime ban, but no formal charges were ever brought against him.

As the most serious scandal ever to rock Major League baseball, the Black Sox incident quickly became a part of America's cultural mythology and has been alluded to and retold in a variety of ways over the decades. Early versions of the story, typified by the famous "Say it ain't so, Joe" cartoon in which a youthful fan implores Jackson to deny the allegations, convey the notion that the greed of the Sox players sullied the innocence of the nation. Late 20th-century films such as *Eight Men Out* and *Field of Dreams* focus on the idea of institutional injustice, painting organized baseball as a villain that exploited the players and then set them up as scapegoats.

David Morrow

FURTHER READING:

Asinof, Eliot. *Eight Men Out.* New York: Henry Holt, 1963.
Carney, Gene. *Burying the Black Sox.* Washington, D.C.: Potomac Books, 2006.
Nathan, Daniel A. *Saying It's So.* Chicago: University of Illinois Press, 2003.

1920 ◆ PONZI SCHEME

From January to July 1920, Italian immigrant Charles Ponzi took in approximately $9.6 million from tens of thousands of investors by promising a 50 percent return on investment in 45 days, or 100 percent in 90. When the initial investors were paid off on time, his claims seemed genuine. This unleashed a frenzy of investing in Boston where Ponzi was based, and he quickly established branch offices of his Security Exchange Company across the Northeast. Although he claimed to be speculating in international postal reply coupons, he was actually executing a classic rob-Peter-to-pay-Paul scheme: The earlier investors were paid off with money from subsequent investors. His operation also functioned on a pyramid basis as each dollar he took in required an additional one and a half dollars to work (not including Ponzi's own "profit" and what he paid

his associates in commissions). Operating largely by word-of-mouth in the early months, Ponzi drew his initial clientele from Boston's Italian-American community and from people of limited financial means. As word of his lucrative offer spread throughout the area, local and state officials grew concerned. However, after questioning Ponzi, they declined to intervene as they could establish nothing illegal about what he claimed to be doing.

Whether Ponzi ever actually believed investing in postal reply coupons could work remains open to question. Regardless, he asserted it would, and it served to cover his tracks. Several months passed before banking and postal officials, aided by the *Boston Post* and financial publisher C. W. Barron, showed that what Ponzi proposed was impossible. Established by the Universal Postal Union in 1906,

FACTBOX

PLACE Boston and the northeastern United States

DATE January–August, 1920

TYPE Financial scam

DESCRIPTION A get-rich-quick scheme operating on the "Peter-to-Paul" principle with the earlier investors paid off with money from those who followed

COST Approximately $4 million in losses for small investors

IMPACT Reform in investment and banking law

international postal reply coupons (IRCs) functioned as international self-addressed stamped envelopes. For instance, a person living in Italy could purchase a coupon and enclose it in a letter to someone living in the United States. That person, in turn, could redeem the coupon for the stamps needed to mail a letter back, thus avoiding the cost of reply postage. The cost of the coupons for different countries was tied to then-current foreign exchange rates. World War I, however, resulted in the devaluation of many European currencies against the U.S. dollar, but the rates of the coupons were never adjusted. This was Ponzi's angle: By buying IRCs in a country like Italy and then redeeming them in the United States, he stood to gain the difference between their cost in Italy and their redemption here. Unfortunately for Ponzi, the practical difficulties outweighed any possible gains. In the first place, the number of coupons needed to realize the millions of dollars he claimed to be making exceeded the number of coupons in existence. There was also the problem of converting millions and millions of stamps back into cash. Nonetheless, postal officials in Europe became so concerned that the coupons were being used for speculation that several countries suspended their sale.

None of this mattered as long as Ponzi continued to redeem his customers' certificates. Hundreds of people lined up daily outside his office on School Street in Boston. His investors included members of the Boston police force, further bolstering the public's confidence. By June, his offices were taking in hundreds of thousands of dollars daily. His admirers called him a financial wizard, and the dapper mon-

eyman proclaimed himself the champion of the little investor. He purchased a home in nearby Lexington and was chauffeured to work in a Locomobile. There were important social and ethnic dimensions to the Ponzi phenomenon. The post–World War I period had seen a dramatic increase in the cost of living, with working-class people most affected. Massachusetts had also experienced significant social tensions beginning with the Boston police strike in 1919 and continuing—at the very same time Ponzi was collecting his millions—with the arrest of Italian anarchists Sacco and Vanzetti. Ponzi appealed to the frustrations of immigrant and working-class groups with his anti–financial establishment posture: By multiplying their investments quickly, he would do for them what the regular bankers and financial kings would not.

His success, however, was his undoing. The massive amounts of money he was receiving increased his public exposure and multiplied the amounts he would shortly have to pay out. In late July, following the publication of a critical article in the *Boston Post*, Ponzi stopped taking in any more funds. Professing his innocence, he voluntarily submitted to an audit and continued to redeem existing customers' certificates. Increased scrutiny, the draining of his cash reserves, and a lawsuit by a former associate that tied up his bank accounts led to the Security Exchange Company's failure in early August. The final blows quickly followed. On August 9, the Massachusetts state banking commissioner ordered Ponzi's bank to stop honoring his checks as his accounts were overdrawn. On August 11, the *Boston Post* published the story of Ponzi's conviction in Montreal for fraud 12 years earlier.

The next day, Ponzi surrendered to federal authorities who arraigned him on charges of mail fraud. The state arraigned him on larceny charges and placed the Security Exchange Company in receivership. His trials dragged on for the next several years, and after serving time for both federal and state convictions, he was deported to Italy in 1934. The receivers' final audit showed that he owed about $4 million to some 12,000 people. The U.S. Supreme Court ruled on the bankruptcy proceedings, and state officials spent until 1930 recovering funds and issuing partial reimbursements to his victims. The *Boston Post* won a Pulitzer Prize for its investigative reporting, and the affair led to some reforms in investment and banking law. Although he died impoverished in Brazil in 1949, Charles Ponzi's amazing run still captures the public's imagination. His name has become synonymous with any swindle operating on a pyramid or multilevel marketing basis. These "Ponzi schemes" have proliferated over the Internet in recent years and continue to bedevil financial regulators.

C. Wyatt Evans

FURTHER READING:

Allen, Frederick Lewis. *Only Yesterday: An Informal History of the 1920s.* New York: HarperPerennial, 2000.

Zuckoff, Mitchell. *Ponzi's Scheme: The True Story of a Financial Legend.* New York: Random House, 2005.

1920 ◆ WALL STREET BOMBING

Shortly after noon on September 16, 1920, a bomb exploded at the corner of Wall and Broad Streets in Manhattan. Thirty-one people were killed instantly, nine more died of injuries within a month, and more than 300 were injured. The bomb, consisting of 100 pounds of dynamite packed with heavy iron weights onto a horse cart, severely damaged numerous structures, including the J. P. Morgan Building, the New York Stock Exchange, and the United States Sub-Treasury Building. The total cost of the damage was estimated at between $1.5 million and $2.5 million.

The attack came near the end of the 1919–20 "Red Scare," a period of strikes, bombings, and mob violence often linked to activities of immigrant anarchists and communists allegedly inspired by the 1917 Bolshevik Revolution in Russia during World War I. Law-enforcement agencies across the country, following the lead of Attorney General A. Mitchell Palmer and the Justice Department's Bureau of Investigation, responded to the violence with a massive campaign of intimidation directed primarily at socialists and immigrants. Hundreds of immigrants suspected of radicalism were deported, and many more were deprived of basic civil liberties in the process of the bureau's surveillance and raids.

Given this recent history of violence, many Americans immediately blamed anarchists or communists for the blast. Both the New York Chamber of Commerce and the *Washington Post* called the bombing an "act of war," and Attorney General Palmer considered it part of a communist plot to destroy capitalism. Although investigators tracked hundreds of leads all across the country, their focus quickly narrowed on followers of Italian anarchist Luigi Galleani. Galleanists, as they were called, had been implicated in several past bombings, and the Bureau of Investiga-

FACTBOX

PLACE Corner of Wall and Broad Streets in New York City

DATE September 16, 1920

TYPE Bombing

DESCRIPTION A bomb, consisting of 100 pounds of dynamite and iron weights packed onto a horse cart, exploded, causing substantial damage to nearby buildings and numerous casualties.

CASUALTIES 40 killed, more than 300 wounded

COST Between $1.5 million and $2.5 million

IMPACT Americans, although shocked at the death and destruction, rejected the fear that the terrorists sought to inspire and rallied around American capitalism.

tion was convinced that they had clear motive for such an attack—revenge for the recent arrest of Galleanists Nicola Sacco and Bartolomeo Vanzetti. Five days before the Wall Street bomb, the two Italian immigrants had been indicted for the robbery and murder of two men in a South Braintree, Massachusetts, shoe factory, the crime for which they would eventually be executed. Fellow Galleanist Mario Buda (alias Mike Boda) fit the description of the man who parked the explosives-laden horse cart on Wall Street. In addition, anarchist pamphlets discovered near the blast site promised further attacks unless "the political prisoners" (likely referring to Sacco and Vanzetti) were released. Despite a $100,000 reward for information on the crime and months of

Beneath the gaze of a statue of George Washington, a scene of chaos unfolds after the bombing of Wall Street on September 16, 1920. *(Library of Congress)*

investigation, all leads eventually ran dry. No one was ever convicted of the crime, and Buda returned to Italy shortly after the bombing without ever being questioned. Historian Paul Avrich, whose research is the most extensive on the subject, has concluded that Buda was indeed the most likely culprit.

Despite the shock of a bomb attack in the heart of America's financial center, and Justice Department accusations of anarchist ties, the blast did not inspire a new wave of anti-communist hysteria. By the end of 1920, the Red Scare had lost its salience as a political issue, particularly as no widespread Bolshevik movement seemed to truly threaten the American political system. When Attorney General Palmer's investigators failed to produce a suspect, his anticommunist pronouncements increasingly fell on deaf ears.

America's response to the Wall Street bombing seemed to signal the country's transition out of the postwar Red Scare and toward the era of "normalcy" in the early 1920s. The New York Stock Exchange confidently opened for business the day after the explosion, putting concerns to rest that anarchists could stop America's nascent financial expansion. In the week following the attack, the *Cleveland Plain Dealer* observed "[s]ociety, government, and industry functioning precisely as if nothing had happened," and the *New York Commercial* noted "a better feeling on Wall Street [than] had been there for some time." Indeed, if the perpetrators of the Wall Street bombing had intended to weaken capitalism, their act had exactly the opposite effect. According to historian Beverly Gage, the attack "solidified national support behind Wall Street, transforming the daily routine of finance into an act of defiance and patriotic affirmation." As the American public increasingly came to associate critics of American capitalism with such acts of violence, "the debate over Wall Street's power grew noticeably more muted. It was in such silences," continues Gage, "that the attack had its most profound national effect."

See also 1919 BOMBING OF ATTORNEY GENERAL'S HOUSE.

William J. Nancarrow

FURTHER READING:

Avrich, Paul. *Sacco and Vanzetti: The Anarchist Background.* Princeton, N.J.: Princeton University Press, 1991.

Gage, Beverly. *The Day Wall Street Exploded: A Story of America in Its First Age of Terror.* Oxford: Oxford University Press, forthcoming.

Murray, Robert K. *Red Scare: A Study in National Hysteria, 1919–1920.* Minneapolis: University of Minnesota Press, 1955.

1926 ◆ MIAMI HURRICANE

The Miami hurricane of September 18, 1926, was a Category 4 storm with peak winds of 138 miles per hour. It has the record as the longest period of sustained 100-mile-per-hour winds in American history. The hurricane, which ravaged much of Florida, killed 373 people and injured 6,381, according to the Red Cross, which is the closest thing to an official death toll. However, there were many reported missing, so the number of casualties may have been higher. As many as 50,000 became homeless, and the damage was estimated at $150 million.

In 1926, more than 300,000 people were living in Miami-Dade County. In addition, there were tens of thousands of tourists visiting the area at the time. Recent arrivals made up the majority of residents, having been drawn to the region by the booming real estate market of the early 1920s which had just collapsed the preceding winter. In all the advertising and promotional literature used to attract settlers to southern Florida, the references to the weather were positive, and none mentioned the threat of violent hurricanes. In September 1926, most Miami residents were therefore unfamiliar with hurricanes and living in hastily built homes with little thought given to a potential massive storm. A smaller hurricane in July 1926 might have given the false impression to the newcomers that hurricanes were not to be feared.

The hurricane that hit Miami on September 18, 1926, started off the coast of Cape Verde, Africa, in the Atlantic Ocean and moved west. After it passed the Bahamas, the United States Weather Bureau believed that the storm would not hit Miami. To complicate matters, the hurricane produced none of the advance warning signs that would have indicated its presence, such as strong winds or large ocean swells.

FACTBOX

PLACE Miami, Moore Haven, and other parts of Florida

DATE September 18–20, 1926

TYPE Hurricane

DESCRIPTION A Category 4 hurricane slammed into the unsuspecting and poorly prepared city of Miami and then struck the towns of Moore Haven and Pensacola, killing scores of people, causing numerous injuries, and damaging buildings and infrastructure in each location.

CASUALTIES 373 deaths

COST Approximately $150 million in damages

IMPACT Plunged Florida into depression three years before the rest of the nation

At 11:30 in the evening on Friday, September 17, the hurricane warning flags were hoisted in the city. Most people, however, were asleep and could not prepare themselves even if they would have known what to do. Miamians received a rude awakening in the early hours of Saturday, September 18, when the intense wind shook their homes and the heavy rains caused flooding. The roofs of some buildings were completely ripped off; others collapsed. The tallest building in Miami, the 17-story Meyer-Kiser building which was supposedly hurricane-proof, was so heavily damaged that the top 10 floors had to be demolished. Infrastructure of the city was likewise damaged. Roads were blocked, the railroad lines severed, and electricity knocked out throughout the storm.

At about 6:10 A.M., the eye of the storm passed over Miami. Thinking that the storm was over, the inexperienced residents left their homes to witness the scene. They found trees and utility poles uprooted, buildings torn apart, ships thrown up on the causeway, and cars strewn about. In less than an hour, the east wall of the eye crossed through Miami, killing many of those who had gone outside. The hospitals overflowed with injured, and hotels became makeshift medical facilities. In all, 113 Miamians lost their lives.

The storm continued its destructive path, triggering a wave on Lake Okeechobee that flooded the town of Moore Haven, Florida, killing 130 people. After hitting southern Florida, the hurricane headed northwest, crossed the Gulf of Mexico, and struck Pensacola, Florida, on September 20. Although weakened, there was additional loss of life, significant coastal flooding, and structural damage to Pensacola. From there, the storm devolved to a tropical depression and moved across Alabama and Louisiana.

Local business and civic leaders tried to put on their best face. They wrote articles in popular magazines downplaying the damage of the storm or describing it as a freak occurrence that had no impact on the rest of the state. "There is no pessimism here," declared the Miami *News* only a couple of days after the storm. The Red Cross publicly charged that the whitewash of the boosters was impeding their fundraising for relief efforts. Money was received from all over the country to relieve the suffering in southern Florida. The federal government provided no funds for relief.

The hurricane caused banks and other businesses to fail. Although the speculative boom in Florida had ended before the hurricane of 1926, the storm plunged Florida into an economic depression three years before the stock market crash dragged down the rest of the nation.

See also 1935 FLORIDA HURRICANE.

Gregory J. Dehler

FURTHER READING:

Emanuel, Kerry. *Divine Wind: The History and Science of Hurricanes.* New York: Oxford University Press, 2005.

Williams, John M., and Iver W. Duedall. *Florida Hurricanes and Tropical Storms, 1871–2001.* Gainesville: University Press of Florida, 2002.

1927 ◆ MISSISSIPPI RIVER FLOOD

On a global scale, only the watersheds of the Amazon and Congo Rivers exceed that of the Mississippi. Rivers and streams from Montana to New York contribute to the Mississippi River's flow as it travels south to the Gulf of Mexico. This massive drainage system encompasses 41 percent of landmass of the lower 48 states, or 1,245,000 square miles. The melting of the great Laurentine Ice Sheet that created the Great Lakes 13,000 years ago also created this extraordinary Mississippi River ecosystem, home to many different species of waterfowl, fish, and aquatic microscopic life and land species needing the river's waters for breeding and sustenance. For humans who entered the region following the Ice Age melt, the watershed and its tributaries provided a ready means of transportation and a source of protein from fishing. The repeated flooding of the river over the millennia created the flat alluvial valley that extended along its banks in the Midwest and the South with a rich and fertile soil for generations of Native American and European American farmers. Today, the Mississippi River and the Gulf Intracoastal Waterway serve as the main outlet for an inland navigable water system about 13,500 miles in length.

Given the volatility of the continent's weather system and the existence of its rich alluvial plain, Mississippi River floods are an important part of the country's history. First noted by Spanish chronicler Garcilaso de la Vega, who recorded the expedition of the explorer Hernando de Soto, the river's prolonged flood in March 1543 lasted about 80 days. With repeated floods throughout the centuries, Congress established the Mississippi River Commission

FACTBOX
PLACE The Mississippi River flood plain from Cairo, Illinois, to New Orleans
DATE April–June 1927
TYPE Flood
DESCRIPTION Flood covered an area the size of New England except for Maine.
CASUALTIES 246 known fatalities
COST An estimated $230 million in property losses
IMPACT Relief efforts conducted mostly by the American Red Cross and volunteers; the Great Flood led Congress to pass the Flood Control Act of 1928, placing levee construction and maintenance under the Army Corps of Engineers. Southern officials responded to the flood in ways that reinforced the region's racial segregation, prompting many African Americans to migrate northward and switch their partisan allegiance from Republican to Democratic.

in 1879 to prevent destructive floods and to promote navigation and commerce along the river. Before the commission's recommendations for levees, floodways, and river channel improvements were implemented, however, the Mississippi flooded again. The 1879 flood, the most disastrous of the 19th century, devastated the South. Despite the efforts of federal agencies, including the Army Corp of Engineers, to construct 1,000 miles of levees, major floods hit the region in 1912, 1913, and again in 1927.

Heavy rainfall in 1926 had raised river and stream levels throughout the midwestern states, including the Ohio Valley, eastern Kansas, and Oklahoma. Sustained rains began again during the first three months of 1927 and caused more than 50 levees to break from Illinois to Louisiana, flooding 28,500 square miles of cropland. These March floods also damaged or destroyed 137,000 homes as well as thousands of public and private commercial and government buildings. If the rains that inundated this extensive area had abated following the March 1927 flooding, damage would have remained extensive but contained. However, humid tropical air from the Gulf of Mexico, excessive rainfall in the Ohio Valley, above normal snowfall in the Great Plains, and rapid warming in the Missouri River basin caused unseasonably high rainfall throughout the spring. As a result, rivers again breached their banks in June, making the 1927 flood a catastrophic event, with 246 known fatalities, injuries to humans and livestock, and losses of property, with $100 million in crops washed away. The total damage was estimated at $230 million.

The Mississippi inundated an area the size of New England, minus the state of Maine. In low spots along riverbanks from Illinois and Missouri to the Gulf coast, water covered the land with depths up to 30 feet. A million people lost their homes and livelihood in 1927, when the nation's population totaled 120 million. Before the flood reached the Mississippi Delta region in the late spring and early summer of 1927, rivers had overflowed their banks in Cairo, Illinois, as early as January. By April 16, 1927, a levee broke south of Cairo, allowing huge volumes of water to surge into surrounding communities. As the flood spread southward, rising waters swamped small towns and large cities, such as St. Louis and Memphis. New Orleans responded to the approach of flood conditions by destroying levees and diverting water into low-lying land populated mostly by African-American farmers. African Americans throughout the Delta region bore the heaviest burden of the rising waters.

Business elites in local communities had drawn flood relief plans for their locales during the months leading up to the flooding. President Calvin Coolidge's secretary of commerce, Herbert Hoover,

As the water rages past, a lone dog sits perched on the roof of a house in Murphy, Mississippi. *(Library of Congress)*

was charged with the responsibility of coordinating these separate efforts into a unified initiative, although he offered no financial assistance from the federal government. Unlike most modern presidents who make a point of traveling to areas struck by natural disasters, Coolidge refused requests to visit the flood scene. He also rejected the use of the $635 million surplus in the federal treasury for relief of citizens victimized by the flood. Private, not public, aid provided needed assistance. The American Red Cross spent nearly $17 million to feed 700,000 flood victims, house them temporarily in tent cities, and rescue individuals stranded on levees (many as high as four stories) and rooftops.

Individuals who lived in the Mississippi floodplain suffered in one way or another from the loss of family members and friends to the destruction of real estate and personal possessions. The treatment of refugees in the tent cities remains a lasting legacy of the Great Flood of 1927. In accordance with social conventions that prevailed in the South, these makeshift camp facilities were segregated by race. African Americans were last to receive food, medical treatment, clothing, and other necessities. Moreover, local white officials established rules that curtailed their freedom of movement. This enforced segregation included the posting of armed guards around the camps. In one instance, armed Boy Scouts were enlisted to prevent freedom of movement. Secretary Hoover, whom the national press labeled as "The Great Humanitarian" for his role in the relief effort, ignored these violations of basic human freedoms.

As the floodwaters receded, thousands of dispossessed residents from Cairo, Illinois, to Greenville,

Mississippi, and beyond returned home to retrieve a life lost in the flood. Others, mostly poor African-American tenant farmers, left the Delta region permanently and became part of the great migration to northern cities. Their lifelong affinity to the Republican Party broken by the actions of President Coolidge and Secretary Hoover, who would be elected president in 1928, these migrants tended to relocate in states where they were allowed to vote. Many of these transplanted African Americans joined the coalition of voters that elected Democrat Franklin D. Roosevelt over incumbent Herbert Hoover as president in 1932. Shortly after the flood, Congress passed the Flood Control Act of 1928, placing levee construction and maintenance under the Army Corps of Engineers, a responsibility still lodged with this organization.

Aside from its impact on government and politics, the flood left an imprint on human emotions. The recollections of Herman Caillouet, an Army Corps of Engineers worker, who used his boat to rescue people caught in the rising flood waters, captures the nearly unimaginable pathos of one moment when he saw a family stranded on a rooftop:

> Back up to a house . . . there was seven people on it. I presume it was wife . . . man, his wife, and five children. And I was heading over to this house. This was my first hauling, the next day after the levee broke. And on the way getting to the house— this house was just moving along [in the river], you know—and all of a sudden it must of hit a stump or something. And the house flew all to pieces. And I searched the boards and things around there for ten minutes, and you know I never saw a soul's hand come up, not a soul.

See also 1993 MISSISSIPPI RIVER FLOOD.

Anthony N. Penna

FURTHER READING:

Barry, John M. *Rising Tide: The Great Mississippi Flood of 1927 and How It Changed America.* New York: Simon and Schuster, 1997.

Daniel, Pete. *Deep'n As It Come: The 1927 Mississippi Flood.* Little Rock: University of Arkansas Press, 1996.

McPhee, John. *The Control of Nature.* New York: Farrar, Straus and Giroux, 1990.

PBS Online. "Fatal Flood: The Film and More." *American Experience.* Available online. URL: http://www.pbs.org/wgbh/amex/flood/filmmore/index.html. Accessed March 26, 2007.

1928 ◆ ST. FRANCIS DAM COLLAPSE

Just before midnight on March 12, 1928, California's St. Francis Dam failed, suddenly releasing 11 billion gallons of water. Over the next four hours, a roaring wall of water made its way 55 miles from the San Francisquito Canyon in northeastern Los Angeles County, through the Santa Clara Valley, and on to the Pacific Ocean near the city of Ventura. The water took with it more than 450 lives, thousands of homes, and millions of dollars' worth of infrastructure and public facilities.

The St. Francis Dam was built by the city of Los Angeles under the aegis of William Mulholland. A self-taught engineer who had fought his way to a position of formidable power, Mulholland was the chief engineer and general manager of the Los Angeles Department of Water and Power. He was personally responsible for the design and construction of much of the city's water system. The St. Francis Dam, completed in 1926, was another element of that system, forming a reservoir for water from the Owens Valley-Los Angeles aqueduct.

On the day of the collapse, the reservoir was completely full. A series of small leaks at the base of the dam had been reported, and Mulholland himself traveled to the site to investigate. All large dams leak to some extent; the important warning sign would be muddy water emerging from around the base and the walls of a structure, which would indicate that material from beneath the dam was being washed away. When his inspection revealed that all of the water flowing from around the dam was clear, Mulholland proclaimed that there was no danger and went home.

The collapse was a genuine shock to the administrators and engineers in charge of the facility. There was no clear emergency or evacuation plan and only limited means of alerting the communities in the path of the flood. The first casualties were workers and their families at a power generating station seven miles from the dam. Floodwater ripped though the villages of the Castaic Junction area of northern Los Angeles County, killing hundreds without warning. It was more than an hour after the collapse of the dam when the first communities in the waters' path got word of the coming flood. Heroic measures on the part of local police and townspeople to awaken and evacuate residents saved thousands of lives in Fillmore, Bardsdale, and Santa Paula.

The official plans for the St. Francis Dam describe a curved, concrete gravity dam. The basic principle behind this type of dam was simple—the mass of the structure had to be great enough to hold against the pressure of the water behind it. However, rock at the dam site, both the red conglomerate rock and sandstone of the western wall of the canyon and the mica schist along the eastern wall, were less than ideal for construction. The conglomerate tended to lose strength when saturated, and the mica was interlaced with fissures and porous rock that made it unstable under pressure. When water seeped into the rock below and alongside these dams, they could experience "uplift"—pressure from beneath them pushed them upward, reducing their effectiveness against the water pushing behind them. There are several ways to counter this effect, but Mulholland used only one technique, installing 10 drainage wells to reduce water in the material beneath the dam. In addition, during construction the width of the dam was decreased and its height increased, although these important design changes were never formally studied or recorded by engineers—presumably, they were ordered and approved by Mulholland verbally. Later study revealed that uplift and unstable rock along the eastern abutment of the dam caused it to give way.

After the collapse, Los Angeles officials wanted to put the disaster behind them as quickly as possible. Because of this, official investigations and hearings were short and cursory. Mulholland publicly announced that he was willing to shoulder all blame but implied that the dam was cursed or had been sabotaged. At the time, he escaped severe criticism and won accolades for his courage and responsibility. It was not until much later that evidence emerged that his hubris and negligence were the root causes of the disaster. Perhaps reflecting his lack of formal education, Mulholland relied more on experience and guesswork than on scientific study and data. He discounted or ignored contemporary knowledge about the dangers of uplift and failed to implement a wide variety of safety measures that were standard for gravity dams at the time. Proud and fiercely independent, Mulholland refused to hire expert consultants, as was the custom on large engineering projects, or to submit to any meaningful independent safety review. His authoritarian management style ensured that none of his subordinates dared question his judgment.

The catastrophe haunted Mulholland, and he retired several months after the collapse of the dam.

FACTBOX

PLACE Southern California

DATE Midnight on March 12, 1928; the main flood reached the Pacific Ocean at dawn on March 13.

TYPE Flood

DESCRIPTION Floodwaters wreaked a 55-mile-long swath of devastation from their origins in the San Francisquito Canyon in northeastern Los Angeles County to the city of Ventura on the Pacific coast. Worst human-made disaster in California history.

CAUSE Inadequate rock foundations and failure to build standard safeguards against hydraulic uplift; arrogance and negligence of Los Angeles engineer William Mulholland

CASUALTIES More than 450 people died

COST Thousands of homes destroyed, millions of dollars in property damage

IMPACT State lawmakers passed the California Dam Act of 1929 to improve dam safety.

Little technical knowledge emerged from the disaster because the causes of the failure were already well understood by engineers, as were the remedies. The most significant outcome was a change in California law; after the passage of the California Dam Act of 1929, city engineers could no longer build dams in the state without the oversight and approval of federal or state engineers.

See also 1874 MILL RIVER DAM COLLAPSE.

Louise Nelson Dyble

FURTHER READING:

Jackson, Donald C., and Norris Hundley, Jr. "Privilege and Responsibility: William Mulholland and the St. Francis Dam Disaster." *California History* 82 (2004): 8–47, 72–78.

Outland, Charles F. *Man-Made Disaster: The Story of the St. Francis Dam, Its Place in Southern California's Water System, Its Failure, and the Tragedy in the Santa Clara River Valley, March 12 and 13, 1928.* Rev. ed. Glendale, Calif.: A. H. Clark, 1977.

1929 ◆ ST. VALENTINE'S DAY MASSACRE

Throughout the 1920s, the city of Chicago, Illinois, became a hotbed of organized crime activity to the extent that underworld violence and corruption have become indelibly associated with the city's image around the world. Funded by the enormous profits from bootlegging liquor during Prohibition, the Chicago gangs employed bribery and coercion of police, politicians, and the judiciary to operate with virtual impunity throughout the city and outlying suburbs. As their dominance of the city progressed throughout the decade, personal rivalry and competition led to increasingly brazen acts of violence, culminating in America's most infamous gangland killing, the 1929 St. Valentine's Day massacre, in which seven affiliates of George "Bugs" Moran's Northside gang were gunned down in the garage of a Clark Street trucking company.

Following the ratification of the Eighteenth Amendment to the U.S. Constitution outlawing the manufacture, transport, and sale of alcoholic beverages in 1919, criminals across the nation set up operations for producing, smuggling, and distributing liquor. In Chicago, career criminal Johnny Torrio, taking a lesson from the oil, railroad, and steel industries, established a trust to control the illicit liquor trade. After arranging the murder of his boss and taking over his Southside gang, Torrio successfully divided the city into territories and fostered an uneasy cooperation among the gangs on mutually beneficial issues such as price fixing and bribery of officials. He discouraged the use of violence except as a last resort,

FACTBOX

PLACE Chicago, Illinois

DATE February 14, 1929

TYPE Gangland murder

DESCRIPTION Execution of several affiliates of George "Bugs" Moran's gang during a failed attempt on Moran's life, assumed to have been ordered by Al Capone

CAUSE Intergang disputes during Prohibition

CASUALTIES 7 deaths (approximately 700 gangland murders occurred in Chicago during Prohibition)

IMPACT Solidified Chicago's worldwide image as a den of organized crime and corruption; use of forensic ballistics during the investigation of the crime fostered acceptance of the science as a standard investigative tool

but squabbles over territory and personal affronts led to an average of 30 gangland killings per year in Chicago during the early 1920s. Many of these were high-profile attacks in public places such as restaurants, flower shops, and street corners that drew considerable attention from the press and public but rarely resulted in convictions.

Torrio retired in 1925 after surviving an attempt on his life and left the operation to his protégé, Alphonse "Scarface" Capone. With Torrio gone, several rivals attempted to increase their territories and profits, and the city saw a sharp escalation in violence, with the annual number of gang killings doubling to 60 in 1925–26. Al Capone proved to be at least Torrio's equal in both business sense and brutality, and by 1927, he had established himself as the undisputed ruler of Chicago's Southside underworld.

Still, the killings continued at a high rate as a way to deal with witnesses, disloyal members within gangs, and hijackings of alcohol shipments by rivals. The latter infraction became a particularly contentious issue between Capone and the Northside gang headed by Bugs Moran. Throughout 1928, Moran intercepted so many of the Southsiders' deliveries that Capone allegedly brought in killers from out of town to end the problem. Their elaborate plan began with a neutral party selling Moran a shipment of premium Canadian whiskey at a bargain price and arranging for a second transaction at a trucking company owned by Moran. On the morning of February 14, 1929, several members of the Northside gang arrived at the location on Clark Street to await the shipment. Lookouts stationed by Capone in an apartment across the street mistook one of the men for Moran and notified the killers of his arrival. Moments later, a police car pulled up to the curb and four men exited, two dressed in officer's uniforms. On entering the garage, they announced a raid, lined the seven men inside up against a brick wall, and then raked them with machine-gun fire and shotgun blasts. The killers exited with the two in uniform pretending to hold the others at gunpoint, creating the impression among bystanders that the gunfire had been a police action resulting in arrest.

While Chicago had long suffered a reputation for vice and corruption even before the start of Prohi-bition, the cold and calculated nature of this mass murder drew the shocked attention of the nation. Commentators and politicians pointed to it as an indicator of everything from the failure of Prohibition to the dehumanization associated with modern urban living. Chicago officials responded by temporarily closing most speakeasies and gambling dens and by launching several independent investigations. They brought in Calvin H. Goddard, one of the leading experts in the little-known field of forensic ballistics, who tested several machine guns—some owned by criminals and some by the police—and finally matched two of the weapons to bullets from the murders. Police were able to partially untangle the weapons' trail of ownership through several gangsters and gun dealers but could not definitively connect any of them to the crime. Goddard's efforts ended lingering suspicions that the killers were actually corrupt Chicago officers, and the attention his methods received during the high-profile investigation helped establish ballistics as a reliable investigative tool. Several arrests were made, but in the end no one was ever tried or convicted for the St. Valentine's murders, and the case remains officially unsolved.

David Morrow

FURTHER READING:

Kobler, John. *Capone: The Life and World of Al Capone.* New York: Da Capo Press, 2003.

Ruth, David E. "Crime and Chicago's Image." In *The Encyclopedia of Chicago.* Edited by James R. Grossman, Ann Durkin Keating, and Janice L. Reiff. Chicago: University of Chicago Press, 2004.

Schoenberg, Robert J. *Mr. Capone: The Real—and Complete—Story of Al Capone.* New York: William Morrow, 1992.

1930 ◆ DEMISE OF THE AMERICAN ELM TREE

In the early 20th century graceful elms adorned American towns from coast to coast. Village improvement movements during the Progressive Era (1900–15) had contributed greatly to the popularity of *Ulmas Americanus,* the Latin name for elms, which Americans had planted in small towns and big cities from Maine to California. In 1930, a blight known as the Dutch elm disease began to kill 100 million of these trees. Eventually, about 90 percent of the country's native elm population died. Within 50 years, a symbol of American culture that had stood for centuries was virtually wiped out.

FACTBOX

PLACE Nationwide, with the largest destruction of elm trees in the northeastern United States

DATE 1930s–70s

TYPE Tree infestation and blight

DESCRIPTION Changed the look and feel of American towns and cities from coast to coast

CAUSE Dutch elm beetle carried spores that blocked vascular systems of American elm trees so that nutrients could not pass through the tree, causing eventual death.

CASUALTIES 100 million trees; 90 percent of the native elm population

IMPACT The biological catastrophe to the American landscape assisted in better urban planning and planting methods as well as experimentation with a variety of insecticides and the hybridization of new varieties of elm trees.

The demise of these majestic trees not only pitted the American landscape but scarred the American psyche as well.

The American elm occupied a prominent place in early American life. Native American tribes used specific elms as council trees for meetings. European colonists found elms poorly suited for their construction needs, as the wood was very difficult to split. It warped when it was used as lumber for homes and roofs. Nor did it dry easily or burn well. Elm wood was odorous, rotted easily, and did not serve any practical purposes. In many cases, colonists built their homes around elms rather than waste time in cutting them down. While lacking practical applications, elms acquired a symbolic place in American life. The homestead and family were central institutions to early colonists, and the elm became a symbol of each. A dowry or wedding gift often consisted of a pair of elms that the newlyweds would plant in front of their new home. The twin plantings tended to grow at approximately the same rate, and their branches would intertwine, symbolizing the strength of marriage. Elms were also planted to mark occasions such as births, deaths, and anniversaries. Some early Americans saw the elm as a sym-

bol of health and good luck. Swedes believed that a pregnant woman who hugged an elm tree would have a healthy delivery—a practice they carried with them to America.

Elms were used as focal points for notable public actions. Colonists and Native Americans signed treaties at landmark elms. The elm at Shackamaxon, Pennsylvania, marked the meeting place where William Penn, the proprietor of Pennsylvania colony, and local Indian tribes signed an agreement in 1683 that kept the peace for 50 years. John Harrod, Daniel Boone, and Richard Henderson met on May 23, 1775, under an elm to discuss the creation of the territory of Kentucky. In the early 1800s, Daniel Boone gathered residents of Missouri under the Justice Tree to proclaim local laws and disseminate news from Washington, D.C. In 1861, Oliver Wendell Holmes immortalized the tree in his poem "Under the Washington Elm." The poem suggests that George Washington had rallied Continental troops against the British under the shade of an elm on Cambridge Common at the beginning of the American Revolution:

Since under the brave old tree
Our fathers gathered in arms, and swore
They would follow the sign their banners bore,
And fight till the land was free.

Elms also symbolized patriotism. The Liberty Tree, a meeting place for Boston's revolutionaries, actually was an elm, planted at the corner of Washington and Essex Streets in 1669. Samuel Adams and Paul Revere would call meetings of the Sons of Liberty by the tree more than a century later to discuss independence and plans to rebel. British soldiers cut down the tree during their departure from Boston in 1775, an offense that contributed to Bostonians' infuriation with their colonial overlords. After the Revolution, the elm became a symbol of democracy and freedom. During the Civil War, Abraham Lincoln planted elms on the White House lawn.

While individual elms have acquired fame, these trees took on added significance as an urban adornment during the late 19th century. Industrialization changed the look of towns and cities across the country, eroding the feel of rural America. Village and urban improvement movements buffered these changes, relying heavily on the American elm to do so. Possessing massive trunks and graceful, overhanging branches, elms reached maturity within 15 to 20 years. The tree spread outward about 20 to 25 feet above ground, creating a vaulted arch over streets and boulevards, with its leaves providing a dappled shade and turning to brilliant hues in autumn. Towns and cities all over the country suspended normal activities to allow residents to adorn their communities by planting trees. New Haven, Connecticut; Springfield, Massachusetts; Portland, Maine; Minneapolis, Minnesota; and Dallas, Texas, are among the cities that had a high concentration of American elms in the early 20th century. These stately trees became a focal point of civic pride until a blight descended in the 1930s that gradually killed most of them during the next 40 years.

Scientists in the Netherlands discovered in 1919 that elm bark beetles carried a deadly fungus, which enters the tree's vascular system. The blight thus acquired the name Dutch elm disease. The fungus produces spores that block nutrient-carrying vessels, causing the tree's leaves to wilt and the wood to yellow. The *Ulmas Americanus* often rotted from the inside out. The disease usually spread from tree to tree through natural root grafts that formed between the trees. The devastation of the elm was exacerbated by the monoculture planting (relying just on elms) and adaptation of fungal spores to other types of elm bark beetles The insect, native to Asia, arrived in Europe through trade contacts, and went on to destroy elms throughout the continent. A French furniture shipment to Cleveland, Ohio, carried the scourge to the United States in 1930.

A variety of treatments have been developed since the arrival of the blight. The most traditional method of prevention was to clear areas of dead and dying elms. Modern methods of preservation include fungicide and insecticide injections that kill the fungus and the elm bark beetle. Disease-resistant hybrids, including the Valley Forge and New Harmony varieties, have been developed during the years. Although these engineered replacements do not fully recapture the glory of the native *Ulmas americanus,* they at least remind Americans of their arboreal heritage. Cities and towns that were once graced with hundreds of elm trees will never recapture the turn-of-the-century look that made them quaint and more livable, but treatment, development, hybridization, and lessons about urban planning can restore some of these glorious trees and help soften the feel of contemporary cities and towns.

See also 1904 AMERICAN CHESTNUT TREE BLIGHT.

Julie Arrison

FURTHER READING:

Campenella, Thomas. *Republic of Shade: New England and the American Elm.* New Haven, Conn.: Yale University Press, 2003.

1931 ◆ SCOTTSBORO CASE

A series of trials that began in 1931 involving nine black teenagers charged with raping two young white women on a train running from Chattanooga, Tennessee, into Alabama became popularly known as the "Scottsboro Boys" case. The ordeal reflected the crisis of homelessness and lack of opportunity facing many young Americans with the onset of the Great Depression. The Scottsboro ordeal highlights the pervasive racial prejudice that plagued Jim Crow America.

By the early 1930s, the nation's overall unemployment rate climbed to a peak of 25 percent and was estimated to be as high as 50 percent among teens and youth. Less than half of all teens remained in classrooms long enough to earn a high school diploma. Even among those that did graduate, work was hard to find. By the end of 1931, an estimated 250,000 adolescents and young adults roamed the nation's railways, highways, and roads. Many were looking for work. Some simply wanted adventure. Others sought to escape abuse and deprivation in volatile families beaten down by the Great Depression. The press and the federal government reported that the situation increased crime rates and threatened national stability. For black transients, old racial stereotypes depicting African-American males as predators threatening white female virtue coupled with the public's growing anxiety about youth crime.

The Scottsboro case started with an incident on a moving railroad tank car on March 25, 1931. A white boy walking across the top of the car stepped on the hand of Haywood Patterson, an 18-year-old black male also hitching a ride on the freight train. Patterson was a veteran transient who began to ride the rails at age 14. He cursed the white boy and a fight broke out between eight whites and 10 blacks as the train pulled into a rail yard. The blacks forced all but one of the whites, Orville Gilley, from the train. In a gesture Patterson probably later regretted, he rescued a falling Gilley by jerking him back into a moving boxcar as the train accelerated out of the rail yard.

The seven white boys left behind told a station master that a gang of blacks had attacked them. The station master notified local authorities who sent a posse after the train. Two white females, 21-year-old Victoria Price and 18-year-old Ruby Bates, were also riding the freight cars that day. Price and Bates told the sheriff's posse that a group of 12 black boys with knives and pistols raped them and attacked their friend Orville Gilley. In response, the Alabama sheriff arrested nine black adolescents found in the train's freight cars and charged them with rape.

Charges of raping a white female were often used to justify the lynching of black males in the post–Civil War South. Souvenir postcards and photographs documented the grizzly events ignored, or worse, enabled by local authorities. The nine young men arrested on the train in Alabama had good reason to believe they would not see justice. The press dubbed the arrested teens the "Scottsboro Boys": Charles Weems (19), Andy Wright (19), Haywood Patterson (18), Clarence Norris (18), Olen Montgomery (17), Willie Robertson (17), Ozie Powell (16), Eugene Williams (13), and Roy Wright (12 or 13 at the time of his arrest). A grand jury indicted the nine youths for rape on March 30, and their trials began on April 6.

The prosecution dubbed Haywood Patterson the group's ringleader. Gilley, Price, and Bates recounted their stories at various times during the trials. According to the *New York Times,* the presiding

FACTBOX

PLACE Scottsboro, Alabama

DATE April 6, 1931, through 1937

TYPE Rape trials and racial conflict

DESCRIPTION The arrest and trials of nine black teens charged with raping two white females on a train. The defendants were sentenced to death based on flimsy evidence.

CASUALTIES Nine individuals wrongly incarcerated

IMPACT Drawing national attention to the plight of transient youth and to the legacy of racism in the United States during the 1930s, the case contributed to a demand for federal programs to help America's adolescents and youth. It also led to two landmark civil rights rulings by the U.S. Supreme Court.

judge instructed the juries that any defendant whom they believed to be in the boxcar at the time of the rapes "was guilty whether [he] had laid hands upon the women or not." Flimsy evidence and testimony by a physician who examined Price and Bates after the alleged incidents showed that it was unlikely the young women had been raped. In addition, the doctor noted that 17-year-old Willie Robertson was severely handicapped by a case of advanced syphilis. The condition made it painful for Robertson to have intercourse, and a bad leg limited his ability to quickly move from the scene of the alleged rape to the boxcar where he was arrested.

Despite the weak evidence, all-white, all-male juries chose to believe the testimonies of Price, Bates, and Gilley. In a series of hasty verdicts offered from April 6 through 9, the juries convicted all nine defendants and sentenced eight to death. Only 12-year-old Roy Wright escaped a death sentence on a legal technicality.

The Scottsboro trials gained international attention as evidence of the rising crime rate in the United States and the country's continuing struggle over civil rights. Within the United States, northern newspapers ran articles that offered some sympathy for the black teens. In addition, lawyers from the International Labor Defense (a Communist Party-led legal group) and the National Association for the

Advancement of Colored People (NAACP) competed for the right to appeal the convictions. Several mothers of the convicted boys toured the United States and Europe demanding justice for their sons. Black and white celebrities also got involved. On top of this groundswell, in January 1932, Ruby Bates changed her story and named the black defendants innocent.

Appealed to the U.S. Supreme Court, the Scottsboro Case led to two landmark legal decisions. In *Powell v. Alabama* (1932), the Supreme Court ruled that the state had not provided the defendants adequate legal counsel and thus overturned the convictions. Alabama tried them and found them guilty a second time, but in *Norris v. Alabama* (1935), the Supreme Court again threw out the convictions on the grounds that African Americans had been unconstitutionally excluded from sitting on the jury. Alabama authorities finally acknowledged the weak evidence against four of the defendants. In July 1937, the state dropped charges against Willie Robertson, Roy Wright, Eugene Williams, and Olen Montgomery. All four left Alabama and settled in the North. But release from prison did not lead to a happy ending for at least two of the four: Olen Montgomery was convicted of raping a black woman at knifepoint in 1940, and Roy Wright killed his wife and committed suicide in 1959.

A second trial for Andy Wright resulted in a sentence of 99 years. Charlie Weems got 75, and Ozzie Powell pleaded guilty in exchange for a 20-year prison sentence. All three were eventually paroled. Clarence Norris was the last Scottsboro defendant released from jail. The infamous segregationist Alabama governor, George Wallace, pardoned Norris in 1976.

The Scottsboro trials provide an important window for viewing the brutal consequences of American racism. The ordeal also revealed the public hysteria surrounding the perceived youth crisis brought on by the Great Depression. A visible army of homeless young men and women wandering the nation's transportation networks led many Americans to call for government intervention. President Franklin Roosevelt's New Deal began with the establishment of the Civilian Conservation Corps in the spring of 1933. Other New Deal programs directly affected the lives of young Americans by helping their families, encouraging teens to stay in school, and establishing the first federal child labor laws under the 1938 Fair Labor Standards Act. The federal government also offered part-time jobs and educational opportunities through the National Youth Administration and built thousands of schools through work-relief efforts. For many Americans, the Scottsboro Case showed the dangers of neglecting the nation's youth. For civil rights activists around the world, it emphasized how racism prevented the United States from living up to its promises of equality and tolerance for all.

Kriste Lindenmeyer

FURTHER READING:

Bienen, Leigh, and Gilbert Geis. *Crimes of the Century: From Leopold and Loeb to O. J. Simpson.* Boston: Northeastern University Press, 1998.

Carter, Dan T. *Scottsboro: A Tragedy of the American South.* Delanco, N.J.: Notable Trials Library, 2000.

Linder, Douglas O. "'The Scottsboro Boys' Trials, 1931–1937." Available online. URL: http://www.law.umkc.edu/faculty/projects/FTrials/scottsboro/SB_acct.html. Accessed April 2, 2007.

1931 ◆ HAWK'S NEST TUNNEL DISASTER

The Hawk's Nest Tunnel disaster was one of the worst industrial tragedies in American history. The catastrophe resulted from the construction of a tunnel along the New River near Gauley Bridge, a small town in south central West Virginia. The three-mile-long tunnel that bored through solid sandstone diverted water to an electrical power station. At least 764 men who worked on the project died from acute silicosis, a disease of the lungs that inhibits the ability to breathe. Union Carbide, the sponsor of the plan, and its subcontractors failed to use standard safety precautions in the drilling operations, yet none of the companies involved was charged with criminal negligence.

Union Carbide, the corporation that would later be involved in the CHEMICAL EXPLOSION IN BHOPAL in 1984, had been formed in West Virginia from a merger of several companies in 1917. By the late 1920s, the corporation created the New Kanawha Power Company in order to produce power that it planned to use in the production of ferro-metals (such as aluminum) at a site below Gauley's Bridge. The proposal required the damming of the New River just below Hawk's Nest, a spectacular overlook on the river, and the construction of a three-mile tunnel through Gauley Mountain that would deposit the rushing water to electrical generators downstream. New Kanawha Power contracted with Rinehart and Dennis Company of Charlottesville, Virginia, to build the tunnel and dam. Tunneling began on March 31, 1930, and progressed at breakneck speed until completed in December 1931. Uncertainty about continued passivity of the Federal Power Commission regarding federal control of the New River may have been one reason

FACTBOX

PLACE New River near Hawk's Nest, West Virginia

DATE March 1930–December 1931 (period of tunnel drilling)

TYPE Occupational disease and industrial negligence

DESCRIPTION A high proportion of men who worked inside Hawk's Nest Tunnel contracted acute silicosis.

CAUSE Dust generated from drilling into silica-laden sandstone and from dynamite blasts

CASUALTIES A conservative estimate of 764 deaths among Hawk's Nest Tunnel workers from acute silicosis

COST Rinehart and Dennis agreed to $200,000 in legal settlements.

IMPACT Acute silicosis was recognized as an occupational disease; by 1937 all states enacted statutes that included acute silicosis under workers' compensation.

that Union Carbide drove hard to finish the project quickly.

Finding workers in Depression-era Appalachia, where numerous coal mines had closed, was no problem. Word spread through the region and farther south that jobs were available at Gauley Bridge. Rinehart and Dennis hired mainly black workers from outside West Virginia; 75 percent of the 1,494 employees used exclusively inside the tunnel (as drillers and mockers—who removed rock debris—and their assistants) were African-American. Another 1,488 workers, again largely African-American, held jobs that involved tasks both inside and outside the tunnel. Workers labored 10 hours a day under the watchful eyes of bosses who used clubs and guns to force ill or unwilling black employees to start each day's work. Black workers were paid in company scrip rather than real money and at lower rates than whites. When dropped from the payroll, they were evicted from company housing and hustled out of town by the Fayette County sheriff.

Neither Rinehart and Dennis nor New Kanawha Power exercised even minimal safety precautions during the tunneling operation, which burrowed through sandstone composed of 99 percent silica. The high-velocity drills that bored cavities in the rock for the insertion of dynamite charges did not spray water on the rock facing, a standard technique to reduce dust. Air ventilation was inadequate, measurement of dust levels in the tunnel were not taken, and portable ventilators were not issued to tunnel workers, although company executives wore them on inspection tours of the project. Moreover, New Kanawha prevented the West Virginia Bureau of Mines from inspecting tunnel operations until spring 1931. Not surprisingly, few workers stayed on the job for long. Sixty percent of blacks worked less than two months on the project; the average was 104 days. But this was long enough to pay a deadly price for signing on at Hawk's Nest.

Between July and December 1932, local attorneys filed suits in West Virginia's circuit court for Fayette County on behalf of 80 workers who had suffered acute silicosis. A type of pneumoconiosis, acute silicosis is a disease caused by the inhalation of fine silica dust. Minute fragments of silica are absorbed by the cells in the lungs, which become damaged by the irritant. The resulting scarring is known as fibrosis, a condition that reduces the capacity to breathe.

When this occurs, the lungs become susceptible to secondary infections, such as tuberculosis. Silicosis (although not its acute form) had been recognized as an industrial disease in the United States since the turn of the century. The United States Bureau of Mines had published warnings in the 1920s about the dangers from using high-speed drills. Acute silicosis, from which death could occur within months of exposure, however, was not a recognized disease in 1930. West Virginia did not classify silicosis as an industrial disease, and the state rejected workers' compensation claims from employees who alleged that they had contracted silicosis at Hawk's Nest.

Facing more than 250 suits that sought $4 million in damages by mid-1933, Rinehart and Dennis settled out of court, agreeing to pay $130,000, half of which went to 157 plaintiffs and half to attorney fees. In accepting the settlement, the plaintiffs' attorneys agreed not to press further suits and to surrender all case records to the defendants. The contractor brokered two additional settlements based on subsequent suits, which eventually totaled 538, with $200,000 paid in awards and attorneys' fees. The average plaintiff received $400, while the defendant took possession of the damaging evidence, including X-rays and medical records of the plaintiffs. Reports circulated that Rinehart and Dennis and its corporate sponsor had bribed witnesses and tampered with juries during the trials prior to settlement. Few records of the afflicted workers remain, apparently by deliberate destruction.

How many workers died in the Hawk's Nest Tunnel tragedy? The real number will never be known, partly because Union Carbide cleansed the historical record, partly because most tunnel workers were dismissed by the end of 1931 and the majority of them, blacks in particular, had scattered throughout the South if they survived, and partly because of the inadequacy of official demographic records. During one of the trials, it was revealed that Rinehart and Dennis had hired a local undertaker to dispose of unclaimed bodies of former workers who had died in the region and were subsequently buried in a field near Gauley Bridge. In 1972, the West Virginia highway department stumbled into 45 of these graves. Martin Cherniack, a medical doctor with a master's degree in public health, reconstructed the epidemiology of the Hawk's Nest tragedy. After painstaking historical research, his "conservative" estimate was that 764 men who worked in the tunnel project died of acute silicosis, which translated into a mortality rate of 63 percent. Blacks constituted 581 (76 percent) of the fatalities.

The Hawk's Nest tragedy forced recognition of acute silicosis as an industrial hazard. A brief and ineffective congressional hearing into the disaster in 1936 helped to focus attention on the condition. By 1937, all states had adopted laws recognizing the disease in some form, although West Virginia's statute was useless because it was written in the interest of the corporations. Dismissed by some in the early 1930s as a product of "mountain gossip" and attorneys feasting on the "silicosis racket," Hawk's Nest now ranks as one of the nation's worst industrial tragedies.

Ballard C. Campbell

FURTHER READING:

Cherniack, Martin. *The Hawk's Nest Incident: America's Worst Industrial Disaster.* New Haven, Conn.: Yale University Press, 1986.

1932 ◆ LINDBERGH KIDNAPPING

Dubbed the "Crime of the Century," the kidnapping of 20-month-old Charles A. Lindbergh, Jr., in 1932 and Bruno Richard Hauptmann's subsequent trial three years later was one of several sensational criminal events of the 1920s and 1930s. The uproar over the Lindbergh tragedy rivaled other famous cases of the era, such as Sacco and Vanzetti (1921), the Leopold and Loeb murder case (1924—also called the "Crime of the Century"), the Scopes "monkey" trial (1925), the Massie affair (1931), and the SCOTTSBORO CASE (1931–37).

FACTBOX

PLACE Hopewell, New Jersey

DATE March 1, 1932 (kidnapping); January 2–February 14, 1935 (trial)

TYPE Kidnapping and murder

DESCRIPTION The child of aviator Charles Lindbergh and his wife, Anne Morrow Lindbergh, was kidnapped and murdered. The subsequent trial of Bruno Richard Hauptmann became a media spectacle.

CASUALTIES 2 deaths: murder of Charles A. Lindbergh, Jr., and execution of Bruno Richard Hauptmann

IMPACT President Hoover signed legislation on June 22, 1932, making kidnapping a federal crime.

Around 10 P.M. on March 1, 1932, nanny Betty Gow found the Lindberghs' infant son missing from his second-story room in the couple's Hopewell, New Jersey, mansion. After quickly searching the house, the baby's father, Charles Lindbergh, found a ransom note demanding $50,000. He also found muddy footprints outside the nursery's open window. He immediately called state and local police. Reporters intercepted police message traffic and within hours the news was broadcast over the nation's radio networks. Lindbergh was a national celebrity, the famed "Lone Eagle," whose daring transatlantic flight in 1927 had riveted the world's attention. His clean good looks and modesty led the media to lionize him as the All-American Hero. The media attention—which Lindbergh detested—only increased after he married Anne Morrow in 1929, and the pair was dubbed "The First Couple of the Air." Rumors of the kidnapping immediately became front-page news.

Together with police, Lindbergh continued the search. Outside, at some distance from the second-story window, they found a homemade extension ladder broken where the sections joined. Both the ladder and the handwritten ransom note would prove to be crucial evidence. By next morning, hundreds of police agents had descended on the normally tranquil country town. They scoured the surrounding area and searched the house and grounds for additional evidence. As the ladder suggested the kidnapper(s) knew beforehand where the baby would be, the baby's nanny and other household servants were closely questioned. Local citizens volunteered their help, and informants told police they had seen a car with New York license plates near the estate the previous evening. Bulletins were quickly sent out across New Jersey and to neighboring jurisdictions including New York City and Philadelphia. Throughout the day, sightseers and reporters arrived at the Lindbergh home, forcing police to establish control points to prevent crowds from inundating the estate.

The next four weeks witnessed the most massive and publicized manhunt in American history. Thousands of law enforcement officers in a half-dozen states searched for the child, established checkpoints to inspect automobiles, interrogated criminals associated with abduction rackets, and pursued hundreds of leads. Houses were searched in Newark and New York City. Hourly radio updates kept the nation informed on the searchers' progress. Congress discussed the kidnapping, and President Herbert Hoover authorized the use of federal enforcement assets to help locate the child. Federal Bureau of Investigation (FBI) director J. Edgar Hoover offered New Jersey State Police superintendent H. Norman Schwarzkopf (father of the Persian Gulf War commander) technical assistance. FBI handwriting experts would later play an important role in establishing the kidnapper's guilt.

While the attention paid to the case was due to Lindbergh's fame and the media portrayal of Charles and Anne as the perfect couple, the case also focused attention on the growing problem of extortion abductions. The week before the child's disappearance, officials had appeared before a congressional committee urging passage of a federal kidnapping statute. Over the two previous years, an estimated 2,000 people had been abducted and forced to pay ransom. Lindbergh's fame as an aviator also worked against him. The massive dragnet made contacting the kidnapper(s) difficult. The crime's celebrity status attracted publicity hounds and hucksters seeking to profit from the couple's plight. Police authorities also deferred to Lindbergh, allowing him to conduct his own investigation and attempt negotiations. On March 9, eight days after the kidnapping, John Condon, a retired principal from the Bronx, told the Lindberghs he had established contact with a person purporting to represent the kidnappers by placing an ad in the *Bronx Home News*. The couple agreed to let him negotiate. A series of meetings ensued with a man who spoke with a German accent and whom Condon—who went by the code name "Jafsie"—referred to simply as "John." On April 2, Condon handed over the $50,000 ransom, which Lindbergh had raised by selling stocks he owned, as Lindbergh waited in a car nearby. "John" handed Condon a note telling him the baby was safe aboard the *Nelly*, a boat located somewhere near Martha's Vineyard. Lindbergh and the police (accompanied by "John") immediately searched for the vessel, but it was never found.

A month later, on May 12, 1932, a trucker's helper on the road between Hopewell and Princeton, New Jersey, found the baby's remains in the woods only a few miles from the Lindberghs' home. The child's skull was fractured and the corpse's decay indicated death occurred on the night of the kidnapping, perhaps in falling off the ladder. The Lindberghs took the news stoically, and police now turned to solving the murder. Fortunately, Treasury agents working with Lindbergh had recorded the serial numbers of the bills used to pay the ransom. The FBI, working with New York City and New Jersey State police, focused their attention on tracking the ransom money. More than two years passed, but in September 1934, their efforts finally paid off. Investigators traced a marked gold certificate to a German-born carpenter named Bruno Richard Hauptmann. They arrested him near his Bronx residence on September 19. On searching the garage adjoining his four-room flat, they found $13,750 in marked bills stashed in the walls and under the floor. Inside the flat they discovered Condon's telephone number written on the inside of a closet door frame. While Hauptmann denied involvement in the kidnapping, he was identified by a cab driver as the person who had handed him a note for Condon. Condon also tentatively identified Hauptmann in a police line-up. The arrest strengthened investigators' suspicions the kidnapping had been a solo affair.

Hauptmann's murder trial—dubbed the "Trial of the Century" by writer Damon Runyon—began on January 3, 1935, in Flemington, New Jersey. It was a media circus beyond precedent, as 60,000 people, including movie stars, society figures, reporters, and writers, descended on the west New Jersey town. Souvenir peddlers sold miniature replicas of the kidnapping ladder. Newsreels of the trial played across the nation, and radio stations carried the proceedings in full. Journalist H. L. Mencken called it "the greatest story since the Resurrection." Novelist Edna Ferber stated of the spectacle, "It made you want to resign as a member of the human race." As Hauptmann never confessed to the crime and there were no eyewitnesses, the prosecution's case depended on circumstantial evidence. The critical pieces included the analysis of Hauptmann's handwriting and the ransom notes, also the analysis of a U.S. Forest Service scientist that the wood from the ladder matched boards found in Hauptmann's attic. Together with the ransom money found on the premises, Condon's testimony, and Hauptmann's lack of an alibi, the evidence proved sufficient. On February 13, the jury found Hauptmann guilty and sentenced him to die.

Doubts surfaced regarding the evidence and Hauptmann's guilt immediately following the trial. Because he feared the political rivalry of David Wilentz, the state's attorney who had prosecuted the case, New Jersey's governor played on the popular misgivings regarding Hauptmann's guilt and granted him a stay of execution. Nonetheless, the petitions to commute Hauptmann's death sentence were denied, and he went to electric chair on April 3, 1936, still maintaining his innocence. To this day, some people hold that Hauptmann was the victim of anti-German prejudice. Various theories on who committed the crime—including that there was no kidnapping at all, or that "the mob" did it, or that Anne Lindbergh's sister Elizabeth committed the deed out of jealousy—have been spun over the years. Hauptmann's widow sued the state of New Jersey twice in the 1980s charging her husband's wrongful death, and the trial is re-created annually in the courthouse where it was originally held. On a more substantial note, the case spurred passage of legislation making kidnapping a federal crime. It also marked a new stage in the sensationalization of crime by the nation's media.

C. Wyatt Evans

FURTHER READING:

Berg, A. Scott. *Lindbergh*. New York: Putnam, 1998.

Davidson, David. "The Story of the Century." *American Heritage Magazine* 27, no. 2 (February 1976).

Fisher, Jim. *The Lindbergh Case*. New Brunswick, N.J.: Rutgers University Press, 1987.

1933 ◆ THE GREAT DEPRESSION

The depression of the 1930s was the worst economic collapse in American history. The depression began after the great stock market crash of 1929, deepened year by year until the economy hit bottom in 1933, and lingered through 1939. Americans did not get fully back to work until the nation fought World War II (1941–45), which triggered a tremendous demand for military goods and agricultural commodities. During the 1930s, hundreds of thousands of businesses failed and millions of families skimped on reduced income, and sometimes none at all. Many individuals never recovered from the psychological stress that came with unemployment, loss of their property, or the deep sense of gloom that had settled over society during the depression years. The rupture of the economy and the social crisis it caused put tremendous pressure on government to lessen the social and commercial distress. Out of this political crucible emerged the New Deal, the collection of laws and policies associated with the first two administrations of President Franklin D. Roosevelt (1933–41) that created a new role for government.

The causes of the Great Depression are complex and continue to generate debate among historians. By most measures, the nation's economy was robust during the 1920s, when industry turned out growing numbers of motor vehicles, washing machines, light fixtures, and other items for the emergent consumer-oriented society. Firms such as General Motors and General Electric not only became household names but also sources of financial investment. Shares of stock in large corporations traded on the New York Stock Exchange and other financial markets, where a speculative boom in stock prices occurred in 1928 and 1929. For many individuals and institutions, including banks, the stock market offered a get-rich-quick plan. Individuals sank millions of borrowed dollars into stock purchases, hoping to reap a profit after repaying the loan. Rising stock prices worried the governors of the Federal Reserve Bank, who tightened credit in 1929, hoping to slow the speculative fever. The bank's action contributed to the stock market "crash" that began in October 1929, although no single event has been pinpointed as its precipitat-

FACTBOX

PLACE The United States and the industrialized world

DATE October 1929 (stock market crash); 1930–39 (depression, with worst years 1932–33)

TYPE Economic depression

DESCRIPTION A severe, prolonged slump in business activity and prices for most commodities thrust the United States into an economic and political crisis.

CAUSE Disputed, with several key factors hypothesized, but most agree that the Stock Market Crash of 1929 played a pivotal role

COST Billions of dollars lost in the collapse of stock values, foreclosed real estate, and failed businesses

IMPACT The adoption of the New Deal, the expansion of the national government and presidential powers, and the beginning of a generation of Democratic Party majorities in national elections

ing spark. Billions of dollars were wiped out within months as the value of stocks declined, losing one-third of their value. The worth of some firms shrank far more.

Several generations of Americans assumed that the stock market crash was the principal cause of the Great Depression. President Roosevelt said as much in his inaugural address on March 4, 1933, in which he blamed the "practices of the unscrupulous money changers" for the economic "crisis" that gripped the country. But economic historians now doubt that the meltdown on the stock market was sufficient in itself to account for such a severe and prolonged economic decline. They point to contributing factors, such as economic troubles abroad. President Herbert Hoover, who took office in March 1929, believed that the depression was largely of foreign origin. According to this reasoning, World War I (1914–18) had ensnared England, France, and Germany in debilitating debts and reparation payments. American loans became crucial to the maintenance of this unstable financial situation. The crash dried up American credit and triggered an implosion of world financial markets. When credit tightened in Europe, foreign orders for American goods declined. Within several years, depression spread around the globe.

Other factors contributed to the economic slowdown. Congress enacted the Smoot-Hawley tariff of 1930, which raised the rate of import duties and triggered retaliatory actions from other countries, which lowered American exports. Like the stock market, banks were lightly regulated. Some institutions had speculated in the stock market with depositors' money. A banking crisis late in 1930 hampered the ability of firms to borrow money and slowed business. Banking crises in Austria and Germany in 1931 further undermined confidence in the economy; in September, the Bank of England abandoned the gold standard by devaluing the pound. The governors of the U.S.'s Federal Reserve Banks, however, rallied around the gold standard. Slow to recognize the emerging catastrophe in the world economy, they resisted a reduction of interest rates at a time when the expansion of credit might have rekindled business growth. In 1932 and early 1933, just before Roosevelt took office, the United States had its own disastrous banking crisis when panicky depositors mobbed financial institutions to cash out their deposits. Many banks were unable to honor these commitments and went bankrupt, sometimes wiping out a family's entire savings in the process. Roughly 4,000 banks closed their doors between 1929 and 1933.

Finally, the actions of the Hoover administration (1929–33) probably helped a modest commercial slowdown grow into a major economic crisis. President Hoover was unwilling to orchestrate aggressive federal intervention into the economy, actions which may have countered the negative psychology that deepened as the conditions worsened. The actions he did approve, such as the Reconstruction Finance Corporation, a loan program, in 1932, were too little too late to stem the magnitude of the economic earthquake.

Whatever its causes, the Great Depression presented the United States with a crisis. Because the word had negative connotations, many contemporaries avoided using the term *crisis*. Republicans and members of the Hoover administration were less willing to acknowledge the scale of the malaise than were Democrats, including Franklin D. Roosevelt (FDR), who was governor of New York prior to assuming the presidency. In his inaugural address in March 1933, Roosevelt referred to the United States as a "stricken nation in the midst of a stricken world." The economic situation, he said, constituted a "crisis," which justified his request for extraordinary powers to "wage war against the emergency." Adolf A. Berle, an aide to FDR, thought that the new administration had an 50-50 chance of stimulating recovery or facing "revolution." At his second inaugural address in 1937, Roosevelt said that the government had the capacity "to protect its people against disasters" and should use this power to overcome "economic epidemics."

This sense of crisis was visible in the way national officials viewed their governing responsibilities. During his first hundred days in office, FDR sent a raft of proposals to Congress to fight the depression. The

The hungry and unemployed stand in the cold for hours to get a cheap meal in New York City. Such sights were common everywhere during the Great Depression. *(FDR Library)*

Agricultural Adjustment Act of 1933, centerpiece of Roosevelt's effort to help ailing farmers, was entitled "An Act to relieve the existing national economic emergency by increasing agricultural purchasing power." FDR had told his agricultural policy makers that if farm prices did not improve, the country stood a chance of witnessing "an uprising or serious social disorders in the west." Henry Wallace, the secretary of agriculture, defended the law's grant of extensive new power to the executive branch on grounds that the "emergency" demanded swift action. The administration's main effort to rekindle economic growth, the National Recovery Act of 1933, also drew on the language of crisis for its justification. In 1935, the Supreme Court rejected the administration's argument that "the grave national crisis" and "Extraordinary conditions" sanctioned the transfer of broad new powers to the government in the act and declared it unconstitutional. Historians also have freely used the term *crisis* and its synonyms to characterize the 1930s. Studs Terkel, whose *Hard Times* (1970) collects personal stories about this difficult decade, called the Great Depression a "disaster" and a "holocaust."

The hard times caused a personal crisis for many individuals. The business slowdown led firms to lay off workers. Bankrupt companies discharged all their employees. At the depression's worst in 1933, nearly 13 million people were out of a job, representing about one-fourth of the workforce. In Chicago and Los Angeles County, the unemployment rate approached 50 percent. Some industries became nearly dormant during the early 1930s. The young, African Americans and other nonwhite groups, women, and the least educated registered the highest rate of unemployment. Joblessness not only reached broadly into society, but it persisted. The rate of unemployment for nonagricultural workers reach 37 percent in 1933 and had fallen only to 21 percent by 1940. A study of the unemployed in Massachusetts found that 63 percent of the unemployed in 1934 had been out of work for a year or more.

At a minimum, unemployment was an inconvenience and an embarrassment. At worst, the loss of a job could throw a family into chaos, trigger desertion, and even prompt suicide. With business lagging, prices dropped and incomes fell. Disposable income in 1933 slipped to one-half of its 1929 level, although lower prices meant that purchasing power declined only 31 percent. Without a job or meaningful work (or to escape parents stressed by their unemployment), many young men and women took to the road, sometime hoboing on freight trains but often on foot. Renters might return home to find their furniture piled on the sidewalk, evicted from their dwelling for nonpayment of rent. Homeowners dreaded the prospect of losing their home to the bank if it decided to foreclose for failure to keep up with the mortgage. Financial institutions seized more than a quarter-million homes and commercial properties in 1933, an action that fed homelessness. Some of the newly dispossessed took up residence in shanty towns, derisively called Hoovervilles, that sprouted up in deserted lots around the nation's cities. The decline in property values played a major role in the closure of banks, whose assets were linked to the value of the mortgaged real estate. Yet individuals lucky enough to have some free cash could buy property at fire sale prices. In these bleak times, people tended to marry later and to have fewer children than in the 1920s.

The hard times put tremendous pressure on local governments to provide emergency relief. The nation's system of public assistance, based in the cities, towns, and counties, could not keep up with the deluge of new supplicants. Numerous big cities experienced hunger marches and other demonstrations demanding public assistance. Local communities, large cities especially, did spend record amounts on aid for the destitute. But with funds declining, largely because of the fall in property values on which local government based its chief tax, many localities went bankrupt. When local welfare officers turned away desperate individuals, some turned to looting.

The rout of the Bonus Marchers from Washington, D.C., in 1932 symbolized this economic pathos and the challenge it posed for public officials. The Bonus Marchers were largely down-and-out World War I veterans who had come to the nation's capital to lobby Congress for an immediate cash payment of a promised "bonus" for their military service. Thousands of veterans and their families occupied vacant buildings near the Capitol and in a makeshift encampment in Anacostia flats just south of the city. After President Hoover and the Senate rejected their demands, city and federal officials gave orders on July 28 to clear the demonstrators from condemned buildings along Pennsylvania Ave-

Unemployment Rate, 1929–1941

Percent unemployed per year

© Infobase Publishing

Unemployment peaked nationwide in 1933 at 25 percent, the highest figure ever recorded in the United States. Source: U.S. Bureau of the Census. *Historical Statistics of the United States to 1970.* Washington, D.C., 1975, series D 86.

nue where reconstruction was planned. When some veterans resisted removal and two were killed by the District police, President Hoover commanded General Douglas MacArthur of the U.S. Army to assist local authorities in removing the squatters. Supported by troops bearing fixed bayonets and firing tear gas, by mounted cavalry, and by tanks, MacArthur exceeded his orders and drove the veterans out of their Anacostia encampment, burning their shanties. MacArthur claimed that communists were the source of the trouble, but the public held Hoover responsible for the army's overreaction, a sentiment that contributed to his failure to win a second term when he ran against Roosevelt in 1932.

Individuals turned to innovative ways to make do. Door-to-door sales grew rapidly, marking the return of the "peddler" and helped to make Fuller Brushes (a large door-to-door retail company) profitable. Tree-sitting came into vogue, as boys perched themselves high in the branches hoping to gain some attention and perhaps cash in on their publicity stunt in some way, perhaps through an advertising appearance. A lasting image of the depression economy was apple selling on city streets, sometimes by unemployed businessmen wearing suits and ties. Pacific coast

growers sponsored this campaign in 1930 as a way to dispose of their surplus.

The backdrop to the story of individual tragedies was the collapse of the economy. Between 1929 and 1933, the Gross National Product declined 30 percent (in constant dollars, which takes account of the price deflation that the depression caused). Disposable personal income was off 45 percent (in current dollars) during the depression years. The floor fell out from under the home construction industry. Corporate profits before taxes dropped more than 100 percent (and thus registered a loss). Some 70,000 factories closed their doors. Small and middle-sized business suffered more than giant corporations, whose large scale permitted flexibility in managing sagging markets. The economic meltdown ravaged the auto industry. Automakers sold nearly 4.5 million cars in 1929 but only 1.5 million in 1933. This collapse dispatched names like Peerless, Stutz, Duesenberg, and Hupmobile to the junkyard of automotive history. General Motors, Ford, and Chrysler, however, weathered the storm and increased market share.

Some businesses actually thrived on hard times, often because they were forced to innovate to survive or because their product fit in with the times. Radio prospered because it offered costless entertainment once a family purchased a receiver. Shows such as *George Burns and Gracie Allen, Amos and Andy*, and the *Lone Ranger* were staples of the depression-era airwaves. By mid-decade, the movie industry was back on its feet, helped by elaborate musicals and theaters that offered "double features." Perhaps Hollywood's most creative year ever was 1939. But live theater, the record industry, and book publishing slumped. IBM remained profitable during the depression, as business and government bureaucracy kept up a demand for office equipment. Major League baseball sponsored its first all-star game in 1933; night games began in 1935. A & P food stores opened their first self-service supermarket in 1936 (saving on the cost of hiring more clerks). Tobacco companies rolled out more cigarettes during the depression. Mason jars (used for home "canning" of vegetables), bicycles, and pawnbrokers were in demand.

Layoffs and wage cuts put labor in a combative mood. Strikes and protest marches proliferated during the early 1930s, as workers demanded public works jobs from government and the acceptance of labor unions as bargain agents from private businesses. Labor had an especially violent year in 1934. Deaths and injuries resulted from the numerous clashes between striking picketers and police, who sometimes were assisted by vigilante groups and company-hired thugs. Major clashes occurred in the auto parts industry in Toledo, in Minneapolis during a trucking strike, and on the waterfront at ports on the West Coast. Strikes among textile workers, who sought union recognition, spawned violence from New England to the South. The restiveness of labor influenced Congress to address the labor question, with the enactment of the National Labor Relations Act in 1935.

Violence was no stranger to rural areas, as the hard times grated on the countryside. Iowa farmers formed a Farmers Holiday Association that withheld their produce from market in protest of abysmally low prices. The Hawkeye state became famous for "penny auctions," at which community residents prevented officials from selling a neighbor's farm (and home) for falling behind in mortgage payments by bidding only a penny at the public auction and repurchasing the property for one cent. These episodes highlight the dramatic fall in the worth of farm property. Nearly one-third of the nation's farms changed hands between 1930 and 1933. Low prices and the DUST BOWL drove migrants from farmlands in Oklahoma and Arkansas, many of whom fled to California. Their trek was immortalized in John Steinbeck's *The Grapes of Wrath* (1939). Before the "Okies" and the "Arkies" arrived on the West Coast, the vegetable fields were a battleground in 1933 and 1934 between migrant worker unions and California growers, who bitterly resisted unionization. Violence impeded the organization of agricultural workers in the South, too. Vigilantes and night-riders attacked members of the interracial Southern Tenant Farmers Union, especially during the union's 1935 strike against cotton planters.

The troubles on the farm, in the factories, among city treasuries, and in business and financial communities were on the mind of FDR and his "brain trust" advisers in the spring of 1933. The Democratic majority in the Congress elected in 1932 enacted a flurry of administration proposals in the first hundred days of the 73rd Congress, christening FDR's New Deal. These actions provided emergency relief for the unemployed and enacted programs designed to help business and agriculture return to economic health. In later years, the New Deal adopted reforms such as governmentally generated electrical power from the Tennessee Valley Authority, public housing, rural resettlement and electrification, and official support for labor unions to bargain collectively on behalf of their members. The crown jewel of Roosevelt's New Deal was the Social Security Act of 1935, which established financial support for retirees, as well as established national programs of unemployment compensation, welfare, and public health. Breaking with precedent, the Roosevelt administration came to accept planned budget deficits as a tool for stimulating business activity. This strategy came to be called Keynesian economics, following the ideas of the British economist John Maynard Keynes.

The Great Depression alone did not cause this new use of government power. Rather, the economic malaise created the occasion—more aptly, an opportunity—for politicians to implement a new approach in government. Modern liberalism emerged from the policy innovations at the state and national levels adopted during the Great Depression. In the process, the national government grew in stature in comparison to state and local governments. Equally important, Roosevelt's active style and proliferation of New Deal programs conditioned the public to expect the president to take the lead in governmental affairs and to steer the nation out of depressions. Despite its unprecedented intervention into commercial and everyday life, the New Deal did not bring about full economic recovery, but it helped enough to keep capitalism afloat. In overseeing this political transformation, Roosevelt was instrumental in preserving the nation's democratic footing, whereas Germany, Japan, and many Latin American countries turned to militarism and fascist regimes during the 1930s.

See also 1907 FINANCIAL PANIC AND DEPRESSION.

Ballard C. Campbell

FURTHER READING:

Hamby, Alonzo L. *For the Survival of Democracy: Franklin Roosevelt and the World Crisis of the 1930s.* New York: Free Press, 2004.

Kennedy, David M. *Freedom from Fear: The American People in Depression and War, 1929–1945.* New York: Oxford University Press, 1999.

Schlesinger, Arthur M. *The Age of Roosevelt.* 3 vols. Boston: Houghton Mifflin, 1957–60.

Terkel, Studs. *Hard Times: An Oral History of the Great Depression.* New York: Washington Square Press, 1970.

Watkins, T. H. *The Hungry Years: A Narrative History of the Great Depression in America.* New York: Henry Holt, 1999.

1935 ◆ DUST BOWL

The dust bowl was one of the worst sustained environmental crises that the United States has ever experienced. Although the dates vary somewhat by location, the dust bowl lasted from 1930 to 1940 and affected most of the Great Plains states from North Dakota to the Texas panhandle. Because it coincided with the Great Depression, it complicated what was already a very difficult situation for farming families throughout the plains.

Around 1930, a severe drought began on the Great Plains. Under the best of circumstances, this was a semiarid region, generally experiencing somewhat dry conditions. The conditions of the 1930s were extreme, and many communities received half or less of their normal rainfall for a decade. Additionally, the summer high temperatures in this area were well above average, with the drought and heat at their worst in 1934 and 1936. The drought, high temperatures, and strong Great Plains winds resulted in dust storms throughout the region that reached their peak in 1935 and 1937. While some of these were only dusty days when a fine haze hung in the air, other storms were terrifying events, with huge, rolling clouds of dust blotting out the sun for hours and even days on end. The southern plains, including parts of Kansas, Oklahoma, Texas, New Mexico, and Colo-

FACTBOX

PLACE The Great Plains

DATE The decade of the 1930s; peak years 1935, 1937

TYPE Drought and dust storms

DESCRIPTION A 10-year drought accompanied by severe dust storms, causing severe erosion of farmland

CAUSE A combination of drought, high temperatures, high winds, and inattention to conservation

COST Loss of agricultural production on 50 million acres of land

IMPACT Led to migration of approximately half of all residents out of the Great Plains and to development of federal programs such as the Soil Conservation Service, Resettlement Administration, and Farm Security Administration; led farmers to invest in irrigation equipment throughout the Great Plains

rado, bore the brunt of the disaster. At the height of the storms, 50 million acres of land—an area greater

A dust storm engulfs Stratford, Texas, on April 18, 1935.
(NOAA George E. Marsh Album)

than the size of New England—experienced severe wind erosion, devastating fields, destroying crops, and making agriculture virtually impossible.

Although the Great Plains had suffered dust storms throughout its recorded history, the storms of the 1930s were particularly severe because of rapid agricultural development after the turn of the century. In 1890, in areas of the southern plains that would become the dust bowl, there were only 5,762 farms and ranches. By 1910, there were 11,422 farms and ranches. What had been grazing land for cattle was transformed into wheat land in the early years of the 20th century. Much of this development occurred with little attention to conservation practices. Farmers plowed their land from fence post to fence post, hoping to plant as much wheat as possible. This was particularly true during World War I, when the U.S. government encouraged farmers to buy more land, invest in more machinery, and expand their production, arguing that "wheat will win the war." Predictably, this increased the erosive potential of already easily eroded lands.

The impact of the dust bowl on agriculture was severe. The drought and dirt storms made it difficult for farmers to put in crops, and those that were planted often did not grow. Farmers slaughtered cattle and swine, unable to grow feed for them. Because the Great Depression had driven agricultural prices to historic lows, the prices farmers received for the crops and animals they did raise failed to meet the costs of production. Farm families faced significant problems in even meeting their subsistence needs because they could not adequately feed chickens and milk cows or keep gardens and fruit trees alive.

Farm income in dust bowl communities fell by 50 to 75 percent. For most families, only funds available through the New Deal farm program allowed them to stay on their farms.

The conditions of the 1930s caused tens of thousands of people to leave the Great Plains. Proportionally, more farmers left than those in other occupations. Most of them headed for California, Oregon, and Washington, although nearly every state in the United States received dust bowl migrants. On average, 25 percent of those living in dust bowl communities chose to leave. Those who left often encountered worse conditions in their new homes than the ones they left behind. Like the fictional Joad family in John Steinbeck's novel, *The Grapes of Wrath,* migrants generally found only very low-wage, menial labor, and discovered that they were ineligible for any kind of state aid because they were not state residents. The vast majority decided to remain in the dust bowl, although there was considerable variation between locations. In some areas with access to irrigation water and sources of employment unaffected by the drought, out-migration was low. In other severely affected agricultural areas, such as Baca County, Colorado, and Morton County, Kansas, 50 percent or more of the population left.

Those who remained endured years of discomfort. The agricultural extension agent in Dodge City, Kansas, kept track of the dust storms. Between 1930 and 1940, he counted more than 700. Dust infiltrated homes, clogged automobile engines, and made life uncomfortable. Even after taping doors and windows shut and cramming every visible crack with rags, there was no way to keep the dust out of homes. Residents suffered through an outbreak of "dust pneumonia" in 1934, respiratory distress caused by inhaling too much dust. For some who became ill, especially the young, the old, or those who were already sick, the results were fatal.

The events of the 1930s caused the federal government to take steps to change the shape of agriculture on the Great Plains. The Soil Conservation Service, part of the New Deal agricultural program, paid farmers to undertake conservation projects, such as planting trees and drought resistant crops and using conservation tillage. Federal money allowed farmers to apply improved techniques to millions of acres of land. The Agricultural Adjustment Administration paid farmers to restrict production of crops such as wheat, and reduce the number of livestock on their farms. The Resettlement Administration relocated approximately 25,000 farm families from the most severely damaged lands to new, model homesteads. The federal government also sponsored the planting of shelterbelts across the West in order to control wind erosion. Some of these reforms would be long-lasting, while others would be abandoned in the U.S. effort to increase agricultural production in order to fight and win World War II.

The conditions of the 1930s also encouraged plains farmers to think more about irrigating their lands. Although a return of the rains in 1941 postponed its implementation, a return of drought conditions in the 1950s led to large-scale use of center-pivot irrigation for wheat, cotton, corn, and other crops. Unfortunately, much of the irrigation on the southern plains depends on a finite water source, the Ogallala Aquifer, and in some areas farmers are reverting to dry land agriculture after several generations of irrigation. What happened in the 1930s has the potential to happen again.

Pamela Riney-Kehrberg

FURTHER READING:

Egan, Timothy. *The Worst Hard Time: The Untold Story of Those Who Survived the Great American Dust Bowl.* Boston: Houghton Mifflin, 2005.

Hurt, R. Douglas. *The Dust Bowl: An Agricultural and Social History.* Chicago: Nelson-Hall, 1981.

Opie, John. *Ogallala: Water for a Dry Land.* Lincoln: University of Nebraska Press, 1993.

Riney-Kehrberg, Pamela. *Rooted in Dust: Surviving Drought and Depression in Southwestern Kansas.* Lawrence: University Press of Kansas, 1994.

Worster, Donald. *Dust Bowl: The Southern Plains in the 1930s.* New York: Oxford University Press, 1979.

1935 ◆ FLORIDA HURRICANE

As Americans struggled with THE GREAT DEPRESSION, movies served as an escape from the harsh realities of the 1930s. In 1937, moviegoers were entertained by *The Hurricane,* Hollywood's adaptation of Charles Nordhoff and James Norman Hall's popular 1935 novel. Directed by the legendary John Ford and starring two of Hollywood's major stars, Dorothy Lamour and Jon Hall, the film was filled with bathing-suit clad performers in action-packed scenes of mayhem, followed by acts of bravery, heroism, and rescue during a violent tropical cyclone. A smash hit, the movie was based on a record-breaking hurricane in 1935 that served as the inspiration for both novelists and the filmmakers, whose art imitated reality.

Florida residents had lived through violent hurricanes in 1926 and 1928, only to be victimized again in 1935. On Labor Day, September 2, 1935, a Category 4 hurricane packing maximum winds of 140 to 150 miles per hour with gusts up to 200 struck the Florida Keys, a series of islands that form an archipelago that bends westward from the foot of Florida

FACTBOX

PLACE Florida Keys

DATE September 2, 1935

TYPE Hurricane

DESCRIPTION Originating in the southeastern Bahamas, a Category 4 hurricane gained velocity quickly as it moved westward toward the Florida Keys, packing estimated winds of 150 to 200 miles per hour and crossed the Keys with gusts approaching 200. From the Keys, it lost strength as it left Florida for the south Atlantic states to the North Atlantic Ocean.

CASUALTIES At least 423 fatalities, 259 of whom were veterans working on a highway construction project

IMPACT Led to state and federal investigations into the causes and reasons for the high number of casualties

to the island of Key West. Originating in the southeastern Bahamas, the storm gained velocity quickly as it moved westward toward the Keys. One of the most intense storms to make landfall in the United States, it destroyed virtually everything in its path, including all buildings, vegetation, and much of the Florida East Coast Railroad that connected most of the Key islands to Florida's mainland. Typical of tropical hurricanes, the storm surge measured 15 to 20 feet, swamping most of the islands.

Despite the Great Depression, the sparsely settled Keys had experienced a real estate boom during the 1930s. Popularized by the residency of the celebrated author Ernest Hemingway, who lived on Key West, the southernmost of the chain, the population on the islands had reached 12,470 in 1935. According to the American Red Cross, at least 423 persons lost their lives in the storm. Officials estimated that many more individuals disappeared, in all likelihood blown into the sea and drowned. Two hundred fifty-nine of the fatalities were veterans of World War I and other campaigns. Most of them were employed by the New Deal's Federal Emergency Relief Administration as workers on U.S. Highway 1. Completed three years later in 1938, the "overseas" highway linked mainland Florida with Key West.

Newly arrived in the Keys and living in hastily built bunkhouses and army tents, the veterans, along with vacationers and locals, were unaware of the storm's power. In the midst of its torrential rains and 200-mile-an-hour winds, attempts to rescue the island residents failed. Writing about the pandemonium caused by the hurricane, a survivor described the scene: "Objects careened through the air with deadly speed. Sheet metal roofs became flying guillotines, decapitating several victims, amputating the limbs of others. Like exploding atoms, pounding sheets of sand sheared clothes and even skin off victims, leaving them clad only in belts and shoes, often with their faces literally sandblasted beyond identification."

Called by one historian the "storm of the century," the hurricane of 1935 holds the record for the lowest barometric pressure—892 millibars/26.35 inches—ever recorded on land in the world. Although limited to the Keys, the storm's extremely low pressure explains the high number of casualties and devastation. As it swept across Tampa, Florida, wind speeds dropped below 75 miles per hour, and the storm lost strength as it traversed the south Atlantic states and ventured into the North Atlantic Ocean. A memorable hurricane had become a tropical storm. Federal and state investigations of the casualties from the storm concluded that the death and destruction of the 1935 hurricane were no one's fault and were caused by "an act of God."

See also 1926 MIAMI HURRICANE.

Anthony N. Penna

FURTHER READING:

Drye, Willie. *Storm of the Century: The Labor Day Hurricane of 1935.* Washington D.C.: National Geographic Books, 2002.

Emanuel, Kerry. *Divine Wind: The History and Science of Hurricanes.* New York: Oxford University Press, 2005.

Scott, Phil. *Hemingway's Hurricane: The Great Florida Keys Storm of 1935.* Camden, Me.: International Marine/Ragged Mountain Press, 2006.

1937 ◆ NEW LONDON SCHOOL EXPLOSION

On March 18, 1937, a tragedy at a school in New London, Texas, ironically highlighted trends shaping modern education for American children and adolescents during the 20th century. New London was a blue-collar community filled with families. Most had been drawn to the East Texas region during the late 1920s and early 1930s as jobs dried up in other parts of the country and the New London region's oil fields expanded. The few rural schools in the area prior to 1937 consisted of tiny buildings, close to children's homes but outdated and ill-equipped. Some employed only one teacher to instruct children from ages six through 14. This situation was typical of many small, one-room

FACTBOX

PLACE New London, Texas

DATE March 18, 1937

TYPE Natural gas explosion

DESCRIPTION Explosion at a large public school campus

CAUSE Improper ventilation of natural gas used to heat the building and water

CASUALTIES 500 deaths, 200 escaped with minor or serious injuries

COST Approximately $1 million in property damage to the school complex

IMPACT Led some Americans to temporarily question the construction of large schools, but ultimately the tragedy did not slow the move toward consolidated, age- and grade-level-based schools

schoolhouses across the country that may seem romantic in retrospect but actually restricted educational opportunities and the application of innovations in curriculum.

With the onset of the New Deal during Franklin Roosevelt's presidency, New London community leaders successfully combined state, county, and federal funding to build a large, new, $1 million school complex. The new facilities offered an up-to-date curriculum for students from the first grade through high school. Consistent with modern educational curriculums of the era, adolescents could choose a vocational or college preparatory path in the later grades. The idea was to keep more students in school longer by offering a diverse curriculum that fit the needs of young people interested in gaining skills to get a job and those headed for college. The New London Consolidated School District's finished campus was a reflection of the New Deal's long reach and a special source of pride for area parents who had generally enjoyed only limited access to school-based education during their own childhoods.

The community's pride and optimism was rocked on March 18, 1937, by a massive explosion that hit the school. Without warning, natural gas used to heat the building and provide hot water ignited,

expanding the walls and lifting the roof off the building, especially over the auditorium. In seconds, the ceiling came crashing down on the 700 children and 40 teachers inside. Flames ignited by the blast quickly died out since the building was fireproof, but the strength of the explosion's concussion and the massive volume of falling debris instantly killed most of the adults and children inside. The *New York Times* reported that a group of mothers gathered for a parent-teachers' association meeting in a cafeteria located about 300 feet away, helplessly watched the building collapse on those inside. The women screamed and raced across the campus, digging for hours to reach victims who were still alive and could be heard crying for help. A crowd of approximately 10,000 area residents quickly gathered at the disaster site, clogging the roads and blocking highways in and out of town.

Most of the dead and injured were children and teachers who had gathered in the auditorium. Some were rescued and cared for in hospitals as far away as Shreveport, Louisiana. However, hopes of finding more survivors dimmed with the onset of nightfall. Illuminated by the school's powerful floodlights surrounding the new state-of-the-art football field, a crowd of grief-stricken parents, relatives, and onlookers stood near a lengthening line of bodies covered by white sheets. Over the next several days morgues and funeral homes throughout East Texas helped to identify and bury the dead. More than 500 students and teachers were killed. Approximately 200 individuals escaped with minor to serious injuries.

In an instant, the New London school that had given the community so much pride became the center of shared heartbreak. An investigation after the blast showed that despite the large initial investment in the project, planners had taken dangerous shortcuts. In order to save money on long-term utility costs, they used natural gas to warm water and heat the building. Safety precautions were not sufficient to prevent the explosion that killed so many on March 18, 1937.

The disaster led some people in New London and beyond to question the wisdom of putting so many children together in large, consolidated schools. But even in the midst of fear and condemnation, it seems that most Americans believed the benefits of modern consolidated schools outweighed the risks. As an article in the *New York Times* three days after the explosion argued, modern consolidated schools were safer than the old-fashioned wooden buildings of the past. The new schools are "made of sand and stone," explained the *Times*. They "have stairways of slate and cement, and are classed as fireproof. Broad corridors, fire towers, fire escapes, sprinkling systems are provided. They furnish a striking contrast to the wooden firetraps still used as schools. No structure, however built, when converted into a holder for inflammable gas . . . can be made to resist explosion." The lack of outcry from the public suggests that many parents and educators agreed with the *Times*'s contention that "the consolidated school is the antithesis of the little red school house." For parents and children living in rural communities, consolidated schools offered facilities comparable to those available to children in urban areas.

The rapid spread of consolidated schools to the rural countryside during the 1930s marked the end of an era shaped by one-room schoolhouses. The terrible loss of life in this East Texas town did not halt the American trend toward higher-quality, grade-level-based schooling for children and adolescents through high school. From the 1930s onward, school districts across the nation benefited from the combination of federal and state funding spent on primary and secondary schools. Such efforts entrenched the idea that public education through high school graduation was a right of modern American childhood.

Kriste Lindenmeyer

FURTHER READING:

Bright, Lorine Zylks. *New London, 1937: The New London School Explosion, 1937: One Woman's Memory of Orange and Green.* Wichita Falls, Tex.: Nortex Press, 1977.

Jackson, Robert Lee. *Living Lessons from the New London Explosion.* Nashville, Tenn.: The Parthenon Press, 1938.

Sealander, Judith. *The Failed Century of the Child: Governing America's Young in the Twentieth Century.* New York: Cambridge University Press, 2003.

Spring, Joel. *Educating the Consumer-Citizen: A History of the Marriage of Schools, Advertising, and the Media.* Mahwah, N.J.: Lawrence Erlbaum Associates, 2004.

1937 ◆ *HINDENBURG* DISASTER

On May 6, 1937, the German zeppelin airship *LZ 129 Hindenburg* burst into flames while descending on Lakehurst, New Jersey. Seven million cubic feet of ignited hydrogen incinerated the dirigible before it hit the earth, killing 35 crew members and passengers and one person on the ground. News of the disaster shocked the world, dealt a blow to Nazi propaganda, and effectively ended the era of lighter-than-air travel.

For half a century, Count Ferdinand von Zeppelin's (1838–1917) inventions had embodied Germany's aeronautical aspirations. Zeppelin drew on the work of several forerunners for his designs, most notably Henry Cavendish, who discovered hydrogen in 1766, and the brothers Montgolfier, who presented a first hot-air balloon to the French public in 1783. Later engineers failed to safely combine the flammable gas with the blimp design but suggested that an elongated envelope would be conducive to a vessel's stability in strong winds. Zeppelin designed a rigid frame that further improved controllability of the *luftschiff,* or airship, and separate gas cells to be filled with hydrogen. He had the first dirigible patented in 1898. For the building of *Luftschiff Zeppelin (LZ) 1*, however, the count's company lacked government funding and had to turn to private shareholders. In 1908, donors had to save the project a second time when *LZ 4* crashed in the German city of Echterdingen. Following models proved more dependable, and airships would soon be used for Arctic exploration, German air raids on London in World War I, and commercial travel. After Adolf Hitler's rise to power in 1933, the Zeppelin lent itself to exploitation by the Nazis: The public perceived the development of

FACTBOX

PLACE Lakehurst, New Jersey

DATE May 6, 1937

TYPE Airship accident

DESCRIPTION While approaching Lakehurst, New Jersey, the Zeppelin airship *Hindenburg* went up in flames and crashed.

CASUALTIES 36 deaths

IMPACT With airplanes increasingly successful, the *Hindenburg* crash contributed to the marginalization of lighter-than-air travel.

the airships as a national rather than an individual achievement, and the dirigibles were not associated with any of the previous systems. Nazi propaganda minister Joseph Goebbels employed the airship in mass events like the Nuremberg rally, and a regular transatlantic service was established in March 1936. Yet what seemed to be the dirigible's ultimate triumph would prove to be a catalyst of its descent into insignificance.

On May 3, 1937, the *Luftschiff Zeppelin 129 Hindenburg* climbed from Rhein-Main airport into the air above Frankfurt, Germany. Its namesake was the recently deceased Paul von Hindenburg, World War I field marshal, president of the Weimar Republic (1925–34), and national idol. The *LZ 129* was 804 feet long, 135 feet in diameter, and weighed approximately 250 tons. To provide the necessary lift, the *Hindenburg's* 16 gas cells still had to be filled with combustible hydrogen, as the United States remained the only country to produce the nonflammable helium. Since its maiden flight in 1936, the *LZ 129* had completed 20 flights across the Atlantic Ocean and broken the previous models' speed records. Under normal conditions, its four 1,050-horsepower Daimler-Benz DB 602 diesel engines accelerated the dirigible to a maximum of 84 miles per hour, but favorable winds had allowed for top speeds of up to 188 miles per hour. A westward trip from Germany to the United States took an average of 63 hours 42 minutes, which was 17.5 hours faster than its predecessor's best time of 81 hours 14 minutes. Although the *Hindenburg* had been built to accommodate 50 to 70 passengers, it carried only 36 travelers in addition to 61 crew members when it embarked on its fatal final flight. The control gondola was the only element to protrude from the body, the passengers resided in 20 heated cabins at the center of the hull's lower decks. Amenities on board included a 528-square-foot dining room, a reading and writing as well as a smoking room, and centrally located sanitary installations with showers. Panoramic windows embedded in the concave hull provided spectacular views for strollers on the promenade deck.

From the outset of the trip, Captains Max Pruss and Ernst Lehmann had to confront numerous adversities, all of them due to bad weather conditions. Storms first kept the airship from crossing the English Channel and then delayed its journey across the Atlantic. Blown off course to Newfoundland, it passed Manhattan behind schedule at 3 P.M. on May 6 and finally reached the U.S. Naval Air Station in Lakehurst, New Jersey, at 6 P.M. Heavy rains kept the airship from initiating landing procedures right away, and it was only an hour later that the storm calmed and the *Hindenburg* approached the mooring mast.

In one of the first disasters captured on film, the *Hindenburg* erupts in flames in Lakehurst, New Jersey. *(Associated Press)*

Various theories have been brought forth about the cause of the spontaneous combustion that occurred at 7:25 P.M. Contemporaries suspected sabotage or a lightning strike, while more recent hypotheses state that maneuvering in the storm might have led to a build-up of static energy in the ship's envelope. An electric discharge may have ignited the hydrogen. As a ball of flames consumed the paneling and the exposed frame crashed on the landing field, the American ground-crews fled in panic. Once the ship hit the ground, those crewmen spun around to pull survivors from the blazing wreckage. The injured were rushed to hospitals, where more succumbed to their wounds, including Zeppelin captain Ernst Lehmann. A column of black smoke rose from the site as the heavy oil engine fuel continued to burn for three hours. A total of 13 passengers, 22 crewmen, and 1 Lakehurst-based navy soldier died in the crash. There were 62 survivors.

Reporting the catastrophe as he witnessed it live, radio reporter Herbert Morrison had exclaimed a tearful "Oh, the humanity!" Added to newsreel footage of the explosion—it was one of the world's first major disasters caught on film—his outcry was heard around the globe. The widely publicized catastrophe and the ensuing reevaluation of lighter-than-air travel helped doom the zeppelin industry, as heavier-than-air flight had already started to eclipse blimps and dirigibles. Inventor Otto Lilienthal had perfected the use of fixed-wing gliders between 1891 and 1896, Orville and Wilbur Wright had pioneered the use of engine-powered airplanes in 1903, and Charles Lindbergh had successfully flown *The Spirit of St. Louis* across the Atlantic in 1927, 10 years before the *Hindenburg* crash. German air minister Hermann Göring consequently shut down the last airship production facilities in 1940, and after World War II ended in 1945, the Allies liquidated the Zeppelin company, which they considered a questionable representation of German nationalism. The airplane's reign of the skies remains uncontested to this day.

Mathias Hanses

FURTHER READING:

Chant, Christopher. *The Zeppelin: The History of German Airships from 1900 to 1937.* London: Amber Books, 2000.

De Syon, Guillaume. *Zeppelin! Germany and the Airship, 1900–1939.* Baltimore: Johns Hopkins University Press, 2002.

Mooney, Michael Macdonald. *The Hindenburg.* London: Hart-Davis, MacGibbon Ltd., 1972.

1937 ◆ MEMORIAL DAY MASSACRE

The Memorial Day massacre, in which 10 striking steelworkers were killed by police during a demonstration in front of Chicago's Republic Steel plant, occurred in 1937—arguably the most tumultuous year in American labor history. The year began with the United Automobile Workers winning recognition as the exclusive bargaining agent for auto workers after organizing headline-grabbing sit-down strikes and continued with violent strikes and altercations in the steel industry as the CIO (Committee for Industrial Organization, later Congress of Industrial Organizations) sought to increase union membership and gain recognition for the SWOC (Steel Workers Organizing Committee). Since 1936, the CIO had made much progress in organizing the steel industry, and by the middle of 1937, about 125 companies had signed union contracts, including Carnegie-Illinois and several other subsidiaries of U.S. Steel, which was known as Big Steel. But the independent steel companies, collectively called Little Steel, held out and refused to recognize the union. Little Steel included Bethlehem Steel, Inland Steel, Youngstown Sheet and Tube Company, and Republic Steel, among others.

On May 26, the SWOC called a strike against Republic, Youngstown, and Inland, primarily because Little Steel refused to recognize the union or its bargaining agent. Prepared for such an event,

Republic president Tom Girdler responded with an army of strikebreakers and local law enforcement personnel. At the Republic plant on Chicago's South Side, local police chief Captain John Prendergast had organized three shifts of policemen, with 90 officers per shift and a 38-man reserve. The police were not only headquartered inside Republic's gates, but they were also fed by the company and supplied with hatchet handles and tear gas. Over the next four days, police beat and arrested striking workers.

On May 30, Memorial Day, the Chicago strikers held their first major rally to protest the constant harassment by police. That afternoon, a crowd of 1,000 to 2,500 workers, supporters, and their families gathered at Sam's Place, a dance hall turned strike headquarters, for a picnic-style rally. Several important union leaders spoke to the crowd, including Joe Weber from the SWOC staff. A motion was passed to establish a picket line at the main gate of the plant, and the group marched toward Republic to form the line. Witnesses reported that some in the group picked up tree branches and rocks from the open field directly in front of the plant, but there was no evidence that any of the strikers had firearms.

The group was met by more than 250 policemen about two blocks from the main gate. Those in front asked permission to proceed to the gate to exercise their right to picket, but the police refused. Accord-

Armed with clubs, guns, and tear gas, police attack strikers and picketers at the Republic Steel plant in Chicago. *(New York Public Library)*

ing to some accounts, the strikers then threw debris at the police, who fired into the air. More debris and tree branches were thrown, prompting the police to fire point blank at the strikers. The police advanced, firing in volleys while hurling tear gas into the crowd. As the strikers ran across the field, the police continued to shoot directly at the strikers while beating the fallen with billy clubs and hatchet handles. They dragged the wounded across the ground, refusing to allow anyone to administer first aid. When the smoke cleared, 10 people had been killed or mortally wounded, including seven who had been shot in the back. Among the wounded were 30 strikers with bullet wounds, 28 with contusions about the head, and 25 to 30 with miscellaneous injuries. About 35 police officers sustained minor injuries.

Immediately, Chicago authorities attempted to assign responsibility for the violence to the strikers. The coroner's verdict determined the deaths to be justifiable homicide, while the *Chicago Tribune* declared that the strikers—whom they speculated were influenced by communists—had been "lusting for blood," implying that the police had been justified in their actions. President Franklin D. Roosevelt—generally perceived to be on the side of labor—condemned both the strikers and the police, which proved to be a blow to the morale of the labor movement.

In the fall of 1937, the SWOC called off the strike against Little Steel, and Republic workers returned to the factory without meeting their goal of union

FACTBOX

PLACE Chicago, Illinois

DATE Memorial Day, May 30, 1937

TYPE Clash between striking steelworkers and police

DESCRIPTION During a rally by steelworkers, police attacked the crowd.

CASUALTIES 10 deaths; about 90 strikers and 35 police officers wounded

IMPACT Although the strike failed, a congressional investigation found police guilty of provoking violence and using excessive force; one in a series of events that eventually led to acceptance of the United Steelworkers union by steel industry

recognition. An official investigation by the U.S. Senate Subcommittee of the Committee on Education and Labor accused the police of provoking the fatal clash and using excessive force. By 1941, the federal government via the National Labor Relations Board had forced Girdler to start to bargain with workers instead of fighting them, and the following year, he signed a contract with the United Steelworkers of America.

Susan Doll

FURTHER READING:

Bernstein, Irving. *Turbulent Years: A History of the American Worker 1933–1941.* Boston: Houghton-Mifflin, 1970.

Cohen, Lizabeth. *Making a New Deal: Industrial Workers in Chicago, 1919–1939.* New York: Cambridge University Press, 1990.

Lauderbaugh, Richard A. *American Steel Makers and the Coming of the Second World War.* Ann Arbor, Mich.: UMI Research Press, 1980.

1937 ◆ DISAPPEARANCE OF AMELIA EARHART

On July 2, 1937, 37-year-old Amelia Earhart and her navigator, Fred Noonan, disappeared over the Pacific Ocean somewhere near Howland Island—roughly halfway between Australia and Hawaii—during what was intended to be the first around-the-world flight by a woman. While previous legs of the flight received moderate press coverage, the search for the wreckage and tributes to Earhart's previous aeronautical accomplishments dominated front pages for weeks. Earhart and Noonan almost certainly perished in the ocean when they ran out of fuel, but because no trace of Earhart's Lockheed Electra aircraft was ever found, the "mystery" of Earhart's ultimate fate continues to generate both scholarly and sensationalized speculation, spawning books, articles, popular films, and documentaries.

Born in Atchison, Kansas, on July 24, 1897, Amelia Earhart left the Ogontz School (a junior college in Rydal, Pennsylvania) in 1917, becoming a nurse's aide in the Spandina Military Convalescent Hospital in Toronto, Canada. The stories by injured World War I military pilots deeply impressed on her the human costs of war (she became a lifelong pacifist) even as they sparked her interest in flying. Earhart made her first solo flight in 1921, earning her National Aeronautics Association license later that year. She flew at various exhibitions, setting the women's altitude record of 14,000 feet (4,300 m) in 1922. The following year, she became the 16th

FACTBOX	
PLACE Unknown, probably in the vicinity of Howland Island, Pacific Ocean	
DATE July 2, 1937	
TYPE Mysterious disappearance	
DESCRIPTION On an intended around-the-world flight, aviator Amelia Earhart and her navigator Fred Noonan disappeared over the Pacific Ocean.	
CAUSE Presumably ran out of fuel searching for an island refueling station	
CASUALTIES Deaths of Amelia Earhart and Fred Noonan	
COST More than $4 million in the fruitless search of the Pacific	
IMPACT The accomplishments as well as the mystery of the final fate of this early feminist have made her an icon in both women's history and the history of flight.	

woman to earn a Federation Aeronautique International license. Rejecting the social dictates that a woman of her age and class could only find happiness and fulfillment through marriage and motherhood, she held a variety of jobs to support her expensive hobby before finally beginning a career as a settlement worker in Boston's Denison House in 1926, selling Kinner aircraft on the side and flying at every opportunity.

On May 20, 1927, Charles Lindbergh piloted *The Spirit of St. Louis* from New York to Paris, becoming the first person to fly solo across the Atlantic Ocean. "Lindy's" feat set off an unprecedented media frenzy and sparked tremendous public interest in the possibilities of air travel. A flurry of record-setting ensued. On June 17, 1928, Amelia Earhart traveled as a passenger aboard the *Friendship*, piloted by Wilmer "Bill" Stultz and Louis "Slim" Gordon. The three departed Trepassy, Newfoundland, making a water landing at Burry Port, Wales, slightly more than 24 hours later. In celebration of her status as the first woman to fly the Atlantic, Earhart was feted in London and given a ticker-tape parade down Broadway. A tremendous amount of attention was paid to Earhart's resemblance to Charles Lindbergh (both were attractive—tall, slim, with short brown hair and a modest yet forthright demeanor). Earhart was immediately dubbed "Lady Lindy."

Earhart was somewhat embarrassed to receive so much attention when she had not even touched the controls during the flight, but she used her sudden fame to promote her passions: aviation, feminism, and pacifism. In 1929, she flew her own Lockheed Vega in the first women's cross-country air derby. She set the first altitude record (18,415 feet [5,613 m]) in the Pitcairn PCA–2 and was the first woman to fly an autogiro (a rotary-wing aircraft that utilizes a propeller for forward motion). Earhart was instrumental in the creation of the women's flying organization, The Ninety Nines, serving as its president, finding jobs for other women pilots.

Earhart married her publicist George Putman in 1931 but remained independent and childless, avidly pursuing her own interests rather than becoming a conventional wife and mother. The following year "Lady Lindy" made her own solo transatlantic flight, from Newfoundland to Ireland, earning the U.S. Distinguished Flying Cross and France's Cross of the Legion of Honor. She continued to set records, to promote aeronautics and world peace, and to celebrate the abilities and accomplishments of women.

According to Hilton Railey, who had been a member of the *Friendship* promotional team, Earhart ulti-mately became caught up in "the hero racket," which "compelled her to strive for increasingly dramatic records, bigger and braver feats that automatically insured the publicity necessary to the maintenance of her position as the foremost woman pilot in the world." On June 1, 1937, Earhart began her second attempt to complete a heavily promoted around-the-world flight. Traveling from west to east, she flew her Lockheed Electra by day, stopping for fuel, rest, food, and repairs by night.

Having flown across the Atlantic from Florida to Africa and then to India and Australia, Earhart and her navigator took off from New Guinea on July 2 (still July 1 in the United States), headed next for Howland Island, 2,556 miles (4,113 km) to the east. Earhart expected the flight to take about 18 hours. Members of the U.S. military had created an airstrip on the tiny (a mile and a half by half a mile) island, located east of the Gilbert Islands along the equator, and were standing by on the Coast Guard cutter *Itasca* to send navigational information and to provide fuel and assistance. Because neither Earhart nor Noonan had the necessary Morse code skills to communicate with the ship, they left behind the marine frequency radio, making it impossible for the *Itasca* to obtain a proper bearing on the plane. The airplane's remaining radio equipment allowed crew members aboard the *Itasca* to only occasionally intercept the increasingly grim messages from Earhart that she and Noonan, unable to locate the island, were running low on fuel. The last message came 20 hours and 14 minutes into the flight.

The most extensive sea hunt in history (a 16-day search of approximately 250,000 miles [650,000 sq km]) yielded no trace of Earhart, Noonan, or the plane. Rumors circulated that Earhart had landed intentionally on an uncharted island in order to pursue a romantic relationship with Noonan; and that the two had made a sea landing, been picked up by a Japanese ship or fishing boat, taken prisoner, and executed. The latter theory was promulgated by the 1943 film *Flight to Freedom* starring Rosalind Russell as a famous pilot who intentionally gets "lost" in order to give the United States an excuse to search Japanese waters.

According to biographer Susan Ware, Amelia Earhart "at least tentatively kept women's advancement on the national agenda at a time when mass-based feminist movements were unlikely to coalesce." With the rise of the modern feminist movement came a renewed interest in this adventurous spirit so eager to enjoy life on her own terms, an intriguing woman whose final fate remains an enduring mystery.

Nancy C. Unger

FURTHER READING:

Butler, Susan. *East to the Dawn: The Life of Amelia Earhart.* Reading, Mass.: Addison-Wesley, 1997.

Rich, Doris L. *Amelia Earhart: A Biography.* Washington, D.C.: Smithsonian Institution, 1989.

Ware, Susan. *Still Missing: Amelia Earhart and the Search for Modern Feminism.* New York: W. W. Norton, 1993.

1937 ◆ ELIXIR SULFANILAMIDE TRAGEDY

The Elixir Sulfanilamide tragedy of 1937 was one of the deadliest medical catastrophes in American history, killing 107 people in little more than a month. People around the nation were shocked that pharmacists could sell a medicine that turned out to be a deadly dose of poison. The backlash from this preventable tragedy was instrumental in the enactment of more effective control over the prescription and sale of drugs in the United States.

The discovery of sulfanilamide represented one of the major medical breakthroughs of the 1930s, proving effective in combating various infections, including gonorrhea and strep throat. The Samuel E. Massengill Company, a small firm in Bristol, Tennessee, that specialized in medicines used by veterinarians, sought to take advantage of the new drug's popularity. As sulfanilamide was available only in capsules and tablets, company president Samuel Massengill instructed his chief chemist, Harold C. Watkins, to develop a liquid form of the drug. After numerous experiments, Watkins found that sulfanilamide dissolved in diethylene glycol, which he chose as the elixir—a flavored solution usually mixed with alcohol that served as a liquid vehicle for medicine. But diethylene glycol was distilled from petroleum (rather than from alcohol) and had proven fatal when given to animals. Watkins apparently was unaware of these reports, nor did he test to see if his concoction harmed people.

On September 4, 1937, the Massengill Company began the distribution of 240 gallons of the raspberry-flavored elixir to pharmacies across the South and Midwest. On October 11, two doctors from Tulsa, Oklahoma, notified the American Medical Associa-

FACTBOX
PLACE 15 states, from Virginia to California
DATE September–November 1937
TYPE Toxic drug
DESCRIPTION Elixir Sulfanilamide, a medicine developed to cure infection, caused illness, intense pain, and often death.
CAUSE Use of diethylene glycol, a toxic agent, as an elixir solution for sulfanilamide, a medicine
CASUALTIES 107 deaths
COST Company fined $26,000
IMPACT The tragedy pressured Congress to pass the Food, Drug, and Cosmetic Act of 1938, which required drug testing, improved labeling, and a doctor's prescription for certain medicines.

tion (AMA) that six of their patients who had taken the elixir had died. By early November, the death toll had grown to 107. Fatalities occurred in 15 states that ranged from Virginia to California, with a concentration in the South and Midwest. Diethylene glycol produced an illness that lasted between seven and 21 days. The disorder attacked the kidneys and liver, destroying their ability to function. As body tissues swelled with fluid, patients became progressively comatose and died, often amid intense pain and convulsions.

Doctors flooded the AMA with inquiries about the medicine. Information about the medicine's formulation was not printed on the label of the bottle because existing law did not require drug manufacturers to divulge their product's ingredients, with exceptions for narcotics and poisons. It was legal to keep the

Food and Drug Administration

The modern U.S. Food and Drug Administration (FDA) began in 1927 when the Bureau of Chemistry's name was changed to the Food, Drug, and Insecticide Administration. Three years later, the agency's name was shortened to Food and Drug Administration. In 1953, the administration was transferred from the Department of Agriculture to the Department of Health, Education, and Welfare, and in 1979 to the Department of Health and Human Services. Through the decades, the agency has grown in size and functions. Its current authority embraces about a quarter of all foods sold in the nation and most prescription drugs and many medical devices. In 2001, the FDA's work cost about $1.3 billion and was undertaken by 9,100 employees, who were stationed in Washington, D.C., 56 regional offices, 20 district offices, and 150 field offices.

The origin of the FDA traces to the investigation of food adulteration by the Division of Chemistry in the Department of Agriculture in the late 19th century. Under the tireless research and lobbying of Harvey W. Wiley, chief chemist from 1883 to 1912, Congress enacted the Pure Food and Drug Act of 1906, one of the federal government's first consumer protection acts. The law prohibited the misbranding of medicines and the use of false or deceptive labeling, and it banned certain hazardous preservatives from food and drugs. Primarily a labeling statute, the law did not require that a drug be safe or mandate that a manufacturer obtain government approval prior to marketing a drug. Following the ELIXIR SULFANILAMIDE TRAGEDY in 1937, Congress enacted the Food, Drug, and Cosmetic Act in 1938. The law's most significant reform prohibited the marketing of new drugs unless manufacturers provided evidence to the FDA that the drug was safe. The law also allowed the FDA to designate that certain drugs required approval by a licensed physician in the form of prescriptions for retail sale. In 1962, the year that the THALIDOMIDE TRAGEDY broke, Congress mandated that the FDA certify that a drug was safe before authorizing its sale and use. In addition to its responsibilities regarding food and drugs, the FDA also has regulatory authority over cosmetics, medical devices, animal feeds, and drugs used by veterinarians. In 1976, Congress broadened the FDA's oversight of medical equipment.

The FDA has a broad regulatory mission, which reaches widely across the foods Americans eat and the health services they receive and which has evolved in response to product development in these fields through the decades (such as new drugs and new medical technologies). In the face of this history, the FDA has been under increased pressure to meet public expectations that it is keeping Americans safe. Complicating this responsibility are the interests of food and drug manufacturers in bringing their products to market and the intervention of their supporters in Congress and among the public. The FDA has faced a stream of controversies concerning its rulings. In part, this tension is inherent in the legislation that requires the FDA to certify that drugs are safe but does not provide resources for the agency to undertake its own testing.

Proposals for FDA regulation of some commodities, tobacco and cigarettes in particular, have generated sharp political controversy. Efforts to classify tobacco as a drug, which would have put the product under the jurisdiction of the FDA, began in 1970 (see 1964 CIGARETTES AND LUNG CANCER). In 1996, the FDA held that smoking is a "pediatric disease," classifying nicotine as an addictive drug. The Supreme Court blocked the decision, ruling in 2001 that Congress had not given the FDA the authority to regulate tobacco products Nonetheless, Americans regard FDA oversight of the food and drug industries as an essential safeguard to their health.

Ballard C. Campbell

formula secret, and most producers did. Moreover, the law did not prohibit sale of drugs to customers who lacked a doctor's prescription. Because of the limited oversight role of the U.S. Food and Drug Administration (FDA, created in 1931) at the time, the AMA functioned as a clearinghouse of information for drugs. Tests ordered by the AMA, not Massengil's public admission, disclosed the toxic compound in the product. Reports of the tragedy galvanized the FDA into action. On October 15, FDA chief Walter Campbell instructed nearly all of his force of 239 inspectors to track down and confiscate the compound. By early November, this search had located and destroyed 99.2 percent of the poisonous potion.

The FDA fined the Massengill Company $26,000, the largest penalty ever levied under the 1906 Food and Drug Act. The fine was not based on the fatalities or even directly on the poisonous nature of the elixir due to the loopholes in existing law but on a technicality concerning the bottle's label. The standard pharmacological reference at the time defined an elixir as containing alcohol, which the Massengill drug did not use. Had Massengil's bottle named its product something other than an elixir, the company might have escaped any penalty.

The Elixir Sulfanilamide tragedy spurred Congress to address the gaps in the nation's drug regulations. The 1906 Food and Drug Act, the first federal effort to ensure drug safety, did not require that the label on a medicine list all its ingredients or that drug companies prove that their products were safe for people to consume. The election of Franklin D. Roosevelt as president in 1932 offered FDA chief Walter Campbell an opportunity to press for stiffer regulations. A reform drug bill was introduced in Congress in 1933, but it languished until the elixir scandal generated pressure on lawmakers to move ahead with the Food, Drug, and Cosmetic Act (52 Stat. 1040) in 1938. This landmark law required that all of a drug's ingredients be listed on the label and banned false and misleading labels. The law's most significant reform prohibited the marketing of new drugs unless manufacturers provided evidence to the FDA that the drug was safe. In administering the new law, the FDA specified that certain medicines could be sold to individuals only if they were prescribed by a licensed physician. This development marked the start of the modern era "prescription drugs," ushering in a fundamental change in the way Americans took their medicine.

See also 1962 THALIDOMIDE TRAGEDY.

Ballard C. Campbell

FURTHER READING:

Jackson, Charles O. *Food and Drug Legislation in the New Deal.* Princeton, N.J.: Princeton University Press, 1970.

Temin, Peter. *Taking Your Medicine: Drug Regulation in the United States.* Cambridge, Mass.: Harvard University Press, 1980.

1938 ◆ GREAT NEW ENGLAND HURRICANE

The great New England hurricane of September 21, 1938, was one of the nation's most devastating storms ever. Measured in terms of its destructive power, it remains one of the top 10 hurricanes to make landfall in the continental United States. It moved northward quickly, aided by a continental low-pressure system that accelerated the storm at speeds unrecorded before or since. Striking the northeastern region of the country without warning, it caused long-term ecological harm, billions of dollars in property damage, and considerable loss of life. Memory of this massive storm became part of folk legend in New York and New England for generations.

The origin of the word *hurricane* derives from the Spanish, *huracan*. As early European explorers of the Caribbean, Mexico, and the West Indies, the Spanish experienced firsthand the tropical cyclones of the region and also learned about them from the creation myths of the Mayan civilizations of Central America. According to these legends, the god whose physical manifestation was the hurricane created the earth and the celestial bodies. According to the Mayans, their god visited often to show his dominating power. In the modern world of science, hurricanes are cyclones that contain rotating winds of at least 74 miles per hour, which form over the tropical Atlantic Ocean and both the eastern North and eastern South Pacific Oceans. From May until October of each year, these regions experience a predictable share of warm ocean breezes and ample sunshine. Rain showers occur frequently but are of short duration.

In recent decades, atmospheric industrial pollutants have accelerated the greenhouse effect for transforming moderate climates into incubators for violent storms. As pollutants trap solar heat energy within the Earth's atmosphere, they heat the surface of the land and raise ocean temperatures. Trapping heat energy in the oceans leads to explosive meteorological events, as the condensation of water vapor into liquid water provides the fuel supply for hurricanes. Under normal tropical weather conditions with average humidity at about 80 percent, warm ocean waters discharge heat energy through evaporation. One way to fathom the energy of a hurricane is to think about what happens to a small particle of water. When a gram of warm tropical water evaporates and then condenses into liquid water in the upper atmosphere, it releases 600 calories of heat. Multiplied billions of times, this phenomenon creates a massive amount of energy. Although the moisture cools down somewhat as it evaporates, rising tropical air continues to fuel this huge energy machine.

The great New England hurricane of 1938 began on September 4 and as almost all begin: with winds blowing off the west coast of Africa in an easterly direction across the Atlantic. When this disturbance reached the tropical waters northeast of Puerto Rico on September 16, the U.S. Weather Bureau classified it a hurricane and warned that its path put it on a collision course with southeast Florida. Four days later, however, the storm slowed and veered northeast, not an uncommon occurrence. At this point, most hurricanes leave the heated waters of the tropics, lose their energy source, and dissipate. What was to become the Great Hurricane of 1938, however, received an energy boost from an unlikely source.

High velocity winds carry cold air from the Arctic southward in search of the warmth and humidity emanating from the Gulf region, a meteorological

---

FACTBOX

PLACE New York and the New England States

DATE September 21, 1938

TYPE Hurricane

DESCRIPTION Originating in the Caribbean, this hurricane was propelled northward by the warm waters of the Gulf Stream and powerful winds from the continent's interior.

CAUSE The combination of a very fast moving storm, exceedingly wet weather in advance of the storm, and the absence of modern weather warning systems. The gravitational pull of the autumnal equinox raised the coastal tides, adding to the storm's devastating power.

CASUALTIES Estimates ranged from 564 to more than 690 deaths.

COST At least $20.8 billion in current dollars

IMPACT Permanently altered the coastline in many areas of New England, destroyed millions of trees and an unrecorded loss of wildlife, destroyed and damaged thousands of properties, and prompted the construction of a system of locks and dams in Providence, Rhode Island, to protect the city from future storm-related flooding

---

phenomenon known as the Great North American Trumpet. The high winds that sweep across central Canada and the Great Lakes region of the United States are evidence of such polar winds pulled southward by tropical conditions. Although this common weather pattern is well documented, the upward movement of air creates strong upper-level troughs. Warm air turns into clouds and rain, and cold air creates dry and clear skies. These troughs obtain their energy from the interplay of warm and cold air moving eastward in the direction of the Gulf of Mexico. By midnight on September 20, 1938, a stronger than normal weather trough with increasing wind velocity over the Caribbean began to propel northward what was to become the Great Hurricane. Despite leaving the warm waters of the Atlantic Gulf Stream for colder northern ocean waters, the jet stream ahead of the trough created what hurricane analysts called the Long Island Express.

The streets of Winchendon, Massachusetts, lie flooded two days after the great New England hurricane. (© Bettmann/CORBIS)

With a forward speed of 70 miles per hour and sometimes higher—the fastest traveling hurricane in recorded history—the storm slammed without warning into Long Island on September 21 at about 3:30 P.M. In 1938, the U.S. Weather Bureau operated without the aid of weather satellites, radar, or ocean buoys outfitted with weather instruments. The bureau posted no storm warnings after the storm had passed Florida. Since television broadcasting did not exist, there was no weather channel. Radio stations continued their regularly scheduled programs and received no weather news worthy of reporting. Coastal weather observation centers and ships at sea provided some tracking information about the storm, yet the coastal Northeast region was unprepared for the events that followed.

As if these circumstances were not alarming enough, a low-pressure frontal system had begun to drop several inches of rain on coastal Long Island and New England for a week before the hurricane arrived. With the land saturated with water and with the rivers, their tributaries, and streams swollen, any additional volume of water would place the region at flood stage. In addition, the autumnal equinox in September caused higher than normal tides in the Northern Hemisphere as the gravity of a new moon tugged at sea levels. These tides reached their height on September 21.

The great hurricane struck Long Island just a few hours before flood tide. With the eye of this category 5 storm 50 miles across, the storm's width spread out 500 miles and packed wind gusts of 180 miles per hour. Coastal Long Island was about to absorb a catastrophic hit. After making landfall, wind velocity dropped, reducing the storm to a Category 3 hurricane yet still very dangerous. The forward motion of the storm propelled by the upper-level jet stream caused it to move so rapidly that many areas in New

York, Connecticut, Rhode Island, and Massachusetts were struck simultaneously. A storm surge with waves of 30 to 50 feet dumped millions of tons of seawater on shocked and unprepared residents along the coastline. The force of the surge was so powerful that it registered on the earthquake seismograph in Alaska, some 4,000 miles away. Tides that were 14 to 18 feet above normal extended along most of the Long Island and Connecticut coast and 18 to 25 feet above normal from New London, Connecticut, to Cape Cod. The downtown section of Providence, Rhode Island, was submerged under a surge of 20 feet, while sections of New Bedford and Falmouth, Massachusetts, were under eight feet of water.

Before heading north to Vermont and New Hampshire, the wind and flooding arrived in Providence, Rhode Island, the state capital, during the evening rush hour. The gushing waters swamped people who were riding buses and trains, driving automobiles, or walking. People trapped in buildings dropped sheets and ropes to those being swept past by the raging waters. More than 90 people died in the city on account of the storm. Faced with massive destruction, officials imposed martial law in Providence to prevent looting. Cleanup operations, using unemployed laborers who were hired at $2 a day, took place soon thereafter. Hundreds of skilled telephone and electrical employees worked to restore communication and power to this hardest hit northeastern city. Later, the city constructed a system of locks and dams to protect it from future storm flooding.

With the loss of hundreds of millions of trees across a six-state area, the environmental impact of the great hurricane was devastating. In addition, the coastlines were changed and in some places new inlets replaced old ones that had been filled with shifting sands and debris from the wind. The damage to the built environment was stunning. The hurricane destroyed at least 8,900 homes, summer cottages, and commercial and public buildings. More than 15,000 others needed substantial repair. The storm destroyed more than 2,600 boats and yachts and damaged another 3,300. Fishing fleets, a regional economic asset, suffered substantially. While the industry recovered in the long run, the hurricane cost fishermen 2,605 vessels, with damages to another 3,369. Calculated in current dollars, property losses from the great hurricane exceeded

$20.8 billion. The storm ranks number eight on the list of the country's most devastating hurricanes (which includes Katrina in 2005).

As with many natural disasters, doubts exist as to the number of storm-related deaths. Some bodies were never recovered, because individuals were swept out to sea, buried beneath the shifting sand and surf, or dismembered by airborne debris. Estimated fatalities range from 564 to more than 690. While these numbers suggest the horror that people faced when confronted with the raging storm, their words do reveal the depths of their despair. One survivor remembered:

"Something hit the house with a terrific thud (I think it was a section of the concrete retaining wall) and the wave brought the back porch down on me, dislocating my left elbow. . . . The wind and the rain and gray spray, filled with sand, came in sheets. There was debris and I decided I had better get out of the churning, shallow water. All fear left me when I hit the water and had to do something to save myself. I was about ready to give up, when a piece of house came by and I crawled onto that; it was like a surfboard. A roof came by upside down, so I crawled into that and lay in the water at the bottom of the V. Flying debris struck the roof first and only me second. My head and face were cut and bruised so, that I could not stand to have my hair touched for four days in the hospital." (*Watch Hill (RI) Hurricane*)

The rapid movement of the hurricane carried it north across New Hampshire and Vermont, destroying part of Jacob's Ladder, the trestle on the Cog Railway to the summit of Mount Washington, New Hampshire, where wind velocity of 163 miles per hour was recorded. By 9 P.M. of September 21, about five and a half hours after first striking Long Island, the Great Hurricane passed into Canada, through Montreal and Quebec and ended its day of destruction in the Arctic. During the next days, cleanup activities commenced and then gave way to reconstruction work. Memories of the Great Hurricane had already been etched into the psyche of New Yorkers and New Englanders.

See also 1900 GALVESTON HURRICANE; 1992 HURRICANE ANDREW; 2005 HURRICANE KATRINA.

Anthony N. Penna

FURTHER READING:

Burns, Cherie. *The Great Hurricane: 1938.* New York: Atlantic Monthly Press, 2005.

Emanuel, Kerry. *Divine Wind: The History and Science of Hurricanes.* New York: Oxford University Press, 2005.

Goudsouzian, Aram. *The Hurricane of 1938.* Boston: Commonwealth Editions, 2004.

Lee, Helen Joy, et al. *Watch Hill Hurricane September 21, 1938.* Watch Hill, R.I.: The Book and Tackle Shop, 1996. ·

Scotti, R. A. *Sudden Sea: The Great Hurricane of 1938.* Boston: Back Bay Books, 2004.

1938 ◆ *WAR OF THE WORLDS* RADIO BROADCAST PANIC

The Orson Welles radio broadcast *War of the Worlds* on October 30, 1938, shocked millions of Americans. Listening to the drama of a supposed Martian invasion in Grover's Mill, New Jersey, convinced a broad spectrum of the population that the world was coming to an end. Welles's dramatic prank was referred in the newspapers at the time as the "Panic Broadcast." Despite the resulting mass hysteria, there were no fatalities attributed to the broadcast. However, this would not be the case with the imitations that followed the original Welles production.

War of the Worlds was directed by Welles and performed by the CBS Mercury Theatre on the Air on the Eve of Halloween. Americans were in a particularly vulnerable state to be manipulated by a radio program. The country was still struggling through THE GREAT DEPRESSION, and now the world was becoming enveloped in a second world war, looming in Europe. Increasingly, the radio connected the public to news of the world. Millions had heard the "fireside chats" of President Franklin D. Roosevelt during the depression. Now with another war on the horizon, people were accustomed to hearing negative news of wartime developments on the radio—and trusting the news they heard.

The format of music entertainment interrupted by pseudo-news bulletins in the Welles production of *War of the Worlds* proved to be too much for the audience. Of the 6 million people who heard the broadcast, 3 million believed it to be true. Of the believers, it is estimated that 1.2 million panicked. The program was convincing enough that many did actually think that the world had been invaded by Martians. Others interpreted the broadcast to be a description of a German or Japanese attack.

FACTBOX

PLACE Listeners of the CBS radio network across the United States. The site of the "invasion" was Grover's Mill in central New Jersey.

DATE October 30, 1938, the eve of Halloween

TYPE Panic induced by the broadcast of *War of the Worlds*

DESCRIPTION The radio broadcast convinced 3 million Americans that the world was going to end.

CAUSE The realism of the Orson Welles radio drama

CASUALTIES Hysteria and small outbreaks of unlawful behavior, but no deaths

COST Originally, millions of dollars in lawsuits were brought against CBS, but all cases were dismissed.

IMPACT The *War of the Worlds* concept became hugely popular in comic books, plays, television, and movies. It was also adapted and imitated by other radio stations, the most notable being a 1949 version in Peru that resulted in the burning down of the radio station and 20 deaths.

The *War of the Worlds* radio show was based on British writer H. G. Wells's classic work *The War of the Worlds* published in 1898. His original story of a Martian invasion was heavily influenced by both Darwinism and European colonization. Welles and the Mercury Theatre on the Air regularly used classic works of literature in their programming. In 1938, they had also adapted for radio Robert Louis Stevenson's *Treasure Island,* Charles Dickens's *A Tale of Two Cities,* and Alexander Dumas's *The Count of Monte Cristo.* On October 23, a week earlier, they had performed Jules Verne's *Around the World in 80 Days.*

The Mercury Theatre on the Air was a small unsponsored radio show prior to their most infamous broadcast. At their time slot, they competed with the *Chase and Sanborn Hour,* featuring the ventriloquist Edgar Bergen and Charlie McCarthy. In the Hooper Ratings, The Mercury Theatre on the Air had a 3.6 percent listening audience compared to the 34.7 percent of the *Chase and Sanborn Hour.*

However, the strength of the Mercury Theatre lay in the dramatic genius of the 23-year-old Orson Welles. Welles was under contract with CBS to produce a 60-minute radio show every week. This week, no one was particularly excited about the upcoming *War of the Worlds* show. Howard Koch, who wrote the script for Welles, thought it was "boring." Welles doubted that people would believe the story, and he pushed to make it more realistic. He had been influenced by the broadcast of Archibald MacLeish's *Air Raid,* and to set the tone for the actors, he had them listen to the radio broadcasts of the *Hindenburg* explosion from 1937.

War of the Worlds began with the announcement: "Orson Welles and *The Mercury Theatre on the Air* in *The War of the Worlds* by H. G. Wells." The announcer continued with the introduction of Welles, who began the program by reading the opening from the original book. These were the only giveaway signs to the listeners that what was taking place was a dramatic production. The show then shifted between the music of Ramon Raquello and his orchestra in New York City to a series of progressively more ominous announcements. Yet the criticisms were accurate. In listening to the broadcast, almost a full 15 minutes passes before the plot action of a Martian invasion begins to materialize.

It was Welles's brilliant manipulation of the relatively new medium of radio that made *War of the Worlds* so effective and dangerous. Welles timed the plot action of *War of the Worlds* with the commercial break of the far more popular *Chase and Sanborn Hour.* Four million listeners switched stations to hear the announcement that a space object had crashed into Earth at Grover's Mill in central New Jersey. These listeners had not heard any of the beginning announcements about the program, and instead of switching back to Edgar Bergen and Charlie McCarthy, they continued to listen.

They then heard a news reporter's frightening description of the extraterrestrial object slowly opening up. At first, it looked like snakes climbing out of the spaceship, but these were actually the tentacles of the "monster." The reporter described it as having eyes that are "black and gleam like a serpent." It also had a threatening looking "v-shaped mouth." However, when the "monster" fully rose out of the spaceship, it was actually a giant machine!

Next, the listeners heard the expert opinion of a Princeton Observatory astronomy professor as he witnessed the space invaders turn violent. The machines were wreaking havoc with their powerful flame throwers. There was horrific news that 40 people had burned to death including six members of the New Jersey state police. The situation was quickly escalating into a total war. The alien machines were not just invading New Jersey, but reports were coming in of more and more of the space ships hitting ground all over the country. The attack at Grover's Mill was just the first in what was becoming a full-scale invasion from Mars.

It appeared there was nothing that could be done to stop the alien invaders. Even the United States Army proved powerless. A witness of the attack on New York City warned that the machines had started to take all survivors as their prisoners. They were going to keep people for horrible experiments. As they listened to these reports of widespread death and destruction, the radio listeners would have also recognized a familiar sounding "Secretary of the Interior" urging everyone to stay calm. In the investigations that followed the broadcast, Welles denied it, but later he admitted that the "Secretary of the Interior" was intentionally made to sound like President Roosevelt.

However, the advice to stay calm was too late as millions of listeners thought they might be next. People screamed and cried. They got down and prayed for their lives. They made desperate phone calls to loved ones. They locked their doors and windows and hid in basements. Others took to the streets, protecting their faces with wet towels. Some jumped in cars and sped off trying to escape. People thought they could see the aliens of the broadcast. Shots were fired at the water tower in Grover's Mill as it appeared to resemble a giant Martian. National guardsmen arrived for duty in New Jersey. The governor of Pennsylvania offered to send troops. Fifteen people were treated for shock in a Newark hospital. Local police departments were flooded with phone calls of frightened people trying to get information.

When the network became aware that a panic was at hand, a CBS supervisor ordered the show to end immediately. Coproducer John Houseman refused, but at the next station break, the audience was reminded that this was a "CBS presentation of Orson Welles and the *Mercury Theatre on the Air* in an original dramatization of *The War of the Worlds* by H. G. Wells." Those that listened through to the end of the program would learn that Earth was safe, the attack was over, and that all the Martians perished due to earthly bacteria. Welles gave the final word in reminding people that this was simply CBS's way of saying "Boo!" on the eve of Halloween. Yet most of the people who panicked were already fleeing before the end of broadcast.

Immediately after the show ended, police raided the CBS studio to investigate. The next day, a press conference was held in which Welles denied that his intention was to scare people, and he claimed he had no idea such a panic had occurred. CBS had to apologize and promise not to create "simulated news broadcasts that could cause harm." The public responses reflected people's reactions. Those who had panicked were generally outraged, and lawsuits were drawn up. Those who knew it was a gag laughed at the susceptibility of others. The Federal Communications Commission received 644 pieces of mail concerning the broadcast, 60 percent of which condemned Welles and the show. The other 40 percent saw it as genius and applauded it.

After the dust had settled and all the lawsuits were dropped, it was off to bigger and better things for Orson Welles and company. The *Mercury Theatre on the Air* was continued, now under the sponsorship of the Campbell Soup Company. Welles received a massive contract with RKO studios, and he moved to Hollywood to direct and star in his masterpiece, *Citizen Kane.* Howard Koch went into film as well, and he received an Oscar in 1944 for the *Casablanca*

screenplay. Even H. G. Wells, who was initially put off by the radio adaptation, changed his opinion and personal impression of Welles when the controversy provoked a renewed interest in the original novel. The *War of the Worlds* concept went on to spawn countless variations in radio imitations, comic books, and movie adaptations. In 2005, Steven Spielberg directed a movie version of *War of the Worlds* starring Tom Cruise.

The notion of an extraterrestrial attack has proved to be popular entertainment throughout history, but some fictional fables about creatures from outer space have caused real tragedy. The deadliest reaction to a broadcast of *War of the Worlds* occurred in 1949 on Radio Quito in Peru, where thousands of people thought that monsters had actually invaded their country. Similar to Welles's broadcast in 1938, some Peruvian listeners believed that their country was under attack from Ecuador or the Soviet Union. Thousands rioted in the streets. Discovering that the broadcast was a prank, mobs attacked the radio station, and Radio Quito was torched, killing 20 people in the blaze.

More recent incidents of people being carried away with the broadcast took place in Buffalo, New York, in 1968, in Providence, Rhode Island, in 1974, and in northern Portugal in 1988. Unlike the Peruvian instance, no deaths occurred in these cases. Still, it is remarkable, given the notoriety surrounding Welles's Halloween show that so many people could be fooled by a radio drama. Radio clearly is a powerful tool, capable of convincing masses of people that their worst fears, such as an invasion from outer space, were indeed coming true. *War of the Worlds* reflects the brilliance of the H. G. Wells's original story, the force of radio as a medium, and the unique genius of Orson Welles to combine both of them.

Curtis C. E. Fazen

FURTHER READING:

Cantril, Hadley. *The Invasion from Mars: A Study in the Psychology of Panic.* London: Transaction Publishers, 2005.

Holmsten, Brian, and Alex Lubertozzi, eds. *The Complete War of the Worlds: Mars' Invasion of Earth from H. G. Wells to Orson Welles.* Naperville, Ill.: Sourcebooks, 2001.

1940 ◆ COLLAPSE OF THE TACOMA NARROWS BRIDGE

During a minor storm on the morning of November 7, 1940, massive undulations tore apart the newly constructed Tacoma Narrows suspension bridge in the state of Washington when winds reached 42 miles per hour. After a half hour of violent twisting, the main section of the concrete roadbed fell into the waters of Puget Sound, along with two automobiles and a hapless cocker spaniel. The disaster ended the career of one of the world's most influential and prolific suspension bridge engineers, Leon Solomon Moisseiff, and shocked a complacent engineering profession into revising the basic tenets of suspension bridge theory. The bridge was a total loss and cost Washington more than $2 million.

At the pinnacle of a distinguished career, Moisseiff designed the Tacoma Narrows Bridge and declared it "the most beautiful bridge in the world." Slender and graceful, it had a two-lane roadbed just more than a half-mile long, and like the recently completed Golden Gate Bridge in San Francisco, on which Moisseiff had consulted, its architecture and proportions were inspired by art-deco design. Its ratio of width to span was 1 to 72, by far the highest in the world. The bridge was very lightweight; Moisseiff had been working for years to reduce the material used in his designs by applying "deflection theory," which held that the longer a bridge was, the more flexible it could be. The bridge was also shallow—Moisseiff specifically recommended that the bridge towers be as short as possible to reduce wind resistance, which actually contributed to the lateral instability of the structure.

Even before the bridge opened, engineers expressed safety concerns about its strength. Theodore L. Condron, who had been hired by financiers to review its design, suggested that Moisseiff widen the roadbed from 39 to 52 feet, but the advice went unheeded. The bridge opened on July 1, 1940, just 19 months after construction began. From the beginning, it was plagued by unusually large and long-lasting oscillations—even in light winds. The bridge was quickly dubbed "Galloping Gertie" by the local press and began to attract joy-riders on windy days as well as complaints about motion sickness from drivers.

FACTBOX

PLACE Narrow channel of Puget Sound dividing the city of Tacoma, Washington, to the east from the Olympic peninsula to the west

DATE November 7, 1940

TYPE Bridge collapse

DESCRIPTION Winds caused the bridge's roadbed to oscillate and fall, crashing into the water below.

CAUSE Aerodynamic instability due to inadequate design, insufficient rigidity, and mass

CASUALTIES One dog killed

COST Completely destroyed a $6.4 million state-owned bridge, though $4 million of the loss was covered by insurance.

IMPACT Profoundly influenced future bridge design

Bridge engineers took a number of ineffective measures to control oscillations and prevent disaster. They added a "dynamic damper" (that bridge maintenance crews damaged) and installed "tie down cables" near each end of the bridge. Although these cables snapped almost immediately in a minor windstorm three months later, they were reinstalled without modification. It was obvious that serious study of the problem was required, and a large scale-model of the bridge was built for testing at the University of Washington under the direction of Professor F. B. Farquharson.

On the fateful morning of disaster, Farquharson and several of his fellow researchers brought a camera to record images of the bridge's movement for study. A cable clamp slipped near the middle of the span at about 10 A.M. as winds reached 42 miles per hour, and for the first time, the roadbed began to twist laterally. Immediately, the bridge was closed to traffic, and drivers abandoned two vehicles on the span as movement became too violent to continue. Farquharson attempted to rescue Tubby, a three-legged cocker

In one of the most stunning disaster pictures ever taken, the Tacoma Narrows suspension bridge plunges into the water amid high winds. Note the automobile moments before it plummeted. *(Library of Congress)*

designed to withstand much stronger winds collapsed under these conditions. While in hindsight the disaster is easy to understand, at the time Moisseiff's work was state-of-the-art. Many of his engineering colleagues were sympathetic to his plight, and Moisseiff continued to work as a behind-the-scenes consultant on bridge projects until his death in 1943.

This spectacular failure of the Tacoma Narrows Bridge transformed suspension-bridge engineering completely and permanently, as scores of old theories and tenets were revised or rejected. The most important change in the field was new attention to aerodynamics, which had been relatively unexamined before. Wind tunnels and scale-model tests, which were rare before the disaster, became de rigueur. The bridge was replaced in 1950 with a much wider, deeper, and more stable suspension span that is still in use today.

Louise Nelson Dyble

spaniel left in one of the vehicles, by walking along the center of the roadway, but before he could reach the vehicle, he saw that lampposts were falling from the bridge, and he turned back. He returned a short time later with more film but was forced to flee to safety when a large section of roadbed fell into Puget Sound at 10:30 A.M. By 11:10 A.M., the entire main span had collapsed, leaving only the side spans and ruined towers hanging at awkward angles.

Moisseiff later remarked that he was "completely at a loss" to explain why a bridge that had been

FURTHER READING:

Petroski, Henry. *Engineers of Dreams: Great Bridge Builders and the Spanning of America.* New York: Knopf, 1995.

Scott, Richard. *In the Wake of Tacoma: Suspension Bridges and the Quest for Aerodynamic Stability.* Reston, Va.: American Society of Civil Engineers, 2001.

Washington State Department of Transportation. "Tacoma Narrows Bridge: Extreme History." Available online. URL: http://www.wsdot.wa.gov/ TNBhistory. Downloaded on April 2, 2007.

1941 ◇ ATTACK ON PEARL HARBOR

At 7:55 A.M. on December 7, 1941, Japanese dive-bombers and minisubs attacked the United States naval base at Pearl Harbor, Hawaii. Seaman Martin Matthews, a metalsmith in training at the Ford Island Naval Air Station, was visiting a friend aboard the USS *Arizona*. After the first wave of dive-bombers and torpedoes hit the battleship, Matthews panicked and dove into the water. From a mooring buoy some 90 feet astern of the ship, he watched the *Arizona* explode, sending steel, oil, fire, decking, and body parts into the water around

him. He was 15 years old, having lied about his age to experience a world of adventure as a sailor. The surprise assault that Matthews witnessed that morning sank or crippled eight battleships, three cruisers, and four other vessels. It destroyed 188 airplanes as well as some vital shore installations, killed 2,403 American soldiers and sailors, and wounded 1,178 more. Some 55 Japanese died in the attack. A day later, President Franklin D. Roosevelt declared the Japanese action "an unprovoked and dastardly attack" and a day "which will live in infamy." Congress voted nearly unanimously to declare war on Japan. On December 11, Germany and Italy, Japan's European allies, declared war on the United States. Pearl Harbor had violently and suddenly brought the world's remaining industrial power and its people into World War II.

The roots of the attack on Pearl Harbor went back years. Deteriorating Japanese-American relations had reached a critical point in July 1937 when Japan renewed its efforts to conquer China. Japanese interests in its continental neighbor as a repository of natural resources dated back to the early 20th-century. A densely populated island nation, Japan relied on goods from abroad to support its modern industrial economy. Manchuria, a region in northern China, offered relative proximity, needed industrial raw materials, and a buffer against Russia. In September 1931, the Japanese army blew up a section of the South Manchurian Railroad provoking a confrontation with the Chinese. The so-called Manchurian incident began Japan's military occupation of China. In 1937, clashes between the Japanese and Chinese nationalist troops near Beijing triggered a second Japanese invasion and a full-scale Sino-Japanese War. While Congress remained committed to a global policy of strict neutrality, President Roosevelt responded to the Japanese incursion by requesting a "quarantine" of aggressor nations and by reinforcing the American military in the Pacific.

The outbreak of World War II in Europe in 1939 served to increase Japanese power. The war drew British, French, Dutch, and Belgian resources away from their colonial territories in the Pacific just as Japan managed to capture much of coastal China. Militarists in Tokyo turned their attention to European holdings in the East Indies and Southeast Asia that were rich in rubber, tin, and petroleum, key ingredients for Japanese industrial and military might. As Nazi Germany overwhelmed the Allied armies in Europe the following year, Japan pressed the opportunity further, signing a formal alliance with Germany and announcing its intention to expand the "East Asian Co-Prosperity Sphere."

The rise of German and Japanese power shifted American attitudes away from neutrality. In 1939 the United States announced its intention to abrogate a U.S.-Japanese treaty that forbade economic sanctions. Then in the summer of 1940, as the Japanese armed forces moved into North Indochina, the Roosevelt administration cut off American sales of

---

FACTBOX

PLACE Pearl Harbor, Hawaii

DATE December 7, 1941

TYPE Surprise military attack

DESCRIPTION Japanese dive-bombers and minisubs attacked the U.S. naval base at Pearl Harbor, Hawaii. The surprise assault sank or crippled eight American battleships, three cruisers, and four other vessels and destroyed 188 airplanes and some vital shore installations.

CAUSE Imperial aggression, strategic miscalculation, diplomatic impasse, intelligence failure

CASUALTIES 2,403 dead and 1,178 wounded Americans, 55 dead and unknown wounded Japanese

IMPACT Drew the United States into World War II

---

aviation fuel to Japan. With relations between Japan and the United States collapsing, the two countries pursued a diplomatic solution during the spring and summer of 1941.

The failure of diplomacy ultimately set the stage for the attack on Pearl Harbor. Despite extensive talks between Japanese ambassador to the United States Kischisaburo Nomura and U.S. secretary of state Cordell Hull, the two countries could not agree on several key issues, including Japan's conquest of China and Southeast Asia, the American embargo of fuel to Japan, and both countries' respective relationships to their warring allies in Europe. Germany's invasion of the Soviet Union in June 1941 all but crushed any chance for compromise. With its Soviet rival now at war in the west, Japan again made plans to extend its conquests in the Pacific. In July 1941, Japanese soldiers moved into South Indochina and prepared to take the oil-rich Dutch East Indies. In response, the Roosevelt administration moved to strengthen its allies and check Japanese expansion. The administration extended Lend-Lease aid to both Britain and the Soviet Union, imposed a complete embargo on Japan, and seized Japanese assets in the United States.

President Roosevelt had known of the Japanese general strategy despite Japanese attempts to keep it secret. The American code-breaking device known as MAGIC had revealed Japan's intentions to move south in the spring of 1941. Japan had only about a 12-month supply of petroleum to fuel its economy and war machine, so the Americans anticipated that their embargo would force the Japanese to act quickly. The only questions they could not answer were when and where.

In October 1941, General Hideki Tojo took over as the premier of Japan and quickened the course for war with the United States. While continuing the diplomatic negotiations in Washington, the premier had plans finalized for an attack on the Americans. Admiral Isoroku Yamamoto masterminded the operation. His plan called for a Japanese air and submarine assault that would knock out the U.S. Pacific Fleet in one bold stroke, buying time for the sweep south that would secure the resources Japan would need to maintain its strength. The attack would be carried out against the main American bases in the Pacific, the American garrison in the Philippines, and the naval installation at Pearl Harbor.

Pearl Harbor had been a major naval base in the American arsenal since before the U.S. annexation of Hawaii in 1898. While the main body of the U.S. Pacific Fleet occasionally conducted war games and other maneuvers at Pearl Harbor, it did not relocate from San Diego to Hawaii until early 1940, after World War II had broken out in Europe. U.S. administrators in Washington hoped that the move would help deter Japanese aggression in the South Pacific. It did not. A huge Japanese task force secretly left for Pearl Harbor in late November 1941. On December 3, the Japanese consulate began to destroy cipher books and secret documents. On December 6, the Japanese formally rejected Secretary of State Hull's latest list of demands on Japan. War warnings went out to American posts in the Pacific, but details about an imminent attack were still sketchy. On December 7, Japanese dive-bombers and minisubs caught the U.S. Pacific Fleet bottled up in Pearl Harbor. For more than two hours, two waves of 180 planes from six Japanese aircraft carriers pounded the American installation.

The initial success of the Japanese attack shook the United States. Hawaii was put under martial law while war scares and air raid drills became commonplace on the California coast. Fearing a fifth-column insurgency, the U.S. government swept more than 110,000 Japanese Americans into internment camps,

The battleships USS *West Virginia* and USS *Tennessee* moments after the Japanese attacked Pearl Harbor on December 7, 1941. The United States declared war the next day. *(NARA)*

depriving them of the most basic citizenship rights. Japan, meanwhile, moved into the South Pacific, capturing the petroleum and metal resources it needed. Japan won every major confrontation with American forces in the first six months of the war, but these victories were short lived and incomplete. Five American aircraft carriers that happened to be out to sea along with Oahu's fuel supplies had been spared in the attack. The U.S. fleet was down but not completely out. War production boomed over the next two years as Americans answered Roosevelt's call for 120,000 new planes and 120,000 new tanks. They rationed what they had for the war effort and went to work in military industry. Others joined the armed services or were drafted. An army of 1.5 million men and women in the summer of 1941 grew to 5.4 million by the end of 1942. As U.S. troops flooded into the Pacific theater with the promise to "remember Pearl Harbor," they eventually forced a long Japanese retreat. After three and a half years of brutal warfare, Japan finally surrendered when the Americans unleashed the world's first nuclear weapons on the Japanese cities of Hiroshima and Nagasaki in August 1945. As Admiral Yamamoto had originally feared, the successful Pearl Harbor assault had unleashed the sleeping giant.

In 1946, the U.S. Congress conducted investigations into the apparent government failure to anticipate the Japanese attack. While the concluding report affixed ultimate responsibility on the Japanese and declared that the Roosevelt administration had neither provoked nor coerced Japan into the attack, it nevertheless found disturbing errors in the evaluation and dissemination of information. Those with access to the most pertinent intelligence in the administration had failed to communicate it, and commanders at Pearl Harbor had failed to comprehend the imminent danger.

The Japanese attack on Pearl Harbor remains among the most infamous days in modern history. The assault drew the United States and Japan into World War II, a war that took tens of millions of lives, catapulted the United States and the Soviet Union to world power, and set the terms of global conflict for more than a generation. Japan's immediate victory would lead to its eventual defeat and the end of its imperial quest. For the Americans, Pearl Harbor was a disaster of both intelligence and diplomacy. For the Japanese, it was a disaster of strategy and ultimately one rooted in the arrogance of power. For individuals such as Seaman Martin Matthews, who went on to see considerable action in the European and Pacific theaters, it was a personal disaster, one that stripped him of his youth and shaped his and his generation's view of the world.

Jeff Woods

FURTHER READING:

Iriye, Akira. *The Origins of the Second World War in Asia and the Pacific.* New York: Longman, 1987.

La Forte, Robert S., and Ronald E. Marcello, eds. *Remembering Pearl Harbor: Eyewitness Accounts by U.S. Military Men and Women.* Wilmington, Del.: Scholarly Resources Books, 1991.

Prange, Gordon. *At Dawn We Slept: The Untold Story of Pearl Harbor.* Boston: McGraw-Hill, 1981.

Wohlstetter, Roberta. *Pearl Harbor: Warning and Decision.* Stanford, Calif.: Stanford University Press, 1962.

1942 ◆ COCOANUT GROVE FIRE

The Cocoanut Grove fire on November 28, 1942, at a popular Boston bistro was the deadliest nightclub fire in the nation's history. The 15-minute inferno in the overcrowded former speakeasy at 17 Piedmont Street in Bay Village just off Park Square killed 492 people. Many victims were soldiers and sailors or football fans celebrating the unexpected loss of the formerly undefeated Boston College to the Holy Cross team at Fenway Park that afternoon. As an army and navy mobilization port, Boston was filled with World War II soldiers and sailors in transit or on leave.

The fire started in the Melody Lounge, located in the basement of the Cocoanut Grove, at about 10:15

FACTBOX

PLACE Boston, Massachusetts

DATE November 28, 1942

TYPE Fire

DESCRIPTION Fire raged through a downtown nightclub.

CAUSE Ignition of flammable interior decorations by an unknown source

CASUALTIES 492 deaths

COST $8 million in personal claims, unpaid, and $22,420 paid for property losses

IMPACT Many cities and states revised or more strictly enforced fire and safety codes, and plastic surgery became more widespread as treatment for burn victims.

P.M. when flammable interior decorations, faux Polynesian palm trees, and a satin ceiling, burst into flames, perhaps sparked by a small electric light or when an employee lit a match while screwing in a bulb. As fire engulfed the entire building, the panicking patrons rushed up the stairs when a fireball of flames, searing heat, and toxic smoke overcame them. Charred bodies blocked the only public exit on the ground floor. Some escaped through the kitchen door, but in minutes, the basement lounge was totally dark and choked with dead or dying bodies. More patrons were trampled in the bedlam or died in their seats from asphyxiation in the upstairs restaurant. Although the fire department arrived by 10:20 P.M., firefighters were forced to crawl over 200 bodies in the doorway to enter the one-and-a-half-story brick building. Fifty military men and 20 employees were among the victims, who included the cowboy movie star Charles "Buck" Jones. The nightclub's revolving doors, inadequate or locked building exits, highly flammable gas in the refrigeration system, and the cramped quarters that were packed with patrons (1,000 people, more than twice the club's licensed capacity of 460) were factors contributing to this tragedy.

Ambulances, taxis, and newspaper trucks transported the victims to Boston hospitals. The nearby Statler and Bradford Hotels supplied blankets and rooms. Hundreds of men and women rushed from local theaters, bars, and restaurants to assist 185 firefighters summoned from the Boston Fire Department's 26 engine, five ladder, and three rescue companies. For 10 days newspapers reported the names of the dead and injured. It took four days to identify all the bodies.

Hundreds of horribly burned victims treated at the Massachusetts General Hospital benefited from new plastic surgery techniques developed by Dr. Branford Cannon (1907–2005), a pioneer in burn treatment and reconstructive surgery. These innovative methods shaped medical treatment across the world and promoted plastic surgery as an established specialty.

Four hundred lawsuits were filed for $8 million, but the club had little insurance, and most survivors or their families received only about $160. Prosecutors indicted 11 men in the aftermath of the tragedy but only convicted the nightclub's owner, Barnett Welansky. Found guilty of 19 counts of involuntary manslaughter and sentenced to 12 to 15 years in prison, Welansky served four years until Governor Maurice Tobin pardoned him. He died two months later. The official investigation determined no single cause for the fire but blamed the massive death toll on gross violations of safety principles. On the day before the fire broke out, a fire department inspection had rated the building as satisfactory. The Cocoanut Grove disaster prompted many American cities and states to revise (or simply enforce) their building and fire codes to require conventional doors alongside revolving doors, emergency lights, nonflammable interior decorations, lighted exit signs, and outward opening doors. A memorial brass plaque embedded in the Piedmont Street sidewalk near the site in 1993 recalls the tragedy that still burns in the imagination of Bostonians.

See also 1903 IROQUOIS THEATER FIRE; 1944 HARTFORD CIRCUS FIRE.

Peter C. Holloran

FURTHER READING:

Benzaquin, Paul. *Fire in Boston's Cocoanut Grove: Holocaust!* Boston: Branden Press, 1967.

Esposito, John C. *Fire in the Grove: The Cocoanut Grove Tragedy and Its Aftermath.* Cambridge, Mass.: Da Capo Press, 2005.

Keyes, Edward. *Cocoanut Grove.* New York: Atheneum, 1984.

Schorow, Stephanie, and Robert J. Allison, eds. *The Cocoanut Grove Fire.* Beverly, Mass.: Commonwealth Editions, 2005.

1943 ◆ LOS ANGELES SMOG CLOUD

On July 9, 1943, thousands of people in downtown Los Angeles, California, were so bothered by burning, stinging eyes that they telephoned the police department to ask if aircraft plants were carrying out smokescreen tests, a frequent occurrence during World War II. The director of war activities of the police department reported that no smoke tests were being conducted. The mysterious airborne irritants quickly dissipated, but less than three weeks later, the city experienced an even worse event. On July 26, 1943, an oppressive brown cloud formed over downtown Los Angeles. It lasted about four hours, so thick that it limited visibility to three blocks and caused a variety of health problems affecting many thousands in the city. Most complained only of eye irritation, but some experienced respiratory difficulties, coughing, sneezing, and vomiting. Initial blame was placed on a plant of the Southern California Gas Company, which was manufacturing butadiene, a substance vital to wartime synthetic-rubber production. Although the plant (which was subsequently closed) spent $1.5 million on an emission clean-up program, instances of smog, termed *gas attacks*, continued. That same year, Los Angeles created the Smoke and Fire Commission to study the problem, and in 1945, the city issued the nation's first air-quality regulation, banning the burning of trash in suburban backyards.

In 1947, pollution control districts were created throughout California. Los Angeles, nestled in a natural basin of some 1,630 square miles, experiences inversion when a layer of air warmed by strong sunshine traps the cooler air below and thus prevents it from moving. In 1950, studies by Caltech biochemistry professor Arie Jan Haagen-Smit showed that the smoke eliminated from that trapped layer in 1945 had been replaced by even more toxic pollutants generated by the "car culture" that quickly came to dominate the greater Los Angeles area after World War II. Haagen-Smit's findings did not immediately lead to strict auto-emission standards, however. Auto manufacturers long resisted scientists' claims that their products were the primary culprits. Citizens in other parts of the country assumed that because they did not share Los Angeles's geographical configura-

FACTBOX	
PLACE Los Angeles	
DATE July 26, 1943	
TYPE Air pollution episode	
DESCRIPTION A thick cloud of smog formed over downtown Los Angeles, limiting visibility and causing health problems.	
CAUSE Auto exhaust and other pollutants trapped by upper layer of warm air	
CASUALTIES Thousands of people experienced eye irritation, respiratory difficulties, and other acute health problems.	
COST The Southern California Gas Company plant, initially blamed for the incident, spent $1.5 million in clean-up costs.	
IMPACT What was assumed to be a one-time, isolated event led to investigations revealing the pervasive problem of air pollution created largely by the emissions of an ever-growing number of cars.	

tion nor its vast car population, they were immune to problems of *smog*—a word that originally meant a combination of smoke and fog but soon became an all-purpose term to describe air pollution visible to the human eye.

Although Los Angeles's natural basin makes the region especially susceptible to smog, scores of other cities began to experience their own air pollution problems. In 1955, the federal Air Pollution Control Act created the first emission standards for new automobiles. It was augmented by the 1963 Clean Air Act. Catalytic converters and other mandatory smog control devices and practices helped to manage but not eliminate the growing pollution problems caused by cars throughout the nation. Even as the average car on American roads emitted fewer pollutants by 1970, the number of vehicles and the number of miles traveled each day continued to grow (from 80 million cars traveling close to 1 trillion miles in

1970, to 128 million cars traveling 2.3 trillion miles in 2000), deepening the continuing pollution crisis.

Rather than developing extensive environmentally friendly subway or light-rail systems, Los Angeles remains heavily dependent on private cars for transportation. This lifestyle, combined with its geography, allows Los Angeles to retain its title as the smog capital of the United States. Visible pollutants are continually being reduced in Los Angeles and elsewhere, but clear air is not always clean air. In the United States, which owns roughly one quarter of the world's cars, the unabated growth of cities, suburbs, roads, freeways, and industries nationwide continues to create new sources and new varieties of air pollution.

On local "Save the Air" Days throughout the country, measurable hazardous air pollutants register so high that the elderly and residents with respiratory problems are urged to stay indoors, and all community members are asked not to barbeque, burn wood in fireplaces, use gas-powered machinery including lawnmowers or leaf blowers, and to keep automobile use to a minimum. As intense and frightening as it was, the 1943 Los Angeles smog event proved to be not a unique, isolated occurrence but rather the first

warning sign of a serious, long-term, and widespread condition.

See also 1948 DONORA SMOG TRAGEDY.

Nancy C. Unger

FURTHER READING:

Allaby, Michael. *Fog, Smog, and Poisoned Rain.* New York: Facts On File, 2003.

Carlin, Alan P., and George E. Kocher. *Environmental Problems: Their Causes, Cures, and Evolution, Using Southern California Smog as an Example.* Santa Monica, Calif.: Rand, 1971.

Davis, Devra. *When Smoke Ran like Water: Tales of Environmental Deception and the Battle against Pollution.* Cambridge, Mass.: MIT Press (Basic Books), 2003.

Lees, Lester. *Smog: A Report to the People.* Pasadena, Calif.: California Institute of Technology, Environmental Quality Laboratory, 1972.

Pennsylvania Department of Environmental Protection. "Donora Smog Kills 20: October, 1948." Fiftieth anniversary commemoration. Available online. URL: http://www.dep.state.pa.us/dep/Rachel_Carson/donora.htm. Accessed April 10, 2007.

1944 ◆ HARTFORD CIRCUS FIRE

On July 6, 1944, the Barbour Street fairgrounds in Hartford, Connecticut, hosted the Ringling Bros. and Barnum & Bailey Circus. Mothers and grandparents brought their young ones for a day of joy and wonderment and to forget about the war overseas. By 2:35 P.M., the day turned into horror and death as fire broke out inside the big-top tent. The ensuing inferno killed 168 people and injured 484. Five bodies still lie unknown and unclaimed in Hartford. The Hartford Circus Fire of 1944 would prove to be one of America's largest tragedies under the big top.

More than 9,000 spectators crowded onto the Barbour Street grounds throughout the early afternoon of July 6. The day was hot and humid. Kids ate hot dogs and cotton candy while mothers purchased tickets for sideshows and rides. Show-goers piled into the tent while the Wonder Band played "The Star Spangled Banner." The animal acts were the first to show, followed by the aerialist troupe, the Flying Wallendas. Animal chutes were extended onto the floor through two exit points. As the animals left the show and the Wallendas were preparing their act 30 feet above the crowd, the call of "Fire!" was shouted.

According to initial reports, the first few minutes after the fire started, there was "little confusion." But cries became more numerous as a football-sized ball of fire rose from the west end of the tent, moving over to the northeast corner. Soon the "entire top became a mass of flames." Burning bits of canvas snowed and liquid paraffin rained onto the panicked crowd, inflicting severe burns onto whomever they struck. The bandleader ordered "Stars and Stripes Forever," the traditional song used in the circus world to warn the performers and circus employees that something was amiss. When the top became fully engulfed in flames, the band proceeded to march calmly from the tent with the hope of encouraging the crowd to do the same. But people became frightened and raced for the exits. Hundreds climbed around parked circus wagons, stumbled over the extended animal chutes, and became stuck in the metal chairs over which they were trying to climb. Parents tossed their children into the open arms of strangers at the bottom of the grandstands. Some of these parents and children left the black smoke unscarred and unscathed. Others were trampled and burned amid the pandemonium.

Sirens screamed at the five alarms triggered, and firetrucks raced to the scene but not in time to rescue many of the people trapped inside: Within 10 minutes of the start of the fire, 125 of the 168 fatalities occurred inside the tent. "Heroes and villains" became apparent in the minutes, hours, days, and weeks following the fire. Some threw chairs at others to remove people from their escape route. Some jumped from the tops of bleachers into a sea of people not knowing if their fall crushed someone or not. Emmett Kelly, one of the clowns, rallied performers to get pails of water and to help whomever they could. Some grabbed lonely,

scared, and crying children and stayed with them until they could be reunited with a loved one.

The aftermath of the fire would prove dismaying. Bodies piled up at the Connecticut State Armory while families filed through, lifting white sheets and attempting to identify charred remains. State and city investigators followed leads about the causes of the fire that ranged from a tossed cigarette, a motor that was running near the tent without oil, and even arson. The likely cause was determined to be a cigarette tossed onto dry grasses by the edge of the tent. The grasses caught fire, and the fire spread to the tent wall. The top of the tent was waterproofed in gasoline-diluted paraffin, the likely cause of the immediate engulfing of the tent. The state investigation listed eight causes of the fire as well as citations to Ringling Bros. for the following: failure to flame-proof, location of animal chutes, insufficiency of personnel, failure to maintain an organization to fight the fire, lack of firefighting equipment, failure to adequately distribute firefighting equipment, absence of supervision, and the location of supply wagons. Five circus employees were charged with manslaughter. Legal claims against Ringling Bros. and Barnum & Bailey totaled $3,916,805.

The story captured the attention of America in 1944, ranking 10th among all stories, according to the Associated Press and the only one not related to the war. The City of Hartford enacted 17 corrective measures for large events, including adequate exit routes, improved signage, better fireproofing and positioning of extinguishing materials, a ban on gasoline-diluted paraffin as a waterproofing material, and prohibition of smoking. Municipalities across the country also enacted improved fire-safety measures, including higher standards for fireproofing tent materials. More than 60 years later, a circus fire support group still exists and meets annually to discuss their memories and how they still cope with the tragedy. The support only extends so far when some discuss the smell of the burning flesh, the touch of a disintegrating body, or the memory of watching the big top flare during what was supposed to be a respite from the world in 1944.

See also 1903 Iroquois Theater fire; 1942 Cocoanut Grove fire.

Julie Arrison

FURTHER READING:

O'Nan, Stewart. *The Circus Fire: A True Story of an American Tragedy.* New York: Anchor Books, 2000.

1945 ◆ AIRPLANE CRASH INTO THE EMPIRE STATE BUILDING

In the summer of 1945, an unusual series of events caused one of the most bizarre air accidents in U.S. history. On the morning of July 28, a two-engine B-25 Army Air Force bomber flying over New York City crashed into the 79th floor of the 102-story Empire State Building, the world's tallest skyscraper at the time. Fourteen people were killed including the pilot and two others aboard, and 25 were seriously hurt in the disaster. The Empire State Building was considered one of the "wonders of the world" when completed in May 1931. Located in midtown Manhattan on Fifth Avenue between 33rd and 34th Streets and rising 1,250 feet, almost a quarter of a mile, the Empire State Building was one of the country's major tourist attractions, drawing 2 million visitors a year to its observation deck. Nearby were two other skyscrapers, the Chrysler and RCA buildings.

The pilot on this unfortunate flight was Air Force Lieutenant Colonel William F. Smith, Jr., a West Point graduate and a highly decorated World War II combat veteran bomber pilot in the European theater. Smith was, however, relatively new to the B-25, having first flown the plane just two days earlier. This aircraft model was a well-tested veteran of the war. Its most famous mission was the bombing raid over Tokyo, commanded by Jimmy Dolittle in April 1942, a symbolic retaliation for the Japanese attack on Pearl Harbor the year before. B-25s weighed 21,000 pounds and could fly at about 225 miles per hour.

On Thursday, July 26, Smith had flown from Sioux Falls, South Dakota, to Newark, New Jersey, by way of Cleveland under supervision of his commanding officer. He then flew solo to Bedford, Massachusetts, to spend two nights with his wife prior to his return to Sioux Falls. On Saturday morning, July 28, Smith set out from Bedford for Newark to pick up his crew and return to Sioux Falls. He left Bedford at 8:55 A.M. with a crew member and a passenger. Since the weather was poor, with a low "ceiling," or cloud cover, he was refused clearance to Newark Airport and instead was directed to fly at a minimum altitude of 4,000 feet to LaGuardia Airport in Queens, a borough of New York City across the East River from Manhattan. Smith contacted the LaGuardia tower at about 9:40 A.M., again request-

FACTBOX

PLACE 79th floor of the Empire State Building, in New York City

DATE July 28, 1945

TYPE Plane crash

DESCRIPTION In thick clouds, a B-25 bomber struck the Empire State Building.

CAUSE Pilot error and poor weather

CASUALTIES 11 office workers and three crew members killed, and 25 others seriously injured

IMPACT The accident demonstrated the hazard of allowing aircraft to fly over cities with tall buildings. Three months later, the Civil Aeronautics Administration set a minimum altitude of 2,500 feet in midtown and lower Manhattan.

ing clearance to Newark. Confusion now occurred, as an argument ensued between the tower controllers, army personnel, and the pilot. Smith was given permission to proceed at an altitude of 1,500 feet with the proviso that if he could not see the top of the Empire State Building, he would change course and proceed to LaGuardia.

The controllers' instructions called for a return across the East River to LaGuardia. The "ceiling" on Saturday morning was approximately 600 feet, with clouds enshrouding New York's skyscrapers. Shortly after 9:40 A.M., the B-25 crashed into the Empire State Building at a height of 913 feet above the ground. The aircraft opened an 18-by-20-foot hole on the 34th Street side of the skyscraper, which was quickly enveloped in smoke. But the structure remained intact—the aircraft carried no bombs, and there were no secondary explosions. Since the crash happened on a Saturday, there were only about 1,500 people in the building. Had the accident occurred on a weekday the structure might have contained 10,000 to 15,000 people.

On impact, the airplane fuel ignited, producing flames from the 65th to the 86th floors. The plane's

Looking down from a ledge on the 81st floor, a photographer took this picture of the Empire State Building just after a B-25 airplane crashed into it. *(Associated Press)*

The elevator plunged hundreds of feet down into a subbasement, and miraculously, the two women survived. One large part of the debris landed as far away as 5th Avenue and 29th Street. Most of the victims of the crash were workers at the War Relief Services of the National Catholic Welfare Conference (now Catholic Relief Services) on the 79th floor. Some of the 11 office workers killed in the mishap died on impact or in the subsequent fire, while others died in hospitals in the next three days. In spite of the death and damage, the Empire State Building was able to reopen for business on Monday morning.

Individuals familiar with aircraft traffic believed that there should have been strict limits in the altitude rules for flights over urban areas. New York mayor Fiorello LaGuardia, a World War I pilot, objected to military flights over the city. New York's fire commissioner urged a total ban on all air travel over congested areas of the city. Three months after the B-25 crash, the Civil Aeronautics Administration set 2,500 feet as the minimum altitude for flying over midtown or lower Manhattan. Yet aircraft continued to smash into New York skyscrapers. In May 1946, a two-engine military C-45 crashed into the 58th floor of a building on Wall Street, killing the pilot and four others, and in October 2006, a plane piloted by New York Yankee pitcher Cory Lidle crashed into a 40-story residential building on 72nd Street near the East River.

Alex Wilson

wings were sheared off; one engine and part of the fuselage went through the building, exiting at the south wall, and fell on top of a penthouse on West 33rd Street. The other engine fell into an elevator shaft and onto an elevator with two women inside.

FURTHER READING:

Tauranac, John. *The Empire State Building.* New York: Scribner, 1995.

1945 ◆ ATOMIC BOMBS DROPPED ON JAPAN

On August 6, 1945, an American B-29 Superfortress bomber nicknamed *Enola Gay* took off from Tinian Island for the six-and-a-half-hour flight to Hiroshima, Japan's eighth largest city. At a little after eight in the morning, a 10,000-pound atomic bomb equivalent to 20,000 tons of TNT detonated 2,000 feet above the city. The explosion sent a mushroom-shaped cloud 40,000 feet into the atmosphere and destroyed virtually everything within a mile and a half of ground zero. The initial blast killed 80,000 people; as many perished later from wounds and radiation. Hearing nothing from the enemy, the United States launched a second nuclear attack on August 9 against the city of Nagasaki that killed at least 55,000. With Japan in a hopeless position, Emperor Hirohito intervened and instructed his government to accept surrender. On August 15, he broadcast the decision to his subjects, most of whom had never before heard his voice. The detonation of the most powerful weapon the world had ever seen had its intended effect. Japan formally surrendered on September 2, 1945, ending World War II. Ironically but perhaps not surprisingly in view of the enormity of the event, the decision to drop the atomic bombs remains controversial.

The atomic bomb emerged from a herculean effort code-name the Manhattan Project. Its origins traced to a committee of scientists, mainly European refugees including Albert Einstein, who had persuaded President Franklin D. Roosevelt in October 1939 to investigate the possibility of turning a nuclear chain reaction into a superweapon. The project advanced further when the Office of Scientific Research and Development, assigned to study the feasibility of atomic weaponry, recommended the development of a bomb. In January 1942, a month after the Japanese ATTACK ON PEARL HARBOR plunged the United States into World War II against Japan and Germany, Roosevelt agreed, placing the project under control of the War Department. At a cost of more than $2 billion, the Manhattan Project put 150,000 employees to work at facilities in Hanson, Washington, and Oak Ridge, Tennessee, making fissionable materials, and at Los Alamos, New Mexico, where the bomb was designed.

President Roosevelt died on April 12, 1945, elevating Harry Truman to the presidency. Despite 10 years in the Senate and three months as vice president, Truman knew nothing about the top-secret Manhattan Project. As scientists neared completion of the atomic bomb, Germany surrendered in May 1945, but the war with Japan continued. Two months later, at the Potsdam Conference in Germany, Truman tried to persuade Soviet premier Joseph Stalin to enter the war against Japan. While at the conference, Truman received a telegram indicating that the first test of the atomic bomb in Alamogordo, New Mexico, had proceeded successfully. Emboldened by the news, he warned Japan on July 26 that it must surrender immediately or face "prompt and utter destruction." Japan refused. By early August 1945, the United States had built two more bombs.

Truman did not hesitate in approving the use of the superbomb. "There was never any doubt that the bomb would be used," he later recorded in his *Memoirs*. "When you deal with a beast you have to treat him as a beast." The president's decision resulted in part from his deference to his military advisers on tactics. Despite reluctance to attack civilian populations, most military leaders favored the deployment of the bomb. Their primary concern was ending the war as quickly as possible and sparing the lives of U.S. servicemen. American forces had suffered a 35 percent casualty rate in subduing the Japanese on Okinawa between April and June 1945. Military planners anticipated that fighting on the mainland would be every bit as bloody, perhaps costing a half-million lives. This prediction was based in part on the belief that the Japanese would fight fervently to the death.

The United States's demand of unconditional surrender made Japanese leaders even more intransigent, as they feared that American terms meant the removal of the emperor. Ethical questions were pushed to the background, if entertained at all. The memory of Pearl Harbor and the cruelty of the Japanese toward American prisoners, especially in the Philippines, weighed on their minds as well. As one air force planner put these sentiments, the United States was at war "with a fanatic enemy whose record of brutality was notorious." Three-quarters of the American public approved of the decision to use the bomb. Memory of Japan's "sneak" attack on Pearl Harbor remained passionate in the United States.

Over the decades since August 1945, scholars and citizens have debated Truman's decision, one of the

FACTBOX

PLACE Hiroshima and Nagasaki, Japan

DATE August 6 and August 9, 1945

TYPE Use of atomic weapons

DESCRIPTION The United States dropped two atomic bombs on Japan.

CAUSE The proximate cause was the hope of avoiding a projected U.S. land invasion of the Japanese mainland during World War II.

CASUALTIES An estimated 215,000 people killed

IMPACT Led to the surrender of Japan and the inauguration of the age of nuclear weapons

most momentous and fateful actions any president has ever made. Some have argued that the use of nuclear weapons against Japan constituted a war crime. Others have argued that the use of the atomic bombs was justified because it saved far more lives than it took. Any assessment of Truman's approval of the nuclear attack should balance its moral implications with the historical context in which the decision was made. World War II had turned the world into a vast killing field. An estimated 50 million people died prematurely during the conflict, over half of them noncombatants. Allied planes subjected civilians in German cities to saturation bombing. The U.S. Air Force firebombed virtually every major Japanese city prior to August 6, 1945, with women representing 60 percent of the casualties. The Holocaust perpetrated by the Nazis killed 6 million Jews, and German soldiers murdered millions of Slavs, gypsies, communists, and anti-German partisans. Poland lost one-fifth of its population. Truman reached his decision in a society that had become dulled to the statistics of mass slaughter, yet retained hatred for a purportedly cruel enemy. Right or wrong, the United States fatefully had entered the atomic age.

Ballard C. Campbell

FURTHER READING:

Frank, Richard B. *Downfall: The End of the Imperial Japanese Empire.* New York: Penguin, 2001.

A mushroom cloud rises over Nagasaki on August 9, 1945, following the U.S. detonation of the second atomic bomb dropped on Japan. *(Library of Congress)*

Rhodes, Richard, *The Making of the Atomic Bomb.* New York: Simon and Schuster, 1986.

Walker, J. Samuel. *Prompt and Utter Destruction: Truman and the Use of Atomic Bombs against Japan.* Chapel Hill: University of North Carolina Press, 1997.

1947 ◆ *GRANDCAMP* EXPLOSION

On April 16, 1947, perhaps the greatest industrial disaster in U.S. history was about to unfold. Early that morning, several bags of ammonium nitrate, part of a large shipment being loaded aboard the *Grandcamp,* a French-owned, American-built Liberty ship docked near Houston in Texas City, Texas, began to smolder in one of the boat's cargo holds. At 9:12 A.M., the *Grandcamp* exploded. The force of the explosion was so great that it registered on a seismograph in Denver, Colorado, 900 miles to the northwest. Texas City's entire waterfront area, the docks, and the adjacent, crowded

Mexican and black enclaves of El Barrio and a part of town known as The Bottom were obliterated. So were a number of oil refineries, storage tanks, and petrochemical plants, including the large Monsanto facility. When the last unrecognizable human body was recovered a month after the blast, the mortality was estimated at 405 identified and 63 unidentified dead. Part of the total number of fatalities of 581 were 113 others who had simply disappeared, and were listed as "believed missing."

When people picked up newspapers the next day, headlines trumpeted the devastation. Wirephotos of

FACTBOX

PLACE Texas City, Texas

DATE April 16, 1947

TYPE Ship explosion

DESCRIPTION While docked near Houston, the Liberty ship *Grandcamp* exploded, destroying the entire waterfront area and surrounding neighborhood.

CAUSE Spontaneous combustion of ammonium nitrate

CASUALTIES 581 fatalities

COST Congress voted awards averaging more than $12,000 to 1,395 claimants.

IMPACT The federal government eventually mandated stronger Coast Guard supervision of dangerous cargo.

thick, black smoke rising above the devastated waterfront gave shocking evidence of the scale of the catastrophe. The force of the blast had hurled the ship's massive 3,000-pound anchor two miles. Huge balls of Mexican sisal—hundreds of them—were transformed instantly from organic plants to deadly meteorites, soaring into the sky. How could a vessel of the *Grandcamp*'s size become a bomb so powerful in the blink of an eye?

The catastrophe happened as the result of a tragic interplay of factors that ultimately and fatally fused on an April morning in this gritty Texas port. It happened because gigantic corporations, such as Humble Oil, Amoco, Monsanto, Union Carbide, and the Santa Fe Railway, among others, wielded irresistible economic leverage and "ran" Texas City their way. The companies used their economic power to exert strong influence in shaping governmental policies, emphasizing their business interests over safety. It also happened because an artificial compound, ammonium nitrate, had been created in 1917 by a German scientist as a potent fertilizer that seemed to give promise of averting, or at least forestalling, widespread starvation. But this same compound is also highly explosive. The chemical had proved indispensable to Allied victory in World War II. Now it was slated to increase crop yields in war-torn

western Europe and thereby enhance the Truman administration's determination to bolster the West's resistance to Soviet influence.

Two more critical causative factors were present. The massive explosion happened because desperately poor longshoremen, who eked out a hardscrabble existence by picking up two or three days of work each week on the docks, had their eyes on a modest paycheck. They dismissed the potential hazards of a cargo such as the ammonium nitrate, which could turn the *Grandcamp* into a floating time-bomb. And finally, the disaster happened because the U.S. Coast Guard, mandated by federal law with regulating vessel movement and the types of cargo loaded, offloaded, or stowed aboard each vessel, was lax in its oversight of hazardous materials. In a deposition later given in connection with a class-action lawsuit against the owners of the *Grandcamp,* brought by Elizabeth Dalehite, whose husband, the Texas City fire chief, was killed in the explosion, and by other plaintiffs, the rear admiral heading the Coast Guard's Office of Merchant Marine Safety said in 1954 that the Coast Guard lacked funds for the inspection of dangerous cargo. Moreover, he stated that the Guard relied on owners or operators to police themselves, as far as compliance was concerned. The Coast Guard also asserted that it did not regularly inspect operations involving dangerous cargo and would do so only when violations were brought to its attention. By the 1960s, new provisions in the Code of Federal Regulations mandated strict Coast Guard supervision in this critical area.

Sixteen hours after the detonation onboard the *Grandcamp,* a second Liberty ship, the *High Flyer,* also laden with ammonium nitrate, exploded. The *High Flyer* had been towed across the channel, away from the doomed *Grandcamp* and away from concentrations of people. Only two additional lives were lost in the second explosion. Within 36 hours of the initial explosion, massive aid began to arrive. Thousands of soldiers from nearby Fort Hood combed the debris for survivors, cleared away the rubble, and patrolled the streets to prevent looting. Hundreds of units of whole blood and plasma were flown in, along with tents, blankets, and other emergency items. With the return of some semblance of civic order, the soldiers were replaced by Salvation Army, Volunteers of America, and Red Cross workers, who undertook longer-term rehabilitative efforts.

Four thousand insurance claims were filed, nearly all of which were settled within three months. The average insurance payment was about $1,000. Hearings held by a Special Subcommittee on the Judiciary of the U.S. House of Representatives in November 1953—six years after the explosion—appeared to many as little more than a whitewash. The Coast Guard, which attempted to shift responsibility for the disaster to the captain and the crew of the *Grandcamp,* was absolved of negligence. The captain and most of the crew died in the cataclysmic explosion, and thus were unable to testify on their own behalf. It was not surprising, therefore, that the U.S. Supreme Court found against Elizabeth Dalehite and the rest of the plaintiffs in a suit filed against the federal government that charged the Coast Guard with negligence. Two years later, however, President Eisenhower yielded to pressure from Lyndon Johnson, Senate majority leader and a Texan, and signed a compensation bill. Elizabeth Dalehite and 1,394 other claimants would now be eligible to receive checks averaging a little more than $12,000.

Of all the horrific experiences seared forever into the minds of those who survived the *Grandcamp* explosion, perhaps none was more terrible than that of one young boy. Seconds after the ship blew up, the boy grabbed the hand of a nearby woman, and the pair began to run away from the hell of the shattered waterfront. As they fled inland, the boy noticed that the woman had begun to wobble, so he glanced anxiously up at her. The woman had been decapitated.

See also 1937 New London school explosion.

John M. O'Toole

FURTHER READING:

Minutaglio, Bill. *City on Fire.* New York: HarperCollins, 2003.

Stephens, Hugh W. *The Texas City Disaster, 1947.* Austin: University of Texas Press, 1997.

U.S. Congress. House of Representatives. Special Subcommittee of the Committee on the Judiciary. *Texas City Disaster Hearings.* 83rd Cong., November 16–18, 1953. Washington, D.C.: U.S. Government Printing Office, 1954.

1948 ◆ DONORA SMOG TRAGEDY

A few days before Halloween 1948, the town of Donora, Pennsylvania, and nearby communities were blanketed in a dense and choking smog that led to the deaths of 20 people and sickened nearly 6,000 others. National media coverage of the tragedy and a yearlong investigation by the U.S. Public Health Service elevated the issue of air pollution from a nuisance to a public-health threat. Donora joined places such as Los Angeles as emblems of a national crisis in air pollution and served as a rallying cry for greater federal involvement, eventually leading to the passage of the first national legislation explicitly aimed at air pollution.

By the late 1940s, air pollution was a familiar problem for urban and industrial areas throughout the country. Despite the ubiquity of the problem, pollution control remained the responsibility of state and local governments. Moreover, air pollution was treated largely as a nuisance rather than as a serious threat to public health. For the tiny industrial town of Donora, 30 miles south of Pittsburgh, smoke and smog were a daily reality. Situated along the Monongahela River, Donora was host to zinc and steel processing plants. Although the plants had been a regular source of odors, smoke, and other noxious air emissions since their establishment in 1915, these industries constituted the major employment for the town. The narrow river valley was also an important route for ships and trains, as well as cars and trucks, resulting in nearly constant heavy traffic. Air pollution was a regular presence, but contaminant-laden fogs, or smogs, were particularly common in the fall.

During the last week of October 1948, an unusually dense and suffocating smog descended on Donora. On Tuesday, October 26, the usual morning pall refused to dissipate. During the next two days, it thickened considerably. By Thursday, traffic on and along the Monongahela River was para-

FACTBOX

PLACE Donora, Pennsylvania

DATE October 1948

TYPE Air pollution episode

DESCRIPTION An intense episode of smog lasting several days in the industrial town of Donora, Pennsylvania, led to widespread illness and deaths.

CAUSE Heavy air pollution combined with unusually stagnant atmospheric conditions led to a toxic concentration of air pollution in the Monongahela valley.

CASUALTIES 20 deaths and 6,000 sickened

IMPACT Donora firmly established air pollution as a threat to public health, not just a nuisance; motivated increased federal support for research on air pollution; and contributed to passage of the first federal legislation on air pollution, the 1955 Air Pollution Control Act.

lyzed. Stranded motorists scrambled to find places to stay. By Friday morning, visibility beyond 100 feet was nearly impossible and was even poor at 30 feet. More ominously, local hospitals were inundated by people complaining of cramping, headaches, and breathing problems. Pharmacists dispensed all manner of prescription and over-the-counter remedies—hypodermics of adrenalin, Benadryl, and morphine. Local volunteer firefighters were dispatched on emergency calls with canisters of oxygen to aid those who could not breathe, though they found it nearly impossible to navigate through the thick, bluish haze that had enveloped the town. The event was not the same for everyone, however. The annual Donora Halloween parade took place as usual, although on-lookers found it difficult to see the children passing before them. The annual football game between Monongahela and Donora High Schools continued, though players ran the ball because they could not see it when it was in the air. By Saturday morning, more than a dozen people had died, and local funeral homes were overwhelmed. On Sunday, October 31, the smog finally dissipated under a light rain, leaving as silently as it had arrived.

News of Donora's deadly smog captured national attention. In response to repeated requests, the U.S.

Public Health Service (PHS) launched the most intensive and exhaustive study on air pollution the nation had ever seen. After a yearlong investigation, the PHS released a report on the Donora smog in October 1949. The final tally of deaths and illnesses from the smog far exceeded initial estimates. Surveys revealed that those most affected were elderly, with preexisting cardiorespiratory problems. Investigators concluded that the smog likely consisted of water droplets, sulfur dioxide, and other atmospheric pollutants. The pollutants reached deadly concentrations when the smog became trapped within the narrow valley due to an atmospheric temperature inversion. A layer of warm air developed above the cooler air near the surface, creating a lid over the valley that prevented the air near the ground—and the pollutants in it—from diluting or dispersing as normally happened. The report recommended that local industries reduce their emissions and that a weather monitoring system be put in place to anticipate similar atmospheric conditions in the future. The report failed to satisfy critics who sought to place blame on the steel and zinc works, but the PHS study succeeded in establishing air pollution as a serious threat to public health.

As momentum gathered for a national response to air pollution, Donora came to symbolize the threat of environmental disaster and the need for action. In May 1950, President Harry Truman convened the first national air pollution conference, citing Donora as an example of the need. Five years later, Congress passed the 1955 Federal Air Pollution Control Act, the first national legislation to explicitly address air pollution. This air pollution legislation was strengthened in subsequent years, and the name *Donora* repeatedly served as a shorthand warning of the costs of inaction.

See also 1943 Los Angeles smog cloud.

Marcos Luna

FURTHER READING:

Davies, J. Clarence, and Barbara S. Davies. *The Politics of Pollution.* 2nd ed. Indianapolis: Bobbs-Merrill Company, 1975.

Kiester, Edwin, Jr. "A Darkness in Donora." *Smithsonian Magazine* (November 1999).

Snyder, Lynne Page. *"The Death-Dealing Smog over Donora, Pennsylvania": Industrial Air Pollution, Public Health, and Federal Policy, 1915–1963.* Unpublished Ph.D. diss., University of Pennsylvania, 1994.

1950 ◆ RETREAT FROM THE YALU

The retreat of U.S. armed forces from their penetration close to the Yalu River in 1950 during the Korean War represented a disastrous defeat for an army that had recently emerged victorious from World War II (1939–45). Despite its incredible brutality, no single combat action of World War II matched the intense casualty rate incurred during the withdrawal from the Yalu, which separated North Korea from China. This setback had a major impact on American military strategy during the remainder of the Korean War (1950–53) and on how Americans viewed the conflict.

On June 25, 1950, the North Korean People's Army (NKPA) stormed across the 38th parallel, the line that divided the Republic of Korea (ROK) in the south from the Democratic People's Republic of Korea in the north. North Korea's immediate objective was Seoul, the capital of the republic and its largest city, which the ROK army was unable to hold. The fall of Seoul made it apparent to American strategists that entry of a U.S. army would be necessary to prevent North Korea from overrunning the entire peninsula. Intensifying concerns, American leaders feared that North Korea's invasion was part of a broader Communist expansion in Asia. President Harry Truman saw the Korean conflict as a direct challenge to his policy of containing Communist advances everywhere in the world. The UN Security Council facilitated American strategy by resolving to defend the Republic of Korea, on June 27th.

U.S. troops (making up 90 percent of the United Nation's soldiers) were unable to halt the NKPA advance deep into South Korea until August, when a front was stabilized in the southeastern corner of the Korean peninsula. On September 15 General Douglas MacArthur, American commander in the Far East, launched a risky but successful amphibious landing at Inchon, thus establishing a beachhead for the recapture of Seoul. Simultaneously, U.S. forces initiated an offensive from their enclave in southeastern Korea. NKPA forces were caught between allied forces advancing from the south and eastward from Seoul. But American strategists misread their success as having neutralized the NKPA capacity to fight. They decided to pursue their foe as they fled northward, back over the 38th parallel.

Truman, the U.S. Joint Chiefs of Staff (JCS), and MacArthur agreed on the plan to pursue the enemy into their own territory. On October 1, ROK troops crossed the 38th parallel and headed north, followed by the Americans several days later. On October 15, MacArthur met with Truman on Wake Island, where they confirmed their strategy. By October 19, the allies occupied Pyongyang, North Korea's capital, and a week later ROK forces advanced close to the Yalu River. As U.S. forces worked their way north toward the border with China, American commanders assumed that the Chinese army would not enter the conflict. And if they did, the Americans believed that air power could handle the incursion. They grievously miscalculated.

ROK forces engaged the Chinese army 40 miles from the Yalu on October 25. Four days later, Chinese forces halted the American X Corps advance. U.S. intelligence had estimated that only 34,000 Chinese troops had crossed the Yalu. In fact, 300,000 Chinese had filtered into North Korea, facing approximately 250,000 U.S. and UN troops. Late in November, MacArthur launched a "final offensive" that ran into uncompromising Chinese resistance. By early

December, American forces began to pull back, evacuating ports on the east coast taken on its drive northward. Major engagements fought at the Chosin Reservoir and along the Chongchon River inflicted heavy casualties on the Americans and South Korean forces, who battled not only "human waves" of Chinese attackers but snow and intense cold. Unit casualty rates above 50 percent were common. Following the death of Eighth Army commander General Walton Walker, who died in a jeep accident, General Matthew Ridgway was appointed as his replacement. MacArthur gave Ridgway full responsibility for field operations. Despite the creation of a new unified American command for Korea, U.S. forces abandoned Seoul by January 6, 1951, but regrouped to hold the Chinese from further advances. By January 24, Ridgway initiated the offensive action that would result in the retaking of Seoul for the final time in mid-March.

Following these dramatic movements up and down the Korean peninsula, the war became stalemated near the 38th parallel for two and a half years. An armistice was reached in July 1953. Total American casualties for the war were 141,000 including 33,741 killed in action and 20,617 killed from other causes; more than 21,300 were killed during the first year of the war. It is estimated that 15,000 soldiers were killed during the retreat from the Yalu in late 1950 and early 1951.

The bloody withdrawal from the Yalu undercut American public support for the Korean War. The retreat also produced an epic confrontation between the strong-willed Douglas MacArthur and the equally tough-minded Harry Truman. MacArthur's fiasco in North Korea and his public criticism of Truman's strategy cost him the support of the president and the Joint Chiefs of Staff. Truman relieved MacArthur of his far eastern command in April 1951. The decision roiled political waters in the United States, where the conservative-minded general had wide political support. Yet the U.S. defeat at the Yalu prompted American strategists to abandon MacArthur's concept of total victory in Korea. Truman and the Joint Chiefs opted for stalemate and containment, a less risky military solution.

The war in Korea had numerous ironies and ambiguities. From the Chinese point of view, their deployment of a "volunteer" army protected their border and permitted survival of the North Korean Communist state to the south. From the American perspective, the Republic of Korea had been preserved and developed into a reliable and increasingly democratic ally. Had its army been defeated, Communist forces would have secured a foothold less than 200 miles from Japan. Despite its victory at the Yalu River, China's Korean campaign may have reduced its military strength sufficiently to prevent an invasion of Taiwan, the breakaway island republic. Yet China's incursion into Korea conditioned American cold war strategists to see developments in Vietnam, another territory bordering China, as part of a larger plan to put all of Asia under Communist rule.

Alex Wilson

FURTHER READING:

Acheson, Dean. *Present at the Creation.* New York: W. W. Norton, 1969.

Blair, Clay. *The Forgotten War: America in Korea, 1950–53.* New York: Doubleday, 1987.

Rees, David. *Korea: The Limited War.* New York: St. Martin's Press, 1964.

1952 ◆ POLIO EPIDEMIC

The year 1952 marked the peak of the polio epidemic in the United States. "Polio season," so named because of the increase in polio cases with the warmer weather, began early that year. Cases were reported prior to Memorial Day, rose steadily through the hot months of July and August, reached a peak in mid-September with more than 4,000 cases reported in one week, and ran well into October. Newspapers kept a box score on their front pages of cases in their communities.

Beaches, parks, and movie theaters were vacant as parents kept their children locked inside to avoid the feared scourge. The year's final tally was 57,879 cases reported nationwide; the illness killed 3,145 people, and 21,269 others suffered some measure of paralysis.

Polio, shortened by space-conscious newspaper headline writers from its formal name, poliomyelitis (from Greek *polio,* "gray"; *myelos,* "marrow" or "cord"; and *itis,* Latin for "inflammation"), is a virus spread by fecal contamination of water and food sources. The virus is apparently an age-old affliction of human populations. A carved image of a priest with the characteristic "dropped foot" of a polio survivor appears on an 18th Dynasty Egyptian stele dating from around 1580 to 1350 B.C.E., and it is likely that the Greek physician Hippocrates described the symptomology of polio in the fifth century B.C.E. Prior to the 20th century, polio was an endemic disease, meaning that it continuously circulated through the human population. The overwhelming majority of people were exposed to the virus at an early age, which generally resulted in a milder course of infection. In addition, maternal antibodies from breast-feeding offered some protection; therefore the vast majority of people survived a polio infection with few noticeable effects.

The late 19th-century sanitation campaigns to separate refuse and sewage from drinking-water sources improved the health of populations in the industrial world by significantly reducing the incidence of water-borne diseases such as typhoid fever and cholera. The success of these sanitary efforts, perversely, had the opposite effect on polio. People were exposed to the polio virus less often because they contacted fecally contaminated water and food sources less often. Consequently the age of infection began to rise, with tragic results. Polio changed from an endemic to an epidemic disease (sudden, widespread infectious outbreak) when the virus was introduced to a population with no previous exposure. Infection at a later age presents a higher percentage of cases that result in paralysis and death. The nations and regions of the world in the forefront of cleaning up their water systems—the United States and Scandinavia—were the first modernized societies to experience polio epidemics.

In 1916, the first large-scale polio epidemic erupted in the United States. Some 27,363 cases were reported nationally, causing 7,179 deaths. New York City was particularly hard hit, suffering 2,448 deaths. Panic in the city prompted thousands to flee only to be met by armed men preventing them from stopping in their towns. Although this 1916 polio peak would only be matched 30 years later—and the mortality total dwarfed by the terrible INFLUENZA PANDEMIC that appeared two years later—polio had entered the public consciousness.

Two events in the following two decades would place polio, then known as infantile paralysis, in the forefront of the public's attention. The first event was the shocking paralysis of Franklin D. Roosevelt. Scion of a wealthy and powerful political family, Roosevelt had run for vice president in 1920 and was vacationing in New Brunswick, Canada, a year later when

Centers for Disease Control and Prevention

The Centers for Disease Control and Prevention is the nation's disease prevention agency. It performs disease surveillance, provides technical assistance to both states and other nations, and is the global center for epidemiologic training. Despite four name changes over a half-century, the institution has always been known as the CDC.

The CDC evolved directly out of the Malaria Control in War Areas (MCWA) program in the Public Health Service. The MCWA was a World War II institution charged with protecting military personnel and workers in the defense industries in the southeastern United States from malaria. In 1946, the MCWA became the Communicable Disease Center. It was a small branch of the Public Health Service relegated to Atlanta because there was not enough room near Washington, D.C. The CDC would eventually define public health practice in the United States and around the world.

Early in its history, the CDC developed the techniques of disease surveillance that became the cornerstone of its mission and one of the defining characteristics of public health practice. Its current mission is to promote health and quality of life by preventing and controlling disease, injury, and disability through surveillance, investigation and corrective action. In addition to disease surveillance, the CDC provides technical assistance and grants to state and local governments. Its Epidemic Intelligence Service, which was formed in 1951 in response to biochemical warfare concerns at the start of the Korean War, is currently the global center for trained epidemiologists.

Three health crises—polio, swine flu, and smallpox—helped establish the credibility of the CDC, particularly the POLIO EPIDEMIC in the 1950s. In 1955, several children who received the recently approved Salk polio vaccine developed polio. The national vaccination program had to be stopped while the CDC investigated. It traced the problem to contamination in one of the manufacturing facilities. The problem was corrected, and the national vaccine program restarted. In 1957, the CDC conducted surveillance of the swine flu epidemic. It used the results to develop guidelines for an effective flu vaccine program. The CDC also played a key role in the global eradication of smallpox. It developed a smallpox surveillance unit in 1962 and refined smallpox vaccination techniques in several countries outside the United States. In Africa, the CDC developed a surveillance and containment strategy which proved to be more efficient and effective than the previous mass-vaccination techniques, and the World Health Organization adopted this strategy elsewhere. Smallpox was eradicated worldwide by 1977.

The CDC has not been without controversy. The Tuskegee syphilis study was initiated by the Public Health Service and other organizations in 1932 and was transferred to the CDC in 1957. The study continued without change until protests about ethical appropriateness compelled the CDC to shut it down in 1972. The Tuskegee syphilis study came to symbolize medical misconduct and highlighted the lack of protections for human research subjects. The CDC learned from this incident and assisted in the development of human subjects guidelines to prevent exploitation of research subjects.

Over time, the CDC underwent several name changes, each change reflecting its evolving and expanding role in public health. In 1970, it became the Center for Disease Control, acknowledging its work in the areas of chronic disease as well as health education. The institution became the Centers for Disease Control after an extensive reorganization in 1981. In 1992, it was renamed the Centers for Disease Control and Prevention, although by law and convention it is still referred to as the CDC.

The CDC comprises 12 separate centers dealing with a variety of health issues including infectious disease, women's and children's health, occupational health and safety, and chronic disease surveillance. It continues to be a global leader in disease surveillance and public health practice by participating in efforts to address polio, malaria, and AIDS around the world.

Neenah Estrella-Luna

he was felled by polio. Roosevelt's advanced age—he was nearly 40—and social status demonstrated that no one was safe from polio. Roosevelt survived, and although he would never walk again unaided, his recovery and remarkable political comeback—he became governor of New York in 1929 and president in 1933—kept polio in the public view, even if few were aware of the lasting effects of his paralysis.

The second event that galvanized public awareness of polio was the creation of the National Foundation for Infantile Paralysis in 1938. Popularly known as the March of Dimes, the foundation used advertising and marketing and created modern fund-raising techniques dedicated to supporting those afflicted with the disease and funding research to prevent it. Under its single-minded director Basil O'Connor, the March of Dimes raised a staggering $622 million between the years 1938 and 1959. The March of Dimes mobilized an army of volunteers who canvassed their neighborhoods and towns to solicit contributions for the cause—frequently a dime at a time—through such gimmicks as encouraging folks to mail dimes to the White House or to create a mile of dimes.

At the heart of the slick March of Dimes publicity campaigns were two themes: sympathy for the afflicted and fear of the virus attacking you or your children. To drum up support for the foundation, the March of Dimes created poster campaigns, drafted national spokespeople, and sent polio survivors to speeches, parades, and rallies, keeping them constantly in the public eye. The March of Dimes also produced movies that illustrated the universal threat of polio. One such example was *The Crippler*, a short film shown before the feature movie at theaters across the country. The film depicted an ominous shadow that loomed over playing children in their homes, at the playground and in the neighborhood swimming hole. The lurking shadow was dispelled by a representative of the March of Dimes. Coupled with these images of polio's threat was the official advice to help avoid polio, which recommended that children not become overtired or suddenly chilled or that they may not mix with new groups. The advice, based on anecdotal evidence of polio infections, in effect, told kids not to be kids.

The palpable images of the disease—children and adults effectively entombed in coffinlike "iron lungs" to help them breathe or walking with braces

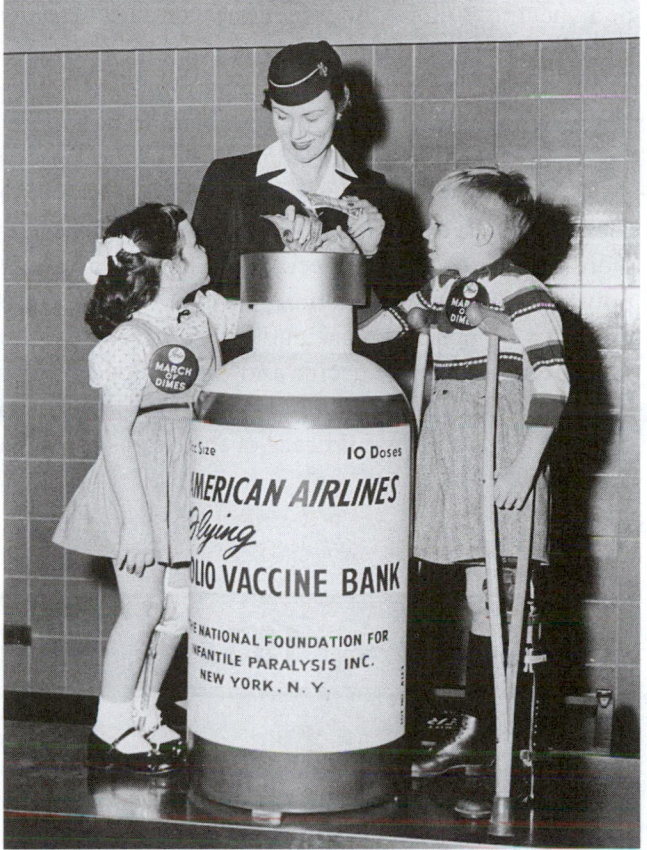

Promoting a "flying vaccine bank," an airline stewardess and two children with polio pose in front of a four-foot replica of a vaccine bottle. *(Library of Congress)*

and crutches—prompted a fear bordering on hysteria during polio outbreaks, despite the statistically small chances of developing a serious or fatal case. Children could be bright and lively one day and fighting for their life the next, and the tragic appeal of these images added poignancy to the ubiquitous March of Dimes poster campaigns. In stark contrast with other diseases which were in retreat due to the success of public health, immunizations, and antibiotics, polio cases continued to rise through the late 1940s and into the 1950s. As the birth rate began to soar after World War II—the early years of the baby boom—so too did polio, threatening the lives and liveliness of these young children. The year 1952 was the worst yet for polio in the United States, and although 1953 had seen a decline ("only" 35,592 cases), there was no guarantee that subsequent years would continue this retreat from the 1952 peak.

Suddenly, the gloom was dispelled. In 1954, the March of Dimes organized the largest field trial ever of a vaccine. Nearly 2 million children were injected with either Jonas Salk's dead-virus vaccine (the virus was chemically killed so that it produced a long-lasting immunity but could not cause the disease), or a placebo in a double-blind study in which neither the participants nor the organizers knew which dose the children received. On April 12, 1955, the results were announced: The vaccine worked. A huge outpouring of relief and emotion greeted this announcement, and Jonas Salk was lauded as a hero. Over the next few years Salk's vaccine and, later, Albert Sabin's live-virus vaccine (the living virus was weakened so that it caused a very mild case of the disease), which could be taken orally, rapidly drove the polio virus into oblivion in the United States. Today, the virus stands on the cusp of being completely eradicated from the planet, joining the dread killer smallpox as the only viral diseases deliberately and permanently eradicated through human intervention.

George Dehner

FURTHER READING:

Oshinsky, David M. *Polio: An American Story.* New York: Oxford University Press, 2005.
Paul, John R. *A History of Poliomyelitis.* New Haven, Conn.: Yale University Press, 1971.

1953 ◆ WORCESTER TORNADO

On Monday, June 8, 1953, an enormous concentration of violent weather moved eastward across the upper Midwest, spawning three deadly tornadoes, one of which took 116 lives in Flint, Michigan. The same system, know as a "super cell," produced numerous towering thunderheads; from one of them, passing over Petersham, Massachusetts, on June 9, a roiling black funnel descended. The tornado, tremendously powerful from the moment of its birth, took no lives in sparsely populated Petersham but began to move southeastward at 30 miles an hour, beginning a path of destruction in central Massachusetts which would stretch for 42 miles, marked by a wide swath of incredible devastation.

Continuing toward adjacent Barre, the tornado exploded a large farmhouse, killing two youthful occupants. Then, in Rutland, another farming community with a small, widely scattered population, it took two more lives, that of a teenage boy and a young father just sitting down to supper with his wife and two young children. His daughter, impaled on the jagged stub of a limb projecting from a still-standing tree, her feet completely off the ground, miraculously survived. In the far more populous town of Holden, a western suburb of Worcester and the next to be struck by the funnel, many homes were virtually

FACTBOX

PLACE Worcester and other central Massachusetts communities

DATE June 9, 1953

TYPE Tornado

DESCRIPTION Winds of more than 300 miles per hour ripped through central Massachusetts, pulverizing homes and destroying towns.

CAUSE Category 5 tornado

CASUALTIES 94 fatalities

IMPACT Sparked massive relief effort

pulverized, including nearly every home in two new developments. In one, there were no fatalities; in the other, five perished. Nearby, a mother and infant son were carried together in the air a distance of 400 feet and then were slammed back to earth. The baby, just two weeks old, was spun aloft once more and whirled to his death. His tiny body would be found, deep in the debris, days later.

When the tornado roared into Worcester at 5:04 P.M., the final funnel had been on the ground for three-quarters of an hour, three times the "life" of most tornadoes. Of more significance, the funnel was now 450 yards wide and rotating like a giant circular saw; its winds were later estimated to have been between 325 and 335 miles per hour. In today's terms, that would put it at the top of the Fujita Scale as a Category 5 tornado with the highest wind speed ever seen. In the course of its 14-minute transit across Worcester, the tornado left in its wake 59 victims dead or dying. As the funnel was crossing Worcester, many people on the northern side of its path saw and felt the fall of large hailstones; the largest were almost the size of tangerines.

Still swirling on a southeasterly course, the tornado plowed across the town of Shrewsbury, where a dozen people perished, including a baby girl who was pronounced dead by the same physician who had delivered her three months earlier. In Westboro, the next community in the funnel's path, six people were killed. Luckily, one young mother and her three children escaped certain injury and perhaps death as they ran to their basement. The bottom step grazed the back of the woman's leg as the stairs and the house to which they were still attached lifted completely off its foundation and was totally pulverized. The woman's husband, meanwhile, survived the funnel in the open, without receiving so much as a single scratch.

After taking a turn toward a northeasterly course, the tornado vented its final fury on the Fayville section of Southboro, where it took three more lives. At 5:40 P.M., the black cloud lifted and dissipated, though bits and pieces of debris sifted to earth all across eastern Massachusetts. One such object was a formal wedding photograph, found floating off Cape Cod more than 100 miles away.

The toll in deaths and devastation was unprecedented in the state's history of natural disasters. Ninety-three lives were lost, making it the 11th deadliest tornado in U.S. history. An electrical company lineman died during repair work on a transformer several days later, adding a 94th life to the toll of fatalities attributable to the storm. Four thousand dwellings were destroyed or damaged, and the number of serious injuries was in the high hundreds. The estimated property loss in 1953 dollars was at least $53 million and perhaps more.

Within five hours of the tornado's passage, the body of every fatality had been removed to a morgue, and most of the injured had received medical attention; some were in surgery, others awaited hospital beds or being treated as outpatients. Doctors and nurses worked around the clock, some for 30 hours or more without rest. Three regiments of National Guard troops were activated for 12 days, controlling access to the storm-stricken areas in Holden, Worcester, and Shrewsbury. During their around-the-clock patrols, they apprehended a number of looters and undoubtedly deterred many more. The Salvation Army, Red Cross, and Catholic Charities worked to help the many hundreds of tornado victims who found themselves with nothing but the clothes in which they stood. Municipal authorities saw to the clearing away of debris—whole structures now reduced to rubble. Governmental disaster relief at the federal level did exist in 1953, but on a far more modest scale than at present. Stricken states looked first to Civil Defense, forerunner to today's Federal Emergency Management Agency. In Worcester's case, air force cargo planes flew in tons of folding cots, mattresses, and blankets within two days of the tornado's passage. Also, some 220 federally owned house trailers were soon located in Wichita, Kansas, and earmarked for shipment to Worcester. Ironically, about 20 of these were destroyed by a low-order tornado while still on the ground in Kansas. The remaining 200 were quickly dispatched to Worcester.

A half-century later, Worcester resident Robert Lee vividly recalled his harrowing encounter with nature. He was driving along West Boylston Street with his mother, Josephine, at the wheel. Unknown to the pair, the tornado had crossed the busy thoroughfare only a few hundred feet ahead of them, as they experienced a fall of large hailstones. Moments later, a number of dead frogs, plucked from a pond by the funnel minutes before, splattered against their front windshield. "Look, Ma!" cried young Bobby excitedly, "it's raining frogs!"

John M. O'Toole

FURTHER READING:

Chittick, William E. *The Worcester Tornado, June 9, 1953*. Bristol, R.I.: privately printed, 2002.

O'Toole, John M. *Tornado! 84 Minutes; 94 Lives*. Worcester, Mass.: Databooks, 1993.

1956 ◆ GRAND CANYON AIRPLANE CRASH

At approximately 10:30 A.M. on Saturday, June 30, 1956, Trans World Airlines (TWA) Flight 2 and United Flight 718 collided over the eastern end of the Grand Canyon in Arizona. All 128 passengers and crew on both airplanes were killed in the accident. The two aircraft involved—TWA's Super Constellation and United's DC-7—were the largest commercial planes in service at the time. The death toll in this horrific collision far outnumbered previous aviation accidents. The disaster spurred the U.S. government to overhaul airline regulation and create the Federal Aviation Administration (FAA).

TWA Flight 2 and United Flight 718 both left Los Angeles International Airport just after 9 A.M. on June 30. TWA 2 was bound for Kansas City and followed a route to the south of United 718, which was headed for Chicago. The planes would come in close proximity at only one point—over the Painted Desert in Arizona, directly above the Grand Canyon. The pilots of both flights communicated with air traffic control as their aircraft gained altitude. In 1956, most civilian flights followed Instrumental Flight Rules (IFR) during and after takeoff, but pilots could switch to Visual Flight Rules (VFR) once they were "on top," that is, above cloud level. Aircraft and crew employed the rudimentary system of "see and be seen" once they switched to VFR, in which case pilots flew primarily by sight. Air traffic control rarely denied the request to fly by VFR. The Civil Aeronautics Agency (CAA), predecessor to the FAA, lacked the funding and facilities to expand the scope of IFR. Consequently, vast areas of uncontrolled airspace prevailed in 1956. Above the clouds, pilots relied on their eyes to fly.

TWA 2 radioed the Los Angeles (LA) Air Traffic Control Center at 9:21 A.M. and requested a climb from 19,000 feet to 21,000 feet. An air traffic controller in Salt Lake City, Utah, recognized that this would intersect the path of the DC-7 and told LA controllers to deny the request. The TWA pilot then asked for 1,000 feet "on top" and a switch to VFR, which LA Air Traffic Control approved. TWA 2 entered uncontrolled airspace at about 21,000 feet. In short, while air traffic control would not approve an elevation climb to 21,000, the switch to VFR in effect permitted it to occur. The pilot of United 718 radioed the LA tower shortly after takeoff, reporting

FACTBOX

PLACE Painted Desert/Grand Canyon, Arizona

DATE June 30, 1956

TYPE Midair collision between two domestic passenger planes

DESCRIPTION Flying under visual flight rules, TWA Flight 2 and United Flight 718 collided over the Grand Canyon.

CAUSE Apparently at least one pilot could not see the other plane due to the position of his cockpit.

CASUALTIES 128 deaths

IMPACT Reform of air traffic control and the creation of the Federal Aviation Agency

that he was "on top." The radio controller granted United 718's request to continue under VFR.

The pilot of each aircraft contacted air traffic control just before 10:00 A.M. At 9:58, United 718 reported an altitude of 21,000 feet over the Needles, a rock formation in Canyonlands National Park, Utah. The pilot estimated that he would pass over the Painted Desert at roughly 10:31. TWA 2's crew reported its position in Las Vegas, Nevada, at 9:59—the Super Constellation had just passed Lake Mohave, Arizona, at 1,000 feet "on top," or 21,000 feet. TWA 2 was also due over the Painted Desert at 10:31. TWA 2 was never heard from again.

The DC-7 issued a final radio correspondence at 10:31 A.M. Aeronautical radio communicators in San Francisco and Salt Lake City could not translate the message, but postcrash analysis revealed the following: "Salt Lake, United 718 . . . ah . . . we're going in!" The CAA issued a missing aircraft alert at 11:51 A.M. No eyewitnesses emerged to guide the search. That evening, a pilot who operated scenic flights spotted wreckage of the TWA Super Constellation. Air force helicopters arrived at the crash sight on July 1, and the CAA's investigation began.

TWA 2 had crashed on the northeast slope of Temple Butte above the Colorado River, which flows through the Grand Canyon. United 718 had struck Chuar Butte opposite the Little Colorado River, a tributary. The CAA investigation panel determined that a collision had taken place in midair. The material evidence showed that paint from the United DC-7 was visible on the TWA, and the propeller incisions on the TWA exactly matched the size of the DC-7's propellers. The planes had been traveling at speeds greater than 300 miles per hour and had plummeted about four miles into the canyon. The investigation disclosed that the left wing of the DC-7 hit the rear fuselage of the TWA aircraft, rendering the aircraft inoperable. TWA 2 suffered more traumatic damage—with the fuselage blown and the rear cabin agape, passengers and luggage flew out the aft of the plane. A mere 30 seconds after the collision, TWA 2 had crashed. United 718 stayed airborne approximately 90 seconds after initial impact, yet lacked the lift to clear Chuar Butte. The sheer force of the plane's collision with the rock wall obliterated aircraft and passengers. Investigators were left with the carnage and debris of TWA 2 strewn across Temple Butte.

The collision exposed many of the flaws that existed in air control in 1956. Air traffic had increased dramatically during the 1950s, straining the CAA's capacity to keep pace. Both the CAA and the Civil Aeronautics Board (CAB) had jurisdiction over phases of air transportation, a situation that hampered regulation. The CAB formulated rules of aviation, while the CAA oversaw their implementation. Safety matters fell to the CAB, even though the CAA was better suited to determine safety guidelines. The military answered to neither agency, further complicating air traffic coordination.

The CAA released its investigation on April 17, 1957, highlighting this regulatory confusion. The most critical part of the report concerned the heavy reliance on VFR, a technique that had become outdated. The "see and be seen" practice had been adequate in an earlier era when the skies were relatively uncrowded. But air travel rose sharply after World War II, significantly congesting the airways. The CAA noted that the technical capability to reduce air collisions existed, but that a lack of funds and personnel had slowed its installation.

President Dwight D. Eisenhower appointed Edward P. Curtis, a veteran of aviation planning, to recommend improvements in air traffic control. Curtis collaborated with the Airways Modernization Board, created by Congress in 1957, in proposing a single agency that would "regulate not only the system of airways, including the nationwide system of electronic aids to navigation," but all safety matters, including the certification of pilots, operators, and aircraft. Congress created the Federal Aviation Agency (FAA) in December 1958, instructing that it create equitable zones of military and civilian airspace. The act empowered the FAA to take over all airway safety matters from the CAB. In 1967, the newly created Department of Transportation absorbed the agency, which was renamed the Federal Aviation Administration. The FAA played an important role in instituting VHF Omni-directional Range (VOR) across the United States during the 1960s. This system gives pilots the electronic capacity to determine the location of other aircraft. The Grand Canyon crash illustrates how bureaucratic inertia can persist until an unthinkable disaster exposes the flaws in a system.

David G. O'Donnell

FURTHER READING:
Aug, Stephen, and Philip Ryther. *Who's Watching the Airways?* New York: Doubleday, 1972.
Conway, Eric. *Echoes in the Grand Canyon: Public Catastrophes and Technologies of Control in American Aviation.* New York: Routledge, 2004.

1957 ◆ LITTLE ROCK SCHOOL DESEGREGATION CRISIS

Little Rock, Arkansas, was an early battleground of the civil rights movement. The backdrop to the conflict was the Supreme Court ruling in *Brown v. the Board of Education* in 1954 that had declared segregation in public schools unconstitutional. Whites throughout the Deep South repudiated and resisted the decision. The situation in Arkansas, however, registered shades of complexity. Whites in western areas of the state, which contained relatively few African Americans, tended to accept the ruling and proceeded to integrate their schools. But in eastern districts of the state, which had a greater political influence in state politics, resistance to the desegregation order was stubborn. Little Rock, the capital located in central Arkansas, emerged as the focal point of this contentiousness in the fall of 1957 when nine African-American students enrolled in Central High School, an all-white institution. Governor Orval Faubus moved to block its integration, deploying the National Guard on September 4 to prevent the nine students from entering the school. In defying the Supreme Court and the federal government, Faubus precipitated a seminal crisis between state and nation over the issue of racial justice.

Governor Faubus had a progressive record on race relations. Elected in 1954, he had approved the racial integration of public transportation and the state colleges. In 1956, however, political winds shifted when Faubus faced James Johnson in the gubernatorial primary. Johnson, a fervent segregationist, ran on a platform resisting all forms of integration and nearly won. Faubus managed to gain reelection but only after pledging to use his office to stymie unpopular such

FACTBOX

PLACE Central High School, Little Rock, Arkansas

DATE September 4–25, 1957

TYPE Political crisis concerning racial integration

DESCRIPTION In defiance of the Supreme Court, segregationists led by Arkansas governor Orval Faubus aimed to prevent the racial integration of Central High School. After a three-week stand-off, President Eisenhower federalized the Arkansas National Guard to enforce the Court's decision to integrate the school.

CAUSE Governor Orval Faubus's decision to defy the ruling of the Supreme Court of the United States and the strength of segregationists in central Arkansas

IMPACT The Little Rock crisis demonstrated the necessity of federal intervention to break the tradition of racially segregated schools in the South

federal policies as school desegregation. This tactic, known as "interposition," would emerge in September 1957 when Faubus defied the Supreme Court.

Central High School began its academic year on September 3, 1957. Faubus faced a difficult choice: Heed the ruling of the nation's highest court or appease a vocal and powerful bloc of segregationists in his state. He tried desperately to avert a decision, arguing on August 29 that integration would incite violence. A local chancery court judge agreed and issued an injunction to delay integration. But Ronald N. Davies, the federal judge for the area, would not be cowed by segregationist pressure. One day after the injunction, on August 30, Davies overruled the local court, opening the way for the integration of Central High.

On Monday, September 2, the day before classes began, Faubus reached his fateful decision. Arguing that integration was "against the overwhelming sentiment of the people," the governor planned to block the move. He commanded the National Guard to surround Central High in order to prevent "widespread disorder and violence." Faubus insisted that the threat of violence forced his hand. Fearing for their children's safety, the parents of the nine African-American students decided to keep their children home on opening day, Tuesday, September 3. Central High remained segregated on the first day of school.

But the next day at 8 A.M., Elizabeth Eckford, a 15-year-old African American, approached Central High School where a segregationist mob and the Arkansas National Guard waited. As members of the crowd shouted derogatory comments, guardsmen refused to let her enter the school. Later that morning, the other black students arrived at Central High, accompanied by several adults, including Harry Bass, a local African-American leader. When the National Guard blocked their path, Bass confronted the commanding officer, Lieutenant Colonel Marion Johnson, asking, "I just want to get this straight, you are doing this on the orders of the governor—is that correct?" Johnson replied: "That is right."

The confrontation in Little Rock received national attention, putting pressure on President Dwight Eisenhower to intercede. On September 11, the president invited Governor Faubus to join him for the weekend at his retreat in Newport, Rhode Island. Although their meeting failed to resolve the impasse, the Justice Department continued its attack on the legality of Faubus's actions. Judge Davies agreed to another injunction hearing scheduled for Friday, September 20. Government lawyer Clark Eadley argued that Faubus was unjustified in mobilizing the guard. Davies agreed. The judge rebuked Faubus and ordered the National Guard to leave Central High. Integration was to resume on Monday, September 23.

Supported by the mayor, the police chief, and the superintendent of public schools, the school board endeavored to proceed with integration. But the crisis persisted because the federal government failed to demonstrate a commitment to enforcing the court order. Predictably, a mob formed on Monday morning, September 23, and blocked the main entrance of Central High. The nine black students entered through an alternative door, which further enraged the demonstrators. Fearing for the students' safety, Superintendent Virgil Blossom sent the nine students home at noon. The African-American children stayed home on Tuesday, September 24, fearful of encountering an angry mob.

Cameramen and journalists had covered the violence in Little Rock, allowing Americans across the nation to witness a chilling scene in which the federal government appeared to be waffling. If local authorities could not protect the rights of children to attend school, then who would? At this momentous juncture, President Eisenhower decided that Arkansas could no longer defy the Supreme Court and the doctrine of national supremacy. He federalized the Arkansas National Guard and ordered the 101st Airborne Infantry Division into Little Rock. The mob assembled again on Wednesday, September 25, but this time the army prevented violence. At 9:30 A.M., an army station wagon pulled in front of the school, and the nine black children emerged. Escorted by 22 armed soldiers, they entered Central High. Under the eye of federal troops, integration finally occurred in Little Rock.

September 25, 1957, was a watershed moment of the civil rights movement. The confrontation in Little Rock led to a victory for racial equality, yet it also indicated the strength of resistance to integration in the South. Moreover, the battle for school integration was not over. In 1958, segregationists pressured Governor Faubus to dissolve the public school system and establish the Little Rock Private School Corporation. Privately funded schools could legally segregate, and

On the orders of segregationist governor Orval Faubus, Arkansas National Guard troops in Little Rock block 15-year-old Elizabeth Eckford from entering Central High School on September 4, 1957. (© Bettmann/CORBIS)

in 1958, 2,200 of 3,700 Little Rock students attended such schools. Despite this effort to circumvent the spirit of the law, Little Rock set an example for other communities to confront racially segregated schools. With the enactment of federal civil rights and school aid laws in the mid-1960s, the national government eventually leveraged substantial progress toward breaking down racial exclusion in southern education. The courage of Elizabeth Eckford and the eight other students to stand up to racism and intimidation became a rallying point for civil rights activists for years to come.

See also 1964 FREEDOM SUMMER CIVIL RIGHTS MURDERS; 1965 SELMA VOTING RIGHTS DEMONSTRATION; 1968 ASSASSINATION OF MARTIN LUTHER KING, JR.

David G. O'Donnell

FURTHER READING:

Ashmore, Harry S. *Civil Rights and Wrongs*. New York: Pantheon Books, 1994.

Blossom, Virgil. *It Has Happened Here*. New York: Harper and Brothers, 1959.

Freyer, Tony. *The Little Rock Crisis*. Westport, Conn.: Greenwood Press, 1984.

1961 ◆ BAY OF PIGS INVASION

On April 17, 1961, a brigade of 1,500 Cuban exiles trained by the United States's Central Intelligence Agency (CIA) landed at the Bay of Pigs in Cuba, expecting to ignite a revolution that would topple Fidel Castro's Communist government. The brigade soon faced several thousand Cuban soldiers and Castro's weakened but still functional air force. The exile brigade appealed to the United States for additional air support, but President John F. Kennedy refused. At the end of two days of fighting, its numbers cut in half and low on ammunition, the exile force surrendered. More than 100 exiles lay dead, along with an estimated 150 to 2,000 Cubans, and 1,189 exiles were taken prisoner. The mission's humiliating and very public failure generated political and diplomatic shock waves throughout the Western Hemisphere and the world.

Cuba had been heavily influenced by the United States since the Spanish-American War ended in 1898. While Cuba was nominally independent, Americans controlled the island's political and economic fate. Fulgencio Batista, the military dictator of Cuba from 1934 to 1959, catered to American businessmen and the island's wealthy plantation owners while neglecting the impoverished masses. In 1959, a young revolutionary nationalist named Fidel Castro led a successful coup against the Batista government in the name of the people. U.S. president Dwight D. Eisenhower recognized the new government just six days after its formation but quickly turned on Castro when the Cuban leader announced he was a Marxist-Leninist and aligned with the Soviet Union.

Emboldened by an insurgency the CIA had successfully launched in Guatemala in 1954, Eisenhower authorized the Bay of Pigs operation as a means of removing Castro and the Communist regime. President John F. Kennedy, elected in November 1960, inherited the plan from Eisenhower. Having criticized Eisenhower for being soft on Castro and convinced by the CIA that the brigade attack would be supported by a popular anti-Castro uprising, Kennedy pressed ahead with the plan despite warnings from presidential adviser Arthur Schlesinger, Jr., and Senate Foreign Relations Committee chairman J. William Fulbright that it could prove disastrous.

FACTBOX

PLACE Bay of Pigs, Cuba

DATE April 17, 1961

TYPE Military disaster

DESCRIPTION 1,500 Cuban exiles trained by the U.S. Central Intelligence Agency invaded Cuba with the intent of overthrowing Fidel Castro's Communist regime but failed after two days of fighting

CAUSE A combination of factors including cold war tensions, poor planning, poor intelligence, and President John F. Kennedy's refusal to provide the exiles with air support

CASUALTIES Some 1,189 members of the exile brigade were taken prisoner, and 114 were killed. Estimates of Cuban defense force losses range from 150 to more than 2,000.

IMPACT Increased cold war tensions in the region and worldwide

Kennedy, in just the third month of his presidency, demanded only one condition from the operation planners: that there be no overt participation by the U.S. armed forces.

Kennedy learned of the Bay of Pigs failure at a white tie dinner in Washington on the evening of April 18. There he rejected further U.S. air cover on the grounds that such overt aggression by the United States against Cuba would undermine goodwill in the region and escalate the conflict to the point that the Soviet Union might decide to intervene. Kennedy was ultimately forced to accept public responsibility for the fiasco anyway when U.S. direct participation became public.

The political backlash in the United States was tremendous. Liberals complained that Kennedy had turned American foreign policy over to the CIA. Conservatives lamented the fact that a Communist government continued to exist just 90 miles off the coast of Florida. The regional fallout was bleak as well. Despite increases in Alliance for Progress aid money for Latin America, U.S. prestige in the Western Hemisphere suffered. Most important was the damage done to U.S.-Soviet relations. It forced both superpowers to harden their diplomatic and military positions and contributed to the general tensions that would play a part in a number of global showdowns, including the building of the Berlin Wall, the Cuban Missile Crisis, and the Vietnam War.

Jeff Woods

FURTHER READING:

Blight, James G., and Peter Kornbluh, eds. *Politics of Illusion: The Bay of Pigs Invasion Reexamined.* New York: Lynne Rienner, 1998.

Higgins, Trumbull. *The Perfect Failure: Kennedy, Eisenhower, and the Bay of Pigs.* New York: W. W. Norton, 1989.

Kornbluh, Peter, ed. *Bay of Pigs Declassified: The Secret CIA Report on the Invasion of Cuba.* New York: New Press, 1998.

1962 ◆ THALIDOMIDE TRAGEDY

The thalidomide tragedy that malformed and killed thousands of babies came to a halt in 1962 when thalidomide was banned in most countries, prompting Congress to enact new legislation to more carefully regulate the U.S. drug market. Thalidomide was originally hailed in the 1950s as a wonder drug for its sedative abilities and was particularly effective in combating morning sickness in pregnant women, causing thalidomide use to quickly spread to nearly 50 countries. As thalidomide use increased, so too did its list of side effects. Today "thalidomide babies"—victims of miscarriage, deafness, blindness, malformed organs, limbs, and more as a result of mothers taking as little as a single dose of thalidomide while pregnant—frame thalidomide's legacy. Surprisingly, thalidomide has since been approved for treating leprosy and multiple myeloma—under the very strictures first prompted by thalidomide in 1962—and may eventually be used to treat other diseases as well.

Thalidomide was first marketed in 1957 by the German Chemie Grunenthal pharmaceutical company in what is now recognized as a scandalous pursuit of profit through irresponsible science and downright deceit. Though little tested and certainly not proven safe, thalidomide was first made available in Germany and distributed via free samples to doctors, accompanied by a massive marketing campaign that provided false assurance of the drug's safety. The successful marketing campaign greatly increased thalidomide sales. With distribution in 46 countries, by the early 1960s thalidomide was sold all over the world under at least 40 different names—but not in the United States.

In 1960, the U.S. Food and Drug Administration (FDA) received a request for approval of thalidomide sales, which was reviewed by Dr. Frances Kelsey, an FDA pharmacologist, using rules from the then-prevailing Food, Drug, and Cosmetic Act of 1938. Because thalidomide did not meet the law's safety requirements, Kelsey denied the request, noting that no information was provided about how the drug affected humans—including pregnant women who Kelsey knew could harm their babies by taking unsafe drugs while pregnant. Kelsey also knew of surfacing anecdotal reports from around the world about thalidomide's side effects. The request for thalidomide approval was resubmitted to the FDA six times but because it did not include any of the additional information Kelsey requested, it was rejected every time. Approximately 20,000 Americans took thalidomide on an investigational basis during this time. When the effects of thalidomide became clear in 1962, Frances Kelsey was hailed as an American heroine and given an award by President Kennedy for her success in preventing further distribution of thalidomide in the United States.

Due to Kelsey's efforts, only 17 American children became thalidomide babies. Elsewhere in the world, thalidomide babies were common, documented in countless thousands of miscarriages and approximately 12,000 malformed births, 5,000 of which survived beyond childhood. The first known

FACTBOX

PLACE United States and 45 other countries around the world

DATE 1956–62

TYPE Toxic drug known for causing birth defects

DESCRIPTION Thalidomide, a sedative used to combat morning sickness in pregnant women, caused miscarriage, infant and child death, and severe disfigurement in babies.

CAUSE Irresponsible actions by drug companies, in selling and marketing thalidomide. As little as one use of thalidomide or any of its 40 aliases by pregnant women could cause death or major harm to the fetus.

CASUALTIES Worldwide, approximately 7,000 infant and child deaths, an additional 5,000 malformed births, and countless thousands of miscarriages

COST Legal settlements cost the manufacturers more than $17 million in North America, $31 million in Germany, $25 million in Britain, and approximately $14 million in Sweden.

IMPACT The disaster led to development of birth defects registries, to allow careful monitoring of birth defects, and resulted in the 1962 passage of the Kefauver-Harris Act that strengthened drug safety measures and approved drug usage rules.

thalidomide baby was born without ears on Christmas day in 1956 to an employee of Chemie Grunenthal who was given samples of the drug that his wife took for morning sickness during pregnancy. Within one year of thalidomide's commercial availability, reports of side effects—including the many different types of birth defects—began to pour into Grunenthal, which the company disregarded. However the picture was clear: Where thalidomide was used, thalidomide babies were born. The otherwise rare condition known as phocomelia, a defect in which limbs fail to form, and hands, feet, or both are directly attached to the body, soon became a signature of the thalidomide baby crisis.

The thalidomide babies disaster resulted in protracted lawsuits around the globe, with families in several countries banding together to seek compensation from thalidomide manufacturers for the high costs of caring for children malformed from thalidomide. In Germany, the thalidomide trial was the largest since the Nuremberg trials after World War II and resulted in Grunenthal making payments of more than $31 million. The North American manufacturer agreed to legal settlements of more than $17 million. In a trial that rocked the British legal system and the press, a settlement valued at more than $25 million was reached. In Sweden, approximately $14 million was initially awarded as a settlement, though as recently as 2003, the Swedish government has continued to authorize *ex gratia* compensation (payments not required by law) for their country's thalidomide victims. In many cases, a single family's share of the legal settlement scarcely covered the lifetime of medical costs families would incur as a result of their child's malformations. None of the manufacturers are believed to have admitted guilt in their negligence in knowingly marketing an unsafe drug, and no jail time was ever served by manufacturing or marketing executives.

The thalidomide tragedy resulted in major changes in the care of fetuses and drug approval processes. By the late 1960s, the monitoring of birth defects began, allowing rare maladies to be spotted quickly and systematically. As early as 1962, many nations adopted new standards for pharmaceutical drug testing to prevent another disaster like thalidomide from happening again. Through passage of the 1962 Kefauver-Harris Act, better evidence of drug efficacy and clearer approved-usage labeling became part of the FDA drug approval process. Because of extensive laboratory and human tests now required, it would take more than eight years on average and cost more than $350 million to obtain FDA approval for a new drug in the early 21st century.

By 1965, researchers discovered thalidomide's usefulness in treating a skin condition common with leprosy, erythema nodosum laprosum (ENL), and began to investigate what other diseases thalidomide could effectively treat. In 1998, the FDA approved thalidomide use for ENL. In 2006, thalidomide was approved for treating multiple myeloma, a major breakthrough for the incurable cancer that previously could only be treated with chemotherapy. With careful oversight, researchers continue to investigate thalidomide's usefulness in treating other dermatological conditions, rheumatological disorders, gastrointestinal disease,

AIDS-related conditions, and several other cancers, which may someday lead to more FDA approvals for thalidomide use. Though thalidomide now gives hope for relieving many diseases, strict rules continue to protect pregnant women from its use.

See also 1937 ELIXIR SURLFANILAMIDE TRAGEDY.

Elaine A. Hills

FURTHER READING:

Knightley, Phillip, Harold Evans, Elaine Potter, and Marjorie Wallace. *Suffer the Children: The Story of Thalidomide.* New York: Viking, 1979.

Stephens, Trent, and Rock Brynner. *Dark Remedy: The Impact of Thalidomide and Its Revival as a Vital Medicine.* Cambridge, Mass.: Perseus, 2001.

1962 ◆ *SILENT SPRING* AND ENVIRONMENTAL DEGRADATION

On September 27, 1962, pioneer ecologist and feminist Rachel Carson dramatically challenged conventional notions of scientific progress and celebrations of prosperity with the publication of *Silent Spring*. Interest in the book, published first as a serial in *The New Yorker*, led to advance sale of 40,000 copies. Another 150,000 copies were sent to the Book of the Month Club. In this lyrically written study that continues to enjoy a large readership, Carson warned that Americans were stunningly oblivious to the dangers of their embrace of all things chemical. Specifically, she questioned governmental wisdom concerning industrial waste and the vast reliance on pesticides, especially DDT. Carson pointed out deadly long-term consequences that far outweighed the short-term profits and consumer benefits.

Carson, who held a master's degree in zoology from Johns Hopkins University, was already the author of five books celebrating the science and the mystery of the natural world, including *The Sea around Us* (1951). In *Silent Spring*, she took a holistic view, evaluating not only the intended but also the unintended consequences of using toxic agents. Paul Hermann Muller, the inventor of DDT (Dichlorodiphenyltrichloroethane), had been awarded the 1948 Nobel Prize in medicine for this pesticide that was so efficient it had cleared the South Pacific islands of malaria-causing insects, saving untold numbers of American troops during World War II. It was also used as an effective delousing powder. Following the war, it was celebrated by gardeners and farmers as an especially efficient way of eliminating crop-destroying pests. An estimated 675,000 tons were applied domesti-

FACTBOX

PLACE United States

DATE September 27, 1962

TYPE An exposé about chemical degradation of the environment

DESCRIPTION The publication of Rachel Carson's *Silent Spring* publicized the damage that pesticides and especially the chemical DDT did to living organisms.

IMPACT By awakening concern about environmental degradation, *Silent Spring* helped give rise to the environmental movement, spurred the creation of the Environmental Protection Agency, and influenced the banning of DDT in 1972.

cally, with the peak year being 1959 when nearly 80 million pounds were used.

Rather than joining the chorus of those singing the praises of this chemical marvel, Carson noted that DDT killed not only the targeted insects but also most life-forms with which it came into contact. Also, DDT, she cautioned, was effective to a fault, remaining toxic for weeks and months even after it had been diluted by water. Following its initial surface application, it seeped into the soil and water and ultimately into the food chain, ingested by birds and animals. Resultant problems in birds included egg shells so thin that they cracked prematurely, exposing to the elements chicks too young to survive. In animals, including humans, it caused cancer and genetic damage.

The book's title came from the opening chapter "A Fable for Tomorrow," forecasting an American town where all life, from song birds to children, had been silenced by this killer unwittingly unleashed by the scientific community. "Future historians may well be amazed by our distorted sense of proportion," Carson warned, "How could intelligent beings seek to control a few unwanted species by a method that contaminated the entire environment and brought the threat of disease and death even to their own kind?"

The first book to clearly lay out the dangers of pesticides, toxic chemicals, and industrial pollution, *Silent Spring* came under immediate attack. In a scathing review, *Time* magazine dismissed it as "hysterically overemphatic." The many denunciations within the popular press of Carson's work as excessively emotional played to the stereotype of women as unscientific and inherently hysterical (a word derived from the Greek word *hystera* for womb). She was initially dismissed contemptuously by most in the scientific community as well. Dr. Robert White-Stevens, a former biochemist and spokesman for the chemical industry during the 1960s, called Carson "a fanatic defender of the cult of the balance of nature" and warned the public, "If man were to follow the teachings of Miss Carson, we would return to the Dark Ages, and the insects and diseases and vermin would once again inherit the earth."

Ezra Taft Benson, an elder in the Mormon Church who had been secretary of agriculture in the Eisenhower administration, suggested to Eisenhower that Carson's marital status disqualified her from making inquiries in the first place. Benson wondered "why a spinster with no children was so worried about genetics" and concluded that Carson was "probably a Communist."

Carson's defenders, however, openly defied arguments that hinged on widely held perceptions of gender and sex. One unidentified woman's praise for Carson denounced the highly touted postwar notion embodied in the title of one of the era's many popular TV shows, *Father Knows Best,* in which a happy, nuclear, middle-class family is shepherded through life's little hazards by a wise and benevolent patriarch: "'Papa' does not always know best. In this instance it seems that 'papa' is taking an arbitrary stand, and we, the people are just supposed to take it, and count the dead animals and birds." When Carson was compared to Carrie Nation, the hatchet-wielding temperance advocate at the turn of the 20th century, the *New York Times* later noted, "This comparison was rejected quietly by Miss Carson, who in her very mild but firm manner refused to accept the identification of an emotional crusader."

Moreover, Carson had already gained a substantial public respectability. *The Sea around Us* had remained on national best-seller lists for 86 weeks and, by the time of the publication of *Silent Spring,* had been translated into 30 languages and garnered several prestigious prizes including the National Book Award. Her critics were finding it hard to persuade the public to reject as just a silly alarmist this considerably renowned and gifted scientist who translated scientific complexities into terms accessible to a nonscientific audience.

When reputable male scientists rose to defend *Silent Spring,* President John F. Kennedy ordered his Science Advisory Committee to investigate the controversy. Carson's painstaking research on the long-term impact of the profligate use of DDT was confirmed, and the pesticide was restricted domestically in 1969. Shortly before her premature death in 1964, Carson suggested to the Senate Committee on Commerce that a commission be established to deal with pesticide issues. This suggestion culminated in the establishment of the Environmental Protection Agency on December 2, 1970. Charged with protecting, developing, and enhancing the environment, the agency has been dubbed "the extended shadow of *Silent Spring.*" It regulates and enforces the protection of water, soils, and animals, including humans. One of its first tasks was to enforce the 1970 Clear Air Act, and on June 14, 1972, it formally banned the use of DDT.

Although the wisdom of even carefully regulated DDT use continues to be debated, Carson's emphasis on the interconnectedness of all life is no longer dismissed as feminine romanticism but accepted as a scientific reality. Through her refusal to adhere to prevailing gender stereotypes of female subservience to male wisdom, Carson made the public aware of attempts by the scientific-industrial complex to manipulate and control nature to the ultimate detriment of all. Her critique of the country's dependence on chemical pesticides helped give rise to the environmental movement and has since been widely recognized as one of the most influential books of the 20th century.

Nancy C. Unger

FURTHER READING:

Carson, Rachel. *Silent Spring.* 40th anniversary ed. Boston: Houghton Mifflin, 2002.

Karaim, Reed. "Not so Fast with the DDT: Rachel Carson's Warnings Still Apply." *American Scholar* 74, no. 3 (June 22, 2005): 53–59.

Lear, Linda. *Rachel Carson: Witness for Nature.* New York: Henry Holt, 1997.

Murphy, Priscella Coit. *What a Book Can Do: The Publication and Reception of* Silent Spring. Amherst: University of Massachusetts Press, 2005.

1962 ◆ CUBAN MISSILE CRISIS

In October 1962, the United States and Soviet Union were on the brink of nuclear war. On October 15 American spy planes produced clear evidence that the Soviets were constructing offensive nuclear weapons facilities in Cuba, a communist nation led by Fidel Castro. A week later, U.S. president John F. Kennedy ordered a "quarantine" of Cuba, which amounted to a naval and air blockade of all ships bound for the island. If the Soviets tried to run the blockade, the United States promised a military response. For four days, the world nervously watched and waited as Soviet ships crossed the Atlantic Ocean toward Cuba. On October 24, the Soviet ships stopped short of the quarantine line. After two more days of intense negotiations between Kennedy and Soviet premier Nikita Khrushchev, the crisis was over. The Soviet Union agreed to remove its missile sites from Cuba in exchange for a U.S. promise not to invade Cuba.

Since Fidel Castro's successful revolution in 1959 and his declaration of allegiance to Marxism-Leninism, the United States's relationship with Cuba had declined precipitously. America's complicity in the disastrous Bay of Pigs invasion in 1961 had further heightened the tension. Then in early 1962 the Kennedy administration had excluded Cuba from Alliance for Progress aid, helped lead an effort that resulted in the expulsion of Cuba from the Organization of American States and imposed an economic embargo on the island. Moreover, President Kennedy approved Operation Mongoose, a Central Intelligence Agency-supervised effort to oust Castro by covert means. Mongoose amounted to a secret war against the Communist leader that included assassination contracts.

Soviet-American relations were little better. Kennedy's apparent reluctance to commit to a full-scale

FACTBOX

PLACE Cuba

DATE October 1962

TYPE Diplomatic crisis; brink of nuclear war

DESCRIPTION On October 14, 1962, American spy planes produced clear evidence that the Soviets were constructing offensive nuclear weapons facilities in Cuba. A week later, U.S. president John F. Kennedy ordered a "quarantine" of Cuba, which amounted to a naval and air blockade of all offensive weaponry bound for the island. Soviet supply ships stopped just short of the quarantine line on October 24, avoiding a direct confrontation that could have potentially led to nuclear war.

CAUSE Cold war anxiety, political miscalculation, nuclear power politics

IMPACT The world learned a hard lesson about nuclear diplomacy, and the United States and Soviet Union temporarily improved communications to prevent further crises and miscalculations.

confrontation with Cuban Communists at the Bay of Pigs simultaneously led Kennedy to become more defensive and Soviet leader Nikita Khrushchev more aggressive. In the summer of 1961, Khrushchev attempted to browbeat Kennedy about German unification at a summit meeting in Vienna and declared his intention to sign a separate treaty with the East Germans. Knowing that such a move would effectively cut off capitalist and democratic West

Berlin, Kennedy took a hard line, declaring that he would stand by the people there even if it meant war. Kennedy upped the military draft, obtained a defense spending increase from Congress, and began a civil defense program that included nuclear fallout shelters. Khrushchev further intensified the crisis in August when he ordered Soviet troops to begin construction of the Berlin wall, the most potent symbol yet of Soviet-American antagonism in the cold war.

With Castro rightfully worried that the United States was planning the violent overthrow of his government and Khrushchev ready to press Kennedy's anticommunist resolve as far as it would go, the Soviet Union began to send weapons and military personnel to Cuba, just 90 miles south of Florida. Included was a complement of offensive nuclear missiles.

As the fall 1962 midterm congressional elections approached, Kennedy and his fellow Democrats were vulnerable to the Republican charge that they

Declassified in 1978, this CIA map shows the distance in nautical miles from suspected missile bases in Cuba to major cities in the United States. *(Kennedy Library)*

had been soft on communism in Cuba. Highlighting the point, Republican senator Kenneth Keating announced that there were 1,200 Russian troops in Cuba as well as what appeared to be rocket installations. With assurances from Soviet ambassador to the United States Anatoly Dobrinin, Kennedy responded to the Republicans with a declaration that no offensive nuclear weapons were in place in Cuba nor would they be tolerated.

The administration nevertheless kept close watch on the island. On October 15, 1962, American U-2 spy planes confirmed that Soviet medium range and intermediate-range ballistic-missile installations were under construction in Cuba. Khrushchev had decided to take the gamble of building nuclear bases there because of his concern that the Americans would topple Castro. He also believed that the missiles strategically countered American nuclear weapons located in Turkey. Kennedy hastily convened a group of top administration officials known as ExComm, short for the Executive Committee of the U.S. National Security Council, to discuss a response. During the week that followed, ExComm considered the options. The two that had the most support were an air strike on the missile installations and a naval blockade of the island that would prevent the Soviets from delivering nuclear warheads. Both options had problems. An air strike might not take out all of the missile sites and would inevitably kill Soviet personnel. Khrushchev might well respond by bombing American missile sites in Turkey or capturing West Berlin. From there, the crisis could easily escalate into a nuclear war. The blockade, on the other hand, was technically an act of war and might have the same disastrous results. ExComm decided in the end to opt for the blockade. They called it a "quarantine" to try to distinguish it from an act of war and in the hope that it allowed Khrushchev a way out short of armed conflict.

On October 22, President Kennedy appeared on national television to announce the presence of the missiles in Cuba and the imposition of the naval quarantine. Khrushchev denounced the move and declared that Soviet ships were to ignore the blockade and continue their supply convoys to Cuba. For two days the world watched and waited. On October 24, just short of the picket line of American ships, the Soviet vessels carrying nuclear missiles changed course to return home. After two more days of negotiation, the Soviet and American leaders found a resolution. To break the impasse Khrushchev sent two contradictory letters to Kennedy. In the first, confidential communication, Khrushchev proposed that the Soviets dismantle the nuclear weapons sites in exchange for a promise from the Americans that they would not invade Cuba. In the second, open letter, the Soviet leader, apparently under pressure from hard-liners in Moscow, demanded that the United States remove its missiles from Turkey as well as promise not to invade before he removed the missiles from Cuba. President Kennedy agreed to the terms of the first communication and ignored the second with the stipulation that the missiles in Turkey could be discussed at a later date. Khrushchev accepted the offer and by the end of the year dismantled the missile sites, as well as withdrawing several nuclear warheads that the Soviets had secreted into Cuba before the quarantine.

During the Cuban missile crisis, the world came closer to full-scale nuclear war than at any other time in its history and for no good reason. Operation Mongoose had unnecessarily heightened Castro's paranoia and convinced Moscow that an invasion was imminent. The Soviets had miscalculated Kennedy's resolve and underestimated the importance of the American political process in the crisis. And both Kennedy and Khrushchev had dangerously let their egos and hard-liner expectations drive the conflict. Perhaps recognizing this fact, Soviet-American relations experienced a slight thaw the following year. The most symbolic gesture in that thaw was the installation of an emergency telephone hotline between Washington, D.C., and Moscow in 1963 that was to be used to avoid misperception and miscalculation in the event of another crisis.

Jeff Woods

FURTHER READING:

Beschloss, Michael. *The Crisis Years: Kennedy and Khrushchev, 1960–1963.* New York: Edward Burlingame Books, 1991.

Blight, James G., and David A. Welch. *On the Brink: Americans and Soviets Reexamine the Cuban Missile Crisis.* New York: Farrar, Straus and Giroux, 1989.

Kennedy, Robert F. *Thirteen Days: A Memoir of the Cuban Missile Crisis.* New York: W. W. Norton, 1969.

May, Ernest R., and Philip D. Zelikow, eds. *The Kennedy Tapes: Inside the White House during the Cuban Missile Crisis.* Cambridge, Mass.: Belknap Press, 1997.

1963 ◆ ASSASSINATION OF PRESIDENT KENNEDY

By the fall of 1963, President John F. Kennedy and his political advisers were becoming increasingly uneasy about the 1964 presidential election. The administration had failed to deliver on medical care for senior citizens or federal aid to education, and unemployment remained too high for political comfort. Most important, the intensifying civil rights movement had polarized public opinion in the South—especially after President Kennedy called racial equality a moral issue in a nationally televised speech in June 1963. It seemed unlikely that JFK could hold onto the seven southern states that were essential to his razor-thin margin of victory in 1960. Conservative senator Barry Goldwater of Arizona, who opposed the administration's civil rights bill (then stalled in Congress), appeared likely to be the Republican candidate. If Goldwater could sweep the South and make inroads among northern whites concerned about racial unrest, JFK's reelection could be in serious trouble. The Kennedy team was convinced that the 25 electoral votes of Vice President Lyndon Johnson's home state of Texas might be decisive. But the Texas Democratic Party was deeply divided between factions led by conservative governor John Connally and liberal senator Ralph Yarborough. The fact that the 1961 special election to fill Johnson's vacated senate seat had been won by a conservative Republican—the first Republican senator elected in Texas since Reconstruction—seemed especially ominous. In an effort to heal the schism among Lone Star State Democrats, Kennedy agreed to go to Texas in late November 1963.

After successful stops in San Antonio, Houston, and Fort Worth, the presidential party, which included JFK, first lady Jacqueline Kennedy, Vice President Johnson, and Governor Connally, flew to Dallas. At about 12:30 on the afternoon of Friday, November 22, as the president's motorcade reached Dealey Plaza in downtown Dallas, several shots rang out. A home movie, made by a local resident standing in the crowd, captured the president's shocked reaction as a bullet struck him in the back of the neck. Within seconds, another bullet blew off much of the back of Kennedy's head. (The president was wearing a rigid brace to ease his chronic back pain. Without the brace, he would probably have been knocked down or off the seat by the nonlethal neck

FACTBOX

PLACE Dallas, Texas

DATE November 22, 1963

TYPE Presidential assassination

DESCRIPTION While riding in a motorcade, President John F. Kennedy was shot and killed.

CASUALTIES Death of President Kennedy; Texas governor Connally wounded

IMPACT Vice President Lyndon Johnson became president; erosion of American confidence and trust in government

shot and thus out of range of any subsequent shots.) Most eyewitnesses believed the gunfire had come from the sixth floor of the adjacent Texas School Book Depository. The president's car raced to nearby Parkland Hospital as Jacqueline Kennedy, her pink suit stained with her husband's brains and blood, cradled the mortally wounded president's head in her arms. The unthinkable news was confirmed within the hour: 46-year-old John Fitzgerald Kennedy had been killed and Governor Connally had been seriously wounded. It was the fourth time in American history that a president had been assassinated. After returning to Air Force One at Dallas's Love Field, with a dazed Mrs. Kennedy standing to his left, Lyndon Johnson took the oath as the 36th president of the United States and flew back to Washington.

Dallas police soon recovered the murder weapon (a mail-order Italian rifle) near the window from which the shots appeared to have been fired. Later that afternoon, Lee Harvey Oswald, a former marine who had once defected to the Soviet Union and was an outspoken supporter of Cuban Communist leader Fidel Castro, was arrested in a Dallas movie theater and charged with the assassination of the president and the subsequent murder of a Dallas police officer. Late that evening, the president's body was returned to the White House. On Saturday, November 23, with a cold, gloomy rain matching the mood in Washington, President Kennedy's body lay in a flag-draped coffin in the East Room of the White House. On Sunday, a horse-drawn caisson carried the casket to the Capitol, where an estimated 250,000 people filed through the rotunda. Finally, on Monday, November 25, the formal state funeral, attended by hundreds of dignitaries and heads of state, was watched on television by the largest audience in history. Indeed, with regular programming and commercials suspended, most Americans spent all their waking hours that weekend in front of their television sets. As a result, when Dallas police attempted on Sunday afternoon to transfer Oswald from downtown headquarters to the county jail, millions witnessed the fatal shooting of the accused assassin by Jack Ruby, a local nightclub owner.

It is almost impossible to capture the shock that gripped the American people, and indeed the whole world, in the wake of these stunning events. Oswald's political background suggested a possible conspiracy involving Cuba or even the Soviet Union. President Johnson was genuinely concerned that evidence of communist complicity could spark a nuclear war. Johnson, nonetheless, initially opposed creating a presidential commission to investigate the assassination. But after the televised murder of Oswald, which he correctly believed had transformed the nation's grief and anger into skepticism and doubt, Johnson recognized that the public would demand more than a routine investigation by the Dallas police or even the FBI.

President Johnson used his prodigious persuasive skills to pressure liberal chief justice Earl Warren to head a presidential commission and to convince conservative Democratic senator Richard Russell of Georgia to serve as well (the two men hated each other). The November 29 appointment of the bipartisan "Warren Commission," as it came to be called, was the first important decision by the new president, and it promptly earned widespread support from the press and the public. Johnson also appointed former CIA director Allen Dulles, former World Bank president John McCloy, Kentucky Republican senator John Sherman Cooper, Michigan Republican representative Gerald Ford, and Louisiana Democratic representative Hale Boggs.

The Warren Commission received unlimited authority to review the evidence and appointed U.S. solicitor general James Lee Rankin as general counsel. The staff of 14 deputy counsels and a 12-member research team worked for 10 months (virtually all the hearings were closed to the public), interviewed more than 500 witnesses, and evaluated written statements from the FBI, the CIA, the State Department, the Secret Service, and other federal agencies. The final commission report was presented to President Johnson in September 1964—in the midst of the presidential election campaign. (The evidentiary material, including transcripts of testimony and declassified documents, filled 26 volumes; most Americans read the one-volume summary report instead.) The Warren Commission found that Lee Harvey Oswald had acted alone in the murders of President Kennedy and a Dallas policeman and found no evidence connecting Oswald and Jack Ruby. In short, there had been no criminal conspiracy and no involvement by foreign governments. The report, at least for the moment, provided a plausible explanation for the assassination. Shortly thereafter, Johnson won a full term by defeating Barry Goldwater by a historic landslide in the November election.

But doubts about the assassination continued to fester. A spate of books appeared, including one by lawyer Mark Lane, that promoted an astonishing range of conspiracies allegedly carried out by right-wing extremists, both in and out of the federal government. In 1967, New Orleans district attorney Jim Garrison claimed to have unraveled a vast government plot; he arrested local businessman Clay Shaw and charged him with involvement in this CIA-sponsored conspiracy to murder President Kennedy. A jury acquitted Shaw in 54 minutes. Garrison's bizarre claims were later revived and popularized in Oliver Stone's 1991 film, *JFK*.

In the 1970s, revelations by the Senate's Church Committee about covert efforts by the Kennedy

Although blurry, this photograph shows President and Mrs. Kennedy in the backseat and Governor and Mrs. Connally in the front seat of the car during the motorcade through Dallas on November 22, 1963. Just after this picture was taken, President Kennedy was assassinated. *(Library of Congress)*

administration to assassinate Fidel Castro, with the aid of the Mafia, riveted the nation. The hearings also revealed that the CIA and the FBI had lied and withheld evidence from the Warren Commission in order to cover up their own incompetence, thus further discrediting the official verdict. The House of Representatives Select Committee on Assassinations concluded in 1979, based on uncorroborated acoustic evidence, that Kennedy "was probably assassinated as a result of a conspiracy . . . [but was] unable to identify the other gunmen or the extent of the conspiracy." This acoustic "evidence" was soon completely discredited. Notwithstanding, these revelations helped spawn an assassination conspiracy "industry" that continues to turn out books and articles, hold conferences with "expert" speakers, and sell a wide variety of assassination-related memorabilia.

Today, more than four decades after that dreadful day in Dallas, a clear majority of the American people believe that the assassination of President Kennedy was the result of a conspiracy. Indeed, many believe that Johnson himself was behind the murder of his predecessor. In November 2003, the 40th anniversary of the assassination, the History Channel broadcast a "documentary" claiming to prove this charge against Johnson. Later, the channel's management was forced to backtrack and aired a withering attack on that baseless claim by three leading historians. Nevertheless, these suspicions remain very much alive.

Recent research, however, has uncovered startling insights into the underside of these conspiracy theories. For example: In the 1960s, the Soviet Union found lawyer Mark Lane's claims about right-wing complicity in the assassination so valuable that the KGB, the Soviet covert intelligence agency, "was secretly underwriting his 'research' and travel." Likewise, Jim Garrison's 1967 prosecution also relied on disinformation planted by the KGB in a communist newspaper in Italy. "Within a matter of months," wrote historian Max Holland in *The Nation* in 2006, "Garrison had succeeded in making the KGB's wildest fantasy come true: an elected public official in America was propagating Moscow's line."

Millions of Americans still recall exactly where they were and what they were doing when they heard the devastating news from Dallas. November 22, 1963, shattered the trust in government and the confidence in the future shared by most Americans at the beginning of the 1960s.

See also 1865 ASSASSINATION OF PRESIDENT LINCOLN; 1881 ASSASSINATION OF PRESIDENT GARFIELD; 1901 ASSASSINATION OF PRESIDENT MCKINLEY.

Sheldon M. Stern

FURTHER READING:

Blakey, G. Robert, and Richard Billings. *The Plot to Kill the President.* New York: Times Books, 1981.

Holland, Max. "The JFK Lawyers' Conspiracy." *The Nation* (February 20, 2006).

———, comp. *The Kennedy Assassination Tapes.* New York: Knopf, 2004.

Lane, Mark. *Rush to Judgment.* New York: Holt, Rinehart & Winston, 1966.

Manchester, William. *The Death of a President.* London: Michael Joseph, 1967.

Posner, Gerald. *Case Closed: Lee Harvey Oswald and the Assassination of JFK.* New York: Random House, 1993.

Report of the President's Commission on the Assassination of President John F. Kennedy. New York: Doubleday, 1964.

1964 ◆ CIGARETTES AND LUNG CANCER

On January 11, 1964, an Advisory Committee on Smoking and Health appointed by the surgeon general of the United States issued a report that cited cigarettes as a prime cause of lung cancer. The committee called cigarette smoking a significant health hazard and urged "remedial action." This announcement inaugurated a long, rancorous battle between government and the tobacco industry over the use of tobacco that has continued into the 21st century. Detrimental effects from smoking were suspected decades before 1964, but scientific credence for the hypothesis did not appear until the 1950s. After 1964, linkages between smoking and lung cancer, cardiovascular disease, and other ailments were conclusively drawn. By the late 1960s, health officials called cigarette smoking a public health "crisis" and smoking-related diseases a major "epidemic." For decades after 1964, cigarette manufacturers denied that they produced a harmful product or that science had proven the toxicity of tobacco. Nonetheless, in 1998, "big tobacco" accepted responsibility for hundreds of thousands of premature deaths and illnesses due to smoking and agreed to pay $206 billion in damages to state governments.

The story of cigarettes and lung cancer begins in the 19th century with the development of the cigarette industry. Tobacco is a product native to the Americas and was introduced to Europeans following their exploration of the Western Hemisphere. Americans in the 19th century smoked tobacco in pipes and cigars, chewed the leaves, or sniffed ground tobacco called "snuff." Cigarettes appeared in the United States after the Civil War (1861–65). Considered an exotic import from Europe, cigarettes gained acceptance slowly, until James Duke, a tobacco manufacturer from North Carolina, entered the market. He began to make cigarettes in 1881 and licensed a newly invented machine in 1884 that transformed the manufacture of cigarettes into a mass-production commodity. Duke advertised his product heavily and, as founder of the American Tobacco Company, moved aggressively to consolidate the industry in the 1890s. In 1911, the Supreme Court cited the American Tobacco Company combination to be in violation of the nation's antimonopoly statute and broke up the corporation, with four companies assuming most of American's assets. Duke also supported opponents of anticigarettes crusaders, who blamed the "weed" for undermining morality, especially among minors. Numerous states banned cigarette sales and use in the early 20th century, on moral rather than health grounds.

The introduction of the cardboard matchbook in 1892, which made lighting a "butt" easier and cheaper, and American entry into World War I in 1917, which drew 4 million men into the armed services, boosted cigarette consumption substantially. The war helped to overcome perceptions that smoking cigarettes was unmanly and unsophisticated. Providing doughboys

FACTBOX

PLACE United States

DATE The first "cancer scare" in the United States occurred in 1954, and the battle between the cigarette industry and health officials continued into the early 21st century. The first surgeon general's report officially linking smoking and lung cancer was made public on January 11, 1964.

TYPE Health crisis

DESCRIPTION The rate of lung cancer increased exponentially between 1920 and 1980.

CAUSE Research demonstrated that 90 percent of lung cancer was attributed to smoking cigarettes, which also was found to contribute to cardiovascular disease and other health ailments.

CASUALTIES The effects of tobacco caused an estimated 400,000 premature deaths a year in the 1990s.

COST Estimates in the mid-1990s put tobacco-related health expenditures at $50 billion a year, about one-half of which was paid by government.

IMPACT Publicity over the health effects of cigarettes led to a diminished rate of smoking among Americans, and the enactment of tobacco control laws, which restricted places of smoking.

in France with cigarettes became official government policy. General John J. Pershing, commander of U.S. forces in Europe, commented: "You ask me what we need to win this war. I answer tobacco as much as bullets." By World War II (1941–45) when military officials stuffed cigarettes in soldiers' knapsacks, cigarettes sales had grown exponentially. Just under 4 billion cigarettes were manufactured in 1900. The figure increased to 48 billion in 1920 and reached 350 billion in 1946. Symbolic of smoking during wartime, Dwight Eisenhower, commander of Allied forces in Europe, was a chain-smoker.

Men predominated among cigarette smokers through the 1940s, but women rapidly closed the gender gap as social mores changed, especially during World War II and in the immediate postwar decades. Smoking became a symbol of the "modern" liberated

"YOU'LL LIVE, BUT NOT AS WELL AS YOU USED TO."

In this drawing by famed cartoonist Bill Mauldin, a doctor examines an ailing cigarette, representing the tobacco industry. *(Papers of Bill Mauldin, Library of Congress)*

women. First lady Eleanor Roosevelt smoked cigarettes, as did her husband, President Franklin D. Roosevelt. A Gallup poll in 1944, the first to survey cigarette usage, found that 41 percent of respondents smoked cigarettes. Gallup's 1949 poll recorded that 44 percent of individuals surveyed smoked, with 54 percent of men and 33 percent of women acknowledging the habit. In 1954, the proportion of smokers had crept up to 47 percent of all adults.

Moral qualms about cigarettes faded as the 20th century progressed, but widespread sentiment that smoking was unhealthy persisted. References to "coffin nails" captured this piece of folk-wisdom and probably contributed to state laws that banned tobacco sales to minors. Gallup's 1949 poll found that 66 percent of nonsmokers and 52 percent of smokers thought that use of cigarettes was bad for health. Health and medical textbooks in the 1930s and 1940s echoed this popular verdict with warnings that cigarettes were habit forming and unhealthy, but establishing a firm linkage between smoking cigarettes

and distinct diseases still lacked solid scientific proof. Lung cancer was not officially classified as a disease until 1923. The creation of two federal agencies, the National Institutes of Health in 1930 and the National Cancer Institute in 1937, set in motion federal investigations of the effects of tobacco.

The rate of lung cancer barely registered on epidemiological charts in 1920 but rose dramatically from the 1930s though 1950. The rates were much higher for men than for women, whose use of cigarettes trailed men historically. Suspicions were articulated in the 1930s and 1940s that cigarettes were a cause of the trend. The hypothesis gained further credence in 1950 with several breakthrough studies. One study, which appeared in *The Journal of the American Medical Association,* reviewed the research of Evarts Graham and his young assistant, Ernest Wynder, at the Washington University in St. Louis. They reported a startling connection between patients with lung cancer and smoking. In 1953, Wynder announced that mice with tobacco tar (an element in cigarette smoke) painted on their backs frequently developed malignant tumors. British researchers came to similar conclusions about the effects of cigarettes in the early 1950s. Britain's health minister told Parliament in 1954 that the nation's "top cancer specialists" concluded that a relationship between smoking and lung cancer was "established." A study by the American Cancer Society, which had taken up the antitobacco crusade around 1950, published a massive survey in 1954 that documented a connection between cigarette smoking and markedly elevated rates of premature death.

The general public did not read the scientific literature, but millions did see the *Reader's Digest,* the nation's best-selling magazine, as well as other popular publications, such as *Life* magazine. The *Digest* was instrumental in bringing the medical findings about the effects of smoking to the attention of Americans. Its article entitled "Cancer by the Carton" in the December 1952 issue of the magazine was a widespread sensation. The *Digest* continued its antismoking campaign with articles such as "The Facts behind the Cigarette Controversy" in July 1954. Such stories in the media generated a "cancer" scare in 1954. Gallup's polls recorded rise of anxiety over these revelations. In his poll of January 1954, 70 percent of the individuals surveyed thought that cigarette smoking was harmful; 41 percent said it caused lung cancer. Eighty-three percent had recently heard or read something that reported cigarettes as a possible cause of lung cancer.

Public qualms about the unhealthiness of smoking spelled trouble for the tobacco industry. Not only did cigarette sales dip in 1954, but that year, Ira C. Lowe of Festus, Missouri, sued four cigarette manufacturers, contending that smoking cigarettes caused him to lose a lung to cancer. His legal challenge failed, but the tobacco industry began a long history of fending off product liability suits. In 1954, cigarette manufacturers and other groups with a financial stake in the product formed the Tobacco Industry Research Committee to counter the negative publicity about smoking. During the next several decades, spokespeople for the industry denied that a causal connection between smoking and lung cancer had been scientifically demonstrated. Its spokespeople argued that statistical studies (epidemiological analysis of biomedical data) of cancer deaths did not prove smoking caused premature death and that the results

of experiments on mice did not hold for people. The industry also responded to health concerns by developing filtered cigarettes, which it alleged reduced tar and nicotine intake, the most usually cited harmful agents in tobacco smoke. Smokers by and large accepted the claim, as filter cigarettes surpassed sales of conventional brands by 1962. By the end of the 1960s, three out of four smokers chose filtered cigarettes, despite the conclusion of medical experts that filters did not significantly reduce the risk of cancer. Filtered cigarettes and the nicotine that tobacco companies purposely added to them—a revelation disclosed by litigation in the 1990s—pushed cigarette sales upward and kept "big tobacco" profitable.

After a brief lull, the tobacco story hit the headlines again in 1957. A Study Group on Smoking and Health formed by the American Cancer Society, the American Heart Association, the National Heart Institute, and the National Cancer Institute reported that "the sum total of scientific evidence established

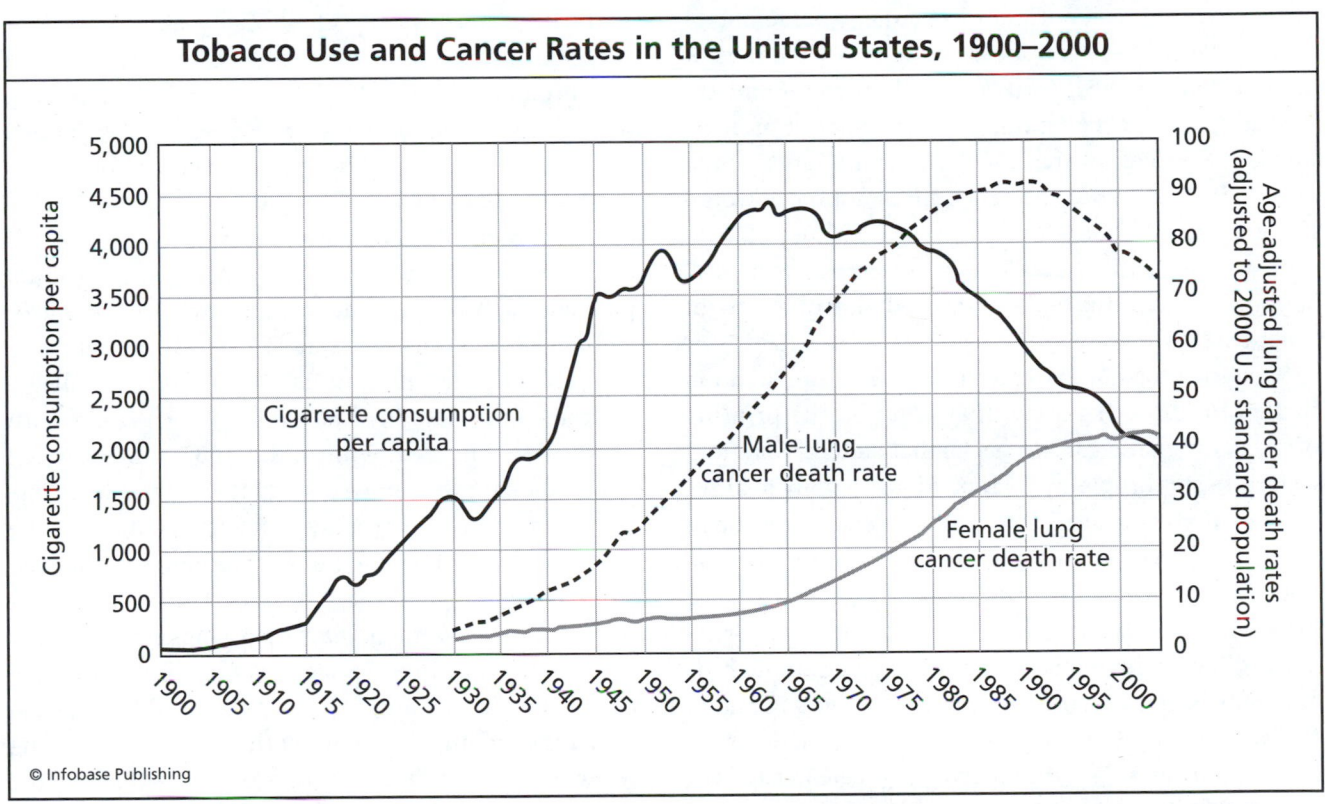

Tobacco Use and Cancer Rates in the United States, 1900–2000

© Infobase Publishing

Cigarette consumption per person peaked in the United States in 1964, the year the Surgeon General released his report on smoking. Lung cancer peaked a generation later. Source: *Death Rates: U.S. Mortality Public Use Tapes, 1960–2003, U.S. Mortality Volumes, 1930–1959*. National Center for Health Statistics Centers for Disease Control and Prevention, 2005. *Cigarette Consumption: U.S. Department of Agriculture, 1900–2003*. Cited in *American Cancer Society 2007. Cancer Statistics, 2007*.

beyond a reasonable doubt that cigarette smoking is a causative factor" in contracting lung cancer. Smoking cigarettes, the group warned, "is an important health hazard." Later in the year, Leroy Burney, the surgeon general of the United States, called attention to the scientific evidence linking cancer to cigarettes. In 1957, Gallup found that 50 percent of individuals polled believed that smoking caused lung cancer.

New research in the late 1950s strengthened the indictment of tobacco, adding heart disease to cancer as a health consequence of smoking. Surgeon General Burney stated in 1959 that cigarettes were the "principal cause" of lung cancer. The American Cancer Society declared that the evidence showed "beyond any reasonable doubt" the damage caused by cigarettes. By the late 1950s, a consensus had formed in the medical and bioscientific communities that smoking was harmful to health and caused lung cancer. Yet cigarette sales increased during these years and into the early 1960s. These dual trends galvanized public health agencies to pressure the federal government for action. In 1962, Surgeon General Luther Terry, appointed by President John F. Kennedy, a Democrat who replaced the Republican Dwight D. Eisenhower as president in 1961, formed an advisory committee to study the issue of smoking. After a year of meeting in secret, the committee concluded in its *Smoking and Health Report* (1964) that cigarette smoking lowered life expectancy, was a prime cause of lung cancer, and was "a health hazard" that warranted remedial action. The committee sidestepped the question of whether cigarettes were "addictive."

Congress took up the committee's recommendation in 1965 by adopting a law that required the printing of a warning on cigarette packs that stated: "Caution: Cigarette smoking may be hazardous to your health." The act also prohibited state governments from enacting stronger regulations of cigarettes. Members of the antitobacco campaign cried foul, claiming that the tobacco industry, which included farmers, advertisers, and retailers, in addition to cigarette manufacturers and southern Democrats whose districts included substantial numbers of tobacco farmers, had gutted the regulations. The antitobacco advocates criticized both the failure to print warnings in advertising and the weakly worded warning. Subsequently, they argued that the warning did little to prevent the start of teenage smoking. Further support for tougher legislation came from antismoking ads run on TV and radio beginning in 1968. This development followed a ruling from the Federal Communication Commission regarding its "fairness doctrine," a decision that opened up airtime for antitobacco advocates. In 1970, Congress enacted new language for cigarette packs: "Warning: The Surgeon General has determined that cigarettes smoking is dangerous to your health." In 1984, Congress adopted a set of four rotated warnings which ranged from a statement that smoking causes lung cancer to a warning that smoking during pregnancy may harm the baby. In the 1970s, rising concern over "second-hand smoke" (cigarette smoke that reached nonsmokers) began to generate restrictions on smoking in public places—public transportation vehicles and public accommodations such as restaurants and bars. Beginning with Arizona in 1973 and California cities in 1983, state and local governments across the nation adopted tobacco control ordinances. By 1995, most companies and public institutions banned smoking in the workplace. In 2006, 14 states had laws that prohibited smoking at work and in public accommodations.

The quarter-century of publicity about the dangers of cigarettes since the "cancer scare" of 1954 had two pronounced effects. First, the rate of smoking diminished after the surgeon general's 1964 report. Between 1966 and 1970, the proportion of adults in the United States who smoked decreased from 43 to 37 percent, and continued to inch downward in succeeding decades. In 1987, the figure fell to 29 percent, with 32 percent of men and 27 percent of women reported as smokers. By 2003, the rate was 22 percent. The rate of smokers among college-educated individuals was half that of people with only high school diplomas. In 1985, virtually all adults thought that smoking caused lung cancer. The death rate from lung cancer in men peaked in the 1980s, although the rate among women, who started smoking later historically, continued to climb. In part because fewer women than men smoke, the female death rate from lung cancer was one-half the male rate. Nonetheless, lung cancer surpassed breast cancer as the leading cause of death from cancer among women in 1986. This gap grew in the 1990s. During the decade, health officials estimated that more than 400,000 premature deaths a year were attributable to smoking. Ninety percent of lung cancer deaths were attributable to smoking. The health cost of smoking to government was estimated at about $25 billion a year in 1993, an amount far greater than the total taxes collected from the sale of tobacco.

The second pronounced effect of publicity surrounding cigarettes is that the tobacco companies faced continuous litigation. One strand of suits came from private citizens who argued that the tobacco companies failed to warn consumers of the hazards of their products. In one breakthrough case brought by Tony Cipollone, a jury ruled in 1988 that the Liggett tobacco company was liable for the death of his wife, Rose Cipollone, a life-long smoker who died of lung cancer. The Supreme Court in 1992 revoked the monetary award to her husband. The cigarette companies spent billions in successfully defending themselves from consumer suits until Brown and Williamson, the makers of Kool and Viceroy, paid a damage award in 2001. The second line of litigation came from governments, which sued to recover monies spent for health care costs attributable to smoking. Beginning with Mississippi in 1994, 46 states filed suit to recover Medicaid expenditures. In conjunction with the litigation, corporate documents surfaced that showed tobacco manufacturers had endeavored for decades to suppress research showing cigarettes to be addictive and carcinogenic. In 1998, the major tobacco firms agreed to pay $206 billion to the states to reimburse medical costs. The following year, Philip Morris, the maker of Marlboros and the nation's largest cigarette manufacturer, acknowledged that smoking carried health risks.

Documents released in 1994, which showed that tobacco companies suppressed information about the effects of smoking, induced the federal government to sue the industry under the Racketeering Influenced and Corrupt Organizations Act (1970). In 2006, a federal district court ruled that the cigarette industry had conspired to deceive the public. Judge Gladys Kessler concluded that big tobacco had "marketed and sold their lethal product with zeal, deception, with a single-minded focus on their financial success and without regard for the human tragedy or social costs that success exacted."

Ballard C. Campbell

FURTHER READING:

Brandt, Allan M. *The Cigarette Century: The Rise, Fall, and Deadly Persistence of the Product that Defined America.* New York: Basic Books, 2007.

Kluger, Richard. *Ashes to Ashes: America's Hundred-Year Cigarette War, the Public Health, and the Unabashed Triumph of Philip Morris.* New York: Knopf, 1996.

Sobel, Robert. *They Satisfy: The Cigarette in American Life.* New York: Anchor, 1978.

Tate, Cassandra. *Cigarette Wars: The Triumph of "the Little White Slaver."* New York: Oxford University Press, 1999.

U.S. Dept. of Health, Education, and Welfare. *Smoking and Health Report of the Advisory Committee to the Surgeon General of the Public Health Service.* Washington, D.C.: U.S. Dept. of Health, 1964.

1964 ◆ FREEDOM SUMMER CIVIL RIGHTS MURDERS

In 1964, a thousand volunteers—mostly college students but also attorneys, clergy, and physicians—descended on Mississippi as part of the civil rights movement's efforts to register black voters, build community centers, and create freedom schools. Planned in 1963 as activists faced exhaustion and escalating white resistance from groups such as the Ku Klux Klan, the Freedom Summer resulted in violence, including the murder of three young volunteers and unprecedented national attention on the struggle for racial justice in Mississippi.

Since the end of Reconstruction in the late 19th century, white southern governments had systematically disenfranchised most African Americans throughout the region, especially in the Deep South. By the early 1960s, rights activists such as Bob Moses of the Student Nonviolent Coordinating Committee (SNCC) concluded that "It was impossible to register Negroes in Mississippi." To overcome this hurdle

FACTBOX

PLACE Philadelphia, Mississippi

DATE June 21, 1964

TYPE Murder and violence over civil rights

DESCRIPTION Murder of three civil rights movement volunteers who were part of a larger effort to use white northern volunteers to advance civil rights for blacks in Mississippi

CAUSE Deep-seated racism and gunshots from members of the Ku Klux Klan

CASUALTIES Three deaths: the murders of James Chaney, Michael Schwerner, and James Goodman

IMPACT Heightened activism and wide-scale publicity surrounding the murders precipitated passage of the Civil Rights Act of 1964, and increased federal involvement in protecting activists and in the prosecution of opponents, such as members of the Klan

civil rights workers recognized that the national media's interest in white northern volunteers would be invaluable in recharging efforts to register local blacks before the 1964 presidential election. Despite concern about the impact of white activists on black leadership within the movement, recruitment efforts began in December 1963. As a result, more than 600 mostly white middle-class students from elite colleges in the North arrived in Oxford, Ohio, in June for a brief orientation, which included Mississippi history and role playing.

Within days, volunteers such as James Chaney, Michael Schwerner, and James Goodman headed south. Chaney, a 21-year-old black man from Meridian, Mississippi, and his friend Schwerner, a white Jewish New Yorker with experience working with the Congress for Racial Equality (CORE), exemplified the goal of creating an interracial community of activists working in Mississippi. Together with Goodman, a white 20-year-old college student from New York and new to the South, they drove to Meridian on June 21 to investigate the burning of a black church that had been targeted by the Klan. Near Philadelphia, Mississippi, Sheriff Deputy Cecil Price arrested the three men for allegedly speeding, held them in jail

for seven hours, and then released them. Price soon stopped them again and turned the volunteers over to Klan members, who shot the three men. Although authorities soon located Schwerner's car, the fate of the activists remained a mystery for the next six weeks. Finally, in early August a tip from an FBI informant revealed their burial in a remote dam.

While civil rights activists and volunteers anguished over their inability to prevent the murders, their predictions of the impact on national opinion proved correct. The summer of 1964 was the most violent in Mississippi since Reconstruction, with 35 shootings, more than 60 cases of arson, and 80 assaults on activists. Regardless, the disappearance of two white northern volunteers and Chaney escalated the interest of the nation and the federal government in the struggle for racial justice in Mississippi. After years of claiming the FBI had little role in protecting the rights of activists in the South, Director J. Edgar Hoover sent six FBI agents to Meridian within days of the murders. By July, Hoover opened a new FBI field office in Jackson that employed more than 150 federal agents by the end of the summer.

The tragic events of the Freedom Summer also shaped the perspectives of both activists and the general public. The white parents of the volunteers created organizations that lobbied both Congress and the U.S. Justice Department on behalf of their children. Such efforts contributed to a new political climate and federal legislation such as the Civil Rights Act of 1964 and the Voting Rights Act of 1965. While Schwerner and Goodman were buried in New York, Chaney's funeral was in Meridian and his eulogy, delivered by activist Dave Dennis, offered a hint as to the anger and frustration that would soon emerge among cries for Black Power and an increasing reevaluation of nonviolence and racial integration. Dennis chastised his fellow activists for their caution and blamed the federal government for the murders. Dennis exclaimed, "I'm sick and tired of going to the funerals of black men who have been murdered by white men."

While the murders of Chaney, Schwerner, and Goodman reflected the violent reemergence of the Ku Klux Klan in Mississippi during the civil rights movement, federal reaction to the crimes resulted in a substantial decrease in the power of the Klan. In the wake of the murders, the FBI increasingly infiltrated the organization and, in 1967, seven men, including Deputy Sheriff Cecil Price and Sam Bow-

Two days after the disappearance of civil rights workers James Chaney, Michael Schwerner, and James Goodman, authorities located the charred remains of Schwerner's car in which they were last seen. *(Library of Congress)*

ers, the imperial wizard of the Klan in Mississippi, were convicted in federal court of violating the civil rights of the three volunteers. After 1964, opponents of the civil rights movement in Mississippi were no longer immune from federal law or the judgment of the American public.

See also 1957 LITTLE ROCK SCHOOL DESEGREGATION CRISIS; 1965 SELMA VOTING RIGHTS DEMONSTRATION; 1968 ASSASSINATION OF MARTIN LUTHER KING, JR.

Richard L. Hughes

FURTHER READING:

Dittmer, John. *Local People: The Struggle for Civil Rights in Mississippi.* Urbana: University of Illinois Press, 1994.

McAdam, Doug. *Freedom Summer.* New York: Oxford University Press, 1988.

Rothschild, Mary A. *A Case of Black and White: Northern Volunteers and the Southern Freedom Summers, 1964–65.* Westport, Conn.: Greenwood, 1982.

1965 ◇ SELMA VOTING RIGHTS DEMONSTRATION

In March 1965, the eyes of the nation fell upon Selma, Alabama. The brutal response of white segregationists to the drive for voting rights by African Americans in this small southern city angered a wide range of Americans, especially outside of the South. Outraged by events in Selma, President Lyndon Johnson and the United States Congress took action to end the disfranchisement of black southerners.

The decision of Martin Luther King, Jr., and the Southern Christian Leadership Conference (SCLC) in late 1964 to come to the aid of civil rights activists in Selma ensured that this city would make national news. King and the SCLC hoped that a Selma

FACTBOX

PLACE Selma and Montgomery, Alabama

DATE March 1965

TYPE Civil rights demonstration and racial violence

DESCRIPTION After attacks on civil rights forces by white segregationists, Martin Luther King, Jr., and other activists mobilized much of the country and the federal government to bring about fundamental change in southern race relations.

CAUSE The dissonance between the humane goals and behavior of the civil rights demonstrators and the racism and brutality of white segregationist forces

CASUALTIES Three deaths (including one the month before at a nearby protest) and at least 100 wounded

IMPACT Federal support for the civil rights movement and passage of the Voting Rights Act

campaign would compel federal voting rights legislation. Recent federal civil rights measures had not secured this elemental right of citizenship for African Americans residing in the South, where many had been disfranchised since the late 19th century.

When King and SCLC activists entered Selma in January 1965, segregation and intimidation still reigned in this city. The local movement, which was bolstered by Student Nonviolent Coordinating Committee (SNCC) organizers, had struggled against a hostile white population, including the sheriff of Dallas County, Jim Clark, who was widely known to hate civil rights "agitators." In February, one local activist, Jimmie Lee Jackson, was killed by a state trooper during an evening protest at the nearby Perry County courthouse.

The reinforced voting rights drive had already attracted some national attention when in March civil rights leaders decided to escalate their protests by marching to Montgomery, the state capital, 50 miles to the southeast. To leave Selma, the demonstrators had to walk across the Edmund Pettus Bridge.

On Sunday, March 7, Hosea Williams of the SCLC and SNCC leader John Lewis crossed the bridge with 600 marchers. On the other side, they ran into a phalanx of law enforcement officers. Governor George Wallace had declared that there would be no march, and Alabama state troopers, backed by Sheriff Clark's possemen, ordered the protestors to turn around. When they did not, the officers attacked the peaceful demonstrators with nightsticks and tear gas, injuring more than 100.

The events of "Bloody Sunday," as it came to be called, unfolded before a large group of reporters. Footage of the beating soon appeared on television sets across the country. ABC interrupted its Sunday evening movie, *Judgment at Nuremberg*, to cover the breaking story. The next day, the nation's leading newspapers featured the brutality in Alabama.

For millions of Americans, the developments in Selma were intolerable. Hundreds rushed to Selma to bear personal witness, thousands joined sympathy protests across the North, while many more contacted their elected officials in Washington. Representatives and senators, moreover, condemned the actions of the Alabama lawmen.

Martin Luther King, Jr., promised to lead a second march across the Pettus bridge. A federal judge, however, issued a decree barring such a march until hearings were held. King now faced a dilemma. He had scrupulously refrained from violating federal injunctions. He did not want to alienate the federal government, which had the power to bring about fundamental change to the South. But he also wanted to fulfill the pledge to march.

On Tuesday, March 9, a large column of demonstrators, led by King, trekked across the Pettus bridge and confronted a line of Alabama state troopers. This time, King stopped and reversed course. To King's critics within the movement, especially within SNCC, his refusal to break the injunction revealed his fundamental timidity.

As civil rights activists plotted their next steps, three clergymen who had come to the city after "Bloody Sunday" were beaten by white segregationists. One of them, James Reeb, soon died. To onlookers outside the South, this death was further evidence of the essential evil of white supremacy.

On Monday, March 15, President Lyndon Johnson responded forcefully to events in Selma. In a nationally televised address, he announced that his administration would introduce new federal legislation, the Voting Rights Act, to protect the right to vote of

Two days after attacking civil rights demonstrators in Selma, Alabama, state troopers block marchers from continuing beyond the Edmund Pettus Bridge. *(© Bettmann/CORBIS)*

southern blacks. He, moreover, directly aligned the federal government behind the cause of freedom in Selma when he concluded his remarks by embracing the words of the civil rights movement, saying, "And . . . we . . . shall . . . overcome."

Six days later, with the federal injunction lifted, King and more than 3,000 activists crossed the Pettus bridge—this time under the protection of the National Guard—on their way to Montgomery. After five days, they reached their destination. In front of the Alabama state capital and 25,000 onlookers, King delivered one of his most stirring speeches. "We are," he said, "on the move now . . . we are moving to the land of freedom."

The forces of reaction did not surrender, however. After the rousing climax of the Selma-to-Montgomery march, a white Detroit housewife, Viola Liuzzo, who had felt compelled to head south to aid the voting rights efforts, was murdered as she helped drive demonstrators back to Selma.

But white segregationists were on their heels. In early August 1965, President Johnson invited King and other civil rights leaders for the signing of the Voting Rights Act. The product of many years of agitation but galvanized by the Selma march, this measure, securing the ballot for African Americans, would mark the high point of the civil rights movement and transform southern politics and race relations.

See also 1957 Little Rock school desegregation crisis; 1964 Freedom Summer civil rights murders; 1968 assassination of Martin Luther King, Jr.

James Ralph

FURTHER READING:

Branch, Taylor. *At Canaan's Edge: America in the King Years, 1965–68.* New York: Simon and Schuster, 2006.

Garrow, David J. *Protest at Selma: Martin Luther King, Jr., and the Voting Rights Act of 1965.* New Haven, Conn.: Yale University Press, 1978.

1965 ◆ WATTS RIOT

Triggered by the California Highway Patrol arrest of a young African-American motorist named Marquette Frye, the Watts riot in South Central Los Angeles, which lasted from August 11 to 17, 1965, permanently shattered the white illusion of black satisfaction with the "California Dream." Because African Americans in Los Angeles had long voted freely, traveled in nonsegregated buses and trains, attended racially integrated schools, and purchased homes on the famously wide, tree-lined streets of the fabled city, whites generally soothed themselves with the notion that African Americans were content. How, they asked, could the unexceptional arrest of a verifiably intoxicated black driver trigger a riot that would destroy more than $40 million in property and cause the deaths of 34 people and the injury of another 1,000? The answer, of course was that it could not: The causes of the riots were much deeper and, for those who cared to address them, much more intractable. Ultimately, the Watts riot was not caused by the arrest of Marquette Frye. Rather, it was the product of at least 20 years of disillusionment in the black community of Los Angeles.

The underlying causes of the Watts riot of 1965 can be traced directly back to World War II. During a period of intense labor demand, the industrial employers of Los Angeles temporarily abandoned their decades-old practice of discriminating against prospective black employees and welcomed them into the workforce, though rarely on equal terms with white workers. Having been relegated almost exclusively to low-paying and often demeaning service occupations prior to the war effort, African Americans in Los Angeles now enjoyed full employment in relatively well-paying and often unionized jobs. This shift—coupled with Hollywood-inspired visions of the city's famous climate and the city's real history of minimal racial violence—triggered an unprecedented wave of migration to the city during and after World War II. Between 1940 and 1970, the black population of Los Angeles grew from 63,744 to 763,000. For those African Americans migrating from racially oppressive conditions in Louisiana,

FACTBOX

PLACE Watts, South Central Los Angeles, California

DATE August 11–17, 1965

TYPE Riot

DESCRIPTION The African-American neighborhood of Watts erupted in a week of violence, causing widespread destruction.

CAUSE Years of racial oppression and discrimination, triggered by the perceived harassment of African-American motorist Marquette Frye on the evening of August 11, 1965

CASUALTIES 34 deaths; more than 1,000 injured

COST $40 million in property damage

IMPACT Creation of McCone Commission, Watts Labor Community Action Committee, and Martin Luther King, Jr./Drew Medical Center; stimulation of "white flight"

Texas, and other states, Los Angeles was a remarkable improvement. Racial discrimination still greatly hampered their efforts to buy housing where they chose or to explore the diverse terrain of the metropolis without chronic harassment from the Los Angeles Police Department (LAPD). But they still believed in the promise of Los Angeles, even as they fought this discrimination in the courts and sometimes on the picket lines.

The children of this "Great Migration generation," however, were not inclined to view their circumstances in the same regionally relative terms as their parents had. They did not compare their opportunities to what their parents had back east in Shreveport or San Antonio but, rather, to those opportunities enjoyed by their white and even Mexican peers to the east, west, and north of South Central Los Angeles. And by these standards, they were clearly still second-class citizens: They were regularly passed over for promotions at work simply because of their race;

they were relentlessly harassed by white officers of the LAPD, whose duties explicitly included the enforcement of invisible racial lines in the city; they lived in relative isolation within the vast metropolis, poorly served by public transportation, public education, or public health facilities. Further aggravating the circumstances of young African Americans was the gradual disappearance of the steady, unionized, industrial work that had been the bedrock of their parents' modest success. California voters had recently invalidated the 1963 Rumford Fair Housing Act, dealing a blow to the black struggle for equality in the state. Finally, in January 1964, President Lyndon Johnson promised Americans that a new War on Poverty would ameliorate the chronic poverty experienced by so many blacks in Los Angeles and elsewhere. But more than a year and a half later, the African Americans of Los Angeles had still not seen a penny of the promised funds, largely because of the foot-dragging of Mayor Samuel Yorty.

In this context, the routine arrest of Marquette Frye easily ignited the tinderbox of Watts, a small community in South Central located in the extreme southeastern portion of Los Angeles County. The violence, however, extended well beyond the soft borders of Watts. After two full days of rioting, it was obvious that the police were vastly outnumbered. Thousands of rioters—many brandishing stolen firearms—flooded the streets, snipers fired at police helicopters, and long stretches of business districts were transformed into "charcoal alleys." After two full days of rioting, the National Guard mobilized in South Central and created a curfew zone, which ultimately extended over 46 square miles of Los Angeles County. The curfew was lifted on August 17 after the governor determined that remaining sporadic skirmishes did not represent a serious threat to public safety. Twenty-eight of the 34 people killed during the riot were African Americans, the vast majority of those at the hands of the LAPD, which was later criticized for its initially slow, and then brutal, response.

Portrayed by many contemporaries as a mindless and aimless rampage, the riot appears to have followed a patterned course: The vast majority of the approximately 400 buildings destroyed in the riot were businesses owned by white—often Jewish—shopkeepers. Many African Americans had long harbored resentment toward the white owners of local liquor stores and "corner" markets because of the perception that they exploited black spatial and commercial isolation in the city by charging extortionate rates. In striking contrast to the Los Angeles riot of 1992 in which even venerable black organizations were burned to the ground in a purposeless frenzy, the targets of the Watts riot appear to have been carefully selected quarry of explicable, if not defensible, black anger.

In response to the Watts riot, California governor Edmund G. "Pat" Brown appointed the McCone Commission to determine the causes of the riot and make recommendations to thwart future rebellions. Ultimately few of the recommendations were enacted, although the county did agree to fund a new hospital in the Watts area, and ground was broken for the hospital—later named Martin Luther King, Jr./Drew Medical Center—in 1968. A visionary and former automobile plant worker named Ted Watkins also founded the Watts Labor Community Action Committee, which provided untold employment training opportunities for black youth and has continued to play a vital role in the African-American community into the 21st century. Perhaps the most enduring legacy of the riot, however, was the flight of the remaining white residents of South Los Angeles and the increased racial isolation of the black population, which had long hoped—but perhaps never truly believed—that Los Angeles could be a racial paradise.

See also 1967 URBAN RIOTS.

Josh Sides

Silhouetted by the streetlights, National Guardsmen patrol the streets of Watts to quell rioting. *(New York Public Library)*

FURTHER READING:

Conot, Robert. *Rivers of Blood, Years of Darkness: The Unforgettable Classic Account of the Watts Riot.* New York: Morrow, 1967.

Fogelson, Robert. *The Los Angeles Riots.* New York: Arno Press, 1969.

Horne, Gerald. *Fire This Time: The Watts Uprising and the 1960s.* Charlottesville: University of Virginia Press, 1995.

Sears, David. *The Politics of Violence: The New Urban Blacks and the Watts Riot.* Boston: Houghton Mifflin, 1973.

1967 ◆ URBAN RIOTS

The summer of 1967 was a high point for racial strife in postwar American cities. This tense period of the nation's history counted 164 "civil disorders" across the country, resulting in 83 deaths. The largest number of fatalities occurred in Detroit, Michigan, and Newark, New Jersey, where riots erupted in July. These two cities accounted for more than one-half of the injuries and $35 million in property lost during these difficult months. The causes of these conflicts varied from city to city, but every riot tapped African-American outrage over police brutality, poor housing, poor education, unemployment, urban renewal, and lack of political power. Black Americans were angry at the stagnation of the civil rights movement and the failure of the Great Society to achieve its announced goals of eradicating poverty and expanding opportunity. Millions of African Americans felt isolated from American democracy and prosperity.

The Newark riot began on the evening of Wednesday, July 12, 1967, when police arrested and beat a black cabdriver named John Smith. As rumor spread that Smith had been killed, an agitated crowd gathered outside the Fourth Precinct police station. Attempting to defuse tension, the police allowed black community leaders into the station to see Smith. When the group determined that Smith needed medical attention, a police car drove him to the hospital. But the crowd that had gathered did not disperse. Instead, they jeered police officers who arrived for the 10:45 P.M. shift. Disregarding pleas from community leaders for calm, people in the mob lobbed Molotov cocktails—bottles containing gasoline and lighted stoppers—at the police station. Other individuals broke into stores next to the station.

FACTBOX

PLACE Newark, New Jersey; Detroit, Michigan; and cities across the country

DATE July 12–17, 1967 (Newark), July 23–27, 1967 (Detroit)

TYPE Race riots

DESCRIPTION Urban riots occurred in Newark, Detroit, and 162 other locations, mainly centered in African-American communities.

CAUSE Local incidents involving police sparked violence in numerous cities, yet a variety of deeper complaints fueled black anger and resentment of the white community and power structure.

CASUALTIES 83 deaths

COSTS An estimated $35 million in property damage

IMPACT The U.S. Riot Commission pointed to the racial division in United States as a profound source of potential instability and recommended that blacks be brought into the mainstream of American life as a way to counter this bifurcation.

On Thursday, July 13, Newark's mayor Hugh Addonizio called the prior evening disturbance an isolated incident. Addonizio's statement, however, did not address the black community's frustration with police brutality. African-American leaders called for a "Police Brutality Protest Rally" to be held Thursday night in front of the Fourth Precinct station. The ingredients for a conflagration were falling into place. Picket lines formed at 7 P.M. At about 7:30 James Threatt, the black director of Newark's Human Rights Commission, announced that Addonizio would create a citizens' group to investigate the Smith incident. Rather than placating the crowd, the statement actually intensified its anger. Demonstrators pelted Threatt with rocks and then turned on the station, hitting it with a barrage of projectiles. Police aggressively dispersed the crowd, which had the effect of spreading the rioting. Soon, all of Central Ward—Newark's predominantly black neighborhood—became the scene of pandemonium. From there, looters moved toward downtown Newark. City police could not neutralize the violence as bands of youths broke into grocery, liquor, clothing, and furniture stores, pawnshops, and other places of business.

Early Friday morning, the mayor mobilized State Police and National Guard units, but the chaos continued, in part because of ineffective coordination between the various law-enforcement groups. Police fired indiscriminately at suspected snipers but on some occasions killed innocent civilians. The inability of police and guardsmen to distinguish between combatants and bystanders fueled the surge of resentment that welled up in the black community. The National Guard eventually quelled the violence, but six days of rioting left 23 people dead, 21 of whom were black, including six women and two children.

Detroit exploded within days after the Newark riot. On Sunday, July 23, police raided an all-night drinking club in the early morning hours. Expecting to find a few revelers, police were surprised to discover 82 people celebrating the return of two black soldiers from Vietnam. The arrest of all 82 patrons drew a crowd to the club. After the last squad car left, several men looted a local clothing store. Then the disorder moved to the 12th Street neighborhood, the center of the black community. By Sunday evening, rioting had spread throughout Northwest Detroit.

Similar to conditions in Newark, hostility toward Detroit's white government, including abusive treatment by its white police force, generated anger and resentment in the black community. Like the beating of John Smith, the arrests at the Detroit club represented a final straw—a threshold had been crossed. At 8:30 A.M. on Monday, U.S. Representative John Conyers, Jr., an African American, attempted to pacify the crowd on 12th Street. His effort at peacemaking was ignored. Violence escalated, resulting in 231 incidents per hour, including 483 fires and 1,800 arrests on Monday alone. Early Tuesday morning, President Lyndon Johnson invoked an obscure 1795 law that permitted the use of military force to combat insurrection against the government. Johnson federalized the 8,000 National Guardsmen, who were deployed in the 12th Street neighborhood. They were joined later by 4,700 paratroopers from the 82nd Airborne Division and 360 state police.

Guardsmen and police used tanks and machine guns to flush out suspected snipers. On one occasion, as two tanks approached an alleged sniper nest, the gunner opened fire when he saw a cigarette lit in a window. The rounds severed a young woman's arm and killed a four-year-old girl. No sniper was found. People witnessed the mayhem on TV in their living rooms as footage showed combat troops and guardsmen engaged in firefights in the street. After five days of rioting, 43 people died in Detroit, 33 of whom were African-American. Some 2,000 buildings burned to the ground, and 7,200 people were arrested.

Riots erupted in cities and towns from coast to coast throughout the summer, signifying an explosion of racial tension stemming from changes in American society. The nation's cities underwent major demographic shifts during and immediately after World War II. Southern migrants, many of them black, flocked north during the war and worked in manufacturing establishments. Urban areas were still predominantly white in 1950, but economic changes were altering ethnic compositions. As cities deindustrialized and jobs were outsourced, those who could afford to leave did so. "White flight" peaked during the 1950s, and as suburbs proliferated around urban centers, conditions in the inner city deteriorated.

Newark and Detroit reflected these demographic trends. There had been 363,000 whites in Newark in 1950. By 1960, their number fell to 266,000; in 1967, only 158,000 whites remained in the city. Conversely, the black population spiked during these years. Newark had been 85 percent white in 1940; in 1967, 55 percent of its inhabitants were black. In Detroit, the black population rose from 303,000 to 487,000 during the 1950s, while the white population declined 23 percent. In both cases, blacks concentrated in blighted sections that were, in effect, racially circumscribed ghettos. Central Ward was Newark's black center; Detroit's was the 12th Street neighborhood.

In the aftermath of the riots, President Johnson appointed a Commission on Civil Disorders, headed by Illinois governor Otto Kerner, and instructed commissioners to investigate the causes of the rioting. Why had so many blacks participated in the violence? Reporting in 1968, the Kerner Commission, as it was called, found that African Americans were alienated from society and politics. The commission accused city officials of marginalizing black schools and cited high unemployment and exorbitant property taxes as factors that perpetuated poverty. The report documented abusive police behavior, especially in Detroit where four-man units called Tac Squads berated black youths. In Newark, Mayor Addonizio had reneged on campaign promises to appoint blacks to prominent posts in his administration. The commission reported that urban renewal projects tended to uproot black homes and businesses. In 1967, for example, Newark officials allocated 150 acres of Central Ward—the heart of the black community—to build a medical school. An area in Detroit called "Black Bottom"—the city's oldest black enclave—was demolished to make way for Interstate 75. Political leaders in both cit-

ies had ignored the voice of the black community. In essence, the Kerner Commission had highlighted inequities that broke along racial lines in the United States. Whites were exiting the city for the suburbs and received governmental assistance for hospitals, highways, and other infrastructure and services. Blacks received far less help. In Detroit, they paid higher prices than whites for shoddier housing. The rate of home ownership among blacks was half that of whites. Faced with inequities and little political recourse or power, black neighborhoods were ready to explode. Only the 1992 LOS ANGELES RIOT surpassed the magnitude of destruction in Detroit.

See also 1965 WATTS RIOT.

David G. O'Donnell

FURTHER READING:

Chikota, Richard. *Riot in the Cities.* Rutherford, N.J.: Fairleigh Dickinson University Press, 1970.

Farley, Reynolds, Sheldon Danziger, and Harry J. Holzer. *Detroit Divided.* New York: Russell Sage Foundation, 2000.

Hayden, Tom. *Rebellion in Newark: Official Violence and Ghetto Response.* New York: Vintage Books, 1967.

The U.S. Riot Commission Report. New York: New York Times Company, 1968.

1968 ◆ TET OFFENSIVE

By 1968, the United States had been at war with Vietnamese insurgents and revolutionaries for more than a dozen years. Taking over from a defeated French colonizer in 1954, the Americans had aimed to create a separate, independent, noncommunist state below the 17th parallel in Vietnam. This nation-building effort met with sustained and capable resistance and eventually grew into large-scale warfare over the whole of southern Vietnam. The United States expanded the war in the mid-1960s as victory became more elusive. U.S. spending mounted to billions annually by the late 1960s as the nation deployed several hundred thousand troops in pursuit of a military victory. Insur-

gent forces combined with aid from North Vietnam met and effectively resisted these escalations of American troops. By the late 1960s, the war had in effect become stalemated. It had also begun to have serious economic and political impact within the United States. Despite serious misgivings and doubts among key advisers and analysts, President Lyndon Johnson, administration officials, and military leaders continued to publicly claim certain victory. They promised an uneasy nation that the enemy was near exhaustion and that American power would prevail. In 1967, the American commander, General William Westmoreland, assured the country of a "light at the end of the tunnel" in Vietnam.

FACTBOX

PLACE Southern Vietnam

DATE January 1968

TYPE Military offensive

DESCRIPTION Large-scale insurgent/revolutionary offensive in more than 100 cities in South Vietnam

CASUALTIES 8,000–15,000 Vietnamese civilians killed, 30,000–40,000 wounded (overwhelmingly civilians); estimated 45,000 insurgent Vietnamese killed

IMPACT Undermined political commitment in the United States to pursue a military solution to the insurgency in Vietnam

The Tet offensive—so named because it began during the Vietnamese New Year holiday known as Tet—occurred in this context. On the morning of January 30, 1968, approximately 70,000 Vietnamese combatants struck in a near simultaneous action across the whole of southern Vietnam. These forces, called the Vietcong, attacked both urban and rural areas, even entering the U.S. embassy compound in Saigon, the capital. More than 100 cities, 36 of 44 provincial capitals, 64 of 242 district towns, and numerous smaller villages and hamlets came under direct attack. The violence unleashed by the Tet offensive resulted in nearly 1 million new refugees, as well as 8,000–15,000 civilians killed and 30,000–40,000 wounded. Most urban centers remained in a state of chaos for months following the attacks. The Agency for International Development, the development aid and assistance arm of the U.S. effort, later reported that in terms of relief to civilians, the country did not recover from Tet until the end of the year.

The Vietnamese economy was also hit hard by this latest round of attacks, profoundly destabilizing the already badly fractured nation-building experiment. Goods remained in warehouses, and importers either reduced orders or stopped placing new orders altogether as business activity came to a virtual standstill. Prices soared on such staples as rice, meat, and fish; the price of the latter increased by more than 300 percent immediately after January 30. Rice shipments from the delta to Saigon, normally on the order of 20,000–30,000 tons per month, shrank to just 456 tons in February. Many Vietnamese families living on the edge of economic disaster were pushed over. Theft, graft, and looting quickly reached crisis proportion.

Aside from the initial success and surprise of the attacks, the Tet offensive is generally viewed as a serious setback for the insurgent and revolutionary Vietnamese forces. With the exception of the old imperial city of Hué, the offensive was beaten back within days at an enormous price. Losses for the insurgent revolutionaries are estimated at approximately 45,000 killed. Furthermore, the insurgency in the south sacrificed its cover among the population that had been vital to its success. The insurgent network, built up over years, was thus exposed and badly damaged.

The offensive is also, however, considered a major setback for the Americans and an important turning point in the war. It is sometimes referred to as a "military victory, and psychological defeat." For example, though the offensive was militarily defeated, it exposed grave problems with the U.S. effort and resulted in a thorough rethinking of the commitment to the war in Vietnam. In the weeks and months following the offensive, the delicate political consensus in the United States that had insured support for the war in Vietnam began to come undone, signaled by President Johnson's stunning announcement in March 1968 that he would not seek reelection. Following the election of Richard Nixon at the end of the year, the United States began to seek a way out of the costly and failed effort in Vietnam.

James M. Carter

FURTHER READING:

Braestrup, Peter. *Big Story: How the American Press and Television Reported and Interpreted the Crisis of Tet 1968 in Vietnam and Washington.* Novato, Calif.: Presidio Press, 1994.

Gilbert, Marc J., and William Head, eds. *The Tet Offensive.* New York: Praeger, 1996.

Oberdorfer, Don. *Tet: The Turning Point in the Vietnam War.* Baltimore, Md.: Johns Hopkins Press, 2001.

Spector, Ronald. *After Tet: The Bloodiest Year in Vietnam.* New York: Vintage, 1994.

1968 ◆ MY LAI MASSACRE

On March 16, 1968, Company C, known as "Charlie" Company, of the United States Army's First Battalion, 20th Infantry Regiment, carried out a massacre of more than 300 Vietnamese civilians, including men, women, and children, at the village of My Lai. The U.S. Army covered up the incident for more than a year, but the story eventually leaked out. Formal inquiries ultimately led to the courts-martial of Lieutenant William Calley and 12 other American soldiers. Only Calley was found guilty of war crimes and sentenced to life in prison. His sentence was reduced in the months after his conviction, eventually culminating in an order by President Richard Nixon in 1974 that effectively granted him parole. The My Lai massacre ranks among the most disturbing atrocities of the Vietnam War and contributed significantly to the decline in public support for U.S. participation in the Southeast Asian conflict.

In March 1968, the U.S. Army was involved in operations to quell enemy attacks by the Vietcong and North Vietnamese in the northernmost region of South Vietnam. The military operations came in the tense period just after the Tet offensive of late January. Charlie Company's role was to enter the hamlet of My Lai in Quang Nam Province to root out Vietcong elements. My Lai was located in Son My village, a reported stronghold of the Vietcong. In recent weeks, Charlie Company had suffered casualties from snipers and land mines, but the company had never engaged directly in combat before. At once green and ready for a fight, Company C soldiers were dropped by helicopter into the hamlet. They did not take any enemy fire and found no active Vietcong in the village, but under the leadership of Captain Ernest Medina and Lieutenant Calley, they rounded up the villagers and killed nearly all of them in cold blood. In one reported instance, dozens of people were driven into a ditch and executed. American soldiers also raped and sodomized as many as 20 women, including girls as young as 10 years old, before shooting them to death. Charlie Company ultimately slaughtered more than 300 and perhaps as many as 500 villagers.

News of the events eventually became public when members of Charlie Company who had refused to take part in the massacre and helicopter pilots who had ferried the troops in and out of My Lai came forward. In 1969, a year after the incident, Lieutenant General William Peers began a formal inquiry. Medina, Calley, and 11 other members of Charlie Company were court-martialed. Only Calley, who was indicted for murdering 109 villagers, was convicted.

When President Nixon essentially granted Calley parole, a U.S. district court took up the case. The court overturned the court-martial's earlier conviction on the premise that Calley had been the victim of unjust publicity. The public outrage over the incident when it was reported had indeed been intense and had come at a time after Tet when American public sentiment in general was turning against the war. Revulsion over the My Lai massacre helped fuel the widening antiwar movement. Calley was released in November 1974 and dishonorably discharged.

Jeff Woods

FACTBOX

PLACE My Lai, Vietnam

DATE March 16, 1968

TYPE Massacre of innocent men, women, and children

DESCRIPTION "Charlie" Company of the U.S. Army killed more than 300 members of the village in cold blood.

CAUSE Poor leadership, improper training, ignorance

CASUALTIES Estimates range between 300 and 500 people

IMPACT Marked a crucial turning point in the U.S. public's perception of the Vietnam War

FURTHER READING:

Anderson, David. *Facing My Lai: Moving Beyond the Massacre.* Lawrence: University Press of Kansas, 1998.

Belknap, Michael. *The Vietnam War on Trial: The My Lai Massacre and the Court Martial of Lieutenant Calley.* Lawrence: University Press of Kansas, 2002.

1968 ◆ ASSASSINATION OF MARTIN LUTHER KING, JR.

The rise to national prominence of Martin Luther King, Jr., in the 1950s can only be understood in the context of more than three centuries of African-American history. From the colonial era to the Civil War, more than 90 percent of black people in America were chattel slaves (marketable property that could be bought and sold), denied basic human rights, and often treated with appalling contempt and cruelty. The free black population in the northern states (as well as the 1 percent of free blacks in the South) was also subjected to severe racial discrimination. After the abolition of slavery in 1865, black Americans endured a century of legal segregation (sanctioned by the Supreme Court in *Plessy v. Ferguson,* 1896); the poverty and exploitation of sharecropping and peonage; organized terror from the Ku Klux Klan and other racist organizations; decades of lynching and racially inspired riots; and many de jure and de facto barriers to earning a decent living, getting an education, shopping or eating in a public facility, and voting.

In its landmark 1954 decision, *Brown v. Board of Education,* the Supreme Court overturned *Plessy v. Ferguson* and ruled unanimously that racial segregation in public schools was illegal and unconstitutional. The following year, the 26-year-old Reverend Dr. Martin Luther King, Jr., emerged on the national scene by leading a successful, nonviolent bus boycott to integrate public transportation in Montgomery, Alabama. King helped form the Southern Christian Leadership Conference in 1957, and for the next decade, he became the dominant national voice of the civil rights movement. In 1963, his campaign of protest marches against segregation in Birmingham, Alabama, his unwavering commitment to nonviolence, and his dramatic "I Have a Dream" speech during the March on Washington galvanized the struggle for racial justice that ultimately resulted in the passage of landmark civil rights and voting rights legislation in 1964 and 1965. As a result, black Americans finally achieved full legal equality for the first time in U.S. history.

A stirring orator and charismatic leader, King won the support of most black Americans, and many whites as well, but he was nonetheless often regarded with suspicion if not outright hatred, espe-

FACTBOX

PLACE Memphis, Tennessee

DATE April 4, 1968

TYPE Political assassination

DESCRIPTION While standing on a hotel balcony, civil rights leader Martin Luther King, Jr., was shot and killed.

CASUALTIES Death of Martin Luther King, Jr.

IMPACT Outbreak of racial violence across the nation; decline of the civil rights movement

cially by southern whites who openly referred to him as "Martin Luther Coon." Attorney General Robert Kennedy agreed to secretly wiretap King's phone in 1963 because of King's association with alleged communists. Federal Bureau of Investigation (FBI) director J. Edgar Hoover called King "the most dangerous man in America" and believed that the civil rights movement was controlled and financed by the Soviet Union. The FBI launched a covert campaign to destroy King by bugging his hotel rooms, taping alleged sexual encounters, and sending the tapes to Coretta Scott King in the hope that her husband would commit suicide or at least forego personally accepting the 1964 Nobel Peace Prize.

King persevered, and after riots in major cities across the nation in 1965 revealed the depth of despair and alienation among young blacks, he turned his attention to the North. But marches and demonstrations he led in the suburbs of Chicago were met with open hatred and violence. King was denounced as a dangerous fanatic and received numerous death threats. He became convinced that the eradication of economic discrimination and poverty were national rather than just southern problems. In 1967, under pressure from militant organizations such as the Black Panthers, which repudiated nonviolence and demanded "Black Power," King founded the Poor People's Campaign. He also broke with President Lyndon B. Johnson over the American war in Vietnam, in part because poor, urban blacks were bearing a disproportionate share of the fighting and dying.

Early in 1968, King went to Memphis, Tennessee, to help black sanitation workers achieve fair treatment and union recognition. On April 3, King spoke prophetically to his followers: "I've seen the promised land. I may not get there with you. But I want you to know . . . [that] I'm not fearing any man. 'Mine eyes have seen the glory of the coming of the Lord.'" The next day, while standing on the balcony of the Lorainne Motel, the 39-year-old King was shot and killed by a sniper firing from a nearby rooming house. President Johnson feared that recent civil rights gains had been wiped out overnight; first lady Claudia "Lady Bird" Johnson described the news of King's death as "one of those frozen moments, as though the bomb had fallen on us." Violence erupted in more than 100 cities across the nation, eventually requiring 50,000 troops to restore order. In Washington, D.C., alone, many downtown buildings were torched, and there were 11 deaths, more than 1,200 injuries, and more than 7,600 arrests. As President Johnson watched the smoke rise over the nation's capital, he remarked that the city looked like a war zone. The civil rights movement never recovered its national cohesion, status, and influence.

The assassination of Martin Luther King, Jr., on April 4, 1968, dealt a major blow to the civil rights movement. (© Associated Press)

The suspected assassin, James Earl Ray, a white supremacist who had escaped from prison a year earlier, eluded Memphis police but was arrested two months later in London, England. After extradition, Ray confessed, entered a guilty plea, and was sentenced to 99 years in prison. (A trial and conviction could have resulted in the death penalty.) However, Ray recanted his confession days later and spent the rest of his life working unsuccessfully with several lawyers to have his case heard in court. He died in prison of liver cancer in 1998.

The King assassination, like that of President Kennedy four and a half years earlier, spawned an extraordinary number of conspiracy theories—most notably the claim that President Johnson and the federal government were behind the killing. In a particularly bizarre development, King's son, Dexter Scott King, met with Ray in prison in 1997. The young King asked Ray if he had murdered his father. Ray denied it, and Dexter King replied, "I believe you, and my family believes you." Dexter King claimed instead that a vast government conspiracy, which included a Special Forces team and the Mafia, had been responsible for his father's assassination.

In the four decades since his death, despite the splintering of the civil rights movement he came to symbolize, Martin Luther King, Jr., has achieved the status of a national icon. More than 650,000 tourists a year, from all over the world, visit the Martin Luther King, Jr., National Historic Site in Atlanta, Georgia, which includes the King Center and Archives, his birthplace, and burial site. The Lorainne Motel, the scene of King's assassination, has become the National Civil Rights Museum, and, since 1986, King's birthday, January 15, 1929, has been a national holiday, celebrated on the third Monday of January.

See also 1957 LITTLE ROCK SCHOOL DESEGREGATION CRISIS; 1964 FREEDOM SUMMER CIVIL RIGHTS MURDERS; 1965 SELMA VOTING RIGHTS DEMONSTRATION.

Sheldon M. Stern

FURTHER READING:

Branch, Tayor. *At Canaan's Edge: America in the King Years, 1965–1968.* New York: Simon and Schuster, 2006.

Garrow, David J. *Bearing the Cross: Martin Luther King, Jr., and the Southern Christian Leadership Conference.* New York: Norton, 1981.

Oates, Stephen B. *Let the Trumpet Sound: The Life of Martin Luther King, Jr.* New York: New American Library, 1983.

Posner, Gerald. *Killing the Dream: James Earl Ray and the Assassination of Martin Luther King, Jr.* New York: Random House, 1998.

1968 ◆ ASSASSINATION OF ROBERT F. KENNEDY

The assassination of Senator Robert F. Kennedy on June 4, 1968, in the Ambassador Hotel in Los Angeles came in the immediate aftermath of his victory over Senator Eugene McCarthy of Minnesota in the crucial California presidential primary. Kennedy's murder was one of the tragic events in the tumultuous year of 1968. That year had already witnessed the TET OFFENSIVE in Vietnam, the "abdication" of President Lyndon Johnson, the ASSASSINATION OF MARTIN LUTHER KING, JR., and unrest on many of the nation's college campuses. Robert Kennedy's death further convulsed the Democrats prior to their Chicago presidential nominating convention. The riots in the streets of Chicago during the Democratic National Convention changed the party dramatically and spurred the resurgence of the Republican Party.

Kennedy was shot by Sirhan Bishara Sirhan, a Palestinian sympathizer from a Christian Arab family. Sirhan's father had lost his job and property following the 1948–1949 Arab-Israeli War. The family had come to the United States in 1957 under the auspices of a United Nations refugee resettlement program. Sirhan Sirhan, who idolized Egyptian leader Gamal Abdel Nasser and his Pan-Arab program, became upset when Kennedy, a United States senator from New York, had strongly committed to the defense of Israeli security earlier in 1968. Sirhan felt the assassination should be timed to mark the first anniversary of the 1967 Six Day War, which resulted in Israel acquiring vast amounts of territory, including the West Bank, Gaza Strip, the Golan Heights, and East Jerusalem.

The 24-year-old-assassin's weapon was a .22 caliber pistol, which was loaded with hollow-nosed bullets. These deadly projectiles were designed to spread or "explode" on impact. Two of the bullets entered Kennedy's body. One was nonlethal, but the one that struck his brain proved fatal, killing Kennedy at 5:01 A.M. on June 6. A team of surgeons had desperately attempted to save his life at Los Angeles's Good Samaritan Hospital. The effort was doomed to failure. In all, Sirhan fired eight shots and wounded four other people. Sirhan was immediately subdued by men surrounding Kennedy including the Olympian Rafer Johnson and professional football player Roosevelt Grier. Sirhan was subsequently sentenced to life imprisonment and remains in the California penal system.

The path to the Los Angeles tragedy was a long yet seemingly inevitable one for Kennedy. He was viewed as the heir to the "Camelot" mystique associated with his martyred brother, President John F.

FACTBOX

PLACE Ambassador Hotel, Los Angeles, California

DATE June 4, 1968 (death on June 6, 1968)

TYPE Political assassination

DESCRIPTION Just after winning the Democratic presidential primary in California, Senator Robert F. Kennedy was shot and killed.

CAUSE Sirhan Sirhan's desire to kill Kennedy for his support of Israel in the wake of the 1967 Six Day War

CASUALTIES Death of Robert F. Kennedy

IMPACT Assured the presidential nominations of Hubert Humphrey and Richard Nixon in 1968. Allowed Nixon to pursue his Southern Strategy, which led to a significant realignment of American politics. Moved the Kennedy supporters more to the left and made Senator Edward Kennedy the heir to a more liberal Kennedy tradition.

Kennedy, who was assassinated in 1963. Robert F. Kennedy, or RFK as he became known, had served in his brother's administration as attorney general and had been elected to the Senate from New York in 1964. His younger brother, Edward Kennedy, had been elected two years earlier as a United States senator from Massachusetts. RFK had originally intended to support Johnson for the Democratic nomination in 1968. However, the Tet offensive had increased opposition to the war in Vietnam and eroded support for Johnson. A relatively unknown senator from Minnesota, Eugene McCarthy, decided to enter the Democratic Party primaries to oppose Johnson and the war. The unheralded McCarthy made an exceptionally strong showing in the nation's first primary in New Hampshire, winning 42 percent of the vote. When polls indicated that the Minnesotan was poised to defeat Johnson in the upcoming Wisconsin primary, Johnson withdrew his candidacy for reelection. The sequence of events also prompted Kennedy to announce his candidacy on March 16. The lateness of his entry into the presidential race meant that Kennedy had to win virtually all of the remaining primaries, including the June 4 contest in delegate-rich California, the most populous state in the country. Previously, McCarthy had unsuccessfully urged Kennedy to be the "antiwar, stop Johnson" candidate. He deeply resented Kennedy's sudden about-face and stubbornly refused to withdraw in favor of the better-known senator.

Kennedy's whirlwind campaign gained him primary victories in Indiana and Nebraska. However, the Kennedy juggernaut was derailed in Oregon where McCarthy defeated him by a 44 to 38 percent margin. This marked the first time (but not the last) that a Kennedy lost an election. RFK then made it clear that a loss in California would end his candidacy.

The California primary of 1968 was the most anticipated in U.S. history to that point. The media coverage was unprecedented. The suddenly beleaguered Kennedy agreed to debate McCarthy on national television prior to the contest. The vote in California gave Kennedy a clear but narrow victory (46 percent RFK, 42 percent McCarthy, and 12 percent "uncommitted"). Kennedy by no means was assured the nomination, but he had gained considerable leverage as he prepared for the Chicago convention. In actuality, he had no more than about 600

to 700 delegates of the 1,312 needed for the nomination, assuming that he won the New York primary, which followed California's. Vice President Hubert Humphrey, the choice of President Johnson and many in the Democratic Party "establishment," had nearly 1,400 tentatively committed delegates—despite entering no primaries. RFK's chance to gain the nomination appeared contingent on a McCarthy withdrawal. Given the animosity between the two, the likelihood of this scenario unfolding seemed slim. The gun of Sirhan Sirhan ended any chance of such a turn of events.

At the National Convention in Chicago in August, the Kennedy delegates generally supported South Dakota senator George McGovern. They desperately hoped that Senator Edward Kennedy at 36 years of age would enter the race, but he did not. As police and protesters clashed outside the convention, delegates nominated Humphrey on the first ballot. He received the nomination with 1,760 votes to 601 for McCarthy and 146 for McGovern. Conventions are designed to provide momentum to a party. Seemingly, the riotous Democratic Convention of 1968 provided much momentum—to the Republicans.

Many argue that the assassination of Robert Kennedy assured the nominations of Democrat Hubert Humphrey and Republican Richard Nixon. Had RFK survived, some moderate Republicans might have turned to Nelson Rockefeller. Most Republican pundits, however, saw Nixon as virtually certain of defeating Humphrey. Kennedy's death also gave Nixon greater flexibility to pursue his "southern strategy" of using guarded racial appeals to pursue white votes in the formerly solid Democratic South. For his vice presidential running mate, Nixon chose Spiro Agnew, the governor of Maryland but hardly a national figure, and made an overt effort to gain the white "backlash" vote in the South. His subtle appeal to race would also cut into traditional Democratic voters among blue-collar union workers and "ethnic" voters in the North. Nixon's narrow victory in November marked a realignment of political parties and the onset of an era of Republican dominance of the White House.

The candidacy and death of RFK also represented a "bridge" in the Kennedy legacy. John F. Kennedy had basically been a centrist, establishment Democrat. Only myth and misperception depict his presidency as a time of liberalism and dramatic reform.

During his presidential bid in 1968, RFK moved to the left and talked of "new politics" that would change the status quo. Senator Edward Kennedy became one of the nation's strongest pillars of liberalism. The transitional link between the John F. Kennedy of the early 1960s and the Edward Kennedy of the 21st century was clearly the RFK campaign of 1968.

William Gudelunas

FURTHER READING:

Gould, Lewis L. *1968: The Election That Changed America*. Chicago: Ivan Dee, 1993.

Schlesinger, Arthur M. *Robert Kennedy and His Times*. Boston: Houghton Mifflin, 1978.

Unger, Irwin, and Debi Unger. *Turning Point: 1968*. New York: Scribner's, 1988.

White, Theodore. *The Making of the President, 1968*. New York: Pocket Books, 1970.

1968 ◆ DEMOCRATIC CONVENTION AND RIOT

Many historians have argued that the most disastrous event in the most riot-filled year in American history was the Democratic convention of 1968 in Chicago. The convention itself ran from August 26 to 30 at the Chicago Amphitheater. The ramifications of the events that occurred inside and on the streets outside the convention had impacts that would influence the nation politically, socially, and culturally for decades into the future.

The election of 1968 may have been decided on the streets of Chicago in August rather than at the polls in November. Gathering to nominate a candidate for president, the Democrats emerged from the Windy City disunited, dispirited, and disoriented. They managed a limited comeback by November but fell short of preventing a Republican victory. In a three-way race, Richard Nixon was able to narrowly defeat the Democratic candidate, Vice President Hubert Humphrey, and the American Independent standard bearer, Governor George Wallace of Alabama. The Republicans managed gains of only five Senate seats and four in the House of Representatives. The Democrats thus retained firm control of both chambers for the next two years. The damage done to the Democrats would become more evident after the next presidential election. The seeds for the "McGovern disaster" in 1972 (when the Democratic nominee carried only one state and Washington, D.C.) were sown in Chicago in 1968.

The omens for the Democrats convening in Chicago had been disconcerting for some time. Houston

FACTBOX

PLACE Chicago, Illinois

DATE August 26–30, 1968

TYPE Riot

DESCRIPTION Disruptions at the Democratic National Convention became "riots" when police moved to quell political demonstrations outside the convention hall.

CAUSE Frustrations of antiwar groups with the Democratic Party and its decision to nominate an "establishment" candidate for president. The Chicago police overreacted to essentially peaceful demonstrations, causing violent confrontations.

CASUALTIES No deaths but many injuries

IMPACT Caused an erosion of public confidence in government and in the Democratic Party, contributing to Republican victory in the 1968 election. Led to reforms in the Democratic Party that abolished winner-take-all primaries and the unit rule at future conventions, and required that more delegates be women and members of minority groups

and Philadelphia had been the front-runners to host the 1968 conclave. Houston's newly opened Astrodome was considered the modern marvel of the world. However, Democratic leaders feared that the city was not yet racially tolerant enough to accept an influx of minority delegates. Philadelphia lacked enough hotel rooms to accommodate the 6,000 delegates and alternates and the thousands of media people scheduled to attend. Chicago was then selected partly because it had a famed, four-time Democratic mayor, Richard Daley, as well as a Democratic governor, Sam Shapiro.

The Democrats were torn apart prior to Chicago by the growing unpopularity of the Vietnam War and their incumbent president, Lyndon Johnson. The Tet offensive, a series of deadly military operations carried out by the Vietcong in February 1968, significantly increased opposition both to the war and to Johnson. After struggling in the New Hampshire primary in March, President Johnson announced at the end of the month that he would not seek reelection. The "establishment" of the party then supported Vice President Humphrey. Senators Robert F. Kennedy of New York and Eugene McCarthy of Minnesota waged heated battles in the remaining primaries. Kennedy, the brother of the martyred president John F. Kennedy, ran slightly ahead of McCarthy but was assassinated after winning the California primary on June 4. Both Kennedy and McCarthy had assumed "dovish" positions on the war, and minorities, antiwar activists, college students, and various factions making up the liberal "New Left" supported them. The death of Kennedy and the inability of McCarthy to galvanize these groups led to heightened frustrations. These tensions climaxed when it became evident that Humphrey would receive a first ballot nomination at the Democratic Convention in Chicago despite having entered no primaries.

Mayor Daley was fully aware that several protest groups were planning demonstrations during the convention. These groups included the "Yippies" (Youth International Party) and MOBE (National Mobilization Committee to End the War in Vietnam). By the opening of the convention, Daley had 12,000 police officers, 5,000 regular army troops, and 6,000 National Guardsmen patrolling Chicago's streets. The *Chicago Sun Times* wrote that "never before had so many feared so much from so few."

Tensions were exacerbated by the fact that a Soviet invasion of Czechoslovakia began on the very eve of the convention. The Communist suppression of young people demanding freedom in "Prague Spring" demonstrations accentuated the events of Chicago. Many commentators began to refer to the city as "Czechago." While Democrats insulted each other on the floor of the convention, the security forces began to restrain the marches on the hall. Most studies now assert that the Chicago police used unnecessary force to quell essentially peaceful demonstrations. This led to open riots and violent confrontations. The events outside the hall were carried on live television. Newscasters Walter Cronkite of CBS and Chet Huntley and David Brinkley of NBC described street violence rather than balloting. On live television, Mayor Daley made an obscene and obvious gesture toward Connecticut senator Abraham Ribicoff when the senator termed the police tactics "Nazi-like" from the podium. Most lip readers also feel Daley uttered an ethnic slur at the Jewish Ribicoff. The Democrats made the nation wonder if they were capable of running a convention—much less a nation.

The most violent day of the week of riots was on Wednesday, August 28. Immediately after the convention rejected a peace plank to its platform, a spontaneous march began about seven miles from the hall. The marchers, largely students and young people, lacked a permit, and this gave police the excuse to launch their most vicious assaults of the week. Using such weapons as tear gas, mace, and clubs, the police attacked both protesters and bystanders. Melees took place at several points as police officers followed protesters into hotels and beat them. The rampage of violence continued into Friday morning. Many groups participated in the resistance to the police including communists, anarchists, and pacifists.

No one was killed during the riots and demonstrations. That very week, more than 300 Americans died in Vietnam. An investigation of the events known as the *Walker Report*, or *A Report on Rights in Conflict*, which commenced immediately after the convention, termed the violence a "police riot." Polls indicated, however, that most Americans initially supported Mayor Daley and his "security forces." The constant turmoil of 1968 caused a backlash effect in an already wary general public.

Several trials resulted from the turmoil. The most publicized involved the "Chicago 7" (originally the "Chicago 8" until a separate trial was ordered for one of the defendants, Bobby Seale). The "7" included

Tom Hayden, Abbie Hoffman, and David Dellinger. All were acquitted on conspiracy charges but five were convicted of intent to incite riot. These convictions were appealed and eventually overturned in 1972 by the United States 7th Circuit Court of Appeals. History and the legal system essentially backed the *Walker Report* and assigned guilt for the riots to Mayor Daley and his police.

The impact of "Chicago '68" on the Democrats lasted for at least a generation. The McCarthy followers pressured for reforms for the 1972 convention. The party adopted many of these, including an end to both winner-take-all primaries and "unit rule" voting at future conventions. The latter prevented forcing a minority of delegates from a state to follow the majority. These were openly designed to lessen the influence of party "bosses" and "professional politicians." These reforms led to the nominations of more liberal—and less electable—candidates such as George McGovern in 1972, Walter Mondale in 1984, and Michael Dukakis in 1988.

The weakening of the Democrats after 1968 enabled Richard Nixon and the Republicans to launch their "southern strategy" and make strong appeals for the white backlash vote in the South and elsewhere. This precipitated mass changes in the politics of the nation, which had not been seen since the early 1930s. By the early 1970s, the Republicans were dominant in the once "solid Democratic South." The Republicans were also emboldened to turn more openly conservative, reducing the influence of the moderate wing of the party for the rest of the 20th century and into the 21st.

William Gudelunas

FURTHER READING:

Farber, David. *Chicago '68.* Chicago: University of Chicago Press, 1988.

Gould, Lewis L. *1968: The Election That Changed America.* Chicago: Ivan Dee, 1993.

Matusow, Allen J. *The Unraveling of America: A History of Liberalism in the 1960's.* New York: Harper & Row, 1984.

Patterson, James. *Grand Expectations: The United States, 1945–1974.* New York: Oxford University Press, 1996.

1969 ◆ SANTA BARBARA OIL SPILL

The 1969 Santa Barbara oil spill was one of those rare events that, though seemingly local, quickly reverberate worldwide. In February 1968, the U.S. Department of the Interior, shunting aside vigorous objections from regional communities, awarded leases to a consortium of oil companies (Union, Mobil, Texaco, and Gulf) to drill in offshore waters of southern California's beautiful Santa Barbara Channel. The department also waived existing safety regulations, including the requirement for casings to protect wells from underwater leaks. On January 28, 1969, a well without casings on Union Oil's Platform A burst open, gushing oil and natural gas. Within days, millions of gallons of crude oil had coagulated into an oil slick stretching over 600 square miles. The rupture soon spread to multiple vents over 50 acres of earthquake-fractured ocean floor, the oil flowing uncontrollably for many months. Driven by tidal and wave action, sticky oil sludge invaded the California coast and offshore islands, smothering rocks and cliffs, prized beaches, boats in marinas, and coastal structures, killing vast numbers of birds, sea mammals, and other coastal fauna, and jeopardizing fragile ecosystems. Record-breaking storms and winds of that fierce winter drove the sludge back and forth, repeatedly blackening the coast, pushing clinging, greasy mists deep into the interior, and forestalling full control and cleanup for more than a year. Residents despaired. "The odor of crude oil reached us like the whiff of a decaying future," recalled famed mystery novelist Ross Macdonald. Even former Secretary of the Interior Stewart Udall admitted he had erred in approving the leases, calling the disaster a "conservation Bay of Pigs."

Ross Macdonald was perceptive when he characterized the spill as "the blowout heard round the

FACTBOX

PLACE Santa Barbara Channel, southern California

DATE January 28, 1969

TYPE Oil spill

DESCRIPTION An offshore oil well burst open, creating an oil slick stretching over 600 square miles.

CAUSE Offshore well drilling for oil without many safety precautions

CASUALTIES No human deaths, but vast killing of birds, sea mammals, and animals, and short-term devastation of coastal ecosystems

COST Many tens of millions of dollars, including long-term losses to the region's major tourist economy

IMPACT Sharp increases in proenvironmental public opinion and organizational activity; unprecedented passage of state and federal environmental regulatory laws

world." Lawsuits—$3.5 billion in damages filed against just Union Oil in the first month alone—dragged on for years, as did the cleanup, but revolutions in public opinion and policy began immediately. The disaster came at a time ripe for change in a state that had hitherto worshiped population growth and economic development with the fervor of a secular religion. Throughout the decade, a spate of disturbing and widely read publications, including California Tomorrow's *California: Going, Going . . .* (1962), Raymond Dasmann's *The Destruction of California* (1965), Richard Lillard's *Eden in Jeopardy* (1966), and William Bronson's *How to Kill a Golden State* (1968), had already spread alarm at the state's fast-vanishing natural resources and beauties in the wake of 20th-century economic booms. Denounced by citizens and public officials across the state irrespective of class, ethnicity, and party allegiance, the Santa Barbara disaster was the last straw.

In its most direct response, the state, historically one of the earliest and foremost petroleum producers, overnight became an aggressive and nationally influential opponent of offshore oil drilling, adopting numerous state and local regulations and, into the 21st century, successfully resisting repeated fed-

eral attempts to reopen drilling. Public opinion polls revealed striking surges in support for general environmental protection, and environmental organizations proliferated and soared in enrollment. The San Francisco–based Sierra Club, for only one example, grew from 30,000 members in 1965 to 150,000 by 1974, with financial resources and lobbying and litigation power now stretching nation- and worldwide; another San Francisco environmental group, Friends of the Earth, dated its very founding to 1969; and a wildly popular, nonpartisan Coastal Alliance (1971) quickly affiliated more than 700 women's, workers', senior citizens', students', conservationist, and civic organizations demanding coastal preservation.

With the Santa Barbara oil spill as a rallying cry, the new conservationist majority, led by burgeoning, militant organizations, over the next few years pushed through the reluctant legislature and administration of Governor Ronald Reagan, never friendly toward environmental protections, a remarkable series of measures revolutionizing California's legal system. In quick succession, through election initiatives or legislative action, the state passed laws establishing a permanent San Francisco Bay Conservation and Development Commission (1969) to protect and restore water quality and shoreline public use in the bay region and, overpowering a prodevelopment bloc in the legislature, creating an interim Coastal Commission (1972, made permanent in 1976), the most powerful agency worldwide to assure public access to the ocean and to regulate coastal development, including shoreline oil refineries and distribution facilities. There were others, including a state Endangered Species Protection Act (1970) and numerous laws cracking down on air and water pollution. Propelled mostly by outrage over the Santa Barbara disaster, the California Environmental Quality Act (CEQA, 1970) required all major construction projects or government actions with potential environmental consequences to complete comprehensive environmental impact studies and empowered state agencies to reject projects on environmental grounds. In the few years after January 1969 and in reaction to the oil spill as symbolic of the eroding of their natural heritage in the service of private profit, Californians created the core of state and local environmental regulatory law, procedure, and institutions.

Nationally, the Santa Barbara disaster proved also to be a quick and explosive catalyst for change. As in the state, public indignation at the government's laxity and the oil companies' careless abuse of the common environment swept the country. Some analysts have credited the oil spill with having caused the remarkable series of federal laws and actions that followed in its wake. More likely, as in California, the disaster served to accelerate an already existing long-term trend. Ecological consciousness and activism had already awakened after World War II, climaxing in monumental reforms, particularly during the Kennedy and Johnson presidential administrations of the early and mid-1960s: the "Mission 66" plan enacted by Congress to upgrade and expand visitor facilities in national parks (1955), Clean Water acts passed in 1960 and 1965, Clean Air acts passed in 1963 and 1967, endangered species protection laws (1964, 1968), the Wilderness Act (1964), the National Wild and Scenic Rivers Act (1968), congressional establishment of Redwood National Park in northern California (1968), and others.

Undeniably, though, the horrendous break at Union Oil's Platform A further broadened and strengthened the environmentalist base in public opinion and energized the movement in subsequent years. One of the inspirations for the convening of the influential first Earth Day celebration in April 1970, the oil spill also helped to propel dozens of laws through Congress, sometimes with the support and leadership of President Richard Nixon's administration, attacking water, air, and toxic pollution, preserving wilderness areas and diverse ecosystems, and providing for more comprehensive environmental regulation and restoration. Notable were the Clean Air Act (1970), Water Pollution Control Act (1972), Endangered Species Act (1974), Coastal Zone Management Act (1972), Eastern Wilderness Act (1974), and Federal Land Policy and Management Act (1976). Most important, the National Environmental Policy Act (1970) established national requirements for environmental impact studies and created the Environmental Protection Agency to enforce federal environmental regulations. In California as in the United States at large, the Santa Barbara oil spill reinforced and popularized a long-term movement toward greater awareness and activism on behalf of resource conservation and environmental protection,

A bird encased in a thick coat of oil, one of the numberless creatures killed by the oil spill off the coast of California in 1969. *(Santa Barbara Historical Society)*

making the late 1960s and early 1970s a remarkable, unprecedented era of nonpartisan environmental reform.

See also 1989 Exxon Valdez oil spill.

Richard J. Orsi

FURTHER READING:

Easton, Robert. *Black Tide: The Santa Barbara Oil Spill and Its Consequences.* New York: Delacorte, 1972.

Freudenburg, William R., and Robert Gramling. *Oil in Troubled Waters: Perception, Politics, and the Battle over Offshore Drilling.* Albany: State University of New York Press, 1994.

Hays, Samuel P. *Beauty, Health, and Permanence: Environmental Politics in the United States, 1955–1985.* New York: Cambridge University Press, 1987.

Kallman, Robert, and Eugene D. Wheeler. *Coastal Crude in a Sea of Conflict.* San Luis Obispo, Calif.: Blake Printing and Publishing Co., 1984.

Keir, A. E., Dean E. Mann, and Phil G. Olsen Nash. *Oil Pollution and the Public Interest: A Study of the Santa Barbara Oil Spill.* Berkeley: University of California Press, 1972.

1969 ◆ DEPLETION OF NEW ENGLAND FISHERIES

Catches in commercial fisheries naturally vary over time. Yet the downturns in catches of cod, haddock, and a variety of flounders, indeed the whole range of the 15 species known as groundfish that have been managed in the northwest Atlantic Ocean by the New England Fishery Management Council since the late 20th century, have been troubling to fishers, scientists, and people dependent on the fishing industry. Similar to the catch trajectory of other groundfish, the world haddock catch peaked in 1969 at 1 million tons but declined to approximately 200,000 tons by 1992. The New England fishing community in particular has suffered from this steady depletion of fish.

Haddock, *Melanogrammus aeglefinus,* is a fine, white-fleshed member of the cod family. Elegant looking, the fish is dark, purple-gray above a black lateral line, silver gray with pink reflections on the sides, and has a white belly. A dark spot below the lateral line is known as "St. Peter's mark" or the "devil's thumbprint." Consumers on both sides of the Atlantic seek haddock in all its guises: fresh, frozen, dried, canned, and smoked (known in Scotland as *Finnan haddie*). Unlike cod (*Gadus morhua*), haddock is not particularly suitable for salting, so its popularity rose following the advent of refrigeration in the late 19th century and the expansion of the fresh fish trade.

FACTBOX

PLACE New England

DATE 1969–2005

TYPE Fishery crisis

DESCRIPTION Haddock and other groundfish were substantially depleted off the coast of New England and elsewhere.

CAUSE Overfishing, due to improved technology and foreign fishing fleets

IMPACT Reduction of commercial fishing stimulated public policies designed to manage New England coastal fisheries; traditional working waterfronts have given way to more taxable residential uses.

In the northwest Atlantic, haddock ranges from the Grand Banks of the coast of New England to Cape Hatteras, North Carolina. The deep water of the Georges Bank-South Channel area, a huge swath of ocean east of Cape Cod, Massachusetts, has long been considered among the most highly productive haddock grounds. Elsewhere in the world, other significant fishing grounds are located around Iceland, in the Barents Sea, around the Faeroe Islands, off western Norway and western Scotland, in the Celtic

Sea, off Ireland in the North Sea, and in the English Channel.

Pursuit of haddock with effective gear has been controversial since 1850 when fishers in coastal Swampscott, Massachusetts, petitioned for a law to prohibit trawling (in this case, referring to 500 hooks on a long line) for haddock in Massachusetts Bay. American landings of haddock exceeded 103,000 tons in 1929, but harvests dropped precipitously from 1930 to 1947. By the mid-1950s through the 1960s, the distant water fleets of Spain, Poland, the Soviet Union, and others were actively fishing on Georges Bank, catching and processing a wide range of species. Whatever was caught was used, filleted and frozen, or converted into fishmeal. Haddock stocks on Georges Bank declined dramatically by 1969, probably due to overfishing.

With the passage of the Magnuson-Stevens Fishery Management and Conservation Act of 1976, a 200-mile exclusive economic zone was established that forced the end of foreign fishing on Georges Bank. The newly established New England Fishery Management Council set quotas, spawning area closures, and minimum mesh sizes for nets in an effort to control fishing on groundfish. Catches of haddock increased between 1977 and 1980 but fell into a steady decline, finally reaching historic lows in the early 1990s. Overfishing is considered the most likely cause of this crisis in commercial fisheries, and echoing the past, technical improvements in gear, including nets, hydraulic systems, engines, and navigational equipment, contributed to the fishing industry's efficiency and the consequent depletion of haddock. Furthermore, since haddock is often caught with some of the more plentiful groundfish species, avoiding it can be difficult.

In 1994, an amendment to the Northeast Multispecies (groundfish) Management Plan imposed regulations such as limiting the numbers of permits, limiting the numbers of days fishers could go to sea, increasing minimum mesh sizes, and increasing closed areas. The measures were intended to progressively cut fishing effort by 50 percent during the following five years. However, a stock assessment indicating that the groundfish stocks were in worse condition than anticipated and a lawsuit demanding even stricter controls on fishing led to a second amendment that moved toward a reduction in fishing effort by 50 percent in two years rather than five. A host of regulations have since been imposed to further control fishing of groundfish.

The effects of the changes in groundfish abundance and the resulting fishing regulations have led to radical changes in the fishing industry and the New England communities that relied on it economically and socially. Traditionally, the northeast fisheries were multifaceted and intertwined. The annual round of fishing often included a wide range of species targeted and a variety of gear used. The region also boasted a predominance of owner-operated boats, as well as a great diversity in vessel size and owners' ethnicity. As the regulations tightened, flexibility was lost, many of the vessels, as well as their owners and crews, left the industry, and the remaining vessels had to specialize in particular gear and target species. The fishing fleet in the region has aged, with few new boats entering and only occasional additions of young men or women. Ownership is beginning to consolidate with some individuals owning multiple boats.

In contrast, high demand for waterfront property, particularly for leisure use or condominiums, has driven up the taxes on fishing-related, waterfront businesses. While some communities are trying to protect their traditional industry in anticipation of the projected recovery of groundfish that will greatly increase landings, others are relinquishing marine-dependent use requirements in favor of higher tax receipts on the use of waterfront property that currently generates the highest income.

The uncertainty associated with frequently changing regulations and supplies of fish has also limited the development and operation of processing facilities and other shoreside businesses such as suppliers of ice and gear. The infrastructure for commercial fishing, once lost, may be difficult to rebuild even when the stocks are fully recovered. The loss of primary industry to small coastal towns with few employment alternatives is daunting. Furthermore, if the fishing industry continues to consolidate, there may be a move toward frozen product with its ease of handling and storing.

Not all is doom and gloom, however. In 1995, haddock catch for the United States was 438.5 tons, but resurgence in the catch began the following year with a catch of 628.5 tons. Despite the regulations that strictly limit fishing effort in the Northeast, by 2004 the catch of haddock was 9,041 tons. Along with a number of the species of groundfish in the Northeast, haddock is no longer considered over-fished and is rebuilding. Interestingly, an analysis of the landing statistics for all commercial fisheries in the continental United States from 1950 to 2004 reflects surprising stability: 609 million tons to 593 million tons. The crises in fisheries may be in part a matter of perception.

Madeleine Hall-Arber

FURTHER READING:

Collette, Bruce B., and Grace Klein-MacPhee, eds. *Bigelow and Schroeder's Fishes of the Gulf of Maine.* Washington, D.C.: Smithsonian Institute Press, 2002.

Goode, George B. *Fisheries and Fishery Industries of the U.S.,* Section V-1. Washington, D.C.: Government Printing Office, U.S. Commission of Fish and Fisheries, 1887.

Stolpe, Nils E. "Full of Sound and Fury, Signifying Nothing." *FishNet USA./June 6, 2006.*

1972 ◆ RAPID CITY FLOOD

On June 9, 1972, heavy rains fell over the eastern Black Hills of South Dakota. In a matter of hours, 15 inches of rain saturated the tiny community of Nemo, with other areas receiving 10 or more inches in as little time. As smaller streams drained into the region's rivers and those rivers into canyons and reservoirs, the waters rose, hurtling toward Rapid City, South Dakota. According to the National Weather Service, water just to the north and west of the city ran 13 feet above normal. The massive downpour caused Canyon Lake Dam to collapse, sending a wall of water surging down Rapid Creek toward Rapid City. The floodwaters struck Rapid City in the early morning hours of June 10, catching many unaware and causing 238 deaths and more than 3,000 injuries.

Scattered showers had fallen in the Black Hills just to the north and west of Rapid City for a week prior to the June 9–10 flood. This precipitation left the soil saturated, leaving little absorption capacity for the rains that would follow. Heat and humidity provided the necessary conditions for heavy rainfall, leading the National Severe Local Storm Forecast Center to predict extreme thunderstorms in the region during the late afternoon and evening.

From 6 P.M. through midnight on June 9, rain fell, often quite heavily. Four inches fell in less than two hours near Galena. Other areas reported similar rates of rain by the early evening. By 7:15 P.M., the National Weather Service issued a flash flood warning for the

FACTBOX

PLACE Rapid City, South Dakota

DATE June 9–10, 1972

TYPE Flash flood

DESCRIPTION A flash flood destroyed Canyon Lake Dam, unleashing a massive wall of water that engulfed Rapid City and its surrounding communities.

CAUSE Torrential downpour of approximately 15 inches in less than 6 hours

CASUALTIES 238 dead; 3,057 injured

COST $160 million

IMPACT Rapid City bore the physical and emotional scars of the horrific flood for decades.

northern Black Hills. Indeed, as rain continued to fall, community after community and family after family made the decision to abandon businesses, schools, churches, and homes for the safety of higher ground. If Canyon Lake Dam failed, it would be too late to evacuate. At appropriately 11 P.M., the dam did breech, sending a surge of water at least 12 feet high down Rapid Creek. Water rushed toward Rapid City, whose population of approximately 44,000 made it the largest community in the path of the wave.

National Weather Service

The National Weather Service (NWS) is one of six entities in the National Oceanic and Atmospheric Administration, a division of the U.S. Department of Commerce. The mission of the NWS is to protect life and property and to enhance the national economy. It issues meteorological, hydrological, and climate forecasts and official weather watches and warnings for the United States, its territories and the adjacent waters. These products are freely available for use by other government agencies, as well as by public and private groups and individuals.

Following the recognition of the weather's contribution to deaths on the Great Lakes by a professor in Milwaukee and the tracing of a winter storm path by the chief of the army's Signal Service, Congressman Halbert E. Paine of Wisconsin proposed a Joint Congressional Resolution in 1869 that required the secretary of war to take weather observations at military stations and to warn of approaching storms. Congress passed the resolution, and President Ulysses S. Grant signed it into law on February 9, 1870. Congress charged the Signal Service, a subdivision of the Department of War, with the operation of the new agency, termed The Division of Telegrams and Reports for the Benefit of Commerce. Observer sergeants took the first weather reports at 24 stations on November 1, 1870. The observing stations, mostly east of the Rocky Mountains, sent their reports via telegraph to the headquarters in Washington, D.C. Military personnel made forecasts by assuming that the weather conditions would simply move with the wind.

On October 1, 1890, the agency became a civilian organization when President Benjamin Harrison signed a law creating the Weather Bureau within the Department of Agriculture. In the first decade of the 20th century, the Weather Bureau began to produce three-day forecasts, delivering and receiving wireless weather reports, and exchanging weather observations with Russia and eastern Asia. By the late 1930s, more advanced techniques and data, including kite experiments, airplane observations, and weather balloons, improved meteorological forecast.

President Franklin D. Roosevelt transferred the Weather Bureau to the Department of Commerce in 1940 after he and others realized its importance to aviation and commerce. The navy gave the Weather Bureau 25 aircraft radars, which were modified for meteorological purposes. In 1967, the Weather Bureau became the National Weather Service. The newly developed National Oceanic and Atmospheric Administration absorbed the NWS in 1970. Advances in computer technology, communication systems, radars, and satellites during the next several decades greatly improved weather observing and forecasting capabilities.

The NWS began a renovation and restructuring during the 1990s. Completed early in the 21st century, the $4.5 billion modernization has resulted in more-advanced and -accurate weather forecasts and warnings. It now has more than 120 field offices or Weather Forecast Offices, 13 River Forecast Centers, and nine National Centers. The agency has approximately 4,800 employees and an annual operating budget of nearly $744 million.

Richard R. Brandt

Many in Rapid City had retired for the night, unaware of the danger hurtling down at them. At 10:30 P.M., Mayor Don Barnett urged those living in low-lying areas to evacuate but mandated no large-scale removal. Whether through stubbornness, disbelief, or simply lack of awareness, few took the mayor's advice. At approximately 12:15 A.M. on June 10, 1972, the flood struck Rapid City. Water ran through the downtown area at an estimated 50,000 cubic feet per second and at an estimated depth of 12 to 13 feet. Five hours later, the water had returned to its placid flow within the banks of Rapid Creek.

Little else, however, was placid in the city. As the community began to assess the damage, they found more and more dead bodies. Some victims were discovered 50 miles downstream from Rapid City; others have never been found. Another 3,057 people were injured. The flood destroyed 1,335 homes and at least 5,000 automobiles, including cars at a dealership that were tossed like toys blocks from their initial locations. Only eight of the 23 bridges that crossed Rapid Creek survived, and most of those that did had severe damage. The flood of 1972 caused approximately $160 million in damages.

The Rapid City flood has been referred to as a 500-year flood, which means that each year there is a 0.2 percent chance of flooding of the same magnitude. Such low probabilities, however, probably have slight impact on the residents of Rapid City.

Rather, each day they are reminded of this horrendous flood by the physical scars that it left on their community.

Kimberly K. Porter

FURTHER READING:

Schwartz, Francis K., L. A. Hughes, E. M. Hansen, M. S. Petersen, and D. B. Kelly. *The Black Hills Rapid City Flood of June 9–10, 1972: A Description of the Storm and Flood.* Washington, D.C.: Government Printing Office, 1975.

1972 ◆ WATERGATE SCANDAL

On June 17, 1972, five men were arrested as they attempted to bug the Democratic headquarters in the Watergate hotel and office complex in Washington, D.C. This break-in, dismissed as a "third-rate burglary" by a White House spokesman, would ultimately ignite a major political crisis and the resignation of President Richard M. Nixon two years later. It was soon discovered that one of the five burglars, James W. McCord, was the director of security for President Nixon's reelection campaign organization, the Committee to Re-Elect the President, known by the acronym, CREEP. Former attorney general John Mitchell, who had resigned to lead the campaign organization, immediately fired McCord and denied knowing anything about the break-in. Investigators learned that E. Howard Hunt and G. Gordon Liddy, both of whom had ties to the White House, had organized the break-in. Despite the fact that Liddy was general counsel to CREEP and that a check made out to CREEP had been deposited in the bank account of one of the burglars, prosecutors were unable to connect the break-in with higher-ups. All but McCord and Liddy pleaded guilty, and in January 1973, two months after President Nixon was overwhelmingly reelected, the two men were convicted. Despite efforts by Judge John J. Sirica to elicit more information, all the defendants stayed mum.

But journalists, especially young *Washington Post* reporters Bob Woodward and Carl Bernstein, dog-

---

FACTBOX

PLACE Washington, D.C.

DATE 1972–74; June 17, 1972 (break-in of Democratic headquarters), and August 9, 1974 (resignation of President Richard M. Nixon)

TYPE Burglary, political scandal, and constitutional crisis

DESCRIPTION Cover-up of criminal activity led to the resignation of President Nixon and jail and prison terms for 25 others.

CAUSE Aggressive use of presidential power and ruthless political tactics led presidential aides to countenance illegal activity and to attempt to cover it up after it was discovered.

IMPACT Congress enacted legislation aimed at recovering power lost to presidents in prior decades.

---

gedly pursued hints of broader Nixon administration involvement in the Watergate break-in. Woodward and Bernstein's secret source, referred to as "Deep Throat" after a pornographic movie of that name, gave them crucial leads that suggested a cover-up, and revelations prompted the Senate to authorize an investigation of the matter in February 1973. (In 2005 it was revealed that "Deep Throat" was Mark

W. Felt, the senior assistant director of the Federal Bureau of Investigation.) Suspecting a broader conspiracy, Judge Sirica kept pressure on the convicted men, and in March, McCord finally broke his silence, informing Sirica that the burglary was part of a larger conspiracy and that he and the others had been paid "hush money" to remain silent. With that discovery, the cover-up began to unravel.

Although the Watergate scandal was precipitated by the June 17, 1972, break-in, its antecedents lay much deeper. It was the culmination of the president's effort to skew American politics through a combination of aggressive claims of executive power and ruthless political tactics. The powers of the president had been growing steadily throughout the 20th century. To deal with the complexities of modern society, Congress had created numerous federal administrative agencies, giving them broad authority to make rules and resolve disputes involving wide areas of American life. Faced with a generally liberal Democratic majority in Congress, Nixon used his power over executive agencies to obstruct the execution of programs he opposed. He claimed the authority to "impound," or withhold, money Congress appropriated to support them.

Nixon was even more expansive in his claims of presidential power over foreign affairs and national defense. Nixon's predecessors as president had claimed and were accorded primary authority over these matters, committing American troops to combat without securing declarations of war from Congress and entering into executive agreements that bypassed the need to secure Senate ratification of treaties. Elected president in 1968, Nixon built on this foundation, claiming sole responsibility for prosecuting the Vietnam War he had inherited from Presidents John F. Kennedy and Lyndon B. Johnson. He took a number of military actions without informing Congress, including a secret invasion of Vietnam's neighbor Cambodia in 1970. He claimed the right as president to order his subordinates to mislead Congress when he believed it necessary to national security, and he insisted that he could exercise an "executive privilege" to order executive department employees to refuse to give information to congressional investigating committees. When Daniel Ellsberg, a former Defense Department employee, leaked secret documents known as the *Pentagon Papers* to the press in 1971, demonstrating that the Johnson administration had purposely deceived the American people about the Vietnam War, Nixon sought a court injunction to block their publication. The case went all the way to the Supreme Court, which ruled against the president.

Embarrassed by the *Pentagon Papers* and other leaks of information, Nixon ordered investigations, insisting that he could ignore constitutional limitations in matters of national security. Without securing necessary warrants, he authorized the infiltration and disruption of antiwar organizations. When the courts ordered a stop to such practices, Nixon created a secret White House investigating group—called "the plumbers"—to stop the leaks, responsible only to him and his closest aides. One of its members was Liddy. Nixon also used his powers to intimidate his political opponents, ordering government agencies to investigate the people on an "enemies list," and hiring political operatives to engage in "dirty tricks" to disrupt the election campaigns of potential Democratic rivals for the presidency in 1972.

All these elements played a role in the Watergate burglary. With the presidential election looming, top Nixon aides feared that the Democrats had uncovered the secret operations of the "plumbers," especially an illegal break-in undertaken to get information about Daniel Ellsberg. Liddy organized the bugging operation at the Watergate Hotel to find out what Democrats knew.

As soon as the burglars were arrested in June 1972, Nixon and his aides began to organize a cover-up of the administration's role in the affair. As the Senate Judiciary Committee began to investigate the burglary the following year, Nixon's aides prepared to lie about their involvement. However, John Dean, general counsel to the president and thus his chief legal adviser, chose to cooperate with investigators. To stem criticism, Nixon fired Dean on April 30, 1973, and accepted the resignations of his top aides, domestic policy adviser John Ehrlichman, chief of staff H. R. Haldeman, and Attorney General Richard Kleindienst—who all still denied knowing about the break-in or engaging in any cover-up. Nixon also named his respected Secretary of Defense Elliot L. Richardson attorney general to take charge of the Justice Department's Watergate investigation. Richardson in turn named former solicitor general Archibald Cox as special prosecutor to take charge of the criminal investigation of the Watergate affair.

Richard Nixon gives one last wave as he leaves the White House on August 9, 1974. Earlier in the day, he had resigned as president because of his involvement in the Watergate scandal. *(Associated Press)*

As Dean testified before the Senate Watergate Committee in June and July that Nixon and his aides had covered up their connection to the Watergate burglars, the senators—along with millions of Americans who watched the hearings on live television—learned that the president, a prolific author and memoirist, had tape-recorded all meetings in his White House office. Realizing that these tape-recorded conversations contained vital evidence, both the Senate committee and the Justice Department investigators requested and then subpoenaed the White House for the tapes and other documents. Claiming "executive privilege," Nixon refused to comply, insisting that he did so to defend the office of the presidency. Judge Sirica and an appeals court rejected Nixon's arguments. Faced with growing public pressure, Nixon offered a "compromise" by which a single senator would consult transcripts of the tapes and summarize them for special prosecutor Archibald Cox. On Saturday, October 20, Cox rejected the offer, and Nixon immediately instructed Richardson to fire him. Both Richardson and his second-in-command resigned rather than comply with the president's order. Finally the number-three Justice Department official, Solicitor General Robert Bork, fired Cox, in what became known as "the Saturday Night Massacre."

Nixon defended his action as the removal of an insubordinate officer, but in light of the questionable activities then coming to light, many people concluded that the president believed himself above the law. Public outrage forced him to retreat. He agreed to turn over some of the tapes, and the Jus-

tice Department named Leon Jaworski as the new special prosecutor to replace Cox, reporting directly to the courts and guaranteed against removal except for extraordinary dereliction of duty. Still defending his actions, Nixon addressed the country directly on November 17 and assured the public, "I am not a crook." Four days later, on November 21, investigators found an 18-minute gap in the tape recordings made at a meeting between Nixon, Haldeman, and Ehrlichman three days after the break-in.

With calls growing for Nixon's resignation, the House of Representatives instructed its Judiciary Committee on February 6, 1974, to investigate whether grounds existed to impeach the president. The urgency of their proceedings increased on March 1, when Jaworski indicted seven top Nixon aides for obstructing justice, naming Nixon as an "un-indicted co-conspirator." Still insisting on his innocence, Nixon continued to refuse to hand over the tapes subpoenaed by the special prosecutor and the House Judiciary Committee, voluntarily giving the committee edited transcripts instead.

Although Democrats controlled Congress, the Constitution required a vote of two-thirds of the Senate to convict the president if he were impeached. With Republicans holding 43 of the 100 Senate seats, Nixon was well aware that no partisan impeachment could succeed. As the president protested his innocence, most Republican members of the House Judiciary Committee continued to defend him, insisting that there was no irrefutable evidence that Nixon had known of the Watergate break-in, cover-up, or wrongdoing. There was, as one of them said, no "smoking gun." But others were clearly shaken as they not only learned more about the break-in itself but about the secret war in Cambodia, the effort to use government agencies to harass political opponents, and the rogue "plumbers" operation.

Meanwhile, the Supreme Court heard the appeal of the lower court's order that Nixon turn over the tapes. Many believed that if the Supreme Court was divided in its decision, Nixon, as the head of a coequal branch of government, would refuse to obey a ruling against him and that no authority could force him to comply. In the view of many Americans, the principle that no one was above the law was at risk. But on July 24, the justices unanimously denied the president's claim of executive privilege in *United States v. Richard M. Nixon.* Faced with a united Supreme Court, Nixon did not dare to disobey. Before receiving the tapes, the House Judiciary Committee voted from July 27 to July 30 to recommend that the House of Representatives bring three articles of impeachment against Nixon—for obstructing the Watergate criminal investigation, abuse of power, and refusal to comply with subpoenas of documents. Seven Republicans voted in favor of the first two articles.

It was almost certain that the House would impeach Nixon on the first two articles. But conviction in the Senate, where Democrats were 10 votes shy of a two-thirds majority, was far from certain. Then on August 5, having lost the Supreme Court's decision, Nixon released the most damaging tapes. One of them contained conversations six days after the burglary demonstrating that he had known that White House officials were involved in the break-in and that he had conspired to deflect an FBI investigation. It was the "smoking gun"—irrefutable evidence that Nixon had obstructed justice and broken the law—that the president's defenders had insisted on. Warned by senior Republican congressmen that impeachment was now inevitable and removal likely, Nixon resigned four days later on August 9, 1974. Special prosecutor Jaworski recommended that he be prosecuted for obstructing justice, but on September 8, Nixon's successor, President Gerald Ford, pardoned him for any and all acts related to the scandal, although many other White House operatives went to jail for their parts in the cover-up.

Many criticized Ford's action, but most Americans believed that events had demonstrated the strength of the nation's constitutional institutions, holding the most aggressive of presidents responsible for abuse of power and criminal behavior. In the aftermath of the Watergate scandal, Congress acted to reclaim some of the powers that had eroded during previous decades. It increased its staff and fact-finding abilities to become more independent of the executive. It passed the Independent Counsel Act, specifying when and how independent investigators would be appointed to search into alleged wrongdoing in the executive branch. It enacted the War Powers Act, requiring the president to notify Congress when committing troops to possible combat and to secure congressional approval to extend the commitment beyond 60 days. Congress passed the National Emergencies Act, specifying procedures presidents must use in declaring them and authorizing Congress to terminate them, and it established procedures to exercise more control over administrative agencies.

The Watergate crisis remains one of the foremost political scandals in American history. It not only forced a president to resign in disgrace but led to jail and prison sentences for 25 men. It also led to a new term in the American lexicon—the suffix –gate added to any word to indicate scandal or misdoing, and equally significant, the Watergate crisis had a major impact on the decline in trust that Americans displayed toward government in the mid- to late 1970s. This souring mood and anger at corruption in the nation's capital led voters to elect two outsiders and non-Washington politicians president: Jimmy Carter in 1976 and Ronald Reagan in 1980.

Michael Les Benedict

FURTHER READING:
Kutler, Stanley I. *The Wars of Watergate: The Last Crisis of Richard Nixon.* New York: Knopf, 1990.
Olson, Keith W. *Watergate: The Presidential Scandal That Shook America.* Lawrence: University of Kansas Press, 2003.

1973 ◆ OIL EMBARGO

On October 20, 1973, Saudi Arabia and other oil-rich nations of the Persian Gulf region embargoed the export of crude oil to the United States. With the supply of petroleum reduced, the price of gasoline and home heating oil spiked upward. Long used to cheap and abundant fuel, Americans were surprised and shocked at these events. More galling, the long lines of drivers at service stations waiting to buy gas during the winter of 1974 demonstrated that the nation had an "energy crisis." The Persian Gulf states lifted the embargo on March 18, 1974, but the impact of the event

FACTBOX

PLACE United States

DATE October 20, 1973–March 18, 1974

TYPE Oil scarcity and economic crisis

DESCRIPTION Petroleum exporters in the Persian Gulf embargoed oil sales to the United States, driving up fuel prices.

CAUSE United States support for Israel during the Yom Kippur War

COST Billions of dollars in increased prices for petroleum-based products

IMPACT In the short run, the national government limited highway speeds to 55 miles per hour and mandated fuel standards for passenger cars. In the long run, the oil embargo ignited the "Great Stagflation," a rise in inflation and unemployment that was an underlying cause of America's political turn to conservatism. The oil embargo also demonstrated America's growing "energy crisis."

radiated throughout American society. The economy stumbled from 1974 to 1982, reeling under record inflation, while incurring several recessions. More alarming, the oil embargo made clear that the United States was now dependent on foreign petroleum. Oil consultant and historian Daniel Yergin goes further, arguing that the crisis of 1973–74 "remade the international economy."

Americans' love affair with their cars set the stage for this new global reality. Since the early 20th century, the automobile offered Americans extraordinary freedom of movement, providing not only flexible transportation but also a sense of personal empowerment—individuals could drive wherever they wanted whenever they wanted. Rising personal incomes after World War II, cheap gasoline, an ever-expanding highway network (interstate highways were authorized in 1956), and spreading suburbs that made cars a necessity for commuting to work put millions more cars on the roads in the 1950s and 1960s. Motor vehicle registrations tripled between 1948 and 1973. American society became largely redesigned around automobility, in which virtually every suburban and rural family owned one car.

Cars also became bigger and went faster, symbolized by the large "muscle" cars of the era. Fuel efficiency dropped, and motor-vehicle fuel consumption more than quadrupled between 1948 and 1973. Demand for petroleum used to heat homes, power factories and agricultural equipment and for manufactured products such as plastics (which are made from petroleum) rose as well. By 1969, domestic petroleum production no longer satisfied American demands. The nation used 17 millions barrels of oil a day in 1973, 36 percent of it imported. Twenty-three percent of foreign oil came from the Middle East (especially Saudi Arabia, Iran, and Iraq), which held the world's largest petroleum reserves.

Oil imports were linked to the volatile relations between Israel and its Arab neighbors. Middle Eastern states had objected to the creation of Israel in 1948 and the subsequent expulsion of Palestinians. The outbreak of the Yom Kippur War on October 6, 1973, when Egypt and Syria attacked Israel, was the latest installment of this ongoing conflict. The Gulf region oil nations, acting within the framework of the Organization of Petroleum Exporting Countries (OPEC, created in 1960) but following the lead of King Faisal of Saudi Arabia, threatened to reduce oil sales to the United States if it continued to support Israel. The United States had established a long-term policy of support for Israel, the only democratic regime in the region. When the United States airlifted a massive infusion of weapons to Israel, whose military situation tottered at the onset of the invasion, OPEC cut off oil exports to the United States. The organization also raised its target price for its oil to $11.65 a barrel, up from $3 before the embargo.

The embargo quickly affected Americans at the gas pumps. Before the embargo, Americans had paid about 36 cents for a gallon of gas. In the winter of 1974, the price jumped to 53 cents a gallon. Some stations jacked up prices to $2 a gallon, prompting states to prosecute price gougers. More troublesome, stations in some areas of the country received smaller supplies than normal, causing motorists to panic. In January and February 1974, long lines of cars formed to fill up at their local gas station, sometimes only to be turned away. When Oregon governor Tom McCall pulled into a station, the attendant responded: "Sorry, Governor, we're only selling to our regular customers." Some states implemented an allocation plan whereby sales were made on even days to cars with license plates ending in even numbers, and plates ending in an odd number could buy on odd days. Getting gas became a national nightmare, leaving some motorists frantic. "These people are like animals foraging for food," one station owner observed.

The oil scarcity unsettled the economy. Prices for many goods and services rose, bumped upward by the rise in the cost of petroleum. The stock market slumped badly in 1973 and 1974 and then again in 1977. The oil disruption helped to push the nation into recession in 1974, which deepened the following year into the worst downturn since the Great Depression 40 years earlier. Unemployment edged up to 8.5 percent in 1975; inflation registered 9.1 percent, a level far above acceptability. The combination of unemployment and inflation, nicknamed *stagflation*, totaled 17.6 percent (on the "Misery" or Stagflation Index) in 1975. Recovery began in 1976, but inflation remained high, and then rocketed upward in 1979 when the revolution in Iran caused a second panic over the availability of Middle Eastern oil. A barrel of petroleum hit $30 in 1979, and a gallon of gasoline jumped to $1.25. For the second time in the decade, tight supplies of fuel produced long lines of drivers awaiting their turn at the gas pump. The second energy shock pushed the Stagflation Index to register 17.5 percent. In 1980, it climbed to 20.6 percent.

The spike in energy costs was not the only factor behind stagflation, but it was key. From 1973 to 1980, the Consumer Price Index rose 86 percent, with fuel costs increasing 308 percent. Inflation had a numbing effect on business and the economy. Real wages (corrected for inflation) fell after 1973, leaving most workers less well off in 1980 than they had been seven years earlier. Despite the energy crunch, such large oil companies as Exxon and Texaco raked in huge profits. In 1973, Exxon, the nation's largest, recorded a record profit for an American corporation of $2.4 billion. Consumer critics such as Ralph Nader wondered if corporations had deliberately engineered the oil shortage to drive up profits.

President Richard Nixon and Congress wrestled with the embargo and oil shortage. Nixon sent Secretary of State Henry Kissinger on a whirlwind of visits to the Middle East on a quest to pacify Arab antagonism. His "shuttle diplomacy" was instrumental in persuading the oil ministers of the Gulf region to lift the embargo. At home, President Nixon opposed price controls on energy production but was faced with the wrath of the American drivers. The oil embargo forced Americans to think more seriously about ways of saving energy. The national government responded to the crisis with a number of short-run steps, such as limiting the speed on main highways to 55 miles per hour, approving an Alaskan pipeline to transport oil from Prudhoe Bay in the Arctic, and instituting daylight saving year round (until 1975). Political disagreements prevented the adoption of emergency energy legislation in 1974, when President Nixon was preoccupied with the WATERGATE SCANDAL. Nixon resigned in 1974, and Gerald Ford became president. In 1975, President Ford signed a law that set new fuel standards for passenger cars (but not trucks), to begin in 1978. But wrangling over the issue of price controls stymied the adoption of a comprehensive federal energy policy for the rest of the decade.

Waiting to fill up their tanks, a line of cars circle a block in Los Angeles. Gas lines were a common sight in 1973–74 and again in 1979. *(Associated Press)*

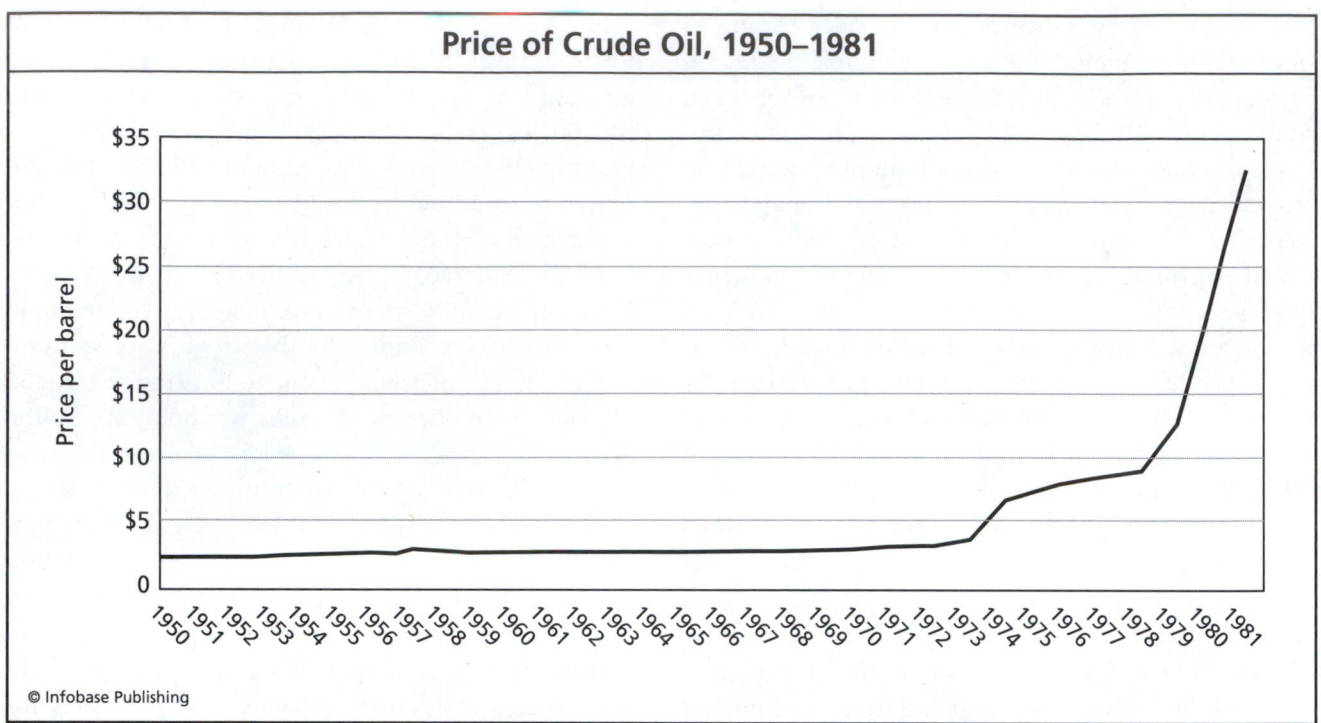

Price of Crude Oil, 1950–1981

© Infobase Publishing

After remaining steady for more than two decades, oil prices shot up in the 1970s. Source: Susan B. Carter et al., eds. *Historical Statistics of the United States Millennial Edition Online*. New York: Cambridge University Press, 2006, Table Db56.

The failure to establish a broad energy strategy compounded uncertainties that festered in the battered economy. Inflation continued to surge upward, causing property values to rise faster than incomes in some states. Higher assessments on real estate increased the amount of property taxes that homeowners owed. When California voters approved Proposition 13 in 1978, a referendum measure that capped property taxes, citizen anguish over the inability of government to remedy the problems of inflation reached Washington. The tax revolt in California and other states greatly complicated the presidency of Jimmy Carter (elected over Ford in 1976) as critics charged his administration with weakness and inaction. Heeding these signs of discontent, lawmakers removed federal regulations from airlines, trucking, banks, and cable TV between 1978 and 1980. Carter appointed Paul Volcker, a tough-minded banker, as chair of the Federal Reserve Board in hopes of reducing inflation. Volcker tamed inflation with higher interest rates, which induced a severe recession in the early 1980s.

By then, Ronald Reagan had captured the presidency and Republicans had gained control of the Senate, setting the stage for a wave of conservative reforms. By fueling the great stagflation and destabilizing the economy, the oil embargo of 1973–74 had been instrumental in triggering a conservative political revolution. Liberalism had become equated with prolonging the economic pain. President Reagan and his conservative supporters were given the opportunity to put the country on a conservative path toward lower federal taxes and greater reliance on an unregulated free market.

Ballard C. Campbell

FURTHER READING:

Hibbs, Douglas A., Jr. *The American Political Economy: Macroeconomics and Electoral Politics.* Cambridge, Mass.: Harvard University Press, 1987.

Small, Melvin. *The Presidency of Richard Nixon.* Lawrence: University Press of Kansas, 1999.

Yergin, Daniel. *The Prize: The Epic Quest for Oil, Money, and Power.* New York: Simon and Schuster, 1991.

1976 ◆ LEGIONNAIRES' DISEASE OUTBREAK

On Tuesday, July 21, 1976, 4,400 delegates and family members of the Pennsylvania chapter of the American Legion, the nation's largest veterans' group, traveled to Philadelphia for their annual meeting. Members from around the state gathered at the stately Bellevue-Stratford Hotel for a raucous celebration of the legion and the nation's Bicentennial. The meeting ended on July 24, and the members dispersed to their hometowns around the state. Just six days later, on Friday, July 30, a physician in the community of Bloomsburg was treating three patients with very high fevers and pneumonia when he realized that all three had been delegates at the legion convention in Philadelphia. He contacted the State Health Department to inquire if cases had been reported from other attendees but was informed that the office was closed for the weekend. Several more cases were reported when the Pennsylvania Health Department opened on Monday, August 2. The Pennsylvania Health Department informed the Centers for Disease Control (CDC) of the association of the convention with a mysterious disease, and the CDC immediately sent in a team of epidemiologists and scientists to aid in the investigation.

Initially, it was feared that the illnesses were caused by swine flu, an influenza strain possibly related to Spanish flu. The federal government had recently authorized creating a massive vaccination campaign to protect its citizens. Although the media would continue to speculate over the connection between the flu and the legionnaires' sickness, influenza was quickly ruled out; 221 patients were soon identified with the illness, and subsequently 34 died. However, the cases were restricted to those who had been in Philadelphia, and there was no indication of secondary spread. This pattern pointed to a common-source exposure as the cause of the sickness. Investigators soon zeroed in on the convention headquarters, the Bellevue-Stratford Hotel. Dozens of CDC investigators descended on the city and the hotel, taking samples from patients, employees, and guests and from various locations in and near the hotel. The CDC investigators broadened their search for cases to the period from July 1 through August

FACTBOX

PLACE Philadelphia, Pennsylvania

DATE July 1–August 18, 1976

TYPE Disease outbreak

DESCRIPTION Attendees at a convention of the American Legion unknowingly inhaled deadly bacteria emitted from hotel air-conditioning ducts.

CAUSE Inhalation of aerosolized bacteria (*Legionella pneumophila*) from modern devices such as air conditioners and showerheads

CASUALTIES 221 stricken with 34 deaths

COST Approximately $2 million in investigating the Philadelphia outbreak; untold millions in outbreaks since then

IMPACT Identification of a bacterium causing numerous localized outbreaks of fever and pneumonia that might be responsible for as much as 2 percent of all pneumonia deaths each year. Identification of the bacteria has prompted doctors to watch for symptoms of the disease so that treatment can be implemented.

18, 1976. The samples were sent to both the Pennsylvania Health Department Laboratories and the CDC laboratories in Atlanta. Eventually nearly $2 million and more than 73,000 person-hours were logged in the investigation.

By the fall of 1976, the fieldwork portion of the investigation ended, and still no cause had been identified. The epidemiological focus on the hotel, and overheated media scrutiny of the investigation branded the Bellevue-Stratford as the cause of the disease. Lodgers stayed away in droves, and on November 18, 1976, the "grand dame of Broad Street," a premier Philadelphia hotel since its opening in 1904, was forced to close its doors. Wild rumors circulated that "Legionnaires' disease" was caused by a chemical attack on the convention by foreign or domestic terrorists. Others suggested the accidental or purposeful release of secret military biological weapons. In the dark days following the Vietnam War and Watergate, many found these theories plausible. The CDC was charged with either complicity or bungling for not identifying the cause. Congressional hearings in the House of Representatives were called to identify what lay behind the CDC's failure to identify the source of the illness.

Then on December 28, 1976, CDC scientist Joseph McDade pulled out some slides he had prepared for a prior test. As he reexamined them he realized that there were some bacteria that he had dismissed previously. McDade managed to culture the bacteria and tested them on samples from people attending the convention. Those who had become ill produced antibodies in reaction to the bacteria; those who were not ill did not. In addition, McDade tested the bacteria against samples from two previous mysterious outbreaks similar to the Philadelphia cases. Both groups demonstrated a positive reaction. McDade had solved the mystery of these outbreaks. The cause was a bacterium dubbed *Legionella pneumophila.*

Subsequently, the bacterium has been found to be ubiquitous, thriving in condensers, faucets, showerheads, grocery produce, misters, and, in the case of the Bellevue-Stratford, the cooling towers of airconditioning units. The bacterium apparently traveled from the cooling towers through the air-conditioning ducts and into the hotel rooms and public spaces where it infected unsuspecting guests and even pass-ersby on the street out front. Since its discovery in 1976, the Legionnaires' bacteria have been traced to numerous outbreaks around the world, especially in hospitals and hotels. The infection is most likely to strike those who are immuno-compromised or with weakened lungs, but anyone may become stricken. Legionnaires' disease requires prompt identification to prevent it from developing into a deadly pneumonia. Prior to 1976, no one knew the bacterium existed. Now doctors around the world can identify the source of *Legionella* outbreaks and begin a proper course of treatment, saving untold numbers of lives. Still, it is estimated that as many as 2 percent of all pneumonia deaths each year could be caused by the bacterium.

George Dehner

FURTHER READING:

Barbaree, James M., Robert F. Breiman, and Alfred P. Dufour. *Legionella: Current Status and Emerging Perspectives.* Washington, D.C.: American Society for Microbiology, 1993.

Fraser, David W., et al. "Legionnaires' Disease: Description of an Epidemic of Pneumonia." *The New England Journal of Medicine* 297, no. 22 (December 1, 1977): 1,189–1,197.

McDade, Joseph E., et al. "Legionnaires' Disease: Isolation of a Bacterium and Demonstration of Its Role in Other Respiratory Disease." *The New England Journal of Medicine* 297, no. 22 (December 1, 1977): 1,197–1,203.

1977 ◆ NEW YORK CITY POWER FAILURE

On the hot, humid night of July 13, 1977, the lights went out in New York City. Although a similar blackout had occurred across the Northeast in November 1965, the failure of New York's power grid thrust the city into one of its most serious crises. The power outage caused 1,037 fires, four deaths, numerous injuries including to dozens of firefighters, and $300 million in economic losses. The disruption had far-reaching consequences for a city already reeling from economic and social problems.

Electricity powers the modern city, making possible a lifestyle of high-rise buildings, subways, traffic and streetlights, and other necessities of a high-density, urban region. The power failure of 1977 demonstrated just how dependent cities had become on electricity. When the power goes off, society can spiral into chaos. The causes of the 1977 failure are still poorly understood. Consolidated Edison, the power distributor, was unable to satisfactorily explain why the outage occurred or convince the public that such an event would not recur.

FACTBOX

PLACE New York City

DATE July 13, 1977

TYPE Electrical power failure; riot

DESCRIPTION A power failure in New York City on a hot summer night led to the breakout of rioting and looting.

CAUSE A combination of crumbling infrastructure, a lightning storm, and official mistakes made by Con Edison

CASUALTIES Four deaths, many injured by broken glass

COST $300 million in property losses

IMPACT The power failure had significant economic consequences, as many shopkeepers in the riot area did not reopen or moved their businesses elsewhere.

The crash of New York's power grid was entangled in a combination of violent weather, human errors, and mechanical breakdowns. Backup generators malfunctioned, and circuit breakers failed at many power plants. Con Edison's central control room lacked a monitoring screen to provide an overview of its power system, a feature that most other power producers had by 1977. The system operator erred in responding to the rapidly developing problem, in part because he was uninformed about the scope of the outage and because he failed to take aggressive actions soon enough. Several lightning strikes, the first at 8:37 P.M., struck a power line connecting the Indian Point number 3 nuclear power plant to New York City, forcing the plant, 35 miles north of the city, to shut down. Due to the difficulty of generating power in the city, much of Con Ed's power was purchased from neighboring companies. The first failure and subsequent problems forced key power conduits to go offline. Procedures put in place after the 1965 blackout made neighboring grid operators more inclined to separate from a troubled grid rather than become entangled in the brewing failure. This policy ensured that the power failure would be confined to a small area but accentuated the trouble in New York City.

In a last-ditch effort, Con Edison imposed an 8 percent power reduction, or "brownout," through-

out the grid to buy time to regroup. At 9:27 P.M., more lightning strikes on the final two feeder cables plunged the city into darkness. Although there was little physical damage to the transmission grid, power was not restored to the city for 25 hours. Ultimately, Con Ed accepted blame for the outage, acknowledging that mechanical failure and human error, not just lightning, caused the blackout.

The power failure coincided with a mid-July heat wave that saw temperatures reach 90°F between July 13 and July 21. The sweltering weather contributed to the violence that erupted when the city went dark. Six times the normal number of blazes broke out that night, precipitating 1,700 false alarms and injuries to 59 firefighters. *Time* magazine reported that firemen were attacked by crowds as they fought the fires. Looting was rampant, sometimes by entire families. One store owner shot the leader of a mob of 30 youths that threatened the business establishment. Jails were seriously overcrowded, unable keep up with the arrests.

City leaders took stock of the rampage the next morning. Businesses located in poorer neighborhoods suffered the most looting and damage. Ronald Gabbini, a shop owner in one of the ravaged neighborhoods, said, "I work twelve hours a day, six days a week for nineteen years, and they destroy everything in ten minutes." Another shop owner pointed out that 25 families would be destitute if he did not reopen. According to *The Economist*, looting during the power failure caused more than $300 million in property damages, including $120 million lost by shopkeepers. The city lost approximately $2.2 million in sales taxes, while it spent $14.6 million on emergency services. Some businesses lost all their records, hindering the task of inventorying stolen goods and claiming insurance. Numerous small shop owners had no insurance coverage. Roughly a quarter of the 2,000 businesses that were vandalized never reopened, a development that contributed to the sense of blight and urban decay in parts of the city.

Numerically and geographically, the 1977 power failure, which cut electricity to 9 million people, was far smaller than the 1965 blackout, which affected eight states and two Canadian provinces and left 25 million people in the dark. Yet the two outages had different consequences. Calm prevailed in 1965, whereas the outage in 1977 brought on a riot. No firm explanation for the different outcomes exists, although the hot, humid weather of mid-July likely contributed. More deep-seated reasons can be traced to the decline in urban infrastructure over the preceding dozen years, along with rising unemployment and inflation, which particularly devastated the nation's cities. One immediate impact of the blackout was on the city's politics, as New York mayor Abe Beame went down to defeat in the Democratic primary in September. The New York City power failure of 1977 came to symbolize the urban decay and social chaos of the mid-1970s.

William Burgess

FURTHER READING:

Goodman, James E. *Blackout.* New York: North Point Press, 2003.

Wolenberg, Ernest H. "'The Geography of Civility' Revisited: New York Blackout Looting, 1977." *Economic Geography* 58, no. 1 (January 1982): 29–44.

1978 ◆ BLIZZARD OF '78

The blizzard of 1978 was the worst winter storm in New England meteorological records. Three air masses combined off the New Jersey coast and moved north while a stationary high pressure air mass over eastern Canada blocked its progress. This unusually severe Nor'easter created the storm of the century, which weather forecasters had underestimated. On February 5–7, 1978, an average of 30 inches of snow fell for 33 hours on much of southern New England as 80- to 100-mph winds combined with a new moon and storm-generated ocean waves to create a devastating tide 15 feet above mean low water on the eastern Massachusetts coast. A snowstorm two weeks earlier had already dumped 21 inches of snow on greater Boston, contributing to the impact of the February 5 blizzard that brought unexpected heavy snow, thunderstorms, and lightning.

By February 7, thousands of homes and vacation cottages at the seashore and especially on Cape Ann and Cape Cod in Massachusetts were destroyed or damaged by the 40-foot waves and gale winds. Cape Cod sand dunes in Nauset were reduced to low mounds as the ocean swept away sand bars, breakwaters, docks, and small islands. Beach erosion was serious on Long Island Sound, and low-lying coastal towns were severely flooded. Thousands of New England motorists were stranded on snow-choked highways for several days, and normal life was suspended for a week as most offices, stores, businesses, churches, and schools closed. Local and state highway departments struggled to plow the 15-foot snow drifts, and homeowners attempted to shovel out their doorways, driveways, and sidewalks. The southern New England interstate highways closed for a week, and more than 3,500 cars and trucks were abandoned on Route 128. About 10,000 people moved into emergency shelters. Paralyzed by the snowfall, Boston (27 inches), Providence (28 inches), Woonsocket (38 inches), and

FACTBOX
PLACE New England
DATE February 5–7, 1978
TYPE Monumental nor'easter storm that moved up the East Coast and was blocked from moving further north by a stationary high-pressure air mass over eastern Canada
DESCRIPTION A blizzard dumped more than three feet of snow on some parts of New England for two days.
CASUALTIES 99 deaths
COST $1.3 billion
IMPACT Impeded normal activities for a week in much of Massachusetts and Rhode Island; improvement in regional planning for natural disasters

Immobilized vehicles lie stranded in Massachusetts. The blizzard of 1978 buried roads and cars across the Northeast. *(Associated Press)*

many other New England cities were eerily quiet as cross-country skiers and sleds replaced automobiles on city streets. Schools were closed for a week. Supermarkets that managed to open soon exhausted supplies and ran short of currency. Ninety-nine people died in this blizzard, with 4,556 injuries, and property losses exceeded $1.3 billion. Massachusetts governor Michael S. Dukakis mobilized the National Guard and banned vehicular traffic for days. President Jimmy Carter declared parts of coastal Massachusetts and Rhode Island federal disaster areas. The police and highway departments towed abandoned cars from snow drifts for one week.

Although blizzards in 1888, 1993, and 1996 surpassed the 1978 snowfall records, the blizzard of 1978 remains New England's most memorable and paralyzing storm of the 20th century. Even the most hardy and weather-wise Yankees recall how they survived the Blizzard of '78. In its aftermath, local and state governments revised mandatory evacuation plans, and many businesses developed conditioned-response policies to close or to send employees home early when severe storms are forecast. Meteorologists reorganized winter storm forecasting methods to avoid similar disasters.

See also 1888 BLIZZARD OF '88.

Peter C. Holloran

FURTHER READING:

Tougias, Michael. *The Blizzard of '78.* Yarmouth Port, Mass.: On Cape Publications, 2003.

———. *Ten Hours Until Dawn: The True Story of Heroism and Tragedy Aboard the Can Do.* New York: St. Martins, 2005.

1978 ◆ LOVE CANAL CRISIS

In the summer of 1978, residents in Niagara Falls, New York, found themselves in the middle of an environmental health crisis. Officials revealed that toxic chemicals buried in the long-abandoned Love Canal posed an imminent threat to those living nearby. The outcry by local residents drew national attention and forced the state and federal government to launch a massive and unprecedented cleanup and relocation process. The crisis—known simply as Love Canal—was a watershed event in the nation's approach to dealing with hazardous waste. Love Canal became a model for grassroots organizing, and it ushered in a new era of governmental and corporate responsibility in the control and disposal of toxic chemicals and other materials.

While the Love Canal crisis erupted in the late 1970s, its development had spanned nearly a century. Love Canal was built by William Love in the 1890s as part of a hydroelectric project. Although never completed, the project left behind a trench 10 feet deep, 80 feet wide, and 3,200 feet long. As the canal filled with water, it became a recreation space until the City of Niagara Falls began to use it as a municipal dump. In 1942, the Hooker Chemicals and Plastics Corporation (now Occidental Chemical Corporation) acquired the canal and the land surrounding it in order to dispose of chemical wastes. Between 1947 and 1952, Hooker dumped more than 22,000 tons of chemical wastes, some sealed in drums, into the canal. In 1953, under pressure from the city which needed space to build a school, Hooker covered the landfill with soil and sold the site and adjacent land to the Niagara Falls Board of Education, though the final sale agreement stipulated that Hooker would not be liable for injury or damage resulting from the chemical wastes buried on the site. Despite protests by Hooker representatives and the board's own engineers, the board erected an elementary school on the site. During the next two decades, the board sold the land adjacent to the buried landfill, which was developed with residential housing, though few residents knew anything about the site's history.

As early as the 1960s, some residents began to complain about noxious fumes and black, oily resi-

FACTBOX

PLACE Niagara Falls, New York

DATE Summer 1978

TYPE Leaking toxic-waste dump

DESCRIPTION Long-buried toxic-waste-contaminated land on which a residential neighborhood and school were later constructed.

CAUSE Improper disposal of hazardous waste and construction of a residential neighborhood atop an uncontrolled toxic-waste site

CASUALTIES Sporadic injuries from direct contact with chemicals and suspected higher than normal rate of miscarriages, birth defects, and other health effects to residents

COST More than $50 million by New York State and the federal government for relocation of families and site remediation; $129 million out-of-court settlement with Occidental Chemical Corporation for cleanup costs

IMPACT Love Canal altered the nation's environmental politics and came to symbolize public fear of ubiquitous environmental toxics. The Love Canal crisis was instrumental in passage of the 1980 Superfund law, the nation's most ambitious and expensive environmental legislation to date.

due seeping into basements. Heavy precipitation in the spring of 1975 literally brought the issue to the surface as the buried canal began to overflow. Properties abutting the canal showed signs of the chemical presence as grass and shrubbery died off, backyards began to sink, and rusting drums became exposed on the canal site. There were also reports of chemical burns to children and pets that had come into contact with chemical residues in and around the site, which included a playground. Following a series of articles by local journalists exposing the history of the Love Canal site, city and state officials launched

Environmental Protection Agency

The Environmental Protection Agency (EPA) is a U.S. governmental agency whose mission is to protect human health and the environment. The agency's primary responsibility is to safeguard the nation's land, water, and air resources. President Richard Nixon established the EPA by executive order on December 2, 1970. Prior to this date, no single government agency had the responsibility for overseeing the various federal antipollution programs. Part of a general governmental reorganization plan that the president submitted to Congress in July 1970, Nixon's proposal for the EPA merged 15 different governmental organizations into a single regulatory body.

The EPA's task was to address the public's growing concerns about the condition of the country's natural resources and the deteriorating quality of the water, air, and land. American rivers and lakes were polluted, factory and car exhaust fumes contaminated the air, and hazardous waste was being buried in the ground. Misgivings about the quality of life in industrial and postindustrial America were growing, and pollution was central to these concerns. The SANTA BARBARA OIL SPILL in 1969 put environmental issues squarely on the nation's political agenda. Later that year, the Cuyahoga River in Cleveland, Ohio, which was coated with oil and debris, burst into flames. Public interest in protecting the environment is captured in the 20

million people who took part in the first Earth Day rally and events on April 22, 1970.

William D. Ruckelshaus, the first head of the EPA, faced huge challenges in shaping the new agency. Ruckelshaus is credited with providing the agency with a sense of mission and with defining the organization's structure. He played a major role in establishing innumerable EPA rules and regulations and also helped to write the Clean Air Act of 1970 and the Clean Water Act of 1972. During his tenure, the EPA banned the use of the pesticide DDT, which was found to be toxic to birds and animals. Ruckelshaus left the EPA in 1973 but returned in 1983 when the agency had lost much of its support from the public and lawmakers.

During the 1980s, the EPA was instrumental in the passage of the Superfund Law. The LOVE CANAL CRISIS in Niagara Falls, New York, where toxic wastes that had contaminated a school and an adjacent neighborhood were discovered in 1978, prompted policy makers to propose a solution for toxic waste dumps. The Superfund Law enacted in 1980 ordered government to clean up polluted sites, funded by taxes on chemical and petroleum industries. During the 1990s, the EPA focused on partnering with companies, such as in the Energy Star program, to improve energy efficiency for electrical appliances and with automobile manufacturers, to upgrade emission stan-

dards. The EPA also undertakes research, promotes environmental education, and publishes information about the environment. Headquartered in Washington, D.C., the EPA includes 10 regional offices and a dozen research laboratories. The agency employs 18,000 people, more than half of whom are engineers, scientists, and policy analysts.

The EPA has been in the middle of numerous political disputes over environmental policy. The agency's handling of the potential health risks of the Ground Zero site in New York City after the 9/11 TERRORIST ATTACKS in 2001 generated considerable controversy. EPA director Christine Todd Whitman asserted that the levels of asbestos, lead, and other particles at the New York City site were safe for human exposure. The claim was refuted by scientists, including personnel within the EPA, and by the thousands of rescue workers who later suffered respiratory illnesses. The EPA has also been criticized for compromising environmental standards in the face of pressure from big business. Beginning in March 2005, state governments filed suits against the EPA for not regulating mercury and carbon-dioxide emissions from factories. Because regulation of the environment tends to trigger conflict among various groups in society, from environmental activists and citizens' groups to manufacturers and mining firms, the EPA often is cast into the middle of heated political debates.

Curtis C. E. Fazen

an investigation, which revealed widespread groundwater contamination.

On August 2, 1978, the New York health commissioner declared a public health emergency. Studies revealed excessive levels of cancer-causing compounds and high rates of miscarriage and birth defects in homes nearest the canal. Over the next two years, President Jimmy Carter made two separate emergency declarations for Love Canal, which established an emergency-declaration area encompassing the 350-acre neighborhood surrounding the Love Canal landfill. The state of New York embarked on a massive cleanup and containment of the Love Canal site, condemning and demolishing the school and adjacent houses and eventually buying out and relocating 950 families from a 10-block area surrounding the site. The cost to the state and the federal government exceeded $50 million. The extensive governmental response was in large part driven by sustained media attention and the unflagging efforts and organization of the Love Canal Homeowners Association (LCHA) and its president, Lois Gibbs. Occidental made an out-of-court settlement of $129 million for cleanup costs.

The Love Canal crisis changed the legal landscape of hazardous-waste management, heightened the public's concern about toxic chemicals in the environment, and exposed the legal and scientific uncertainty surrounding the handling of industrial hazards. In the wake of Love Canal, Congress passed the Comprehensive Environmental Response, Compensation, and Liability Act, commonly known as "Superfund," in December 1980. This was by far the most expensive environmental legislation ever. The law established a $1.6 billion trust fund for cleaning up abandoned or uncontrolled hazardous-waste sites, created a tax on the chemical and petroleum industries, and provided for strict liability for persons responsible for releases of hazardous waste to these sites. Lois Gibbs went on to found the Citizens Clearinghouse for Hazardous Waste (now the Center for Health, Environment and Justice), an organization dedicated to helping communities in similar situations. In 2004, the Environmental Protection Agency declared cleanup activities at Love Canal complete. A 40-acre site, including the canal itself and immediately adjacent properties, remain off-limits in perpetuity. However, approximately 260 houses in the surrounding area were resold to new residents, and a new community—now going by the name Black Creek Village—has sprung up in the once-abandoned neighborhood. Nevertheless, the name *Love Canal* remains an infamous reminder of the complexities of toxic-waste generation and disposal.

Marcos Luna

FURTHER READING:

Layzer, Judith A. "Love Canal: Hazardous Waste and the Politics of Fear." In *The Environmental Case: Translating Values into Policy.* Washington, D.C.: CQ Press, 2006.

Levine, Adeline Gordon. *Love Canal: Science, Politics, and People.* Lexington, Mass.: Lexington Books, 1983.

1979 ◆ ACCIDENT AT THREE MILE ISLAND

The March 28, 1979, melt-down of reactor number 2 at the Metropolitan Edison (ME) nuclear-power facility on Three Mile Island (TMI) on the Susquehanna River near Goldsboro, Pennsylvania, is the worst disaster of its type in American history. No lives were lost due to the immediate event, although 144,000 people evacuated from within a 15-mile radius of the plant. The TMI disaster stopped the expansion of the nuclear power industry in the United States.

Throughout the 1970s, nuclear power had received increasing attention as an inexpensive renewable energy source. The administrations of Presidents Richard Nixon, Gerald Ford, and Jimmy Carter promoted greater reliance on nuclear energy. Prior to the TMI disaster, polls consistently showed that 60 percent of Americans supported greater usage of nuclear power. However, the antinuclear movement also grew throughout the decade

FACTBOX

PLACE Three Mile Island in the Susquehanna River of Pennsylvania, 11 miles southeast of Harrisburg

DATE March 28–April 3, 1979

TYPE Nuclear disaster

DESCRIPTION Human error, lack of training, and mechanical failure led one of the nuclear reactors to overheat when 32,000 gallons of contaminated water coolant was discharged into an auxiliary building. Radioactive gases were released into the atmosphere.

COST Approximately $1 billion to clean up the disaster. In addition, an uncalculated amount probably totaling several billions of dollars was lost due to the evacuation of 144,000 people during the crisis. The Nuclear Regulatory Commission fined the owners of TMI $155,000.

IMPACT Expansion of nuclear power industry effectively halted although plants already under construction continued.

of the 1970s. The antinuclear forces were an eclectic group of environmentalists, local activists, and scientists. As a whole, they were concerned with radiation, toxic-waste disposal, poor training of engineers, lack of federal oversight of the plants, and uncorrected but recognized design flaws. The movie *China Syndrome*, released on March 16, 1979—coincidentally, just 12 days before the TMI disaster—depicted a worst-case scenario in a sensationalized account that fueled fears concerning the dangers of nuclear power.

At 4 in the morning on Wednesday, March 28, 1979, alarms in the control room at the TMI facility indicated a problem. However, there was nothing in the more than 700 lights and alarms on the control panel that guided the engineers to a specific problem or how to fix it. The engineers struggled unsuccessfully for the next two hours to determine the nature of the alarms. In addition to the confusing control panel, they had limited training for such emergencies.

The disaster was triggered by a combination of mechanical failure and human errors. At the con-

clusion of routine maintenance, two valves that had been shut off were not reopened. A backup valve also failed to operate as designed, and the pumps that sent water to cool the reactor were erroneously shut down. In the meantime, 32,000 gallons of contaminated water had flooded an auxiliary building, which was not designed to contain nuclear waste. Without the water, the reactor overheated. At 6:56 A.M., a state of emergency was declared at the TMI facility, and the Pennsylvania Emergency Management Agency (PEMA) was notified.

As events during the next several days showed, it was difficult to manage the crisis adequately without a full understanding of what was happening inside the reactor. ME gave misleading information to the media and to PEMA. Within a few hours of the crisis, PEMA no longer trusted ME. The Nuclear Regulatory Commission (NRC) was equally confused. The regional office based in Baltimore gave contradictory assessments from the headquarters in Washington, D.C. In either case, the NRC was not designed to manage a nuclear crisis but only to license power plants. In Harrisburg, Pennsylvania, just 11 miles from TMI, Governor Richard Thornburgh had to base crucial public-safety decisions on poor quality information. Governor Thornburgh felt an unnecessary evacuation could cause more casualties than none at all, but without a full understanding of the situation, this became a difficult decision.

Throughout Wednesday and Thursday, March 28 and 29, officials grappled with the confused situation. No appreciable amount of radiation was detected in areas surrounding TMI, but evacuation plans were prepared for a 15-mile radius. The reactor remained overheated despite the efforts of the engineers to cool it.

On Friday, March 30, the situation worsened. Engineers, with approval of the NRC, released radioactive gas to relieve pressure in the reactor. Still, conditions had not significantly improved, and when a civil defense alarm inexplicably went off in Harrisburg that morning, the public became jittery. In response to the conflicting signals from ME and the NRC, Thornburgh advised pregnant women and children to leave the immediate area, and all schools in a five-mile radius were closed. In all, 144,000 people in a 15-mile radius from TMI

Located on the Susquehanna River in Pennsylvania, the Metropolitan Edison nuclear-power facility on Three Mile Island became the site of the nation's worst nuclear disaster when the plant released radioactive gases into the atmosphere. *(National Archives)*

evacuated. The closest town to TMI, Goldsboro, was almost deserted.

On Saturday, the reactor finally began to cool, but a new crisis developed as a 3,000–cubic-foot hydrogen bubble developed inside the reactor chamber. While the engineers were puzzled as to the cause or solution to this problem, an Associated Press story reporting that the bubble could explode like a hydrogen bomb caused panic in the Harrisburg area. A visit on Sunday by President Carter to TMI stabilized the public mood. Meanwhile, the hydrogen bubble started to dissipate, and by Tuesday, April 3, it was completely gone. Although it would not be until April 27 that the reactor had stabilized enough to be safely shut down, the immediate crisis was over.

Critics of nuclear power seized on the crisis at TMI to illustrate their concerns. "This is the beginning of the end of nuclear power in this country," consumer activist Ralph Nader declared. Nader alleged that ME willfully endangered the public safety when it rushed reactor 2 online in December 1978 in order to get tens of millions of dollars in tax write-offs before the end of the year. Antinuclear ral-

lies were held throughout the nation on the weekend of April 7. The Union of Concerned Scientists called for a thorough revamping of the engineer training program and a moratorium on the licensing of any new nuclear power plants.

The NRC, President Carter, and Congress all conducted inquiries. These reports failed to meet the demands of the antinuclear advocates but did result in better training for engineers. The NRC fined ME a total of $155,000.

Cleaning up TMI took almost a decade and cost $1 billion. The 32,000 gallons of contaminated water was allowed to slowly evaporate into the atmosphere. In 1987, scientists were surprised to learn that 70 percent of the core had been damaged and 45 percent melted. Studies conducted since the disaster have not found any increased health risks to the population living in the areas surrounding TMI.

The nuclear-power industry was heavily damaged by the disaster at Three Mile Island, and further expansion was effectively halted. Although orders for nuclear-power plants stopped as a result of TMI, construction for those already ordered did not. There were about 70 nuclear plants operating in the United States in 1978, and the number peaked at 111 in 1991. The amount of power generated by nuclear plants increased from about 300 billion kilowatt-hours in 1978 to 800 billion kilowatt-hours in 2004. As the nation considers alternative fuel policies in the early 21st century, expansion of nuclear power remains a controversial issue.

Gregory J. Dehler

FURTHER READING:

Ford, Daniel F. *Three Mile Island: Thirty Minutes to Meltdown.* New York: Penguin, 1981.

Houts, Peter S., Paul Cleary, and The-Wei Hu. *The Three Mile Island Crisis: Psychological, Social, and Economic Impacts on the Surrounding Population.* University Park, Pa.: Pennsylvania State University Press, 1988.

Stephens, Mark. *Three Mile Island: The Hour by Hour Account of What Really Happened.* New York: Random House, 1980.

Walker, J. Samuel. *Three Mile Island: A Nuclear Crisis in Historical Perspective.* Berkeley: University of California Press, 2004.

1979 ◆ CRASH OF AMERICAN AIRLINES FLIGHT 191

The worst single-airplane disaster in American history on U.S. soil and one of the most horrifying in the annals of aviation took place in Chicago on May 25, 1979. American Airlines Flight 191 took off from O'Hare International Airport en route to Los Angeles just after 3 P.M. Moments later, the left engine on the McDonnell Douglas DC-10 fell off and plummeted to the ground. With the aircraft's hydraulic system fatally compromised, the plane stalled, banked into an uncontrollable 112-degree dive, and plunged wing-first 400 feet into a nearby field, instantly killing 258 passengers, 13 crew members, and two persons on the ground in the fiery explosion.

It was a perfect day preceding the long Memorial Day weekend, with a clear blue sky and warm spring weather. As usual, O'Hare was packed with passengers as Flight 191 prepared for take-off from Runway 32-R. As the plane rose into the sky, tower controllers halfway through the two concrete miles of runway observed the appalling sight of the main engine on the left wing falling away from the DC-10, flying up and over the wing, and plunging to the ground. The engine separation disabled the aircraft's hydraulic system, making it impossible to control both the retractable slats necessary for take-off and landing and the captain's electrical controls, which were not duplicated in the copilot's instrumentation. Since the engines were not visible from the cockpit windows of the plane, the pilots knew only that something was wrong but not what. It would not have mattered. After 31 seconds in the air at about 400 feet, the DC-10 banked to the left in a dizzying dive, memorably captured by an amateur photographer in one of the most dramatic photographs ever taken. Flight 191 crashed into a field 4,600 feet beyond the runway near the Touhy Mobile Home Park in Des Plaines, Illinois. The explosion and fire killed everyone on board, as well as two persons on the ground. The cockpit voice recorder contained one exclamation: "Damn!"

One observer tending his garden reported hearing a loud explosion and then feeling fire raining down on him. A fire department officer on the scene said that in an odd way, it was somehow less appalling

FACTBOX

PLACE Chicago, Illinois

DATE May 25, 1979

TYPE Airplane crash

DESCRIPTION In the deadliest airplane crash involving a single airplane on U.S. soil, American Airlines Flight 191 crashed left wing first into a field near O'Hare Airport.

CAUSE Separation of engine no. 1 on left wing on take-off

CASUALTIES All 258 passengers and 13 crew members killed, as well as two people on the ground

IMPACT Congress enacted legislation allowing family members to visit airplane-crash sites, assigning employees to assist survivors with counseling, informing them of progress in the investigation, and arranging and paying for funerals.

that there was virtually nothing recognizably human in the devastation. At the time, it was possible for passengers to watch on closed-circuit television their flight's take-off and landing. A lingering nightmare is the idea that the passengers spent a few horrific moments watching the crash about to happen.

The National Transportation Safety Board (NTSB) sprang into action and released its report seven months later on December 21, 1979. Early on, investigators eliminated possible causes such as terrorism, bad weather, other aircraft, and pilot error. Since there had been three other fatal crashes of DC-10's, they focused on the aircraft itself, finding in short order a broken bolt from the mount connecting the wing to the engine that fell off. Then two mechanics discovered metal dust on the engine mount of a United Airlines DC-10 and cracks behind access panels with broken rivets and other defects. The Federal Aviation Administration (FAA) ordered all 138 American DC-10s to be grounded, causing chaos in the air travel industry.

A riveting 2004 documentary on *The History Channel* titled "The Crash of Flight 191" details the shrewd detective work of NTSB metallurgist Michael Marx, who discovered the real problem to be a maintenance procedure that had been performed in Tulsa, Oklahoma, on the doomed aircraft. Instead of separately removing and reinstalling the engine and its mount, mechanics had performed the procedure in a single step to save time and money. A forklift used to hold the engine up was left untended for a while, and a hydraulic problem caused the tilting of the engine, creating enough pressure on the mount to develop a fracture. This problem worsened over two months of flights, until the mount virtually disintegrated upon take-off of Flight 191. The head mechanic responsible for the maintenance procedure committed suicide hours before his NTSB testimony.

Surviving family members, interviewed in 2004 for the 25th-anniversary commemoration in the *Chicago Tribune,* detailed their callous treatment by American Airlines in the disaster's aftermath. One survivor even noted that the airline was so insensitive, possibly to lessen the number of lawsuits, that even more survivors actually did sue. But the airline learned some valuable lessons and survived the calamity, slowly instituting procedures that are now mandated by federal law, such as allowing family members to visit the crash site, assigning employees to assist survivors with counseling, informing them of progress in the investigation, and arranging and paying for funerals. Perhaps the magnitude of this horror helped to mitigate family members' pain after future airplane crashes.

There are numerous legends about Flight 191, including TV *Bionic Woman* actress Lindsay Wagner having a premonition before boarding and deciding not to fly. Author Arthur C. Clarke reported on the TV series *World of Strange Powers* the story of Ohio resident David Booth, who had recurring nightmares about a plane in a steep bank prior to a fatal crash. On May 22, 1979, three days before the flight, he telephoned the FAA, American Airlines, and a psychiatrist in Cincinnati. Whether he was presumed crazy or taken seriously, nothing was done before May 25.

As one survivor quoted in the *Tribune* on May 26, 2004, observed, "The pain never leaves, ever. Maybe I'm up to about 10 minutes now, but there is no more than a 10-minute span that goes by that I don't somehow think of my mother and father."

Kyle Renick

FURTHER READING:

"The Crash of Flight 191." *Chicago Tribune,* May 25, 2004, 18.

Davis, Jon. "Flight 191 Crash Visit Relatives of Victims Gather in Field to Remember, Grieve, Heal." Chicago *Daily Herald,* May 26, 2004, 3.

Meyer, H. Gregory. "Pain of Tragedy Lives on Long After; Reunion Ceremony Pays Tribute to the Hundreds Who Died in Worst Aviation Accident." *Chicago Tribune,* May 26, 2004, 1.

St. Clair, Stacy. "At Long Last Families Get Their Time at Scene." Chicago *Daily Herald,* May 23, 2004, 1.

1979 ◆ IRAN HOSTAGE CRISIS

The streets of Teheran (Tehran) were alive with thousands of protesting students on Sunday morning, November 4, 1979. As the massed procession filed past the American embassy in the Iranian capital, two women raised a banner reading "Allah-o-Akbar." This was a signal for a group of students to approach the embassy and instruct the Iranian police guarding the gate to step aside. After the guards complied, several women removed bolt-cutters concealed beneath their long garments: The chains around the embassy gates were quickly severed. One hundred and fifty members of a radical group called the Muslim Students Following the Line of the Imam swarmed into the embassy compound and began to take Americans captive. By the end of the day, the invaders had seized 66 hostages. Fifty-two remained in captivity for 444 days. The Iran Hostage Crisis riveted the attention of Americans, who wondered

FACTBOX

PLACE Teheran (Tehran), Iran, and the United States

DATE November 4, 1979–January 20, 1981

TYPE Hostage and diplomatic crisis

DESCRIPTION Iranian college students took 66 Americans in the United States embassy hostage and held 52 of them for 444 days.

CAUSE Iranian anger at American support of the shah

CASUALTIES 8 servicemen killed in aborted rescue mission

IMPACT The crisis contributed to President Jimmy Carter's defeat in the election of 1980 and symbolized the onset of America's confrontation with radical Islamic politics.

how a bunch of religious radicals could hold the most powerful nation on earth at bay. The fallout over this question helped to defeat President Jimmy Carter in his bid for reelection in 1980.

The roots of the crisis lay in the history of U.S.-Iran relations since 1953, when the United States aided a coup against the elected government of Mohammad Mossadegh and helped to install Mohammad Reza Pahlavi, the shah, as the ruler of the oil-rich country. American policy makers saw the shah as a key link in the nation's cold war struggle with the Soviet Union. American military aid helped keep the shah in power, along with his dreaded secret police, the SAVAK. Reza Pahlavi's vision of building a secular Iran and his pro-American leaning antagonized religious traditionalists, including Ayatollah Khomeini, a prominent Islamic leader, who galvanized opposition to the shah's regime. Khomeini was arrested and exiled in 1965 but labored incessantly against the shah and the "Great Satan," as he called the United States.

By 1979, anti-shah resistance in Iran had reached the boiling point, forcing the shah to flee to Morocco and opening the way for the return of Khomeini, who became a central authority within a country wracked with revolution and political chaos. President Carter's approval of the admission of the shah to the United States for treatment of cancer prompted the ayatollah and his loyalists to proclaim that Amer-

icans were continuing to conspire against Iran and Islam. On November 4, the Muslim Students Following the Line of the Imam, acting on their own, stormed the American embassy. The group of both men and women blindfolded their victims, tied their hands, and led them outside into the embassy courtyard. "I thought we were going to go in front of a firing squad," one hostage recalled. But no one was killed. Khomeini gave his blessing to the enterprise and instructed the student leaders to demand that the United States return the shah to Iran to stand trial as the condition for the release of the hostages.

Refusing to extradite Reza, President Carter desperately sought a diplomatic solution to the impasse. The media in the United States made the crisis daily headlines, reinforcing Carter critics who charged his administration with ineptitude and weakness. Khomeini fanned these flames by releasing 13 black and female hostages in late November; in July 1980, a hostage suffering from multiple sclerosis was freed, leaving 52 remaining hostages. U.S. citizens around the country demonstrated support for the captives and their families. Penne Laingen, the wife of Bruce Laingen, chargé d'affaires (chief officer) at the U.S. embassy in Iran, tied a yellow ribbon to an oak tree in her yard. She vowed to leave it there until her husband returned to the United States to remove it. Bruce Laingen had been visiting the Iranian Foreign Ministry at the time of the hostage taking but was not taken captive. He remained at the Foreign Ministry until he slipped out of the country. Americans took Penne Laingen's cue and placed yellow ribbons on trees, on their bumpers, and in their lapels.

Rebuffed diplomatically, Carter authorized a military rescue mission in spring 1980. The plan was to insert a special forces team of 118 men in Teheran, who would link up with operatives in the city and free the hostages at the American embassy. The mission was a disaster. A dust storm caused mechanical failure to three of the eight helicopters launched from the aircraft carrier *Nimitz* in the Gulf of Oman, leading the commander to abort the mission. Further tragedy occurred when one of the remaining helicopters collided with a refueling plane in the desert rendezvous location and burned, killing eight servicemen. Khomeini exploited the fiasco, proclaiming that "those sand particles were divinely commissioned." The rescue mission prompted the Iranians to disperse their captives around the country.

Fortuitous events moved the crisis toward resolution. The shah, who was unceremoniously hustled out of the United States when his medical condition stabilized, died in Egypt on July 27. The Iraq-Iran war broke out on September 22. With the shah now removed from consideration, Khomeini shifted his demands to delivery of weapons for which the shah had contracted and the release of Iranian assets that the United States had impounded. More concerned with repelling the Iraqi forces of Saddam Hussein than with milking further propaganda from his American prisoners, Khomeini consented to release of the hostages, who were freed January 20, 1981, the day that President Ronald Reagan took office.

Historian Erwin Hargrove observed that President Carter became "totally absorbed" by the Iran hostage crisis, which added a huge weight to a presidency already burdened with bad news and political obstacles. His inability to resolve the crisis contributed to his loss to Ronald Reagan in the presidential election of 1980. Carter's public opinion rating had spiked upward in the immediate aftermath of the embassy takeover, but his approval rating sank thereafter. The failure of his administration to return the hostages swiftly reinforced public sentiment that the national government lacked resolve and effectiveness. Carter as much as the 52 Americans in Iran had become a prisoner of Ayatollah Khomeini. This reality signaled to Americans that the United States now confronted a new international challenge. Before 1979, few Americans knew much about the Middle East. After the hostage crisis, conflict with Islamic nationalism and Muslim terrorists emerged as a central element of American foreign policy.

Ballard C. Campbell

FURTHER READING:

Farber, David. *Taken Hostage: The Iran Hostage Crisis and America's First Encounter with Radical Islam.* Princeton, N.J.: Princeton University Press, 2005.

Hargrove, Erwin C. *Jimmy Carter as President.* Baton Rouge: Louisiana State University Press, 1988.

1980 ◆ MARIEL BOATLIFT EXODUS

Between April and September 1980, Cuban dictator Fidel Castro unleashed uncontrolled emigration from Cuba to the United States, leading to the Mariel boatlift crisis. In small overcrowded boats, some 125,000 Cubans made a perilous journey across the Florida Straits. This massive exodus caught President Jimmy Carter, then running for reelection, unprepared and created both a humanitarian and political crisis.

In 1979–80, Cuba was suffering severe economic problems. At the same time, many Cuban Americans were visiting Cuba due to improvement in U.S.-Cuban relations during the Carter administration. As Cubans learned from these visits of the affluence and personal freedom of the Cuban-American community, disillusion grew with the Castro regime, which had been in power since 1959. This discontent manifested itself in desperate attempts to leave Cuba. An incident on April 1, 1980, particularly enraged Castro. Asylum-seeking Cubans crashed a bus through the gates of the Peruvian Embassy in Havana, the nation's capital, killing one of the Cuban guards. When Peru granted the Cubans asylum, Castro retaliated. Cuban radio announced that any "scum" who wanted to leave Cuba could go to the embassy. Within 48 hours, 10,800 desperate people invaded the Peruvian legation. This huge response generated negative publicity, embarrassing Castro. To regain control of the situation, he decided to manipulate it to his advantage by getting rid of the discontented elements in Cuban society. On April 20, he announced that the port of Mariel near Havana would be opened for anyone who wanted to leave. He then invited Cuban Americans to come there to collect their relatives who wished to leave.

Cuban Americans quickly responded, hiring a "freedom flotilla" of small and midsized crafts to sail to Mariel. By the end of May, more than 90,000

FACTBOX

PLACE From Mariel, Cuba, to the United States through south Florida

DATE April–September 1980

TYPE Challenges created by the sudden and rapid exodus of 125,000 destitute and undocumented Cubans across the Straits of Florida in a flotilla of small boats

DESCRIPTION Fidel Castro opened the port of Mariel, Cuba, as a point of debarkation for discontented Cubans, forcibly adding criminals and others to the departing masses. The ferrying operation by small boats created a safety crisis, while the sudden arrival of 125,000 destitute and undocumented Cubans seeking political asylum strained governmental and charitable resources.

CAUSE Castro's desire to rid Cuba of malcontents and those he deemed politically and socially undesirable while also dealing with unemployment; lack of a clear, prompt, and effective response from the U.S. government

CASUALTIES 26 confirmed deaths, but many more were feared lost in the Florida Straits. The Cuban government refused to release the number of people embarking from the port of Mariel.

COST As much as $1 billion to federal, state, and local governments as well as humanitarian groups. The *Miami Herald* estimated the cost to state and county governments in Florida alone at $100 million.

IMPACT Change in America's "open door" policy to Cuban immigrants, significant change in the demography of both the Cuban-American community and the population of south Florida, political fallout for the Carter administration and other Democrats

Cubans had arrived in Florida. Many of the boats were overcrowded, had insufficient life-saving equipment, and were only marginally seaworthy. Storms in the Florida Straits further endangered the boats and their passengers. The United States Coast Guard, assisted by the navy, was ordered to provide escort and rescue services for flotilla boats. Hundreds of lives were saved and only 26 deaths officially recorded, but many more were feared lost on the treacherous journey. The true number cannot be known because Cuban authorities would not disclose the exact number of *marielitos,* as the emigrants who embarked from Mariel were called.

The Mariel boatlift caught the Carter administration off guard. Its early response was neither consistent nor effective. Initially, Carter welcomed the *marielitos.* Soon, however, he declared an emergency and had the federal government take over organizing the relief effort from local groups in Florida. By mid-May, in response to both humanitarian concerns and political pressures to control the immigration, Carter prohibited any more boats from going to Cuba. He ordered the Coast Guard to impound vessels and prosecute boat owners who violated the order. Despite these efforts, tens of thousands more Cubans arrived before Castro closed down the port of Mariel on September 25.

Unlike other post-1959 undocumented Cuban emigrants, who could easily receive legal residency in the United States, the *marielitos* were not welcomed as political refugees. Someone had to provide not only for their registration and processing as applicants for political asylum but also for housing and feeding them. Because they were forced to surrender their papers and possessions as the price of leaving Cuba, most lacked even basic identification. The "boatlift Cubans," typically young, male, blue-collar workers who came without families, were more difficult to resettle in American society than their predecessors, mostly white, middle- and upper-class Cuban families. Additionally, to validate his claim that Cuban dissidents were "scum" and to embarrass the U.S. government and Cuban-American community, Castro used the boatlift to empty prisons and mental hospitals of persons he did not want in his country. The Cuban and American media highlighted this element, which caused the American public—even Cuban Americans—to feel threatened by the *marielitos.* The cost of the escort and rescue operation combined with the resettlement program for *marielitos* approached $1 billion; state and county governments in Florida alone spent an estimated $100 million.

South Florida, which like the rest of the United States was in an economic recession, could not immediately absorb 125,000 people. About half were flown to processing camps at military installations as far away as Arkansas and Wisconsin. Those awaiting placement grew frustrated as the resettlement process bogged down in the hot summer of 1980. This led to violence in the camps and more bad publicity. In the short run, some Americans blamed the Mariel influx for housing shortages, rising unemployment, and a crime wave in south Florida. However, only about 2 percent of *marielitos* were ultimately classified as "excludables" and subject to deportation to Cuba. Most boatlift Cubans settled in and became productive members of American society.

The Mariel boatlift signaled the beginning of a change in U.S. policy toward Cuban immigrants: After 1980, political asylum and permanent residency were no longer extended automatically to people who left Cuba. More than two-thirds of the expatriates settled in south Florida, making Cubans a near majority in Miami, a demographic shift that would have long-term political, social, and cultural effects. The Mariel influx also created political fallout for the Democratic Party. Members of labor and minority groups already resented competition from immigrants for jobs and social services during a recession. These groups wanted the government to curb all immigration and decried the Carter administration's ineffectiveness in stopping the boatlift. Those favoring immigration criticized the government for not helping more, and the backlash from the Mariel boatlift contributed to the defeat of President Jimmy Carter and Arkansas governor Bill Clinton in 1980.

Victoria H. Cummins

FURTHER READING:

Cros Sandoval, Mercedes. *Mariel and Cuban National Identity.* Miami, Fla.: Editorial SIBI, 1986.

Fernández, Gastón. *The Mariel Exodus Twenty Years Later: A Study in the Politics of Stigma and a Research Bibliography.* Miami, Fla.: Ediciones Universal, 2002.

Masud-Piloto, Felix. *From Welcomed Exiles to Illegal Immigrants: Cuban Migration to the U.S., 1959–1995.* London: Rowman and Littlefield, 1996.

1980 ◆ ERUPTION OF MOUNT ST. HELENS

On May 18, 1980, the symmetrical cone of Mount St. Helens in Washington State erupted in the largest known debris avalanche in recorded history. The eruption killed 57 people and at least 7,000 deer and elk (and countless smaller animals), devastated more than 230 square miles of lush forest, and filled lakes and rivers with mudslides and logjams. The profile of the mountain itself was obliterated, reduced in the blast from a pre-eruption summit of 9,677 feet to a hollowed-out 8,363 feet dominated by a huge crater and the collapsed north face of the mountain. Two-thirds of a cubic mile of rock either cascaded or was blown from the mountain in a blast with an energy equivalent to 27,000 Hiroshima-sized atomic bombs detonating sequentially over a span of nine and half hours. Ash fall created havoc across Washington, Idaho and Montana as the sky turned black at midday.

An estimated 40,000 to 50,000 years old, Mount St. Helens is the youngest of the five volcanoes in western Washington State's Cascade Range. The volatile nature of the mountain was well known to native tribes, and when explorers, missionaries, and early settlers moved into the area in the 19th century, they witnessed dozens of small eruptions, the last one of note occurring in 1857. Although geologists were aware of the potential for a large eruption, the general public primarily knew Mount St. Helens as a scenic recreation area—the region's lakes, streams, and forests found favor with outdoor enthusiasts.

In March 1980, Mount St. Helens stirred after 123 years of relative quiet. Throughout March and April, the mountain sporadically spewed ash-laden steam while minor earthquakes rumbled within. The burst of activity attracted scientists from the United States Geological Survey (USGS) and various universities, as well as reporters and sightseers. Scientists installed extensive new monitoring equipment to track the activity, and residents, tourists, and outdoors enthusiasts were warned to avoid the most dangerous areas. The activity was nearly constant: The snowy summit turned black with ash, lightning caused by static electricity rocketed down the slopes, and an eerie blue flame was seen burning in

FACTBOX

PLACE Mount St. Helens, in the Cascade Range of southwestern Washington State

DATE May 18, 1980

TYPE Volcanic eruption

DESCRIPTION During the eruption of Mount St. Helens, more than 1,000 feet of the mountain's summit was obliterated. More than 230 square miles of forest was destroyed, mudslides and logjams choked rivers, and an ash plume blotted out the sun as it rose to 100,000 feet in the stratosphere. Ash falling across eastern Washington, the Idaho panhandle, and western Montana brought human activity to a standstill.

CASUALTIES 57 people were killed, along with 7,000 deer and elk and countless smaller animals.

IMPACT The eruption decimated the physical environment, reducing a lush wilderness to a moonscape within minutes. At least $1 billion in economic damage was reported.

a recently opened vent. Explosions were common (93 recorded on a single day), ash plumes were ejected to 100,000 feet above the summit, and new vents were expanding.

At the end of April 1980, the mountain appeared to grow silent. Eruptions ceased, but a swelling on the north flank, referred to as "the bulge," was monitored to be growing laterally at a rate of five to six feet per day. By the middle of May, this bulge had grown by 450 feet. Geologists saw the bulging north flank as the most immediate danger, as its collapse could set in motion an eruption. By May 11, the volcano resumed activity. Explosions resumed, as did the release of ash. Rising magma continued to push against the bulge.

At 8:32 Sunday morning, May 18, the forces building up inside the mountain found sudden and catastrophic release. A magnitude 5.1 earthquake either caused the debris avalanche, or the avalanche caused the earthquake—it is impossible to know which event preceded the other. A second earthquake occurred minutes after the first. The north side of the summit of St. Helens broke into three separate blocks of material, avalanching downslope at

an estimated velocity of 155 to 180 miles an hour. As the first landslide block moved north, it unleashed an eruption that was to continue uninterrupted for nine and a half hours. The hot blast of steam, ash, and dust came down the mountain at temperatures above 600°F.

Despite warnings to avoid the danger area, dozens of people were within the blast zone when the eruption occurred. The most famous of the local residents who refused to evacuate was Harry Truman (no relation to the former president), the 84-year-old owner of a lodge on nearby Spirit Lake. Like many others who had lived in the shadows of this seemingly harmless mountain, Truman refused to take the volcanic threat seriously. After the blast, Truman's home was buried beneath hot mud, water, and broken forest debris. David A. Johnston, a 30-year-old geologist-volcanologist with the USGS, witnessed the eruption from a ridge five miles north of the summit. As the eruption began, Johnston radioed the temporary USGS base in Vancouver, Washington to report that an eruption was underway. "Vancouver! Vancouver! This is it!" Johnston was never heard from again. Likely killed in the lateral blast, no trace of Johnston or his observation post (including a four-wheel-drive vehicle and a camp trailer) has ever been found.

More lives would undoubtedly have been lost if the eruption had not occurred on a Sunday—it was a day off for Weyerhaeuser timber crews that worked within what became the blast zone. Some victims who witnessed the debris avalanche and the subsequent eruption unsuccessfully tried to outrace the cataclysm and were found dead in or near their cars, unable to escape the cyclonic force. Although some victims perished due to burns, most who died were asphyxiated by the overwhelming ash. Lucky survivors, mostly from the margins of the blast zone, described conditions of total darkness, unbearable heat, and a suffocating lack of oxygen.

The eruption destroyed 123 buildings and everything in the Toutle Valley, including bridges, roads, and any other signs of human habitation. It was the most impressive and deadly volcanic eruption seen by modern Americans in their own country. Mudflows and debris cascading down surrounding waterways scoured the riverbeds, removing bridges and roads in their wake. The North Fork of the Toutle River was filled with a debris flow 600 feet thick for 17 miles down the valley leading away from Mount St. Helens. Sediment from the volcano reduced the

In the largest eruption of debris ever recorded, Mount St. Helens sent a plume of ash and smoke 100,000 feet into the stratosphere. *(NOAA National Geophysical Data Center)*

depth of the Columbia River from 40 feet to 10 feet within 24 hours of the eruption. As fallen trees accumulated downstream, a 20-mile-long logjam plugged the Columbia River, and the water was heated to 85°F.

As the leading edge of the volcanic plume moved across eastern Washington and the Idaho panhandle, life came to a standstill. The ash fall reduced visibility to zero and plugged the engines of motor vehicles. Airports and highways were closed as 1.7 billion to 2.4 billion cubic yards of fine ash fell on towns, farms, forestland, and the open range across Washington, Idaho, Montana, and beyond. Almost 50 percent of the territory in Washington State received visible ash fall, with the deepest amounts recorded at 2 to 3 inches.

Much of Washington's fruit crop was destroyed as the thick ash inhibited photosynthesis, but the ash was beneficial to wheat crops, acting as a mulch. The insect population was heavily injured; both bees and grasshoppers in the ash fall area were wiped out. Ports on the Columbia River were closed for 13 days, and it took three months to restore shipping traffic. Millions of dollars in port revenue was lost. Modest estimates put the total damages from the volcanic eruption somewhere near a billion dollars.

Aaron Christopher Schab

FURTHER READING:

Harris, Steven L. *Fire Mountains of the West.* Missoula, Mont.: Mountain Press Publishing Company, 2005.

Rosenfeld, Charles, and Robert Cooke. *Earthfire.* Cambridge, Mass.: MIT Press, 1982.

1980 ◆ DEADLY HEAT WAVE

In the summer of 1980 a deadly heat wave killed an estimated 10,000 people in the United States. With the nation sweltering in the grip of temperatures of more than 100°F for days on end, drought caused economic losses of approximately $20 billion. The epicenter of this deadly weather catastrophe lay in the southeastern United States. Most of the deaths in this region occurred in urban areas, particularly among the poor, the elderly, and minority communities.

A heat wave is a prolonged period of uncomfortable and abnormally hot, humid weather lasting anywhere from several days to several weeks. These periods of abnormal temperatures can be dangerous, and indeed fatal when high heat coupled with high humidity overtaxes the body. The body cools itself through sweating, which is the evaporation of water caused by blood flow to the skin. During periods of intense heat, heavy sweating can take an inordinate amount of blood from the vital organs, which can lead to heat exhaustion. Another potentially fatal result of extended exposure to high temperatures is dehydration, which causes heat cramps. There is also the potential of heat stroke, occurring when the body reaches 106°F and lacks adequate water to produce the sweat needed to cool itself. Cities are especially vulnerable to heat waves because asphalt and concrete absorb heat during the day and release it at night, creating a hot-box effect. Heat in urban areas increases air pollution, which impairs breathing.

The heat wave of 1980 was particularly devastating for urban areas in Missouri, Tennessee, and Texas. In

Memphis, Tennessee, there were 83 heat-related deaths in July 1980 compared to none the previous summer. The incidence rates of heat strokes in Missouri were 26.1 per 100,000 in St. Louis, and 17.6 per 100,000 in Kansas City, significantly higher than normal. There was a strong socioeconomic gradient in these rates, whereby lower-income individuals were six times more likely to be affected than more affluent groups.

In 1981, the Centers for Disease Control and Prevention (CDC) established a summer mortality surveillance project to review mortality rates in St. Louis and Kansas City. In the aftermath of the project, St. Louis instituted several preventive measures to lessen the effects of another heat wave, especially among poor and low-income families. These steps included air-conditioner loans and energy assistance for low-income families, a program to weatherize homes for the poor and disabled, and emergency shelters, offered through the St. Louis Homeless Network. Other cities have followed this model.

With temperatures rising every year in the United States, heat waves continue to pose a threat to health and survival. Recent estimates from the CDC indicate that, on average, 688 people die from heat-related illnesses each year due to exposure to excessive heat, or hyperthermia. The most vulnerable are the elderly, low-income families, males, and minorities. The tragic outcome of the heat wave of 1980 led to increased educational outreach programs. The media now issues more warnings about spikes in temperature, and com-

FACTBOX

PLACE Central and eastern United States

DATE Summer 1980

TYPE Heat wave and drought

DESCRIPTION A deadly heat wave and drought struck much of the country.

CAUSE High temperatures

CASUALTIES Approximately 10,000 deaths

COST $20 billion

IMPACT More coordinated efforts and outreach programs to the elderly, poor, and other vulnerable populations to reduce mortality associated with heat waves. These include air-conditioner loan programs, energy assistance, and emergency shelters.

munity programs target the elderly and the poor with information about how to keep cool during abnormally hot months. This heightened awareness of the real dangers of heat-related illnesses has reduced the mortality associated with more recent heat waves.

Diana S. Grigsby

FURTHER READING:

Noji, E. K. *The Public Health Consequences of Disasters.* New York: Oxford University Press, 2002.

1981 ◇ AIDS EPIDEMIC

The world was forever changed in 1981 when a cluster of otherwise healthy men in New York and California were diagnosed with unusual infections and cancers associated with an unknown condition that was eventually labeled the Acquired Immune Deficiency Syndrome (AIDS). From its inception, AIDS baffled the public health and medical communities, prompting a scurry of medical detective work and an ultimately unsuccessful race to ward off an epidemic. By 2005, more than 65 million people had been infected with the Human Immunodeficiency Virus (HIV), the virus that causes AIDS, and more than 25 million had died from AIDS, making it one of the world's worst ever global pandemics. The effects of HIV/AIDS have transcended biology, sparking an epidemic of fear that has revealed social, racial, economic, and gender-based divisions of societies. The biosocial impacts of HIV/AIDS continue as this medical and public-health catastrophe continues to take 8,000

FACTBOX

PLACE First diagnosed in New York and California before spreading all over the world

DATE 1981–present

TYPE Pandemic caused by infection from human immunodeficiency virus (HIV)

DESCRIPTION Widespread infection with HIV, a virus that causes severe immune dysfunction that, when unchecked, eventually results in the acquired immune deficiency syndrome (AIDS) and death

CAUSE AIDS is caused by HIV, which can be transmitted through bodily fluid during birth, breast-feeding, and sexual intercourse, the use of contaminated intravenous drug equipment, or infected blood transfusions. The ongoing AIDS/HIV epidemic is the result of poverty, faulty policy, ineffective public-information campaigns, and unequal distribution of antiretroviral drugs and other resources.

CASUALTIES More than 530,000 deaths in the United States and approximately 25 million deaths worldwide thus far

COST Untold billions in prevention, treatment, medical discovery, and societal costs

IMPACT One of the worst pandemics known to humankind and the most studied illness ever, the AIDS epidemic has ravaged communities worldwide, bred fear and discrimination against those infected, and prompted changes in sexual behavior and public-health policy.

lives a day, reshaping social and economic spheres around the globe.

The early 1980s will forever be remembered for the HIV/AIDS medical mystery and public health disaster that sent shockwaves throughout the world. For then unknown reasons, rare cancers and illnesses associated with severe immune deficiency were first observed by doctors in the United States, who watched as a small cluster of mostly young, gay, male, otherwise healthy patients began to die quickly in 1981. By the year's end, similar reports surfaced among intravenous drug users and among similar populations in the United Kingdom.

The medical and public-health communities were frantic, facing what appeared to be a new disease that was spreading rapidly—but nobody knew how it spread or how to stop it. AIDS cases steadily cropped up across the map, among men, women, injecting drug users, and hemophiliacs and their sexual partners, in rich countries and in poor countries. Providing scientists clues about what fueled the epidemic and what hope might exist for stopping it, all signs pointed to what eventually became known as fact: HIV was spreading sexually, through the blood supply, among intravenous drug users, and from mothers to children.

In hopes of averting or slowing a public health disaster, scientists worked feverishly to solve the HIV/AIDS medical mystery, but it was not until 1983 and 1984—in France and the United States, respectively—that they isolated the virus that causes AIDS. By 1985, scientists had developed a test for the AIDS virus so that blood donations could be screened for it. Scientific disputes stalled agreement on a single name for the newly identified virus until 1986, when HIV was chosen. Excitement flurried again in 1986, when scientists discovered that azidothymidine (AZT), an antiretroviral drug, was effective in slowing HIV's progress. Though not a cure for HIV, the AZT discovery was a major breakthrough that gave hope for greater progress in the HIV/AIDS struggle. More antiretroviral drugs and a combination of related drugs that slow HIV's progression to AIDS have since been developed, though no cure has been found. Potential vaccines to prevent HIV infection have also been tested, though none has yet been shown effective.

Despite many scientific breakthroughs on HIV/AIDS, the epidemic has continued to spread from its original epicenters to all corners of the world. During the 1980s, the number of known AIDS cases in the United States quickly soared from single digits to the hundreds, thousands, and tens of thousands. By the end of the decade, AIDS was documented in many more than 100 countries—encompassing every continent except Antarctica—and the World Health Organization reported more than 100,000 AIDS cases worldwide. Global estimates pegged the total number of HIV-infected individuals in the late 1980s—those confirmed by testing and those not yet discovered—well into the millions.

Fear and uncertainty have accompanied the spread of HIV, producing confusion, prejudice, disinformation—and grave consequences. With the first recognized AIDS cases among gay men, discrimination accompanied public perceptions of the disease and fueled a stereotype that HIV/AIDS was a disease of gay men, leading some newspapers to use the label "gay-related immune disease" before AIDS had been named. By 1982, the name AIDS was chosen in place of earlier titles to clearly indicate the disease was not restricted to homosexuals. Nevertheless the stereotype of AIDS being a "gay disease" held, as did accompanying prejudices about homosexuality. Similarly, when health officials incorrectly speculated that AIDS emerged from Haiti, the epidemic of fear from misinformation was further fueled. Consequently, the Haitian tourist industry and economy were hampered, and Haitians everywhere were discriminated against. In 1985, 13-year-old Ryan White made headlines when he was banned from his school after local officials learned he had contracted AIDS from a contaminated blood transfusion; other HIV-positive children suffered a similar fate in the 1980s. Such practices have consistently accompanied the spread of HIV, prompting many countries to implement laws intended to protect people with HIV/AIDS from discrimination.

The patterning of HIV transmission and access to treatment highlights social cleavages, showing inequities domestically and globally in access to public-health resources. For instance, in the United States in 2005 African Americans comprised 12 percent of the population but accounted for 50 percent of new HIV diagnoses, and African-American women were more than 12 times more likely to contract HIV than white women. Despite this striking risk of HIV infection, African Americans were half as likely to receive antiretroviral treatment as other segments of the U.S. population, causing nearly twice as many African Americans to die of HIV as whites. Globally, resource-poor countries struggle for assistance from rich countries to help combat the HIV epidemic. Recent legal battles have been waged in which poor countries have been forced to sue for access to affordable generic HIV treatments to which drug companies in rich countries hold the patents. Unequal access to these resources has led to a global picture in which antiretroviral drugs today reach only one of every five HIV-positive people who need them. Additional shortages persist in dissemination of much-needed HIV prevention information, and global funds continue to fall short for these efforts.

The AIDS epidemic has spurred a wave of activism and changes in public-health policy. Activist groups such as the Gay Men's Health Crisis, Project Inform, ACT UP, and the National Association of People with AIDS have formed to demand more HIV/AIDS research and better medical treatment, as well as to educate the public and promote safer behaviors and practices that could help prevent HIV's spread and reduce the stigma that is still often associated with HIV/AIDS. Many governments have responded to the epidemic with public-health measures such as mandatory HIV testing of the blood supply, surveillance monitoring of new HIV and AIDS cases and AIDS deaths, and education campaigns about preventing HIV transmission and encouraging HIV testing. Public health-prevention messages have centered around promoting condom use during sexual intercourse. Though the promotion of safe sex—as opposed to no sex at all—has been controversial among some religious groups, more controversial yet have been needle exchange programs for injecting drug users, which provide clean needles in order to prevent HIV transmission via injecting drug use.

Today HIV is a leading cause of adult mortality worldwide, though considerable disparities exist in national experiences. Globally, one in 100 adults have HIV. In sub-Saharan Africa, the world's most affected region, nearly 1 in 16 adults is HIV-positive, though in some of these countries as many as one in three adults have HIV. The scale of AIDS deaths in sub-Saharan Africa has reduced average life expectancy in many countries by 12–17 years and has created a generation of orphaned children as well as a drastically reduced workforce. In other areas of the world, HIV is rising, such as in eastern Europe and central Asia where there has been a recent 20-fold increase in the number of people living with HIV.

More than a quarter-century after the AIDS epidemic began, nearly 8,000 AIDS deaths and 11,000 new HIV infections still occur daily worldwide. In its first 25 years, the HIV/AIDS disaster has taken more lives than all the 20th century's war deaths. To this day, the spread of HIV reveals social, racial, and gender disparities that expose larger societal inequities, bearing social, psychological, and economic impacts that remain enormous, both in the United States and around the world.

Elaine A. Hills

FURTHER READING:

Irwin, A. C., J. Millen, and D. Fallows. *Global AIDS: Myths and Facts: Tools for Fighting the AIDS Pandemic.* Cambridge, Mass.: South End Press, 2003.

Marlink, Richard G., and Alison G. Kotin. *Global AIDS Crisis: A Reference Handbook.* Santa Barbara, Calif.: ABC-CLIO, 2004.

Shilts, Randy. *And the Band Played On: Politics, People, and the AIDS Epidemic.* New York: St. Martin's Press, 1987.

UNAIDS. *2006 Report on the Global AIDS Epidemic: A UNAIDS 10th Anniversary Special Edition.* Geneva, Switzerland: UNAIDS, 2006.

1983 ◆ BOMBING OF U.S. MARINE BARRACKS

The suicide bombing of the United States Marine barracks in Beirut, Lebanon, on Sunday, October 23, 1983, killed 241 American marines and naval personnel. It was the most devastating loss of life by the U.S. military since the Vietnam War. The tragedy resulted in withdrawal of U.S. military forces from Lebanon, which left a political vacuum in the region filled by Syria and Israel. Of equal significance, the attack shocked Americans into the realization that they were not immune to terrorism.

Lebanese are Arabs, most of whom are Muslims (divided into three main sects: Sunni, Shia, and Druse), with a minority of Christians (divided into two main groups: Maronite Catholic and Greek Orthodox). After the fall of the Ottoman Empire following World War I, Lebanon and Syria were granted to France as a League of Nations mandate. When Lebanon gained its independence in 1945, the population was roughly split between Muslims and Christians. A political understanding of 1943, known as the National Pact, stipulated that a Maronite would be president, parliament would have a six to five Christian majority, the prime minister would be a Sunni Muslim, and the Speaker of Parliament would be a Shia. By the 1970s, however, the Muslims had gained a clear majority of the population, with the Christians slipping to a third. Maronite Christians resisted Muslim attempts to change the National Pact to reflect this demographic shift. Adding further complications to the situation were the substantial number of Palestinians who lived in refugee camps in Lebanon. Most Palestinian refugees supported the Palestine Liberation Organization (PLO), which sought to reclaim Israel. These factors led to the outbreak of civil war in 1975. Beirut, the country's prin-

FACTBOX

PLACE Beirut, Lebanon

DATE October 23, 1983

TYPE Bombing

DESCRIPTION A suicide bomber drove a truck carrying six tons of dynamite into the four-story U.S. Marine barracks, and the resulting explosion destroyed the building.

CAUSE Perception of many Lebanese and Hezbollah members that the United States had intervened on the side of the Lebanese army in an internal Lebanese struggle.

CASUALTIES 241 U.S. Marines and naval personnel killed.

IMPACT U.S. forces withdrew from Lebanon four months later, diminishing U.S. influence in the region; people in the United States realized that they could be victims of a terrorist attack.

cipal city, had been a very attractive urban center, known as "the Paris of the East" with its mixture of French and Arabic culture. Now wartorn, Beirut became divided into the Muslim west and the Christian east along a street known as the "Green Line."

In 1978, Israel invaded southern Lebanon, remaining until a United Nations peacekeeping force was installed on the border between the two countries. A second Israeli invasion in June 1982 was intended to break PLO power. The Israelis reached Beirut, routed the PLO forces through shelling and cluster bombing (with munitions provided by the United States), and forced the PLO to evacuate by sea. By prior agreement, U.S. Marines were part of a multi-national force (MNF) brought into Beirut to insure that the evacuations were successful.

But Lebanon continued to spiral into chaos. Bashir Gemayel, Lebanon's recently elected Maronite president, was assassinated by a Syrian National Party member. On September 18, 1982, the Maronite militia massacred roughly 1,000 Palestinians in the Shia neighborhood of Sabra and the Shatila refugee camp. Israeli forces under General Ariel Sharon made no effort to stop the bloodshed. As a result 1,200 U.S. Marines returned as part of the MNF on September 29. The marines bivouacked at the Beirut airport, south of the city. In April 1983, the U.S. embassy in Beirut was bombed with 63 killed, 17 of whom were Americans. The United States mission in Lebanon became confused and conflicted. Shia Muslims saw the United States as intervening in favor of Christian forces who dominated the Lebanese army. The U.S. Navy, cruising off the coast of Beirut, fired shells into the eastern mountains, ostensibly to help the Lebanese army but actually resulting in putting the marines in great danger. By mid-October, the marines had become the targets of isolated attacks, including sniper fire and car bombs.

This was the scene on October 23 when a yellow Mercedes truck turned toward the front of the four-story marine barracks housing many of the marines at 6:20 A.M. The truck, which had a driver and no passengers, carried six tons of dynamite. As the vehicle reached the gate the driver sped into the lobby of the building, and the truck exploded. The roof of the barracks collapsed, bringing down all four floors and trapping many American personnel in the rubble. The attack killed 241 U.S. military personnel.

Minutes later, a second explosion four miles away destroyed a command post of French members of the MNF, killing 58.

Iran and Syria came under immediate suspicion of complicity in the bombing though no hard evidence was presented to confirm this hypothesis. The evidence appeared to implicate a new Shia group called Hezbollah (Party of God) that had forces in the Bekka Valley near Syria as the agents that carried out the attack. Based on this supposition, U.S. and French authorities planned to bomb Hezbollah sites. President Ronald Reagan approved the plan. The French carried out their part of the mission, but Caspar Weinberger, the United States secretary of defense, cancelled the operation without Reagan's approval.

Although western leaders reiterated their commitment to a peace process in the Middle East. President Reagan withdrew the remaining U.S. Marines in February 1984. The removal of American forces and the failure to retaliate against Hezbollah weakened the influence of the United States in the region. This outcome suggested to radical Muslims that the United States was a "paper tiger" that chose retreat before incurring further casualties. Moreover, the bombing of the marine barracks introduced Americans to the horror of terrorism. The 1983 Lebanon bombing was a gruesome reminder of the inherent instability of the Middle East.

Alex Wilson

FURTHER READING:

Friedman, Thomas L. *From Beirut to Jerusalem.* New York: Farrar, Straus and Giroux, 1989.

Mackey, Sandra. *Lebanon: Death of a Nation.* New York: Congdon & Weed, 1989.

Wright, Robin. *Sacred Rage.* New York: Simon and Schuster, 1985.

1984 ◆ CHEMICAL EXPLOSION IN BHOPAL

On December 3, 1984, the world's worst industrial disaster struck the city of Bhopal, India. In the middle of the night, a pesticide plant owned by the American company Union Carbide accidentally released deadly methyl isocyanate (MIC) gas into the crowded city, killing thousands and condemning tens of thousands to debilitating injury and illness for years to come. The disaster shocked the world and raised questions about government and corporate responsibility for

FACTBOX

PLACE Bhopal, India

DATE December 3, 1984

TYPE Release of toxic gas from a pesticide plant

DESCRIPTION An accidental release of deadly methyl isocyanate gas from a pesticide plant explosion resulted in thousands of deaths and tens of thousands of permanent injuries.

CAUSE Inadequate safety equipment and maintenance and poor planning and training allowed water to come into contact with methyl isocyanate, initiating an uncontrolled chemical reaction.

CASUALTIES More than 20,000 deaths and 100,000 serious injuries

COST Union Carbide Corporation paid $470 million to the government of India.

IMPACT Bhopal changed practices of the chemical industry worldwide and contributed to passage of the first federal legislation in the United States specifically designed to prevent major chemical accidents: the Emergency Planning and Community Right-to-Know Act of 1986, and the Clean Air Act Amendments of 1990.

industrial accidents. In the United States, the Bhopal tragedy prompted new policy for public oversight in the handling of hazardous materials to prevent a similar tragedy from happening at home. After more than two decades, Bhopal continues to be a potent reminder of the dangers of modern industrial activity and the unresolved issue of international justice.

The Union Carbide Corporation (UCC), the same company involved in the HAWK'S NEST TUNNEL DISASTER in 1931, established a pesticide-manufacturing plant in Bhopal, India, in 1969 as part of the "Green Revolution"—an effort in which high technology was applied to agriculture in developing nations in order to increase crop yields and thus make food more abundant and affordable. The Bhopal plant began to manufacture the pesticide Sevin in September 1977, using imported MIC. By February 1980, the plant was manufacturing and storing MIC as well as other chemicals on-site. Declining sales of the pesticide

in the 1980s, however, led to a number of cost-cutting measures which set the stage for disaster: inadequate maintenance, use of inappropriate equipment and methods, and lack of proper training and preparation. A densely populated urban area had grown around the plant since its establishment, but there was little public awareness of the potential hazard and there was no plan in place to deal with emergency situations.

In the late hours of December 2, 1984, a leak allowed water to enter one of the storage tanks containing MIC, which initiated an uncontrolled chemical reaction. Just after midnight on December 3, 54,000 pounds of MIC and another 26,000 pounds of unidentified reaction products exploded from the plant as a thick white cloud that flowed along the ground and enveloped the neighboring community. Without warning, residents awoke to painful burning of eyes and skin. The gas caused people to cough and choke, and some to vomit. As news of the deadly cloud spread, families fled from their homes in blind panic. Thousands died in the streets, asphyxiated as their lungs filled with phlegm and fluid, and their eyes were burned shut. Many of those who died were young children. Some would-be rescuers were themselves poisoned as they inhaled the gas while administering mouth-to-mouth resuscitation. By sunrise the gas had largely dissipated, and local officials were confronted by a massive public-health crisis. There were thousands of dead and dying people, as well as the carcasses of more than a thousand cattle and other domestic animals that littered a two-square-mile area. The sheer number of human corpses required mass burials, sometimes entire families, which prevented identification of many bodies. Between 7,000 and 10,000 people died within three days of the gas leak. A further 15,000 died in the following years. About 100,000 people continue to suffer chronic and debilitating illnesses. Many of the ailments involve chronic respiratory problems and eye injuries, as well as gynecological problems and nervous system disorders. Investigators estimate that as many as 500,000 people were actually exposed to the chemicals.

The Bhopal tragedy, along with other less severe incidents in the United States (one of which occurred at Bhopal's sister plant in Institute, West Virginia, in 1985), led to major changes within the U.S. chemical industry. A series of federal laws and regulations were subsequently passed in an effort to prevent major chemical accidents and to mitigate any that do occur. These laws and regulations include the Emergency Planning and Community Right-to-Know Act of 1986 and the Clean Air Act Amendments of 1990, which established both the Environmental Protection Agency's (EPA) Risk Management Program, and the Occupational Safety and Health Administration's Process Safety Management (OSHA PSM) standard. The EPA Risk Management Program and the OSHA PSM standard were the first national regulations specifically designed to prevent major chemical accidents that could harm workers, the public, and the environment.

The Bhopal tragedy remains unresolved as local community and international activists continue to petition for more adequate compensation and assistance for survivors, as well as legal and moral accountability by UCC (acquired by the Dow Chemical Company in 2001) and individuals responsible for the Bhopal plant. In 1989, UCC settled with the government of India for $470 million. Indian courts reinstated criminal charges against UCC's CEO, Warren Anderson, but he has refused to appear before the Indian courts, and both the governments of India and the United States have made no effort at extradition. Since acquiring UCC, Dow Chemical Company has rejected any responsibility for the Bhopal tragedy.

Marcos Luna

FURTHER READING:

Belke, James C., and Deborah Y. Dietrich. "The Post-Bhopal and Post-9/11 Transformations in Chemical Emergency Prevention and Response Policy in the United States." Paper presented at the International Conference on the 20th Anniversary of the Bhopal gas tragedy, "Bhopal Gas Tragedy and its Effects on Process Safety," Indian Institute of Technology Kanpur, India 2004. Available online. URL: http://yosemite.epa.gov/oswer/ceppoweb.nsf/ae2ff10ca577b18b85256b83007b7db9/85256b9f0072443385256f7e00550b2a!OpenDocument. Accessed April 10, 2007.

Clouds of Injustice: Bhopal Disaster 20 Years On. London: Amnesty International Publications, 2004. Available online. URL: http://web.amnesty.org/pages/ec-bhopal-eng. Accessed April 10, 2007.

Gunn, Angus M. "Pesticide Leak, Bhopal, India, December 3, 1984." In *Unnatural Disasters: Case Studies of Human-Induced Environmental Catastrophes,* 113–118. Westport, Conn.: Greenwood Press, 2003.

1986 ◆ SHUTTLE *CHALLENGER* EXPLOSION

The space shuttle *Challenger* had been scheduled for launch from the Kennedy Space Center at Cape Canaveral, Florida, on January 22, 1986. Space Transportation System (STS) mission 51-L was NASA's 10th operational flight utilizing the orbiter *Challenger*. Assigned to the mission were seven crew members: Mission Commander Richard Scobee, pilot Michael Smith, astronauts Ellison Onizuka, Judith Resnik, and Ronald McNair, aerospace engineer Gregory Jarvis, and Christa McAuliffe, a New Hampshire elementary school teacher. Selected after a long nationwide search, McAuliffe was assigned was to teach elementary school students from space. As the first NASA "volunteer," her responsibility gave the mission its popular "Teacher in Space" appellation and was meant to symbolize that space operations had become both normal and safe. Because slips in the launch schedules of earlier missions had raised questions about the reliability of NASA schedules, pressure had grown to get this mission, with its very public face, off as near to schedule as possible. But *Challenger*'s launch had already been delayed several times until January 26. Then a mechanical problem and increasing crosswinds pushed the launch date back again to January 28. Finally, at 11:38 A.M., the space shuttle lifted off. Seventy-three seconds later, while traveling at a Mach rate of 1.92, at an attitude of about 48,000 feet,

FACTBOX

PLACE In space, approximately nine miles above Florida

DATE January 28, 1986

TYPE Space shuttle explosion

DESCRIPTION 73 seconds after STS 51-L blasted off, a fireball erupted, enveloping the *Challenger* in a cloud of smoke and debris. All members of the crew died as the orbiter plunged back to the earth.

CAUSE The O-rings that sealed the sections of the solid booster rockets lost their resiliency in the cold weather, permitting ignited gas blow-by in the right rocket booster, which set the fuel tanks on fire.

CASUALTIES All seven shuttle crew members died.

IMPACT Shuttle launches were suspended for two and a half years, during which time investigations were undertaken and improvements in design and procedures implemented.

however, the *Challenger* exploded, killing all seven people onboard.

Weather forecasters for January 26 had predicted clear skies but with abnormally low temperatures—much colder than was considered safe by NASA engineers. Based on analyses of earlier cold-weather launches, engineers were aware of erosion to the rubberlike Viton O-rings that sealed the joints of the assembled case sections of the solid rocket boosters, which powered the shuttle into orbit. On the night of January 27, NASA managers contacted Morton Thiokol-Wasatch, their Utah-based manufacturer, and requested that its engineers evaluate the impact of a cold-weather launch on the boosters. The managers were worried that the cold might reduce the ability of the rings to properly seal the tiny intersectional gaps. Failure of the rings might permit "blow by" of hot gases, which could ignite the shuttle and threaten the safety of the mission. Several teleconferences between NASA and Thiokol personnel reviewed the engineers' recommendations, as well as conflicting data from earlier launches. As a result of these conversations, a "managerial" recommendation for a launch

was made. Simultaneously, a NASA Inspection Team observed ice formation on the orbiter itself. NASA asked its prime contractor, Rockwell International, for an opinion about how surface ice on the rockets might affect the launch. Rockwell reported that it did not know and refused to vouch for the integrity of the shuttle under icing conditions.

Based on this information and reports from NASA's Ice/Frost Inspection Team which had ordered deicing and antifreezing procedures performed on the STS, NASA decided at 9 A.M. on January 28 to launch the *Challenger* that morning. The temperature stood at 36°F. Two and a half hours later, the *Challenger* lifted off the ground. One minute and 13 seconds into the flight, a fireball erupted in the sky some nine miles above the Earth's surface, enveloping the orbiter in a cloud of smoke and debris. Moments later, the air force safety officer destroyed the wildly careening solid rocket boosters. All members of the crew perished as the orbiter plunged to the earth. That night, President Ronald Reagan mourned the loss of the orbiter and its crew in a televised address to the nation. He praised the crew for its pioneering bravery and promised that "we'll continue our quest in space. There will be more shuttle flights and more shuttle crews and, yes, more volunteers, more civilians, more teachers in space. Nothing ends here; our hopes and our journeys continue."

A month after the *Challenger* disaster, President Reagan created a presidential commission headed by former secretary of state William Rogers to investigate the disaster. NASA and the Committee on Science and Technology of the U.S. House of Representatives also undertook their own investigations of the tragedy. Their findings determined that the proximate cause of the disaster was the failure of the O-ring seals, which had lost their resiliency in the cold, thus permitting ignited gas blow-by in the right solid rocket booster. The resulting lateral thrust broke the strut connecting it to the external fuel tank. The flame then breached the tank and ignited its volatile liquid hydrogen and oxygen contents, which erupted in fire. The crew compartment remained intact as the orbiter broke apart and fell into the Atlantic Ocean, crashing at 200 miles per hour. The O-rings were determined to be a design flaw in the boosters, a condition first recognized in 1977. According to the *Presidential Commission Report,* this weakness, combined with "the effects of temperature, physi-

Moments after the *Challenger* exploded, all that remained visible in the sky was an expanding plume of smoke. *(NASA)*

cal dimensions, the character of the materials, the effects of reusability [of the booster], processing, and the reaction of the joint to dynamic loading," caused the tragedy. A contributory factor was "faulty information flows" resulting in a "flawed decision making process" throughout the NASA hierarchy.

Behind this specific diagnosis lay an institutional culture within NASA that routinely compromised safety in order to meet other mission priorities. NASA had become so segmented and rigidly hierarchical that it had disregarded the advice of technical specialists on aspects of its projects. America's space program also suffered from more embedded problems. A series of political and design trade-offs made years earlier had created an orbiter smaller than originally planned. In this process, the military had insisted on the inclusion of a large cargo capacity. Further, a change was made to power the shuttle by solid fueled boosters, which were considered

less safe than liquid-fueled rockets but required less development time. More rapid turnaround between launches appealed to military and commercial customers. But the redesign lacked an escape pod for its crew, a precaution built in to prior manned capsules. To cut costs in an attempt to make the project self-supporting, the boosters were built in pieces, a procedure used on previous rocket boosters. The Morton Thiokol-Wasatch booster design had been selected because its bid was substantially lower than were those of its three competitors. Rumors of political patronage in the design decision have persisted, although several investigations failed to confirm the allegation.

NASA suspended shuttle launches until September 1988, when it sent *Discovery* into space. A year earlier, Congress had authorized the construction of a replacement for *Challenger*. Christened the *Endeavor*, the new space vehicle was built partly from scratch and partly from spare parts intended for repairs to the remaining shuttles. *Endeavor* made its first flight in May 1992. The *Challenger* explosion was the deadliest accident in space history in the 20th century.

See also 2003 SHUTTLE COLUMBIA DISASTER.

Gerald Herman

FURTHER READING:

Fahey, Kathleen. Challenger *and* Columbia. Milwaukee, Wis.: Gareth Stevens Publishers, 1995.

Heppenheimer, T. R. *The Space Shuttle Decision, 1965–1972.* Washington D.C.: Smithsonian Institution Press, 2002.

Tomkins, Phillip. Apollo, Challenger, Columbia: *The Decline of the Space Program.* Los Angeles: Roxbury, 2005.

Vaughan, Diane. *The* Challenger *Launch Decision: Risky Technology, Culture and Deviance at NASA.* Chicago: University of Chicago University Press, 1996.

1988 ◆ YELLOWSTONE FIRES

Fires in Yellowstone National Park in the summer of 1988 burned through nearly half of the United States's first and most popular national park. This massive conflagration also ignited a debate over fire suppression and forest management in America's public lands. In a summer when forest fires threatened a larger swath of the American West than at any time since the early 1900s, Americans were forced to reevaluate the legacy of nearly a century of fire suppression on public lands. The controversial decision to "let it burn" resulted in an uproar from the general public, which watched flames cut through Yellowstone on national television and listened to ecologists who tried to explain the rationale. The fires of 1988 tested America's ideas about wilderness, wildfires, and the public's relationship to nature.

On June 14, 1988, a lightning strike started a fire in Montana's Custer National Forest, north of Yellowstone National Park. Officials decided to let it burn, expecting that it would exhaust itself over time. However, on June 23, a lightning strike in the southwest corner of the park ignited stands of old lodgepole pines that had been devastated by mountain pine beetles. Multiple subsequent fires broke out in late June and early July, the worst of which was started by a group of woodcutters who discarded a lit cigarette into dry grass on the park's border. Committed to a program of natural fire management, Yellowstone officials decided to fight some fires while letting others burn. Scientists felt this was a unique opportunity to observe natural fire behavior in a wil-

FACTBOX	
PLACE	Yellowstone National Park
DATE	Summer 1988
TYPE	Wildfires
DESCRIPTION	Fire ravaged much of Yellowstone National Park in the summer of 1988
CAUSE	Primarily lightning, with one fire sparked by a discarded cigarette
CASUALTIES	Two human deaths, along with 345 elk, 36 deer, 12 moose, nine bison, and six black bears
COST	More than $130 million
IMPACT	45 percent of Yellowstone National Park burned during the fires and 67 structures were destroyed. Nearly 1.2 million acres burned within Yellowstone and the surrounding national forests. Sparked an ongoing debate on fire suppression and forest management

derness setting. Outside of populated areas and not an immediate danger to humans and most wildlife, the fires burned steadily throughout June, July, and early August. Eleven of 20 early season fires died out without human intervention.

But on Sunday, August 20, 1988, high winds generated by the fires themselves caused the burn area to double in size. The explosive growth of the fires overwhelmed the resources of Yellowstone and National Forest officials to control the blazes. A nation raised on Smokey the Bear and taught about the inherent evil of fire could not understand why officials had done so little to control the burn. Although it seemed that the entire park was aflame, officials struggled to keep Yellowstone open for tourists while closely monitoring the situation. In a moment of high drama, the fires raged within yards of the Old Faithful Inn, which was protected by a sprinkler system installed on its roof. President Reagan was so disturbed by the television reports from Old Faithful that he sent a team to the park to investigate. National Park Service officials called in more than 9,400 firefighters, the largest firefighting force ever assembled to date in one place. Although 25,000 firefighters rotated through the Yellowstone fires during the 1988 season, not one was killed until the fires were nearly gone. Fire crew pilot Don Kykendell died on September 11 when his plane crashed, and firefighter Ed Hutton was killed on October 11 by a falling tree.

A snowstorm on September 11, followed by cooler weather and increased humidity, deprived the flames of their power, although the fire smoldered in places until November. The Old Faithful Inn survived, as did all of Yellowstone's landmark buildings. Forty-five percent of Yellowstone National Park burned during the fires. Nearly 1.2 million acres burned within Yellowstone and the surrounding national forests—an area larger than the entire state of Rhode Island. Little commercial timber was destroyed because the bulk of the burned area was wilderness and off-limits to timber interests. Sixty-seven structures were destroyed, 18 of which were employee and guest cabins. Biologists determined that 345 elk (out of 40,000–50,000), 36 deer, 12 moose, six black bears, and nine bison died in the Greater Yellowstone area as a direct result of the fires. Streams heated by the fires or contaminated by fire retardant resulted in some small fish kills. Total damages from the fire exceeded $130 million.

Debate over how to manage forest fires continued for years. Yellowstone National Park continues to have a wildland fire-management plan but with stricter guidelines under which naturally occurring fires will be allowed to burn. While the general public felt that fire should be eliminated or significantly controlled within the national park, many park officials and fire ecologists preferred to allow natural cycles to run their course. Common to both sides of the controversy, however, was the notion that humans could control the fires if necessary or desirable. The 1988 Yellowstone fires overwhelmed human capacities in the same way that floods, hurricanes, and volcanoes can.

Aaron Christopher Schab

FURTHER READING:

Barker, Rocky. *Scorched Earth: How the Fires of Yellowstone Changed America.* Washington, D.C.: Island Press, 2005.
Wallace, Linda L. *After the Fires: The Ecology of Change in Yellowstone National Park.* New Haven, Conn.: Yale University Press, 2004.

1989 ◆ *EXXON VALDEZ* OIL SPILL

Four minutes after midnight on March 24, 1989, the oil tanker *Exxon Valdez* ran aground on Bligh Reef in Alaska's Prince William Sound, setting into motion the worst confirmed oil spill in U.S. history. More than 11 of the more than 50 million gallons of crude oil in the ship's hold flowed onto the water, creating a massive slick spread by winds and currents. Within days, oil covered a huge swath of Alaska's south-central coast, fouling beaches and killing fish and wildlife in astronomical numbers. While the physical effects of this disaster are still being felt, perhaps its greatest impact has been forcing the recognition that oil spills of this magnitude are impossible to control, giving rise to improved prevention efforts and broader awareness of the need for environmental protection.

FACTBOX

PLACE Bligh Reef, Prince William Sound, Alaska

DATE March 24, 1989

TYPE Oil spill

DESCRIPTION An oil tanker hit submerged rocks, causing its hull to crack or rip open and spill more than 11 million gallons of oil.

CAUSE Immediate cause of tanker running aground was human error, but the spill ultimately resulted from a combination of policy violations, navigational mistakes, and the industrywide failure to implement promised safety precautions.

CASUALTIES Devastating losses to plant, fish, and animal communities

COST More than $3 billion in clean-up costs

IMPACT Recognition of uncontrollable nature and devastating long-term effects of a major oil spill, leading to greater environmental concern and to enhanced protection measures

A pool of at least 8 million barrels (336 million gallons) was discovered on Alaska's Arctic slope in 1968. Promising the U.S. Congress that it would spare no effort to protect the environment, a consortium of oil companies spent more than $8 billion building a pipeline stretching 800 miles from Prudhoe Bay at the edge of the Arctic Ocean to Valdez on Prince William Sound. Oil began to flow through that pipeline and into waiting tankers in 1977, quickly transforming Alaska's economy by generating 85 percent of state revenues. Alaska's state income tax was abolished, and each resident received an annual "windfall" check of about $800.

Accidents and near accidents involving tankers in Alaskan waters suggested that a major spill would eventually happen. The *Exxon Valdez* disaster confirmed this likelihood, resulting from a combination of policy violations, navigational mistakes, and the industrywide failure to implement promised safety precautions, such as using only double-bottom ships to reduce the possibility of spills. Much attention has been paid to the fact that *Exxon Valdez* captain

Joseph Hazelwood had been drinking alcohol on the night of the accident. Nine hours after the grounding, Hazelwood's blood alcohol registered .06, below the legal limit, but indicating that it had been much higher at the time of the accident. In the five years preceding the event, Hazelwood's automobile driver's license had been suspended three times for alcohol-related violations, despite participation in an alcohol treatment program. To simplify this catastrophe into a cautionary tale against drunk driving, however, ignores the fact that Hazelwood had left the ship's bridge, the post from which the ship is navigated, approximately 10 minutes before the incident. Third Mate Gregory Cousins, who had repeatedly assured Hazelwood that he was comfortably in control, did not notice until it was too late that the captain had taken the ship off course. Cousins was at the helm when the ship ran aground.

When the *Exxon Valdez* hit the submerged rocks of Bligh Reef, 600 feet (183 m) of its hull either cracked or ripped open, rupturing eight of the ship's cargo compartments. During the crucial first hours when conditions allowed the greatest ability to either skim large quantities off the surface or drop chemical dispersants, neither people nor necessary equipment were available in sufficient quantities to be effective. The remoteness of the accident site in Alaska was not to blame for this delay. Harvard University professor James Butler, who had chaired a National Research Council study group, stated, "A spill of this magnitude is virtually impossible to respond to adequately." The oil ultimately contaminated 1,500 miles (2,400 km) of shoreline—about the length of the California coast. Accounts of the devastation vary: Some include only the immediate impact, while others factor in predicted long-term effects on fish and animal populations. Even immediate-impact figures vary, depending on whether only the actual carcasses of birds and animals that came to shore are counted or if estimates of the wildlife that disappeared into the sea are included. Even the most conservative death tallies include more than 1,000 otters and 37,000 birds, with projected estimates at three to 10 times those numbers.

Photographs of birds, including rare bald eagles, rendered flightless by a thick coating of oil, and otters dying even as volunteers tried to clean their matted fur made for horrific television footage, as did scenes of Alaska's formerly ruggedly beautiful beaches transformed into lifeless, grotesque landscapes. These images dominated the news for several days, making it clear to the general public that the preparations for such an eventuality had been woefully inadequate and bringing into question the ability of even the best-prepared plan to clean up such a widespread and destructive mess. William K. Reilly, head of the federal Environmental Protection Agency, called the Alaska spill "the San Francisco earthquake of ecological catastrophes." The president of the National Wildlife Federation, the nation's largest environmental organization, claimed that "the long-term environmental consequences of the Prince William Sound oil spill will far exceed those of Chernobyl or Bhopal" (two of the world's worst environmental catastrophes, also set into motion by simple human error). Such dire predictions about the long-term effects of the spill turned out not to be exaggerations. Although the Exxon corporation spent nearly $2 billion on clean-up efforts in the first year of the disaster alone, it recovered only 3 to 13 percent of the oil spilled. The remaining oil destroyed countless fish and invertebrates (such as mussels) and disrupted their reproduction patterns, severely affecting not only commercial fishers but also Alaskan Natives who lived a subsistence lifestyle.

This event was not only unprecedented among oil spills because of the destruction it caused but also because of the intense scientific, legal, economic, and social scrutiny the accident received, not to mention the extensive efforts to combat its effects. Captain Joseph Hazelwood was convicted of negligence (a misdemeanor), fined $50,000, and sentenced to 1,000 hours of community service. Third mate Gregory Cousins pled no contest to civil charges of failing to navigate the tanker properly, and the Coast Guard suspended his license for nine months. As part of the 1991 settlements in both civil and criminal courts between Exxon, Alaska, and the federal government, the corporation funded restoration programs at a total cost of approximately $1 billion over the next 11 years. Even after these vast expenditures, Alaskans continue to file new lawsuits as recovery remains slow despite Exxon's claims to the contrary. The seal population decline continues. Certain bird, mammal, and invertebrate populations may never fully recover.

The long-term effects of the *Exxon Valdez* oil spill foster the recognition of the human limitations in controlling the environmental disasters they create. The most effective of the legislative efforts to ensure greater prevention and accountability is the requirement that every company and individual involved in a spill can be held personally liable for the damage caused. Ongoing concerns about future disasters have slowed subsequent resource extraction plans, including the proposal to carry out oil drilling in the Arctic National Wildlife Refuge, a delicate ecosystem that is home to wildlife including thousands of caribou. The chain of events set into motion by a single ship running aground culminated in an environmental disaster that caused many Americans to question the limits of technology in controlling nature and the ability of nature to repair itself.

See also 1969 Santa Barbara oil spill.

Nancy C. Unger

Rescue workers spent more than a decade trying to clean up the millions of gallons of oil that spilled when the *Exxon Valdez* tanker ran aground in Alaska's Prince William Sound. (*New York Public Library*)

FURTHER READING:

Davidson, Art. *In the Wake of the* Exxon Valdez*: The Devastating Impact of the Alaska Oil Spill.* San Francisco: Sierra Club Books, 1990.

Keeble, John. *Out of the Channel: The* Exxon Valdez *Oil Spill in Prince William Sound.* Cheney, Wash.: Eastern Washington University Press, 1999.

Leacock, Elspeth. *The* Exxon Valdez *Oil Spill.* New York: Facts On File, 2005.

Ott, Riki. *Sound Truth & Corporate Myth$: The Legacy of the* Exxon Valdez *Oil Spill.* Cordova, Alaska: Dragonfly Sisters Press, 2005.

1989 ◆ LOMA PRIETA EARTHQUAKE

On October 17, 1989, at 5:04 P.M., a 25-mile segment of the San Andreas Fault 11 miles below the surface of the earth ruptured and slipped, shaking Northern California for just under 15 seconds. The quake was named after the Loma Prieta Mountain above its epicenter, part of the Santa Cruz mountain range, in the Forest of Nisene Marks State Park. The tremor measured 7.1 on the Richter scale and could be felt in Oregon, Nevada, and as far south as Los Angeles. It caused the most devastation in the urban areas 60 miles to the north, particularly in the cities of San Jose, San Francisco, and Oakland. The earthquake took 62 lives, sent thousands to emergency rooms, and destroyed vital infrastructure. The event crippled the economy of a major metropolitan region and resulted in approximately $7.4 billion in physical damage.

Although this was the largest earthquake on the San Andreas Fault since the SAN FRANCISCO EARTHQUAKE of 1906, it was far from unexpected and quite moderate compared to forecasts. The Bay Area is a well-known danger zone, and advanced seismic engineering had been applied in the construction of most of the region's buildings and infrastructure. In general, the outcome of the event proved the efficacy of these measures—structures that were constructed and maintained according to modern standards for seismic safety fared exceptionally well. Fortunately for those injured, not a single hospital was seriously damaged. Most of the region's schools weathered the event with no more than cosmetic injury. Electrical outages were minimal, with power restored to San Francisco within seven hours and to the rest of the region within two days. Other service infrastructure, including water and gas systems, performed better than expected. Modern high-rises and office buildings in downtown San Francisco, Oakland, and San Jose were among the safest structures to inhabit during the event.

Where engineering standards were outdated, the tremor wreaked havoc. For decades, California Department of Transportation officials had routinely deferred maintenance and seismic improvements on bridges and freeways in response to budget shortfalls, and their performance in the Bay Area freeways reflected years of neglect. The single most deadly event caused by the earthquake was the col-

FACTBOX

PLACE Epicenter in the Forest of Nisene Marks State Park, just south of Loma Prieta Mountain near Santa Cruz, California. The earthquake caused major damage in the San Francisco Bay Area and was felt in Nevada, Oregon, and Southern California.

DATE October 17, 1989

TYPE Earthquake

DESCRIPTION An earthquake struck California, destroying part of the San Francisco–Oakland Bay Bridge, freeways, and other structures.

CAUSE Sudden rupture of a 25-mile section of the San Andreas Fault.

CASUALTIES 62 deaths, 3,757 injuries

COST An estimated $7.4 billion in damage to property and infrastructure, including the complete destruction of approximately 1,300 buildings

IMPACT Raised public awareness of earthquake safety and vindicated existing procedures and codes

lapse of a mile-long section of the Cypress Street viaduct of the I-880 freeway in Oakland. The collapsed roadway crushed automobiles on the lower deck of the thoroughfare, killing 42 motorists. Many more would have died on another day—traffic was unusually light because game three of the World Series was about to begin at San Francisco's Candlestick Park (the Series was postponed for 10 days, though the stadium suffered no serious damage). Sections of the Central and Embarcadero Freeways in San Francisco also collapsed. Probably the most costly transportation failure for the economy of the region was the collapse of the upper deck of the San Francisco–Oakland Bay bridge. A vital route for commuting San Francisco workers, repairs delayed its reopening for more than a month, and a safer replacement span is still under construction.

Property owners also suffered significant losses in the quake. The liquefaction of unstable, sandy soil

A crane mounted on a barge begins repair on the upper deck of the San Francisco–Oakland Bay Bridge, damaged by the Loma Prieta earthquake of 1989. *(Associated Press)*

was a major problem throughout the region, most notably in the South-of-Market and Marina districts of San Francisco. There, as in many hard-hit neighborhoods, the Bay had been "filled" with relatively loose and sandy soil to create land for development. Most of the buildings damaged were older, wood-frame structures, and many had supporting walls or foundations made of unreinforced masonry or brick, which were also vulnerable. All in all, approximately 27,000 buildings were damaged or destroyed, approximately 1,300 completely. The quake rendered more than 11,500 residences uninhabitable, the vast majority of which were in multifamily dwellings in low-income neighborhoods. Watsonville and Santa Cruz to the south suffered the greatest proportionate housing losses, amounting to nearly 10 percent of residential units.

Certainly, the 1989 quake raised public awareness of earthquake safety in San Francisco and danger zones around the world. However, state and local governments were not quick to respond with improved planning and seismic safety. The 1993 Northridge earthquake in Los Angeles revealed that the freeways of California remained hazardous and unreliable. The epicenter of that 6.8 magnitude

quake was in an urban area, and it resulted in $25.7 billion in property damage, though it took slightly fewer lives than did the 1989 tremor. Neither earthquake provided significant new knowledge or major revelations to experts; they did more to confirm previous ideas and to vindicate existing procedures and codes. Research on seismic safety and building codes continued as before, and expert recommendations were implemented without any substantial change in urgency, efficiency, or administrative procedure.

See also 1906 SAN FRANCISCO EARTHQUAKE AND FIRE.

Louise Nelson Dyble

FURTHER READING:

Comerio, Mary. *Disaster Hits Home: New Policy for Urban Housing Recovery.* Berkeley, Calif.: University of California Press, 1998.

Housner, George W. *Competing Against Time: Report to Governor George Deukmejian from the Governor's Board of Inquiry on the 1989 Loma Prieta Earthquake.* Sacramento, Calif.: State of California Office of Planning and Research, 1990.

National Research Council. *Practical Lessons from the Loma Prieta Earthquake.* Washington, D.C.: National Academy Press, 1994.

1992 ◆ LOS ANGELES RIOT

Known also as the Rodney King riots, the Los Angeles riot of 1992 was the largest civil disturbance in the history of California and one of the most destructive in the history of the United States. Spanning almost six days from April 29 to May 4, 1992, the riot in South Central Los Angeles exacted a deadly toll: 55 killed, more than 4,000 injured, and more than $1 billion in property damage. The immediate cause of the riot was the acquittal of four white Los Angeles Police Department (LAPD) officers—Stacey C. Koon, Theodore J. Briseno, Timothy E. Wind, and Laurence M. Powell—of all charges stemming from the 1991 beating of an intoxicated motorist named Rodney King, an African-American parolee who led officers on a short, high-speed pursuit. In many respects, the beating of Rodney King was entirely unexceptional: African Americans in Los Angeles had been the victims of racially motivated and totally unchecked police violence since the late 19th century. The difference in this case was that a plumber named George Holliday was testing out his new video camera and captured most of the beating on videotape. The Holliday video, which showed a crouching King absorbing more than 50 baton blows, seared the national conscience as it was broadcast on televisions nationwide.

Traditionally understood as a race riot, the Los Angeles Riot of 1992 was considerably more complex. On one hand, it was indisputably about race. The high-profile beating of an African American confirmed longstanding—but difficult to verify—antiblack racism within the LAPD. And for many African Americans, the acquittals also seemed to confirm their suspicions that the courts regarded them as less deserving of justice than whites. Intensifying these sentiments was the murder of 15-year-old African-American Latasha Harlins by a Korean-American grocer named Soon Ja Du, also captured on videotape and also aired nationally only weeks after the King beating was televised. Despite shooting the unarmed Harlins in the back of the head as she left the store, Du was only charged with voluntary manslaughter and sentenced to community service. Finally, most of the violence during the riot was clearly motivated by racial animus. Most sensationally, white truckdriver Reginald Denny was

FACTBOX	
PLACE	South Central Los Angeles
DATE	April 29–May 4, 1992
TYPE	Race riot
DESCRIPTION	Riot consisting of widespread looting and physical violence
CAUSE	Acquittal of four white police officers who were videotaped beating black motorist Rodney King
CASUALTIES	55 killed; more than 4,000 injured
COST	More than $1 billion
IMPACT	Intensified capital flight from South Central Los Angeles; spurred federal civil-rights-violation charges against officers; and prompted formation of the Rebuild L.A. campaign to spark investment and job growth

pulled from his stalled tractor trailer at the intersection of Florence and Normandie and brutally beaten by African Americans for no other reason than that he was white.

It was difficult to conceal the class-based nature of the riot. Though the officers' acquittals were the ostensible trigger of the crisis, the economic context of South Central Los Angeles in the early 1990s clearly shaped its outcome. Battered by a national recession, South Central was also particularly hard hit by the massive industrial plant closures of the 1980s, which left a rising proportion of the population—particularly young black men—unemployed and frustrated. Simultaneously, South Central—which had been solidly black since the 1960s—was beginning a historic shift into a predominantly Latino community. (By the early 21st century, Latinos would outnumber blacks in South Central.) Though African Americans often overstated the degree of competition between blacks and Latinos, the arrival of the new immigrants did in fact represent a source of labor competition in low-paying services and manufacturing jobs. For their part, the influx of Latinos into the overcrowded and impoverished Pico-Union District intensified existing gang problems and stretched limited resources even thinner. To the surprise of whites, blacks, and established Latinos alike, a slim majority of those arrested for looting during the riot were in fact Latino, not black. Aerial video footage and photographs from the riots—in which Latinos can be seen carrying diapers, shoes, and foodstuffs through broken windows—suggested that the motivation of Latino looters was not political but practical, a function of their economic situation rather than their ethnic or racial makeup.

Aside from the massive property destruction it wrought, the Los Angeles riot of 1992 did not lead to significant changes in the circumstances of residents of South Central. The immediate effect, in fact, was negative in that it accelerated the flight of remaining capital investment in the region. The retrial of the four officers on federal civil rights violations charges and the conviction of two restored some sense of faith in the judiciary among blacks. Most promising was the ambitious Rebuild L.A. campaign, which sought to spur investment and job growth in South Central. But despite good intentions—and the capable stewardship of former baseball commissioner and head of the 1984 Olympic Committee, Peter Ueberroth—Rebuild L.A. was not able to reach its goals and disbanded in 1997.

Josh Sides

FURTHER READING:

Cannon, Lou. *Official Negligence: How Rodney King and the Riots Changed Los Angeles and the LAPD.* New York: Crown, 1998.

Gooding-Williams, Robert, ed. *Reading Rodney King, Reading Urban Uprising.* New York: Routledge, 1993.

Los Angeles Times Staff. *Understanding the Riots: Los Angeles Before and After the Rodney King Case.* Los Angeles: Los Angeles Times, 1992.

1992 ◆ HURRICANE ANDREW

Nobody could predict the damage and destruction that loomed when a small cluster of clouds formed on August 14, 1992, off the west coast of Africa. But over the next week, as the cluster moved west across the Atlantic Ocean, it grew to become Hurricane Andrew, the third most intense hurricane to strike the United States since 1900. Winds topped 160 miles per hour, with gusts exceeding 175 miles per hour. The storm killed 65 people, damaged or destroyed over 200,000 homes, left more than 160,000 people homeless, and caused over $26 billion in damage.

The early stages of Andrew seemed innocent, although the warm waters of the Atlantic Ocean lay in the system's path. By August 17, winds reached 40 miles per hour, strong enough to classify the system as Tropical Storm Andrew. The storm changed very little over the next four days. Winds increased to 75 miles per hour early on August 22, and Andrew officially became a hurricane. Over the next day and a half, winds strengthened to more than 160 miles per hour.

The Bahamas was the first place to feel the full wrath of Hurricane Andrew. Strong winds and heavy rain battered the islands. There were numerous reports of funnel clouds, and rain poured in torrents. The storm surge pushed water levels to 16 feet

One of the fiercest hurricanes in American history, Andrew left a trial of destruction across Florida and neighboring states. *(New York Public Library)*

FACTBOX

PLACE Southern Florida (especially Homestead and Dade County), Louisiana, Mississippi, Alabama, and Georgia

DATE August 24–25, 1992; its full lifecycle spanned August 14–28

TYPE Hurricane

DESCRIPTION Massive winds and rains struck Florida, then crossed the Gulf of Mexico and struck the Gulf states before weakening and turning northward

CAUSE A storm formed off the west coast of Africa and developed into a Category 5 hurricane in the Caribbean.

CASUALTIES 65 people killed

COST Damage estimated at more than $26 billion

IMPACT The storm caused extensive environmental damage in southern Florida and Louisiana; Florida adopted hurricane safeguards and established a new statewide building code in 2002; insurance companies dropped hazard coverage or doubled their rates.

clouds and tornadoes were common in Louisiana, Mississippi, Alabama, and Georgia. Many locations recorded more than three inches of rain. One site in Louisiana measured nearly 12 inches of rain. The remnants of Andrew turned northward, then northeastward, and merged with a low-pressure system over the mid-Atlantic states on August 28.

Andrew was one of the costliest natural disasters in American history. There were 26 direct fatalities, while 39 were indirect, including electrocution and accidents during cleanup. Massive evacuations prior to Andrew, including 1.25 million people in Louisiana, 1.23 million in Florida, 650,000 in Mississippi, and 250,000 in Texas, probably reduced the death toll. There was significant damage to, or total destruction of, more than 200,000 residences, leaving more than 160,000 people homeless. Approximately 82,000 businesses were damaged or destroyed, resulting in 86,000 jobs lost.

Andrew damaged or destroyed 21,000 homes in Louisiana and ruined at least 25 percent of the state's sugar crop. The hurricane knocked down 22 oil and natural-gas structures and significantly damaged 65 others in the Gulf of Mexico, spilling approximately 500 barrels of oil. In Louisiana's Atchafalaya River Basin, Andrew knocked down 80 percent of the trees near the coast and 30 percent of the inland trees. An estimated 50 to 75 percent of the area's young squirrels died as a result. The large amount of sediment in the Mississippi River killed 182 million freshwater fish, valued at $160 million. Nearly 9.4 million saltwater fish, valued at $7.8 million, also died.

The worst damage occurred in Florida, most from Andrew's powerful winds. Residents filed 725,000 insurance claims. Nearly 80 percent of the state's farms suffered damage. In Homestead, winds destroyed 50,000 homes and hurled steel-reinforced tie beams several blocks. About 99 percent of the mobile homes in the city were completely destroyed. Total destruction occurred in 90 percent of mobile homes in all of Dade County. There was significant damage to boats in the area. Farther off the coast, a 350-ton barge loaded with 1,000 tons of concrete lost large sections of steel-plate siding as winds moved it 700 feet.

Winds leveled or caused major damage to many of the region's trees. In southern Dade County, 90 percent of the native pinelands, mangroves, and undergrowth suffered various levels of damage. Severe damage also occurred in nearly 25 percent of the palm trees in Everglades National Park. The trees and shrubs that survived sprouted new growth within three weeks.

above mean sea level in the town of Little Bogue. Andrew next set its sights on Florida.

Andrew made landfall near Homestead in Dade County about 25 miles south of Miami on the morning of August 24, with powerful winds, a 17-foot storm surge, and heavy rain. Original estimates of sustained wind speeds were 145 miles per hour. The National Hurricane Center in Miami measured a wind gust of 164 miles per hour, while a gust at a private home reached 177 miles per hour. A later reevaluation placed maximum sustained winds at 165 miles per hour, officially making Andrew only the third category 5 storm to hit the continental United States. Andrew weakened slightly during its three-hour trek across southern Florida. During this time, residents reported funnels clouds, and more than seven inches of rain fell in the path.

Andrew regained strength over the Gulf of Mexico and turned northwestward. Another landfall occurred on the central Louisiana coast on the evening of August 25, with 140-mile-per-hour winds and an eight-foot storm surge. Reports of funnel

In Biscayne National Park, nearly 33 percent of the coral reefs suffered structural damage. Most fish and wildlife in the two parks escaped harm.

Approximately 100,000 residents of southern Dade County permanently left after Hurricane Andrew. Those who remained or came after saw prices rise significantly as a result of the storm. Officials established hurricane safeguards in 1994 and implemented a new statewide building code in 2002, which can add up to $20,000 to the cost of a new home. Many insurance companies either dropped their coverage or increased their rates by up to 100 percent. One of the most destructive and costliest storms in American history, Hurricane Andrew has continued to affect life into the 21st century.

See also 1900 GALVESTON HURRICANE; 1938 GREAT NEW ENGLAND HURRICANE; 2005 HURRICANE KATRINA.

Richard R. Brandt

FURTHER READING:

Ahrens, C. Donald. *Meteorology Today: An Introduction to Weather, Climate, and the Environment.* 8th ed. Belmont, Calif.: Thomson Higher Education/ Brooks-Cole, 2007.

Gore, Rick. "Andrew Aftermath." *National Geographic* 183.4 (April 1993): 2–37.

Lutgens, Frederick K., and Edward J. Tarbuck. *The Atmosphere: An Introduction to Meteorology.* 10th ed. Upper Saddle River, N.J.: Pearson/Prentice Hall, 2007.

1992 ◆ SILICONE BREAST IMPLANT CRISIS

The silicone breast implant crisis has divided medical scientists, legal advisers, corporate interests, and the public. In 1992, the Food and Drug Administration (FDA) banned implants because they had not been proven safe for use—despite 40 years of prior use in the United States. Medical debates surged around the silicone breast implant issue, with accusations lodged that corporate-funded and "junk" science had supported what some saw as poor decisions by the FDA. Lawyers have been accused of predatory behavior for representing women in case after multimillion dollar case. Manufacturers of silicone gel implants have wrangled with scientists, the law, the FDA, and the public, often under charges of secrecy, neglect, and greed. All the while, the public has perhaps suffered the most. Hundreds of thousands of implant recipients have experienced extensive health problems for unknown reasons. Some women have so desperately believed that these problems resulted from their implants, they took razors to their breasts to remove the implants themselves. Yet in 2006, the FDA shocked many by again approving silicone-filled gel implants for use.

Most women have opted to receive breast implants for cosmetic reasons, fueled in large part by changing cultural norms that emphasize the importance of female breast size. Many breast cancer survivors have also received implants for breast reconstruction after mastectomy.

The first use of silicone for breast enlargement is believed to have occurred in Japanese women who were trying to impress U.S. servicemen in the 1940s. Liquid silicone gel was injected by syringe directly into women's breasts, along with paraffin and other substances. In the 1950s, women in the United States began to undergo the same procedures. The first modern, enveloped silicone gel-filled breast implant was placed in a Houston woman in 1962 after the invention was produced by manufacturer Dow Corning. Silicone gel implants increased in popularity in subsequent decades. By 1992, it is estimated that 1 million to 2 million women had received silicone gel implants.

Scattered individual medical case reports and case series, or small groups, of silicone-related illnesses associated with breast implants were published throughout the decades that implants became increasingly popular. In the early 1960s, Japanese medical journals began to document rheumatic illnesses associated with breast implants. By the late 1970s, British and American medical journals documented similar health issues. In subsequent decades, anecdotal reports continued to appear in the medical literature of affluent nations where

FACTBOX

PLACE United States

DATE 1962 (first use in the United States), 1992 (FDA ban on silicone implants), 2006 (FDA rescinding of ban on silicone implants)

TYPE Health crisis

DESCRIPTION Silicone gel-filled breast implants are believed by many to cause the wide range of health problems known as silicone disease, a condition disputed by some scientific studies.

CAUSE Some contend that silicone gel implant leaching and rupture cause silicone disease, but debate on the issue continues.

CASUALTIES Hundreds of thousands of diseased women

COST Untold billions in legal settlements, medical, and societal costs

IMPACT In 1988, the FDA classified breast implants as a potentially dangerous device for regulatory purposes and banned the use of implants in 1992. The agency reversed its ban in 2006, rekindling controversy in the ongoing legal and scientific debate over breast implants and corporate responsibility for the health ailments that stem from them.

the costly implants were popular. Women began to report health problems including connective tissue disease, inflammation and muscle pain, joint pain and swelling, swollen lymph nodes, gastrointestinal symptoms, chronic fatigue, decreased sex drive, depression, and more. Symptoms were reported anytime from immediately after implantation to decades later. However, the growing list of ailments, collectively named *silicone disease,* did not immediately prompt government investigation into implant safety or regulation of use.

A loophole in U.S. laws governing medical devices, such as silicone breast implants, did not require the FDA to act on the growing literature that documented safety and health concerns believed associated with implants. In fact, the FDA was not required to provide any oversight of implants or other medical devices until the 1976 passage of the Medical Device Amendments to the Federal Food,

Drug, and Cosmetic Act. The amendments required that, at the discretion of the FDA, manufacturers of new devices submit an application to the FDA for pre-marketing approval. Approval applications were to entail safety and effectiveness data from both animal and human studies prior to medical device sales. But because breast implants were marketed prior to passage of the amendment and presumably assumed fit for sale, they were exempted from the 1976 rules.

Increasing public pressure to regulate implant sales mounted, not only from the growing list of medical reports documenting problems believed to be associated with breast implants but also from the increasing numbers of women who felt they were adversely affected by their implants and thus sought legal justice. Notable legal cases include the 1984 jury case that awarded nearly $2 million to one woman for her implants; in 1991, a federal jury awarded Mariann Hopkins $7.34 million when she argued that her implants caused a rare mixed connective tissue disease; and one Texas woman received $25 million in her 1992 implant case. Lawsuits were ultimately filed by thousands of women across the country who were desperate for answers about their health problems and increasingly demanded compensation from surgeons and device manufacturers.

As concerns about the safety of silicone implants grew, the FDA began to act. First, in 1982, the FDA put forth a proposal to classify implants as a potentially dangerous, Class III device. By 1988, the proposal was approved, and the FDA increasingly scrutinized implant safety studies and reports of device failures. By the early 1990s, the FDA began to crack down on silicone implant manufacturers. This included a formal warning to one manufacturer who was then providing false and misleading statements about the safety of implants in response to customer inquiries. The FDA declared that scientific studies had not been able to definitively back safety reassurances and required that all implant manufacturers submit evidence of product safety. This led to lengthy reviews of the manufacturers' safety evidence by FDA advisory panels, which ultimately recommended that silicone-filled gel implants be removed from the market, except under extremely exceptional circumstances. On April 16, 1992, FDA commissioner David Kessler accepted the panel's decision.

For many of the 1–2 million women who had already received silicone breast implants, the FDA ban incited alarm. Yet for others, the ban was a symbol of vindication after years of legal struggles with implant manufacturers. Indeed, the silicone implant legal battles had often been successful and continued to be after the 1992 ban. In 1994, with the exception of Dow Corning, all of the implant companies agreed to a $4.25 billion class-action settlement. At the time, it was the largest class-action settlement in history. Though originally the suit intended for payments of up to $1.4 million for women, few ever received more than $50,000, and some received as little as $700. The Dow Corning Company set up a separate $3.2 billion settlement plan in 1998 for the thousands of women who received their implants but declared bankruptcy soon after, sending the case to bankruptcy court.

Meanwhile, the scientific community, which had not uniformly supported the legal rulings on implants, continued to investigate the health issues surrounding them. In 1999, the Institute of Medicine (IOM), in a report commissioned by Congress, concluded that there was not sufficient evidence to link implants to serious illness. Scientists affiliated with advocacy groups strongly disagreed with the IOM findings, noting that funding sources of some of the more prominent implant studies came directly from implant manufacturers.

Despite an onslaught of public concern over the safety of breast implants and the medical-legal controversies they sparked, in late 2006 the FDA approved for use the very same silicone gel-filled breast implants that they had previously banned. Some believe the medical evidence supports the approvals though, as with virtually all scientific controversies, studies remain ongoing. At least one corporate scientist-turned-whistleblower formerly employed by one of the companies whose implants were recently reapproved for use has publicly accused his former employer of hiding critical safety information about the implants from the FDA. However, in early 2007, the FDA dismissed the whistleblower's complaint. Nevertheless, the FDA has urged women considering breast implants to make careful and informed decisions about implantation, in part because the available scientific data about implants may be incomplete. The FDA warns that implants are likely to lead to complications that will require additional surgeries later in life. Moreover, silicone-filled implants are subject to rupture that can occur with or without symptoms; implants may also rupture during routine mammogram screening for breast cancer. Women are urged to have an MRI to screen for rupture three years after implantation and every two years thereafter. Given the risks, the FDA's approvals require ongoing studies of the long-term effects of implants.

Indeed, the breast implant controversy is a critical reminder that individuals are trusted to make informed decisions, even when the available scientific data about a product may be incomplete and even when scientific tools for assessing problems may not be able to provide all the answers. The controversy may be far from over.

Elaine A. Hills

FURTHER READING:

Angell, Marcia. *Science on Trial: The Clash of Medical Evidence and the Law in the Breast Implant Case.* New York: W. W. Norton, 1996.

Bondurant, Stuart, Virginia Ernster, and Roger Herdman, eds. *Safety of Silicone Breast Implants.* Washington, D.C.: Institute of Medicine, 2000.

Vasey, Frank B., and Josh Feldstein. *The Silicone Breast Implant Controversy: What Women Need to Know.* Freedom, Calif.: Crossing Press, 1993.

1993 ◆ WORLD TRADE CENTER BOMBING

Shortly after noon on February 26, 1993, terrorists detonated a bomb at the World Trade Center in New York City, killing six people and injuring more than 1,000. The World Trade Center not only was an engineering marvel—at the time of their construction in 1973, the two 110-story buildings were the tallest skyscrapers in the world—but also a prominent symbol of American power, almost as conspicuous as the Statue of Liberty located two miles south in New York Harbor. The 1993 bombing shocked many Americans into the realization that terrorism could now happen in the United States.

FACTBOX

PLACE World Trade Center, New York City

DATE February 26, 1993

TYPE Terrorist bombing

DESCRIPTION A car bomb detonated in a basement parking level of the North Tower of the World Trade Center.

CAUSE An act of terrorism by militant Muslims in retaliation for U.S. support for Israel

CASUALTIES Six people killed and more than 1,000 injured

COST $591 million

IMPACT Shocked Americans into the realization that terrorism could happen in the United States

Owned by the Port Authority of New York and New Jersey, the World Trade Center occupied a 16-acre plot of land in Lower Manhattan, the heart of New York City's financial district. In addition to the twin towers, built at a cost about $750 million, the Port Authority operates the Holland and Lincoln Tunnels; the George Washington Bridge; Kennedy, LaGuardia, and Newark Airports; and the Path rail system that connects New York City with the ports of Newark and Elizabeth, New Jersey.

The blast in 1993 occurred on level B-2 of the North Tower One, an area used mostly for parking. Law-enforcement authorities determined that a car had been used to deliver the explosives. The blast occurred directly below the police and fire communications control center, creating a crater of about 11,500 square feet and rendering the towers' public safety systems useless. The explosion also knocked out the buildings' telephone lines and power systems, caused smoke to rise up through both towers, destroyed the ceiling of a nearby subway line, and paralyzed much of Lower Manhattan. The World Trade Center complex suffered an estimated $591 million in damages and business to Trade Center tenants. The bombers had hoped that the blast would topple the North Tower and cause it to collapse onto the South Tower. However, the integrity of the structures remained, and the towers remained standing.

Coinciding with the explosion, one of the defendants sent a letter to the *New York Times* stating that the attack was in retaliation for U.S. support of Israel and U.S. policies toward the Middle East. Beginning with the arrest of Mohammed A. Salameh, a Muslim fundamentalist, in Jersey City, New Jersey, on March 4, the FBI investigation tracked the bombing plot to radical Islamists living in the United States. By August, seven suspects had been charged in the bombing, all of whom were described as Arab militants. Trials began in New York City on October 4, and 10 conspirators eventually received jail sentences.

In June 1993, the FBI discovered that the bombing was part of a wider terrorist campaign that included a plot to bomb other landmarks in New York City, including the United Nations building. Public officials, including UN Secretary-General Boutros Boutros Ghali and Egyptian President Hosni Mubarak, had also been targeted for assassination. A federal grand jury indicted Sheik Omar Abdel Rahman, a radical Muslim cleric, for orchestrating these plans and the World Trade Center plot, as well as the 1990 murder of Rabbi Meir Kahane, a militant pro-Israel advocate, in New York City. Rahman had been in U.S. custody since July 2, 1993, on charges that he had violated American immigration laws. He received a life sentence for his involvement in the plot. The mastermind bomber, Ramzi Yousef, had fled the country on the evening of February 26. He was later captured in Pakistan at a safe house run by al-Qaeda, the radical Islamic terrorist organization, and extradited to the United States, where he was tried, convicted, and imprisoned.

A controversy soon arose on how to prosecute the bombers. During the administration of President Bill Clinton, federal officials decided to treat them like domestic disaster felons as was later done with the defendants in the OKLAHOMA CITY BOMBING in 1995 and to try them in the American courts. In the wake of 9/11 TERRORIST ATTACK in 2001, however, President George W. Bush viewed terrorism as an act of state sovereignty directed by foreign leaders like Iraqi dictator Saddam Hussein and al-Qaeda leader Osama bin Laden. Under the new interpretation, terrorists would be tried under articles of war. Thus, the 1993 World Trade Center bombing was a precursor to the 9/11 attack, which dramatically changed U.S. approaches to terrorism.

Frank T. Colon

FURTHER READING:
Caram, Peter. *The 1993 World Trade Center Bombing: Foresight and Warning.* London, England: Janus, 2001.

Mylroie, Laurie. *Study of Revenge, The First World Trade Center Attack and Saddam Hussein's War Against America.* Washington, D.C.: AEI Press, 2001.

1993 ◆ SUPERSTORM

Anyone who experienced the 1993 Superstorm is certain to remember it, whether the name conjures up memories of strong winds, heavy precipitation, or cold temperatures. Also known as the Storm of the Century, the Great Blizzard of 1993, and the No-Name Storm, it directly affected more than 100 million people in the eastern United States and parts of Mexico, Canada, and several Caribbean countries and closed every major East Coast airport.

The Superstorm began as a weak low-pressure system near the coast of Texas on March 12. It rapidly intensified over the Gulf of Mexico and the southeastern United States on the morning of March 13. It moved up the East Coast and strengthened further that day. The central pressure was equivalent to a category 3 hurricane at one point. The storm weakened as it moved northeastward on March 14, although it remained much stronger than most winter storms.

The 1993 Superstorm delivered wild and record-setting weather to much of the eastern United States. Coastal flooding, heavy rain and snow, strong winds, intense thunderstorms, tornadoes, and very cold temperatures were widespread. Coastal flooding in Cuba and along the U.S. Gulf coast resulted from the system's storm surge. Water levels rose up to 12 feet above mean sea level in parts of Florida.

Heavy precipitation covered an extensive area. The region from eastern Texas to the central Great Lakes and eastward to the coast received at least one inch of precipitation. Up to six inches of rain fell in parts of Texas. Some meteorologists called the aerial coverage of the snowfall "the most extensive distribution of heavy snow across the eastern United States in modern times." Seven states recorded snowfall exceeding 40 inches, the greatest of which was 56 inches at Mount LeConte, Tennessee. Snowdrifts

> ## FACTBOX
>
> **PLACE** Eastern third of the United States, along with parts of Mexico, Canada, and the Caribbean
>
> **DATE** March 12–14, 1993
>
> **TYPE** Storm
>
> **DESCRIPTION** Strong winds, heavy precipitation, and freezing temperatures wreaked havoc across much of the nation.
>
> **CASUALTIES** 270 deaths, hundreds of injuries in the United States, nearly 40 deaths in Canada, and three in Cuba
>
> **COST** $3 billion to $6 billion
>
> **IMPACT** Closed every major airport on the East Coast and shut down business, travel, trade, and communication in the region; precipitated economic slump

topped six feet throughout the region. The total snowfall was equivalent to the volume of water that flows over Niagara Falls in 100 days.

Strong winds also accompanied the storm. Locations from the Gulf Coast to New England recorded wind speeds over 70 miles per hour. The strongest gusts were at Mt. Washington, New Hampshire, where the wind whipped at 144 mile per hour, and Grand Etang, Nova Scotia, where it blew at 131 mile per hour. The wind caused ocean swells up to 65 feet off the coast of Nova Scotia.

Severe weather occurred in Mexico, Florida, and several Caribbean nations. Intense thunderstorms spawned multiple tornadoes, which left over 5,000 people homeless in far northeastern Mexico. A line of thunderstorms generated 27 tornadoes across Florida.

Very cold air overtook the region during and after the Superstorm. Temperatures plummeted by 45°F in 18 hours in northern New Brunswick as the storm passed. In the United States, 70 records for low temperatures were set on March 14, and another 75 record lows occurred on March 15.

The 1993 Superstorm caused approximately 270 deaths in the United States alone. Nearly 100 deaths were directly associated with the storm, including loss of life due to tornadoes or other severe weather and drowning from the storm surges. Another 170 deaths were indirectly associated with the storm, such as heart attacks caused by overexertion while shoveling snow. Nearly 40 deaths occurred in Canada, with three more deaths in Cuba.

The wintry weather wreaked havoc from Florida to New England, shutting down every major airport on the East Coast at some point, a first in American history. This resulted in the cancellation of nearly 25 percent of flights nationwide, leaving thousands of people stranded. Until the cancellation of flights after the attacks of September 11, 2001, eight years later, the storm caused the most extensive disruption of air travel in aviation history. Ground travel was nearly impossible in many locations. The snow closed major interstates and highways and secondary and local roadways from Atlanta northward. Emergency personnel in North Carolina and Tennessee rescued more than 200 hikers, and officials set curfews after declaring states of emergency.

The massive scale of the 1993 Superstorm was unprecedented. Twenty-six of the nation's 50 states experienced some impact, including nearly 90 million U.S. residents, more than one-third of the nation's population. This storm ranks as one of the most costly winter storms in American history, with damage estimates ranging from $3 billion to $6 billion. The Department of Commerce credited most of the economic slump in the first quarter of 1993 to this storm, which interrupted business, travel, trade, and communication.

Richard R. Brandt

FURTHER READING:

Aguado, E., and James E. Burt. *Understanding Weather and Climate.* 4th ed. Upper Saddle River, N.J.: Pearson/Prentice Hall, 2007.

Ahrens, C. Donald. *Meteorology Today: An Introduction to Weather, Climate, and the Environment.* 8th ed. Belmont, Calif.: Thomson Higher Education/ Brooks-Cole, 2007.

Bramer, Daniel, David Wojtowicz, Steven E. Hall, Bob Wilhelmson, Mohan Ramamurthy, and the Department of Atmospheric Sciences at the University of Illinois–Urbana-Champaign. "Superstorm 1993: A Case Study." Available online. URL: http://ww2010.atmos.uiuc.edu/(Gh)/arch/cases/930312/home.rxml. Updated on September 13, 1997.

Kocin, P. J., P. N. Schumacher, R. F. Morales, Jr., and L. W. Uccellini. "Overview of the 12–14 March 1993 Superstorm." *Bulletin of the American Meteorological Society* 76, no. 2 (February 1995): 165–182.

1993 ◆ RAID ON BRANCH DAVIDIAN COMPOUND

An assault by federal officials turned a Branch Davidian settlement near Waco, Texas, on April 19, 1993, into a fiery inferno that killed about 82 members of the religious sect, including many children. The incident culminated a siege that had begun on February 25 when agents of the Bureau of Alcohol, Tobacco, and Firearms (ATF), an agency of the U.S. Treasury Department, raided the Branch Davidians' compound in an attempt to search for illegal firearms and explosive devices and to arrest the group's leader, David Koresh. Federal agents had surrounded the compound and demanded that Koresh and his followers surrender, but the confrontation ended in a gun battle in which four ATF agents and six Branch Davidians were killed. After a 51-day standoff, federal officials launched a military-style assault that reduced the compound to charred rubble.

Born Vernon Howell, David Koresh was a high school dropout who at times claimed to be Jesus Christ. He had joined the Branch Davidians in the 1970s and assumed its leadership in 1987. The Branch Davidians are an offshoot of the Davidians, a religious sect that had split from the Seventh-Day Adventists in the 1930s. Branch Davidians believe that this world belongs to Satan and that it will soon end. Federal law-enforcement officials regarded the Branch Davidians as a criminal organization that paraded under the guise of religion. This was the basis of the ATF's attempt to search the Davidian settlement.

The Federal Bureau of Investigation (FBI) assumed control of the situation after the shoot-out and prepared to wait out the crisis. During the stalemate, Koresh told the authorities that he would surrender. When he did not, some members who had left the compound, stated that Koresh believed his group was fated to engage in a fiery confrontation with officials, an event that would signal the end of the world. During the siege, Koresh made several extravagant and often incoherent prophecies.

After weeks of fruitless negotiations, federal authorities assaulted the compound on April 19. Armored vehicles punched large holes in the side of the structure of the compound and sprayed tear gas for hours, hoping to flush out the holdouts inside. By afternoon, several buildings in the compound burst into flames. The main building, an expansive wooden structure, burned to the ground in 30 minutes with nearly all the remaining church members, including Koresh, still inside.

Argument subsequently ensued between FBI agents and surviving cult members concerning who started the fires. The FBI claimed the cult members set the fires on Koresh's orders. Branch Davidians stated that Koresh had no plans for mass suicide and that the fires must have been caused by the government's assault tactics. A government investigation of the incident released in October 1993 supported the FBI's position. A prior report, however, issued in September, had sharply criticized the ATF for mishandling the February raid, charging that supervising agents on the scene ordered the attack to proceed despite knowledge that the cultists knew about an impending raid. ATF officers were accused of covering up their mistakes. Treasury Secretary Lloyd M.

FACTBOX

PLACE Waco, Texas

DATE February 25–April 19, 1993

TYPE Federal assault on a religious sect

DESCRIPTION After a 51-day standoff following a gun battle between federal agents and the Branch Davidians, who had blocked a federal search of their settlement, the FBI assaulted the compound, and several structures burst into flames.

CAUSE Fire of unknown origins destroyed the main building that housed the Branch Davidians.

CASUALTIES Approximately 92 deaths: six members of the Branch Davidians and four federal agents killed during the shootout on February 25; approximately 82 members of the Branch Davidians killed during the FBI raid on April 19.

IMPACT The raid heightened fears among survivalists, private militias, and religious sects of growing federal power.

Bentsen, Jr., replaced ATF Director Stephen E. Higgins and suspended five officials who had directed the raid. Some observers criticized the October report as a whitewash because it exonerated Attorney General Janet Reno, who had consented to the FBI request to launch an assault.

The assault represented one of several incidents in the early 1990s involving religious sects, survivalists, and private militias fearful of growing federal authority. Two years after the Waco raid, terrorist Timothy McVeigh cited the siege as part of his motivation for the OKLAHOMA CITY BOMBING. Some religious writers believe that Koresh was following the Sixth Seal of the Seven Seals of the Book of Revelation that Babylon would be destroyed in a fiery inferno. For Koresh, perhaps, Waco became a self-fulfilling prophecy.

Frank T. Colon

FURTHER READING:
Faubion, James D. *The Shadows and Lights of Waco: Millennialism Today.* Princeton, N.J.: Princeton University Press, 2001.

1993 ◆ MISSISSIPPI RIVER FLOOD

Flooding in the upper and middle Mississippi River valley devastated the region from April to August 1993, causing the greatest and costliest flood in American history. Before the waters receded, nearly $20 billion in economic damage occurred, hundreds of levees broke, 10,000 homes were totally destroyed, 100,000 more suffered damage, and 52 individuals lost their lives. Only the great MISSISSIPPI RIVER FLOOD of 1927 rivals the scale of this devastation. But 1993 also brought other weather disasters, especially in the Southeast, which suffered drought and a heat wave.

The flood of the millennium started in the winter of 1992–93. Heavy fall rains saturated the soil, and harsh temperatures froze the land to unusual depths. Such conditions left little room for the natural spring runoff, let alone any extraordinary precipitation. However, extraordinary precipitation started early in 1993 with exceptionally heavy snowfalls throughout the upper Midwest, and extraordinary precipitation continued in the months to come.

For example, portions of eastern Iowa received 48 inches of rain between April and August 1993, while the traditionally dry Dakotas contributed 12 inches of precipitation to the drainage basin from June through August. Massive rainfall also hit Kansas, Nebraska, Wisconsin, Minnesota, Missouri, Illinois, and Indiana. Rainfall totals for the upper Midwest were approximately two to three-and-a-half times above normal for the four months between April and July 1993.

Scholars have suggested the reasons for the spring/summer deluge lie with unusual weather patterns, including a stationary high-level trough that established itself over the interior West and upper Midwest. Simultaneously, southerly low-level winds poured a flow of moist air from the Gulf of Mexico into the Midwest. As the two flows met above the upper Midwest, continuous, drenching rains fell, ultimately making their way to the Mississippi River. By June, the streams of the upper Midwest flowed bank high. With continuing persistent rains of the early summer, the tributar-

FACTBOX
PLACE Upper Mississippi River basin: North Dakota, South Dakota, Iowa, Minnesota, Nebraska, Wisconsin, Missouri, Illinois, Kansas, and Indiana
DATE April through August 1993
TYPE Flood
DESCRIPTION The greatest flood in recorded American history devastated the upper Midwest, resulting in vast financial and human cost.
CAUSE Unusual weather patterns, anomalous rainfall, and soil saturation in the river basin
CASUALTIES 52 deaths
COST Estimated $20 billion
IMPACT Long-term environmental damage, including soil erosion, chemical spills in fields, and hypoxic conditions in the Gulf of Mexico

ies to the Mississippi filled in Minnesota, Wisconsin, Iowa, Missouri, North and South Dakota, and Illinois. The waters then drained into the Mississippi River, leading to a flood that is rivaled only by the great flood of 1927 in terms of its duration, the square miles flooded, persons displaced, crop and property damage, and number of record river levels. In some categories, it surpassed the famed flood 66 years earlier.

River cities all along the upper Mississippi River set new records for flooding. From the Quad Cities of Iowa and Illinois (Bettendorf, Davenport, Moline, and Rock Island) to Hannibal and St. Louis, Missouri, the river rose to heights never before seen. The major tributaries flooded as well, leaving communities such as Kansas City, Missouri, on the Missouri River and Hardin, Illinois, on the Illinois River with flood levels beyond even old-timers' memories. Des Moines, Iowa, on the Raccoon River crested at seven feet over its previous all-time record. Due to the flooding, the city's water-treatment plant was forced to close, leaving its 250,000 citizens without potable water for 12 days. Alton, Illinois, and St. Joseph, Missouri, also lost their water-treatment plants to high water.

Floodwaters displaced people and destroyed homes all along the upper portion of the Mississippi River. While 10,000 homes were totally ruined by the flood, another 100,000 incurred significant damage, generally to groundwater or sewer backup. The number of displaced persons remains unknown due to some individuals leaving peremptorily, some staying away only a day or two, and others residing with friends and family members for months. At least 52 individuals lost their lives to the flood of 1993.

As the floodwaters stayed high for weeks, and even months in some areas, the pressure on the levees protecting farm fields, small towns, and large cities finally gave way to the pressures placed upon them. Forty of the 226 federal levees in the river basin either failed or were overtopped, as did 1,043 of 1,345 nonfederal levees. Breaks in the levees not only flooded towns but also farmland. Of the 17 million acres flooded—an area larger than the entire state of West Virginia—slightly more than 10 million acres of farmland submerged beneath the brackish water. More than 35 million acres could not be planted in 1993 due to flooded or saturated fields. Agricultural losses, not including real property, exceeded $5 billion. Nearly every variety of farm animal perished in the rising waters.

Also thrown asunder were the nation's transportation systems. Barge traffic all but ended on the Missouri and Mississippi Rivers during the summer of 1993. More than 5,000 barges halted in place on a 600-mile portion of the Mississippi River with an estimated $3 million per day in lost revenues accruing. Similarly, a 535-mile stretch of the Missouri River closed from its confluence with the Mississippi River to Sioux City, Iowa.

Airports and railroads suffered as well. At least 11 commercial airports closed for a portion of the flood, and more than 4,000 miles of railroad track were either flooded or idled due to the waters, accruing more than $200 million in damages and lost revenue. Given the damages to so many sectors of the economy, many regions were declared

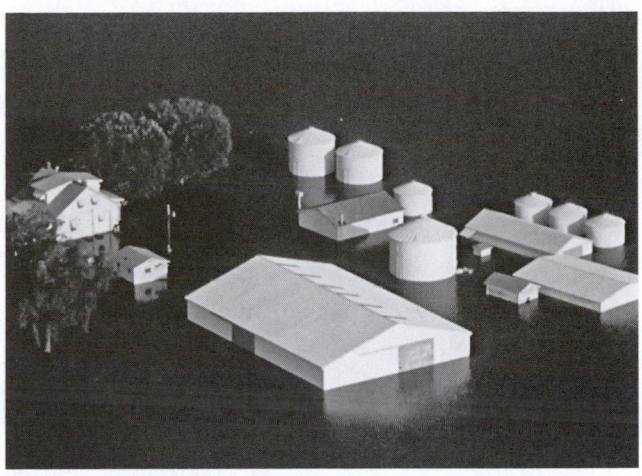

A farm in Missouri sits submerged in water during the Mississippi River flood of 1993, one of the most devastating floods in U.S. history. *(© Les Stone/Sygma/Corbis)*

federal disaster areas, including the entire state of Iowa, 62 percent of Missouri, 58 percent of Wisconsin and North Dakota, 52 percent of South Dakota, 46 percent of Nebraska, 25 percent of Illinois, and 22 percent of Kansas.

Estimates of the financial damages wrought by the Mississippi River flood of 1993 accrued to approximately $20 billion. This figure included not only lost homes and businesses but also lost crops and transportation and approximations of lost financial opportunities owning to the flood itself and efforts to withstand it. No dollar figure can be determined for the long-term impact to the natural environment: erosion, fields damaged by chemical spills, or warm, nutrient-rich water reaching the Gulf of Mexico resulting in hypoxic conditions.

Kimberly K. Porter

FURTHER READING:

Josephson, D. H. "The Great Midwest Flood of 1993: Natural Disaster Survey Report." Silver Spring, Md.: National Oceanic and Atmospheric Administration, National Weather Service, 1994.

Larson, Lee. "The Great USA Flood of 1993." Paper presented at the IAHS Conference, Anaheim, Calif.: June 24–28, 1996. Available online. URL: http://www.nwrfc.noaa.gov/floods/papers/oh_2/great.htm. Downloaded April 10, 2007.

1995 ◆ OKLAHOMA CITY BOMBING

At 9:02 A.M. on April 19, 1995, a truck bomb exploded outside of the nine-story Alfred P. Murrah Federal Building in Oklahoma City. The blast was tremendous in its power and devastating in its effects. It destroyed the Murrah building, with its north side turned instantly into a pile of rubble. As a result, 168 people lost their lives, and hundreds were injured. That death toll made this bombing the worst single act of domestic terrorism in U.S. history. Among those killed were 19 children at America's Kids Day Care, housed on the second floor of the building. The horror of this event was, in fact, encapsulated with a picture of firefighter Chris Fields carrying the body of one of these children, one-year-old Baylee Almon, from the building. The rescue operation itself proved exceptionally difficult given falling debris, a bomb threat, and late afternoon rain, with one rescuer, Rebecca Anderson, killed on this day. Rescue efforts continued until May 4.

On the afternoon of the bombing, President Bill Clinton labeled the act one of "cowardice" and "evil." He promised that the federal government would "find the people who did this" and exact "swift, certain, and severe" justice. Unbeknown to the president and the country at the time, the chief perpetrator of this act, Timothy McVeigh, was already behind bars. State Trooper Charlie Hanger had arrested McVeigh that morning, about 60 miles north of Oklahoma City, on a weapons charge after noticing that McVeigh's car lacked license tags. Fast and good detective work enabled the authorities to realize that McVeigh was "their man" before his release.

Just two blocks from the detonation point, federal agents had quickly discovered a twisted scrap of metal bearing the vehicle identification number of a Ryder rental truck which had contained the bomb. With the identification number, investigators were able to trace the truck ultimately to a shop in Junction City, Kansas, where two men had rented it. These men became known as John Does #1 and #2. While these men had used false identification, the clerk was able to provide a description of them. Armed with the sketches, federal agents soon discovered that John Doe #1 had stayed at a local motel and had identified himself as Timothy McVeigh. When that name was

run through their database, agents noted the recent arrest. The search for John Doe #2 and any other accomplices did not go as easily. The address on McVeigh's license led agents to James Nichols's farm in Decker, Michigan. Terry Nichols, the brother of James, was an army buddy of McVeigh's and would later be implicated in the bombing. However, neither the Nichols brothers nor Michael Fortier, another army buddy of McVeigh's who later admitted knowledge of the plot, matched the description of John Doe #2, whose identity remains a mystery.

One important clue to McVeigh's motive comes from the date of the attack itself, April 19. It was on that date in 1993 that federal agents had initiated a RAID ON THE BRANCH DAVIDIAN COMPOUND in Waco, Texas, after a 51-day siege. Eighty Davidians, including 21 children, and four Alcohol, Tobacco and Firearms agents were killed in the raid as the Davidians set fire to the premises. Antigovernment groups blamed the federal government for the deaths. According to acquaintances, McVeigh was especially irate about Waco. This incident convinced many in antigovernment groups that the U.S. government was engaged in a conspiracy to disarm the populace and turn the country over to foreigners. To protect their rights from this perceived threat, many adherents of this view formed militias. The Nichols brothers associated with one such militia in Michigan and introduced a willing McVeigh to it. Following his release from the army in 1991 after failing to qualify for Special Forces, McVeigh reportedly became obsessed with guns and feared the government's intent to disarm him.

While estimates vary, the militias numbered about 100,000 people in 30 states at this time and peaked at approximately 858 groups in 1996. These groups tended to be survivalist, strongly supportive of gun rights, and fearful of government conspiracies and the United Nations. Many had racist or anti-Semitic overtones. In fact, the Oklahoma City bombing was remarkably similar to a fictional attack portrayed in *The Turner Diaries,* a novel by white supremacist William Pierce that sympathetically describes the story of a group engaged in terrorist acts against a Jewish-controlled U.S. government. In the book, a truck fertilizer bomb destroys a federal building. McVeigh's bomb contained 4,800 pounds of ammonium nitrate fertilizer mixed with fuel oil. What is more, McVeigh had a copy of *The Turner Diaries* with him when he was arrested and spoke highly of the book to his friends. Because April 19 also happens to be Patriot's Day, celebrating the start of the Revolutionary War, some speculate that McVeigh hoped to spark a revolution similar to the one in the book with this attack.

On the contrary, however, one consequence of this crime was to discredit the militias, which experienced a decline in membership in subsequent years. At first, however, the attack was blamed not on domestic extremists but on foreigners, specifically foreign Muslims. In its immediate aftermath, mosques were vandalized, and Muslims were physically assaulted in the United States. Interestingly, the antiterror legislation that President Clinton signed on April 24, 1996, mainly focused on immigration and external terrorist threats. That legislation, formally known as the Anti-Terrorism and Effective Death Penalty Act, streamlined the deportation process for noncitizens convicted of crimes and made it easier for the federal government to deny entry to foreigners. Not solely focused on foreign terror, the bill had several other provisions, including limitations on federal appeals in death penalty cases and expansion of federal jurisdiction over terrorism.

The Alfred P. Murrah Federal Building in Oklahoma City lay in ruins after terrorists exploded a truck bomb on April 19, 1995. *(New York Public Library)*

In the criminal case against Timothy McVeigh, lead prosecutor Joseph Hartzler convinced a jury to convict McVeigh of 11 counts of murder, conspiracy, and using a weapon of mass destruction. Sentenced to death on August 15, 1997, McVeigh became the first federal prisoner executed in 38 years on June 11, 2001. A federal judge sentenced Terry Nichols to life in prison on July 5, 1998, after his conviction on manslaughter charges. Although the state of Oklahoma tried and convicted Nichols of multiple counts of murder in 2004, a deadlocked jury did not sentence him to death.

Despite McVeigh's swift capture, the Oklahoma City bombing shattered any sense of invulnerability held by the people at home. If a bombing could happen in the nation's heartland, people reasoned, it could happen anywhere, anytime. Physical changes at federal facilities across the country reminded its citizens of this newfound threat. The most significant and symbolic of these was the closure of a section of Pennsylvania Avenue in front of the White House to vehicular traffic.

In Oklahoma City, a new federal facility opened a block from the old one in 2004. At the site of the bombing, a memorial now stands for the victims. That memorial includes 168 stone chairs, one for each victim, with the children's chairs smaller than the others. It additionally includes a reflecting pool, with two monuments or entryways on each side. One notes the time as 9:01 and the other 9:03, with the pool symbolizing 9:02, the time of transformation from an ordinary day to catastrophe.

Julie Walsh

FURTHER READING:

Linenthal, Edward T. *The Unfinished Bombing: Oklahoma City in American Memory.* New York: Oxford University Press, 2001.

Oklahoma Bombing Investigation Committee. *Final Report on the Bombing of the Alfred P. Murrah Building,* 2001.

Serrano, Richard. *One of Ours: Timothy McVeigh and the Oklahoma City Bombing.* New York: W. W. Norton, 1998.

1995 ◆ FEDERAL GOVERNMENT SHUTDOWN

A deadlock between President Bill Clinton and Republicans in the House of Representatives over the budget led to two shutdowns of the federal government in 1995–96, the longest such episode in U.S. history. The first six-day shutdown in November 1995 affected 800,000 workers across the country, or roughly half of the federal workforce. The second shutdown at the end of the year, which lasted almost three weeks, caused about a third as many to stay home. The impact of these extraordinary events influenced Clinton's approach to domestic policy for the remainder of his presidency.

The shutdown resulted from the government's lack of authority to spend money in fiscal year 1996, which began October 1, 1995. Because Congress had not finished work on all of the 13 appropriations bills for the new fiscal year, a continuing resolution had been necessary to keep the government funded and operating. That continuing resolution expired November 14, sparking the first shutdown. The lack of spending authority, in turn, resulted from a political "game of chicken," as one observer put it, played out between congressional Republicans and Democrat Bill Clinton. Republicans, who had gained control of both houses of Congress in the 1994 midterm elections, wished to capitalize on their advantage by compelling the president to sign off on a series of conservative budgetary reforms, including a cap on the growth of Medicare and agreement on a plan to balance the federal budget in seven years. The president refused to sign a budget bill that included the Republicans' demands, declaring that Speaker of the House Newt Gingrich and congressional Republicans had put "ideology ahead of common sense and shared values."

During the first shutdown, only nonessential government employees were sent home. Air traffic controllers and the Coast Guard remained on the job, for example, and postal workers still delivered mail. New applicants for Social Security, however, were forced to wait for processing, passport offices were shut, and government medical research was put on hold. National parks and museums were closed. In the nation's capital, roughly 150,000 workers were affected.

The shutdown ended November 19 with a temporary compromise. President Clinton accepted commitment to the Republican aim of balancing the federal budget by 2002, and Congress accepted that the budget must include sufficient funding for social programs such as Medicaid, education, and environmental protection. The November agreement, however, was temporary and only resulted in another continuing resolution until December 15, the new deadline for completing the budget.

A month later, Republican congressional leaders and President Clinton remained at an impasse concerning the balanced-budget plan. Republicans refused to pass another temporary spending bill unless the president made a proposal that included serious budget cuts. The president said that deep cuts in Medicare and Medicaid were unacceptable. With six of the 13 annual appropriations bills still uncompleted, another partial shutdown of the government began December 16 and lasted into the first week of the new year. Some 760,000 federal workers did not receive their full pay during the shutdown (though Congress eventually approved back pay for them), and nearly 100,000 applied for unemployment benefits.

By January 1996, the congressional Republicans' shutdown gambit had produced a decidedly mixed payoff. President Clinton had acceded to their demands for a seven-year balanced budget plan that incorporated the less optimistic economic estimates of the Congressional Budget Office and thus forced the administration to consider more serious cuts in order to reach balance. Indeed, in his State of the Union address in January 1996, Clinton announced that the "era of big government is over." But the public disapproved of Congress's handling of the issue by nearly four-to-one, while the president's overall approval rating remained at about 50 percent. By the end of January, Republicans had abandoned thoughts of further government shutdowns and agreed to a series of continuing resolutions, eventually 13 in all, that kept the government running while they negotiated with the president.

FACTBOX

PLACE Washington, D.C.

DATE November 1995–January 1996

TYPE Political crisis over federal budget

DESCRIPTION During this two-month period, parts of the federal government closed for several weeks due to lack of funding. Hundreds of thousands of federal employees were affected, and many government services were interrupted.

CAUSE Deadlocked on federal spending issues, the Republican-led Congress and Democrat Bill Clinton both decided to let the government close rather than make unacceptable concessions.

IMPACT Republicans eventually made President Clinton commit to a balanced budget as well as cuts in spending but faced severe public disapproval as a result of their actions.

Nearly seven months after the fiscal year began, President Clinton signed a $160 billion spending bill that put the 1996 budget to bed. Republicans succeeded in cutting $23 billion in discretionary spending from the budget, though they compromised with the president on restoring some funding for some education, child care, and environmental protection programs. Thanks in large part to a booming national economy, the goal of a balanced budget actually was achieved ahead of schedule in 1998. But the budget imbroglio had dealt a body blow to the Clinton administration, which thereafter responded with caution and restraint on domestic issues.

Dante J. Scala

FURTHER READING:

Rubin, Irene. *Balancing the Federal Budget: Eating the Seed Corn or Trimming the Herds?* Washington, D.C.: CQ Press, 2002.

———. *The Politics of Public Budgeting: Getting and Spending, Borrowing and Balancing.* New York: Seven Bridges Press, 2000.

Schick, Allen. *The Federal Budget: Politics, Policy, Process.* Washington, D.C.: Brookings Institution Press, 2000.

1996 ◆ EXPLOSION OF TWA FLIGHT 800

On the evening of July 17, 1996, 212 passengers bound for Paris gathered at Gate 27 of the Trans World Airlines (TWA) terminal at Kennedy Airport (JFK) in New York City for a transatlantic crossing on TWA flight 800. In less than two hours, everyone onboard the flight would be dead in the most publicized air disaster in U.S. history. A catastrophic explosion of the central fuel tank likely destroyed the aircraft, which plunged into the ocean and snuffed out the lives of 230 people. Despite a monumental effort to reconstruct the shredded aircraft and a lengthy investigation, the full cause of the disaster remains undetermined.

The doomed aircraft was a Boeing 747–100, bearing tail number N93119. The plane had been one of the first 747s to fly, put in use by TWA in late 1971. Number 93119 had flown more than 93,000 miles prior to July 17. The craft had started the day at Hellenikon Airport in Athens and arrived at JFK airport as TWA 881 in New York City shortly after 5:00 P.M., one hour late. The aircraft was scheduled to depart JFK for Paris as Flight 800 at 7:00 P.M. Baggage problems delayed takeoff until 8:18 P.M.

The pilot had logged 5,000 hours on 747s, but this flight was his first flight as captain of a 747. An instructor-pilot with 2,800 hours as captain flew as copilot. Two flight engineers and 14 attendants made up the rest of the crew, and many of the flight's 212 passengers were TWA employees. Takeoff was routine. Flight 800 followed a route over the Atlantic south of Long Island, climbing at 287 miles per hour and then increasing its speed to 344 miles per hour. By 8:25 P.M., ground supervision of the flight had been passed to controllers in Boston, who gave permission to climb to 13,000 feet; they raised the ceiling to 15,000 feet five minutes later. At 8:31, the aircraft reached 13,760 feet at 40 degrees 40 minutes north latitude and 73:39 west longitude.

Moments later, an explosion engulfed the plane, shredding the fuselage and dispersing bodies and debris over a wide area. The aircraft disaster would immediately be known through witnesses on the ground, on water, and in the air, as well as the tracking of the radar system. Within an hour, boats hoping to conduct rescue operations arrived on the scene

FACTBOX
PLACE Over the Atlantic Ocean, east of Kennedy Airport, south of Long Island, at an altitude of 13,760 feet
DATE July 17, 1996
TYPE Airplane explosion
DESCRIPTION En route from New York to Paris, TWA Flight 800 exploded in midair, killing everyone onboard.
CAUSE Most likely a spark, perhaps from the plane's wiring, ignited vapors in the central fuel tank.
CASUALTIES 230 deaths (212 passengers and 18 crew members)
IMPACT Ten years after the crash, the Federal Aviation Administration proposed a rule that would order the installation of systems to reduce the risk of fuel tank explosions.

some 10 miles off East Moriches in Suffolk County. There were no signs of life anywhere; dead bodies were evident in the water. By daybreak, some 100 dead had been taken to a mortuary in East Moriches. It was obvious to rescuers that there were no survivors. Relatives of the passengers were beginning to gather at JFK and nearby motels.

Recent terrorist activities, including the bomb explosion aboard Pan American Flight 103 over Lockerbie, Scotland, in December 1988, the WORLD TRADE CENTER BOMBING in Lower Manhattan in February 1993, and the destruction of an American military residence at Khobar Towers in Saudi Arabia in June 1996, immediately raised the suspicion the explosion was the work of terrorists. This supposition was reinforced by the ongoing trial in New York of the alleged (later convicted) mastermind of the 1993 World Trade Center bombing.

Two government agencies, the Federal Bureau of Investigation (FBI) and the National Transportation Safety Board (NTSB), played major roles in the investigation of the accident. Suspicions that terrorists caused the explosion led the FBI to dominate the early stage of the probe. The investigation included a long, arduous process of salvaging flight 800's elements, many of which were on the ocean floor. Eventually, nearly every part (98 percent) of the plane was retrieved, and the aircraft was meticulously reassembled at Calverton hangar on Long Island. After checking various leads that a bomb or a missile had brought the aircraft down, the FBI found no evidence to substantiate these claims.

The NTSB is the agency responsible for determining the cause of aircraft accidents. Its investigators established that the explosion occurred in the central fuel tank, one of three on the plane. At takeoff, Flight 800's central tank was almost empty, with only 50 gallons of fuel remaining. The two wing tanks contained sufficient fuel to make the trip to Paris. Virtually empty, the central fuel tank posed an extremely small risk of an explosion triggered by a static electricity spark. Nonetheless, the NTSB investigation concluded that a spark had ignited the vapors in the center fuel tank, causing the explosion. The NTSB speculated that the source of the spark lay somewhere in the plane's wiring. To reduce the possibility of such explosions, safety experts had suggested the installation of nitrogen in all 747s' fuel tanks. This safeguard, called Onboard Inert Gas Generating System, had been under study for some time for commercial planes and was installed on military aircraft. The NTSB suggested keeping the center fuel tanks filled on eastbound transatlantic flights, shutting off the air conditioning while the aircraft rested on the tarmac, and using inert nitrogen as an additive to fuel. The Federal Aviation Administration (FAA) did not accept the recommendations but instituted other procedures including a review of fuel tank design on commercial aircraft.

Despite the massive and prolonged investigations of the TWA Flight 800 disaster, the failure to provide a definitive explanation for the cause of the explosion left many of the families of the victims in a state of suspended grief. Lacking a final resolution of the disaster, many relatives were critical of the various inquiries. In 2006, the FAA proposed a rule that would implement the NTSB's recommendation for safeguarding the fuel tanks on commercial 747s.

Alex Wilson

FURTHER READING:

Milton, Pat. *In the Blink of an Eye.* New York: Random House, 1999.

Negroni, Christine. *Deadly Departure.* New York: HarperCollins, 2000.

1999 ◆ COLUMBINE SCHOOL SHOOTING

On April 20, 1999, two teenagers went on a shooting spree at Columbine High School in Littleton, Colorado, and then killed themselves. The rampage at their Jefferson County school in suburban Denver left 15 individuals dead and 24 wounded. Shocking the entire country, the Columbine school shooting prompted a nationwide focus on why school killings occur and how to prevent them, renewed debate on gun control, and raised concerns about how violence in the media was affecting young people. It also, tragically, prompted several copycat killings.

The attack on Columbine High School by Eric Harris, 18, and Dylan Klebold, 17, is considered the deadliest public school shooting in U.S. history and the second deadliest attack on a U.S. school after the May 18, 1927, Bath School disaster. In that episode, a disgruntled school board member named Andrew Kehoe, upset by a tax to help build a new school, bombed the Bath Consolidated School in Bath Township, Michigan, killing 45 people and injuring 58. The Virginia Tech massacre in Blacksburg, Virginia, in which 32 people were murdered on April 16, 2007, by a student who took his own life, occurred on a college campus.

The Columbine attack occurred on the anniversary of Adolf Hitler's birthday and one day after the anniversary of both the Waco disaster (1993),

FACTBOX

PLACE Columbine High School in Littleton, Colorado

DATE April 20, 1999

TYPE School shooting

DESCRIPTION Armed with guns and bombs, two teenaged students went on a killing rampage at their high school.

CASUALTIES 15 deaths (including the two shooters), 24 wounded

IMPACT Nationwide focus on school outcasts who become enraged; heightened school security measures; gun control debate; copycat killings

in which 76 members of the Branch Davidian sect died in a fire after a 51-day standoff with federal officers (see 1993 RAID ON BRANCH DAVIDIAN COMPOUND), and the OKLAHOMA CITY BOMBING (1995). Apparently, Harris and Klebold wanted to do something "bigger" than either of those disasters.

On the morning of the tragedy, Harris and Klebold came to school dressed in long black trenchcoats with an arsenal of guns and homemade bombs they had spent a year amassing. They placed a duffel bag with bombs inside the cafeteria and set them to explode. The bombs had enough power to cause massive destruction in the cafeteria and the library on the floor above. Harris and Klebold waited for the bombs to go off outside in separate cars. Their original plan was to open fire on students fleeing from the explosion. But the bombs did not detonate. Then, at about 11:30 A.M., the teens, armed with sawed-off shotguns and other weapons, started to kill. They shot at students first outside the school and then moved inside, shooting and throwing pipe bombs in hallways, near the cafeteria, and in the library. Students and teachers who could flee the school got out; others hid in bathrooms, storage rooms, or under tables.

On their way to the library, Harris and Klebold shot a teacher, Dave Sanders, as he was trying to lead students to safety. Sanders died later that day. In the library, where 55 students, three library staff, and a teacher were hiding, they terrorized and taunted students, brutally killing several. They returned to the cafeteria, where Harris attempted unsuccessfully to detonate one of the failed bombs. Then they went back upstairs, shooting randomly. They returned to the library, but it had been evacuated of all living students except for two injured students, one unconscious, one playing dead. Harris and Klebold shot out the windows at police officers who had been called to the scene, but they did not hit anyone. Then, roughly 45 minutes after they started their rampage, they shot themselves.

Securing the building took more than four hours. SWAT teams did not know the killers were dead or how many there were, so they took time to search carefully for shooters or bombs. Also, as police escorted shaken and injured students from the building, they checked each one for bombs or weapons. At about 4 P.M., police found the bodies of the two killers with guns in their hands and explosive devices hidden under their coats.

In the wake of the killings, people in the Littleton area and around the nation spent months trying to understand what had motivated Harris and Klebold. Questions arose about whether anything could have been done to prevent the tragedy, whether law enforcement acted properly during the disaster and its aftermath, and what could be done to prevent similar tragedies from occurring in the future. It was learned that Harris and Klebold had become angry and bitter after years of being bullied and scorned. In addition to their arsenal of explosives, ammunition, and weapons, they had also built up an arsenal of rage against some of their classmates: jocks, girls who had rejected them, and others who had insulted them. They had developed a taste for a violent videogame called *Doom* as well as for Nazi culture. They also wanted to be famous.

According to their journals and videotapes, the teens had much more in mind than just shooting up their school. They hoped that after setting off bombs in the cafeteria, they would rampage through the school and shoot any survivors and then continue their attack on surrounding houses. That plan did not materialize because their main explosives did not detonate. But if they had—and if they had survived—they even envisioned hijacking a plane and crashing it into New York City.

In the wake of the tragedy, the Littleton community was wracked with questions and accusations. The Jefferson County sheriff's department was blamed for taking too long to secure the building. Police were also criticized for failing to follow up on pre-attack warnings, such as complaints from one family that Harris had threatened their son and Harris's Internet site that openly discussed his plans to carry out an attack at the high school and gave details of experiments with pipe bombs. Harris and Klebold had been arrested in 1998 for breaking into a van and stealing several items and were also known to police through several other incidents. It also came to light that Harris had told both counselors and a parole officer of his difficulty in controlling violent thoughts. A grand jury investigated whether or not there had been a police cover-up.

In spite of the warning signs—and in spite of the fact that one police officer pursued a potential search warrant of the Harris household—no action was taken ahead of time. Harris and Klebold had apparently convinced the adults around them that they were trying to get on the right track. They had taken care to hide their cache of weapons in their own homes, as well as to deceive their parents.

Lawsuits were filed against school officials, law-enforcement officials, the manufacturer of an anti-depressant that had been prescribed for Harris, gun dealers, friends of the killers who had helped them obtain guns, and the killers' parents. There were nationwide ramifications as well. Schools introduced a host of new security measures, such as see-through backpacks, metal detectors, and security guards. They instituted anti-bully policies and zero tolerance for weapons or threatening behavior. They tried to learn more about behaviors that could alert them to potentially dangerous students. Among educators and policy makers, there was much discussion about high school cliques, bullying, the impact of violent movies and video games on U.S. youth, and teen depression and isolation. Also, police departments worked to beef up training for potential Columbine-like situations.

The Columbine killings also greatly intensified the national debate about gun control. Laws were passed making it a crime to buy guns for criminals and children. The tragedy produced controversy about the ease of buying weapons at gun shows—which was how Klebold and Harris had obtained some of their guns via a friend. There was massive cultural impact as well, as the incident spread like wildfire through the media, inspiring music, literature, a controversial computer game, and films, such as Michael Moore's *Bowling for Columbine*, which examined violence and gun culture in the United States, and the name *Columbine* came to be a word that means, simply, "school shooting."

Karen Feldscher

FURTHER READING:

Hasky, Judy L. *Columbine High School Shooting: Student Violence.* Berkeley Heights, N.J.: Enslow, 2002.

Watson, Justin. *The Martyrs of Columbine: Faith and the Politics of Tragedy.* New York: Palgrave Macmillan, 2002.

2000 ◆ PRESIDENTIAL ELECTION STALEMATE

The U.S. presidential election of 2000 turned out to be too close to call, even after all the votes had been cast. Vice President Al Gore, the Democratic candidate, had won the national popular vote and at one point on election night seemed all but certain to triumph, according to television network projections. But in the wee hours of the morning after election day, the Republican challenger, Texas governor George W. Bush, apparently held a bare majority in the electoral college that decides presidential elections, thanks to his success in carrying Florida and its 25 electoral votes, which gave him 271 electoral votes out of 538.

Early on election night, Tuesday, November 7, exit poll projections indicated that Gore would carry the Sunshine State. A couple hours later, though, the networks' polling agency had retracted its call, and the networks hastily followed. After 2 A.M., the networks called Florida again, this time for Bush. Shortly thereafter, Gore called Bush to concede and prepared to make a concession speech to his supporters. In the meantime, however, the vice president's top campaign operatives realized that the networks once again had called the race prematurely and that Gore actually was pulling even in Florida. Whoever prevailed in Florida would win the presidency. Gore called Bush again, this time to retract his concession. The initial statewide tally showed that Bush was ahead by 1,784 votes out of more than 5.8 million cast.

The next day, Florida election officials automatically began a machine recount because the margin of victory was so close. By the end of the week, Bush's lead had shrunk to 327 votes. Gore and his campaign team believed that more voters in Florida had intended to vote for him than for Bush. In Palm Beach County, for instance, there were widespread reports of Gore voters mistakenly casting ballots for third-party conservative candidate Patrick Buchanan because of the confusing format of that county's "butterfly ballot." These ballots had candidates' names on two facing pages; arrows directed the voter from the names to the punch holes in the center. Gore's campaign officials thought that their candidate could overtake Bush in the Florida vote count if undervotes—ballots on which a vote for president had not been recorded by machine—were examined more closely. They called for a recount by hand in four counties representing about 30 percent of Florida's vote, arguing that every reasonable step should be taken to ensure that all votes were counted. The Bush campaign attempted to stop the hand counts, but the federal courts refused to intervene on its behalf.

The extra votes Gore needed to pull ahead proved elusive. Not all the county boards were eager to conduct a countywide recount. Those that were amenable faced daunting deadlines strictly enforced by Florida's secretary of state, Katherine Harris, a Republican. Harris's goal was to certify the results as quickly as possible, and she made plans to do so on November 18, 11 days after the election. She refused to extend the deadline for recounts in the four counties Gore had targeted. However, the Florida Supreme Court, dominated by Democrats, ordered Harris to delay certification of the results and then ruled unanimously that hand-recounted votes could be submitted to the secretary of state until Sunday, November 26.

As national audiences watched with bemusement on cable-television news programs, county boards began the arduous task of a hand recount. The Florida Supreme Court had stated that the "fundamental purpose" of the state's election laws was to ensure

FACTBOX

PLACE Florida

DATE November 7 (election day)—December 12, 2000

TYPE Disputed election and political crisis

DESCRIPTION Disputes about the certification of presidential ballots in Florida delayed the outcome of the 2000 presidential election until the U.S. Supreme Court blocked further recounts of the votes.

CAUSE Conflict concerning the legitimacy of ballot markings and the processing of absentee ballots

IMPACT George W. Bush became president of the United States. Both Congress and the state of Florida passed legislation to improve voting procedures.

that each voter was able to express his or her will at the polls. Central to the task, then, was discerning the intent of the voter in cases when the physical ballot left that intent open to question. The court, however, did not lay down guidelines for this task, leaving those decisions to county election boards. The ensuing debate introduced the term *chad*—the rectangle punched out by a punch-card voting machine to indicate the voter's choice—into the national vocabulary. In Broward County, for example, the board decided that not only should hanging chads (chads hanging off the ballot by one or two corners) count as proof of voters' intent but also pierced chads and dimpled chads (which only showed an indentation). By the time the Broward recount was complete, Gore had gained 567 votes.

Republicans cried foul at the Florida Supreme Court's decision. James Baker, the representative of the Bush campaign in Florida, accused the court of changing the rules for counting votes "after the game has been played." He strongly suggested that the Bush campaign might ask the Republican-controlled state legislature to rectify the situation. On November 22, Bush took his case to the U.S. Supreme Court, requesting that the Court review the Florida ruling, and on the ground in Miami-Dade County, Republican anger boiled over when the election board moved its proceedings into a room with limited public access. A few dozen protesters (mainly congressional staff members and other volunteers from Washington, D.C., who were down to observe the recount) demanded that the media be allowed access and shouted, "Stop the count! Stop the fraud!" A few hours later, the board decided to halt the recount because it could not meet the November 26 deadline, causing serious damage to the Gore strategy to overtake Bush with hand-recounted votes.

Meanwhile, the Bush campaign had found its own cache of votes as well as a public-relations victory in the absentee ballots that remained to be counted. These ballots included votes from military personnel serving overseas. The Gore campaign, aware that overseas military mostly would vote Republican, decided to follow Florida election law to the letter and challenge all overseas ballots without a postmark. In all, it questioned four of 10 military ballots. Republicans seized on the issue, accusing the Democrats of scheming to prevent servicemen and women from having their votes counted—an especially telling charge given the Gore campaign's insistence that its only goal in the recount was to make sure that all voters had their voices heard. On national television, Democratic vice presidential candidate Joseph Lieberman undercut his campaign's strategy by insisting that he and Gore never would want to put extra burdens on service members overseas who wished to vote. The Gore campaign soon relented, and the overseas absentee ballots padded Bush's overall lead by more than 600 votes.

On November 26, the Sunday after Thanksgiving, Katherine Harris certified Bush as the winner of Florida's election with a lead of 537 votes. Of the four counties where Gore had requested recounts, only two submitted results in time. Palm Beach County was still counting that Sunday, but Harris refused to grant county officials an extension. After Harris's announcement, Bush asserted his victory on television.

Harris's certification, however, ended only the first phase of the postelection process. In the protest phase, Gore only had been able to challenge results in front of the county election boards. Certification concluded this phase and started the contest phase in which Gore could file suit in Florida's Leon County circuit court regarding alleged problems. The judge possessed significant authority to implement solutions necessary to fix the problems as he saw fit. Thus, Gore filed suit the very next day, asking for a recount of thousands of disputed ballots in three Florida counties. On the same day, he gave a speech to the country, asking for continued patience with the ongoing proceedings. Independent of public opinion, the Gore campaign had just a few weeks remaining before federal law stated that Florida's electors had to cast their votes in the electoral college.

Later that week, the transition team for the new Bush administration opened its office for business, and Bush met with Republican congressional leaders at his Texas ranch, and in the U.S. Supreme Court, justices listened to arguments from Bush's lawyers that they should overturn the Florida Supreme Court's decision to authorize recounts. A few days later the Court set aside the Florida court's decision, returning it to the state court for clarification, citing uncertainty as to the grounds for its decision.

On the same day, December 4, Leon County circuit court judge N. Sanders Sauls declined to overturn Bush's certification as the winner of the Florida election. The Gore campaign offered no credible evidence, he stated, that the proposed recounts would change the results. The Gore campaign immediately appealed the decision, and the Florida Supreme Court once again found the dispute under its jurisdiction. Four days later, in a 4-3 vote, the court reversed Sauls's decision, stating that the Florida legislature "expressly recognized the will of the people of Florida as the guiding principle for the selection of all elected officials." The court ordered that all 43,000 "undervotes" in the state of Florida be examined for evidence of voter intent. With just days left before the federal deadline for choosing Florida's electors who would cast the state's votes for president in the electoral college, the Florida Supreme Court ordered the Leon County court to oversee the undervote count. In addition, the Florida court ordered that hand counts already conducted in Florida Palm Beach and Miami-Dade counties be included in the certified results. As a result, as the undervote count began, Bush's lead shrank to fewer than 200 votes. The Bush campaign returned to the U.S. Supreme Court the same day to appeal the decision.

Counting of the "undervotes" began the following day, Saturday, December 9, with plans to finish before the weekend was over. But hours later, in a 5-4 decision, the U.S. Supreme Court ordered a halt to the recount in response to Bush's appeal. Three days later, the Court overturned the Florida Supreme Court, declaring that the recount did not have procedures in place that would ensure that all voters were treated in a nonarbitrary manner. This decision on December 12 awarded Bush the presidency and effectively ended the five-week dispute. Seven justices agreed that because standards for counting punch-card ballots varied from county to county, the process violated both the due process and equal protection clauses of the Constitution. Two of the seven, David Souter and Stephen Breyer, argued that the remedy should be to continue the recount until December 18, the date the electors of the electoral college were scheduled to meet. The other five, however, argued that Florida's electors to the electoral college needed to be chosen by December 12, after which they could be challenged in Congress. As a result of this deadline, the five justices concluded, the recount was impossible to complete.

Dissenters stated that the court had ignored basic constitutional principles by refusing to defer to a state high court's interpretation of its own state's law. "Although we may never know with complete certainty the identity of the winner of this year's Presidential election," wrote Justice John Paul Stevens, "the identity of the loser is perfectly clear. It is the nation's confidence in the judge as an impartial guardian of the rule of law."

The next evening, Gore conceded the election while expressing his disagreement with the court's decision. Shortly afterward, Bush made his belated victory speech, stating that "Our nation must rise above a house divided . . . I was not elected to serve one party, but to serve one nation." Bush's two terms in office, however, were marked by fierce partisanship on both sides of the aisle, despite the temporary unity created in response to the September 11 terrorist attacks. Congress approved funding for improvement of the country's electoral machinery and created standards for election administration. The state of Florida itself spent millions of dollars on new voting machines and instituted reforms such as a statewide voter database, vote-counting standards, and provisional balloting. The possibility of another Florida in some future election, however, remains quite plausible, and public doubt remains about the reliability of the electoral process.

See also 1800–1801 PRESIDENTIAL ELECTION CRISIS; 1824–1825 PRESIDENTIAL ELECTION DEADLOCK; 1876–1877 CONTESTED PRESIDENTIAL ELECTION.

Dante J. Scala

FURTHER READING:

Correspondents of the *New York Times*. *36 Days: The Complete Chronicle of the 2000 Presidential Election Crisis*. New York: Times Books, 2001.

Political Staff of the *Washington Post*. *Deadlock: The Inside Story of America's Closest Election*. New York: PublicAffairs, 2001.

Sabato, Larry, ed. *Overtime! The Election 2000 Thriller*. New York: Longman, 2002.

2001 ◆ 9/11 TERRORIST ATTACK

At 8:46 on the morning of Tuesday, September 11, 2001, American Airlines Flight 11 slammed into the North Tower of the World Trade Center in New York City. It struck the 93rd through 99th floors of the 110-story building, dooming all those trapped on the floors above. Just 17 minutes later, at 9:03, United Airlines Flight 175 crashed into the South Tower, hitting the 78th through 85th floors. If there were any doubts that the first crash was intentional despite the clear skies on this September morning, these doubts were removed with the second. The United States was under attack.

The tragic events of this day, which quickly came to be identified as 9/11, were far from over. Already, American Airlines Flight 77, flying from Washington, D.C., to Los Angeles, had veered from its designated flight plan. At 9:12, Renee May, a flight attendant, used a cell phone to report to her mother that the plane had been hijacked. For the first time ever, at 9:26, the Federal Aviation Administration initiated a national ground stop, forbidding takeoffs and requiring all planes to land as soon as reasonable. At 9:27, Tom Burnett, a passenger on board United Flight 93 flying from Newark to San Francisco, was the first of many to use his cell phone to

FACTBOX

PLACE New York City; Arlington, Virginia; and near Shanksville, Pennsylvania

DATE September 11, 2001

TYPE Terrorist attack

DESCRIPTION Working under the direction of the terrorist group, al-Qaeda, 19 hijackers crashed two planes into the Twin Towers of the World Trade Center, one plane into the Pentagon, and one plane in a field near Shanksville, Pennsylvania.

CASUALTIES At least 2,973 victims died, as well as the 19 hijackers.

IMPACT Transformed U.S. foreign policy to focus on fighting terrorism, led to passage of the USA PATRIOT Act, and led to U.S. invasion of Afghanistan and Iraq

hopelessness of the situation, many jumped from these floors to their death. At 9:59 A.M., less than an hour after it was struck, the South Tower collapsed, spreading dust and debris over downtown Manhattan and the surrounding area. Firefighters and emergency personnel were heading up the steps of the tower to rescue people and were trapped inside when the building fell. The North Tower then collapsed at 10:28 A.M. Ultimately, 343 firefighters, 23 police officers, and 37 Port Authority officers sacrificed their lives. Much later, a full accounting placed the total death toll, including those on the two flights, in New York at 2,759, at least. At the time, however, no one had any idea how many had been killed. Speculation ranged in the tens of thousands. The final death toll for all four attacks was put at 2,973 (plus the 19 hijackers), making it the deadliest attack ever on U.S. soil.

There was also great concern that more attacks were to come. The media aired several false reports about additional hijackings and other attacks. Such

report that this plane too had been hijacked. Flight 77 crashed into the Pentagon in Arlington, Virginia, at 9:37, killing all 64 on board and 125 people on the ground. United Flight 93 crashed in a field near Shanksville, Pennsylvania, some 80 miles southeast of Pittsburgh at approximately 10:06, killing all 44 persons on board. There is evidence that passengers, aware from cell phone conversations of the other crashes, stormed the cockpit, struggled with the hijackers, and thereby prevented this plane from crashing into yet another symbol of America, such as the Capitol.

Four hijackers were aboard Flight 93, while five perpetrators were on board each of the other three planes. Mohamed Atta, the Egyptian who flew Flight 11 into the North Tower of the World Trade Center, was considered the leader of this group of 19. All of the hijackers were of Middle Eastern descent, with 15 tracing their roots to Saudi Arabia. Based on phone calls from passengers, an authorized study concluded that knives, some noxious spray such as mace, and bomb threats were the means used to take over these flights.

On the ground in New York City, it proved impossible to rescue anyone from the floors above the crash impact in both towers. Recognizing the

Airplanes hijacked by terrorists crashed into the two 110-story skyscrapers of the World Trade Center in New York City on September 11, 2001. Both towers collapsed later that morning, killing more than 2,750 people. *(Associated Press)*

The remains of the World Trade Center at Ground Zero, a month after the attack. *(Andrea Booher/FEMA News Photo)*

reports contributed to an atmosphere of terror and hysteria. By 11 A.M., however, all flights were either grounded or complying with restrictions from controllers. American airspace would remain closed until September 13. Across the country, skyscrapers, government buildings, and tourist attractions were evacuated. As might be expected, New York City mayor Rudolph Guiliani, who won plaudits for his actions on this day, ordered the evacuation of Lower Manhattan at 1:02 P.M. The New York Stock Exchange, located just blocks from the World Trade Center, had already closed and would not reopen until September 17.

President George W. Bush, who was visiting an elementary school in Florida at the time of the attacks, spent much of the day in transit. Because of security concerns and possible threats to Air Force One, the president's airplane, which were later disputed, he did not return to Washington, D.C., until 6:54 P.M. and then addressed the nation at 8:30. By this time, Building Seven of the World Trade Center complex had also collapsed. In his address to the nation that

evening, President Bush assured Americans that the functions of government would "continue without interruption" and that the "full resources" of the government would be directed toward finding those responsible for the attack. In this quest, the president noted that the United States "would make no distinction between the terrorists who committed these acts and those who harbor them." In his address to a joint session of Congress the following week, President Bush characterized the attack as an act of war. Already, the North Atlantic Treaty Organization for the first time ever had invoked Article 5 of its charter that said an attack on one member is an attack on all.

In the hours, days, and weeks after the attacks, there was a surge of patriotism across the United States, both in its positive and negative forms. Americans generously donated blood and money to victims' relief funds. Flags could be seen everywhere, on lapels, cars, trucks, and homes. Yet because the hijackers were Muslims, there were attacks on innocent Muslims and Sikhs, mistaken for Muslims. At least nine people were murdered in retaliation for the attacks. The political context was tense as well, with few in the media or opposition party willing to offer critical commentary about the U.S. government's response to the attack.

Almost immediately, experts speculated that the terrorist group, al-Qaeda, was responsible for the attack. Formed by Osama bin Laden in the late 1980s to serve as an organizational base for a radical Islamic crusade, al-Qaeda—its name means "the base"—soon turned its wrath toward the United States. Ironically, bin Laden had tacit American support throughout the 1980s in his struggles against the Soviets, who had invaded Afghanistan in 1979. Bin Laden, who had inherited millions of dollars on his father's death, left his native Saudi Arabia to join the resistance to the Soviet forces in Afghanistan. There he proceeded to impress the guerrillas with his wealth and acquired notoriety among Muslims. Influenced by a radically puritanical and extremist version of Islam called Wahhabism, bin Laden renounced the secular world and called for a return to the original text of the Koran. In so doing, he abandoned the tradition of Islamic scholarship and, according to most, distorted Islamic teaching. All 19 of the hijackers were adherents of this radical version of Islam and willing to sacrifice their lives for it. Because of his beliefs, bin Laden found the presence of American troops in the Muslim holy cities of Mecca and Medina, Saudi Arabia, especially offensive. These troops were stationed there in the aftermath of the 1990–91 Gulf War. Labeling the presence of these troops a crime against Islam itself, he issued a fatwa, or religious ruling, declaring a holy war on "Americans occupying the land of the two holy places" in 1996 and then, via another fatwa, extended that war to all Americans in 1998.

These were not idle threats. On August 7, 1998, terrorists bombed American embassies in Kenya and Tanzania, Africa, killing 224 people. President Bill Clinton responded to these attacks by ordering air strikes against a Sudanese factory and al-Qaeda training camps in Afghanistan, which, after Soviet withdrawal in 1989, was now under the control of the Islamic radicals, the Taliban. At the time, the United States claimed that the Sudanese factory was used to make weapons, but that claim was disputed. U.S. authorities suspected bin Laden's network in other attacks as well, such as the 1993 bombing of the World Trade Center and the 2000 bombing of the USS *Cole,* an American naval ship harbored in Yemen. Clearly, then, bin Laden and al-Qaeda were enemies of the United States well before September 11, 2001. In this sense, the attack was not a complete surprise.

Indeed, in the days and months before September 11, an extraordinary number of warnings were passed to the U.S. government. Many were general in nature, but some threats specifically mentioned the use of planes. Credible sources, such as the British and Russian governments, gave information to the United States about the danger of an impending attack. To understate the matter grossly, controversy exists about the explanation for the lack of sufficient attention to these threats. The State Department issued an alert on September 7, but it identified only overseas facilities and military personnel as potential targets. The presence of these myriad warnings, together with the response time on the morning of September 11, has fueled a plethora of conspiracy theories and alternative explanations. Although some of these are fantastic, weaving stories on the basis of no or faulty evidence, others raise legitimate questions, such as why the second and especially third and fourth planes were not intercepted by fighter jets. After much prodding, specifically by families of those killed in the attack, the government formed a commission to answer such questions and to describe comprehensively the events of the day. Although the National Commission on Terrorist Attacks Upon the United States, known popularly as the 9/11 Commission, issued its findings on July 22, 2004, the report did not end the controversies.

The attacks on September 11, 2001, were quickly identified as transformative events, with modern history henceforward to be categorized into pre-9/11 and post-9/11 periods. Congress immediately provided President Bush with authorization to use "all necessary and appropriate force" against the perpetrators of the attacks, their sponsors, and those who protect them. On October 7, 2001, President Bush acted on this authority and ordered the bombing of Afghanistan, whose Taliban rulers had refused to produce bin Laden. Since Bush had warned that no distinctions would be made between terrorists and those who harbor them, Afghanistan was an obvious target. On the ground, U.S. troops supported the Northern Alliance in its efforts to overthrow the Taliban. By December 17, 2001, the Northern Alliance was able to claim victory and a new ruler, Hamid

Karzai, assumed power shortly thereafter. However, bin Laden and other members of al-Qaeda had escaped into the mountainous region along the Pakistani border. As of this writing, the new regime in Afghanistan confronts insurgents who are attempting to restore Taliban rule in the border regions.

To be sure, hundreds of Taliban and al-Qaeda fighters were captured in the course of the war in Afghanistan. The treatment of these detainees soon became a controversial issue, as the Bush administration refused to apply to them the Geneva Conventions, a series of treaties that dictate conditions for prisoners of war. Claiming that these individuals were "unlawful enemy combatants," the Bush administration ultimately held many of them at the U.S. military base at Guantánamo Bay, Cuba. Additionally, the administration authorized the use of interrogation techniques that would be classified as torture under international laws, such as the 1984 Convention Against Torture. To justify the treatment of these detainees, including plans to try them in military tribunals, the administration relied on the congressional authorization to use force against the 9/11 perpetrators. Opponents of these policies, including some members of Congress, contested this interpretation. In June 2006, the Supreme Court, in a 5-3 ruling, agreed with the administration's critics and declined to accept either this interpretation of the authorization or the treatment itself. However, acceptable rules for the treatment and disposition of the remaining detainees have yet to be determined.

In the United States, too, well over 1,000 immigrants were rounded up and secretly detained in the weeks following the attack. On October 26, 2001, Congress passed sweeping legislation, known as the USA PATRIOT Act (an acronym for Uniting and Strengthening America by Providing Appropriate Tools Required to Intercept and Obstruct Terrorism), that enhanced executive authority and specifically provided more discretion to the attorney general in detaining immigrants. While the bill passed with large majorities, a number of provisions proved controversial. For example, authorities were given permission to search suspects' home without giving notice of such searches. Those sections expanding the surveillance powers of the government had "sunset provisions," or expiration dates, but most were subsequently renewed. Given the climate of fear at this time, public opinion polls indicated strong support for this enhancement of executive authority.

To protect the United States better from another attack, the government created the Department of Homeland Security. When Congress formalized this largest reorganization of government in contemporary history on November 25, 2002, the newly created department, led by former Pennsylvania governor Thomas Ridge, consolidated nearly 170,000 workers from 22 agencies, including the Customs Service, federal security guards in airports, and the Coast Guard, but not the FBI or the CIA. The omission of these two agencies, central players in preventing terrorism, led many to question how effective the new department would be in centralizing information and overcoming turf wars. One of the main features of this reorganization was the change in status of airport screeners from private to public employees. This new arrangement was intended to enhance airport security.

Additionally, Congress passed a $1.5 billion federal aid package to help the airlines financially in the aftermath of the attacks and also established a fund to compensate the relatives of those killed in the attacks so long as they waived their rights to sue the airlines or other parties. It was not only the airline industry that needed economic help after the attacks. The entire economy of Lower Manhattan had ground to a virtual halt. When the New York Stock Exchange reopened on September 17, it experienced its largest one-day point drop ever of 678.52 (though this was not among the top 10 biggest daily percentage drops). Property damage from the attacks exceeded $20 billion. Many service workers lost their jobs. Later, it was learned that those in lower Manhattan also were subjected to unhealthy air from the dust and debris. This particularly affected those working at the site itself, known as Ground Zero.

The immediate consequences of the 9/11 attack were thus clearly monumental. Beyond direct effects, this attack transformed the political context as well and played an important role in the onset of the Iraq War. Prior to September 11, President Bush had a weak mandate given the contested nature of his election in 2000. With this attack, citizens rallied behind him, and his approval ratings soared. He used that political capital to make the case for expanding the war against al-Qaeda and the Taliban to Iraq. In his 2002 State of the Union address, he alluded to an "axis of evil" comprised of Iraq, Iran, and North Korea. In the following year, the administration focused on Saddam Hussein's Iraq, arguing that it had weapons of mass destruction and links to terrorist groups, possibly al-Qaeda. Bush sought to invade Iraq to preempt it from attacking the United States or its allies with weapons of mass destruction, but he was unable to win support from the United Nations. Indicative of its willingness to act unilaterally, the United States, together with a few allies, nonetheless invaded Iraq on March 20, 2003. Arguably, Congress and the American people were much more receptive to Bush's rationale of preemptive attack in the aftermath of September 11. No weapons of mass destruction were found in Iraq, and no ties to al-Qaeda were ever conclusively proven. Given those facts, the large number of American deaths, and the lack of an exit strategy, the Iraq war proved controversial. Whatever the final outcome, it is sure to have long-term ramifications for the distribution of power in the Middle East.

It remains to be seen if the trends unleashed, such as the enhancement of executive authority and unilateralism in foreign policy, as a result of September 11, will continue unabated. Amid the controversies about those policies, it is important to remember the magnitude of the tragedy that took place that day. For the 2,973 known victims, life ended on September 11, 2001, and for all of their loved ones, life would never be the same.

Julie Walsh

FURTHER READING:

Coll, Steve. *Ghost Wars: The Secret History of the CIA, Afghanistan, and Bin Laden, from the Soviet Invasion to September 10, 2001.* New York: Penguin, 2004.

Dudziak, Mary L., ed. *September 11 in History: A Watershed Moment?* Durham, N.C.: Duke University Press, 2003.

Kean, Thomas H., and Lee Hamilton. *Without Precedent: The Inside Story of the 9/11 Commission.* New York: Knopf, 2006.

Leone, Richard C., and Greg Anrig, Jr., eds. *The War on Our Freedoms: Civil Liberties in an Age of Terrorism.* New York: Century Foundation, 2003.

McDermott, Terry. *Perfect Soldiers: The Hijackers.* New York: HarperCollins, 2005.

National Commission on Terrorist Attacks Upon the United States. *The 9/11 Commission Report.* New York: W. W. Norton, 2004.

Thompson, Paul, and the Center for Cooperative Research. *The Terror Timeline.* New York: HarperCollins, 2004.

Wright, Lawrence. *The Looming Tower: Al Qaeda and the Road to 9/11.* New York: Knopf, 2006.

2001 ◆ ENRON SCANDAL

The fall of Enron in late 2001 produced the biggest corporate bankruptcy in American history. From its inauspicious origins as a mid-sized energy pipeline company in 1986, Enron reinvented itself into a global energy-trading conglomerate over the next 15 years. By 2001, it had been transformed into a giant with $70 billion in market value and sales that ranked it seventh among American corporations. Its stock price made the corporation the darling of Wall Street. *Fortune* magazine called Enron the most innovative company in the country. Enron symbolized the go-go atmosphere of the 1990s, when stock prices soared and bigger and bigger corporate mergers were daily headlines. By the same token, Enron's fall mirrored the implosion of the stock market and the wave of accounting scandals in 2001–02. Enron's bankruptcy led to criminal convictions for numerous individuals, financial devastation for thousands of Enron employees, and new accounting standards for Americans corporations.

Enron's story is entwined with the aspirations of Kenneth Lay, who built the corporation and infused its employees with a mission of the firm's potential greatness. Born in Tyrone, Missouri, in 1942, Lay earned a Ph.D. in economics from the University of Houston and went to work for a pipeline company in

FACTBOX

PLACE Houston, Texas

DATE December 2001

TYPE Corporate scandal

DESCRIPTION Enron corporation declared bankruptcy, and its top executives were convicted of accounting fraud and securities conspiracy. The company's 20,000 employees lost their jobs, and many lost all of their retirement savings. The scandal also doomed Arthur Andersen, forcing 80,000 out of their jobs.

CAUSE Personal greed, lax accounting regulation

COST Enron's market capitalization of $70 billion collapsed to virtually nothing.

IMPACT Congress enacted the Sarbanes-Oxley Corporate Fraud Act of 2002 to provide closer oversight of accounting procedures.

Florida. In 1984, Lay became chairman of Houston Natural Gas, a pipeline company which InterNorth acquired in 1985. Within six months, Lay became the chairman of these merged pipeline companies, which he renamed Enron in 1986 and headquartered in Houston, Texas. To help him transform the staid pipeline carrier into the leader in energy, Lay hired Jeffrey Skilling in 1990. A graduate of Harvard Business School and a daring entrepreneur who shared Lay's vision, Skilling was willing to take chances and, so it appears, bend the rules. He got to work as the economy emerged from the recession of 1991 and gathered momentum in the business expansion of the 1990s, a surge spearheaded by the Internet, wireless communications, and the dot-com boom. Rising to CEO, Skilling shaped Enron to fit the new economy, as some observers styled this period of merger mania, proliferation of high-tech startups, and booming stock market.

Lay and Skilling transformed Enron by the acquisition of other businesses, such as power plants, and purchase and sale of power. They pushed aggressively for deregulation of electrical and natural gas markets, which facilitated Enron's plan of trading natural gas and electricity. In a few years, they reinvented Enron from a company dedicated to transporting natural gas into a multidimensional, globally based corporation whose forte was trading energy supplies and power resources. Enron even invested in broadband, a high-speed communications venture that flopped, costing the company billions. It was all part of the corporation's whirlwind of deals that spread Enron into new fields and many countries. The fly in this ointment was debt. To block an attempt to buy control of Enron in 1985, Lay had saddled the company with a large debt financed by high-interest "junk" bonds. Enron continued to borrow in the 1990s as it bought assets and expanded operations. But debt was a red flag to Wall Street stock analysts, who wanted to see growing profits on each quarterly financial statement.

To satisfy these goals—controlling debt while increasing profits—Skilling and Lay turned to Andrew Fastow, a young banker who rose to become Enron's treasurer. Fastow's talent lay in creating versatile Special Purpose Entities (SPEs), which in theory were independent partnerships that entered into contractual relations with another business. So long as a company owned less than half of the partnership, accounting rules allowed the company to keep the SPEs' debt and losses off the corporate books. SPEs had to have a minimum of 3 percent outside investment ("equity"), allowing the partnership to borrow the rest of its capital. Bending the rules, Fastow turned SPEs, such as LJM1, into cash cows for Enron. They provided the firm with fresh funds and purchased assets from Enron, taking the corporation's stock in payment. It was all very cozy, especially since Fastow personally ran these off-the-books operations, pocketing $30 million or more for his effort. Neither Enron's board of directors nor its accounting consultant, Arthur Andersen, one of the nation's "big 5" accounting firms, blew the whistle on this blatant conflict of interest and these questionable financial dealings.

LJM1 and other Fastow hedging operations enabled Enron to satisfy Wall Street profit expectations. Enron's stock literally soared. Between January 1993 and August 2000, the price of its stock went from $10 a share to $90, a run that included a two-for-one split of shares in 1999. The attention of Enron executives was riveted on the price of their stock, not only because the corporation's strategy hinged on it, but also because the top managers received lavish compensation in Enron stock. Employees who cut profitable deals reaped huge rewards and lived like princes in Enron's glitzy environment. Enron orchestrated a blitz of media hype, handing out lavish consulting contracts and generous donations to politicians to polish its image and gain influence. It was a powerfully seductive elixir.

Enron energy traders were the untamed cowboys of this new business model, and they played fast and loose with the nation's energy supply. With considerable help from Enron lobbying, California partially deregulated electric energy in 1996, effective in 1998. Rate caps remained on the price consumers paid, but electric companies were set free to buy power on the open market and distribute it to customers. Enron traders took advantage of this vulnerability, manipulating the market to cause scarcities and brownouts—temporary, localized shutdowns of power availability—which drove up prices. These prices skyrocketed eightfold between 1998 and 2001, earning Enron enormous profits in the process. California's power companies went bankrupt, local business operators worried about their survival, and the state government acquired a huge debt from subsidizing emergency power purchases. The political fallout over the energy crisis directly contributed to the recall of California governor Gray Davis and the election of Arnold Schwarzenegger in 2003.

The burst of the stock market bubble and the economic slowdown in 2001, developments that the TERRORIST ATTACKS of September 11 fanned, triggered the unraveling of Enron's tangled financial empire. Lower stock prices placed the SPEs in financial jeopardy and hindered Enron's ability to hedge its energy trading operations. When analysts demanded full accounting of its financial concoctions, Enron revealed in October 2001 that it had lost $618 million in the third quarter and had unreported debts in prior years. Unable to pay its debt or finance its hedge funds that protected its trading operations, Enron's stock plummeted. The company declared bankruptcy in December 2001 when its stock hit zero. Most of the corporation's 20,000 employees were terminated; many lost all of their retirement money, which they had been encouraged to invest entirely in Enron stock.

Apprehensive of their role in the unfolding accounting scandal, Arthur Andersen employees shredded documents regarding their client. Convicted of obstruction of justice in April 2002, Arthur Andersen, founded in 1913, closed its doors soon afterwards, sending its 80,000 employees looking for work elsewhere. In searching for explanations for this scandal, Congress subpoenaed Lay, Skilling, Fastow, and other Enron executives to testify in Washington. When Illinois senator Peter G. Fitzgerald told Lay that he was "the most accomplished confidence man since Charles Ponzi"—originator of the PONZI SCHEME in 1920—he was simply reflecting a sentiment shared widely in the United States. In 2002, Worldcom, Adelphi, Tyco, Qwest Communications, and even Martha Stewart, diva of the home-decorating industry, made news for fraudulent financial manipulation. In response to the accounting scandals, Congress adopted the Sarbanes-Oxley Corporate Fraud Act, which established the Public Company Accounting Oversight Board to regulate the auditing of publicly traded companies and barred accounting firms from providing consulting services to clients they audited. CEOs were required to certify the accuracy of their corporation's financial statements, and stiff criminal penalties for corporate fraud were enacted. Federal prosecutors indicted or secured guilty pleas from more than 20 Enron employees. In May 2006, a jury convicted Ken Lay of fraud and conspiracy; he died on July 5 before sentencing. Skilling was given a 24-year sentence in federal prison, an extraordinary harsh penalty for white-collar crime, and Fastow received a six-year jail term. These sentences mirrored the deflation of public confidence in corporate executives.

The economist Joseph Stiglitz saw the Enron saga as "emblematic of all that went wrong in the roaring Nineties—corporate greed, accounting scandals, public influence mongering, banking scandals, deregulation, and the free market mantra, all wrapped together."

Ballard C. Campbell

FURTHER READING:

Fusaro, Peter C., and Ross M. Miller. *What Went Wrong at Enron.* Hoboken, N.J.: Wiley, 2002.

Stiglitz, Joseph E. *The Roaring Nineties: A New History of the World's Most Prosperous Decade.* New York: W. W. Norton, 2003.

Swartz, Mimi, with Sherron Watkins. *Power Failure: The Inside Story of the Collapse of Enron.* New York: Doubleday, 2003.

2002 ◆ CATHOLIC CHURCH SEX ABUSE SCANDAL

The Catholic Church sex abuse scandal that began to unfold in January 2002 may be the biggest crisis the church has faced since the Reformation. Beginning in Boston, Massachusetts, allegations that priests had sexually abused children quickly spread both nationally and internationally and eventually forced the resignation of Cardinal Bernard Law, one of the most powerful American Catholic prelates, caught the attention of the Vatican, and promoted significant reform and prevention efforts by the United States Council of Catholic Bishops. In addition, it prompted the formation of one of the most coordinated dissent groups in the history of the modern church, Voice of the Faithful (VOTF), and significantly eroded the laity's trust of the Catholic hierarchy.

The linchpin in breaking the scandal of 2002 involved the declassification of archdiocesan documents. Prompted by litigation against the archdiocese involving defrocked priest John Geoghan, *The Boston Globe* launched an investigation into the church's response to the pedophilic priest, and, as a result, hundreds of previously classified documents were made public. Although Geoghan was accused of sexual abuse by more than 100 people, the most striking aspect of the unraveling story involved Geoghan's repeated reassignment into new parishes after fresh allegations of abuse were made. Documents indicated that Cardinal Law had been aware of Geoghan's offenses since 1984 but waited nearly 12 years to remove him from active duty. Even then, no sanctions were imposed; instead, he was placed on "senior priest retirement status." A criminal trial of Geoghan also proceeded in early 2002, and although the church itself was not on trial for its complicity, the spotlight brought the actions of both Geoghan and his superiors to center stage. Geoghan was found guilty and sentenced to nine years. The judge cited both his lack of remorse and propensity for reoffending as grounds for the maximum sentence. Not long after his incarceration, Geoghan was murdered in prison.

Within a few months, more than 70 priests in the archdiocese were implicated in the scandal. The evidence disclosed a clear pattern of secrecy within the church, limited or no treatment for the priests accused of molesting parishioners, and repeated

FACTBOX

PLACE Initially, the Roman Catholic Archdiocese of Boston; eventually spread across the country and the world

DATE Scandal broke January 2002

TYPE Priest sexual abuse scandal

DESCRIPTION First in Boston and then elsewhere, thousands of people made allegations of sexual abuse of children by priests that spanned several decades. Priest sexual abuse is arguably partially responsible for victims' psychological problems and countless suicides.

CAUSE Although debated, most people agree that church leaders' mismanagement and, at times, indifference allowed sexual predators easy access to children.

IMPACT The church paid out more than $1 billion in settlement costs and related counseling fees. The U.S. bishops implemented new policies to prevent such abuse in the future, but widespread mistrust of the Catholic Church hierarchy continued.

reassignment of the accused priests. Notably, the majority of abuse reported was perpetrated against boys (both pre- and postpubescent), a curious fact given boys' well-established underreporting of childhood sexual abuse. By the end of April 2002, the allegations of sexual abuse attracted the attention of the Vatican. The pope called an emergency summit for cardinals regarding the crisis in the American church. By the end of the year, 552 people in Boston filed suit against the archdiocese, marking an unprecedented action against any archdiocese.

Investigations revealed that priests' sexual abuse of parishioners had spanned decades and that the church had long covered up such behavior. Over and over, the response to victims had been more legal than pastoral. Many of these survivors suffered significant trauma, the effects of which often manifested themselves in a variety of dysfunctional behaviors, including drug and alcohol abuse and difficulties in interpersonal relationships. Victims found the church's lack of response frustrating and infuriating. As one victim cogently summed up the reason so many survivors litigated:

> We absolutely thought that if we told a priest, a bishop, a vicar general, anyone from the Church, that they would jump on this situation and do what was right. They could have prevented the litigation in 90 percent of the cases if they had given a simple, decent, human response to the victims. I don't mean to oversimplify, but if someone had looked at us face to face and said, "I'm so terribly sorry," it could have changed things. . . . Time after time, the responses were cold, bureaucratic, and hairsplitting.

By the end of 2002, Cardinal Law resigned his position in Boston. Under Archbishop Sean O'Malley's direction, the Boston cases were collectively settled in the fall of 2003, notably without any secrecy clauses, for $85 million, a figure unprecedented at the time but soon surpassed by other settlements across the country. By 2006, conservative estimates placed the total financial damages in the United States (which include legal fees, settlements, and funds for counseling) to well over $1 billion.

While the financial implications were steep, the cost to the erosion of trust in church hierarchy may have proven even more consequential. Although allegations of sexual abuse and concomitant litigation had been publicized in the national media since the mid-1980s, one of the main differences between pre- and post-2002 cases involved the groundswell of support for survivors by fellow Catholics. Previously, such lawsuits were bound by "no talk" rules in settlement, and outside support for civil action was limited. After 2002, however, lay Catholics became more closely connected to one another through the Internet. Already existing tensions between the laity and the hierarchy on such issues as the church's position on priestly celibacy, birth control, and homosexuality came to the forefront. Within 18 months of VOTF's inception, 200 chapters were incorporated worldwide, suggesting the scandal tapped into deep mistrust by the laity of church management.

With its epicenter in Boston, allegations of priest sexual abuse within the Catholic Church quickly spread across the world in the early 21st century. The U.S. bishops ultimately implemented new policies aimed at preventing such abuse before it occurred and hastening pastoral responses once charges were made. The impact of these reforms is not yet known. While it is difficult to predict the long-range consequences of the scandal, the revelations of priestly sexual abuse and the church's secrecy and mishandling of such cases called into question the fundamental benevolence of the church's leaders with regard to the protection of children.

Jennifer M. Balboni

FURTHER READING:
Muller, John E., and Charles Kenney. *Keep the Faith, Change the Church.* Emmaus, Pa.: Rodale Press, 2004.
Steinfels, Peter. *A People Adrift: The Crisis of the Roman Catholic Church in America.* New York: Simon and Schuster, 2003.

2003 ◆ SHUTTLE *COLUMBIA* DISASTER

On January 16, 2003, NASA, the National Aeronautics and Space Administration, launched Space Transportation System (STS) mission 107 from the Kennedy Space Center at Cape Canaveral, Florida. The shuttle launch system was carrying the space shuttle *Columbia* on its 28th operational flight. *Columbia* had been part of the first STS mission into space in 1981. Now 22 years old, it carried seven crew members: Mission Commander Rick D. Husband, pilot William C. McCool, and mission specialists—payload commander Michael P. Anderson, Kaplana Chawla, David M. Brown, Laurel Blair Salton Clark, and Israeli astronaut Ilan Ramon, who would perform a variety of scientific experiments on the STS-107 "Spacelab Research Double Module," which it carried into space in its cargo bay. The *Columbia* astronauts divided into two teams and engaged in the most intensive round-the-clock basic and applied commercial scientific research program ever undertaken in space, completing some 90 experiments during *Columbia's* 16-day mission. But tragedy awaited their return to Earth.

During the launch of STS mission 107 from Cape Canaveral on January 16, a small piece of foam insulation measuring 20 by 10 by 6 inches and weighing just 1.7 pounds had broken off from the external fuel tank and penetrated a two-square-foot section of Panel 6 of the shuttle's reinforced carbon-carbon protective heat tiles on the leading edge of the left wing. NASA engineers in Florida noticed the mishap, but based on similar, although not disastrous, foam strikes during earlier STS missions (particularly on *Atlantis* during STS-112 the previous October), mission managers downplayed any danger, classifying the problem as a "maintenance-level concern." They rejected engineer requests for in-flight satellite imaging or crew observation of the wing. This decision would prove fatal.

FACTBOX

PLACE In space 45 miles over the southwestern United States

DATE February 1, 2003

TYPE Space shuttle explosion

DESCRIPTION The space shuttle *Columbia* disintegrated upon its reentry into the earth's atmosphere at 238,000 feet.

CAUSE Foam insulation that had been dislodged during the launch ruptured the protective heat tiles on the leading edge of the left wing, rendering it unable to resist the high temperatures generated as the space vehicle reentered Earth's atmosphere.

CASUALTIES All seven crew members died.

IMPACT Shuttle launches were suspended until July 2005, technical improvements in the shuttle were implemented, reforms in shuttle procedures were adopted, and the shuttle program was drastically curtailed.

After completing their mission, the seven astronauts strapped themselves into *Columbia* on Saturday, February 1, to begin their journey back to Earth. *Columbia* left the space station that morning at 8:15 A.M. Eastern Standard Time. One hour and 42 minutes later, at about 9:00 A.M., the space shuttle began its reentry into the earth's atmosphere. As the vehicle descended and approached a peak speed of 6,000 miles per hour, superheated air flowed into and through the damaged left wing, producing temperatures of 5,000°F in the wing's structural support, whose melting point was just 2,500°F. Lacking protection from the heating tiles, *Columbia* literally fell apart 45 miles over the southwestern United States. As the crew module separated from the shuttle body, it lost its integrity and plummeted to Earth in thousands of pieces. All seven crew members inside died from hypoxia and blunt force trauma, making it the deadliest accident in space since the *Challenger* disaster of 1986. The explosion showered 87,000 pounds of debris over an area of roughly 2,000 square miles of east Texas and Louisiana. It would take more than 25,000 searchers 100 days to recover the pieces, which ranged from inch-square shards to 800-pound shuttle chunks.

After the disaster, NASA quickly formed a 13-member Columbia Accident Investigation Board (CAIB). Headed by retired navy Admiral Harold Gehrman, the CAIB concluded that an institutional culture of complacency and compartmentalization within the space agency had hindered communication and produced flawed analysis. Safety concerns and experts were, despite NASA's contrary belief, never given priority, as scheduling, production, cost-cutting, and efficiency concerns competed with other decision-making concerns. Moreover, the CAIB identified eight instances where imaging and observation of *Columbia's* damaged wing had been suggested and rejected. The CAIB's report concluded that "Twice in NASA's history, the agency embarked on a slippery slope that resulted in catastrophe. Each decision, taken by itself, seemed correct, routine, and indeed, insignificant and unremarkable, yet the cumulative effect was stunning. . . . The echoes of *Challenger* in *Columbia* have serious implications."

The CAIB made several recommendations to improve shuttle operations and safety, including a retrofit of improved external fuel tank foam, the creation and deployment of improved sensors and observation systems, and the development of in-flight repair equipment and techniques. NASA administrator Sean O'Keefe accepted them all. Shuttle flights were suspended pending the development and adoption of these solutions, and Russian Soyuz space capsules were used to maintain and resupply the International Space Station (*ISS*) during the interim. After two and a half years, shuttle flights resumed with the launch of *Discovery* on STS-114 in July 2005. Although its mission to test shuttle safety and repair procedures and to make needed repairs to the *ISS* was successful, foam divots continued to separate from the tank, posing potential danger to the shuttle and exacerbating doubts about the shuttle program's future.

See also 1986 SHUTTLE *CHALLENGER* EXPLOSION.

Gerald H. Herman

FURTHER READING:

Cabbage, Michael, and William Harwood. *Comm Check: The Final Flight of Shuttle* Columbia. New York: Free Press, 2004.

Tomkins, Phillip. Apollo, Challenger, Columbia: *The Decline of the Space Program.* Los Angeles: Roxbury, 2005.

2005 ◆ HURRICANE KATRINA

Hurricane Katrina was the costliest natural disaster in U.S. history. Striking the Gulf states in late August 2005, it affected more than 90,000 square miles along the coastal regions of Alabama, Louisiana, and Mississippi, including the city of New Orleans. The human cost of the storm is estimated at more than 1,400 deaths. More than 250,000 buildings were destroyed. The economic cost is hard to calculate but will greatly exceed the $110 billion the federal government pledged to spend in the year following Katrina. Above and beyond the financial and human costs, Hurricane Katrina exacted a high psychological cost on Americans who felt embarrassed by the inability of all levels of government to manage the emergency. Moreover, Katrina reopened the question of race in American society in a dramatic and unexpected way.

Katrina officially became a hurricane on August 24, 2005, near the Bahamas. The following day, it moved across southern Florida between Miami and Fort Lauderdale, causing flood damage, destroying buildings, and killing nine people before it passed out to the Gulf of Mexico as a category 1 storm. On the Gulf, Katrina gained strength at an astonishing rate. As Katrina grew in intensity, it moved north toward New Orleans. On Friday, August 26, Governor Kathleen Blanco issued a state of emergency for Louisiana. By Saturday, it was becoming clear that the storm's path would take it close, if not directly

FACTBOX

PLACE New Orleans and other parts of Louisiana, as well as Florida, Mississippi, and Alabama

DATE August 25–30, 2005

TYPE Hurricane and flood

DESCRIPTION Massive winds and rain destroyed levees around New Orleans, causing water to pour in and flood the city. The hurricane also caused heavy damage along the Gulf coast.

CASUALTIES Approximately 1,400 deaths

COST 250,000 buildings; it is too early to know the financial cost, but it will greatly exceed the $110 billion the federal government has pledged, making it the costliest natural disaster in U.S. history.

IMPACT The city of New Orleans may never be the same. With tens of thousands of evacuees not returning, the population has plunged from 485,000 to about 200,000.

over, New Orleans. Saturday evening, Max Mayfield, director of the National Hurricane Center in Miami, Florida, conducted a conference call with Blanco, New Orleans Mayor Ray Nagin, and Mississippi Governor Haley Barbour in which he urged

A U.S. Coast Guard boat searches for survivors in New Orleans. *(Associated Press)*

them to issue mandatory evacuations to all areas in Katrina's path.

Later that evening, Mayor Nagin issued a voluntary evacuation order for New Orleans, and authorities made all lanes of traffic on the interstate highways open to northbound vehicles only. On Sunday, August 28, Katrina was upgraded to a category 5 hurricane with winds of 170 miles per hour. While over 80 percent of New Orleans's population of 460,000 followed Mayor Nagin's advice and evacuated, many of the city's poorest citizens remained, including the sick and the elderly. As best they could, those left behind migrated to the Superdome or Convention Center, the officially designated shelters of last resort. At 10:00 Sunday morning, after receiving a National Weather Service advisory that predicted severe flooding, Mayor Nagin issued a mandatory evacuation for the entire city. But it was too late. City plans for using school buses and Amtrak trains to evacuate New Orleans were not fully implemented. While some buses ferried citizens to the designated

shelters of last resort, the failure of a large number of drivers to report because they had already evacuated or the city to post designated pickup locations greatly blunted the effectiveness of the operation. Neither the Superdome nor the Convention Center were prepared for the onslaught of over 30,000 people who came seeking shelter. Both facilities lacked adequate space, medicine, food, and water.

Between 2001 and 2005, a number of well-publicized disaster scenarios had predicted a massive hurricane that could cause significant flood damage to New Orleans, a city that is mostly below sea level and protected by 18-foot-high levees that hold back the canals, the Mississippi River, and Lake Pontchartrain. Some of these models, such as the fictional "Hurricane Pam," bore an eerie resemblance to Katrina. Stories about these scenarios appeared in the *New Orleans Times-Picayune,* which won a Pulitzer Prize for a series of articles, and *National Geographic* magazine, among others. However, complacency gripped many New Orleans residents who had seen several hurricanes, including Ivan in 1998, suddenly change course and skirt past the city. With tourism as the primary industry, Mayor Nagin and city leaders were fearful of scaring off visitors or damaging the economy by issuing a mandatory evacuation.

At 4:00 Sunday afternoon, the first rain fell in Louisiana and continued all night. On Monday, August 29, the full force of Katrina ripped through coastal Louisiana devastating Plaquemines and Saint Bernard Parishes before slamming into New Orleans. Approximately 8 to 10 inches of rain and 120 mile-per-hour winds swelled Lake Pontchartrain and overwhelmed the levees, causing them to fail for two reasons. First, they were overtopped by waves of water stemming from the rain and the high-velocity winds. Second, and more serious, the levees breached, or broke open, filling New Orleans like an empty bowl as water from the canals and Lake Pontchartrain poured in. The breeches created storm surges that measured as high as 17 feet, decimated all in their path, and led to rapid flooding. The lower Ninth Ward, the poorest area of New Orleans, quickly lay under eight feet of water. About 80 percent of the city was flooded during Katrina.

After hitting New Orleans, Katrina moved north and brought its destructive power to the coastal regions of Mississippi and Alabama. Biloxi and Gulfport, Mississippi, were both hit hard. In addition to the destruction of homes and businesses, all 13 of Biloxi's casinos were destroyed. Some were thrown off their moorings and moved several blocks by the sheer force of Katrina's winds.

Lack of communication between local and federal officials hampered efforts to manage the storm. For example, on National Public Radio, Michael Chertoff, Secretary of Homeland Security, the department that oversees the Federal Emergency Management Agency (FEMA), which handles disaster relief, stated that he had no knowledge of the thousands who were trapped in the New Orleans Convention Center, even though that story had been widely reported the day before by all the major television networks. Two days later, President George W. Bush congratulated FEMA head Michael Brown for "doing a heckuva job." To many, it seemed undue praise for a man who had bungled the federal rescue operations from the start. With Brown drawing too much

heat, President Bush replaced him on September 9 with Coast Guard Vice Admiral Thad Allen.

Scenes from New Orleans and the Gulf Coast were horrifying, and the nation watched in shock as these events unfolded. The floodwaters rushed in so quickly that many residents could only escape to the upper floors or attics of their homes. Helicopters and boats rescued people trapped on roofs and treetops, sometimes using axes or chainsaws to get to those in attics. Lower floors of hospitals were flooded, and patients had to be moved to the upper levels. In Saint Bernard Parish, 34 residents at St. Rita's nursing home were killed by floodwaters. Many people were stranded on the overpasses of highways without water, food, or protection from the blazing sun as temperatures soared into the upper 90s and the humidity level remained above 100 percent. Looting was rampant but also exaggerated. Rescue workers could not tell if gunshots were snipers or pleas for help from trapped residents. Floating bodies drifted in the floodwaters. Fearing the worst, Mayor Nagin ordered 25,000 body bags, and Governor Blanco announced that the National Guard had authority to shoot looters or those hampering rescue operations on site. Uncontrolled fires, chemical contamination of the floodwater, sewage, piles of garbage, rotting bodies, concern for alligators, snakes, and disease all added to the dangerous and toxic environment in the city. Homes were leveled in New Orleans and Mississippi to such an extent that some compared the scene to Hiroshima or Nagasaki, Japan, after

The costliest disaster in American history, Hurricane Katrina killed approximately 1,400 people, displaced hundreds of thousands more, and caused untold destruction. (*Marvin Nauman/FEMA*)

the atomic bombs of August 1945. Rescue workers searched through homes and spray painted the number of bodies found inside on the exteriors of buildings. Katrina damaged oil refineries, off-shore drilling facilities, and pipelines, causing a nationwide spike in gasoline prices.

Conditions in the Superdome and Convention Center rapidly deteriorated. With failing electricity, poor

Federal Emergency Management Agency

President Jimmy Carter created the Federal Emergency Management Agency (FEMA) by executive order in 1979. His action merged several federal agencies into a single organization. Among the units folded into FEMA were the Federal Insurance Administration, the National Fire Prevention and Control Administration, the National Weather Service Community Preparedness Program, the Federal Preparedness Agency of the General Services Administration, and disasters agencies from the U.S. Department of Housing and Urban Development. Charged with supervising the federal government's disaster policy, FEMA balances a variety of functions. Its mission includes providing advice on building codes and flood-plain management, help in equipping local and state emergency preparedness, the coordination of federal responses to disasters, the training of emergency managers (for instance, state government personnel), and the administration of the national flood and crime insurances programs. In 2003, FEMA was merged into the Department of Homeland Security, which was created in the wake of the TERRORIST ATTACK of September 11, 2001. FEMA employed 2,500 full-time workers in 2006 and could call on 5,000 stand-by employees.

FEMA represents the culmination of a long history of federal involvement with disasters. During most of the past two centuries, these actions took the form of individual congressional laws enacted in response to particular disasters. Between 1800 and 1949, Congress passed 128 such statutes. In 1950, Congress authorized the president to declare disaster areas in the cases of flood, fires, hurricane, earthquake, drought, and storm. Additional natural disasters, including tsunamis and landslides, were added to this authority in 1970 and 1974. Declaration of a disaster authorizes federal agencies such as the U.S. Department of Agriculture, the Department of Housing and Urban Development, and the Small Business Administration to provide assistance to state and local officials. During the 1950s and 1960s, agencies of the Department of Agriculture offered assistance to farm families and others following numerous natural disasters, including a tornado in Kansas (1955), an earthquake and landslide in Montana (1959), Hurricane Carla (1961), and a grasshopper invasion in North Dakota (1961).

FEMA's chief preoccupation during the administrations of Presidents Ronald Reagan (1981–89) and George H. W. Bush (1989–93) revolved around cold war issues, such as training civil-defense officials in the event of a nuclear attack. In the eyes of critics, the agency's emphasis on defense weakened its ability to prepare for responses to natural disasters and catastrophic accidents. Criticism was particular sharp following FEMA's responses to Hurricane Hugo and the LOMA PRIETA EARTHQUAKE in San Francisco in 1989. While the agency learned from these events, its preparation for domestic disasters was diverted again by 9/11 and the agency's relocation to the Department of Homeland Security. FEMA's handling of Hurricane Katrina in 2005 intensified criticism of the agency. When TV cameras pictured victims of Katrina isolated on rooftops in New Orleans and packed into the city's civic center without proper assistance, the public blamed FEMA for the bungled response. The intensity of the criticism led to the resignation of its director, Michael Brown, who had had no prior disaster experience when he took control of the agency two years earlier. In fairness to FEMA, a 2006 congressional report on responses to the Katrina crisis faulted Louisiana state government and New Orleans city government as well as the federal disaster team for poor preparation and haphazard responses to the catastrophe.

Ballard C. Campbell

ventilation and sanitation, and inadequate supplies, lawlessness prevailed, including cases of assault and rape. White sheets covered elderly invalids who were found dead in their wheelchairs from want of medical care. While the police department attempted to protect the public good, many officers abandoned the city and did not show up for duty. With little disaster training and breakdown at the highest level of the department, the remaining officers on the street were not in a position to provide much help.

On Friday, September 2, the National Guard arrived at the Superdome and Convention Center with food, water, and supplies. Buses followed, and mass evacuations began. Evacuees were taken to Baton Rouge, Louisiana, and to the Astrodome in Houston, Texas. Eventually Katrina refugees would be dispersed throughout the United States to such places as Dallas, Texas; Kalamazoo, Michigan; and Denver, Colorado. Often it took weeks or months for evacuees to locate friends and family.

Katrina left as much controversy as destruction in its wake. Immediately, questions emerged as to the lack of preparedness. The situation in New Orleans led the city and state officials to blame the federal government for the shortcomings of disaster relief. State officials launched a litany of charges against the Bush administration, including defunding levee repair, leaving Louisiana without sufficient National Guard troops, and a lack of leadership. In an interview with the *Wall Street Journal,* Mayor Nagin declared that the city's plan for the hurricane was to "get the people to higher ground and have the feds and the state airlift supplies to them." The city, however, had several emergency plans that were never implemented.

The Bush administration and Republicans in Congress responded that the state and city governments did not follow their own emergency plans and misdirected federal grant money for disaster preparedness. In fact, all levels of government were overwhelmed. Many Americans asked how national leaders could be so unprepared for a large-scale emergency four years after the terrorist attack of September 11, 2001.

Speaker of the House Dennis Hastert, among others, questioned the wisdom of rebuilding a city so vulnerable to flooding. Environmentalists called a number of practices into question including the elaborate system of unnatural levees which have destroyed tens of thousands of acres of wetlands that might have buffered the impact of Katrina. President Bush put the matter of rebuilding to rest on September 15, 2005, when in a televised address to the nation from Jackson Square in New Orleans, he pledged federal assistance to rebuilding from the hurricane.

Katrina exacerbated racial tensions as well. Nearly 68 percent of New Orleans was black and disproportionately poor. Many blacks felt that they did not get the help they needed from the national government because of their race. President Bush's publicized trip to the destroyed home of white Mississippi Senator Trent Lott and his failure to make a similar trip to the devastated areas of New Orleans led many blacks to consider that reconstruction of their homes was at the bottom of the administration's recovery priorities.

Controversy plagued other aspects of the federal recovery effort as well. When FEMA provided debit cards valued at $2,000 to over 900,000 victims of Katrina, examples of fraud and mismanagement made headlines across the nation. Suspension of federal contract and wage regulations in favor of large national firms at the expense of local businesses also led many to question federal priorities. Finally, Mississippi, which had a powerful delegation in Congress, received disproportionately more in aid than harder-hit Louisiana.

The levee breaches were repaired on September 5, and, after seven weeks of pumping, New Orleans was declared dry. While many residents trickled back to their homes, more remained away. Entire neighborhoods in New Orleans and Mississippi remained piles of rubble one year after Katrina hit. Mayor Nagin attempted to lift the spirit of the city by conducting business as normal. In 2006, the Mardi Gras and Jazz Festival celebrations went on according to their normal schedule. Nagin also created the 17-member Bring New Orleans Back Commission to build excitement around rebuilding. But with one-quarter of the prehurricane tax base, one-third the student body in the public schools, power shortages, and tens of thousands not yet returned, Katrina has left a scar that will heal slowly, if at all.

See also 1900 GALVESTON HURRICANE; 1938 NEW ENGLAND HURRICANE; 1992 HURRICANE ANDREW.

Gregory J. Dehler

FURTHER READING:

Brinkley, Douglas. *The Great Deluge: Hurricane Katrina, New Orleans, and the Mississippi Gulf Coast.* New York: HarperCollins, 2006.

Cooper, Christopher, and Robert Block. *Disaster: Hurricane Katrina and the Failure of Homeland Security.* New York: Times Books, 2006.

Dyson, Michael Eric. *Come Hell or High Water: Hurricane Katrina and the Color of Disaster.* New York: Basic Books, 2006.

Heerden, Ivor van, and Mike Bryan. *The Storm: What Went Wrong During Hurricane Katrina The Inside Story from One Louisiana Scientist.* New York: Viking, 2006.

Horne, Jed. *Breach of Faith: Hurricane Katrina and the Near Death of a Great American City.* New York: Random House, 2006.

Syzerhans, Douglas, ed. *Federal Disaster Programs and Hurricane Katrina.* New York: Nova Science Publishers, 2006.

◆ APPENDIX A ◆

DISASTER MOVIES

The 1970 movie *Airport,* based on a best-selling novel by Arthur Hailey, scored $45.2 million on its initial box-office release. A series of disaster-driven dramas, including *The Poseidon Adventure* (1972) and *Earthquake* (1974), followed in its wake, launching a full-fledged genre. Though derived from the historical epic and science-fiction genres, disaster movies are distinguished by plots that are propelled solely by natural or human-made catastrophes. Like all genres, the disaster movie ebbs and flows in popularity in response to current events and issues.

Generally derided by film reviewers, disaster movies are often popular with audiences in part because they exemplify one of the basic appeals of the cinema—its ability to flaunt spectacle. From the earliest days of cinema at the dawn of the 20th century, films exploited the spectacle of mass destruction through actual footage of the aftermath of such famous disasters as the 1900 GALVESTON HURRICANE and the 1906 SAN FRANCISCO EARTHQUAKE as well as simplistic recreations of those disasters by novice moviemakers.

A few years later, as the cinema rapidly developed the conventions and techniques that defined it as an art form, a cycle of films from Italy used disaster as a key narrative element. From 1908 to 1914, a series of Roman epics, including two versions of *The Last Days of Pompeii* (1908 and 1913), *The Fall of Troy* (1910), and *Cabiria* (1914), influenced director D. W. Griffith to produce films that exceeded the standard one-reel and gave U.S. viewers a taste for historical epics. A massive disaster generally provided the climax or turning point in these films, often serving as a punishment for the characters' or society's moral breakdown. For decades after, the spectacle of catastrophe and mass destruction could generally be found as a key part of the ancient history epic, though the narratives did not revolve around that disaster.

During the 1930s, a cycle of Hollywood dramas with recent historical settings emerged, incorporating a natural or human-made disaster as the momentous climax. Less epic in scope, these dramas involved fewer characters and focused on romance, not history. Two areas of technological advancement heightened the spectacle of the disasters depicted in these films. Synchronized sound and the improved quality of special effects made the rumbling earthquakes that concluded *Deluge* (1933) and *San Francisco* (1936) resonate more deeply, the howling winds in *The Hurricane* (1937) more palpable, and the crackling fires in *In Old Chicago* (1937) spark with life.

In the 1950s, scale and breadth returned to the historical narrative boosting it from mere drama to epic. Once again, the Hollywood industry's adoption of certain technologies increased the element of spectacle in the movies. The use of widescreen processes such as CinemaScope and VistaVision and an increased dependence on color, particularly Technicolor, enhanced the large-scale catastrophes that were hallmarks of such ancient and biblical epics as *Quo Vadis* (1951) and *The Ten Commandments* (1956). Another genre dependent on massive destruction, the science-fiction film, also developed during this time, serving as a direct precursor to the disaster genre. Monster movies and stories of alien invasions such as *War of the Worlds* (1953; remade in 2005), often incorporated the destruction of major cities as part of their iconography and then focused on the survival of that destruction as part of the story line.

Unlike historical epics that place massive disasters in the past, and science-fiction films that are futuristic, improbable, or far-fetched, the disaster film uses relatively believable disasters that not only occur in the present but are relevant to it. Also different is the central role of the disaster in the narrative—it propels the story, motivates the characters, and prompts the themes of redemption, survival, and responsibility.

The disaster portrayed in *Airport* in 1970 was modest in scale—a mad bomber blows a hole in the side of an airplane that attempts to land during a snowstorm—but later films featured increasingly sensational catastrophes with the potential for mass destruction. A huge tidal wave literally turned the world of the characters upside down in *The Poseidon Adventure,* a multistory fire wreaked havoc in a modern skyscraper in *The Towering Inferno,* and deafening seismic traumas (in Sensurround) rocked Los Angeles in *Earthquake.* The enormous box-office success of these films reflected their popularity with the public, if not reviewers, and guaranteed that other disaster dramas would follow. From 1970 to 1980, over 50 disaster films were released.

Producer Irwin Allen, who loved the disaster genre and produced some its most famous 1970s examples, including *Poseidon* and *Inferno,* did much to establish the conventions of the genre. In the disaster film, a large cast of major movie stars play archetypal characters placed in perilous situations. A cross section of society from ordinary folk to the privileged wealthy is represented, with one or more persevering heroes leading the characters to survival. The sensational events in the film are paralleled by melodramatic acting, which is in keeping with the scale of the events. Generally, not all of the characters survive, making the disaster film one of the few genres in which major stars are killed off. In the disaster genre, the hallmarks of civilization—from moral codes to personal relationships to technological advancements—are tested and, generally, a combination of cultural values and social institutions are the reasons for survival. Those who make their way out of the rubble often declare a renewed perspective on traditional values and ideals.

Large-scale special effects also characterize the disaster genre. Special effects technology has changed over time—from stop-motion animation to an intricate combination of matte painting and models to computer-generated imagery—but the visual splendor of disaster films has always been part of their appeal. Often, easily recognizable landmarks such as the Statue of Liberty, the Empire State Building, and the Eiffel Tower are destroyed as part of the catastrophe, and special effects are crucial in depicting that destruction.

As with other popular genres, disaster films are acutely reflective of social, cultural, and political developments of the era in which they are produced. The disaster genre is considered conservative because traditional values are generally drawn on during the course of the film or because characters representing social institutions or social classes—police officers, firefighters, priests, doctors, even mechanics—commit heroic deeds, thereby validating the strength of those institutions and classes. It is no accident that the genre was developed during the 1970s, the era of the Vietnam debacle, Watergate, social unrest, racial tensions, and rapid inflation. The doubt and distrust generated by these events split American society by generation, and disaster films reflected a desire to find faith in old values and ideals. Likewise, Hollywood was split by generation in the 1970s with young college-educated directors making films of rebellion featuring a new wave of gritty method-style actors. Disaster films were the Hollywood industry's reaction to the innovative work of the film-school generation. The genre was a throwback to old-fashioned moviemaking with big stars, big spectacle, and big budgets.

The initial wave of disaster films fizzled out in about 1980 because of repetition and imitation. In the mid-1990s, the genre returned with such films as *Twister* (1996), *Volcano* (1997), *Deep Impact* (1998), and *The Perfect Storm* (2000). End-of-millennium jitters may have prompted the new cycle, as indicated by the title *Armageddon* (1998), but it was undoubtedly boosted by advancements in computer-generated special effects, which intensified the scale of the destruction and disaster in each of these films. *Titanic* (1997), the ultimate version of the real-life disaster that has been depicted on film almost every decade since it sank in 1912, validated the genre with audiences and critics when it became the highest-grossing film of all time ($1.2 billion worldwide) and won 11 Academy Awards.

Just as it appeared to wane, the disaster film was revived with the release of *The Core* (2003) and *The Day After Tomorrow* (2004). The threat of terrorism after the events of September 11, 2001, is generally credited with influencing this revival, as well as sparking a return to airplane-related thrillers such as *Red Eye* (2005), *Flight Plan* (2005), *Snakes on a Plane* (2006), and three films directly about the 9/11 terrorist attack, *United 93* (2006), *Flight 93* (TV, 2006), and *World Trade Center* (2006).

Ultimately, the disaster genre reflects our society's neuroses regarding traditional values and social institutions, especially a need to have our faith restored in them. According to the disaster genre, values, ideals, and institutions when tested should not only protect and revitalize us but also define us.

Susan Doll

FURTHER READING:

Fry, Ron, and Pamela Fourzen. *The Saga of Special Effects.* Englewood Cliffs, N.J.: Prentice Hall, 1977.

Kay, Glenn, and Michael Rose. *Disaster Movies.* Chicago: Chicago Review Press, 2006.

Keane, Stephen. *Disaster Movies: The Cinema of Catastrophe.* London: Wallflower Press, 2001.

Sackett, Susan. *Box Office Hits: Hollywood's Most Successful Movies.* New York: Billboard Books, 1990.

Sontag, Susan. "The Imagination of Disaster." P. 4 in *Against Interpretation and Other Essays.* London: Andre Deutsch, 1965.

◆ APPENDIX B ◆

"WORST OF" LISTS: THE WORST DISASTERS, ACCIDENTS, AND CRISES IN AMERICAN HISTORY*

NATURAL DISASTERS

Fatalities

- 1980 Deadly Heat Wave (10,000)
- 1900 Galveston Hurricane (6,000–10,000)
- 1906 San Francisco Earthquake and Fire (estimated 3,000)
- 1871 Peshtigo Fire (1,200–2,400)
- 2005 Hurricane Katrina (more than 1,400)
- 1938 Great New England Hurricane (564–690)
- 1935 Florida Hurricane (at least 423)
- 1888 Blizzard of '88 (around 400)
- 1926 Miami Hurricane (373)
- 1993 Superstorm (270)
- 1927 Mississippi River Flood (246)

Cost

- 2005 Hurricane Katrina (up to $200 billion)
- 1992 Hurricane Andrew ($26 billion)
- 1993 Mississippi River Flood ($20 billion)
- 1938 Great New England Hurricane ($20.8 billion in estimated current dollars)
- 1906 San Francisco Earthquake and Fire ($400 million, $8.2 billion in estimated current dollars)

SHIP AND MARITIME ACCIDENTS

Fatalities

- 1865 Explosion of the *Sultana* (1,700–1,800)
- 1912 Sinking of the *Titanic* (1,503–1,517)
- 1904 *General Slocum* Disaster (1,021)
- 1915 Capsizing of the *Eastland* (844)
- 1947 *Grandcamp* Explosion (581)
- 1860 Wreck of the *Lady Elgin* (around 400)

- 1854 Sinking of the *Arctic* (296)
- 1853 Sinking of the *San Francisco* (220)
- 1898 Sinking of the *Portland* (192)
- 1838 Explosion of the *Moselle* (at least 150)

OTHER ACCIDENTS

Fatalities

- 1889 Johnstown Flood (2,209)
- 1931 Hawk's Nest Tunnel Disaster (764)
- 1903 Iroquois Theater Fire (602)
- 1937 New London School Explosion (more than 500)
- 1942 Cocoanut Grove Fire (492)
- 1928 St. Francis Dam Collapse (more than 450)
- 1871 Great Chicago Fire (around 300)
- 1979 Crash of American Airlines Flight 191 (273)
- 1909 Cherry Mine Disaster (259)
- 1996 Explosion of TWA Flight 800 (230)
- 1944 Hartford Circus Fire (168)
- 1911 Triangle Shirtwaist Factory Fire (146)

Note: 1899 First Auto Fatality (3 million through 2005, with a peak of over 55,000 in 1969)

EPIDEMICS

Fatalities

- 1492 Decimation of Native Americans by European Diseases (estimated 48 million)
- 1918 Influenza Pandemic (675,000 Americans; 50–100 million worldwide)

- 1845 Irish Famine (up to 1 million)
- 1981 AIDS Epidemic (530,000 Americans; 25 million worldwide)
- 1832 Cholera (estimated 50,000–150,000)
- 1964 Cigarettes and Lung Cancer (estimated 400,000 premature deaths a year in the 1990s)
- 1878 Yellow Fever Epidemic (20,000)
- 1793 Yellow Fever Epidemic (close to 5,000)
- 1952 Polio Epidemic (3,145 in 1952)

STRIKES AND RIOTS

Fatalities
- 1892 Lynching Tragedy (4,700 between 1882–1964)
- 1831 Nat Turner Slave Rebellion (over 160)
- 1863 New York City Draft Riots (over 100)
- 1877 Great Railroad Strike (over 100)
- 1967 Urban Riots (83)
- 1919 Chicago Race Riot (38)

OTHER DISASTERS

Fatalities
- 1945 Atomic Bombs Dropped on Japan (estimated 215,000)
- 1984 Chemical Explosion in Bhopal (over 20,000)
- 1950 Retreat from the Yalu (estimated 15,000 U.S. servicemen)

- 1838 Trail of Tears (4,000–6,000)
- 1675 King Philip's War (estimated 4,000 Algonquians and 2,000 colonists)
- 1755 Exile of the Acadians (at least 5,000 during the deportation)
- 2001 9/11 Terrorist Attack (2,973 victims plus 19 hijackers)
- 1941 Attack on Pearl Harbor (2,403 U.S. servicemen; 55 Japanese in attacking force)
- 1915 Sinking of the *Lusitania* (1,198, including 128 Americans)
- 1836 Battle of the Alamo (189 Texans and approximately 600 Mexicans)
- 1861 Battle of Bull Run (481 Union and 387 Confederate soldiers)
- 1622 Great Massacre at Jamestown (at least 347 settlers)
- 1898 Explosion of the USS *Maine* (274)
- 1876 Battle of Little Bighorn (263 American soldiers and 60 Native Americans)
- 1995 Oklahoma City Bombing (168)
- 1864 Sand Creek Massacre (150 Native Americans and 9 Colorado Volunteers)
- 1775 Battles of Lexington and Concord (73 British soldiers and 49 American colonists)

*Only events included in this book are listed.

BIBLIOGRAPHY

Acheson, Dean. *Present at the Creation.* New York: W. W. Norton, 1969.

Ackerman, Kenneth D. *Dark Horse: The Surprise Election and Political Murder of President James A. Garfield.* New York: Carroll & Graf, 2003.

Adams, Charles Francis. *Notes on Railroad Accidents.* New York: G. P. Putnam's Sons, 1879.

Aguado, E., and James E. Burt. *Understanding Weather and Climate.* 4th ed. Upper Saddle River, N.J.: Pearson/Prentice Hall, 2007.

Ahrens, C. Donald. *Meteorology Today: An Introduction to Weather, Climate, and the Environment.* 8th ed. Belmont, Calif.: Thomson Higher Education/Brooks-Cole, 2007.

Allaby, Michael. *Fog, Smog, and Poisoned Rain.* New York: Facts On File, 2003.

Allen, Frederick Lewis. *Only Yesterday: An Informal History of the 1920s.* New York: HarperPerennial, 2000.

Allen, James, et al. *Without Sanctuary: Lynching Photography in America.* Santa Fe, N.Mex: Twin Palms, 2000.

Ambrose, Stephen J. *Nothing Like It in the World: The Men Who Built the Transcontinental Railroad, 1863–1869.* New York: Simon and Schuster, 2000.

Anderson, David. *Facing My Lai: Moving Beyond the Massacre.* Lawrence: University Press of Kansas, 1998.

Angell, Marcia. *Science on Trial: The Clash of Medical Evidence and the Law in the Breast Implant Case.* New York: W. W. Norton, 1996.

Ashmore, Harry S. *Civil Rights and Wrongs.* New York: Pantheon, 1994.

Asinof, Eliot. *Eight Men Out.* New York: Henry Holt, 1963.

Atkins, Annette. *Harvest of Grief: Grasshopper Plagues and Public Assistance in Minnesota, 1873–1878.* St. Paul: Minnesota Historical Society Press, 1984.

Aug, Stephen, and Philip Ryther. *Who's Watching the Airways?* New York: Doubleday, 1972.

Avrich, Paul. *Sacco and Vanzetti: The Anarchist Background.* Princeton, N.J.: Princeton University Press, 1991.

Backelder, Peter Dow. *Four Short Blasts: The Gale of 1898 and the Loss of the Steamer* Portland. Portland Me.: Provincial Press, 2003.

Bailey, Thomas A., and Paul B. Ryan. *The* Lusitania *Disaster: An Episode in Modern Warfare and Diplomacy.* New York: Free Press, 1975.

Bailyn, Bernard. *The Ideological Origins of the American Revolution.* Cambridge, Mass.: Belknap Press, 1967.

———. *The Ordeal of Thomas Hutchinson.* Cambridge, Mass.: Belknap Press of Harvard University Press, 1974.

Bain, David Haward. *Empire Express: Building the First Transcontinental Railroad.* New York: Viking, 1999.

Banner, James M. *To the Hartford Convention: The Federalists and the Origins of the Party Politics in Massachusetts, 1789–1815.* New York: Knopf, 1970.

Barbaree, James M., Robert F. Breiman, and Alfred P. Dufour. *Legionella: Current Status and Emerging Perspectives.* Washington, D.C.: American Society for Microbiology, 1993.

Barker, Rocky. *Scorched Earth: How the Fires of Yellowstone Changed America.* Washington, D.C.: Island Press, 2005.

Barry, James P. *Ships of the Great Lakes.* Holt, Mich.: Thunder Bay Press, 1996.

Barry, John M. *The Great Influenza: The Epic Story of the Deadliest Plague in History.* New York: Penguin Books, 2004.

———. *Rising Tide: The Great Mississippi Flood of 1927 and How It Changed America.* New York: Simon and Schuster, 1997.

Beard, Patricia. *After the Ball: Gilded Age Secrets, Boardroom Betrayals, and the Party That Ignited the Great Wall Street Scandal of 1905.* New York: HarperCollins, 2003.

Beckey, Fred. *Range of Glaciers: The Exploration and Survey of the Northern Cascade Range.* Portland: Oregon Historical Society Press, 2003.

Belke, James C., and Deborah Y. Dietrich. "The Post-Bhopal and Post–9/11 Transformations in Chemical Emergency Prevention and Response Policy in the United States." Paper presented at the International Conference on the 20th Anniversary of the Bhopal Gas Tragedy "Bhopal Gas Tragedy and Its Effects on Process Safety," Indian Institute of Technology, Kanpur, India 2004. Available online. URL: http://yosemite.epa.gov/oswer/ceppoweb.nsf/ae2ff10ca577b18b85256b83007b7db9/85256b9f0072443385256f7e00550b2a!OpenDocument. Downloaded April 10, 2007.

Belknap, Michael. *The Vietnam War on Trial: The My Lai Massacre and the Court Martial of Lieutenant Calley.* Lawrence: University Press of Kansas, 2002.

Benedict, Michael Les. *The Impeachment and Trial of Andrew Johnson.* 1973. Reprint, New York: W. W. Norton, 1999.

———. "Southern Democrats in the Crisis of 1876–1877: A Reconsideration of *Reunion and Reaction.*" *Journal of Southern History* 46 (November 1980): 489–524.

Bennett, William Edward [Warren Armstrong, pseud.]. *The Collins Story.* London: R. Hale, 1957.

Benzaquin, Paul. *Fire in Boston's Cocoanut Grove: Holocaust!* Boston: Branden Press, 1967.

Berg, A. Scott. *Lindbergh.* New York: Putnam, 1998.

Bernstein, Irving. *Turbulent Years: A History of the American Worker 1933–1941.* Boston: Houghton Mifflin, 1970.

Bernstein, Iver. *The New York City Draft Riots.* New York: Oxford University Press, 1990.

Berry, Chester D., ed. *Loss of the* Sultana *and Reminiscences of Survivors.* Rev. ed. Knoxville: University of Tennessee Press, 2005.

Beschloss, Michael. *The Crisis Years: Kennedy and Khrushchev, 1960–1963.* New York: Edward Burlingame Books, 1991.

Biel, Steven, ed. *American Disasters.* New York: New York University Press, 2000.

Bienen, Leigh, and Gilbert Geis. *Crimes of the Century: From Leopold and Loeb to O. J. Simpson.* Boston: Northeastern University Press, 1998.

Billington, Ray Allen. *The Protestant Crusade, 1800–1860.* Chicago: Quadrangle Books, 1964.

Birkland, Thomas A. *After Disaster: Agenda Setting, Public Policy, and Focusing Events.* Washington D.C.: Georgetown University Press, 1997.

Bixel, Patricia Bellis, and Elizabeth Hayes Turner. *Galveston and the 1900 Storm.* Austin: University of Texas Press, 2000.

Blair, Clay. *The Forgotten War: America in Korea, 1950–53.* New York: Doubleday, 1987.

Blake, John B. *Public Health in the Town of Boston, 1630–1822.* Cambridge, Mass.: Harvard University Press, 1959.

Blakey, G. Robert, and Richard Billings. *The Plot to Kill the President.* New York: Times Books, 1981.

Blewett, Mary H., ed. *Surviving Hard Times: The Working People of Lowell.* Lowell, Mass.: Lowell Museum, 1982.

Blight, James G., and David A. Welch. *On the Brink: Americans and Soviets Reexamine the Cuban Missile Crisis.* New York: Farrar, Straus and Giroux, 1989.

Blight, James G., and Peter Kornbluh, eds. *Politics of Illusion: The Bay of Pigs Invasion Reexamined.* New York: Lynne Rienner, 1998.

Blossom, Virgil. *It Has Happened Here.* New York: Harper and Brothers, 1959.

Bodle, Wayne. *The Valley Forge Winter: Civilians and Soldiers in War.* University Park: Pennsylvania State University Press, 2002.

Bollet, Alfred Jay. *Plagues and Poxes: The Impact of Human History on Epidemic Disease.* New York: Demos, 2004.

Bonansinga, Jay. *The Sinking of the* Eastland*: America's Forgotten Tragedy.* New York: Citadel Press, 2004.

Bondurant, Stuart, Virginia Ernster, and Roger Herdman, eds. *Safety of Silicone Breast Implants.* Washington, D.C.: Institute of Medicine, 2000.

Bonwick, Colin. *The American Revolution.* Charlottesville: University Press of Virginia, 1991.

Bourdain, Anthony. *Typhoid Mary: An Urban Historical.* New York: Bloomsbury, 2001.

Boyer, Dwight. *True Tales of the Great Lakes.* New York: Dodd, Mead, 1971.

Boyer, Paul. *The Legend of John Brown.* New York: Knopf, 1973.

Boyer, Paul, and Stephen Nissenbaum. *Salem Possessed: The Social Origins of Witchcraft.* Cambridge, Mass.: Harvard University Press, 1974.

Bradford, William. *Of Plymouth Plantation.* Edited by Samuel Eliot Morison. New York: Knopf, 1970.

Bradsher, Keith. *High and Mighty: SUVs, The World's Most Dangerous Vehicles and How They Got That Way.* New York: PublicAffairs, 2002.

Braestrup, Peter. *Big Story: How the American Press and Television Reported and Interpreted the Crisis of Tet 1968 in Vietnam and Washington.* Novato, Calif.: Presidio Press, 1994.

Branch, Taylor. *At Canaan's Edge: America in the King Years, 1965–68.* New York: Simon and Schuster, 2006.

Braun, Mark S. *Chicago's North Shore Shipwrecks.* Polo, Ill.: Transportation Trails, 1992.

Brigham, William Tufts. *Historical Notes on the Earthquakes of New England.* Boston, 1871.

Bright, Lorine Zylks. *New London, 1937: The New London School Explosion, 1937: One Woman's Memory of Orange and Green.* Wichita Falls, Tex.: Nortex Press, 1977.

Brinkley, Alan. *American History: A Survey.* Boston: McGraw Hill, 1999.

Brinkley, Douglas. *The Great Deluge: Hurricane Katrina, New Orleans, and the Mississippi Gulf Coast.* New York: HarperCollins, 2006.

Brockmann, R. John. *Exploding Steamboats, Senate Debates, and Technical Reports: The Convergence of Technology, Politics and Rhetoric in the Steamboat Bill of 1838.* Amityville, N.Y.: Baywood Publishing Company, 2002.

Brody, David. *Steelworkers in America: The Nonunion Era.* Cambridge, Mass.: Harvard University Press, 1960.

Brown, Alexander Crosby. *Women and Children Last: The Loss of the Steamship* Arctic. New York: Putnam, 1961.

Brown, D. Alexander. "The Great Peshtigo Fire." *American History Illustrated* 3, no. 10 (1969): 26–32.

Brown, John Kennedy. *Limbs on the Levee: Steamboat Explosions and the Origins of Federal Public Welfare Regulation, 1817–1852.* Middlebourne, W.Va.: International Steamboat Society, 1988.

Brown, Roger. *Redeeming the Republic: Federalists, Taxation, and the Origins of the Constitution.* Baltimore: Johns Hopkins University Press, 1993.

Browne, Ray B., and Arthur G. Neal, eds., *Ordinary Reactions to Extraordinary Events.* Bowling Green, Ohio: Bowling Green State University Popular Press, 2001.

Bruce, Robert V. *1877: Year of Violence.* New York: Bobbs-Merrill, 1959.

Brundage, W. Fitzhugh. *Lynching in the New South: Georgia and Virginia, 1880–1930.* Urbana: University of Illinois Press, 1993.

Brust, Beth Wagner. *The Great Molasses Flood.* Mahwah, N.J.: Troll Communications, 1998.

Bullion, J. L. *A Great and Necessary Measure: George Grenville and the Genesis of the Stamp Act, 1763–1765.* Columbia: University of Missouri Press, 1982.

Burke, John C. "Bursting Boilers and the Federal Power." *Technology and Culture* 7 (1966): 1–23.

Burns, Cherie. *The Great Hurricane: 1938.* New York: Atlantic Monthly Press, 2005.

Butler, Jonathan, and Ronald Numbers, eds. *The Disappointed: Millerism and Millenarianism in the Nineteenth Century.* Bloomington: Indiana University Press, 1987.

Butler, Susan. *East to the Dawn: The Life of Amelia Earhart.* Reading, Mass.: Addison-Wesley, 1997.

Cabbage, Michael, and William Harwood. *Comm Check: The Final Flight of Shuttle* Columbia. New York: Free Press, 2004.

Cable, Mary. *The Blizzard of '88.* New York: Atheneum, 1988.

Cahn, William. *Lawrence 1912: The Bread and Roses Strike.* New York: Pilgrim Press, 1977.

Cameron, Ardis. *Radicals of the Worst Sort: Laboring Women in Lawrence, Massachusetts, 1860–1912.* Chicago: University of Illinois Press, 1993.

Campenella, Thomas. *Republic of Shade: New England and the American Elm.* New Haven, Conn.: Yale University Press, 2003.

Cannon, Lou. *Official Negligence: How Rodney King and the Riots Changed Los Angeles and the LAPD.* New York: Crown, 1998.

Cantril, Hadley. *The Invasion from Mars: A Study in the Psychology of Panic.* London: Transaction Publishers, 2005.

Caram, Peter. *The 1993 World Trade Center Bombing: Foresight and Warning.* London: Janus Publishing Co., 2001.

Carlin, Alan P., and George E. Kocher. *Environmental Problems: Their Causes, Cures, and Evolution, Using Southern California Smog as an Example.* Santa Monica, Calif.: Rand, 1971.

Carney, Gene. *Burying the Black Sox.* Washington, D.C.: Potomac Books, 2006.

Carp, E. Wayne. *To Starve the Army at Pleasure: Continental Army Administration and American Political Culture, 1775–1783.* Chapel Hill: University of North Carolina Press, 1984.

Carson, Jane. *Bacon's Rebellion, 1676–1976.* Virginia: The Jamestown Foundation, 1976.

Carson, Rachel. *Silent Spring.* 40th anniversary ed. Boston: Houghton Mifflin, 2002.

Carter, Dan T. *Scottsboro: A Tragedy of the American South.* Delanco, N.J.: Notable Trials Library, 2000.

Carter, Susan B., and Richard Sutch. "Great Depression of 1890s: New Suggestive Estimates of the Unemployment Rate, 1890–1905." *Research in Economic History* 14 (1992): 347–76.

Channing, Steven A. *Crisis of Fear: Secession in South Carolina.* New York: Norton, 1974.

Chant, Christopher. *The Zeppelin: The History of German Airships from 1900 to 1937.* London: Amber Books, 2000.

Chase, Marilyn. *The Barbary Plague: The Black Death in Victorian San Francisco.* New York: Random House, 2003.

Cherniack, Martin. *The Hawk's Nest Incident: America's Worst Industrial Disaster.* New Haven, Conn.: Yale University Press, 1986.

Chernow, Ron. *The House of Morgan: An American Banking Dynasty and the Rise of Modern Finance.* New York: Atlantic Monthly Press, 1990.

Chicago Commission on Race Relations. *The Negro in Chicago: A Study of Race Relations and a Race Riot.* Chicago: University of Chicago Press, 1922.

Chikota, Richard. *Riot in the Cities.* Rutherford, N.J.: Fairleigh Dickinson University Press, 1970.

Chittick, William E. *The Worcester Tornado, June 9, 1953.* Bristol, R.I.: privately printed, 2002.

Clark, Jerome. *1844: Intellectual, Social, and Religious Movements.* Nashville, Tenn.: Southern Publishing Association, 1968.

Clouds of Injustice: Bhopal Disaster 20 Years On. London: Amnesty International Publications, 2004. Available online. URL: http://web.amnesty.org/pages/ec-bhopal-eng. Accessed April 10, 2007.

Coben, Stanley. *A. Mitchell Palmer, Politician.* New York: Da Capo Press, 1972.

Cohen, Daniel. "Passing the Torch: Boston Firemen, 'Tea Party' Patriots, and the Burning of the Charlestown Convent." *Journal of the Early Republic* 24, no. 4 (Winter 2004).

Cohen, Lizabeth. *Making a New Deal: Industrial Workers in Chicago, 1919–1939.* New York: Cambridge University Press, 1990.

Coll, Steve. *Ghost Wars: The Secret History of the CIA, Afghanistan, and Bin Laden, from the Soviet Invasion to September 10, 2001.* New York: Penguin, 2004.

Collette, Bruce B., and Grace Klein-MacPhee, eds. *Bigelow and Schroeder's Fishes of the Gulf of Maine.* Washington: Smithsonian Institution Press, 2002.

Columbus, Christopher. *The Four Voyages of Christopher Columbus.* Edited and translated by J. M. Cohen. New York: Penguin, 1969.

Comerio, Mary. *Disaster Hits Home: New Policy for Urban Housing Recovery.* Berkeley: University of California Press, 1998.

Conot, Robert. *Rivers of Blood, Years of Darkness: The Unforgettable Classic Account of the Watts Riot.* New York: Morrow, 1967.

Conway, Eric. *Echoes in the Grand Canyon: Public Catastrophes and Technologies of Control in American Aviation.* New York: Routledge, 2004.

Cook, Adrian. *The Armies of the Street: The New York City Draft Riots of 1863.* Lexington: University Press of Kentucky, 1974.

Cook, Noble David. *Born to Die: Disease and New World Conquest, 1492–1650.* New York: Cambridge University Press, 1998.

Cooper, Christopher, and Robert Block. *Disaster: Hurricane Katrina and the Failure of Homeland Security.* New York: Times Books, 2006.

Corn, Jacqueline K. *Response to Occupational Health Hazards: A Historical Perspective.* New York: Van Nostrand Reinhold, 1992.

Correspondents of The New York Times. *36 Days: The Complete Chronicle of the 2000 Presidential Election Crisis.* New York: Times Books, 2001.

Cowan, David. *Great Chicago Fires: Historic Blazes That Shaped a City.* Chicago: Lake Claremont Press, 2001.

Craven, Avery Odelle. *The Growth of Southern Nationalism, 1848–1861.* Baton Rouge: Louisiana State University Press, 1953.

Cros Sandoval, Mercedes. *Mariel and Cuban National Identity.* Miami: Editorial SIBI, 1986.

Crosby, Alfred W. *America's Forgotten Pandemic: The Influenza of 1918.* New York: Cambridge University Press, 1989.

——. *Ecological Imperialism: The Biological Expansion of Europe, 900–1900.* New York: Cambridge University Press, 1986.

Crouthamel, James L. "The Springfield Race Riot of 1908." *The Journal of Negro History* 45 (July 1960): 164–181.

Cutler, Carl C. *Queens of the Western Ocean: The Story of America's Mail and Passenger Sailing Lines.* Annapolis, Md.: U.S. Naval Institute, 1961.

Daniel, Pete. *Deep'n As It Come: The 1927 Mississippi Flood.* Little Rock: University of Arkansas Press, 1996.

Davidson, Art. *In the Wake of the* Exxon Valdez*: The Devastating Impact of the Alaska Oil Spill.* San Francisco: Sierra Club Books, 1990.

Davies, J. Clarence, and Barbara S. Davies. *The Politics of Pollution.* 2d ed. Indianapolis: Bobbs-Merrill, 1975.

Davis, Devra. *When Smoke Ran like Water: Tales of Environmental Deception and the Battle Against Pollution.* Cambridge, Mass.: MIT Press (Basic Books), 2003.

Davis, Donald Edward. *Where There Are Mountains: An Environmental History of the Southern Appalachians.* Athens: University of Georgia Press, 2000.

Davis, Thomas. J. *A Rumor of Revolt: The "Great Negro Plot" in Colonial New York.* New York: Free Press, 1985.

Davis, William C. *Battle at Bull Run: A History of the First Major Campaign of the Civil War.* Mechanicsburg, Pa.: Stackpole, 1995.

——. *Three Roads to the Alamo: The Lives and Fortunes of David Crockett, James Bowie, and William Barret Travis.* New York: HarperCollins, 1998.

Demarest, David P., Jr., ed. *"The River Ran Red": Homestead 1892.* Pittsburgh: University of Pittsburgh Press, 1992.

Demos, John. *The Unredeemed Captive: A Family Story from Early America.* New York: Knopf, 1994.

Denevan, William M., ed. *The Native Population of the Americas in 1492.* Madison: University of Wisconsin Press, 1976.

Dennison, George M. *The Dorr War: Republicanism on Trial, 1831–1861.* Lexington: University of Kentucky Press, 1976.

de Syon, Guillaume. *Zeppelin! Germany and the Airship, 1900–1939.* Baltimore: Johns Hopkins University Press, 2002.

Detzer, David. *Donnybrook: The Battle of Bull Run, 1861.* Orlando, Fla.: Harcourt, 2004.

Dittmer, John. *Local People: The Struggle for Civil Rights in Mississippi.* Urbana: University of Illinois Press, 1994.

Donald, David Herbert. *Lincoln.* New York: Simon and Schuster, 1996.

Drake, James. *King Philip's War: Civil War in New England, 1675–1676.* Amherst, Mass.: University of Massachusetts Press, 1999.

Dray, Philip. *At the Hands of Persons Unknown: The Lynching of Black America.* New York: Random House, 2002.

Drye, Willie. *Storm of the Century: The Labor Day Hurricane of 1935.* Washington D.C.: National Geographic Books, 2002.

Dudziak, Mary L., ed. *September 11 in History: A Watershed Moment?* Durham, N.C.: Duke University Press, 2003.

Duffy, John. *A History of Public Health in New York City: 1625–1866.* New York: Russell Sage Foundation, 1968.

Dumond, Dwight Lowell. *The Secession Movement, 1860–1861.* New York: Negro Universities Press, 1968.

Dwight, Theodore. *History of the Hartford Convention: With a Review of the Policy of the United States Government Which Led to the War of 1812.* 1833. Reprint, Freeport, N.Y.: Da Capo Press, 1970.

Dyson, Michael Eric. *Come Hell or High Water: Hurricane Katrina and the Color of Disaster.* New York: Basic Books, 2006.

Eastman, Joel W. *Styling vs. Safety: The American Automobile Industry and the Development of Auto-*

motive Safety, 1900–1966. Lanham, Md.: University Press of America, 1984.

Easton, Robert. Black Tide: The Santa Barbara Oil Spill and Its Consequences. New York: Delacorte, 1972.

Eaton, John P., and Charles A. Haas. Titanic: Destination Disaster. Rev. and exp. ed. New York: W. W. Norton, 1996.

Egan, Timothy. The Worst Hard Time: The Untold Story of Those Who Survived the Great American Dust Bowl. Boston: Houghton-Mifflin, 2005.

Egerton, Douglas R. He Shall Go Out Free: The Lives of Denmark Vesey. Madison, Wis.: Madison House, 1999.

Eggert, Gerald G. Richard Olney: Evolution of a Statesman. University Park: Pennsylvania State University Press, 1974.

Elkins, Stanley, and Eric McKitrick. The Age of Federalism: The Early American Republic, 1788–1800. New York: Oxford University Press, 1993.

Ellis, John Hubert. Yellow Fever and Public Health in the New South. Lexington: University of Kentucky, 1992.

Emanuel, Kerry. Divine Wind: The History and Science of Hurricanes. New York: Oxford University Press, 2005.

Errington, Sara. "Wonders and the Creation of Evangelical Culture in New England, 1720–1820." Ph.D. diss., Brown University, 2000.

Esposito, John C. Fire in the Grove: The Cocoanut Grove Tragedy and Its Aftermath. Cambridge, Mass.: Da Capo, 2005.

Estes, J. Worth, and Billy G. Smith, eds. A Melancholy Scene of Devastation: The Public Response to the 1793 Philadelphia Yellow Fever Epidemic. Canton, Mass.: Science History Publications/USA, 1997.

Fahey, Kathleen. Challenger and Columbia. Milwaukee: Gareth Stevens Publishers, 1995.

Faragher, John Mack. A Great and Noble Scheme: The Tragic Story of the Expulsion of the French Acadians from Their American Homeland. New York: W. W. Norton & Company, 2005.

Farber, David. Chicago '68. Chicago: University of Chicago Press, 1988.

———. Taken Hostage: The Iran Hostage Crisis and America's First Encounter with Radical Islam. Princeton, N.J.: Princeton University Press, 2005.

Farley, Reynolds, Sheldon Danziger, and Harry J. Holzer. Detroit Divided. New York: Russell Sage Foundation, 2000.

Faubion, James D. The Shadows and Lights of Waco: Millennialism Today. Princeton, N.J.: Princeton University Press, 2001.

Faulkner, Harold U. The Decline of Laissez Faire, 1897–1917. New York: Rinehart and Company, 1951.

Feer, Robert A. Shays's Rebellion. New York: Garland Press, 1988.

Feldberg, Michael. The Turbulent Era: Riot and Disorder in Jacksonian America. New York: Oxford University Press, 1980.

Fernández, Gastón. The Mariel Exodus Twenty Years Later: A Study in the Politics of Stigma and a Research Bibliography. Miami: Ediciones Universal, 2002.

Fischer, David Hackett. Paul Revere's Ride. New York: Oxford University Press, 1994.

Fisher, Jim. The Lindbergh Case. New Brunswick, N.J.: Rutgers University Press, 1987.

Fiske, John. The Critical Period of American History, 1783–1789. Boston: Houghton, Mifflin and Co., 1888. Reprint Whitefish, Mont.: Kessinger Publishing, 2004.

Flayhart, William Henry III. Perils of the Atlantic: Steamship Disasters, 1850 to the Present. New York: W. W. Norton, 2003.

Fleming, Thomas. Washington's Secret War: The Hidden History of Valley Forge. New York: Smithsonian Books/Collins, 2005.

Flexner, James. George Washington and the New Nation, 1783–1793. Boston: Little, Brown: 1970.

Fogel, Robert W. The Union Pacific Railroad: A Case of Premature Enterprise. Baltimore: Johns Hopkins University Press, 1960.

Fogelson, Robert. The Los Angeles Riots. New York: Arno Press, 1969.

Foner, Eric. Reconstruction: America's Unfinished Revolution. New York: Harper and Row, 1988.

Foner, Philip S. The Great Labor Uprising of 1877. New York: Monad Press, 1977.

Ford, Daniel F. Three Mile Island: Thirty Minutes to Meltdown. New York: Penguin, 1981.

Fradkin, Philip L. The Great Earthquake and Firestorms of 1906: How San Francisco Nearly Destroyed Itself. Berkeley: University of California Press, 2005.

Frank, Richard B. Downfall: The End of the Imperial Japanese Empire. New York: Penguin, 2001.

Fraser, David W., et al. "Legionnaires' Disease: Description of an Epidemic of Pneumonia."

The New England Journal of Medicine 297, no. 22 (December 1, 1977): 1,189–1,197.

Fraser, Walter. *Charleston! Charleston! The History of a Southern City.* Columbia: University of South Carolina Press, 1989.

Freehling, William W. *The Road to Disunion: Secessionists Triumphant, 1854–1861.* New York: Oxford University Press, 1990.

Freudenburg, William R., and Robert Gramling. *Oil in Troubled Waters: Perception, Politics, and the Battle over Offshore Drilling.* Albany: State University of New York, 1994.

Freyer, Tony. *The Little Rock Crisis.* Westport, Conn.: Greenwood Press, 1984.

Friedman, Thomas L. *From Beirut to Jerusalem.* New York: Farrar, Straus and Giroux, 1989.

Fry, Ron, and Pamela Fourzen. *The Saga of Special Effects.* Englewood Cliffs, N.J.: Prentice Hall, 1977.

Fuller, Myron L. "The New Madrid Earthquakes." Cape Girardeau, Mo. Ampere Press. First published as Bulletin 394, Department of the Interior, Government Printing Office, 1912.

Fusaro, Peter C., and Ross M. Miller. *What Went Wrong at Enron.* Hoboken, N.J.: Wiley, 2002.

Gage, Beverly. *The Day Wall Street Exploded: A Story of America in Its First Age of Terror.* Oxford: Oxford University Press, forthcoming.

Garrow, David J. *Bearing the Cross: Martin Luther King, Jr. and the Southern Christian Leadership Conference.* New York: W. W. Norton, 1981.

———. *Protest at Selma: Martin Luther King, Jr., and the Voting Rights Act of 1965.* New Haven, Conn.: Yale University Press, 1978.

Gasparini, D. A., and Melissa Fields. "Collapse of the Ashtabula Bridge on December 29, 1876." *Journal of Performance of Constructed Materials* 7, May 1993: 109–125.

Gess, Denise, and William Lutz. *Firestorm at Peshtigo: A Town, Its People, and the Deadliest Fire in American History.* New York: Henry Holt, 2002.

Gettleman, Marvin E. *The Dorr Rebellion: A Study in American Radicalism.* New York: Random House, 1973.

Gilbert, Marc J., and William Head, eds. *The Tet Offensive.* New York: Praeger, 1996.

Goode, George B. *Fisheries and Fishery Industries of the U.S.,* Section V-1. Washington, D.C.: GPO, U.S. Commission of Fish and Fisheries, 1887.

Gooding-Williams, Robert, ed. *Reading Rodney King, Reading Urban Uprising.* New York: Routledge, 1993.

Goodman, James E. *Blackout.* New York: North Point Press, 2003.

Gore, Rick. "Andrew Aftermath." *National Geographic* 183, no. 4 (April 1993): 2–37.

Goudsouzian, Aram. *The Hurricane of 1938.* Boston: Commonwealth Editions, 2004.

Gould, Lewis L. *1968: The Election That Changed America.* Chicago: Ivan Dee, 1993.

———. *The Presidency of William McKinley.* Lawrence: University Press of Kansas, 1980.

Greene, Casey Edward, and Shelly Henley Kelly. *Through a Night of Horrors: Voices from the 1900 Galveston Storm.* College Station: Texas A&M University Press, 2000.

Greene, Jerome A., and Douglas D. Scott. *Finding Sand Creek: History, Archeology, and the 1864 Massacre Site.* Norman: University of Oklahoma Press, 2004.

———. ed. *Lakota and Cheyenne: Indian Views of the Great Sioux War, 1876–1877.* Norman: University of Oklahoma Press, 1994.

Greenwald, Richard. *The Triangle Fire, the Protocols of Peace, and Industrial Democracy in Progressive Era New York.* Philadelphia: Temple University Press, 2005.

Grob, Gerald N. *The Deadly Truth: A History of Disease in America.* Cambridge, Mass.: Harvard University Press. 2002.

Gross, Robert A. *The Minutemen and Their World.* New York: Hill and Wang, 1976.

Guggenheim, Charles. "The Scene of the Crime." *American Heritage* (November 1992): 120–127.

Gunn, Angus M. "Pesticide Leak, Bhopal, India, December 3, 1984." In *Unnatural Disasters: Case Studies of Human-Induced Environmental Catastrophes.* Westport, Conn.: Greenwood Press, 2003, 113–118.

Haefeli, Evan, and Kevin Sweeney. *Captors and Captives: The 1704 French and Indian Raid on Deerfield.* Amherst: University of Massachusetts Press, 2003.

Haines, Francis. *The Buffalo: The Story of American Bison and Their Hunters from Prehistoric Times to the Present.* 1970. Reprint, Norman: University of Oklahoma Press, 1995.

Hamby, Alonzo L. *For the Survival of Democracy: Franklin Roosevelt and the World Crisis of the 1930s.* New York: Free Press, 2004.

Hamilton, Holman. "Democratic Senate Leadership and the Compromise of 1850." *Mississippi Valley Historical Review* 41 (December 1954): 403–418.

——. *Prologue to Conflict: The Crisis and Compromise of 1850.* Lexington: University of Kentucky Press, 1964.

Hammond, Bray. *Banks and Politics in America from the Revolution to the Civil War.* Princeton, N.J.: Princeton University Press, 1957.

Hanchett, William. *The Lincoln Murder Conspiracies.* Urbana: University of Illinois Press, 1983.

Hansen, Gladys C., and Emmet Condon. *Denial of Disaster: The Untold Story and Photographs of the San Francisco Earthquake and Fire of 1906.* Edited by David Fowler. San Francisco: Cameron and Co., 1989.

Hardin, Stephen L. *Texian Iliad: A Military History of the Texas Revolution.* Austin: University of Texas Press, 1994.

Hargrove, Erwin C. *Jimmy Carter as President.* Baton Rouge: Louisiana State University Press, 1988.

Harris, Steven L. *Fire Mountains of the West.* Missoula, Mont.: Mountain Press Publishing Company, 2005.

Hasky, Judy L. *Columbine High School Shooting: Student Violence.* Berkeley Heights, N.J.: Enslow, 2002.

Hatch, Thom. *Black Kettle: The Cheyenne Chief Who Sought Peace but Found War.* Hoboken, N.J.: Wiley, 2004.

Hayden, Tom. *Rebellion in Newark: Official Violence and Ghetto Response.* New York: Vintage, 1967.

Hays, Samuel P. *Beauty, Health, and Permanence: Environmental Politics in the United States, 1955–1985.* New York: Cambridge University Press, 1987.

Heerden, Ivor van, and Mike Bryan. *The Storm: What Went Wrong During Hurricane Katrina—The Inside Story from One Louisiana Scientist.* New York: Viking, 2006.

Heppenheimer, T. R. *The Space Shuttle Decision, 1965–1972.* Washington D.C.: Smithsonian Institution Press, 2002.

Hibbs, Douglas A., Jr. *The American Political Economy: Macroeconomics and Electoral Politics.* Cambridge, Mass.: Harvard University Press, 1987.

Hickey, Donald. *Don't Give up the Ship! Myths of the War of 1812.* Urbana and Chicago: University of Illinois Press, 2006.

——. *The War of 1812: A Forgotten Conflict.* Urbana: University of Illinois Press, 1989.

Higgins, Trumbull. *The Perfect Failure: Kennedy, Eisenhower, and the Bay of Pigs.* New York: W. W. Norton, 1989.

Hilton, George W. *Eastland: Legacy of the* Titanic. Stanford, Calif.: Stanford University Press, 1995.

Hodder, Frank H. "The Authorship of the Compromise of 1850." *Mississippi Valley Historical Review* 22 (March 1936): 525–536.

Hoffer, Peter Charles. *The Devil's Disciples: Makers of the Salem Witchcraft Trials.* Baltimore: Johns Hopkins University Press, 1996.

Hoffman, Charles. *The Depression of the Nineties: An Economic History.* Westport, Conn.: Greenwood, 1970.

Hoig, Stan. *The Sand Creek Massacre.* Norman: University of Oklahoma Press, 1961.

Holland, Max. "The JFK Lawyers' Conspiracy." *Nation* (February 20, 2006).

——. comp. *The Kennedy Assassination Tapes.* New York: Knopf, 2004.

Holmsten, Brian, and Alex Lubertozzi, eds. *The Complete War of the Worlds: Mars' Invasion of Earth from H. G. Wells to Orson Welles.* Naperville, Ill.: Sourcebooks, 2001.

Hopkins, James F. "The Presidential Election of 1824." In *History of American Presidential Elections,* Vol. 1, edited by Arthur J. Schlesinger, Jr., and Fred L. Israel, 349–409. New York: Chelsea House, 1971.

Horne, Gerald. *Fire This Time: The Watts Uprising and the 1960s.* Charlottesville: University of Virginia Press, 1995.

Horne, Jed. *Breach of Faith: Hurricane Katrina and the Near Death of a Great American City.* New York: Random House, 2006.

Hough, Susan E. *Earthshaking Science: What We Know (and Don't Know) about Earthquakes.* Princeton, N.J.: Princeton University Press, 2002.

Housner, George W. *Competing against Time: Report to Governor George Deukmejian from the Governor's Board of Inquiry on the 1989 Loma Prieta Earthquake.* Sacramento: State of California Office of Planning and Research, 1990.

Houts, Peter S., Paul Cleary, and The-Wei Hu. *The Three Mile Island Crisis: Psychological, Social, and Economic Impacts on the Surrounding Population.* University Park: Pennsylvania State University Press, 1988.

Hughes, Patrick. *American Weather Stories.* Washington, D.C.: U.S. Department of Commerce, 1976.

Hult, Ruby El. *Northwest Disaster: Avalanche and Fire.* Portland, Oreg.: Binford and Mort, 1960.

Humphreys, Margaret. *Yellow Fever and the South.* Rutgers, N.J.: University Press, 1992.

Hunter, Louis C. *Steamboats on the Western Rivers: An Economic and Technical History.* Cambridge, Mass.: Harvard University Press, 1949.

Hurt, R. Douglas. *The Dust Bowl: An Agricultural and Social History.* Chicago: Nelson-Hall, 1981.

Huston, James L. *The Panic of 1857 and the Coming of the Civil War.* Baton Rouge: Louisiana State University Press, 1987.

Iriye, Akira. *The Origins of the Second World War in Asia and the Pacific.* New York: Longman, 1987.

Irwin, A. C., J. Millen, and D. Fallows. *Global AIDS: Myths and Facts: Tools for Fighting the AIDS Pandemic.* Cambridge, Mass.: South End Press, 2003.

Ise, John. *Sod and Stubble: The Story of a Kansas Farm.* Lawrence: University Press of Kansas, 1996.

Isenberg, Andrew. *The Destruction of the Bison.* Cambridge: Cambridge University Press, 2000.

Jackson, Charles O. *Food and Drug Legislation in the New Deal.* Princeton, N.J.: Princeton University Press, 1970.

Jackson, Donald C., and Norris Hundley, Jr. "Privilege and Responsibility: William Mulholland and the St. Francis Dam Disaster" *California History* 82 (2004): 8–47, 72–78.

Jackson, Robert Lee. *Living Lessons from the New London Explosion.* Nashville, Tenn.: The Parthenon Press, 1938.

Jobb, Dean. *The Cajuns: A People's Story of Exile and Triumph.* New York: Wiley, 2005.

Johnson, Michael P. "Denmark Vesey and His Co-Conspirators." *William and Mary Quarterly* 58 (October 2001): 915–976.

Johnston, Arch C. "A Major Earthquake Zone on the Mississippi." *Scientific American* 246, no. 4 (April 1982): 60–68.

Jones, Susan. *Valuing Animals: Veterinarians and Their Patients in Modern America.* Baltimore: Johns Hopkins University Press, 2003.

Josephson, D. H. "The Great Midwest Flood of 1993: Natural Disaster Survey Report." Silver Spring, Md.: National Oceanic and Atmospheric Administration, National Weather Service, 1994.

Kahn, Judd. *Imperial San Francisco: Politics and Planning in an American City, 1897–1906.* Lincoln: University of Nebraska Press, 1979.

Kallman, Robert, and Eugene D. Wheeler. *Coastal Crude in a Sea of Conflict.* San Luis Obispo, Calif.: Blake Printing and Publishing Co., 1984.

Karaim, Reed. "Not So Fast with the DDT: Rachel Carson's Warnings Still Apply." *American Scholar* 74, no. 3 (June 22, 2005): 53–59.

Kars, Marjoleine. *Breaking Loose Together: The Regulator Rebellion in Pre-Revolutionary North Carolina.* Chapel Hill: University of North Carolina Press, 2002.

Kauffman, Michael W. *American Brutus: John Wilkes Booth and the Lincoln Conspiracies.* New York: Random House, 2004.

Kawashima, Yasuhide. *Igniting King Philip's War: The John Sassamon Murder Trial.* Lawrence: University Press of Kansas, 2001.

Kay, Glenn, and Michael Rose. *Disaster Movies.* Chicago: Chicago Review Press, 2006.

Kean, Thomas H., and Lee Hamilton. *Without Precedent: The Inside Story of the 9/11 Commission.* New York: Knopf, 2006.

Keane, Stephen. *Disaster Movies: The Cinema of Catastrophe.* London: Wallflower Press, 2001.

Keeble, John. *Out of the Channel: The Exxon Valdez Oil Spill in Prince William Sound.* Cheney, Wash.: Eastern Washington University Press, 1999.

Keir, A. E., Dean E. Mann, and Phil G. Olsen Nash. *Oil Pollution and the Public Interest: A Study of the Santa Barbara Oil Spill.* Berkeley: University of California Press, 1972.

Keller, Morton. *The Life Insurance Enterprise, 1885–1910: A Study in the Limits of Corporate Power.* Cambridge, Mass.: Belknap Press, 1963.

Kelly, Alfred H., Winfred A. Harbison, and Herman Belz. *The American Constitution.* New York: W. W. Norton, 1991.

Kennedy, David M. *Freedom from Fear: The American People in Depression and War, 1929–1945.* New York: Oxford University Press, 1999.

Kennedy, Robert F. *Thirteen Days: A Memoir of the Cuban Missile Crisis.* New York: W. W. Norton, 1969.

Kenny, Kevin. *Making Sense of the Molly Maguires.* New York: Oxford University Press, 1998.

Keyes, Edward. *Cocoanut Grove.* New York: Atheneum, 1984.

The Kheel Center, Catherwood Library, ILR School at Cornell University. *The Triangle Factory Fire.* Available online. URL: http://www.ilr.cornell.edu/trianglefire/. Accessed April 10, 2007.

Kiester, Edwin, Jr. "A Darkness in Donora." *Smithsonian Magazine* (November 1999).

Kindleberger, Charles. *Historical Economics: Art or Science?* New York: Harvester/Wheatsheaf, 1990.

Klein, Maury. *The Union Pacific: Birth of a Railroad, 1862–1893.* New York: Doubleday, 1987.

Kluger, Richard. *Ashes to Ashes: America's Hundred-Year Cigarette War, the Public Health, and the Unabashed Triumph of Philip Morris.* New York: Knopf, 1996.

Knightley, Phillip, Harold Evans, Elaine Potter, and Marjorie Wallace. *Suffer the Children: The Story of Thalidomide.* New York: Viking, 1979.

Kobler, John. *Capone: The Life and World of Al Capone.* New York: Da Capo Press, 2003.

Kocin, P. J., P. N. Schumacher, R. F. Morales, Jr., and L. W. Uccellini. "Overview of the 12–14 March 1993 Superstorm." *Bulletin of the American Meteorological Society* 76, no. 2 (February 1995): 165–182.

Koeppel, Gerard R. *Water for Gotham: A History.* Princeton, N.J.: Princeton University Press, 2000.

Kolata, Gina. *Flu: The Story of the Great Influenza Pandemic of 1918 and the Search for the Virus That Caused It.* New York: Farrar, Straus and Giroux, 1999.

Kornbluh, Peter, ed. *Bay of Pigs Declassified: The Secret CIA Report on the Invasion of Cuba.* New York: New Press, 1998.

Krause, Paul. *The Battle for Homestead, 1880–1892.* Pittsburgh: University of Pittsburgh Press, 1992.

Krist, Gary. *The White Cascade: The Great Northern Railway Disaster and America's Deadliest Avalanche.* New York: Holt, 2007.

Krohe, James, Jr. *Summer of Rage: The Springfield Race Riot of 1908.* Springfield, Ill.: Sangamon County Historical Society, 1973.

Kuntz, Tom, ed. *The* Titanic *Disaster Hearings: The Official Transcripts of the 1912 Senate Investigation.* New York: Pocket Books, 1998.

Kupperman, Karen Ordahl. *Roanoke: The Abandoned Colony.* Savage, Md.: Rowman and Littlefield, 1984.

Kutler, Stanley I. *The Wars of Watergate: The Last Crisis of Richard Nixon.* New York: Knopf, 1990.

La Forte, Robert S., and Ronald E. Marcello, eds. *Remembering Pearl Harbor: Eyewitness Accounts by U.S. Military Men and Women.* Wilmington, Del.: Scholarly Resources Books, 1991.

Lane, Mark. *Rush to Judgment.* New York: Holt, Rinehart & Winston, 1966.

Larson, Erik. *Isaac's Storm: A Man, a Time, and the Deadliest Hurricane in History.* New York: Crown, 1999.

Larson, Lee. "The Great USA Flood of 1993," paper presented at the IAHS Conference, Anaheim, Calif., June 24–28, 1996. Available online. URL: http://www.nwrfc.noaa.gov/floods/papers/oh_2/great.htm. Accessed April 10, 2007.

Laskin, David. *Braving the Elements: The Stormy History of American Weather.* New York: Anchor Book, 1993.

Lauderbaugh, Richard A. *American Steel Makers and the Coming of the Second World War.* Ann Arbor, Mich.: UMI Research Press, 1980.

Lawson, Thomas. "Lawson and His Critics." *Everybody's Magazine* 11 (December 1904): 72. Reprinted in *The Muckrakers,* Arthur and Lila Weinberg, eds, 286–96. Urbana: University of Illinois Press, 2001.

Layzer, Judith A. "Love Canal: Hazardous Waste and the Politics of Fear." In *The Environmental Case: Translating Values into Policy.* Washington, D.C.: CQ Press, 2006.

Leacock, Elspeth. *The* Exxon Valdez *Oil Spill.* New York: Facts On File, 2005.

Lear, Linda. *Rachel Carson: Witness for Nature.* New York: Henry Holt, 1997.

Leavitt, Judith Walzer. *Typhoid Mary: Captive to the Public's Health.* Boston: Beacon Press, 1996.

Lee, Helen Joy, et al. *Watch Hill Hurricane September 21, 1938.* Watch Hill, R.I.: The Book and Tackle Shop, 1996.

Leech, Margaret, and Harry J. Brown. *The Garfield Orbit.* New York: Harper & Row, 1978.

Lees, Lester. *Smog: A Report to the People.* Pasadena, Calif.: California Institute of Technology, Environmental Quality Laboratory, 1972.

Lender, Mark, and James Kirby Martin. *A Respectable Army: The Military Origins of the Republic, 1763–1789.* Arlington Heights, Ill.: H. Davidson, 1982.

Leone, Richard C., and Greg Anrig, Jr., eds. *The War on Our Freedoms: Civil Liberties in an Age of Terrorism.* New York: Century Foundation, 2003.

———. *The Name of War: King Philip's War and the Origins of American Identity.* New York: Knopf, 1999.

Lepore, Jill. *New York Burning: Liberty, Slavery, and Conspiracy in Eighteenth-Century Manhattan.* New York: Knopf, 2005.

Levine, Adeline Gordon. *Love Canal: Science, Politics, and People.* Lexington, Mass.: Lexington Books, 1983.

Linder, Douglas. *Famous Trials: The Triangle Shirtwaist Fire Trial 1911.* Available online. URL: http://www.law.umkc.edu/faculty/projects/ftrials/triangle/trianglefire.html. Accessed April 10, 2007.

Lindsey, Almont. *The Pullman Strike: The Story of a Unique Experiment and of a Great Labor Upheaval.* Chicago: University of Chicago Press, 1942.

Lord, Walter. *A Night to Remember.* New York: Bantam Books, 1956.

Los Angeles Times Staff. *Understanding the Riots: Los Angeles Before and After the Rodney King Case.* Los Angeles: Los Angeles Times, 1992.

Lutgens, Frederick K., and Edward J. Tarbuck. *The Atmosphere: An Introduction to Meteorology.* 10th ed. Upper Saddle River, N.J.: Pearson/Prentice Hall, 2007.

Lutts, Ralph H. "Like Manna from God: The American Chestnut Trade in Southwestern Virginia." *Environmental History* 9 (July 2004): 497–525.

Mackey, Sandra. *Lebanon: Death of a Nation.* New York: Congdon & Weed, 1989.

Manchester, William. *The Death of a President.* London: Michael Joseph, 1967.

Mann, Charles C. *1491: New Revelations of the Americas Before Columbus.* New York: Knopf, 2005.

Mashaw, Jerry L., and David L. Harfst. *The Struggle for Auto Safety.* Cambridge, Mass.: Harvard University Press, 1990.

Masud-Piloto, Felix. *From Welcomed Exiles to Illegal Immigrants: Cuban Migration to the U.S., 1959–1995.* London: Rowman and Littlefield Publishers, 1996.

Matusow, Allen J. *The Unraveling of America: A History of Liberalism in the 1960's.* New York: Harper and Row, 1984.

May, Ernest R. *Imperial Democracy: The Emergence of America as a Great Power.* New York: Harper and Row, 1973.

May, Ernest R., and Philip D. Zelikow, eds. *The Kennedy Tapes: Inside the White House during the Cuban Missile Crisis.* Cambridge, Mass.: Belknap Press, 1997.

McAdam, Doug. *Freedom Summer.* New York: Oxford University Press, 1988.

McCardell, John. *The Idea of a Southern Nation: Southern Nationalists and Southern Nationalism, 1830–1860.* New York: W. W. Norton, 1979.

McClain, Charles. *In Search of Equality: The Chinese Struggle against Discrimination in Nineteenth-Century America.* Berkeley: University of California Press, 1994.

McClymer, John F. *The Triangle Strike and Fire.* Fort Worth, Tex.: Harcourt Brace College Publishers, 1998.

McComb, David. *Galveston: A History.* Austin: University of Texas Press, 1986.

McCraw, Thomas K. *Prophets of Regulation.* Cambridge, Mass.: Harvard University Press, 1984.

McCullough, David. *The Johnstown Flood: The Incredible Story Behind One of the Most Devastating "Natural" Disasters America Has Ever Known.* New York: Simon and Schuster, 1968.

McDade, Joseph E., et al. "Legionnaires' Disease: Isolation of a Bacterium and Demonstration of Its Role in Other Respiratory Disease." *The New England Journal of Medicine* 297, no. 22 (December 1, 1977): 1,197–1,203.

McDermott, Terry. *Perfect Soldiers: The Hijackers.* New York: HarperCollins Publishers, 2005.

McPhee, John. *The Control of Nature.* New York: Farrar, Straus and Giroux, 1990.

McShane, Clay. "Gelded Age Boston." *New England Quarterly* 74 (August 2001): 274–301.

McShane, Clay, and Joel A. Tarr. "The Centrality of the Horse to the Nineteenth Century American City," In *The Making of Urban America,* edited by Raymond Mohl, 103–130. Rev. ed. Wilmington, Del.: Scholarly Resources, 1997.

Mercantini, Jonathan. "The Great Carolina Hurricane of 1752." *South Carolina Historical Magazine* 103 (October 2002): 351–365.

Millas, J. C. *Hurricanes of the Caribbean and Adjacent Regions.* Miami: Academy of the Arts and Sciences of the Americas, 1968.

Miller, Kerby. *Emigrants and Exiles: Ireland and the Irish Exodus to North America.* Oxford: Oxford University Press, 1985.

Miller, Ross. *American Apocalypse: The Great Fire and the Myth of Chicago.* Chicago: University of Chicago Press, 1990.

Millett, Allan R., and Peter Maslowski. *For the Common Defense: A Military History of the United States.* New York: Macmillan, 1994.

Mills, Frederick C. *Economic Tendencies in the United States.* New York: J. J. Little and Ives Co., 1932.

Milton, Pat. *In the Blink of an Eye.* New York: Random House, 1999.

Minutaglio, Bill. *City on Fire.* New York: HarperCollins, 2003.

Mokyr, Joel. *Why Ireland Starved: A Quantitative and Analytical History of the Irish Economy, 1800–1850.* London: George Allen & Unwin, 1983.

Mooney, Michael Macdonald. *The Hindenburg.* London: Hart-Davis, MacGibbon Ltd., 1972.

Morgan, Edmund S., and Helen M. Morgan *The Stamp Act Crisis: Prologue to Revolution.* 3rd ed. Chapel Hill: University of North Carolina Press, 1995.

Morgan, H. Wayne. *William McKinley and His America.* Kent, Ohio: Kent State University Press, 2003.

Morison, Samuel Eliot. *Harrison Gray Otis, 1765–1848: The Urbane Federalist.* Boston: Houghton Mifflin, 1969.

Morris, Richard B. *The Forging of the Union, 1781–1789.* New York: Harper and Row, 1987.

Mulcahy, Matthew. *Hurricanes and Society in the British Greater Caribbean, 1624–1783.* Baltimore: Johns Hopkins University Press, 2006.

Muller, John E., and Charles Kenney. *Keep the Faith, Change the Church.* Emmaus, Pa.: Rodale Press, 2004.

Munson, Howard. *The Triumph of the American Spirit: Johnstown, Pennsylvania.* Lanham: Johnstown Flood Museum and American Association for State and Local History Library, 1989.

Murphy, Jim. *An American Plague: The True and Terrifying Story of the Yellow Fever Epidemic of 1793.* New York: Scholastic, 2004.

Murphy, Priscella Coit. *What a Book Can Do: The Publication and Reception of* Silent Spring. Amherst: University of Massachusetts Press, 2005.

Murray, Robert K. *Red Scare: A Study in National Hysteria, 1919–1920.* Minneapolis: University of Minnesota Press, 1955.

Mylroie, Laurie. *Study of Revenge, The First World Trade Center Attack and Saddam Hussein's War Against America.* Washington, D.C.: AEI Press, 2001.

Nader, Ralph. *Unsafe at Any Speed: The Designed-In Danger of the American Automobile.* New York: Grossman, 1965.

Nasaw, David. *Andrew Carnegie.* New York: Penguin, 2006.

Nathan, Daniel A. *Saying It's So.* Chicago: University of Illinois Press, 2003.

National Commission on Terrorist Attacks upon the United States. *The 9/11 Commission Report.* New York: W. W. Norton, 2004.

National Research Council. *Practical Lessons from the Loma Prieta Earthquake.* Washington, D.C.: National Academy Press, 1994.

Negroni, Christine. *Deadly Departure.* New York: HarperCollins, 2000.

Nettels, Curtis. *The Emergence of a National Economy, 1775–1815.* New York: Harper and Row, 1962.

Nevins, Allan. *The American States During and After the Revolution, 1775–1789.* New York: Macmillan, 1924.

———. *The Emergence of Modern America, 1865–1878.* New York: Macmillan, 1927.

Noji, E. K. *The Public Health Consequences of Disasters.* New York: Oxford University Press, 2002.

Norton, Mary Beth. *In the Devil's Snare: The Salem Witchcraft Crisis of 1692.* New York: Knopf, 2002.

Ó Gráda, Cormac. *The Great Irish Famine.* New York: Cambridge University Press, 2000.

O'Connor, Thomas H. *Boston Catholics: A History of the Church and Its People.* Boston: Northeastern University Press, 1998.

O'Donnell, Edward T. *Ship Ablaze: The Tragedy of the Steamboat General Slocum.* New York: Broadway Books, 2003.

O'Nan, Stewart. *The Circus Fire: A True Story of an American Tragedy.* New York: Anchor Books, 2000.

O'Toole, John M. *Tornado! 84 Minutes; 94 Lives.* Worcester, Mass.: Databooks, 1993.

Oates, Stephen B. *Let the Trumpet Sound: The Life of Martin Luther King, Jr.* New York: New American Library, 1983.

——. *To Purge This Land with Blood: A Biography of John Brown.* New York: Harper and Row, 1970.

Oberdorfer, Don. *Tet: The Turning Point in the Vietnam War.* Baltimore: Johns Hopkins Press, 2001.

Offner, John L. "McKinley and the Spanish-American War." *Presidential Studies Quarterly* 34, no. 1 (2004): 50–61.

Olson, Keith W. *Watergate: The Presidential Scandal That Shook America.* Lawrence: University of Kansas Press, 2003.

Opie, John. *Ogallala: Water for a Dry Land.* Lincoln: University of Nebraska Press, 1993.

Oshinsky, David M. *Polio: An American Story.* New York: Oxford University Press, 2005.

Ott, Riki. *Sound Truth & Corporate Myth$: The Legacy of the* Exxon Valdez *Oil Spill.* Cordova, Ark.: Dragonfly Sisters Press, 2005.

Outland, Charles F. *Man-Made Disaster: The Story of the St. Francis Dam, Its Place in Southern California's Water System, Its Failure, and the Tragedy in the Santa Clara River Valley, March 12 and 13, 1928.* Rev. ed. Glendale, Calif.: A. H. Clark, 1977.

Ovington, Mary White. "The National Association for the Advancement of Colored People." *The Journal of Negro History* 9 (April 1924): 107–116.

Packard, A. S., Jr. *Report on the Rocky Mountain Locust and Other Insects Now Injuring or Likely to Injure Field and Garden Crops in the United States.* Washington, D.C.: United States Geological Survey, Department of the Interior, 1877.

Papanikolas, Zeese. *Buried Unsung: Louis Tikas and the Ludlow Massacre.* Salt Lake City: University of Utah Press, 1982.

Paquette, Robert L. "From Rebellion to Revisionism: The Continuing Debate about the Denmark Vesey Affair." *The Journal of the Historical Society* 4, no. 3 (Fall 2004): 291–334.

Parsons, Lynn Hudson. "The Election of 1824." In *American Presidential Campaigns and Elections,* edited by William G. Shade and Ballard C. Campbell, 214–231. Armonk, N.Y.: M. E. Sharpe, 2003.

Patterson, James. *Grand Expectations: The United States, 1945–1974.* New York: Oxford University Press, 1996.

Paul, John R. *A History of Poliomyelitis.* New Haven, Conn.: Yale University Press, 1971.

PBS Online. "Fatal Flood: The Film and More." *American Experience.* Available online. URL: http://www.pbs.org/wgbh/amex/flood/filmmore/index.html. Accessed March 26, 2007.

Peet, Stephen D. *The Ashtabula Disaster.* Chicago: J. S. Goodman, 1877.

Pennsylvania Department of Environmental Protection. "Donora Smog Kills 20: October, 1948." Fiftieth anniversary commemoration. Available online. URL: http://www.dep.state.pa.us/dep/Rachel_Carson/donora.htm. Accessed April 10, 2007.

Perdue, Theda, and Michael D. Green. *The Cherokee Removal: A Brief History with Documents.* 2d ed. Boston: Bedford/St. Martin's Press, 2005.

Perez, Louis A., Jr. "The Meaning of the *Maine*: Causation and Historiography of the Spanish-American War." *Pacific Historical Review* 58, no. 3 (1989): 293–322.

Perley, Sidney. *Historic Storms of New England.* Beverly, Mass.: Memoirs Unlimited, 2001. First published by Salem Press Publishing, 1891.

Pernin, Peter. "The Great Peshtigo Fire: An Eyewitness Account." *Wisconsin Magazine of History* 54, no. 4 (1971): 246–272.

Peskin, Allan. *Garfield: A Biography.* Kent, Ohio: Kent State University Press, 1978.

Petroski, Henry. *Engineers of Dreams: Great Bridge Builders and the Spanning of America.* New York: Knopf, 1995.

Philbrick, Nathaniel. *Mayflower.* New York: Viking, 2006.

Phillips, William D., Jr., and Carla Rahn Phillips. *The Worlds of Christopher Columbus.* Cambridge, England: Cambridge University Press, 1992.

Pinkowski, Edward. *John Siney: The Miners' Martyr.* Philadelphia: Sunshine Press, 1963.

Pitch, Anthony S. *The Burning of Washington: The British Invasion of 1814.* Washington, D.C.: Naval Institute Press, 1998.

Polakoff, Keith Ian. *The Politics of Inertia: The Election of 1876 and the End of Reconstruction.* Baton Rouge: Louisiana State University Press, 1973.

Political Staff of The Washington Post. *Deadlock: The Inside Story of America's Closest Election.* New York: PublicAffairs, 2001.

Pope, Daniel. "American Economists and the High Cost of Living: The Progressive Era." *Journal of the History of Behavioral Science* 17 (1981): 75–87.

Posner, Gerald. *Case Closed: Lee Harvey Oswald and the Assassination of JFK.* New York: Random House, 1993.

———. *Killing the Dream: James Earl Ray and the Assassination of Martin Luther King, Jr.* New York: Random House, 1998.

Post, John D. *The Last Great Subsistence Crisis in the Western World.* Baltimore: Johns Hopkins University Press, 1977.

Potter, Jerry O. *The* Sultana *Tragedy: America's Greatest Maritime Disaster.* Gretna, La.: Pelican Publishing, 1992.

Powell, John H. *Bring Out Your Dead: The Great Plague of Yellow Fever in Philadelphia in 1793.* Reprint, Philadelphia: University of Pennsylvania Press, 1993.

Powell, William S., James K. Huhta, and Thomas J. Farnham, eds. *The Regulators in North Carolina: A Documentary History, 1759–1776.* Raleigh, N.C.: State Department of Archives and History, 1971.

Prange, Gordon. *At Dawn We Slept: The Untold Story of Pearl Harbor.* Boston: McGraw Hill, 1981.

Preston, Diana. Lusitania: *An Epic Tragedy.* New York: Berkley, 2002.

Price, David A. *Love and Hate in Jamestown.* New York: Knopf, 2003.

Puleo, Stephen. *Dark Tide: The Great Boston Molasses Flood of 1919.* Boston: Beacon Press, 2004.

Pyne, Stephen J. *Fire in America: A Cultural History of Wildland and Rural Fire.* Seattle: University of Washington Press, 1997.

Quinn, David Beers. *Set Fair for Roanoke: Voyages and Colonies, 1584–1606.* Chapel Hill: University of North Carolina Press, 1985.

Quitt, Martin H. "Trade and Acculturation at Jamestown, 1607–1609: The Limits of Understanding." *William and Mary Quarterly* 52, no. 2 (April 1995): 227–258.

Ramsay, David. Lusitania: *Saga and Myth.* New York: W. W. Norton, 2001.

Raper, Arthur F. *The Tragedy of Lynching.* Chapel Hill: University of North Carolina Press, 1933.

Rauchway, Eric. *Murdering McKinley: The Making of Theodore Roosevelt's America.* New York: Hill and Wang, 2003.

Rees, David. *Korea: The Limited War.* New York: St. Martin's Press, 1964.

Reeves, J. E. "The Eminent Domain of Sanitary Science and the Usefulness of Boards of Health in Guarding the Public Welfare." *Journal of the American Medical Association* 1, no. 21 (1883): 612.

Rehnquist, William H. *Centennial Crisis: The Disputed Election of 1876.* New York: Knopf, 2004.

———. *Grand Inquests: The Historic Impeachments of Justice Samuel Chase and President Andrew Johnson.* New York: Morrow, 1992.

Report of the Joint Committee of the Senate and Assembly of the State of New York Appointed to Investigate the Affairs of Life Insurance Companies. Albany, N.Y.: Brandow Printing Co., 1906.

Report of the President's Commission on the Assassination of President John F. Kennedy. New York: Doubleday, 1964.

Reynolds, David S. *John Brown, Abolitionist: The Man Who Killed Slavery, Sparked the Civil War, and Seeded Civil Rights.* New York: Knopf, 2005.

Rezneck, Samuel. "Distress, Relief, and Discontent in the United States During the Depression of 1873–78" *Journal of Political Economy* 58 (1950): 494–512.

———. "Unemployment, Unrest, and Relief in the United States during the Depression of 1893–1897." *Journal of Political Economy* 61 (1953): 324–345.

Rhodehamel, John, and Louise Taper, eds. *"Right or Wrong, God Judge Me": The Writings of John Wilkes Booth.* Urbana: University of Illinois Press, 1997.

Rhodes, Richard, *The Making of the Atomic Bomb.* New York: Simon and Schuster, 1986.

Rich, Doris L. *Amelia Earhart: A Biography.* Washington, D.C.: Smithsonian Institution, 1989.

Richards, Leonard R. *Shays's Rebellion: The American Revolution's Final Battle.* Philadelphia: University of Pennsylvania Press, 2002.

Riney-Kehrberg, Pamela. *Rooted in Dust: Surviving Drought and Depression in Southwestern Kansas.* Lawrence: University Press of Kansas, 1994.

Risse, Guenter B. "The Politics of Fear: Bubonic Plague in San Francisco, California, 1900." In *New Countries and Old Medicine: Proceedings of an International Conference on the History of Medicine and Health,* edited by Linda Bryder and Derek Dow, 1–19. Auckland, N.Z.: Pyramid Press, 1995.

Roberts, Randy, and James S. Olson. *A Line in the Sand: The Alamo in Blood and Memory*. New York: Free Press, 2001.

Rosenberg, Charles E. *The Cholera Years: The United States in 1832, 1849, and 1866*. Chicago: University of Chicago Press, 1962.

———. *The Trial of the Assassin Guiteau: Psychiatry and the Law in the Gilded Age*. Chicago: University of Chicago Press, 1968.

Rosenfeld, Charles, and Robert Cooke. *Earthfire*. Cambridge, Mass.: The MIT Press, 1982.

Rothbard, Murray N. *The Panic of 1819: Reactions and Policies*. New York: Columbia University Press, 1962.

Rothschild, Mary A. *A Case of Black and White: Northern Volunteers and the Southern Freedom Summers, 1964–65*. Westport, Conn.: Greenwood Press, 1982.

Rubin, Irene. *Balancing the Federal Budget: Eating the Seed Corn or Trimming the Herds?* Washington, D.C.: CQ Press, 2002.

———. *The Politics of Public Budgeting: Getting and Spending, Borrowing and Balancing*. New York: Seven Bridges Press, 2000.

Russell, Robert R. "What Was the Compromise of 1850?" *The Journal of Southern History* 22 (August 1956): 292–309.

Rust, Claude. *The Burning of the* General Slocum. New York: Elsevier/Nelson Books, 1981.

Ruth, David E. "Crime and Chicago's Image." In *The Encyclopedia of Chicago*. Edited by James R. Grossman, Ann Durkin Keating, and Janice L. Reiff. Chicago: University of Chicago Press, 2004.

Sabato, Larry, ed. *Overtime! The Election 2000 Thriller*. New York: Longman, 2002.

Sackett, Susan. *Box Office Hits: Hollywood's Most Successful Movies*. New York: Billboard Books, 1990.

Salvatore, Nick. *Eugene V. Debs: Citizen and Socialist*. Urbana: University of Illinois Press, 1982.

Sammarco, Anthony M. *The Great Boston Fire of 1872*. Dover, N.H.: Arcadia, 1997.

Samuels, Peggy, and Harold Samuels. *Remembering the* Maine. Washington, D.C.: Smithsonian Institute Press, 1995.

Sarasohn, David. *The Party of Reform: Democrats in the Progressive Era*. Jackson: University of Mississippi Press, 1989.

Scanlan, Charles M. *The* Lady Elgin *Disaster*. Milwaukee, Wis.: Charles M. Scanlan, 1928.

Schechter, Bernard. *The Devil's Own Work: The Civil War Draft Riots and the Fight to Reconstruct America*. New York: Walker, 2005.

Schick, Allen. *The Federal Budget: Politics, Policy, Process*. Washington, D.C.: Brookings Institution Press, 2000.

Schlebecker, John T. "Grasshoppers in American Agricultural History." *Agricultural History* 27 (July 1953): 85–93.

Schlesinger, Arthur M. *The Age of Roosevelt*. 3 vols. Boston: Houghton Mifflin, 1957–60.

———. *Robert Kennedy and His Times*. Boston: Houghton Mifflin, 1978.

Schoenberg, Robert J. *Mr. Capone: The Real—and Complete—Story of Al Capone*. New York: William Morrow, 1992.

Schorow, Stephanie. *Boston on Fire: A History of Fires and Firefighting in Boston*. Beverly, Mass.: Commonwealth Editions, 2003.

Schorow, Stephanie, and Robert J. Allison, eds. *The Cocoanut Grove Fire*. Beverly, Mass.: Commonwealth Editions, 2005.

Schrier, Arnold. *Ireland and the American Emigration 1850–1900*. Chester Springs, Pa.: Dufour Editions, 1997.

Schultz, Duane. *Month of the Freezing Moon: The Sand Creek Massacre, November 1864*. New York: St. Martin's Press, 1990.

Schultz, Nancy Lusignan. *Fires and Roses: The Burning of the Charlestown Convent, 1834*. New York: Free Press, 2000.

Schwartz, Francis K., L. A. Hughes, E. M. Hansen, M. S. Petersen, and D. B. Kelly. *The Black Hills Rapid City Flood of June 9–10, 1972: A Description of the Storm and Flood*. Washington, D.C.: U.S. Government Printing Office, 1975.

Scott, Phil. *Hemingway's Hurricane: The Great Florida Keys Storm of 1935*. Camden, Me.: International Marine/Ragged Mountain Press, 2006.

Scott, Richard. *In the Wake of Tacoma: Suspension Bridges and the Quest for Aerodynamic Stability*. Reston, Va.: American Society of Civil Engineers, 2001.

Scotti, R.A. *Sudden Sea: The Great Hurricane of 1938*. Boston: Back Bay Books, 2004.

Sealander, Judith. *The Failed Century of the Child: Governing America's Young in the Twentieth Century*. New York: Cambridge University Press, 2003.

Sears, David. *The Politics of Violence: The New Urban Blacks and the Watts Riot*. Boston: Houghton Mifflin, 1973.

Senechal, Roberta. *The Sociogenesis of a Race Riot: Springfield, Illinois in 1908*. Urbana, Ill.: University of Chicago Press, 1990.

Sharp, James Roger. *American Politics in the Early Republic: The New Nation in Crisis*. New Haven, Conn.: Yale University Press, 1993.

Sharpe, Elizabeth M. *In the Shadow of the Dam: The Aftermath of the Mill River Flood of 1874*. New York: Free Press, 2004.

Shaw, David W. *The Sea Shall Embrace Them: The Tragic Story of the Steamship* Arctic. New York: Free Press, 2002.

Shilts, Randy. *And the Band Played On: Politics, People, and the AIDS Epidemic*. New York: St. Martin's Press, 1987.

Small, Melvin. *The Presidency of Richard Nixon*. Lawrence: University Press of Kansas, 1999.

Smith, Mark M. *Stono: Documenting and Interpreting a Southern Slave Revolt*. Columbia: University of South Carolina Press, 2005.

Snow, Edward Rowe. *Great Storms and Famous Shipwrecks of the New England Coast*. 3rd ed. Boston: Yankee Publishing, 1946.

Snyder, Lynne Page. "*The Death-Dealing Smog over Donora, Pennsylvania": Industrial Air Pollution, Public Health, and Federal Policy, 1915–1963*. Unpublished Ph.D. diss., University of Pennsylvania, 1994.

Sobel, Robert. *They Satisfy: The Cigarette in American Life*. New York: Anchor, 1978.

Sontag, Susan. "The Imagination of Disaster." In *Against Interpretation and Other Essays*. London: Andre Deutsch, 1965.

Spector, Ronald. *After Tet: The Bloodiest Year in Vietnam*. New York: Vintage, 1994.

Spring, Joel. *Educating the Consumer-Citizen: A History of the Marriage of Schools, Advertising, and the Media*. Mahwah, N.J.: Lawrence Erlbaum Associates, 2004.

Stackpole, Edouard A. *The Wreck of the Steamer* San Francisco. Mystic, Conn.: Marine Historical Association, 1954.

Stampp, Kenneth M. *And the War Came: The North and the Secession Crisis, 1860–1861*. Baton Rouge: Louisiana State University Press, 1950.

Standiford, Les. *Meet You in Hell: Andrew Carnegie, Henry Clay Frick, and the Bitter Partnership that Transformed America*. New York: Crown, 2005.

Steeples, Douglas, and David O. Whitten. *Democracy in Desperation: The Depression of 1893*. Westport, Conn.: Greenwood Press, 1998.

Stein, Leon. *The Triangle Fire*. Philadelphia: Lippincott, 1962.

Steinburg, Theodore. *Acts of God: The Unnatural History of Natural Disaster in America*. New York: Oxford University Press, 2000.

Steinfels, Peter. *A People Adrift: The Crisis of the Roman Catholic Church in America*. New York: Simon and Schuster, 2003.

Stephens, Hugh W. *The Texas City Disaster, 1947*. Austin: University of Texas Press, 1997.

Stephens, Mark. *Three Mile Island: The Hour by Hour Account of What Really Happened*. New York: Random House, 1980.

Stephens, Trent, and Rock Brynner. *Dark Remedy: The Impact of Thalidomide and Its Revival as a Vital Medicine*. Cambridge, Mass.: Perseus Publishing, 2001.

Stewart, George R. *Ordeal by Hunger: The Story of the Donner Party*. Lincoln: University of Nebraska Press, 1986.

Stiglitz, Joseph E. *The Roaring Nineties: A New History of the World's Most Prosperous Decade*. New York: W. W. Norton, 2003.

Stolpe, Nils E. "Full of Sound and Fury, Signifying Nothing." *FishNet USA./June 6, 2006*

Stommel, Henry, and Elizabeth Stommel. *Volcano Weather: The Story of 1816, the Year Without a Summer*. Newport, R.I.: Seven Seas Press, 1983.

Stout, Steve. "Tragedy in November: The Cherry Mine Disaster." *Journal of the Illinois State Historical Society* 72 (February 1979): 57–69.

Stowell, David O. *Streets, Railroads, and the Great Strike of 1877*. Chicago: University of Chicago Press, 1999.

Stromquist, Shelton. *A Generation of Boomers: The Pattern of Railroad Labor Conflict in Nineteenth-Century America*. Urbana: University of Illinois Press, 1987.

Swartz, Mimi, with Sherron Watkins. *Power Failure: The Inside Story of the Collapse of Enron*. New York: Doubleday, 2003.

Syzerhans, Douglas, ed. *Federal Disaster Programs and Hurricane Katrina*. New York: Nova Science Publishers, 2006.

Szatmary, David P. *Shays' Rebellion: The Making of an Agrarian Insurrection.* Amherst: University of Massachusetts Press, 1980.

Tate, Cassandra. *Cigarette Wars: The Triumph of "the Little White Slaver."* New York: Oxford University Press, 1999.

Tauranac, John. *The Empire State Building.* New York: Scribner, 1995.

Taylor, George Rogers. *The Transportation Revolution, 1815–1860.* New York: Holt, Rinehart, and Winston, 1951.

Temin, Peter. *The Jacksonian Economy.* New York: W. W. Norton, 1969.

———. *Taking Your Medicine: Drug Regulation in the United States.* Cambridge, Mass.: Harvard University Press, 1980.

Terkel, Studs. *Hard Times: An Oral History of the Great Depression.* New York: Washington Square Press, 1970.

Thomas, P. D. G. *British Politics and the Stamp Act Crisis: The First Phase of the American Revolution, 1763–1767.* New York: Clarendon Press, 1975.

Thompson, Paul, and the Center for Cooperative Research. *The Terror Timeline.* New York: HarperCollins, 2004.

Thornton, John K. "African Dimensions of the Stono Rebellion." *American Historical Review* 96 (October 1991): 1,101–1,113.

Thornton, Russell. *American Indian Holocaust and Survival: A Population History Since 1492.* Norman: University of Oklahoma Press, 1990.

Tidwell, William A., James O. Hall, and David Winfred Gaddy. *Come Retribution: The Confederate Secret Service and the Assassination of Lincoln.* Jackson: University Press of Mississippi, 1988.

Timberlake, Richard H., Jr. *The Origins of Central Banking in the United States.* Cambridge, Mass.: Harvard University Press, 1978.

Tintori, Karen. *Trapped: The 1909 Cherry Mine Disaster.* New York: Atria Books, 2002.

Tobriner, Stephen. *Bracing for Disaster: Earthquake-resistant Architecture and Engineering in San Francisco, 1838–1933.* Berkeley, Calif.: Heyday Books, 2006.

Tomkins, Phillip. *Apollo, Challenger, Columbia: The Decline of the Space Program.* Los Angeles: Roxbury, 2005.

Tougias, Michael. *The Blizzard of '78.* Yarmouth Port, Mass.: On Cape Publications, 2003.

———. *Ten Hours Until Dawn: The True Story of Heroism and Tragedy Aboard the* Can Do. New York: St. Martins, 2005.

Trefousse, Hans L. *Impeachment of a President: Andrew Johnson, the Blacks, and Reconstruction.* 1975. Reprint, New York: Fordham University Press, 1999.

The Triangle Shirtwaist Factory Fire, March 25, 1911: A Memorial Compilation and Testament to the 146 Victims, Their Families and Those Heroic Immigrants Whose Labor and Sacrifice Made America Great. Albany, N.Y.: New York State Senate, 2006.

Tuttle, William M., Jr. *Race Riot: Chicago in the Red Summer of 1919.* New York: Atheneum, 1970. Reprint, Chicago: University of Illinois Press, 1996.

UNAIDS. *2006 Report on the Global AIDS Epidemic: A UNAIDS 10th Anniversary Special Edition.* Geneva: UNAIDS, 2006.

Unger, Irwin, and Debi Unger. *Turning Point: 1968.* New York: Scribner, 1988.

Unruh, John D. *The Plains Across: The Overland Immigrants and the Trans-Mississippi West, 1840–1860.* Urbana: University of Illinois Press, 1979.

U.S. Congress. House of Representatives. Special Subcommittee of the Committee on the Judiciary. *Texas City Disaster Hearings.* 83rd Cong., November 16–18, 1953. Washington, D.C.: U.S. Government Printing Office, 1954.

U.S. Dept. of Health, Education, and Welfare. *Smoking and Health Report of the Advisory Committee to the Surgeon General of the Public Health Service.* Washington, D.C.: U.S. Dept. of Health, 1964.

The U.S. Riot Commission Report. New York: New York Times Company, 1968.

Utley, Robert M. *Cavalier in Buckskin: George Armstrong Custer and the Western Military Frontier.* Rev. ed. Norman: University of Oklahoma Press, 2001.

Van Vleck, George W. *The Panic of 1857: An Analytical Study.* New York: Columbia University Press, 1943.

Vasey, Frank B., and Josh Feldstein. *The Silicone Breast Implant Controversy: What Women Need to Know.* Freedom, Calif.: Crossing Press, 1993.

Vaughan, Alden T. "'Expulsion of the Salvages': English Policy and the Virginia Massacre of 1622." *The William and Mary Quarterly* 35, no. 1 (January 1978): 57–84.

Vaughan, Diane. *The* Challenger *Launch Decision: Risky Technology, and Deviance at NASA.* Chicago: University of Chicago University Press, 1996.

Verano, John W., and Douglas H. Ubelaker, eds. *Disease and Demography in the Americas.* Washington, D.C.: Smithsonian Institution Press, 1992.

Von Drehle, David. *Triangle: The Fire That Changed America.* New York: Atlantic Monthly Press, 2003.

Wade, Wyn Craig. *The Titanic: End of a Dream.* Rev. ed. New York: Penguin, 1986.

Walker, J. Samuel. *Prompt and Utter Destruction: Truman and the Use of Atomic Bombs Against Japan.* Chapel Hill: University of North Carolina Press, 1997.

———. *Three Mile Island: A Nuclear Crisis in Historical Perspective.* Berkeley, Calif.: University of California Press, 2004.

Wallace, Anthony F. C. *The Long, Bitter Trail: Andrew Jackson and the Indians.* New York: Hill and Wang, 1993.

———. *St. Clair: A Nineteenth-Century Coal Town's Experience with a Disaster-Prone Industry.* New York: Knopf, 1987.

Wallace, Linda L. *After the Fires: The Ecology of Change in Yellowstone National Park.* New Haven, Conn.: Yale University Press, 2004.

Ware, Susan. *Still Missing: Amelia Earhart and the Search for Modern Feminism.* New York: W. W. Norton, 1993.

Warner, Sam Bass, Jr. *The Private City: Philadelphia in Three Periods of Its Growth.* Philadelphia: University of Pennsylvania Press, 1968.

Washburn, Wilcomb. *The Governor and the Rebel: A History of Bacon's Rebellion in Virginia.* Chapel Hill: University of North Carolina Press, 1957.

Washington State Department of Transportation. "Tacoma Narrows Bridge: Extreme History." Available online. URL: http://www.wsdot.wa.gov/TNBhistory. Downloaded on April 2, 2007.

Watkins, T. H. *The Hungry Years: A Narrative History of the Great Depression in America.* New York: Henry Holt, 1999.

Watson, Bruce. *Bread & Roses: Mills, Migrants and the Struggle for the American Dream.* New York: Viking, 2005.

Watson, Justin. *The Martyrs of Columbine: Faith and the Politics of Tragedy.* New York: Palgrave Macmillan, 2002.

Webb, Stephen Saunders. *1676: The End of American Independence.* New York: Knopf, 1984.

Weems, John Edward. *A Weekend in September.* 1957. Reprint, College Station: Texas A&M University Press, 1989.

Weigley, Russell F. *A Great Civil War: A Military and Political History, 1861–1865.* Bloomington: Indiana University Press, 2000.

Welch, James, and Paul Stekler. *Killing Custer: The Battle of the Little Bighorn and the Fate of the Plains Indians.* New York: W. W. Norton, 1994.

Wells, Robert W. *Fire at Peshtigo.* Englewood Cliffs, N.J.: Prentice Hall, 1968.

Werstein, Irving. *The Blizzard of '88.* New York: Crowell, 1960.

West, Delno. "Christopher Columbus and His Enterprise to the Indies: Scholarship of the Last Quarter Century." *William and Mary Quarterly* 49 (April 1992): 254–277.

White, Richard. "Information, Markets, and Corruption: Transcontinental Railroads in the Gilded Age." *Journal of American History* 90, no. 1 (June 2003): 19–43.

White, Theodore. *The Making of the President, 1968.* New York: Pocket Books, 1970.

Williams, John M., and Iver W. Duedall. *Florida Hurricanes and Tropical Storms, 1871–2001.* Gainesville: University Press of Florida, 2002.

Williams, Lee E. *Anatomy of Four Race Riots: Racial Conflict in Knoxville, Elaine (Arkansas), Tulsa, and Chicago, 1919–1921.* Hattiesburg: University and College Press of Mississippi, 1972.

Willison, George F. *Saints and Strangers.* New York: Reynal and Hitchcock, 1945.

Winocour, Jack, ed. *The Story of the* Titanic *as Told by Its Survivors.* New York: Dover, 1960.

Winslow, Ola Elizabeth. *A Destroying Angel. The Conquest of Smallpox in Colonial Boston.* Boston: Houghton Mifflin, 1974.

Wohlstetter, Roberta. *Pearl Harbor: Warning and Decision.* Stanford, Calif.: Stanford University Press, 1962.

Wolenberg, Ernest H. "'The Geography of Civility' Revisited: New York Blackout Looting, 1977." *Economic Geography* 58, no. 1 (January 1982): 29–44.

Wood, Peter H. *Black Majority: Negroes in Colonial South Carolina from 1670 through the Stono Rebellion.* New York: Knopf, 1974.

Woodham-Smith, Cecil. *The Great Hunger: Ireland 1845–1849.* London: Penguin, 1991.

Woodward, C. Vann. *Reunion and Reaction: The Compromise of 1877 and the End of Reconstruction.* 1951. Reprint with new preface, New York: Oxford University Press, 1999.

Worster, Donald. *Dust Bowl: The Southern Plains in the 1930s.* New York: Oxford University Press, 1979.

Wright, Lawrence. *The Looming Tower: Al Qaeda and the Road to 9/11.* New York: Knopf: 2006.

Wright, Robin. *Sacred Rage.* New York: Simon and Schuster, 1985.

Yergin, Daniel. *The Prize: The Epic Quest for Oil, Money, and Power.* New York: Simon and Schuster, 1991.

Youngs, Robert L. "'A Right Smart Little Jolt': Loss of the Chestnut and A Way of Life." *Journal of Forestry* 98 (February 2000): 17–21.

Zabin, Serena. *The New York Conspiracy Trials of 1741: Daniel Horsmanden's Journal of the Proceedings, with Related Documents.* Boston: Bedford/St. Martin's, 2004.

Zangrando, Robert. *The NAACP Crusade against Lynching, 1909–1950.* Philadelphia: Temple University Press, 1980.

Zinn, Howard. *The Twentieth Century: A People's History.* New York: Harper and Row, 1984.

Zobel, Hiller. *The Boston Massacre.* New York: Norton Library, 1970.

Zuckoff, Mitchell. *Ponzi's Scheme: The True Story of a Financial Legend.* New York: Random House, 2005.

◆ INDEX ◆

◆ ABOUT THE AUTHOR ◆

Ballard C. Campbell, Ph.D., is professor of history and of public policy in the Law, Policy, and Society Program at Northeastern University. He is president of the New England Historical Association and the author of numerous books, including *The Growth of American Government: Governance from the Cleveland Era to the Present*, *Representative Democracy: Public Policy and Midwestern Legislatures in the Late Nineteenth Century*, and *The Human Tradition in the Gilded Age and Progressive Era*. He also coedited the three-volume encyclopedia *American Presidential Campaigns and Elections*. He has served as associate editor of *American National Biography* and as a Distinguished Lecturer for the Organization of American Historians.